NORTH CAROLINA TRIAD
BEER

 A History

RICHARD COX, DAVID GWYNN
AND ERIN LAWRIMORE

AMERICAN PALATE

Published by American Palate
A Division of The History Press
Charleston, SC
www.historypress.com

Front cover: Downtown Greensboro. *Grant Evan Gilliard, UNC Greensboro.*

First published 2021

ISBN 9781540248480

Library of Congress Control Number: 2021937158

Notice: The information in this book is true and complete to the best of our knowledge. It is offered without guarantee on the part of the authors or The History Press. The authors and The History Press disclaim all liability in connection with the use of this book.

"Treier's *Introducing Evangelical Theology* treats the gamut of evangelical theological categories. He seeks to maintain Scripture's preeminent place as the authoritative source for theological formulation and its evaluative power for faith and practice. In the course of engaging theological and social questions and issues inside and outside the church, Treier consistently demonstrates a respect for centuries of church theological reflection done by sinful people who received the grace of Holy Spirit–empowered reasoning. This volume will no doubt become a standard work for the theological training of professional and lay church leadership."

—**Bruce Fields**, Trinity Evangelical Divinity School

"Alert to theology's doctrinal, moral, and spiritual dimensions; deeply informed by classical and contemporary approaches to the matters at hand; and irenic in its survey of a broad theological landscape, Treier's *Introducing Evangelical Theology* offers a faithful and creative account of Christian teaching that both students and teachers will appreciate and that further distinguishes the author as one of our most gifted theologians."

—**Scott R. Swain**, Reformed Theological Seminary, Orlando

"*Introducing Evangelical Theology* is biblically rooted, historically informed, ecclesially located, and spiritually formative. While readers will not agree with every conclusion, Treier has given us an introduction to Christian theology that is eminently accessible, richly stimulating, grounded in the Christian tradition, and committed to evangelical distinctives—a rare feat. This book will benefit students, pastors, and academic theologians alike."

—**Matthew Y. Emerson**, Oklahoma Baptist University

"In making introductions, first impressions count: according to a Harvard study it takes only seven seconds to size up a new acquaintance. *Introducing Evangelical Theology* makes a good impression in the first seven pages, where we meet a movement that is equally concerned with intellectual, moral, and spiritual formation; ecumenically orthodox and rooted in the great creeds; yet distinctly Protestant in its insistence that the gospel retain its glorious freedom to renew and reform. By the end of the book, readers will also have formed a good lasting impression of evangelical theology and an appreciation for Treier's clear, fair, and winsome exposition of the trinitarian narrative of the gospel and its interpretive traditions. Each chapter includes theses, definitions of key terms, and a set of learning objectives—everything one needs to learn the grammar of evangelical faith. This is not simply an introduction to but an education in evangelical theology, and one to which I will be enthusiastically introducing students for years to come."

—**Kevin J. Vanhoozer**, Trinity Evangelical Divinity School

"In these pages Treier offers a truly remarkable combination of Scripture, tradition, ethics, doctrine, historic debates, and contemporary challenges as he explores one essential topic after another. Trinitarian in both content and structure, the book could not be more thoughtfully ordered and presented. I know this book's pages will be dog-eared and its binding worn by many a college student, pastor, graduate student, and academic, for whom it will quickly become an invaluable and treasured resource."

—**Kristen Deede Johnson**, Western Theological Seminary

"What a great teacher! Treier is a master of summarizing the expansive, explaining the complicated, and highlighting the central. Here we encounter an invitation to experience the breadth of the Christian tradition while standing within the best of the spirit of evangelical theology. Treier is fair, judicious, generous, and wise. Learn to theologize like him not only for the good of your heart but also for the good of God's church and world. This volume will surely be a great gift to a generation of readers."

—**Kelly M. Kapic**, Covenant College

Introducing

EVANGELICAL THEOLOGY

DANIEL J. TREIER

Baker Academic
a division of Baker Publishing Group
Grand Rapids, Michigan

© 2019 by Daniel J. Treier

Published by Baker Academic
a division of Baker Publishing Group
PO Box 6287, Grand Rapids, MI 49516-6287
www.bakeracademic.com

Printed in the United States of America

Library of Congress Cataloging-in-Publication Data
Names: Treier, Daniel J., 1972– author.
Title: Introducing Evangelical theology / Daniel J. Treier.
Description: Grand Rapids : Baker Publishing Group, 2019. | Includes bibliographical references and index.
Identifiers: LCCN 2018044330 | ISBN 9780801097690 (pbk.)
Subjects: LCSH: Evangelicalism. | Reformed Church—Doctrines.
Classification: LCC BR1640 .T74 2019 | DDC 230/.04624—dc23
LC record available at https://lccn.loc.gov/2018044330

ISBN 978-1-5409-6158-7 (casebound)

19   20   21   22   23   24   25   7   6   5   4   3   2   1

To my daughter, Anna.
May you continue to radiate joy
as you grow in the grace and knowledge
of the Triune God (2 Pet. 3:18).

Contents

Acknowledgments

The roots of this book begin with the seeds of biblical faith that my parents and grandparents planted in my formative years. Professors and peers nurtured this faith in my young adulthood. Mentors and friends have constantly strengthened its roots. Deep thanks to the many people who pray for me and support my vocation. This particular project received helpful exhortations and vital encouragement from Michael Allen, Mark Bowald, Kevin Hector, Beth Felker Jones, Kelly Kapic, Timothy Larsen, Scott Swain, and Kevin Vanhoozer.

Thanks to friendly colleagues, faithful students, and supportive administrators at Wheaton College, who have helped me to find my theological voice; needing special mention from the past are Jeff Greenman, Mark Husbands, Alan Jacobs, Roger Lundin, Mark Noll, Dennis Okholm, and Ashley Woodiwiss. Seventeen other colleagues joined me in a survey course on Christian doctrine during 2014–15, funded by the Faith and Learning program. Their gracious interaction made the present book much better than the teaching notes that legions of students previously encountered.

The book also improved thanks to Sunday school interaction at my home church, Immanuel Presbyterian in Warrenville, Illinois, where we have tackled material from the first few chapters. For a decade, Pastor George Garrison has faithfully proclaimed the primacy of Jesus Christ, which I hope has left a mark on this book. In addition, the Creation Project Regional Discussion group at Trinity Evangelical Divinity School prompted me to revise the sixth chapter; Sharm Davy, whom I met at an Evangelical Theological Society meeting, challenged me to revise the treatment of angels and demons; and Tom McCall graciously answered my eleventh-hour plea for troubleshooting on the doctrine of sin and refinements regarding Wesleyan theology.

Other friends whose comprehensive reading improved the manuscript include colleagues Marc Cortez and Jon Laansma, along with several graduate students: Craig Hefner, Dustyn Keepers, Ty Kieser, Jeremy Mann, and Nimrod Tica. Gerardo Corpeño, Michelle Knight, and Chris Smith made helpful comments on particular portions. Katherine Goodwin, Dustyn Keepers, Ty Kieser, Jeremy Mann, and Anna Williams provided crucial research help during the writing process. Long ago, Barry Jones and Darren Sarisky drafted helpful research for my course notes.

Much of what I learned from professors, pastors, the Basement Boys, and the Dead Theologians Society has undoubtedly made its way into my teaching. In my earliest years, Steve Spencer and Kevin Vanhoozer shared their course notes liberally, and I borrowed from them gratefully. I have acknowledged specific debts that I can remember, but no set of footnotes could fully identify, let alone repay, what I owe.

For permission to reuse previous material, thanks to:

1. InterVarsity Press: (a) Portions of chapter 14 appeared previously in "Who Is the Church?," in *Theology Questions Everyone Asks*, edited by Gary M. Burge and David Lauber, 156–67. Copyright © 2014 by Gary M. Burge and David Lauber. Used by permission of InterVarsity Press, P.O. Box 1400, Downers Grove, IL 60515, USA. www.ivpress.com. (b) Aspects of chapter 4 are reworked from (with thanks to my coauthor David Lauber) the introduction to *Trinitarian Theology for the Church*, edited by Daniel J. Treier and David Lauber. Copyright © 2009 by Daniel J. Treier and David Lauber. Used by permission of InterVarsity Press, P.O. Box 1400, Downers Grove, IL 60515, USA. www.ivpress.com.

2. Zondervan: Brief portions of chapter 13 are from "The Freedom of God's Word: Toward an 'Evangelical' Dogmatics of Scripture," in *The Voice of God in the Text of Scripture*, edited by Oliver D. Crisp and Fred Sanders (Grand Rapids: Zondervan, 2016), 21–40. Used by permission.

3. Baker Publishing Group: (a) Portions of chapters 1 and 6 are from articles in *Evangelical Dictionary of Theology*, edited by Daniel J. Treier and Walter A. Elwell, 3rd ed. (Grand Rapids: Baker Academic, 2017). (b) Portions of chapter 8 draw from "Jesus Christ, Doctrine of," in *Dictionary for Theological Interpretation of the Bible*, edited by Kevin J. Vanhoozer et al. (Grand Rapids: Baker Academic, 2005), 363–71. (c) Portions of chapters 8 and 9 are from "Incarnation," in *Christian Dogmatics: Reformed Theology for the Church Catholic*, edited by Michael Allen and Scott R. Swain (Grand Rapids: Baker Academic, 2016), 216–42.

Ironically (let the reader understand!), we suffered a major house fire as I was drafting the final chapter, on eschatology. I am very grateful to the folks at Baker for their kindness and patience amid the serial delays that followed. Jim Kinney and especially Dave Nelson are responsible first for making this book possible and then for making it better. Paula Gibson labored patiently to craft a cover by which to judge the book. My longtime friend Brian Bolger and his editorial team still have their fine-toothed combs in good working order.

Finally, words fail to express the debt of gratitude I owe to my wife, Amy, and daughter, Anna. Their ordinary kindness is a delightful reflection of the gospel. During the months of rebuilding our house, their patience was herculean, especially in moments when I fretted over this book rather than household details. More prosaically, Amy brought some of this material closer to understandable English when we taught a confirmation class together a decade ago. And Anna remained constantly in mind as I tried to articulate a clear and winsome account of evangelical theology. The reason for completing these acknowledgments on Trinity Sunday will, I hope, be obvious throughout the book.

Trinity Sunday 2018

Abbreviations

ANE   ancient Near East

ANF   *The Ante-Nicene Fathers*. Edited by Alexander Roberts and James Donaldson. 10 vols. 1885–87. Reprint, Peabody, MA: Hendrickson, 1994.

CD   *Church Dogmatics*. By Karl Barth. Edited by G. W. Bromiley and T. F. Torrance. Translated by G. W. Bromiley, G. T. Thomson, et al. Four volumes in 13 parts. Edinburgh: T&T Clark, 1936–77.

LW   *Luther's Works: American Edition*. Edited by J. Pelikan and H. Lehmann. 55 vols. Philadelphia: Fortress, 1955–86.

NPNF[1]   *The Nicene and Post-Nicene Fathers*, Series 1. Edited by Philip Schaff. 14 vols. 1886–89. Reprint, Peabody, MA: Hendrickson, 1994.

NPNF[2]   *The Nicene and Post-Nicene Fathers*, Series 2. Edited by Philip Schaff and Henry Wace. 14 vols. 1890–1900. Reprint, Peabody, MA: Hendrickson, 1994.

"One Carries It Around Within"

Brett Foster

Doctrine can never be belief. Doctrine
is one means only to register belief,
like a job interview conducted briefly
or census taker who never sees the tin
of steaming tamales, much less tastes them.
He makes his tallies, door to door without relief.
Sometimes doctrine is most felt as a grief,
hard in the bones or sorrow's marrow when
prodigious clumps of cells become prolific.
The other part is like a funny gift,
there in your bones as well, but lonelier, late,
sent from a shipping station far in the distance.
Opened but barely known, it still irradiates
your every admiration for existence.

Brett Foster (1973–2015), my friend and colleague in Wheaton's English department, authored
this poem early in his untimely battle with cancer. In his hospital room we discussed the possibility of including it in this book. I am grateful for permission to do so from Brett's wife,
Anise, and from John Wilson of *Books & Culture*, where it was previously published. If nothing
else, this poem conveys the mysterious reason for healthy Christian doctrine: staking our entire
lives—in all their glory and agony—on a gracious God.

The Nicene Creed

I
We believe in one God,
the Father, the Almighty,
maker of heaven and earth,
of all that is, seen and unseen.

II
We believe in one Lord, Jesus Christ,
the only Son of God,
eternally begotten of the Father,
God from God, Light from Light,
true God from true God,
begotten, not made,
of one Being with the Father;
through him all things were made.
For us and for our salvation
he came down from heaven,
was incarnate of the Holy Spirit and the Virgin Mary
and was made man.
For our sake he was crucified under Pontius Pilate;
he suffered death and was buried.
On the third day he rose again
in accordance with the Scriptures;
he ascended into heaven
and is seated at the right hand of the Father.
He will come again in glory to judge the living and the dead,
and his kingdom will have no end.

III

We believe in the Holy Spirit, the Lord, the giver of life,
who proceeds from the Father [and the Son],
who with the Father and the Son is worshipped and glorified,
who has spoken through the prophets.
We believe in one holy catholic and apostolic Church.
We acknowledge one baptism for the forgiveness of sins.
We look for the resurrection of the dead,
and the life of the world to come. Amen.[1]

---

1. This version of the Nicene Creed was adopted at the Council of Constantinople in 381, as explained in chap. 8. The translation here is available at the English Language Liturgical Consultation, http://englishtexts.org/ELLC-Documents/Survey-of-Use#thenicenecreed, and reprinted here with permission, with one alteration: the ELLC translation reads "became truly human" instead of "was made man," which is more precise.

Chapter Theses

1. Christian theology is a communicative practice of faith seeking understanding, in response to the Word of the Triune God accompanied by the Holy Spirit.
2. Christian beliefs are integrated with behavior, extending Israel's moral tradition from the Ten Commandments to root human community in the love of God and neighbor.
3. Christian beliefs are integrated with belonging as well as behavior, reforming Israel's spiritual tradition to inaugurate a community of grace among Jesus's followers, as epitomized in the Sermon on the Mount and especially the Lord's Prayer.
4. Christian orthodoxy teaches that the one true God is triune, existing in three persons—Father, Son, and Holy Spirit—who are undivided in the external works that reveal the divine identity.
5. From creation to consummation, providence reveals the Triune God's perfections of power, wisdom, love, and holiness; the drama of redemption is the setting in which the Bible addresses the mystery of divine sovereignty and human responsibility along with the meaning of evil.
6. Creation out of nothing is an article of Christian faith according to which the Triune God has spoken the world into existence—granting dignified life, dependent freedom, and delightful fellowship to creatures in their materiality, sociality, and temporality.
7. Human beings are uniquely created to commune with God and to communicate what God is like; for this calling God has made them embodied souls and relational selves, with each person and culture having dignity

rooted in God's love and their diversity being an occasion of divine delight.

8. The orthodox identity of Jesus Christ involves the hypostatic union: in the incarnation the fully divine Son of God has assumed a fully human nature, to serve as the one Mediator of revelation and redemption.

9. Jesus Christ's ministry of reconciliation as the Mediator between God and humanity is signaled by his virginal conception; continues throughout his earthly ministry as messianic prophet, priest, and king; climaxes in his atoning passion; and commences a newly exalted phase in his resurrection and ascension.

10. All of Adam and Eve's descendants are born dead in sin, which is rooted in idolatry and inevitably results in injustice. The Spirit's application of Jesus's reconciling work brings salvation from sin's past, present, and future effects; justification removes sin's penalty, regeneration removes sin's power, and glorification removes sin's presence from those who are united with Christ.

11. The gospel takes cultural form in Orthodox Christianity, emphasizing a tradition of *theosis*; in Catholic Christianity, emphasizing the sacramental renewal of creaturely being; and in seven major traditions of Protestant Christianity, emphasizing the gospel's freedom for biblical reform.

12. The Holy Spirit is the divine Giver of creaturely life, pouring out common grace, and the divine Giver of new life, applying Christ's redeeming grace as God's empowering presence—fostering conversion, consecration, assurance and perseverance, and shared ministry.

13. The authority of Holy Scripture emerges from God's final Word having been spoken in Jesus Christ; by the Holy Spirit, the written words and message of the prophets and apostles faithfully proclaim divine truth and powerfully rule over the church—even, with appropriate nuance, through various translations and the process of interpretation.

14. The Bible identifies the church as God's people in Christ; the Spirit graciously uses various practices for shaping the church as a community of worship, nurture, and witness; along with Word and "sacrament," institutional order marks the church, yet traditional models of polity require wise modern implementation and humble acknowledgment of communal brokenness.

15. The vital Christian hope that God will make all things new has both cosmic and personal dimensions: cosmically, involving the return and

reign of Christ as anticipated in biblical prophecy; personally, involving resurrection of the body and final judgment. This hope is already inaugurated but not yet completely fulfilled, thus serving as an impetus for mission and an incentive for martyrdom in whatever form becomes necessary.

Introduction

E vangelical theology" announces a primary theme: the gospel. This good news of the Triune God's love for sinners and redemption of the whole creation is the heart of the Bible's story. This drama has its climax in the self-giving life of Jesus Christ and the empowering presence of the Holy Spirit. Usually we hear this gospel from those who already believe. By whatever means, though, the good news evokes faith in Christ as a person cries out for salvation (Rom. 10:9–17). In this saving announcement—a Word that God literally speaks in person—we encounter the *Logos (note that glossary terms are marked with an asterisk), which holds together all creation (John 1:1–18; Col. 1:15–20). The Spirit prompts us to express our faith by seeking theological understanding, wanting to know more fully the God who first loves us.

Introducing Evangelical *Theology*

Christian theology has a trinitarian and narrative structure. The drama of redemption involves four glorious unions: the Trinity—one God in three persons; the incarnation—the two natures of divinity and humanity in the one Son of God; the atonement—reconciliation between sinners and God; and the covenant—the communion of the saints with God.[1]

This trinitarian, narrative structure is reflected in the present book, which follows the Niceno-Constantinopolitan Creed (the *Nicene Creed for short)— the most widely embraced consensus, or *ecumenical, expression of Christian faith. The Nicene Creed's original form stems from the Council of Nicaea

---

1. I learned this framework from Scott Swain.

(AD 325), when the church first insisted on the full divinity of Jesus Christ in opposition to the "Arian" heresy. This creed's present form dates to the Council of Constantinople (AD 381). There, after much intervening struggle, the church reiterated the Son's full deity and more adequately acknowledged the Holy Spirit. Matching this creed's three *articles, or sections, the present book has a trinitarian and narrative structure: first, especially in the person of the Father, the Almighty Lord, God creates and rules; second, especially in the person of the Son, the Logos, God is personally present to redeem; and third, especially in the person of the Holy Spirit, the Life Giver, God pours out the love that brings creation toward its consummation.

In sections 2, 3, and 4 the present book explores these three creedal articles. The first section introduces a classic pattern of *catechesis—basic teaching of the faith. Given its first element, the Creed, chapter 1 introduces "theology" as faith seeking understanding. A *creed is an ordered account of fundamental *beliefs* that intersect with personal *behavior* and communal *belonging*.[2] *Credo* says, "I believe . . . ," within a chorus of voices joined across time and place. "I" commit to seek shared understanding of these beliefs with others who have heard God's good news in Jesus Christ. Hence most of the present book explores creedal beliefs in detail.

Belonging to communities identified with these beliefs, we seek to embody them in our behavior. Not only do personal identities and congregational liturgies bear witness to these beliefs; church life also sustains us in confessing them. Mere "knowledge" of God easily withers into practical atheism or warps into hypocrisy and arrogance. When Psalms 14 and 53 depict fools saying in their hearts that there is no God, they do not portray pagans; rather, some among God's people live as if God were not real. It is possible to have knowledge that only puffs up (1 Cor. 8:1) without acting in love (James 4:17). Therefore, the church catechizes and, as necessary, disciplines believers in order to nurture genuine and growing faith.

Accordingly, chapters 2 and 3 introduce two other elements of classic catechesis. First, the Ten Commandments focus on moral formation, tethering the church to God's way of addressing all creation through the people of Israel. The Ten Commandments resonate with many cultures, yet they keep Christian moral theology attached to God's self-revelation within the Old Testament.[3]

---

2. This rhetorical triad appears in Bass, *Christianity after Religion*, but previously and more importantly in Kreider, *Change of Conversion*.

3. An informal study (Brannan, "Writing a Systematic Theology") recently drew attention to how infrequently systematic theologies cite Old Testament texts. Indeed, the dominance of Pauline texts and minimal exposition of biblical foundations for monotheism and ethics can be problematic. Yet Old Testament foundations undergird Christian doctrine just as they do

Second, the Lord's Prayer focuses on spiritual formation, incorporating us within Jesus's ultimate renewal of Israel and unique knowledge of God as Father. The Sermon on the Mount, the wider context of the Lord's Prayer, resonates with the Ten Commandments yet intensifies their Godward focus. The Sermon on the Mount goes beyond outlining moral formation for any and every community to highlight spiritual formation in the church.

The God of Israel, honored in the Ten Commandments, is the same God revealed in Jesus Christ, honored in the Lord's Prayer. The Creed teaches the identity of that Triune God, revealed in a unified story of creation and redemption. These three elements of catechesis integrate belief, behavior, and belonging by unfolding the unity of the old covenant, the Christ-event, and the new covenant—the anticipation, unveiling, and aftermath of Jesus as the center of creation's history. The present book introduces these key biblical texts early and extensively, thus integrating theological ethics and spiritual theology with its exposition of Christian doctrine.

Introducing *Evangelical* Theology

The present book is an evangelical introduction, not a creative interpretation. More advanced than some textbooks yet shorter than others, this introduction explains as many important concepts and evangelical debates as possible. Therefore, despite inevitable overlap, this introduction has a different focus than those of other excellent texts. In particular, this book does not focus primarily on the practices embedded in Christian doctrine, on the biblical theology undergirding it, on a particular tradition, or on the most basic and inclusive account. Each of those approaches already has worthy champions. The focus here is on introducing a theological vocabulary and grammar that will help students to embrace an ecumenically orthodox and evangelical heritage.

This theological heritage is "evangelical" in two senses. First, the present book prioritizes *the gospel* as expressed via the Creed, the Ten Commandments, and the Lord's Prayer. Obviously, no book should claim too much in this regard. Yet the size and focus of many theologies can diminish the centrality or the scope of the biblical gospel. This introduction presents creation as foundational, and new creation as climactic, for the drama of redemption, which centers on God's mighty act in Jesus Christ. Ecumenical Christian orthodoxy, as expressed in the Creed, shares faith in the Triune God of that

---

the New Testament, and recovering classic catechesis helps to make these foundations visible. Furthermore, it is one-sided to evaluate the biblical dimensions of a systematic theology merely by counting citations.

gospel drama. The present book celebrates and communicates this shared faith that is heralded in the Scriptures.

Second, the present book prioritizes *a specific Protestant theological culture*, even if debates about that "evangelical" identity seem interminable. Evangelical "theology" is not much easier to identify than "evangelicalism"; popular practice can be broadly theological even when it is not academically disciplined. Yet although evangelical theology is an essentially contested concept, it remains functionally essential.[4] Accepting both the promise and pitfalls of evangelicalism—that is, orthodox, pietist Protestant ecumenism—the present book must be selective about what to engage, and willing to generalize. Characterizations of evangelical theology—for instance, regarding quantity ("some"; "many"; "most"), time ("traditionally"; "today"), and membership (characterizing scholarly versus popular differences; including Pentecostals but excluding nontrinitarian groups)—inevitably reflect my background, commitments, interests, and social location, even in ways that I cannot see. Reviewers will debate these judgment calls, and readers must be discerning about them. I sincerely hope that most people will notice my effort to describe others as neutrally or even generously as possible, even where we disagree. In any case, the present book does not speak to evangelicals alone, nor does it speak for all "evangelicals," as if anyone could!

David Bebbington influentially characterizes *evangelicalism as activist, biblicist, conversionist, and crucicentrist Christianity. This fourfold characterization remains helpful, once the ensuing network is located historically in the Anglo-American revivals of the 1730s.[5] Further characterizing evangelicalism is emphasis upon the Holy Spirit, along with the breadth of contemporary networks associated with those earlier revivals.[6] How to label precursors among post-Reformation, Continental European pietists remains debatable.[7] The crucial issue involves whether evangelicalism requires intentionally transdenominational activity (in which case the earlier pietists might not qualify) or merely renewal efforts (such as the pietists opposing dead orthodoxy or heresy within existing churches).[8] Solving that historical debate

---

4. Abraham, "Church and Churches," 303.

5. Bebbington, *Evangelicalism in Modern Britain*, 2–17.

6. Larsen, "Defining and Locating Evangelicalism."

7. See the profile of W. R. Ward by Noll and Hindmarsh, "Rewriting the History of Evangelicalism," 8.

8. John G. Stackhouse Jr. emphasizes transdenominational cooperation (see "Generic Evangelicalism"). Bebbington responds that this additional factor fails to account for contradictory historical evidence such as Church-of-England-only evangelicals ("About the Definition of Evangelicalism," 5). Part of the difference apparently lies in speaking of "evangelical" as a primary identity (attachment to an institutional or cultural network) versus a secondary theological

is beyond the purposes of this introduction; so are contemporary sociological and theological debates about precise evangelical boundaries. Moreover, some Catholic and Orthodox Christians, not to mention still others, share "evangelical" characteristics without claiming a "Protestant" identity. Despite such complications, it remains possible to characterize an "evangelical" theological subculture.[9]

In that light, the present book introduces both shared commitments and perennial debates within evangelical theology.[10] Evangelicals tend to do theology using primarily the language of the Bible, which can be both helpful and harmful. The obvious help lies in making theology accessible for all of God's people who read the Scriptures. Hence this introduction frequently references biblical texts and periodically discusses them at length. The potential harm of evangelical biblicism lies in tempting us with false expectations of theological clarity or naive understandings of the Bible's sufficiency. Excessive biblicism falls into *proof-texting—appealing to Scripture passages in support of a theological claim without adequately addressing their contexts. Hence this introduction tries to avoid that pitfall by citing fewer biblical references in parentheses, focusing instead on key texts with awareness of their context. Still, the need to represent how evangelicals have supported theological claims from Scripture requires periodically providing parenthetical references.

The present book presents longer-standing evangelical consensus and debates rather than referencing every current issue or trend. The *Evangelical Dictionary of Theology* (*EDT*), for which I spent several years producing a new edition, provides a helpful companion to supplement the glossary included here.[11] The *EDT* offers short, readable overviews on numerous subjects, as well as recommendations for further reading. Resources like the *EDT* remind us to keep current evangelical flaws and fragmentation in perspective. For several decades, faithful teachers have provided basic, biblical, evangelical theology to help pastors and laypersons bear gospel witness in the modern world. Similarly, the Lausanne movement has called

---

descriptor (an approach taken within a denominational framework). For instance, some in the Church of England may be evangelical in the latter sense without attaching themselves to the evangelical subculture in the former sense.

9. Alasdair MacIntyre's account of traditions (MacIntyre, *After Virtue*, 186–87)—as socially embodied arguments, extended over time, about the meaning of foundational texts—is useful here. Even if disagreement itself characterizes evangelical theology, such disagreements may have a coherent shape, stemming from an underlying "imagination" or set of commitments and concerns. On that score, see Worthen, *Apostles of Reason*.

10. For my own accounts, see briefly Treier, "Evangelical Theology"; more fully Vanhoozer and Treier, *Theology and the Mirror of Scripture*.

11. Treier and Elwell, *Evangelical Dictionary of Theology*.

evangelicals to global awareness and holistic mission rooted in the love of the Triune God.[12] Although ongoing reform is necessary in practice, I continue to embrace in principle the "evangelical" project: orthodox, pietist, Protestant ecumenism.

At this point the present book may be controversial for introducing evangelical theology in terms of classic catechesis and especially the Creed. Yet the creedal structure does not privilege orthodoxy over pietism. First, whether or not they are noncreedal, pietist evangelicals generally embrace trinitarian faith. Second, the Creed does not compete with Scripture's final authority but rather helps to communicate its teaching. Third, some pietist theologians have been leaders in calling evangelicals to recover their trinitarian heritage.[13] Fourth, some forms of Protestant orthodoxy do not prioritize the ecumenical creeds any more than pietism. Fifth, the present book's catechetical approach both champions a heritage and calls for reform—as evangelical theologies naturally do. The heritage championed here integrates ecumenical orthodoxy and evangelical piety. The reform called for integrates a trinitarian presentation of the gospel and a biblical foundation for piety—rooted in teaching the Ten Commandments and the Lord's Prayer alongside the Creed.

To draw these reflections together, I offer ten summary theses and brief representative readings that attempt to put evangelical theology in historical perspective.

1. *Introduction.* Evangelical theology faces increasing perceptions of fragmentation. In what sense are these perceptions an opportunity for reform and renewal, and in what sense are they a dangerous form of self-fulfilling prophecy?[14]

2. *Pietism.* Evangelical theology arises from, and seeks to guide, Protestant movements of personal renewal. These renewal movements pursue spiritual affinities across various churchly boundaries.[15]

3. *Puritanism.* Evangelical theology arises from, and seeks to guide, Protestant movements of ecclesial renewal. These renewal movements pur-

12. Most recently, see *Cape Town Commitment.* Its theme is Love. Part 1 is "For the Lord We Love: The Cape Town Confession of Faith" while part 2 is "For the World We Serve: The Cape Town Call to Action."
13. E.g., Grenz, *Rediscovering the Triune God.*
14. In the summer of 2015 I taught a ten-day course on evangelical theology at Regent College in Vancouver, for which I prepared these thesis statements and selected these readings. I learned much from the interaction. The issues raised by this introductory question are addressed further in Vanhoozer and Treier, *Theology and the Mirror of Scripture.*
15. E.g., Wesley, "Christian Perfection."

sue corrective actions that generate and perpetuate various churchly boundaries.[16]

4. *Protestant orthodoxy.* Some strands of evangelical theology focus on Protestant doctrinal renewal. These theological strands find it most important for evangelicals to perpetuate the material commitments of the Reformation regarding justification by faith alone and the formal commitments of the Reformation regarding Scripture alone as the final authority over faith and practice. In the process, these theological strands have been most successful at fostering academic biblical interpretation and formal doctrinal systems.[17]

5. *Revivalism.* Other strands of evangelical theology focus on promoting evangelism and Protestant spiritual revival. These revivalist strands find it most important for evangelicals to pursue the salvation of the lost and the holiness of the saved. In the process, these revivalist strands have been most successful at fostering practical mission and ministries of social justice, as well as leadership opportunities for women and other marginalized groups.[18]

6. *Fundamentalism and "neo"-evangelicalism.* Modern American evangelical theology emerges from "fundamentalist" institutional retrenchment. These "neo"-evangelicals generally retained the doctrinal commitments of *The Fundamentals* but slowly shed cultural isolation in favor of societal reengagement.[19]

7. *"Postconservative" evangelical theology?* Later modern Anglo-American evangelical theology, having generally and slowly shed cultural isolation in favor of societal reengagement, has become increasingly divided over which "culture" to prioritize—"modern" or "postmodern"—and how such philosophical strands helpfully reform or dangerously put at risk evangelical identity.[20]

8. *Evangelicalism goes "glocal"?* Contemporary evangelical theology is more diverse than ever, due to globalization and immigration along with awareness of particularity. Though still slow to acknowledge and celebrate this diversity, evangelicals are beginning to recognize and wrestle with the opportunities and challenges that it presents. Some of today's

16. E.g., Edwards, "Treatise Concerning Religious Affections."

17. E.g., Warfield, "Idea of Systematic Theology."

18. E.g., Finney, "Lectures on Revivals"; Palmer, "Way of Holiness."

19. E.g., Henry, "Evaporation of Fundamentalist Humanitarianism"; Henry, "Method and Criteria of Theology."

20. E.g., Grenz, "Evangelical Theological Method"; in contrast with Carson, "Domesticating the Gospel."

leading evangelical theologians themselves embody this increasing variety of backgrounds and perspectives.[21]

9. *Evangelicalism and the "Great Tradition"?* At the same time that contemporary evangelical theology diversifies with respect to place and background, it is also increasingly diverse with respect to time. Many evangelicals have increasing interest in the liturgical and spiritual practices of the "Great Christian Tradition"; among these evangelicals, some are increasingly committed to this classic tradition's surrounding theological heritage—the creeds and possible dogmatic consensus surrounding them. Yet still other evangelicals are critical of particular doctrines or practices from the classic tradition, making "*sola scriptura*" and "the church is always reforming" their rallying cries.[22]

10. *Conclusion.* As complex and essentially contested as evangelical theology is, the adjective "evangelical" and the noun "evangelicalism" still do cognitive work. The noun designates an ongoing movement or network of institutions, and the adjective can be used not only to describe what that movement's theology is but also to propose what it should aspire to be—theology that accords with and focuses on the biblical gospel of Jesus Christ.[23]

Through evangelical sisters and brothers—often through our differences—I have learned more living and active, locally diverse, globally connected, ecumenically creedal, deeply biblical, and therefore dramatically trinitarian, theology. May God use this book to edify the church with such teaching (Eph. 4:11–16).

---

21. E.g., Chan, "Preface," "Methodological Questions," and "Epilogue," in *Grassroots Asian Theology*, 7–46, 203–4; also Yong, "Preface," "Prologue," "Evangelicalism and Global Theology," "Legacy of Evangelical Theology," "Toward a Global Evangelical Theology," and "Epilogue," in *Future of Evangelical Theology*, 11–13, 17–66, 98–124, 217–49.

22. E.g., McDermott, "Emerging Divide in Evangelical Theology"; in contrast with Roger E. Olson's response in Olson, "My Response."

23. E.g., Noll, "What Is 'Evangelical'?"; Vanhoozer, "Scripture and Hermeneutics"; Abraham, "Church and Churches."

PART 1

Knowing
THE TRIUNE GOD

— 1 —

The Creed

Faith Seeking Understanding

THESIS

Christian theology is a communicative practice of faith seeking understanding, in response to the Word of the Triune God accompanied by the Holy Spirit.

LEARNING OBJECTIVES

After learning the material in the introduction and this chapter, you should be able to:

1. *Define briefly* the key terms introduced here (marked with an asterisk and included in the glossary).
2. *List and recognize* the following: (a) David Bebbington's four characteristics of evangelicalism; (b) two elements of Christian faith; (c) four theological contexts.
3. *Describe and compare* the following: (a) four basic views of general revelation; (b) four periods' approaches to special revelation.
4. *Identify and illustrate* the relationships and distinctions between the following: (a) four sources for theology; (b) five theological disciplines.
5. *Explain* the following: (a) the contrast between Christian and modern views of faith and reason; (b) the complexity of selecting relevant biblical texts and synthesizing their theological implications for contemporary questions; (c) the holistic nature of theology as faith seeking understanding.

The Letter to the Romans offers Exhibit A of this chapter's theme: Christian theology is faith seeking understanding. Romans provides the Bible's most orderly account of the gospel. Yet the letter remains pastoral, not a modern "systematic" theology. Paul presents his gospel in an effort to reconcile Jewish and gentile Christians while gaining support for missionary travels to Spain. The "Romans Road" of chapters 1–8 heads toward chapters 9–11 as the gateway to its practical destination in chapters 12–16. Prompted by faith, pursuing pastoral encouragement (Rom. 1:12), Paul provides theological understanding.

Paul's Romans road is paved by Isaiah, which, along with Deuteronomy and Psalms, preoccupies New Testament citations of the Old Testament. Isaiah advances the biblical gospel: looking back to the grandeur of creation and the tragedy of the fall, as embodied in Israel; looking forward to a new creation, another redeeming exodus. Through God's ultimate Servant the redemption of Israel, God's unfaithful servant, would fully reveal the identity of *Yhwh—the Sovereign Creator who formed a saving covenant with Israel, and before whom every knee will finally bow.[1] Romans echoes Isaiah when Paul says he is not "ashamed" of the gospel (Rom. 1:16; e.g., Isa. 54:3–5), which reveals God's righteousness promoting faith (Rom. 1:17).

In the background is the story of Ahaz, an unfaithful descendant of King David who refused to believe that God would defend Judah. Instead, Ahaz made a disobedient foreign alliance. As a sign of God's judgment over Ahaz and Israel's eventual deliverance, Isaiah 7:14 announced a special child: "Immanuel," God with us. Prior to that announcement, God told Ahaz, "If you will not believe, surely you will not be established," or, as Augustine (354–430) read in Latin, "Unless you believe, you shall not understand" (Isa. 7:9).[2] Christian theology as "faith seeking understanding" echoes the story of Ahaz's downfall and the Christ-centered hope that followed. Ahaz was not established in God's blessing because he did not trust God's promise. Refusing to hear God, he was misled by apparent signs of his time. By contrast, faith is the impetus behind all Christian theology: trusting God's Word enough to seek fuller understanding of its perennial meaning and present significance. Without exercising faith, we cannot rightly hear the

---

1. Yhwh, often translated as "the Lord" and pronounced as "Yahweh," is the personal name with which the covenant people were invited to address God (as narrated beginning in Exod. 3:14). Gradually, out of reverence, Israel began to leave this name unspoken or else to pronounce it with different vowels. Here, with a Christian understanding of divine self-revelation on the one hand, and respect for the Jewish people on the other, the word appears without the vowels being printed.

Another introductory note about speaking of God: The present book uses "masculine" English pronouns for God when necessary. The divine essence is spiritual, with no body and therefore no biological sex. The divine essence also transcends human, culturally constructed, gender. Nevertheless, given "Father" and "Son" proper naming in the Trinity, the use of grammatically masculine pronouns seems to be the most biblical approach, even if we must remember not to project cultural notions of masculinity onto God.

2. Augustine, "Tractate 29.6," 184.

Word by which to know God; without seeking understanding, like Ahaz we twist Scripture to line up with whatever delusional "faith" we have in the world or ourselves.

The present chapter examines more carefully the shape of Christian belief—what it means for faith to seek theological understanding. This chapter addresses *prolegomena: the first words with which theology indicates how it will proceed from faith toward understanding. In *faith* we hear God's speech; in *seeking* we prayerfully contemplate the sources of this divine revelation; in pursuit of *understanding* we practice theological disciplines.

Faith: Hearing God's Speech

Faith comes by hearing (Rom. 10:17)—hearing divine revelation, its "theological counterpart."[3] In Scripture, hearing and obeying overlap enough that hearing is a metaphor for obedience. Beyond bare listening, biblical hearing begins the journey of trusting and obeying God. By modern times, however, "revelation" became a source of knowledge in the philosophical sense—one alternative among others, such as reason or observation. Soon revelation seemed like a doubtful source when compared to what people could see and what science could produce. God, humans, and the natural world became competitors in a winner-take-all contest: rather than hearing God speak through creaturely realities, many "Western" people came to think that revelation threatens their integrity, reducing them to puppets. Revelation appeared rational only if it lost its specifically Christian God and pointed to generic "religious" experience.[4] Reason became a universal human project, claiming to be as neutral as possible. By proclaiming divine intervention in history, today Christian faith may seem irrational.

Personal Knowledge

Yet Christian *faith is "firm and certain knowledge of God's benevolence toward us."[5] Faith is a personal form of knowledge: knowledge, because God's

---

3. Webster, "Criticism," 2.

4. "Modern" and "Western" are complex terms. "Western" frequently means "Northern" in contrast to the "Majority World" (previously the "Two-Thirds" or "developing" world) and the "Global South" Christianity rapidly growing today. As those regions "modernize"—both by choice and by "globalization"—*modernity and *Western culture do not overlap completely. Yet in its early history, modernity involved Western figures and nations thinking that they reached a fundamentally new stage of civilization ("modern" means "new"), which they would spread throughout the world.

5. Calvin, *Institutes* 3.2.7 (1:551).

benevolence has a meaningful history; personal, because we apprehend God's benevolence toward us.[6] Hence Christian faith involves both the public truth of God's speech—"the faith"—and the personal response of trust and loyalty.[7] Faith as *trust* relates the future to the past: biblical faith anticipates, based on a history of faithfulness, the fulfillment of God's gracious promises (Heb. 11:1, 6). Faith as *loyalty* relates the past and future to the present: biblical faith responds to God's self-communication over time, expressing itself in obedient love (Rom. 1:5; Gal. 5:6; James 2).

Accordingly, faith involves the whole person—intellect (belief), affections (confidence), and will (trusting loyalty). Its characteristic posture is prayer, calling on the Lord's name (Rom. 10:9–13). Such prayer is trinitarian: the Spirit prompts believers to call on God as Father with confidence that in Jesus Christ they are beloved children (Rom. 8:14–17). Genuine prayer includes being broken over sin and seeking the *shalom—peaceful flourishing—of all creation. In calling for repentance, the Old Testament prophets establish the proper connection between faith and love: good works are an expression of faith, not a condition of God's favor, yet genuine faith includes grief over sin. Persisting in idolatry and injustice eventually raises this question: Are such "believers" really calling on the Lord with trust and loyalty?

Faith seeks understanding because believers await the unseen fulfillment of God's promises. Tensions inevitably arise between faith and modern reasoning, which operates by sight. Believers cannot avoid dealing with the way the world currently runs, since divine revelation addresses all the relationships defining our lives—not only communion with God but also harmony with other humans and the rest of creation. Thus, Christian theology cannot give up the connection between divine revelation and human reason, as if God communicates only inner experiences or ideas with no implications for the rest of life. Yet God's self-communication involves particular actions in creation and salvation, beyond what human reason could figure out on its own.

---

6. Eric Springsted, in his preface to *The Act of Faith*, tells of surveying students and discovering that "the vast majority thought faith was 'believing something without proof'" (ix). They remained unable to grasp the concept of trust: instead, "Faith was a 'personal' choice (albeit in a shallow sense of 'personal'). . . . The idea of faith as knowledge gained by interpersonal dealings, or as a matter of being linked to a tradition, a history, or a community, didn't make sense because traditions, history, and communities didn't make sense at any deep level" (x). Springsted notes that "in the modern world Mark Twain could get a laugh by claiming in the mouth of a schoolboy that 'faith is believing what you know ain't true'" (6). While a medieval person "would not have gotten the joke" (6), modern philosophy of religion implied that faith could be rational only if we provide grounds for God's existence and evidence for revelation (11).

7. The technical terms are *fides qua*, the "subjective" faith we exercise, and *fides quae*, the "objective" faith we embrace. See further Treier, "Faith."

Because seeing is not yet fully believing, to know the True Way of Life we must listen to God's Word, led by God's Spirit.

Tensions between faith and modern reason tempt theologians to treat "prolegomena" as nontheological words spoken *before* beginning to do theology. Sometimes "apologetics" among Protestants and "fundamental theology" among Catholics become nontheological prolegomena. These approaches try to demonstrate theology's intellectual credibility according to external methods and standards. Instead, truly Christian theology begins by faith and seeks to understand the gospel's distinctive logic and divine mystery. Prolegomena must be the first theological words *in* doing theology. *Theological* prolegomena seek initial clarity about the proper response of rational creatures to divine revelation. Prolegomena articulate what conditions enable, and which criteria settle, Christian teaching. These prolegomena already introduce the Triune God's perfect character and gracious action. God's actions in creation and redemption speak volumes; God's words are living and active.

Divine Self-Disclosure

*Revelation is God's self-disclosure—communication to establish communion with us. Revelation is "the eloquence of divine action."[8] This eloquence echoes at various times and places from creation until the completion of redemption. God has spoken to everyone in some ways, and to particular people in special ways, which Scripture records to share with others. Hence divine revelation goes beyond the eloquence of all divine activity; as the Creed claims in its third article, God the Holy Spirit has spoken specifically "through the prophets." This book does not fully address the revelatory authority of Scripture until a later chapter, when it returns to the Holy Spirit's work in detail. For now, *communicative action offers a helpful concept for integrating revelation with the rest of God's activity: God's speech actively establishes covenant relationship with us, while this saving activity communicates what God is like. Hearing the good news of God's mighty grace is at the heart of understanding divine self-revelation.

This revelation addresses two barriers to knowing God: finitude and fallenness. *Finitude means that human beings have inherent limits that render us incapable of knowing the Infinite God on our own. The Creator graciously condescends to speak with us. God condescended initially by creating us with capacities for fellowship, as bearers of the divine image. Now, having fallen, humans have rendered themselves incapable of truly knowing and

8. Webster, "Criticism," 3.

representing the Creator. Although God eloquently condescends, we refuse to listen and fail to understand. Hence the fullness of God's self-disclosure involves our salvation. The Holy Spirit helps us to hear God's Word in Jesus Christ, interrupting our self-destruction and interpreting God's work on our behalf.

Seeking: Contemplating God's Revelation

Human finitude and fallenness partially correspond to the widespread distinction between "general" and "special" divine revelation. So-called *general revelation focuses on God's self-disclosure in the gracious activity of creating and providentially sustaining the cosmos. Created to bear God's image, humans have a calling to represent God in the world. This calling opens us to divine self-communication and obligates us to obey divine commands. *Special revelation addresses our need to know God as Redeemer, not just Creator, through the Spirit's ministry of the Word at particular times and places. For humans have failed to hear God's speech in faith and to represent God in loving obedience. After the fall, God must not only unveil the divine character but also remove the veil covering our eyes. Sinful humans often seek to fill a God-shaped void in their hearts, but they stumble around blindly until the Light of the world shines upon them.

"General" Revelation in Creation

The physical world, the cycles and flow of history, personal conscience, cultural expression, social orders—traditionally understood, these may somehow be vehicles of general revelation. But modern debates emerged about how the Christian understanding of God should specifically relate to broader theism. Thus, current approaches to general revelation reflect four basic tendencies.

FOUR BASIC VIEWS

A first, *Catholic*, view broadly characterizes the church's pre-Reformation history. Fundamentally, this Catholic approach affirms that general revelation provides some nonsaving, natural knowledge of God. Humans may attain knowledge of God from creation, even developing a modest yet public *natural theology—not just experiential but conceptual knowledge of God. This modest knowledge is not enough for salvation, but it can prepare someone to seek salvation. In the "Thomistic" version from Thomas Aquinas (1225–74), this knowledge involves the existence of an all-powerful, perfect, First

Cause; human immortality; our resulting moral obligation; and the like. We can know and speak of this First Cause because of the *analogia entis* or "analogy of being." The gift of existence includes participation, as creatures, in the Creator's perfections. Such participation enables human language to communicate about God by analogy—with modest similarities and greater dissimilarities—between ourselves and the One whose image we bear. Strictly speaking, Thomas's so-called five ways of proving God's existence were not philosophical proofs, since they built upon some theistic assumptions of the time. Nevertheless, the Catholic tendency is to connect theology with philosophical commitments based on the doctrine of creation.

A second, *classic Protestant*, view stems from the Reformers. Fundamentally, this classic Protestant approach affirms that general revelation establishes accountability before God and encourages study of creation. Unbelievers suppress the knowledge of God that general revelation makes available, while believers may encounter truth about God in creation that is confirmed by Scripture. This modest knowledge is not enough for salvation or even for natural theology, at least publicly in the Catholic sense, because of human idolatry; general revelation does not even prepare anyone for salvation apart from special divine grace. Reformer John Calvin (1509–64) made the knowledge of God as Creator and Redeemer his starting point for Christian instruction.[9] Calvin interpreted Romans 1:18–31 as teaching the revelation of God as Creator; objectively, creation with its resulting history is the theater of God's glory. Subjectively, every human has a *sensus divinitatis*, a seed planted in the heart that should grow into faith. In Augustine's famous words, "Our heart is restless until it rests in you [God]."[10] Yet Calvin quickly emphasized that fallen humans suppress any general knowledge of God (Rom. 1:18–20). The classic Protestant tendency is to emphasize that humans distort what God has made plain.

A third, *Deist*, view emerged from early modern rationalism. Fundamentally, this Deist approach affirms that human *religion—devotion to something sacred beyond oneself, typically involving shared rituals—is accountable to natural reason. Knowledge of God from creation is possible, but such "revelation" does not involve particular divine self-communication; the Creator does not intervene in history. In one sense, this natural knowledge of God is not modest but as exhaustive as possible. In another sense, though, natural theology must be fairly minimal to be universally accessible. Rationally governed experience provides whatever religion is necessary, if

9. Note the structure of Calvin's *Institutes*: book 1 follows Rom. 1 at key points.
10. Augustine, *Confessions* 1.1.1 (p. 3).

any, for moral living; "salvation" in the traditional Christian sense is not at stake, because promoting the social good lies at the heart of God's kingdom. Even if Jesus is special, as deistic "liberal" theologies have taught, he basically manifests a general truth about God's love or a human example to follow. Religious experience is privately suitable within public norms for what is reasonable. A Deist approach might seem implausible today, since early modern rationalism lies in the rearview mirror and globalization surrounds us with cultural relativism. Yet this tendency lingers in the "moralistic therapeutic deism" of some Western cultures, and in aspects of theological liberalism.[11]

A fourth, *Barthian*, view is the opposite of Deism. Fundamentally, this Barthian approach denies the category of general revelation. Creation offers no actual knowledge of God apart from salvation; any natural theology would simply be idolatry. Believing exploration of creation does not depend on its potential to reveal God, and human "religion" is a declaration of independence from God's self-revelation in Jesus Christ. Germany's liberal "cultural Protestantism" supported World War I and later the Nazi regime in World War II. In that context, Karl Barth (1886–1968) radicalized Calvin's approach to Romans 1. Because human religion is idolatrous (here Barth follows Calvin), it can only mislead, to such an extent that "revelation" is only special (here Barth goes farther than Calvin). Barth famously responded "Nein!" (No!) when Emil Brunner (1889–1966) attempted to maintain a cultural "point of contact" for the gospel, rooted in humans being created as God's image-bearers. Although Barth insisted on the uniqueness of divine revelation, eventually he acknowledged the possibility of learning from non-Christian beliefs and practices. But these secular "parables"[12] offer only indirect parallels to God's Word in Jesus Christ; they do not count as revelation.

EVANGELICAL QUESTIONS

Obviously, evangelical theology rejects the deistic tendency to separate the knowledge of God from the gospel of Jesus Christ. Generally, despite growing diversity, evangelical theology follows the classic Protestant tendency to maintain the category of general revelation. Some—especially those who emphasize human freedom—take this category in a Catholic direction, while others now lean in a Barthian direction. For philosophical or missional reasons, many affirm that God uses elements of every culture as preparation

11. As chronicled by C. Smith and Denton in *Soul Searching*.
12. An aspect of Barth's approach to public engagement in *CD* IV.3.1, esp. 112–13.

for the gospel. A classic Protestant perspective, however, distinguishes such cultural presence from religious preparation for personal salvation. Several key questions further shape evangelical approaches.

Of course, the first question concerns *the teaching of Scripture* itself. Romans 1:18–32 is a crucial text, but theology must address its larger biblical context. What does it mean to say that the heavens declare God's glory (Ps. 19), that God sends rain on the just and the unjust (Matt. 5:45; Acts 14:16–18), that pagans somehow connect in their ignorant worship with the true God (Acts 17:22–31)? On whose hearts is God's law written: just believers' or also pagans' (Rom. 2:12–16)?

A second question concerns *the nature of revelation*. The more "personal" revelation is, emphasizing the event of God's self-disclosure (as in Barth's definition), the less general revelation will be affirmed. The more "propositional" revelation is, emphasizing the content of God's self-disclosure (as in classic Catholic and Protestant definitions), the more general revelation will be affirmed. The personal definition emphasizes the successful reception of revelation; divine self-communication establishes *communion* if "revelation" happens at all. The propositional definition emphasizes the presentation of *propositions, namely, truth claims; divine self-communication establishes *cognitive contact*, which counts as "revelation" whether humans receive or resist the truth.

A third question concerns *the implications for *apologetics*, the defense of Christian faith. Early "apologists" like Justin Martyr (c. 100–165) appealed to the Logos as theological justification for engaging Greco-Roman culture, in particular philosophy. Naysayers like Tertullian (160–220)—employing the rhetoric of his day—offered this pungent rejoinder: "What has Jerusalem to do with Athens?" Later Thomas Aquinas attempted to reconcile Augustine's cautious appropriation of Greco-Roman culture with an emerging renaissance of Aristotle's thought. While that medieval synthesis shaped the dominant Catholic tendency, the Deist tendency triumphed once modern plausibility structures—especially science—became dominant. Nowadays the Western intellectual drift toward atheism, combined with religious variety across global cultures, challenges the enterprise of natural theology.

Protestant approaches to apologetics vary despite affirming general revelation. "Liberal" theologies have frequently reflected Deist sympathies. They have even defined themselves by apologetically correlating core doctrines with modern emphases such as human freedom. Among non-Calvinist evangelicals, some "rationalists" have promoted Christian faith based on technical philosophical arguments, while "evidentialists" have appealed to an even wider array of evidence. Some Calvinist evangelicals have also pursued those rational strategies. Others, "presuppositionalists," have emphasized that all non-Christian starting points reflect holistic opposition toward God. In that case, apologetic activity focuses defensively on answering objections to Christian faith and highlighting the problems with unbelieving alternatives. Somewhat like Barth, who denied general revelation, a presuppositional approach champions proclaiming God's authoritative Word rather than responding to human reason. Now that postmodernity complicates appeals to reason, these three evangelical categories of apologetics are increasingly giving way to more person- and situation-specific approaches.

A fourth question concerns the relation between general revelation and *nontheological realms of study*. Evangelical support for liberal arts education often appeals to the maxim "All truth is God's truth." However, general revelation may not be the best way to authorize "integration" of faith and learning. One potential problem is defining "revelation" too broadly: not all truths come from God in the same way or speak about God as directly. If studying biology or sociology depends primarily on general revelation, then several spheres of human knowledge reduce to theological claims in trivial ways. As the ultimate source of all knowledge, the Creator is not one source among others or a gap-filler standing behind other knowledge. A broad definition of revelation may not only foster rivalry with other sources of knowledge but also lose its focus—God. A second potential problem with using general revelation to authorize wider learning is related: narrowing the motivation for nontheological learning. If studying biology or sociology depends primarily on general revelation, then several spheres of human knowledge reduce to the means for serving "spiritual" ends. Truths about physical life or human society seem interesting only for what they indirectly reveal about God's character. God becomes not just a rival source of knowledge but even rival subject matter. Theology then creates the impression that God does not care very much about the created world or its cultural histories. By contrast, special revelation teaches that learning about the creation honors its loving Creator.

The limitations of general revelation signal the final authority of special revelation. In principle, the physical world, providence in history, conscience, and culture say something about our Creator. In practice, however, finite and fallen humans need "special" forms of God's self-disclosure. We need forgiveness in Jesus Christ to restore communion with the Triune God; we need the Holy Spirit's help to embrace the cross as true wisdom rather than clinging to foolish idols (1 Cor. 1:18–2:16). God addresses these needs in special revelation by Word and Spirit.

"Special" Revelation in Redemption

Special revelation meets our need for redemption without nullifying human freedom. The Word and the Spirit make spiritual seeking meaningful, fulfilling our search for divine Light. Once we have encountered the Triune God in Jesus Christ, the Spirit uses the Scriptures to shine further light on our spiritual path (Ps. 19:8; Eph. 1:17–18). The authority of Scripture rests in God's gracious communication of who we are in Christ and what we are becoming by his Spirit. Authority is "the objective correlate of freedom." *Freedom involves "purposive action" in response to various "grounds" of authority that make our actions intelligible to others.[13] So God's authority is not tyrannical power but rather is the gracious environment in which human freedom flourishes. In this environment Christian believers seek to understand God's past faithfulness, future promises, and present claims upon our lives. Theology fosters such understanding by ministering the authority of special revelation.

Most biblical passages associated with "revelation" actually use the vocabulary of divine *speech*.[14] Jesus Christ, the Logos, is God's ultimate way of communicating *himself* to us in history (John 1:1–18; Heb. 1:1–2). Yet not everyone lived in Jesus's earthly context; not everyone who did could encounter him in person; and not everyone who did encountered him in faith. Thus, special revelation, particularly in Scripture, makes God's Word in Jesus Christ simultaneously more widespread and more personal through the Holy Spirit. Divine speech, the theological "norm" of special revelation, is heard and faithfully understood through four theological "sources"—Scripture, tradition, reason, experience—that have a complex history.

Early Christianity. Christian doctrine reflected the final authority of special revelation from the beginning, since Jesus Christ fulfilled the authoritative forms of Old Testament faith: from Torah to prophecy, priesthood, and kingship. The church fathers' basic practices of Scripture reading creatively followed the New Testament writers' reading of the Old Testament. A generation or two after the apostles, "gnostic" heresies set the God of Old Testament Israel in opposition to the One revealed in Jesus Christ—sometimes even dicing up what we know as the New Testament into authoritative and nonauthoritative portions. In response, some of the church fathers appealed to a *regula fidei* or "Rule of Faith" as an authoritative guide to Scripture's unified revelation. The Rule summarized the overall "scope" of the Bible's story, identifying the Creator God of Israel with the Redeemer God revealed in Jesus Christ. The Rule operated informally through verbal summaries

---

13. O'Donovan, *Resurrection and Moral Order*, 122.
14. Cameron, "Revelation, Idea of."

until it became formalized in the Nicene and Apostles' Creeds. Without worrying about technical theories, the Rule upheld Scripture's authority by clarifying its basic contents while acknowledging the necessity of right churchly reading.

The Middle Ages. In the medieval period faith gradually became more distinct from reason. Growing philosophical sophistication distinguished matters of "proof" from personal knowledge that depended directly upon divine revelation. Likewise, Scripture and tradition became more distinct as the rational means and plural results of interpretation intensified. The Bible functioned as the preeminent written tradition, but other written traditions gained authority. Unwritten traditions—such as liturgical practices—gained authority too, along with bishops and church institutions. The split between Eastern and Western Christianity, made official in 1054, emerged from several factors, but the crucial dispute concerned the pope's authority vis-à-vis the creeds. Eventually the Reformation period in the West crystallized disputes over binding tradition, church authority, and Scripture's supremacy.

The Reformation. Traditional Protestants emphasized special revelation by Word and Spirit. Scripture is the final authority (though not the sole source) for theology. The Spirit enables sinful humans to hear God's authoritative Word in faith. Tradition, though not revelatory, could guide Scripture's interpretation. Tradition helped to identify the canonical books of Scripture, based not on the church's determination but on the discovery of what God revealed: the Spirit, not the church, bears the ultimate witness regarding the Word. The Catholic ("Counter") Reformation, associated with the Council of Trent (1545–63), hardened a contrary perspective. Trent formalized a scriptural canon that included not only the Old and New Testaments but also books known as the *Apocrypha, which primarily reflect the interaction of intertestamental "Judaism" with its pagan environment. Trent also appeared to formalize a developing view that scholars call "Tradition II": Tradition as an independent source of revelatory authority alongside Scripture.[15] The Protestant Reformers worried that this view enabled "tradition" to contradict, not just interpret, biblical teaching. Moreover, they worried that this view enabled the church's *magisterium, its teaching office, to replace the complexity and insight of classic tradition with authoritative contemporary interpretations. Vatican Council I (1869–70) intensified that Protestant worry by formalizing *papal infallibility—the belief that the pope cannot err when speaking *ex cathedra*, from his authoritative chair, on matters of faith or practice.

---

15. Placing this label from Oberman ("Quo Vadis?") in a larger theological context is Lane, "Scripture, Tradition and Church."

Modernity. At the dawn of the modern age "Enlightenment" figures opposed church authority and subordinated or rejected revelation in favor of reason.[16] Rationalism (focused on ideas) and empiricism (focused on observation and experience) became competing ways to seek universally available, "scientifically" verifiable knowledge. Enlightenment thinkers hoped to promote social harmony and to reduce warfare provoked by religion; some promoted reason or reduced church authority due to their own sense of Christian commitment. Meanwhile, traditional Protestants developed their *Scripture principle more formally: the Bible is the *inspired,* thereby *canonically written* and *infallible* record and channel of *revelation* so that it is the supreme *authority* for theology.

Like Catholics, traditional Protestants addressed early modern epistemology by championing a view of revelation as *doctrine*—making propositional truth claims—as represented by evangelical Carl F. H. Henry (1913–2003). By contrast, Protestant liberals championed revelation as *experience*—generating religious meaning, symbolically expressed in doctrine—as represented by Friedrich Schleiermacher (1768–1834). The traditional approach risks reducing divine revelation to the static provision of knowledge. The liberal approach risks reducing divine revelation to dynamic experience, reducing theology to the study of "God-talk" that lacks knowledge of God at all.

The twentieth century also saw the rise of revelation as *dialectical presence*—providing events of personal encounter that simultaneously unveil and veil the divine being—as represented by Barth. For the Infinite God to take finite form in Jesus Christ definitively unveiled the divine identity; only in finite form could God be known by humans. Yet any finite form necessarily veils the divine identity, by definition. This view was sometimes labeled *neoorthodoxy, but Barth rejected that label and distanced himself from others to whom it was applied.

Recent theologies of revelation try to integrate these emphases in light of the biblical focus: hearing the divine Word accompanied by the Holy Spirit. The different concepts highlight moments in the biblical narrative of God's self-disclosure: *preservation* of creation as the sphere of religious experience; divine *action* in history, ultimately in Jesus Christ; *inspiration* of Scripture, conveying doctrinal truths; and *illumination* by the Holy Spirit, whether more institutionally (as in traditional Orthodoxy and Catholicism) or dynamically

---

16. For an overview, see Treier, "Scripture and Hermeneutics" (2012). For analysis of how the traditional Scripture principle is tied to salvation history (from those who reject a traditional account), see Farley and Hodgson, "Scripture and Tradition."

(as in Holiness and Pentecostal movements).[17] To some degree these concepts could be complementary. But adherents of some views perceive others to be obscuring the authoritative truth of God's Word. Consequently, special revelation garners further discussion in terms of theology's sources and norms.

Theological Sources

Christian theology rarely theorized about its sources until medieval- and Reformation-era scholasticism emerged. Then modern theologians began to address their sources with *hermeneutics, the study of human understanding, and/or a philosophical *epistemology, a theory of knowledge, ordering their relationships. These academic discussions, though, intersect with different Christian traditions' approaches to authority.

SCRIPTURE AND TRADITION

(Eastern) Orthodoxy continues to designate Tradition as its fundamental authority; Scripture is preeminent within Tradition, as its initial source. Revelation involves the ecumenical creeds' binding dogma. Otherwise, Orthodoxy places more emphasis on liturgical mystery and less on propositional truth. At Vatican Council II (1962–65) the (Roman) Catholic account of Scripture and Tradition became friendlier to Protestant concerns. *Dei Verbum*, the Vatican II document on divine revelation, moved away from a "Tradition II" understanding of the Council of Trent. Instead of treating Scripture and Tradition as potentially independent sources, *Dei Verbum* took a "Tradition I" approach: revelation in Jesus Christ is the ultimate authority; Scripture is its preeminent source; Tradition is its essential interpretative guide. This approach restrains Tradition's official authority to operate independently of Scripture. Nevertheless, the magisterium may still offer infallible teaching. Contrary to Protestant accounts, the formal—if not material—insufficiency of Scripture remains. In other words, even if all the knowledge of God that is necessary for Christian faith were contained within Scripture, this material content could not be reliably understood without the church's formal guidance.

By contrast, Protestant theology affirms *sola scriptura* ("Scripture alone") as the final arbiter of truth claims, the norming norm (*norma normans non normata*). This Scripture principle does not entail that theology lacks other sources or even subordinate norms. Yet special revelation by Word and Spirit

---

17. On these moments, see Fackre, *Doctrine of Revelation*. For an influential survey that resists treating the views as mutually exclusive, see Dulles, *Models of Revelation*.

is theology's primary source. *Scripture is the verbal witness of prophets and apostles concerning God's ultimate speech in Jesus Christ (Heb. 1:1–4; 4:12–13). Protestant theology emphasizes the patristic concept of the *analogia fidei* ("analogy of faith")—the practice of relating difficult biblical texts to clearer ones and to the canonical message as a whole. Then, according to the "Magisterial" Reformation traditions such as Lutheranism and Calvinism, *tradition—all Christian witness, verbal and nonverbal, faithful and false—provides another vital guide, a "ministerial" norm, for biblical interpretation. In particular, the ecumenical creeds minister an authoritative Rule of Faith, a providential identification of Scripture's Triune God. *Confessions of faith add another aspect of Protestant tradition by stating a particular church's beliefs; *catechisms help church members to learn those beliefs in a question-and-answer format. These subordinate norms shape how believers understand the orthodox Christian teaching derived from Scripture, the norming norm.

In contrast with traditional Protestants, "Radical" Reformation and "pietist" movements are usually noncreedal. Of course, these movements still operate with subordinate norms, at least in practice; they implicitly have "traditions," even if not by name. Moreover, in practice such evangelical movements affirm trinitarian *orthodoxy—the basic, church-identifying dogma (the opposite of which is *heresy) that the true God is Father, Son, and Holy Spirit, definitively revealed in the incarnation of Jesus Christ as the God-man.

REASON AND EXPERIENCE

A crucial precursor to the modern discussion was the "three-legged stool" of Anglican Richard Hooker (1554–1600), which included "reason" alongside Scripture and tradition in its account of theological authority. The subsequent *Wesleyan quadrilateral of sources, adapted from John Wesley (1703–91) and now widely standard, incorporates "experience" as a fourth authority. Wesley's emphasis, that true interpretation of Scripture manifests itself in authentic spiritual experience, echoes a similar link in Martin Luther (1483–1546). Traditional Protestants treat reason and experience as important influences but subordinate sources that should not exert authority over Christian teaching in the same sense as Scripture or even tradition.

*Reason is a God-given cognitive and linguistic faculty by which we communicate and seek coherent understanding. Treating "reason" primarily as a distinct source of beliefs may credit disciplines like philosophy or science with more consensus than they have. Still, both "tradition" and "reason" can designate not just activities but also their products. As the product of tradition, ecumenical creeds present the biblical consensus that most decisively impinges upon Christian understanding. The first step in the activity of reason is making distinctions,[18] which is necessary for interpreting Scripture and tradition. This activity is also vital for interacting with the disciplines of modern learning, and the current products of that interaction comprise reason as a theological source.

*Experience too involves both human processes and their products. Experience is not really a human faculty; reason is the key faculty by which we have experiences. While emotions arise in connection with experience, our faculties for feeling and thinking are interwoven.[19] The products of raw experience are rarely, if ever, coherent or public enough to serve as a direct source of theological authority. But that hardly makes emotions unimportant! Instead, experience is what the "renewal of our mind" (Rom. 12:1–2) transforms. Experience ceaselessly raises questions that return believing reason to Scripture and tradition, but it cannot provide authoritative answers on its own. Its subordinate authority lies in unsettling some interpretations and helping to confirm others.

Reason and experience intersect in the context of "culture," particularly through language. *Culture harvests, then plants fresh seeds, from cultivating human freedom to express meaning. Cultural expression connects the physical context of "nature" with social contexts. Reason and experience should celebrate God's universal witness as Creator, so that all of creation and every culture may bring contextual insight to theological contemplation. As the intersection and expression of the two, culture reminds us neither to separate reason and experience nor to pit them against each other.

If earlier modernity overemphasized reason, today's world usually overemphasizes experience: "Adding a fourth leg to a three-legged stool often makes it unstable."[20] Taken to extremes, making experience an authority licenses everyone doing what is right in their own eyes (Judg. 21:25). Even Scripture, tradition, and reason are not like three different bookshelves to search for answers: "Rather, scripture is the bookshelf; tradition is the memory of what people in the house have read and understood (or perhaps misunderstood) from the shelf; and reason is the set of spectacles that people wear in order to make sense of what they read." Experience is actually what Scripture has authority over:

> "Experience" is what grows by itself in the garden. "Authority" is what happens when the gardener wants to affirm the goodness of the genuine flowers

18. Sokolowski, *God of Faith and Reason*, 4.
19. Nussbaum, *Upheavals of Thought*, helpfully suggests thinking of emotions as pointers to deeply held reasons, rather than splitting the two apart as modern culture often does.
20. For the quotations in this paragraph, see N. T. Wright, *The Last Word*, esp. 100–105.

and vegetables by uprooting the weeds in order to let beauty and fruitfulness triumph over chaos, thorns and thistles. An over-authoritarian church, paying no attention to experience, solves the problem by paving the garden with concrete. An over-experiential church solves the (real or imagined) problem of concrete (rigid and "judgmental" forms of faith) by letting anything and everything grow unchecked, sometimes labeling concrete as "law" and so celebrating any and every weed as "grace."

Of course, specifying sources and norms will not automatically solve theological problems. Nevertheless, Christian doctrine must bear faithful witness regarding God's speech and action: evangelical theology emphasizes Scripture's final authority in order to keep Christ as its foundation, the gospel at its heart. Churches and their surrounding cultures inevitably, often helpfully, influence the Bible's interpretation. Yet no humans fully grasp the gospel; we bear witness only by the Spirit to the Word.

Understanding: Practicing Theological Disciplines

Christian "theology," then, is the integrating discipline that studies how the church may bear enduring, timely, and truthful witness to the Triune God revealed in Jesus Christ. In other words, *theology is disciplined pursuit of Christian *wisdom, the most germane biblical concept for knowledge of God. Knowledge of God is relational, involving the whole person within God's covenant community. Such knowledge is contextual, incorporating freedom for discernment about obedient discipleship. Christian wisdom is worshipful, not merely instrumental, inviting us to contemplate who God is and not just to "apply" knowledge. Our minds are renewed in Christian wisdom as we offer ourselves to the Triune God as living sacrifices. Responding in faith to divine revelation, the community of faith seeks understanding of God and God's will for all of life, aided in this form of worship by God-given teachers (Rom. 12:1–3).

Prayerful Wisdom

The earliest Christian "theologians" mostly were bishops communicating in sermons, catechesis, liturgies, and letters. Origen (c. 185–254) and his school were a partial exception to this rule, but spiritual devotion still characterized them. *Theology proper spoke of God's character, distinct from the *economy of divine activity that discloses God's character in the world. Theology focused on contemplatively practicing the means of grace.

As Evagrius Ponticus (345–99) insisted, one who prays is truly a theologian, and vice versa.[21] Accordingly, premodern theologians proceeded chiefly as prayerful students and pastoral teachers of Scripture. Promoting Christian virtue helped interpreters to distinguish biblical truth from error.[22] This integral relation between theory and practice cautions against viewing theology as "practical" in terms of instant application, a set of "how-to" steps for accomplishing spiritual goals. When modern people think that theology is impractical, sometimes they reveal theology's failure to realize its classic aims, getting lost in scientific jargon. At other times, however, they may reveal the wrong expectation: a one-way movement from "theory" to immediate usefulness. Sometimes, instead, theology best shapes "practice" by telling us what God has done or by changing our expectations.

Beginning in the later Middle Ages, biblical exegesis, prayer, and other aspects of the theological art became increasingly distinct. Monasteries preserved the Scriptures and perpetuated the Christian tradition. As universities emerged, monks grew concerned that the technical arguments and bawdy lifestyles that took place therein threatened theology's heart, competing with prayerful contemplation of classic texts. The humanist learning of medieval universities complicated theology's unity. Soon modern universities formalized distinctions between theology's subdisciplines—notably, between biblical studies and dogmatics. Modern ideals of objectivity distanced theology's knowing subjects from its subject matter: now God, as an increasingly inaccessible Object of knowledge, could be studied apart from prayer. In other words, theology's social location changed: Pope Gregory I (the Great; c. 540–604) as both bishop and monk embodies the medieval transition from the bishop's chair to the monk's cloister; then Luther as both monk and professor embodies the later transition from the monk's cloister to the professor's classroom.[23] Medieval and post-Reformation scholasticism fostered coherent teaching, but also it set the stage for modern obsessions with intellectual procedure and scientific status.

Theology addresses Christian *witness or communicative action—whatever people say or do with reference to God, whether good or bad—seeking to speak truly, clearly, and harmoniously. We are all "amateur" (i.e., for the love of it) theologians, like it or not, know it or not. Theology as a professional academic discipline rests on spiritual and intellectual practices of faith seeking

---

21. Evagrius Ponticus, *Treatise on Prayer* 61, in *Evagrius of Pontus: The Greek Ascetic Corpus*, 199.

22. As detailed by Charry, *Renewing of Your Minds*. See also Alasdair MacIntyre's definition of a "practice," discussed in Treier, *Virtue and the Voice of God*, 22–23.

23. As Jaroslav Pelikan famously mentioned in *Emergence of the Catholic Tradition*, 5.

understanding that, to varying degrees, are incumbent upon everyone. The following sections introduce key categories for that academic discipline.[24]

Theological Concepts

"Theology" can be a general term, covering all the disciplines that study sacred texts and religious practices. More specifically, the term can indicate *systematic theology, which emphasizes intellectual coherence. The adjective "systematic" is widespread in evangelical circles, used to emphasize presenting the Bible's unified truth. *Constructive theology emphasizes creativity and cultural relevance; this term was initially prominent in liberal circles but now appears among evangelicals as well. *Dogmatic theology emphasizes the church's "Great Tradition" or a particular confessional tradition; this term is preferred among those who root theology in the exposition of *dogma— authoritative church teaching.

How systematic should theology aspire to be?[25] Historically, most theology has appeared in occasional treatises rather than full-scale systems. Systematic thinking—avoiding obvious contradictions and aspiring to coherent reflection—expresses faith in one God of one gospel. Yet theology should minister biblical revelation, not replace the Scriptures with a human system. Today "dialogical" approaches promote more flexible notions of systematic theology that incorporate dialogue between the multiple genres and frameworks in Scripture itself. The Bible's different forms of literature, emerging within different eras of redemptive history, together relate theological language to life in a "dramatic" fashion. Theology helps people to participate faithfully in redemption's drama by relating biblical forms of understanding to one another and to our current scenes.[26]

Language changes over time via *metaphor: thinking of what is difficult to name by bringing to mind features of more familiar terms.[27] The shock value of a new term recedes over time, and if commonly used it becomes a "dead" metaphor or *concept: a standard habit of relating words to objects or ideas. So, for example, "revelation" is a *concept*, which reflects the underlying

24. Much of the following material appears in Treier, "Systematic Theology," and is used here with permission.

25. See further A. N. Williams, *Architecture of Theology*, esp. the introduction; Gunton, "A Rose by Any Other Name?"

26. See further Vanhoozer, *Drama of Doctrine*; Vanhoozer and Treier, *Theology and the Mirror of Scripture*.

27. On metaphor, see Soskice, *Metaphor and Religious Language*. See also Treier, "Concept"; Treier and Sarisky, "Model"; Treier and Hill, "Philosophy"; Treier, "Proof Text"; Treier, "Scripture, Unity of"; Treier, "Theological Hermeneutics, Contemporary"; and Treier, "Wisdom."

metaphor of unveiling (that simultaneously, in this case, veils). Concepts foster making judgments and then communicating those claims in different contexts or even languages: Formulated as true-or-false claims ("propositions"), these *judgments are basic to theology's intellectual practice. So, for example, the concept of "revelation" reflects the *judgment* that God's self-communication is the authoritative basis for making theological truth claims.

Theologians develop one or more concepts into *models: smaller-scale representations with which humans teach and learn aspects of revealed truth. So, for example, "revelation as doctrine" is a *model*, which preserves a central insight (cognitive content) but sometimes neglects other aspects (experience or mystery). Theologians combine models into *systems: networks of concepts and models that convey judgments about not only particular truths but also special emphases. Systems, however large, reflect particular judgments or root metaphors. So, for example, some evangelicals made "propositional revelation" not only into a model addressing theology's basis but even into its fundamental principle and theme: propositional revelation defined a theological *system* in which concepts like the inerrancy of Scripture coherently followed from that basic principle. The risk, of course, is that systems eventually marginalize aspects of biblical teaching. The alternative risk of not trying to relate concepts and judgments coherently, though, is that our teaching will fail to reflect the ordered beauty of God and the gospel.

Theological Disciplines

Among theology's intellectual disciplines, evangelical Protestants prioritize *exegesis of the Bible, the discipline of understanding "the way the words run."[28] Some treat theology largely as the result of biblical interpretation; they emphasize inductive study of particular texts. Others treat theology equally as a resource for understanding Scripture texts; they emphasize synthetic interaction with other biblical passages and broader themes.

*Biblical theology is a related discipline that pursues historical and literary understanding of how Scripture's parts relate to its overall teaching. Although difficult to define, biblical theology can foster integration with Christian doctrine as it emerges from and contributes to exegesis. Biblical theology seeks doctrinal concepts and connections that reflect Scripture's own language and internal structures.

Similarly, *historical theology oscillates between detailed interpretation of texts and doctrinal integration. Its immediate focus is not the Bible but

---

28. This phrase, summarizing a traditional stance associated with Thomas Aquinas, apparently stems from B. Marshall, "Absorbing the World," 90–97.

Christian tradition. So historical theology will reflect commitments regarding tradition's levels or lack of authority. Historical theology pursues responsible analysis of the past. But such analysis is inevitably selective—regarding materials to access, subjects to study, questions to ask, and authorities to honor or critique.

*Pastoral or *practical theology, by various names and specializations (e.g., missiology, spirituality), brings experience of Christian living and church ministry to bear on doctrinal concepts. In this way an intentional feedback loop raises fresh questions about current understandings of Scripture and tradition.

Systematic theology stands at the intersection of these biblical, historical, and pastoral tasks. While theological authority moves one way, from Scripture through church witness to the contemporary world, the practice of theological inquiry involves blurry lines and nonlinear movement.[29] Obvious parallels exist between these disciplines and particular sources: *Scripture* vis-à-vis exegesis and biblical theology; *tradition* vis-à-vis historical theology; *reason* vis-à-vis systematic theology; *experience* vis-à-vis pastoral theology. Sometimes systematic theology unfolds in a particular mode as *philosophical theology, interacting with philosophy of religion.[30] Since theology and philosophy both seek wisdom as integrating disciplines, their boundaries are blurry, with a checkered past: philosophy sought to dethrone theology, the medieval "queen of the sciences," as the two became more distinct in modernity. On this side of heaven, theology, starting from revelation, needs to be provoked by philosophy, pursuing reason as far as it will go; thus provoked, however, theology needs to steal philosophy's weapons and defend some territory of its own.[31]

The interplay of these theological disciplines can be illustrated with the doctrine of revelation. Early on, this chapter's account of faith appealed to *exegesis* of key texts in Romans and Isaiah that emphasize hearing God's Word. *Biblical theology* influences and emerges from such exegesis. Its historical dimension highlights the movement from relatively infrequent appeals to "faith" in the Old Testament, through the emergence of this theme in Isaiah, to its prominence in Paul's Epistles: the identity of Jesus Christ as God's final Word is lurking in that redemptive-historical trajectory. The literary dimension of biblical theology highlights the association of "revelation" with apocalyptic literature and conversely the prominence of "speech" in texts traditionally associated with revelation. This chapter's emphasis upon God's communicative action by Word and Spirit is lurking in that literary trajectory.

---

29. Carson, "Unity and Diversity."

30. Mapping the two streams in philosophy of religion, with corresponding theological implications, is W. Wainwright, *God, Philosophy, and Academic Culture*.

31. Gunton, "Indispensable Opponent."

Nearly this entire chapter could be viewed as *historical theology*: retrieving the most important elements of the past, good and bad—both consensus about Scripture's basic teaching and divisive or mistaken categories—to inform theological reflection today. Certainly the effort to retrieve integration between "faith" and "reason" in a doctrine of revelation reflects commitment to learning from the past, without assuming that modern learning is simply pathological. The questions of *pastoral theology* that energized this chapter may not rest on the surface. Addressing tensions between "theory" and "practice," however, is one example of an implicitly pastoral concern that shaped its engagement with biblical and historical theology. Indeed, those tensions are not just academic; the spiritual aftermath of seminary education made Ellen Charry's account of classic Christian doctrine personally compelling. Of course, this chapter surveys historical theology out of *systematic* interest: in the present case, sketching Christian theological prolegomena within the framework of "faith seeking understanding."

Theological Contexts

Theology takes different forms depending on its primary *public—that is, what community's context and goals raise the questions that people of faith are addressing.[32] So theology focuses on *celebration* in the context of the church, helping us to encounter God together in faithful worship. Theology focuses on *communication* in the context of society, helping us to encounter other Christians in catechesis and pastoral care. Theology focuses on *criticism* in the context of the university and the media, helping us to encounter the world in humble yet fruitful witness. Sometimes public opinion needs to hear gentle defenses of the gospel. At other times, though, public objections really concern the church's unfaithfulness to that gospel, so theological criticism may reshape the church's celebration and communication. Finally, theology encourages *cultivation* in the context of the physical world, helping us to encounter God's other creatures with care and delight. Of course, the influence of these publics will reflect particular times and places as well as other aspects of cultural context—social class, economic resources, gender, race, and so forth. God's self-revelation does not change, but the contexts of theological understanding are as diverse and dynamic as the people to whom God lovingly speaks.

Beyond a professional academic discipline, then, theology involves *communicative praxis: the way in which Christian practices, directly and indirectly,

---

32. The following account appropriates the prologue of R. Williams, *On Christian Theology*, on theological "styles," with David Tracy's account of "publics" in the background.

enact a drama—learning and speaking of God in response to mighty acts of salvation. Faith seeks holistic understanding, "a set of capacities for action in relation to something."[33] Theological understanding includes and influences the actions-in-relationship described above: celebration, communication, criticism, and cultivation. Theology includes and influences Christian worship, nurture, witness, and creation care. Theology is too important to leave to professionals, yet too influential to take lightly.

33. See Kelsey, *To Understand God Truly*, 124–29.

— 2 —

The Ten Commandments
𝒜 Community's Moral Formation

THESIS

Christian beliefs are integrated with behavior, extending Israel's moral tradition from the Ten Commandments to root human community in the love of God and neighbor.

LEARNING OBJECTIVES

After learning the material in this chapter, you should be able to:

1. *Define briefly* the key terms introduced here (marked with an asterisk and included in the glossary).
2. *List and recognize* the following: (a) the Ten Commandments; (b) three views of the essence of ethics; (c) three aspects of the Mosaic law.
3. *Describe and compare* the following: (a) three uses of the law; (b) four basic approaches to natural law.
4. *Identify and illustrate* the basic significance of each of the Ten Commandments.
5. *Explain* the following: (a) the relationship between negative commands and positive values; (b) your own tentative approach to theological ethics.

Christian teaching integrates beliefs with belonging and behavior. While the Creed focuses on beliefs, the Ten Commandments and the Lord's Prayer focus on behavior and belonging. The Ten Commandments, the focus of this chapter, express God's character in providing instruction for human behavior. These commands apply to all people—believers and nonbelievers alike—yet Christian theologies explain this application variously.

35

Labeling this application "moral" theology connects the Ten Commandments with "general" revelation. "Spiritual" theology, developed especially from the Lord's Prayer, connects more directly with God's "special" revelation in Jesus Christ. Even so, the contrast between moral and spiritual formation should not be simplistic—as if the former solely addresses personal behavior while the latter addresses communal belonging. Both the Decalogue (Ten Commandments) and the Pater Noster (Lord's Prayer) form God's covenant community. The Decalogue inaugurates the formation of God's redeemed people with a moral focus, establishing a foundation for communal flourishing. Yet this foundation calls people to worship, not just generally obey. Hence there are various theological approaches to the Ten Commandments.

The Decalogue: The Foundation of Biblical Law

Christian traditions number the Ten Commandments differently.[1] Numbering aside, though, the Ten Words (the Hebrew term) do not begin immediately with the prohibition against other gods. First they set this prohibition in the context of grace: "I am the LORD your God, who brought you out of Egypt, out of the land of slavery" (Exod. 20:2; Deut. 5:6). God claims the covenant people's exclusive allegiance (in the "first" commandment) by saving them. From there the numbering system used below distinguishes the prohibition of idolatry from the prohibition of images, while synthesizing one prohibition of coveting (whatever the object). This approach sets forth the most coherent, distinct tracks of ethical teaching.

The Decalogue often faces criticism for being "negative" due to its several prohibitions. But negative commands make space for positive action as long as people do not violate the specific prohibition. A prohibition actually provides freedom and encouragement to pursue something precious. So, for example,

1. Three basic systems need attention. The *first* comes from the Septuagint (LXX), the major Greek translation of the Old Testament; later this order (followed below) became standard among Orthodox and Reformed Christians.

A *second* system comes from the Jewish Talmud, the major compendium of ancient rabbinic teaching. The Talmud influenced Augustine, whose order became standard for Catholic Christians. In that system the prohibition of other gods and the prohibition of making images combine as the first commandment. Not coveting a neighbor's wife is ninth, and not coveting a neighbor's other possessions is tenth—following Deut. 5:21 rather than Exod. 20:17.

A *third* system is Lutheran. Its first through eighth commandments are the same as Augustine's. Then, while distinguishing two aspects of not coveting for its ninth and tenth commandments (like Augustine), it follows Exodus rather than Deuteronomy for their order (unlike Augustine): thus, ninth, not coveting a neighbor's house; tenth, not coveting a neighbor's wife or anything else.

"no killing" signals that God treasures life. Humans not only exercise freedom in separate acts involving life or death dilemmas; in truly free acts they also develop character, forming people and communities who promote life.

Having No Other Gods

The first commandment demands the loyalty of faith: having no other gods before YHWH. In light of God's gracious claim, the covenant people must fear and worship God alone (Isa. 44:9–10). *Idols comprise not just statues of wood or stone, but anything in life that draws allegiance away from the Creator. Humans owe God total obedience, never allowing another ruler to supplant God. Accordingly, God's people trust God, not themselves, for all their needs (Matt. 6:31–33).[2] Throughout history, idolatry has included trusting in ways of saving ourselves—ability to live righteously, or to manipulate religion for getting what we want. Ancients who idolized the sun and stars, or objects of wood and stone, hoped to secure some advantage, maybe by magic. Modern idolaters supposedly despise magic and rituals, but we still worship physical objects and ultimately ourselves. Efforts to use spirituality for selfish ends are a perennial form of idolatry.

No Making Graven Images

*Worship proclaims God's worth. Done in words, often set to music, *praise* focuses on who God is; *thanksgiving* focuses on what God has done for us. Worship also embraces *service*, devoting all of life to God like a sacrifice (Rom. 12:1–2; Heb. 13:15). Communal worship gathers the covenant people to engage with their God—to hear God speak; to offer praise and thanksgiving; to intercede for ourselves and others; and to return time, talent, and treasure to their Giver. As reflected in these tangible gifts, all that humans are and have is a divine gift, remaining under God's ownership; earthly possession is simply *stewardship*. Covenant engagement with God reorients life, both weekly and annually, as Christian rhythms of ordinary time unfold within the divine drama of redemption.

Christians disagree over the use of images within worship. Christians agree that this commandment prohibits idolatry: it is forbidden to direct worship toward any fixed, physical representation of what humans think God is like. People become like what they worship; correspondingly, idols reflect, and reshape humans into, their images of the divine.[3] Controversy arose, however,

---

2. Luther, "Large Catechism," 386–92.
3. Beale, *We Become What We Worship*.

regarding *icons—objects picturing Jesus Christ or Mary or various saints and used as vehicles for worship. *Iconoclasts argued that use of icons was idolatrous, whereas *iconodules favored "venerating" icons in order to "worship" God. Iconodules argued that the incarnation of God in Jesus Christ authorized iconic rendering of the divine in human form, and this position was victorious at the Second Council of Nicaea (AD 787). Catholic, Orthodox, and many Protestant Christians today treat icons as reflectors, like the moon to the sun, of the divine light. Yet other Protestants, especially in the Reformed tradition, do not allow icons, although they remain open to worship's use of many, including visual, arts.

Iconoclasts appeal not only to the second commandment but also to the uniqueness of the incarnation: Jesus Christ, the true image of God, reflects perfectly what God is like, but not due to particular details of his physical form. Instead, his revelation of God's character became possible through his embrace of human flesh. Through this one Mediator between God and humanity, our prayer and praise participate in Jesus's human worship of God and the Son's divine adoration of his Father: he is the true temple, sacrifice, priest, and son who fulfills the human vocation of imaging God (Col. 2:9–10; cf. Gen. 1:26–28). Israel's idolatry with the golden calf is instructive (Exod. 32:1–4). God has authorized no earthly representation other than human beings! The physical form of these bearers of the divine image represents God, who is Spirit, only indirectly. Israel's tabernacle and temple worship never incorporated arts and objects as divine likenesses to venerate. Israel's God is unique as One who lovingly authorized human representation of the divine character.

Whatever one's approach to icons, what does worship centrally involve? First, since even the physical world praises God, humans should care for the rest of creation as a reflection of the divine glory. Second, church gatherings praise and thank God through music and prayer; read Scripture to hear God speak and learn its teaching; offer mutual encouragement; and celebrate baptism and the Lord's Supper. Third, since worship is covenant engagement with God, Christians participate in an unfolding drama—integrating communal gatherings with everyday service (see, e.g., Rom. 15:27; Phil. 2:25), increasingly reflecting Jesus Christ as the true divine image.

No Misusing God's Name

Like the first two, the third commandment focuses on responding to God. The importance of God's name lies in the ancient association of a name with character: to claim something by someone's name powerfully invokes that person's very being, as oaths testify. Invoking the divine name means being in covenant relationship with God, claiming to be God's people. Proper bearing of God's name begins with various forms of speech, then broadly addresses all representation. Our character bears either true or false witness regarding the God we claim to serve. The Bible speaks of God's name facing *blasphemy—scornful misuse, implying disgrace or disbelief—among pagans on account of God's people (Isa. 52:5; Rom. 2:24). This third commandment can be violated broadly and narrowly at the same time.

Its traditional focus on speech may stem from lifting up God's name liturgically, in public ritual. Accordingly, "We are to fear and love God, so that we do not curse, swear [in the sense of taking a false oath], practice magic, lie or deceive using God's name, but instead use that very name in every time of need to call on, pray to, praise, and give thanks to God."[4] God's people call on God's name in prayer not just through external acts or rote sayings but ultimately with an internal disposition of humility (Luke 18:9–14). Human speech should thank God and build up others (Eph. 4:29; 5:4). Yet the danger of *hypocrisy—saying one thing but thinking and doing another—is all too real: the same mouth often praises God and curses other people, who are God's image-bearers (James 3:9–10). The ninth commandment highlights further that speech is important, yet no one can tame the tongue (James 3:3–6). Beyond hypocrisy, human speech is often guilty of pagan "babblings" (Matt. 6:7), as if length or sound might manipulate a deity. Such efforts at manipulation imply that God is not really benevolent, not already like a loving Father. A call for sincerity also undergirds the prohibition of oaths in the Sermon on the Mount; a person's word should be trustworthy without needing special proofs to convince others.

Of course, the content of prayer matters to God (e.g., James 4), likewise revealing the heart's sincerity. Selfish requests are a form of idolatry, befriending the world and becoming God's enemy. To invoke God's name, appealing to covenant relationship, requires worshiping the Creator rather than any creature. Yet invoking God's name does not preclude acknowledging the breadth and depth of human sinfulness. God promises not to despise a "broken and contrite heart" (Ps. 51:17); God knows the difference between begging for mercy as a sinner and claiming the divine name while cherishing bloodstained hands (Isa. 1:10–15).

Hallowing the Sabbath

While principally concerned with God's honor, the third and fourth commandments also imply commitments to fellow humans. The third commandment

---

4. Luther, "Handbook," 352.

expands bearing the divine name beyond liturgical speech into the aims of prayer and the representation of God's character. Similarly, the fourth commandment begins by addressing worship but then orients our time and work accordingly. On that basis all of life is shaped by rhythms of praising God, enjoying rest, and showing mercy.

*Sabbath designates the seventh day of the Jewish week: Saturday (on a schedule of sundown to sunset). Among Christians, Seventh-Day Adventists are the most prominent group that retains the Saturday commitment inherited from the Old Testament. By contrast, an increasingly large class of Christians operates at the other end of the spectrum: they draw a sharper contrast between the Old and New Testaments, honoring no such special day. They typically attend church on Sundays and enjoy provision for family or leisure activities; however, these are echoes of a dying cultural heritage, not principled commitments to keeping Sabbath. They interpret Pauline texts about not needing to observe days or seasons (Rom. 14:5–9; Col. 2:16–17) as abrogating the Sabbath, not just making Jewish festivals optional. In between these two ends of the spectrum, other Christians have traditionally associated Sunday worship with Sabbath observance.

Biblical theology presents complications for all three approaches—strict, modified, and nonsabbatarian. The historical evidence shows no clear relation between the Sabbath command and the early Christian emergence of Sunday worship. By contrast, the Lord's Day was clearly associated with the Lord's Supper, in celebration of Christ's resurrection. One reason why the Sabbath command may not have generated Sunday worship is that most early Christians had to work on Sunday.[5] Yet Sabbath appears in scriptural passages that may reach beyond the specific salvation-historical context of Israel. The Sabbath appears from the start, in the creation narrative. The rhythms of Israel's week and the nature of Israel's covenant relationship with God reflect God's design from the beginning. At minimum, then, the Sabbath may have significance tied to creation in general and not just Israel's redemption in particular. If so, then that creational significance somehow has contemporary application. Of course, like the other Ten Commandments, Sabbath now confronts the church with moral instruction rather than a civic obligation like it gave to Israel; therefore, its implementation would vary.

Theological systems have also affected Christian appeals to the Sabbath command. The other nine commandments all boast fairly direct repetition in the New Testament. So, one way or another, various traditions acknowledge their enduring moral authority. The Sabbath command not only lacks clear

---

5. Laansma, "Lord's Day." See also Laansma, "Rest (Work)."

New Testament repetition but also faces possible evidence of abrogation, as noted above. Accordingly, modern Protestant systems for understanding salvation history—sketched later in this chapter—manifest particular differences regarding Old Testament law when they handle this command.

In the meantime, the Sabbath's primary moral significance is threefold. First, the Sabbath sanctifies time, focusing on *worship*. Such days are offered "to" the Lord, indicating that no work—however regular and time-consuming—ultimately governs human life. Just as fasting fosters devotion to prayer, so Sabbath is a holy day, belonging especially to worship. Second, the Sabbath focuses on *rest*. The Creator sanctifies this gift by example (Gen. 1:31–2:3). Rest is God's promise, pointing to the fullness of salvation (Heb. 4:1–11). A preliminary taste of ultimate rest in Christ's immediate presence teaches about grace: God's provision, not human work, is primary, whether physically or spiritually. Third, far from selfish quietism, the Sabbath focuses on *mercy and justice*—honoring God and serving others. Many people are tempted to put on a good show of worshiping God while simultaneously indulging selfish unrighteousness (Isa. 58). By contrast, Jesus healed on the Sabbath, indicating that humans honor the Sabbath when they love God by loving others (Matt. 12:1–14).

Jesus said that the Sabbath was made for people, not the reverse (Mark 2:27), and he initiated a salvation-historical change in the relationship of God's people to the Torah. Since the extent of that change is debated, the nature of Sabbath obligation today is ambiguous. At least the specific manner of Sabbath observance seems to count as *adiaphora*—a "disputable" matter (Rom. 14). On such matters of disputed biblical principle, the paramount emphasis should be personal accountability to the Lord for stewardship of Christian freedom. Hence Sabbath-keeping today does not involve a simple list of what may or may not be done. Sabbath rest underscores that God created human work to good purpose, but work should not consume or define us. From beginning to end the week belongs to God. Christ's resurrection renews human activity yet indicates its limited significance: only God can redeem. The Bible does not clearly legislate Sabbath prescriptions and proscriptions for the present age, but it sanctifies positive priorities—locating true rest in worshiping God and serving others.

Honoring Parents

While connected with the Decalogue's initial focus on God, the fifth commandment turns to focus increasingly on human relationships. Its root concern, linking the two foci, is authority, as much of the subsequent exposition learns from Luther's catechisms: "We are to fear and love God, so that we neither despise nor anger our parents and others in authority [princes and pastors], but instead honor, serve, obey, love, and respect them."[6] This is the first and greatest among neighbor-focused commandments because of the special role God has given to parents. All people should be loved as neighbors, and some or many as friends; parents (and, by extension, other authority figures) should also be honored, because they represent God's loving authority and provision within human community.

Obeying parents is the primary "good work" that God gives young people to do. As we grow, it becomes easy to forget the care of parents and other authorities just as we neglect God's pervasive care. But this commandment calls for more than obeying and showing gratitude, or even attempting reciprocal care later in life (1 Tim. 5:8). It calls for showing lifelong honor and embracing the covenant faith of godly parents through adulthood. All parents, even unbelievers, should be honored as representing God's authority and care. Proverbs and other wisdom texts closely identify human instruction with God's because God cares for people as in a household.[7] The fifth commandment is "the first commandment with a promise—'so that it may go well with you and that you may enjoy long life on the earth'" (Eph. 6:2–3; cf. Exod. 20:12; Deut. 5:16). Put critically, "Why do you think the world is now so full of unfaithfulness, shame, misery, and murder? It is because all want to be their own lords, to be free of all authority, to care nothing for anyone, and to do whatever they please."[8]

This commandment poignantly illustrates the Decalogue's broad application and spiritual intensification: all people should discern their obligation to honor authority figures by virtue of creation; within the covenant community, these relationships should reflect deeper realities of redeeming grace. Society includes "fathers" and "mothers" by blood, of a household (e.g., adoptive parents, other relatives, and schoolteachers), of a nation (e.g., monarchs), and in a spiritual sense (e.g., pastors, worthy of "double honor" according to 1 Tim. 5:17). These authorities must not act as "tyrants," yet they should be obeyed unless they command direct disobedience to God (Acts 5:29).

"Family," then, transcends the "nuclear" family: various household arrangements have existed in Bible times and throughout Christian history, often with "extended" family members living together. In addition, "celibate" singleness

6. Luther, "Handbook," 352.
7. Treier, *Proverbs and Ecclesiastes*, 109–15.
8. Luther, "Large Catechism," 407–8.

is a valid, even ideal, calling for some (1 Cor. 7). Marrying and raising children remain central to God's created design (Matt. 19:4–6). In the end, though, the church is "first" family, since loyalty to Jesus and solidarity with God's people take priority over earthly bonds (e.g., Matt. 13:45–50; 19:29), creating a newly reconciled humanity (Eph. 2; 4).

No (Unjustified?) Killing

The sixth commandment shifts the primary focus onto duties toward neighbors, proscribing killing and promoting life. We should harm no one with either actions or speech. Verbal violence is as sinful as murder, albeit not deadly in quite the same way (Matt. 5:21–26; James 3:1–4:3). People should not even remain angry at others, including enemies (Matt. 5:38–48; Eph. 4:26). Positively, this commandment calls for doing good toward neighbors (Matt. 25:42–43). As Proverbs 24:11–12 indicates, those who are able ought to rescue the perishing. This call to help even enemies, leaving judgment in God's hands, is finally rooted in the first commandment, like all the others: as our God, Yhwh "wishes to help, comfort, and protect us, so that he may restrain our desire for revenge."[9]

This commandment reflects the view, first, that *life is a gift*, by the Creator's constant sustenance (Gen. 2:7; Rom. 4:17): "How many are your works, Lord! In wisdom you made them all; the earth is full of your creatures. . . . When you take away their breath, they die and return to the dust" (Ps. 104:24, 29). Second, life is a gift *shared with other creatures*—with animals and even plants (Gen. 1:29–30). Third, because God cares for human lives (since, after all, God even cares for sparrows; Matt. 6:25–34), *we should not worry*. Fourth, *long life* is typical, though not surefire, evidence of God's favor (Exod. 20:12; Ps. 21:4; 91:16; Prov. 10:27). Humans "choose life" by obeying God (Deut. 30:11, 15, 19; Matt. 7:24–27), despite having no guarantees—as Job and Jesus (along with texts like Isa. 57:1) testify. Fifth, *God is the primary giver and taker of life* (Job 1:21), while making use of secondary human and creaturely causes. Suicide, abortion, and euthanasia count as murder because they unnaturally intervene to stop human life before it has realized God-given fullness. Heroic medical intervention may also be inappropriate or at least unnecessary; humans should not operate as if they can or must maintain life forever on their own. Sixth, by associating life with "breath," the Bible shows that God is present through the Holy Spirit: *life is not just physical but also has a "spiritual" dimension.*

---

9. Luther, "Large Catechism," 413.

A lingering conundrum concerns human violence. While debate continues, there is substantial evidence that early Christians leaned in the direction of *pacifism or nonviolence—that is, rejecting all participation in killing, including military combat. At minimum, early Christians frowned on service as a Roman soldier. We can only speculate about how they might have viewed modern policing; some of their opposition to soldiering surely involved improper allegiance to the Roman Empire, not simply killing.[10] Nevertheless, Jesus's teaching and practice of peace called forth an alternative community characterized by self-sacrificing love, giving enemies maximal opportunities for repentance.[11]

As Christianity became the established religion of the Roman Empire, though, Christians more clearly began claiming that God expects governmental authorities to restrain people from harming others. Augustine appropriated classical theory to develop a Christian *just war tradition—a set of criteria for determining a government's proper use of restraining or defensive force. Such criteria address *ius ad bellum*, the right to go to war, and *ius in bello*, right conduct in war. The former involves criteria such as a just cause, competent authority, right intention, probable success, proportionality, and last resort. Criteria for the latter include protection of noncombatants, proportionality, and military necessity. According to this tradition, the sixth commandment does not prohibit absolutely all killing, but only unjustified killing or, in other words, murder.

The just war tradition exerted moderating influence over Western culture, including military practice. The medieval Crusades raise many historical complexities, and views of religious coercion from Augustine onward certainly differ from the modern West. Nevertheless, in principle crusading is distinct from the Christian just war tradition, which does not authorize violence for promoting religious transformation. Just war criteria may not even authorize self-defense as such; their governmental focus is upon protecting neighbors while pursuing just peace as ethically and quickly as possible. Accordingly, much Christian just war thinking has moved away from defending capital punishment. Broad parallels remain between national defense and civic policing; however, unlike earlier eras that lacked prison systems, contemporary societies can protect citizens without taking additional life. Meanwhile, capital punishment has frequently been administered unjustly, not meeting biblical criteria for establishing clear guilt.

10. See the complex summary of the introductory comments regarding "The Patristic Age," in O'Donovan and O'Donovan, *From Irenaeus to Grotius*, 2–3. Texts like Luke 3:14 do not portray Jesus as forbidding military service outright.

11. For recent access to the evidence, see Kalantzis, *Caesar and the Lamb*; Sider, *Early Church on Killing*.

During the Protestant Reformation, many Anabaptists claimed to recover early Christian teaching about nonviolence. Most Anabaptist movements have been pacifist, although some promoted *nonresistance or noncombat stances: These alternatives allowed for fulfilling military obligations and helping others without participating directly in killing. At minimum, the enduring Anabaptist witness regarding Christian nonviolence reminds the mainstream Christian just war tradition of its proper focus: pursuing peace, not justifying warfare.

No Committing Adultery

The seventh commandment prohibits adultery, promoting the integrity of marriage. Like other neighbor-focused commandments, it has an implicit theological dimension. Marriage is a major motif for God's relationship with the covenant people. Old Testament Wisdom literature places parents and teachers at the forefront of God's pedagogy, and the prophets place marriage at the forefront of God's lawsuit against the unfaithful. As Hosea dramatically demonstrates, YHWH is like a cuckolded husband who longs to reclaim a wayward bride. Malachi insists that YHWH hates divorce (2:16)—for the sake of not only particular marriages but ultimately the revelation of God's covenant faithfulness.

The New Testament extends this trajectory. Jesus rooted one-flesh union between male and female in God's created design (Matt. 19:3–10). Concerning divorce, Jesus's teaching was more restrictive than permissive alternatives in his day. He upheld the sanctity of the marriage covenant and restricted legitimate divorce (whether or not remarriage is permissible) to situations when that covenant has been fundamentally violated. Paul upheld Jesus's teaching as he addressed the Corinthians. In that context, he also reaffirmed the distinctive vocation of celibate singleness for advancing God's kingdom (1 Cor. 7:25–40). Fundamentally, human marriage reflects the mystery of Christ's self-giving love for the church (Eph. 5:25–33).

Further questions over human sexuality resurface in a later chapter on theological anthropology. Here it is worth noting that the sanctity of marriage includes but transcends childrearing. Sexual union involves the formal possibility of parenting, and the Bible relishes this gift as normally accompanying marriage. Yet marriage reflects God's covenant love whether or not a particular couple conceives a child. The Bible celebrates physical, emotional, and relational delights of human marriage (e.g., Prov. 5:19). Given these unitive and procreative ends of marriage, the proper form of conjugal openness to conceiving children is debated. Traditional Roman Catholic teaching, as promulgated in *Humanae Vitae* (1968)—and typical among earlier Protestants—insists that openness to children precludes artificial means of contraception. Modern Protestants, once those means became readily available, have generally rejected that claim. If the Catholic position struggles to define what counts as "artificial" vis-à-vis techniques such as natural family planning, then perhaps modern Protestants struggle to maintain the biblical embrace of children as a divine gift of marriage.

No Stealing

The eighth commandment protects the integrity of human property. This commandment still assumes that God owns everything; humans hold property only as stewards. God provides for life (no killing), family (no adultery), and property (no stealing). This provision is broad rather than narrow, addressing numerous ways by which people wrongly take what belongs to another: "We are to fear and love God, so that we neither take our neighbors' money or property nor acquire them by using shoddy merchandise or crooked deals, but instead help them to improve and protect their property and income."[12] Laziness on the job, overcharging for goods, paying unjust wages, misusing wealth or power, taking advantage of ignorance—these are examples of how thievery goes far beyond pickpocketing.

Positively, God "commands justice and charity in the care of earthly goods" and the fruits of labor.[13] Of course, notions of property vary among cultures. Generally, however, stewarding goods is appropriate for meeting basic needs, as well as expressing human dignity in responsible agency. Stewardship should foster "natural solidarity," since God's original gift of the earth makes everyone neighbors. "Stewards of Providence" seek to make property fruitful and share its benefits with others.[14] Given the "cultural mandate" (Gen. 1:28–31), humans must care for the nonhuman creation; animals and the rest of the physical environment are a gift to all on earth from the God who delights in them.

This call to stewardship further implies that *slavery is a sin against human dignity. No human can truly own another, for all belong to God as responsible agents. Admittedly, the Decalogue's initial context contained forms of slavery that God regulated rather than immediately abolished. As with divorce, though, God tolerated and regulated those forms on account of human wickedness, and those regulations gave no space for the race-based and terrorizing forms of

12. Luther, "Handbook," 353.
13. *Catechism of the Catholic Church*, 577, §2401.
14. *Catechism of the Catholic Church*, 578, §2404.

modern slavery. The New Testament then equalized slaves and masters as brothers and sisters in Christ (e.g., in Philemon), and early Christianity challenged Roman culture's treatment of female slaves as sexual property. Eventually the church more fully and consistently recognized the injustice at stake in slavery. Put positively, the call for responsible stewardship implies that freely pursued work is a good gift from the Creator, necessary for obtaining food (2 Thess. 3:10; 1 Thess. 4:11). Unless the Lord blesses, human labor is in vain; yet those who will not work refuse God's appointed means for obtaining daily bread. Those to whom work is denied feel an understandable loss of their human dignity.

God's purpose behind human property is not to uphold the rich but to lift up the poor, so that they too can have the means of helping others (Eph. 4:28).[15] Proverbs 30:8–9 models the proper request: "Give me neither poverty nor riches, but give me only my daily bread. Otherwise, I may have too much and disown you and say, 'Who is the LORD?' Or I may become poor and steal, and so dishonor the name of my God." In the Lord's Prayer, Jesus makes this request a staple of Christian piety, while expanding its reach—from "give me only my daily bread" to "give us today our daily bread." This communal emphasis, as well as the surrounding emphasis on God's care (Matt. 6:25–34), links human stewardship with divine provision.

No Bearing False Witness

The ninth commandment fits the ongoing pattern: shaping human life to reflect divine love. Now God promotes truth and justice by protecting reputations. The implications of testimony can be vital: a judicial system depends on honesty, affecting not just livelihoods but lives. Witnesses and jurists must be people of integrity, wisdom, and courage. Yet this command's judicial focus should not mislead: its ancient context was not a courtroom but rather a village gate or town square, entangled with communal life as a whole. So, while the absolute prohibition of lying is debated in the Christian tradition,[16] here God at least prohibits any lying that harms others.

Positively, this commandment promotes verbally caring for others: "We are to fear and love God, so that we do not tell lies about our neighbors, betray or slander them, or destroy their reputations. Instead we are to come to their defense, speak well of them, and interpret everything they do in the best possible light."[17] God is true (John 14:6; Rom. 3:4), so the "Golden Rule" (Matt.

---

15. Luther, "Large Catechism," 419.

16. In his book *Lying*, Paul J. Griffiths sets Augustine's absolute prohibition of lying in its context. The absolute prohibition is now a minority view in biblical scholarship.

17. Luther, "Handbook," 353.

7:12) must shape human speech. Loving one another means not only refusing to dishonor others but even refusing to make unnecessary comparisons or judgments about one another (James 4:11–12). When discernment is necessary, "Truthfulness keeps to the just mean between what ought to be expressed and what ought to be kept secret: it entails honesty and discretion."[18]

Undoubtedly this commandment confronts media conduct and consumption: falling victim to the vice of curiosity expands the reach of false witness. To promote speaking the truth in love, this commandment confronts all sins of the tongue, such as backbiting and slander (Eph. 4:15, 23–25). When people know damaging truths, Jesus's guidelines preclude immediately telling others and instead require addressing sin as privately as possible (Matt. 18:15–17). Both production and consumption of gossip are forbidden—not just falsehood or damaging truth but even information that people do not need to know. What's more, boasting violates this commandment, misleading ourselves and others by taking credit for what God's grace makes possible. By contrast, this commandment finally promotes martyrdom. Martyrdom, from the Greek terminology for bearing witness, indicates life wholly devoted, no matter the cost, to God's truth (Phil. 4:8–9).

No Coveting

The final commandment cuts to the heart. Not just actually taking another's life or spouse or property is unlawful; even desiring them for oneself is unrighteous. Not just wanting to have as much as possible—that is, *jealousy over what others have—is forbidden. Still more insidious is *envy—wanting others not to have what is theirs, or wanting to have it in their place. As Jesus underscored to the rich young man, this tenth commandment especially confronts those whom the world considers most upright (Matt. 19:16–30; Mark 10:17–31; Luke 18:18–30). The Ten Commandments are for everybody, equalizing all sinners before God, who knows the heart.

Prohibition of coveting circles back to the first commandment: having no other gods but God. Only fear of God, and faith that God will take care of us, leads to fully loving others. A fundamental choice lies between desiring God or worldly riches (Matt. 5:8; 15:19; 6:19–24; 1 John 2:15–17). The dangers of envy are poignantly displayed by Saul in the Old Testament and the rich fool in the New Testament (2 Sam. 12:1–10; Luke 12:16–21). Envy is a form of sadness and refusal of love, coming from pride and leading to loneliness. Desire as a human possibility can be good in itself, along

---

18. *Catechism of the Catholic Church*, 592, §2469.

with its objects, for God created the world; recognizing creation's goodness praises the Creator. Sin, however, distorts desire beyond God's limits on what and when and how much people should want. Such limits enhance proper enjoyment of God's gifts by fostering true joy in God. The virtue of temperance involves modesty in promoting desire among others, and moderation in pursuing our own earthly desires. Temperance thus opposes capital vices such as envy, greed, and lust. The Ten Commandments can foster earthly *shalom* at a basic level by regulating behavior to establish a moral community. At another level, though, the Decalogue should foster loyal love in covenant relationships—the spiritual fullness of having no other gods besides Yhwh.

Instruction: The Heart of Divine Law

Christians have consistently appropriated the Ten Commandments as a framework for moral formation. Yet this approach to theological ethics has generated several debates, each with its own categories, ultimately revolving around how the Old Testament law applies beyond its initial context from the nation of Israel. Before tracing those theological categories, however, we must glance at the basic categories that have dominated modern philosophical ethics—raising the question of how law relates to ethics in the first place.

The Essence of Ethics

Three categories have dominated modern accounts of ethics. These categories shape how people evaluate possible actions in order to reach personal and communal goals. While the categories may not be mutually exclusive, they convey tension regarding what is ethically primary.

1. *Deontological theories claim that *commands* are ethically fundamental. To be ethical is to have one's act(s) follow a rule. At the very least, an act must not violate a prohibition. Although modern deontological ethics bears the marks of Immanuel Kant (1724–1804) and other philosophers, many Christians opt for deontological theories because the Bible is full of commands. What makes an act good or bad, finally, must be God's approval or disapproval. Modern Christian deontological theories have come from traditional Catholic and evangelical sources, as well as recent variations from theologians influenced by Søren Kierkegaard (1813–55). Following Kierkegaard, Barth emphasized the infinitely demanding yet gracious "command of God" that comes to followers of Jesus Christ. This personal divine demand may

set aside external laws; accordingly, these divine command accounts are not deontological in the usual philosophical sense.

2. *Consequentialist theories claim that *consequences* are ethically fundamental. To be ethical is to have one's act(s) produce maximal good and minimal or no harm. The resulting calculations may involve quantitative good—the number of people affected or the amount of some good for one or more persons. The qualitative good informing these calculations may involve various values, such as pleasure (as in hedonistic theories) or freedom (as in modern liberal theories). Traditional Christians rarely adopt consequentialist theories due to the prominence of divine commands in the Bible. They worry about the "utilitarian" tendency to treat ethics as humanly constructed. The Bible does, however, include teleological elements that focus on the ends or goals of action, as in Paul's appeal to what is spiritually beneficial (1 Cor. 6:12–20). An influential Christian version of consequentialist ethics emerged in the modern "situation ethics" of Joseph Fletcher (1905–91), which illustrates how theologically consequentialist ethics prioritize "love" as their key criterion.

3. *Virtue theories claim that *character* is ethically fundamental. To be ethical is to have one's act(s) produced by and producing virtues—enduring dispositions of the heart that provide the impetus for living well. The four classic *cardinal virtues—prudence, justice, temperance, and fortitude—inform Catholic, along with some Orthodox and Protestant, accounts of the moral life. The three *theological virtues—faith, hope, and charity—specify spiritual aspects of the moral life. Recent Christian versions of virtue ethics have their momentum from Stanley Hauerwas (1940–), who promotes a "community of character" that learns to practice the "Christian non-violence" of Jesus. More broadly, philosophical attention to virtues has accompanied the "postmodern" turn to narrative. Such virtue theories notice that the meaning of human actions arises in context—in the context of our life stories and their social relations with others.

The Bible's aim of character formation is obvious—not least in the Old Testament's Wisdom literature and in the New Testament's Pauline and Catholic Epistles. Yet this aim assumes the broad boundaries established by divine commands, and sometimes the need for situation-specific discernment of our decisions' consequences. Admittedly, focusing on decisions about particular acts can be a distinctly modern approach. And operating in terms of only one theory may be unnecessary, leaving us unable to develop adequately holistic biblical ethics. As the exposition above illustrates, the Ten Commandments establish obligations before God, affect discernment regarding consequences, and form character that represents God's design for humanity.

Application of the Mosaic Law

In the New Testament itself, Christians struggle to discern the relation between the *Torah—the law revealed to Moses in the Pentateuch—and the inauguration of the new covenant in Jesus Christ. Jesus did not abolish one iota of the Torah (Matt. 5:17–20); the Torah is holy, righteous, and good (Rom. 7:12). Yet the Torah identifies sin without restraining it (Rom. 7:7–11); the old covenant gives way to the new covenant, which underlies a better priesthood (Heb. 7:12). What then is the relation of the Torah to "Christ's law" (1 Cor. 9:21), the "law of the Spirit who gives life" (Rom. 8:2)? One classic approach, notably formulated by Thomas Aquinas, distinguishes between three aspects of the old law—grouping its precepts according to relevance for Christian practice.[19]

Moral law addresses how people should live according to God's will and character. The Decalogue constitutes its initial heart. Subsequent laws provide detail on how love for God and neighbor applies to particular cases.

Judicial law in the Torah addressed how Israel should live as an earthly nation. Particular laws or dimensions of law composed a civil code for Israel's early theocracy. By analogy, "civil" law can inform present-day ethical reflection, although it cannot constitute a full civic code for contemporary nations.

Likewise *ceremonial* law present in the Torah was Israel-specific, in order for Israel to serve as God's representative society in the world. Ceremonial laws or dimensions of law addressed how Israel should worship God before the coming of Jesus Christ, who "fulfilled" these shadows by being the true light.

Uses of God's Law

As the Protestant Reformers engaged these questions, they distinguished between uses of God's law.[20] They agreed regarding the first two but not the third.

One, "political," use of God's law is to *protect community* by hindering sin and its harmful effects (1 Tim. 1:9–10). Here, for Lutherans, God's law confronts the fallen human condition without being directly grounded in the doctrine of creation. God surely desired from the beginning that humans would depend upon divine grace and flourish in healthy community, but the first two uses of the law could be construed as merely provisional ways by which God addresses the fall.

---

19. Thomas's treatise on law comprises questions 90–108 of *Summa theologica*, Ia IIae (first part of the second part, in 2:993–1119); question 99 introduces this threefold distinction.

20. For Calvin's treatment, see *Institutes* 2.7 (1:348–66). For Luther's, see particularly "Smalcald Articles," 311–12. Various Reformers order the political and the theological uses differently. Luther and Lutherans typically place the political first.

Another, "theological," use of God's law in addressing the fall is to *convict humans* of their sinfulness and their helplessness to redeem themselves apart from God's grace (Rom. 3:20; 7:7). Even if humans could keep many behavioral laws about loving their neighbors, at minimum after the fall they cannot fully keep the first and last commandments: they substitute idolatrous desires for worship of the one true God.

The third, "didactic," use of God's law is to teach God's will, *to foster human obedience by grace* (Ps. 19:7–8; 119:5, 105). Like the first, this third use is more personal than the second, although implications remain for the church community. In principle the law teaches God's will for all humans, but in practice this third use is distinctively possible for God's covenant people. Along with classical, Orthodox, and Catholic Christianity, Reformed and pietistic forms of Christianity embrace this third, sanctifying use of the law. Dispensationalist Christians, distinguishing somewhat sharply between the old and new covenants, tend to restrict or even reject this use of the law, restricting it to New Testament commands and perhaps select Old Testament laws (most readily, those repeated in the New Testament).

Lutherans debate and often reject this third use of God's law, even for the New Testament: the dialectic of law and gospel cuts across the two Testaments. The Lutheran worry is that the law's third use could convince humans—even Christians who initially entrust their justification to Jesus Christ by faith alone—to ground sanctification partly in cooperation with God's grace. Doing so would reenact the fall all over again, grasping after moral life on our own. Luther himself, though, sometimes appealed to biblical commands as indicators of God's will, and his catechisms teach from the Ten Commandments on fearing and loving God. Therefore, using God's law for Christian formation does not automatically betray the gospel.

Paul and the Law

Contemporary debate over moral law in Scripture centers on Paul's theology. It would be impossible to trace this debate in detail. Even the definition of the so-called *new perspective on Paul is contested, depending heavily upon which figures are highlighted.

Most evangelicals have broadly followed the Protestant Reformers' insistence that Paul teaches justification—God declaring sinners righteous—by grace alone, in Christ alone, through faith alone (e.g., Rom. 4). They saw Paul drawing a decisive contrast: the teaching of the "Judaizers," such as requiring circumcision for gentile converts, amounted to justification by works because of a focus on fulfilling divine conditions. The apparent tension between

Romans 4 and the critique of justification by "faith" in James 2 generates various responses.[21] Yet Christ's atoning work ends any justifying or condemning relationship to the law by undergoing its penalty and fulfilling its demands on behalf of believers. This traditional Protestant account has several labels among contemporary critics: the "Lutheran" Paul, a "contractualist" theory of salvation, and so on.

More access and greater attention to sources led twentieth-century scholars to a different understanding of Second Temple Judaism. E. P. Sanders insisted that the Jews of Paul's day did not promote "justification by works" but rather *covenantal nomism—the idea that Israelites were already in covenant with God by grace, needing to respond with obedience to remain in covenant blessing.[22] Accordingly, scholars associated with this "new perspective" began reinterpreting the "works of the law" that Paul rejected for salvation. No longer did such works designate self-righteous efforts to earn merit before God—as suggested by Luther's analogy between the Judaism of Paul's day and the Catholicism of his own. Instead, these works focused on boundary markers of Israel as God's people. On this newer account, Paul rejected the exclusionary implications of these identity-marking works. They barred the gentiles' participation in Christ's benefits, and perhaps indirectly reflected excessive optimism about Jewish covenant fidelity. So Paul was not preoccupied "anthropologically" with the salvation of individuals who cannot keep moral law adequately; instead, Paul was preoccupied with the salvation of the covenant people and the inclusion of gentiles.[23]

Even more recently, "apocalyptic" accounts have emphasized the future eschatological age breaking into and dialectically confronting the present. This eruption of God's final future into the present disrupts all stable identities and contrasts (between, say, Jewish covenant people and gentile pagans) through universal reconciliation in Christ.[24] The apocalyptic view critiques the contractual nature of the traditional picture: supposedly, the traditional Protestant picture of Christ's atoning work simply replaces law-keeping with

21. Luther famously dismisses James as an "epistle of straw" in "Preface to the New Testament." Calvin interprets "justification" in James regarding not God's verdict (as in Paul) but "the manifestation of righteousness by the conduct," in *Commentaries on the Epistle of James*, 315.

22. E. P. Sanders, *Paul and Palestinian Judaism*.

23. A helpful introduction is Westerholm, *Perspectives Old and New*. The most significant recent book, which critiques both the "new perspective" and the traditional view at points, is Barclay, *Paul and the Gift*. Barclay shows that while the Jews appealed to divine grace in covenant (so the new perspective), they did so quite variously. Paul's emphasis on the unconditional nature of God's gift was comparatively unique (so the traditional view).

24. Most audaciously, Campbell, *Deliverance of God*. For a helpful, if forceful, critique see Allen, *Justification and the Gospel*.

"faith" as the new condition for receiving divine benefits. According to the apocalyptic emphasis, the whole point is that God has done away with conditions and the categorical thinking that generates them.

These scholarly trends offer important corrections. First, they correct misleading portrayals of Second Temple Judaism and possibly Old Testament faith, not to mention—for Protestants—analogies with Catholicism. In the ongoing wake of the Holocaust, it is vital to repudiate Luther's anti-Semitic attitudes and to ensure that they do not distort interpretation of the Bible. Plus, understanding more accurately what Paul critiques can help believers to realize how subtle is justification by works: people must not merely avoid blatant appeals to human merit; they must more subtly recognize how conditions affect belonging to the covenant community. Second, these trends correct misleading popular portrayals of justification and atonement in contractual rather than covenantal terms. If faith operates simply as a condition of God's favor, then our gospel falls into a form of justification by works.

These corrections, however, do not actually require rejecting the traditional Protestant doctrine of justification. Indeed, the Protestant Reformers worked hard to avoid treating faith as a work, as if it fulfills a contractual condition. Their readings of Paul's opponents and of Catholic practices in their day plausibly recognized some common assumptions about relationship with God. And Paul disagreed sharply with his opponents over basic principles in the light of Christ. Debate will continue over particular texts and the larger pattern of Pauline theology. But it remains unproven that these contemporary insights preclude, rather than refine, the classic Protestant doctrine—which reappears in later chapters concerning salvation.

Natural Law

Beyond approaches to biblical law, Christian theological ethics has debated the concept of *natural law: moral requirements that people of good conscience can or at least should discern from the nature of the world God created. Approaches to natural law correlate broadly with positions concerning general revelation.

The *Catholic* tradition developed an account of natural law that is often associated with Thomas Aquinas. On this account, people of good conscience can naturally discern certain obligations. For instance, people should see that God values life and that murder is wrong. To some degree, cultural recognition of natural law makes society possible. Personal recognition of natural law provides no guarantee of obedience, and merely formal obedience to an external standard does not count as a fully good work. Thus, in a Catholic account, natural law in itself offers no form of salvation. As with general revelation, natural law may prepare people to respond appropriately, but it does not provide full understanding or adequate motivation.

Classic Protestant figures are not typically associated with natural law, yet recent scholarship indicates that they retained a form of it. Both Luther and Calvin affirmed that God made an ordered creation. They assumed from earlier tradition that the Decalogue contains in miniature the moral heart of God's law, which appears more widely throughout creation. But they remained less optimistic than the Catholic tradition about human moral ability after the fall. As with general revelation, natural law establishes accountability, but people do not recognize it and respond appropriately.

Modern *liberal* theologians, often associated with loosely *Deist* "cultural Protestantism," sought to correlate Christian and public ethics, whether or not they appealed directly to natural law. In the twentieth-century German context, the concept of "orders of creation"—such as the state, the family, and work—was misused. Cultural Protestants used these orders as a rationalist substitute for traditional natural law, justifying their nation's war efforts as part of the Creator's providence.

Radical Christian approaches have periodically challenged the other three. As noted previously, Tertullian opposed apologetic appeals to philosophy in the early church. In the Reformation era, more "radical" Protestants usually denied or ignored natural law, championing Scripture's direct authority in believers' lives. Then Barth and others resisted modern cultural Protestantism; notably, in the Barmen Declaration of 1934 they insisted on fidelity to God's revelation in Jesus Christ against Hitler's regime. Such radical accounts believe that natural law betrays the gospel and its divine authority. Yet the Lutheran Dietrich Bonhoeffer (1906–45), although involved with the Barmen group, urged Protestants not simply to reject the concept of creation order(s) but also to develop an account of "the natural" as a reality in Christ, authorized by the gospel.

Today, some Protestants share the Catholic embrace of natural law in ethics, appealing to *creation*. Other Protestants still resist natural law in ethics, appealing to God's redemptive *kingdom* revealed in Christ. John Howard Yoder (1927–97) and Hauerwas are influential "neo-Anabaptist" champions of kingdom ethics, calling for Jesus's disciples to form an alternative community of virtue, particularly Christian nonviolence.[25] Although Barth did not emphasize either the church's distinctiveness or human virtue as neo-Anabaptists have done, he certainly has influenced kingdom ethics as well.

25. See especially Yoder, *Politics of Jesus.*

Oliver O'Donovan (1945–) attempts to surmount the divide between creation and kingdom ethics by appealing to Christ's *resurrection*. As the next chapter explores further, Christ's resurrection reaffirms God's commitment to redeem the created order from its present curse. This redemption involves both continuity and transformation.[26] Accordingly, creation's moral order is an "ontological" reality, yet fallen humans face strong enough "epistemological" challenges in recognizing this reality that natural law theories are thwarted.[27] A key question for this debate concerns "promulgation": What further step of divine communication is required, if any, for the created moral order to count as "law"? That will shape how much Christians expect fallen humans or their societies to acknowledge God's moral order.

Ethics: The Application of Divine Instruction

While internal debates about Christian moral teaching likely will continue, attention to the character of law in Scripture may be helpful. Regarding both particular verses containing commandments and broader sections containing legal or moral codes, associating biblical "law" with modern statutes could convey the wrong impression. The Torah does not primarily present exact prescriptions. Instead, given its covenant context, "instruction" might be a more accurate term. God's law graciously teaches how to live according to God's design for human flourishing. Such instruction is not primarily a list of dos and don'ts with accompanying benefits or penalties. Instead, with a set of principles and practical cases Scripture teaches the way of *shalom*: "Observe them carefully, for this will show your wisdom and understanding to the nations. . . . What other nation is so great as to have their gods near them the way the LORD our God is near us whenever we pray to him?" (Deut. 4:6–7).

God's instruction in the Torah is authoritative, to be sure. But its authority operates by fostering wise interpretation, so that instruction presented within a particular language, time, and place can apply to a host of circumstances. Christian ethics must attend to this authoritative instruction in a way that helps to form wise character and thereby communal *shalom*. The next chapter explores further how ethics and theology relate by reflecting on the third instrument of classic Christian catechesis: the Lord's Prayer.

26. O'Donovan, *Resurrection and Moral Order*.

27. Beyond widespread evidence of creation order as a concept in the Wisdom literature, there are also, e.g., "oracles against the nations" in the prophets. These oracles confront nations outside Israel for their violence, evil that they should have avoided despite lacking the written Torah. Additionally, passages like Lev. 18:24–30 suggest pagan accountability for evil practices that defile their dwelling places.

— 3 —

The Lord's Prayer
The Church's Spiritual Formation

THESIS

Christian beliefs are integrated with belonging as well as behavior, reforming Israel's spiritual tradition to inaugurate a community of grace among Jesus's followers, as epitomized in the Sermon on the Mount and especially the Lord's Prayer.

LEARNING OBJECTIVES

After learning the material in this chapter, you should be able to:

1. *Define briefly* the key terms introduced here (marked with an asterisk and included in the glossary).
2. *List and recognize* the following: (a) the elements of the A-C-T-S model; (b) the petitions of the Lord's Prayer; (c) two aspects of God's will; (d) three tempters from which God delivers us.
3. *Describe and compare* the traditions of interpreting the Sermon on the Mount.
4. *Identify and illustrate* the basic significance of each petition in the Lord's Prayer.
5. *Explain* the relationship between obedience and dependence in prayer.

Christian catechesis integrates belief, behavior, and belonging. If the Creed focuses on *belief* and the Ten Commandments on *behavior*, now the Lord's Prayer focuses on *belonging* to the people who pray to God as "our Father" in Jesus Christ. The Sermon on the Mount is the larger context containing the Pater Noster ("Our Father"). Jesus's Sermon, with the Prayer at its heart, has crucially shaped Christian accounts of how ethics and spirituality intersect. The variety in these accounts runs parallel with approaches to general revelation and natural law that we have already encountered.

Eventually this chapter addresses spiritual formation specifically with the petitions of the Lord's Prayer. First, it is worth establishing a threefold context for how Christians relate moral and spiritual formation: the history of interpretation of the Sermon on the Mount; the relationship between ethics and theology in light of Christ's resurrection; and the relationship between obedience to God and dependence upon God that is anchored in prayer.

Moral Theology and Spiritual Formation

Relating moral and spiritual formation involves clarifying how Christian persons and churches should engage social ethics. The previous chapter sketched some relevant factors in terms of biblical law and natural law. Now the Sermon on the Mount highlights another factor: how Jesus's teaching and work of redemption "fulfill" the Decalogue's instruction and God's work of creation.

The Sermon on the Mount

The Sermon presents a summary (what Augustine called an "epitome") of Jesus's ethical teaching. In Luke's Gospel the Sermon on the Plain appears soon after Jesus programmatically identifies his mission in fulfillment of Isaiah 61:1–2 (Luke 4:14–21). In Matthew's Gospel the longer Sermon on the Mount is the first of five teaching discourses, suggesting a parallel with the five books of the Pentateuch.

OVERVIEW

The Sermon on the Mount, in Matthew's Gospel, has been historically dominant; there, Jesus, the new prophet greater than Moses, presents the Torah's true fulfillment. The famous *Beatitudes (Matt. 5:3–12) introduce the material with blessings that characterize living in God's favor. The "righteousness" involved—for which people should hunger and thirst (5:6), for which Jesus's disciples are persecuted (5:10), which surpasses that of the Pharisees (5:20), which distinguishes God's people from pagans (5:45) but should be practiced for God's sake and not social status (6:1), which we should seek above everything else (6:33)—this righteousness preserves the world and reflects God's glory (5:13–16). Such righteousness involves obedience from the heart (5:17–20), even to the point of loving enemies (5:21–48). Being focused on God's glory, the righteous seek treasure in heaven rather than on earth, trusting God to take care of their true needs (6:1–34; 7:7–11). Focusing on

God frees Jesus's disciples from judging others, to deal first and foremost with our own sin (7:1–6) and to seek others' good (7:12).

The Sermon on the Plain, in Luke's Gospel, repeats "now" four times, especially in the Beatitudes (Luke 6:21a, 21c, 25a, 25c). This immediacy supports Luke's emphasis upon taking up one's cross and following Jesus daily (e.g., 9:23).[1] Four "woes" correspond to the Beatitudes (6:20–21, 24–26). These woes emphasize the contrast between desperately needy and complacent people, highlighting Jesus's concern for the poor.

Influential early commentators include Augustine and John Chrysostom (c. 349–407), the East's most famous preacher. In the Middle Ages, Thomas Aquinas and Hugh of St. Victor (c. 1096–1141) were notable. Among these interpreters and later Protestants as well, certain questions have persisted: Does Jesus simply interpret or more fundamentally clarify the law of Moses? What is the relationship between Matthew 5–7 and Paul's gospel of grace? To whom is the Sermon addressed: people in general or committed followers of Jesus? Are all parts of the Sermon to be interpreted literally or are some hyperbolic? Does the Sermon present an ethical code or a broader set of principles or attitudes? To what extent are particular sayings dominated by the expectation of the end times approaching?

TRADITIONS OF INTERPRETATION

Perhaps the chief question concerns whom Jesus calls to follow this blessed way of life. How generally does the Sermon spread "the fatherhood of God and the brotherhood of man" versus specifically gathering a redeemed community of Jesus followers? As Creator, God calls everyone to live justly and lovingly. Appealing to creation in that way, some align the Sermon as much as possible with the Old Testament, from which they highlight divine instruction, human wisdom, and prophetic critique to uphold a broad moral vision. As Redeemer, though, Jesus Christ calls a particular community to bear witness to God's saving love and just rule. Appealing to mission in that way, others find less alignment between the Sermon and the Mosaic law, or between Jesus's disciples and the wider world. Within the church they may even distinguish sharply between committed disciples and others. After all, throughout history the Sermon's demands have often provoked resistance, even to the church's status quo.[2]

---

1. Stanton, "Sermon on the Mount/Plain," 737. Stanton's article informs this section's discussion of the Sermon, especially the five key questions. Greenman, Larsen, and Spencer, *Sermon on the Mount*, profiles influential interpreters mentioned here.

2. Betz, *Sermon on the Mount*, 3. Betz's account of the history of interpretation, while focused on modern figures and critical issues, further informs this section. Intriguingly, he suggests

So the four major tendencies regarding "general revelation" (chap. 1) and "natural law" (chap. 2) align broadly with tendencies regarding the Sermon—and thus regarding how the church should form disciples in relation to culture.

Within the *Catholic* tradition, speaking of a single approach is almost always an oversimplification, and there is plenty of variety concerning the Sermon on the Mount. Within the variety, though, a particular tendency is notable. For instance, two early commentators, Augustine and Chrysostom (who is often associated with later Orthodoxy), both saw the Sermon as addressing all Christians. They also reflect the beginnings of a later tendency, however: understanding aspects of the Sermon in terms of an ideal spirituality.

Augustine stressed continuity between the Old Testament law and this "new" law when opposing "gnostic" dualism. Early Christians denied that good and evil were locked in an eternal struggle, or that matter was simply evil, or that the New Testament God was fundamentally opposed to the God of the Old Testament. Otherwise, though, Augustine reflected a fairly sharp distinction between the Old and the New. He saw the Sermon as calling mature Christians to higher things (Jesus addresses us from a mountain) rather than primarily addressing beginners. Chrysostom stressed the Sermon's application to all Christians, but in doing so he tried to democratize spiritual ideals, such as calling everyone to renounce wealth very strongly. Thus, he reflected a surrounding theological culture that celebrated *asceticism, a strong emphasis on self-denial.

Medieval interpretation was not monolithic. Many expositions of the Sermon still addressed all believers, even (in a Christendom context) all humans. Desiderius Erasmus (1466–1536) read the Sermon as reflecting ideals for human society, as did Geoffrey Chaucer (c. 1343–1400), who connected personal repentance with social action. By contrast, Dante Alighieri (1265–1321) appealed more minimally to the Sermon as he focused on mystical purging of sins. If those figures represent an array of Catholic approaches, Hugh of St. Victor represents a wider pedagogical tendency. He developed an elaborate series of five groups of seven: *vices* to be addressed by *petitions*, in response to which God gives *gifts*, which produce *virtues* leading to *beatitudes*. These groupings helped with remembering the Sermon's key elements. Such pedagogical devices could make praying the Sermon, especially through the Lord's Prayer, more accessible to all believers. Thus, the ascetic ideals of the Middle Ages did not always involve monastic forms or spiritually elite audiences. Much Catholic interpretation tried to take a fairly holistic approach to the Sermon.

---

that the development from the disciples as the audience in Matt. 5:1 to the mention of the crowds in 7:28–29 may indicate "progress": the core of Jesus's teaching became public knowledge.

Yet Thomas Aquinas distinguished between the new law's "commands," which are necessary for salvation, and its more optional "counsels," which assist with assurance. This distinction contributed to what Luther saw as a two-tiered spirituality. When Catholicism or Orthodoxy reflected a two-tiered view, ideally spiritual believers would pursue self-denial by separating from the world (whether as desert hermits or eventually in monasteries). Ordinary believers in the world would obey God in accordance with natural and biblical law (epitomized in the Ten Commandments) while they pursued transforming grace through the sacraments. But they could not attain the life of prayerful contemplation that monks (and to some degree priests) undertook on behalf of the church. Or so Protestants perceived, anyway.

The *classic Protestant* approach rejected this medieval Catholic tendency. Luther read the Sermon in terms of a battle against satanic deception: the Sermon is neither "law" (detailing what to do for merit before God, which we cannot attain) nor "gospel" (detailing what God has promised to do for us in Christ). Instead, the Sermon depicts the fruit that grows from saving faith. While Jesus provided the true meaning of Old Testament instruction for all walks of life—for properly Christian worldliness—Luther retained a sharp contrast between law and gospel. That contrast did not run between the Old and New Testaments as such; rather, people encounter God in two different ways within a passage of Scripture: condemning and promising. Luther thought that Anabaptists committed another version of the Catholic error, obscuring the gospel with law: Anabaptists simply applied the monastic ideal of separation from worldly society to all believers.

Calvin's approach was similar to Luther's but more moderate. Like Luther, he retained a version of natural law that saw the Decalogue as summarizing God's moral expectations. In principle, the Ten Commandments applied to all people everywhere, rooting moral life in worship. Like Luther, Calvin rejected monastic withdrawal from the world. Somewhat like Luther, he moderated the Sermon's apparent demands about not protecting oneself, swearing oaths, and the like. In some cases, though, Luther used a sharper law-gospel or two-kingdoms contrast to address such matters. For instance, an ordinary Christian should not act in self-defense (as a heavenly citizen) but might defend someone else out of love for neighbor (in the temporal sphere); a Christian should not kill as an ordinary person (in the light of gospel mercy) but might be permitted or even expected to do so as a magistrate or a soldier (in the realm of law). Calvin, by contrast, tended simply to moderate the Sermon's demands in light of other Scripture texts that apparently permit violence in certain cases. Calvin distinguished law from gospel in support of justification by faith alone, yet he saw strong continuity between the Old Testament law and Christ's instruction for his people.

In the Reformation's aftermath, evangelicals tended to read the Sermon in a twofold way. First, especially early in the Beatitudes, the Sermon confronts sinners with their need for God's grace. Then, especially in the antitheses beginning at Matthew 5:21 and culminating in the call for "perfection" at 5:48, the Sermon calls redeemed people to holiness. These evangelical tendencies appear in diverse figures like John Wesley and Jonathan Edwards (1703–58). The early Wesley, like Anglican moralists, read the Sermon in relation to Micah 6:8 and what the Lord requires of everyone: justice, mercy, and a humble walk with God. The mature Wesley, like Edwards and other mainstream evangelicals, related the Sermon to the heart—the heart of any believer who is sanctified by God's justifying grace. Even a Calvinistic Baptist like Charles Haddon Spurgeon (1834–92) appealed to medieval Catholic mystics regarding the Sermon's focus on the heart, although he spread that appeal more clearly to all Christians. In sum, the classic Protestant tendency is to oppose spiritual elitism by moderating certain demands of the Sermon, yet to intensify its focus upon the heart.

A distinct *liberal* tendency is to focus on the Sermon's import for social justice. Such modern accounts have sometimes appealed to Jesus's Sermon, along with his example, in support of nonviolent approaches to social transformation. They often highlight elements of the Sermon that appeal to non-Christians, such as the "Golden Rule" (Matt. 7:12) of doing unto others what we would have them do unto us. The Golden Rule has parallels elsewhere, although those parallels are stated negatively and not positively. Liberal accounts have noted that non-Christians like Mohandas (honored as "Mahatma") Gandhi (1869–1948) admired elements of Jesus's teaching and example that are epitomized in the Sermon.

The influential approach of Reinhold Niebuhr (1892–1971) partially overlapped with such wider appeals to the Sermon but remained distinct. Niebuhr understood the Sermon to promote ideals of love so high that they were impossible to realize within the present earthly order. Accordingly, he advocated "Christian realism" to promote whatever temporary justice is possible for "moral man" within "immoral society." Niebuhr's justice-love contrast somewhat parallels Luther's law-gospel contrast, with a more liberal context: focusing on the church's social responsibility rather than its distinct proclamation of the gospel or call to discipleship. The liberal tendency is not to be nervous if Jesus's ideals apparently conflict with elements of the Old Testament, because the priority is not to present a unified account of Scripture's authoritative teaching. Instead, the priority is to assess how Jesus's ideals promote contemporary social transformation.

A more *radical* tendency does not directly include a "Barthian" approach, since Karl Barth did not give the focused attention to the Sermon that he gave to other passages. However, Barth's basic response concerning general revelation and natural law—No!—parallels the Anabaptist tradition here, which presents the church as an alternative community. Stanley Hauerwas, an influential champion of such a radical approach, directly critiques Niebuhr's more liberal approach. Along with Barth, standing behind Hauerwas's neo-Anabaptist approach are the Anabaptist John Howard Yoder and the Lutheran Dietrich Bonhoeffer.

Both Bonhoeffer and Yoder emphasized the church's visibility (in light of Matt. 5:13–16, for instance). Hence *Christendom—the Christian synthesis of the church and the late Roman Empire that shaped the Catholic, Orthodox, and early Protestant traditions—seemed very problematic. "Christendom" hid whether or not someone was a Christian by having nearly all infants baptized and making earthly citizenship virtually equivalent to church membership. Committed disciples of Jesus became difficult to recognize; the concept of the "invisible church" distinguished true and false believers. Hence, what distinguished true disciples became something inward rather than concrete practices. The church became so connected to the empire that it became complicit in violence, thus violating a key aspect of Christ's teaching and practice.

Bonhoeffer's famous treatment of the Sermon in *Discipleship* certainly made Barth nervous.[3] The exact contours of Bonhoeffer's commitment to nonviolence remain debatable. Thus, neither the Bonhoeffer-Barth link nor the Bonhoeffer-Yoder link is airtight. Bonhoeffer remained Lutheran and upheld elements of a law-gospel, two-kingdoms view, even if he criticized its perversion after Luther. Sometimes Bonhoeffer sounded broadly Calvinistic, emphasizing God's transformative lordship over all of reality unified in Christ. Yet Bonhoeffer championed the church's visibility in his interpretation, with the "extraordinary" mark of Jesus's disciples being love for their enemies. The broader radical tendency follows: distinctly emphasizing the Word of God made personal, to the point of a sharp break with the prevailing cultural order.

Already the question of natural law highlighted tension between "creation" and "kingdom" ethics.[4] In response, the next section examines the "evangelical" ethics of Oliver O'Donovan, who addresses this tension by drawing out the implications of Christ's resurrection.

---

3. Bethge, *Dietrich Bonhoeffer*, 555.
4. Beyond sources already mentioned see the kingdom-oriented account of Stassen and Gushee, *Kingdom Ethics*.

Christ's Resurrection and Christian Ethics

In creation-oriented ethics (such as the Catholic commitment to natural law and the mainline Protestant social gospel), the foundation is nature and/or culture. In kingdom-oriented ethics (such as the Barthian focus on God's command and the neo-Anabaptist focus on Christian nonviolence), the foundation is redemption. Another form of kingdom-oriented ethics appears in *liberation theology, which identifies Jesus with the broader biblical struggles of oppressed humanity, confronting structural evil along with personal sin. Kingdom-oriented ethics worries that natural law and creation order can be tools for maintaining the social status quo, and that creation-oriented ethics domesticates "the politics of Jesus" in the Sermon on the Mount.[5] Creation-oriented ethics worries in return that kingdom-oriented ethics pits Jesus against the Old Testament rather than treating the Sermon in terms of its fulfillment.

Christians have not only struggled to discern the relationship between the Sermon on the Mount and the Old Testament generally or creation specifically. They have also struggled to discern the relationship between the Sermon and the eschatological future of God's kingdom. An illustration of that struggle is the tendency among early dispensationalists to interpret the Sermon as ethics for the future kingdom and not the present church. *Dispensationalism is a difficult tradition to define, although chapter 15 of this book traces its major strands in more detail. At minimum, dispensationalists typically have emphasized the different ways that God administers his relationship with human beings in different eras of salvation history. This emphasis on discontinuity led many dispensationalists to minimize the Sermon's application to the church. If restricting the Sermon to Israel was a mistaken extreme, still dispensationalism can highlight another factor to consider: The Sermon presents Jesus's call to discipleship prior to the cross and resurrection. The church traditionally has read the Sermon in light of the completion of Jesus's earthly mission, but we must discern carefully how to do so.

O'Donovan's influential account of "evangelical" ethics takes the resurrection as its starting point.[6] Christ's resurrection is the moment when the possibility of liberated human action is restored. The resurrection triumphed over human death, but not by redeeming us out of creation. The resurrection redeemed creation by inaugurating Christ's ultimate rule. A crucial distinction between ontology and epistemology correlates with the distinction between

---

5. Emphasizing the need for a Protestant account of the natural is Bonhoeffer, "Natural Life."
6. This section distills crucial claims from O'Donovan, *Resurrection and Moral Order*, as well as O'Donovan, *Self, World, and Time*.

creation and fall. Ontologically, an objective moral order really exists by virtue of creation. Epistemologically, though, subjective human recognition of creation's moral order is broken and sporadic by virtue of the fall. As the Holy Spirit brings the power of the resurrection to bear upon present existence, the new humanity begins to enjoy true freedom in Christ. The resurrection proclaims God's triumph in a way that invites all humans to embrace this freedom.

*Ethics in general evaluates the projects of human freedom—the rightness of particular decisions and the goodness of ways of living. Ethics arises from moral awareness, as humans awake to their indebtedness. They encounter the world, their own being within it, and therefore living in time. The discipline of ethics must address these three elements—world, self, and time—in order to connect our happiness with our duty. Ethics should help us to connect the rightness of our duty with the goodness of reality; recognizing how these two fit together offers the possibility of true happiness. "Practical" reasoning in this way incorporates both "reflection" about what is real and "deliberation" about what to do. Because ethical reasoning involves particular lives in numerous contexts, it generates personal disagreements and different traditions. Some of this variety is simply a matter of right and wrong, but not all; people may develop good character while having different vocations, and various cultures may legitimately celebrate different values.

Ethical responsibility should lead humans to prayer. Healthy practical reasoning coordinates the present ("give us today our daily bread"), the past ("forgive us our trespasses"), and the future ("lead us not into temptation, but deliver us from evil"). Longing to participate in the new creation ("your kingdom come"), Christians pray for God's healing of our agency. We pray as members of communities, longing to see others enjoy true freedom ("your will be done, on earth as it is in heaven"). Freedom: we do not try to control others but rather lift them up to God while pursuing our own repentance (dealing first with the log in our own eye; Matt. 7:1–5). True freedom: we try to help others learn obedience through various forms of moral communication (discerning what is appropriate; Matt. 7:6).

Moral communication does not focus on specifying individual decisions, because circumstances are particular and regularly change. Instead, moral communication addresses the frameworks with which we reflect and deliberate. Often Scripture itself presents broad commands that promote virtue— "love your neighbor as yourself"—rather than spelling out a specific action for every scenario. Even Torah typically presents case law that is designed to foster wise application in changing circumstances.

Thus, above all, Christian moral communication teaches how to pray and what to pray for. Traditional Christian worship flowers from the Lord's Prayer into healthy integration of "I" and "we," as the Holy Spirit grafts those who pray "Our Father" into the community of faith—"the 'we' within which each and every 'I' can realize itself."[7] Philosophical ethics can help Christians to clarify alternatives for action. But ethics should ultimately be theological, because moral life depends upon God as the world's Creator, the self's Judge, and time's Lord.

To summarize: First, Christian moral theology bears witness to *the objective reality of created order*. God has made various *kinds* of creatures, and human beings can realize their ultimate end in God by pursuing various proximate *ends* as they interact with the rest of God's creation. Christ's resurrection redeems the history of this created order so that moral learning is possible. Accordingly, second, Christian spiritual theology invites people to embrace *the subjective reality of creaturely freedom*. The Spirit makes redemption present and authoritative, healing the alienation of human reason and wills from each other and from God. Third, therefore, Christian moral and spiritual theology fosters growth in wisdom so that we can properly engage *a set of opportunities for action*. Wisdom helps us to recognize opportunities that we are truly free to enact and the ways that enacting those opportunities may affect ourselves and others. The opportunities that we take both reflect larger patterns in our lives and influence our character. They also reflect and influence the communal contexts that shape our character.

Moral life is spiritual life, ultimately, because it deals with ordering our loves for God and neighbor. Unbelievers who lack the fear of God, which is the beginning of wisdom (Prov. 1:7), can still align their lives with parts of the created order that Christ's resurrection has reaffirmed. But they cannot align the totality of their lives with the fullness of God's wisdom. Only by trusting in the promise of God's final "Yes" in Christ can we actually love God and neighbor with hope of enjoying love's reward. Because moral life is finally spiritual, and spiritual life hopes in the Spirit who raised Christ from the dead for what we do not yet see, the reordering of our loves is rooted in prayer—in the heart's cry for God. "Our heart is restless until it rests in you."[8]

Obedience and Dependence in Prayer

Prayer begins with God's call, inviting human response. *Prayer is the heart's response to God, crying out for deeper communion in light of divine revelation. Thus rooted in faith—calling upon the Lord's name, claiming God's covenant promises—prayer is an obedient response of childlike

---

7. O'Donovan, *Self, World, and Time*, 64–65.
8. Augustine, *Confessions* 1.1.1 (p. 3).

supplication.[9] Regardless of what prayer might accomplish in the world, believers cry out to God as Father in Jesus's name by the Holy Spirit. God promises to hear because the Son has already provided the response in which disciples participate as prompted by the Spirit. Perhaps it seems odd for God to command what is rooted in our hearts' desire. In fact, however, such is the dynamic involved throughout the Christian life: "Grant what you command, and command what you will."[10] God instructs us regarding what we truly need in order to flourish. Then God gives us what we need, enabling the very obedience that is expected. God fosters our obedience through the very fellowship that God initiates in calling us to prayer.

Prayer helps believers to recognize their genuine needs.[11] Out of the depths believers cry to God (Ps. 130:1), begging for mercy like the tax collector who knew himself to be an unworthy sinner (Luke 18:9–14). Jesus offers to quench our desperate thirst with God's gift of "living water" (John 4:10). Far too often we walk on in our own flagging strength. The purpose of the Lord's Prayer, in the context of the Sermon on the Mount, is to reeducate our desires so that we may follow Jesus's teaching throughout our lives. It is worth remembering that Jesus himself prayed the Psalms as he embraced the fullness of our humanity. So the Lord's Prayer teaches Jesus's followers the core grammar from the poetic school of the Psalms, where God's people learn their language for dealing with all of life.[12] Despite being rooted in God's gracious self-communication and unfolding in covenant communion, prayer remains demanding for redeemed sinners. The demand involved, however, is to ask, seek, and knock (Matt. 7:7–12): learning, by accepting Jesus's easy yoke and light burden (Matt. 11:28–30), to desire God's kingdom above all else (Matt. 6:33).

The Lord's Prayer

As disciples learn to desire God's kingdom in verbal prayer, Jesus provides a model. The widely known *A-C-T-S* acrostic is fitting: in *adoration* we cry out

9. For a practical exploration of prayer that emphasizes the freedom of childlike honesty and humility, see Miller, *Praying Life*. Bonhoeffer discusses childlike supplication as the essence of Christian prayer in *Discipleship*, 154. Similarly, in his chapter on prayer (*God, Christ and Us*, chap. 18), McCabe underscores that there is no use in pretending before God, and that acknowledging infantile desires in prayer may be part of how God helps us to grow up.

10. Augustine, *Confessions* 10.29 (p. 202).

11. See Luther, "Large Catechism," 443–44.

12. Emphasizing the earthy, poetic rhythms of the Psalms is E. Peterson, *Answering God*. The Psalms address the full range of human experience, as Jesus did, including betrayal, suffering, and despair, not just celebration and praise.

regarding God's perfections; in *confession* we cry out regarding our sin; in *thanksgiving* we cry out regarding God's kindness toward us; in *supplication* we cry out to God regarding the needs of ourselves and others. The Lord's Prayer has a slightly different order: Adoration and thanksgiving appear back to back, since supplication for daily bread implies thanksgiving; the request for forgiveness implies confession at the end, although we have already acknowledged God's greatness and our longing for God's kingdom right from the beginning. In any case, neither A-C-T-S as a broadly biblical order nor the Lord's Prayer presents itself as a rigid, sequential model. Both of them place our encounter with God's holiness front and center, while reorienting our desire around God's will.

In supplication, we "petition" for our own needs and we "intercede" for others. In asking for "our" daily bread, we acknowledge common life with others whom God has given us to love. In community, we remain particular persons: we plead for forgiveness as we forgive others who sin against us. The blessings of God's kingdom involve all the benefits of being God's children: the faithful Giver of all good gifts (James 1:17) meets all kinds of needs, physical and spiritual.

"Our Father"

The Lord's Prayer indicates from the beginning—"Our Father"—that Jesus's followers pray to the Triune God, not the philosophers' generic god. Of course, as the next chapter of this book examines in detail, a complete *trinitarian theology does not appear directly on Scripture's surface. Nevertheless, the Lord invites us to cry "Our Father" with him: Christians pray by participating with Jesus, the God-man, in his prayer to God the Father. We do not approach God on our own. We pray through the one Mediator, Jesus Christ (1 Tim. 2:5), so we need not fear that sin or inadequacy will keep us from God. Hebrews encourages drawing near with boldness (Heb. 4:14–16; 10:19–25) because of the Son's intercession (Heb. 5:7–9). Christians pray "in Jesus's name," and today his heavenly intercession continues his earthly practice of prayer (e.g., Mark 1:35; 6:46; Luke 5:16; as well as several times during his passion).

Christians pray to God as Father because they are prompted to cry "Abba" by the Holy Spirit (Rom. 8:14–17). This Holy Spirit knows the will of God the Father (1 Cor. 2:10–11) and enables believers to develop the mind of Christ (1 Cor. 2:12–16). Abiding in Christ by the Spirit, Christians conform their desires to the divine will, so God grants what they ask for (John 15:7). The Holy Spirit intercedes for these disciples along with the Son. The Spirit's intercession is distinctively immanent: the Spirit is so personally present within believers as to identify with their most intimate groanings, offering these to God even when they cannot pray in words (Rom. 8:26–27).

When we pray personally, we draw near to God with all who are "in Christ." Jesus prayed the psalms as an Israelite long before later generations of disciples, who can pray in solidarity with others even if they do not share the same immediate circumstances. So, for instance, we lament with persecuted Christians using psalms that cry out "How long, O Lord?" even when we are not presently suffering. As Jesus identifies with his people in prayer, so should we.[13] This Christ-shaped, communal dimension of prayer is fitting in light of trinitarian theology. As people "in Christ," Christians gain a creaturely share in the Triune God's life of loving fellowship. Such a trinitarian, relational account of prayer is consistent with Old Testament precursors. The Psalms manifest prayer deepening for others, not ourselves alone; these prayers are inseparably very personal and communal. Other biblical prayers, such as those of Nehemiah, Daniel, and other Old Testament saints who confessed the sin of Israel as if it were their own, reflect such interwoven personal and communal identities. These prayers are sometimes initially spontaneous yet they soon join the liturgy. They are simple and beautiful alike, befitting both temple buildings and the temple of the human heart.

God's Name

Prayer's first priority is to obey the third commandment and seek its fulfillment in others: hallowing God's name. "Hallowed" means to be treated as holy, uniquely set apart. As Creator, God is Wholly Other than all creatures, not just the source but the epitome of all perfections. Having seen God's grandeur, Isaiah saw himself as a person of unclean lips, among a people of unclean lips (Isa. 6). Similarly, the heavenly throne room manifests extraordinary grandeur in Revelation 4—jewels, a rainbow, lightning and thunder, blazing lamps, a sea of glass, and strange creatures covered with eyes. Day and night they repeat, "Holy, holy, holy is the Lord God Almighty, who was, and is, and is to come" (Rev. 4:8).

God's name, however, is not yet hallowed as it should be: not yet by all God's creatures, and not on earth as in heaven. As God's children, Christians long for their heavenly Father to receive the earthly honor that is due. Of course, God is not needy for praise; asking God to advance the honor of the divine name manifests the Almighty's blessedness, as we participate in the

---

13. See Bonhoeffer, *Life Together*, 141–81.

very worship for which we pray. As previously noted regarding the third commandment, "name" was associated with identity, reputation, and character in the ancient world. Hence this petition expresses our desire that everyone acknowledge God's utter perfection. Sacredness involves comprehensive allegiance, not marginal separation: hallowing makes God's name centrally revered, not off limits. In expressing this longing for everyone to honor God's unique lordship, we acknowledge our duty to seek first God's kingdom, as the next petition expresses further.

God's Kingdom

It seems counterintuitive to plead with the Sovereign of the universe, "Thy kingdom come." It seems stranger still that the Lord Christ taught his disciples to pray in this way, when he brought God's kingdom into their midst (e.g., Luke 17:20–21). Hebrews 2:8 expresses the other side of the story: "we do not [yet] see everything subject to" him. If the first three petitions mutually define one another, then the hallowing of God's name means the kingdom of God coming in fullness, which means the will of God being done on earth as in heaven. That is not yet fully happening.

An increasing consensus in evangelical biblical theology speaks of *inaugurated eschatology to name this dialectical, "already and not yet," tension. God's kingdom is *already* present from the beginning in the Creator's cosmic sovereignty. God's kingdom is *already* present in a new way with the first advent of Jesus Christ: the messianic Servant has come to redeem God's people and reestablish God's personal rule among them. The entire drama of the Christ event—from his miraculous birth through his baptism, public ministry, and passion to his resurrection and ascension—presents and establishes God's rule anew. Jesus regathered and redefined the people of God in himself. But God's kingdom is *not yet* present in fullness—not even in the church, a community of redeemed sinners, let alone in the world at large.

This petition implies three aspects of the *kingdom of God. There is a *Ruler*: the core concept involves God's activity of reigning. There are the things and people that are *ruled*: as Creator and Sustainer, God ultimately reigns over everything and everyone; as Redeemer, God is restoring a people who willingly submit to, even welcome, this reign. There are also *realms*: God ultimately reigns over everything and everyone, but we are praying for God's reign over human beings and the earth to take a renewed and ultimate form. Put differently, God is always entitled to reign; through Jesus, God has reclaimed this title on earth; someday, God will be fully acknowledged as King. In Christ, God has begun to reign in the hearts and the gatherings of a new humanity, extending the victory of the resurrection from Jerusalem to Judea and Samaria and the uttermost parts of the earth. Until Jesus returns to complete that earthly extension of his victory, his followers continue to pray for God's reign to be fully realized—starting with themselves.

God's Will

Praying for God's will to be done on earth as in heaven makes a personal commitment. With confidence that God hears and guides us, we can seek first God's kingdom and righteousness. There is no need to worry about anything else, since God has promised to meet the true needs of ourselves and others. God's glory encompasses our ultimate good, inviting joyful submission to the providential unfolding of God's will. The Lord's Prayer highlights what will characterize the fullness of God's reign: like beloved children, people immediately and joyfully obeying God, who cares for them like a heavenly Father. Of course, focusing on God's will in the present raises acute questions about how human freedom intersects with God's providential purposes.

While models of divine providence appear later on (in chap. 5), here two dimensions of God's will predominate. First, God's will is *sovereign*: God always and already rules over history, working to bring in the kingdom's fullness. Understanding how and why God exercises this sovereignty in and through human failure will always remain mysterious. God's sovereign will incorporates patience, from an earthly standpoint: God kindly makes space and time for humans to repent (Rom. 2:4; 2 Pet. 3:9). The mystery of this divine patience indicates a second, *moral*, dimension of God's will: since God's kingdom has a history, God's will includes human freedom to obey or disobey the divinely revealed instruction for living. The obedience for which God makes time and space is not mechanical or slavish but rather is heartfelt and joyful.

God's goal is to reign over everything—not just history in general, but each person's heart and each community's life—in harmonious fellowship. Because God's knowledge and rule are comprehensive, Christians understandably have been tempted to conclude that God also has a "personal" will: one right or best job to prepare for, spouse to pursue, place to settle down, church to join, and so forth. On this account, there are numerous biblical examples of specific divine guidance for which to expect parallels today; by responding to such guidance we locate ourselves in the "center" of God's will.

To the contrary, though, as a King, God is a gracious shepherd, not a tyrant micromanaging every decision. The Bible emphasizes human growth in wisdom, to an extent that leads many to reject the concept of God's personal will altogether. These wisdom-oriented approaches limit God's will to its sovereign and moral dimensions—within which we enjoy God-given freedom to discern what is best or even simply to choose between alternatives.[14] Scripture's numerous examples of specific divine guidance generally reflect particular occasions of salvation history, so they may not be paradigmatic for everyone. Many modern decisions differ considerably from those depicted in biblical narratives, when people were not choosing a college or a job or a spouse in the same way. The concept of a comprehensive personal will of God probably stretches the scriptural evidence.

At the same time, there may be biblical support for the notion of personal callings to church leadership. Biblical forms of leadership are not identical with modern ministry professions, but New Testament accounts of spiritual gifts may have relevant implications. Somehow God sets apart gifted leaders for the church. Additionally, for Christian decision-making in general, the application of wisdom to morally permissible alternatives may not say enough: perhaps not all morally permissible alternatives are equal in particular contexts for particular people. For instance, Philippians 1:9 has Paul praying for Christians to discern in love what is best. Texts like 1 Corinthians 6:12–20 imply a distinction between what is permissible and what is particularly excellent or spiritually expedient to pursue. Therefore, while acknowledging the mystery of how God's sovereign will intersects with human decisions—in all their dimensions—and focusing upon obedience to God's moral will, we must develop the character necessary for charitable discernment. Even when we cannot discern one clearly superior path on which to walk, we can trust that God's providence still leads us and God's presence accompanies us. That faith expresses itself in acts of self-giving love.

Our Daily Bread

The next petition turns to more tangible, immediate concerns. Praying for daily bread addresses a specific example of the fullness of God's kingdom: all will have their basic needs met—food, clothing, and the like. The surrounding context exhorts believers not to worry, because God cares for human needs (Matt. 6:25–34)—even beyond God's routine care for animals and plants. Freedom from worry does not lie in having barns—or savings accounts, the modern equivalent—so full that needs could be met without ever working another day (Luke 12:16–21). Instead, people should pray for enough that

14. E.g., Friesen, with Maxson, *Decision Making and the Will of God*; Meadors, *Decision Making God's Way*.

they are not tempted to steal, but not so much that they forget their constant dependence upon God (Prov. 30:8–9).

This petition concerns others, not just ourselves: "Give us today *our* daily bread." When celebrating the Lord's Supper, we look forward to the banquet in God's kingdom, when everyone will have enough to join the feast (Isa. 25:6–9). Such sharing at table looks backward to Jesus's practice of fellowship, even with tax collectors and sinners.[15] Therefore, this petition reminds us to share "the gifts of God for the people of God" in the present, honoring the Lord who has saved us and anticipating the fullness of that salvation.

This petition covers more than food, extending to everything needed for earthly life. However "spiritual" other petitions seem to be, people cannot do God's will on earth without trusting God for physical life. Basic necessities upheld by other biblical texts—clothing, health, good neighbors, protection from war, and so on—are part of the fatherly care that God invites us to pray for.[16]

Again, this petition asks for what God already gives. God cares for everyone, believers and unbelievers alike (Matt. 5:43–48). But God delights in being asked and thanked for these gifts. It is good to learn dependence upon our Creator in this way. Not only may we ask God for "our" daily bread; we participate in God's answers to these prayers. As Ignatius of Loyola (c. 1491–1556) urged, "Pray as if everything depended on God and work as if everything depended on you."[17] Perhaps God intends to answer prayers for starving people by having us give them bread.

Our Forgiveness

The fifth petition treats spiritual need as a concrete part of earthly existence. Particular persons need to request and receive regular forgiveness so that they might live in the joy of ongoing fellowship with God (1 John 1:9). Yet this petition goes further: challenging us to advance God's kingdom by extending forgiveness to others, it highlights the inconsistency of trying to hoard God's forgiveness for ourselves. Peter thought that "seventy times seven" reflected a generous amount of willingness to forgive. Even how to interpret this number (is it seventy-seven?) remains unclear, powerfully making the point that there is no proper limit. God has generously forgiven a multitude of sins—and an unholy state of sin—over and over, so we hardly grasp this gift if we refuse mercy to others. Frequently, though, we do precisely that, for very minor offenses (Matt. 18:15–35).

15. Moberly, *Bible, Theology, and Faith*, 62–63.
16. Luther, "Large Catechism," 450–52.
17. This attribution appears in *Catechism of the Catholic Church*, §2834 (680n122).

Therefore, this petition goes beyond addressing particular persons in their relationships with God and others. We long to be a community of ambassadors of reconciliation (2 Cor. 5:14–21). The language is again plural—"our"—pointing toward reciprocity in the request. The request is not strictly conditioned, as if a certain amount of forgiveness is a minimal requirement for earning or keeping God's favor. We could never forgive others as expansively as we need God to forgive us! If we tried to meet such a condition, we would not be seeking forgiveness from God but rather absolution or approval. The point is not to fulfill a condition of forgiveness, but rather to embody genuine understanding of forgiveness genuinely received.

Different texts and translations reflect the complexity of biblical metaphors for sin. One, "forgive us our debts," still relates to "sins" (or "trespasses") but introduces a monetary, justice-oriented aspect. Sin often takes concrete forms affecting earthly goods. Sin obligates people to God and others, owing something they cannot repay. Hence God's forgiveness encompasses past, present, and future. The full debt for past sin is removed when one embraces the good news of Jesus Christ. This removal of debt, though, begins to transform people in the present, so that they will want to make restitution for the wrong and reconcile relationships to whatever extent they can (e.g., Luke 19:1–10). The removal of debt secures the future too: repentant sinners will ultimately be forgiven at the final judgment. Without overstretching the analogy, this reality is like school: one might know something after studying it, but this knowledge is confirmed after taking an exam; one who studies but forgets before the exam does not receive the credit—an unfortunate reality that, when it comes to salvation, theological traditions handle in various ways.

The means for resting in the preliminary reality of God's forgiveness is *confession of sin, acknowledging our sin and need of grace in Christ. Confessing sins personally day by day, and communally in public worship, helps to restore unhindered fellowship with God. Failure to confess does not violate a formal condition for retaining forgiveness; failure to confess, however, hinders our embrace of forgiveness already encountered. Forgiveness is not merely a set of words. Its words point to ongoing practices of embodied relationship.[18] So it may be possible to have forgiveness in terms of final salvation without fully experiencing forgiveness in terms of present fellowship. Confession of sin fosters the humility and comfort that makes fellowship a reality—not just for ourselves but also for others.

If we cannot love our brother or sister, whom we can see, we cannot love God, whom we cannot see (1 John 4:20). And we are to forgive enemies, not

18. L. Jones, *Embodying Forgiveness.*

just our friends (Matt. 5:43–48). Forgiveness is not just saying words to someone ("I forgive you") or trying (impossibly?) to forget wrongs and get rid of bad feelings. Forgiveness involves seeking restored relationship in action. Of course, the proper enactment of forgiveness depends on context. On this earth, full reconciliation may not be possible or appropriate. For instance, someone who is physically abused needs to forgive the abuser, but the victim should not be placed back in harm's way. Restored relationships—even with God—may not undo the consequences of our actions. God—and even human victims—may forgive a sin such as drunk driving while the perpetrator rightly lands in prison. To clarify a principle behind such illustrations: forgiveness should be offered unconditionally, but forms of reconciliation depend on repentance. Consequences may have to remain for the sake of justice rather than simply being removed in the name of love.[19] Praying the Lord's Prayer, then, neither ignores earthly consequences nor usurps God's heavenly judgment. Instead, we ask for forgiveness while committing ourselves to sharing that blessing with others as practically as possible.

Our Deliverance

As we have seen, the petitions of the Lord's Prayer may be profoundly personal, but they reflect a communal dimension as well: we pray "us" and "our," not just "me" and "mine." Here the vocabulary of temptation adds another layer of complexity. "Temptation" doubles for trials or tests as well as temptation toward sin. According to James 1:2–12, God brings "trials" into our lives for good: such tests strengthen us with encouragement that our faith is genuine. "Temptation," on the other hand—and the Greek vocabulary is the same, in a complex play on words—comes from God's enemies and our mistaken responses to trials, not directly from God (James 1:13–15).

The three basic tempters are the world, the flesh, and the devil (1 John 2:13–17). The world, in the sense of the creation and culture outside us, is a good gift, but it can take our love away from God. We are made to be *in* the world, but not *of* it: the world is not supposed to be "in" us. The flesh, in the sense of the physical body, is another good gift of God, but it can also take our love away from God. As instruments for action in the world that become identified with our very selves, bodies reinforce the desires they make it possible to implement. As enacted desires reflect human weakness and worldly attachment, our bodies reinforce them by accumulating habits—in the case of sin, habits of desiring created things in an excessive measure or an evil manner.

---

19. For sophisticated treatment of these issues, see Volf, *Exclusion and Embrace*.

Like the world and the flesh, then, the devil and demons must have been part of God's good creation. But somehow they turned to prideful rebellion. The adversary, the Satan, now deceives people into thinking that God does not love them and is not good for them. This deceiver promotes "the lust of the flesh, the lust of the eyes, and the pride of life" apart from God (1 John 2:16). The heart of God's armor for resisting this adversary (Eph. 6:10–18) rests in prayerful appeals to God's Word.

God promises not to let any temptation arise—in the sense of a test or trial—without providing a way to defeat or escape its pull toward sin (1 Cor. 10:12–13). Jesus paradigmatically defeated temptation by praying and knowing Scripture (Matt. 4:1–11; 26:36–44). Trials are not only occasions of direct temptation to sin; trials are also tests of believers' perseverance, including when we suffer from natural or relational evils. Accordingly, this petition seeks the Lord's deliverance from evil through moment-by-moment protection from harm—physically and emotionally as well as spiritually. Of course, this prayer comes in the context of preeminent commitment to God's kingdom—from beginning to end. Sometimes the petition for God to deliver from evil will be answered by God's care during suffering (e.g., John 17:15), since God's kingdom may be advanced by our endurance—even in ways that are impossible for us to understand.

The prayer closes with "Amen"—"so be it"—affirming in faith that, "Yes," God will answer. It is tempting to doubt, "Why should I be so bold as to boast that God hears my prayer? I am only a poor sinner."[20] But such doubt neglects God's promise; our focus should not rest on our own works (or unworthiness) rather than God's love. "Deliver us, Lord, we beseech you, from every evil and grant us peace in our day, so that aided by your mercy we might be ever free from sin and protected from all anxiety, as we await the blessed hope and the coming of our Savior, Jesus Christ."[21] The way in which fatherly mercy is at the heart of who God is—"God is love," as reflected in this prayer—becomes clearer as the next chapter explores the doctrine of the Trinity.

---

20. Luther, "Large Catechism," 456.
21. *Catechism of the Catholic Church*, 687, §2854.

PART 2

Father, THE
THE ALMIGHTY
LORD

—— *4* ——

The Triune Name of God

THESIS

Christian orthodoxy teaches that the one true God is triune, existing in three persons—Father, Son, and Holy Spirit—who are undivided in the external works that reveal the divine identity.

LEARNING OBJECTIVES

After learning the material in this chapter, you should be able to:

1. *Define briefly* the key terms introduced here (marked with an asterisk and included in the glossary).
2. *List and recognize* the elements of orthodox trinitarian doctrine, including creedal rules and crucial concepts.
3. *Describe and compare* the narrative of a twentieth-century trinitarian renewal and critiques of this narrative.
4. *Identify and illustrate* the contemporary significance of trinitarian theology.
5. *Explain* the relationship between orthodox trinitarian doctrine and key Scripture texts.

The Ten Commandments ground moral instruction in Israel's worship of the one true Creator; the Sermon on the Mount orients spiritual community around Jesus's unique prayer to God as Father. Once God raised Jesus from the dead by the Holy Spirit, he instructed his church to baptize future disciples into a trinitarian name—Father, Son, and Holy Spirit (Matt. 28:18–20). The church's understanding of its faith, as we have seen from the beginning, is a response to God's self-revelation through the Word and the Spirit. The orthodox doctrine of the Trinity gives voice to this biblical mystery of how the one true God has been definitely revealed in Jesus Christ.

The present chapter first expounds the orthodox doctrine before explaining some ongoing debates and illustrating its contemporary significance.

Admittedly, trinitarian theology seems scandalous to modern people who desire a religion that is universally accessible and readily acceptable to natural reason. No one would ever imagine such a god on their own and expect everyone else to embrace their logic. It makes sense, however, that the true *God* should be beyond the grasp of human understanding. Since God *is* love (1 John 4:8, 16), the revelation of the trinitarian communion at the heart of God's identity is understandably mysterious but not impossible to believe. Indeed, as redeemed bearers of the divine image in Jesus Christ, we have been invited into communion with the Father, the Son, and the Holy Spirit—communion that overflows into fellowship with one another. As our fellowship deepens, we reflect the love of the Triune God in the world (John 13:34–35; 17:3, 20–26).

The Orthodox Doctrine

Rooted in Jewish monotheism, the doctrine of the Trinity flowered gradually. Early Christians struggled to understand the God of Israel in relation to Jesus Christ. Hence trinitarian doctrine implied respect for human limits in understanding the divine mystery. The early Christians discerned those limits both by developing concepts for presenting trinitarian claims and by developing creedal boundaries for restraining theological speculation. Even if the church cannot fully understand who God is, at least it can avoid idolatrous errors.

One True God

The first essential aspect of trinitarian doctrine is the confession that there is one and only one true God. The basic pattern of this biblical teaching starts with God's unique act of creation in Genesis 1:1 and leads to the *Shema* of Deuteronomy 6:4: "Hear, O Israel: The LORD our God, the LORD is one." How were early Christians to understand worshiping Christ in light of Old Testament teaching—the Bible as they knew it? To what degree was New Testament "worship" acknowledging Jesus as fully divine?[1] Church fathers used the phrase *lex orandi lex credendi* to say that the "law of prayer" should

---

1. See further Bauckham, *Jesus and the God of Israel*; Hurtado, *Lord Jesus Christ*; Rowe, "Biblical Pressure and Trinitarian Hermeneutics"; Yeago, "New Testament and the Nicene Dogma."

be the "law of faith": creedal affirmations about God should correspond to Christian worship. If Jesus Christ received worship as God's Son, and only the Creator deserves worship, then New Testament Christians were identifying Jesus with the God of Israel. That is the orthodox logic. But modern scholars often allege that the trinitarian theology of the Nicene Creed stems from concepts imposed by Greco-Roman philosophy, which overwhelmed the biblical simplicity of Jewish monotheism. In such critiques of trinitarian orthodoxy, Jesus went from being a messianic figure who acted on God's behalf to being (mistakenly) identified with the divine nature.

An orthodox response can begin by recognizing that the New Testament ardently maintains the oneness of YHWH while identifying this God with Jesus. First Corinthians 8:4–6 is representative, alluding to the *Shema* when insisting that there is only one God (8:4). Moreover, "following patterns of discourse present in Second Temple Jewish literature, the New Testament employs the language of Greek 'natural theology' to distinguish the nature of the one true God—immortal, invisible, immutable, 'having neither beginning of days nor end of life' (Heb. 7:3; Rom. 1:20, 23; 1 Tim. 1:17; Heb. 11:27; James 1:17; Rev. 1:4)—from so-called gods 'that by nature are not gods' (1 Cor. 8:5; Gal. 4:8)."[2] At the same time, 1 Corinthians 8 represents New Testament triadic thinking about God as Father, Son, and Holy Spirit. There is only one God, yes, the Father, who creates and sustains all life; yet there is also only one Lord, Jesus Christ, through whom the Father creates and sustains (1 Cor. 8:6). While the Holy Spirit is not mentioned immediately given the focus of that context, the preceding passage appeals to the Spirit of God (1 Cor. 7:40), and fairly soon Paul insists that "no one can say, 'Jesus is Lord,' except by the Holy Spirit" (1 Cor. 12:3), who reveals this divine truth by virtue of unique participation in the reality (1 Cor. 2:10–16).

Three Divine "Persons"

Such triadic material points to the second essential aspect of trinitarian doctrine: the confession that the Father, Son, and Holy Spirit are three divine "persons"—loving relations within the being of the one God. Texts such as 2 Corinthians 13:14 and 1 Peter 1:2, among numerous others, clearly evince some "divine" identification of the Son and Spirit with God the Father, thus rendering God's name threefold. The baptismal formula of Matthew 28:18–20 epitomizes this trinitarian naming: claiming all authority in heaven and on earth, Jesus instructs his disciples to baptize in the name of the Father and

2. Swain, "Divine Trinity," 86.

of the Son and of the Holy Spirit. As noted in previous chapters, ancient cultures took names to be deeply intertwined with character, so that "God's *name* is the mode of revelation that most fully and faithfully indicates the inexhaustible reality of God's *being*."[3] Put differently, God's name functions like an "audible sacrament."[4]

The identification of the three persons of the Trinity with the singular name makes a veiled reference to the *Tetragrammaton, the four-consonantal name of God in Hebrew. God revealed this personal name, YHWH, specially to the covenant people Israel (Exod. 3:14: "I AM WHO I AM"). The name of YHWH is then applied explicitly to the Son and Spirit in the New Testament. Texts such as 2 Corinthians 3:18 ("the Lord, who is the Spirit") and Philippians 2:11 ("Jesus Christ is Lord") make this connection via the Greek "surrogate," *Kyrios*, which represented YHWH.[5] Jews of Jesus's day avoided speaking God's personal covenant name, using substitutes out of reverence; in the *Septuagint (LXX), the Greek translation of the Old Testament, *Kyrios* is the substitute. The Tetragrammaton's association with other names throughout the Old Testament identifies God as both the Creator of everything and the covenant Lord of Israel. The New Testament use of this name identifies the Creator of Israel as the Father, Son, and Holy Spirit.

The New Testament draws on Old Testament hints about divine relationality, reflected in God's self-expression toward the created order: Wisdom, Word, and Spirit are especially prominent. Of course, the Old Testament cannot be explicitly trinitarian, for if that were the case, the biblical narrative of redemptive history would make no sense; the revelation of God's triune identity involved the Son's becoming incarnate, and being powerfully accompanied by the Holy Spirit, for our salvation. Yet while the Old Testament can only hint at God's triune identity, such hints are present. Take the involvement of Word and Spirit at creation in Psalm 33:6: "By the word of the LORD the heavens were made, their starry host by the breath of his mouth." John's Gospel (in places such as 1:1–18 and 8:58) explicitly identifies Jesus with the Creator's Word. From Jesus's and their own experience, the early Christians soon recognized that the Spirit, associated with divine breath in the Old Testament, participates personally in the divine identity, not just operating as an impersonal power. Acts 5:3 and Romans 8:14–16 indicate the Spirit's divine personhood in terms of communicative agency: the Spirit is personal in speaking and being spoken to.

3. Swain, "Divine Trinity," 83 (emphasis original).
4. Soulen, *Distinguishing the Voices*, 3.
5. On this concept of a surrogate see Soulen, *Distinguishing the Voices*, 10.

Creedal Rules

The third essential aspect of trinitarian doctrine moves from the material to the formal contribution of the ecumenical creeds: they express a Rule of Faith, a grammar that regulates faithful Christian speech about God. The Rule of Faith is not a grammar in the sense of just talking about talk. The metaphor of a grammar is useful, however, to emphasize that talking about the Triune God is mysterious. Participating in the church's worship is a bit like learning a language; the purpose of formal rules is to acquaint us gradually with an intuitive relational sensibility. The creeds do not explain how God can be triune or even describe the trinitarian relations very much. Far from threatening to reduce the mystery of the Triune God, they actually preserve that mystery. For the heresies excluded by the creeds arise from attempts to solve apparent theological problems—attempts that privilege one aspect of the mystery at the expense of another. In the present context, heresies either privilege God's oneness at the expense of the three persons' full divinity or else they privilege the three persons' full divinity at the expense of God's unified being. As a regulative grammar, the creeds help us to bear faithful but indirect witness to the truth of the love that God is.

One set of creedal rules addresses the identity of Jesus Christ, which will be examined more thoroughly in chapter 8. To summarize briefly for now: the church must (1a) *honor Jesus as fully divine*—neither merely human as the Ebionites said, nor a partly divine mediating creature as the Arians said. The church must also (1b) *acknowledge Christ to be fully human*—neither solely divine as the docetists said, nor just partly human as the Apollinarians said. Furthermore, the church must (1c) *maintain the personal unity of Jesus Christ* without confusing his divine and human natures. The incarnation of God in Jesus Christ does not remove the distinction between the Creator and dependent creatures. The integrity of Christian worship is at stake in that distinction. The church's understanding of the Holy Spirit as a fully divine person follows from this understanding of Jesus Christ.

Another set of rules more broadly addresses the identity of God as Father, Son, and Holy Spirit. On the one hand, the church must (2a) *avoid forms of *tritheism*: there are not three gods, or even three separate persons who share a "divine" nature. No Christians directly advocate tritheism, of course, but it is possible to fall unintentionally into such error. One form would use a modern concept of "person" that overemphasizes individuality for each of the three. Another form would overemphasize distinctive traits for each divine person, rather than rooting personal distinctions in the relations of origin that underlie their missions. Even providing an example of tritheism is inherently controversial, since modern "social" forms of trinitarianism regularly face this accusation—on which, more later.

On the other hand, the church must (2b) *avoid forms of *modalism*: the three "persons" in God are not a matter of mere appearance; they are real, not just masks. Chronological forms of modalism have God merely appearing in three different modes at different moments of salvation history: for instance, as Father in the Old Testament, as Son in the Gospels, and as Spirit from the rest of the New Testament onward. Functional forms of modalism have God merely acting in three different forms: for instance, as Father in being the transcendent Creator, as Son in being the Incarnate Lord, and as Spirit in being immanent divine power or presence. One early form of modalism, *Sabellianism, became associated with *patripassianism, the idea that the one God and Father suffered and died on the cross since the Son was not a distinct divine person. A contemporary, subtler form of modalism is *Oneness Pentecostalism.[6] If tritheism particularly threatens the integrity of Christian worship, then modalism threatens the integrity of salvation: this gift comes from the Living God through the variegated work of Father, Son, and Holy Spirit in a historical economy. Only the Son became incarnate, and he died by virtue of his human nature, remaining personally united with the Father and the Spirit in the divine being. If the divine missions do not manifest corresponding divine processions, then salvation may be a mere appearance and not the reality of God's triune love. There might be a hidden God behind the history of salvation with whom humans remain out of favor. For salvation to involve knowing the true God revealed in Jesus Christ, the Father, Son, and Holy Spirit must be proper names for divine persons, not just alternative masks that the one God wears.

Crucial Concepts

A fourth essential aspect of trinitarian doctrine involves key concepts that inform Christian speech about God—with allowance for their varied use across

---

6. Oneness Pentecostalism arose on the margins of evangelicalism. But F. Sanders ("Oneness Pentecostalism") has shown that Oneness teaching began by marginalizing Matt. 28:19 due to passages regarding baptism "in the name of Jesus." Oneness teaching approaches Col. 2:9, "in Christ all the fullness of the Deity lives in bodily form," with a strict understanding of Old Testament monotheism. The result is failing to distinguish between Jesus *exhausting* the fullness of God (as Oneness claims) and Jesus being *the revelatory embodiment of* the fullness of God (as orthodoxy claims). Claiming that God undertook a new mode of existence in Jesus (and again in the Spirit) without remainder, Oneness raises the problems of patripassianism once again. Passages in which the Father, Son, and Spirit communicate with one another must be drastically reinterpreted (either to deny personal distinctions or else to reflect temporary phenomena that end with personal reabsorption when the Son and/or the Spirit return to heaven).

languages and cultures. After the creedal rules initially acknowledged the incarnation of God in Jesus Christ via the Nicene Creed, additional trinitarian
and christological concepts emerged from the Cappadocian fathers Basil of
Caesarea (330–79), Gregory of Nazianzus (329–90), and Gregory of Nyssa
(335–94), along with Augustine and other "pro-Nicene" theologians. Eventually the Council of Chalcedon (451) shaped trinitarian theology by solidifying
christological orthodoxy. The Chalcedonian Definition clarified the nature
of the *hypostatic union of the divine and human natures in the one person
(*hypostasis*) of Jesus Christ.

From this clarification comes the first set of concepts, especially the Greek
distinction between *ousia* (one: substance or essence or being) and *hypostasis* (three: persons or subsistences). The Latin *Trinitas* (*Trinity), used
much earlier by Tertullian, designates not simply threeness but rather triunity.
Whatever the language, the grammar of trinitarian theology involves the
oneness of God in the three "persons" of Father, Son, and Holy Spirit. The
one substance or essence or being of God—what the three share—does not
exist independently of the persons, as if it were a fourth entity. The *ousia*
(Greek) or *substantia* (Latin) names this one being of the Triune God. The
Nicene Creed confessed that the Son is *homoousion* (the same in being)
with the Father, and this term eventually applied to the Spirit as well. The
three persons share one essential nature as God; in christological teaching,
the one person of the Son has two natures, having assumed a human nature
in the incarnation.

For the three "persons," *hypostasis* (Greek), a basic particular, corresponds
roughly to Tertullian's earlier use of *persona* (Latin). *Persona* denoted someone's role in a drama, for which the player wore a mask. As this terminology
developed theologically, the point was not mere appearance or play-acting;
that would land in modalism. Instead, as Augustine eventually noted, Christians need a way to refer to three "persons" even if whatever human term is
used there will not apply clearly to God.[7] Somehow the chosen term must
indicate that the Father, Son, and Spirit are "distinct in relations over against
one another as well as distinct in missions in relation to the world."[8] Hence
Thomas Aquinas defined a divine person as a "subsisting relation":[9] when
Christians predicate characteristics such as "love" to Father, Son, and Spirit,
they address God's essential being; the only way to predicate distinctions
between the persons is to address their relations of origin. The Father is God,

7. Augustine, *Trinity* 7.11 (p. 229).
8. C. Hall and Olson, *Trinity*, 3.
9. Thomas Aquinas, *Summa theologica*, Ia, q. 30, 2co, provides perhaps the most direct
statement to this effect; the foundational discussion appears in Ia, q. 29, 4co (1:158–64).

the Son is God, and the Holy Spirit is God; yet the Father is not the Son, the Son is not the Spirit, and the Spirit is not the Father or the Son.[10]

These relational distinctions are *internal* to God, not *external* as if they were defined by creation. The Father is Father with reference to the Son; the Son is Son with reference to the Father; and so forth. The Father's personal property is "paternity," as the unbegotten One from whom the Son is eternally generated and the Spirit eternally proceeds. The Son's personal property is "filiation," as the eternally begotten One. The Spirit's personal property is "procession," as the One eternally spirated by the Father (and, perhaps, the Son). The missions of the divine persons in the scriptural economy of salvation signal these distinct relations of origin to which the proper names testify.

A second crucial concept, *perichōrēsis* (coinherence or mutual interweaving of being), eventually expressed the three divine persons' communion. This aspect of the Cappadocian legacy remains disputed. While the term has widely been related to the movement of a dance, a dance that humans imitate at some level, that background is questionable.[11] Originally the term applied to the personal union of the divine and human natures in Jesus Christ, likened to the mysterious union of body and soul. Subsequently the term was transposed into trinitarian theology. As with other aspects of trinitarian doctrine, *perichōrēsis* is fundamentally a placeholder: rather than providing an explanation, it expresses a dynamic of God's life that is wondrously beyond our understanding. The one being of the Triune God does not involve a static substance void of dynamic relationship; to the contrary, God exists in restful yet lively communion, which human beings are invited to enjoy rather than imitate.

These first two trinitarian concepts, the person/nature distinction and *perichōrēsis*, address the internal life of Father, Son, and Spirit: that is, *ad intra*, without any necessary regard to the economy of God's relations with creation. The third concept, *appropriation, addresses the work of Father, Son, and Spirit *ad extra*: outside of the Triune God's inner life, in engagement with creation. Appropriation builds upon a commitment to "the unity of divine action" (*opera Trinitatis ad extra indivisa sunt* = the external works of the Trinity are undivided). This unity of divine action *ad extra* is essential to maintaining biblical monotheism; otherwise there would be more than one sovereign actor in the world. Appropriation addresses the internal economy of the unified external acts of God: it is proper to associate particular aspects of a divine act with particular persons. The incarnation is the preeminent

---

10. See, e.g., Augustine, *Trinity* 7.9 (p. 227).
11. Humphrey, "Gift of the Father," 95n9.

example: the Son became incarnate, whereas the Father and the Spirit did not. Yet the Father and the Spirit were intimately involved in the divine act of the incarnation: the Father sent the Son, while the Spirit empowered the Son's mission from conception to ascension and beyond.

This internal economy of divine action, signaled by the incarnation, can expand in two general directions. One direction is creedal, involving the basic flow of salvation history: the creeds especially associate creation with the Father's initiative, redemption with the Son's incarnation, and consummation with the Spirit's indwelling empowerment. The other direction is structural, involving the basic order of divine acts: biblical patterns and the divine persons' proper names associate the Father with planning particular works, the Son with expressing and executing particular works, and the Spirit with enabling and perfecting particular works. Viewed from the other side, the picture of this structural pattern is consistent: when Christians pray, they are prompted by the Holy Spirit, they approach God in the name of the Son Jesus Christ, and they address God as Father.

Sometimes appropriation extends even further, from divine action to divine perfections: "In appropriation some divine characteristic, activity, or effect that belongs equally to all three Persons is thought and spoken of as belonging to one of the three." So, for instance, the Bible may especially associate divine wisdom with the Son in texts like 1 Corinthians 1:24. In such cases, "The basis for attribution usually is a similarity between a divine perfection, action, or effect and a characteristic proper to one of the Persons. Something in the Person Himself calls for the appropriation. The appropriations fall into a pattern with certain things seen usually in relation to one Person, as, for example, goodness, peace, joy to the Holy Spirit."[12] This aspect of appropriation is questionable, however, since the perfections—like divine acts *ad extra*—deal with the being that all the persons share. So, for instance, 1 Corinthians 1:24 also labels Christ as the power of God, yet the rest of Scripture associates divine power especially with the Father at some times (in the Old Testament) and the Spirit at other times (in both Testaments). The Holy Spirit even has holiness especially by name, yet the Bible associates holiness with God the Father from the very beginning. Hence, when it comes to divine perfections rather than actions, appropriation must be handled with great care.

The essential trinitarian concepts are correspondingly few. They reflect the mystery of the divine life and the modesty of the church's response to divine self-revelation. The crucial concepts developed not to replace the interpretation of Scripture but rather to express its complex naming of God. The early

---

12. Endres, "Appropriation," 1:606.

Christians adopted Greco-Roman philosophical language not naively but creatively. They sought to identify the God of Israel in the light of Jesus Christ and thus to oppose explanations that split them apart. Traditional trinitarian concepts do not "represent" God directly; no human concept could adequately do so. Instead, by analogy trinitarian concepts "signify": "They give us true knowledge of God, all the while respecting his incomprehensibility."[13] Trinitarian doctrine does not explain the mystery of God but more modestly provides a grammar for the church's worshipful speech.

Ongoing Debates

Once orthodoxy stabilized officially, the church still contemplated enduring mysteries of trinitarian theology. A particular narrative of that contemplation became prominent in the latter half of the twentieth century, but it now faces significant critiques in contemporary scholarship. As a result, even the history of trinitarian doctrine is subject to theological controversy. To engage this controversy, first we need to hear the prominent textbook narrative, largely without interruption; then, the recent criticisms that raise the possibility of revisionist history.

A Prominent Narrative

According to the narrative that has dominated recent textbooks, Western trinitarian theology became a set of complex footnotes to Augustine's thought, emphasizing the oneness of the Godhead. Augustine developed a series of what have been called "psychological" analogies, which related the Trinity to the human person: for example, the oneness-with-distinction of memory, understanding, and will; or, a lover, the beloved, and the bond of love between them. By contrast, the Cappadocian fathers influenced Eastern Christianity with more "social" analogies: for instance, Peter, James, and John were persons who shared a single, common humanity, and could form a community.[14] Whereas the West emphasized the equality of the three divine persons, the East emphasized the monarchy of the Father along with the distinctness of the three persons.

The resulting dispute over the *filioque* clause in the Nicene Creed led to formal division between the Eastern and Western churches (AD 1054).

13. Emery, *The Trinity*, 98. On concepts serving Scripture interpretation and forming a "grammar," see further S. Holmes, *Quest for the Trinity*, esp. 108, 198.
14. Gregory of Nyssa, "On Not Three Gods" (*NPNF*² 5:455).

Influenced by Augustine, public worship in the West gradually added "and the Son" (*filioque*) to the third article of the Creed (so that the Spirit "proceeds from the Father and the Son"). The pope mandated this increasingly common practice, but the Eastern churches rejected this unilateral Western move as schismatic. Politics aside, theologically the East worried that the *filioque* weakened the monarchy of the Father as well as the full personhood of the Spirit, who seemed to become merely an impersonal "bond of love" between Father and Son.

Western trinitarianism is then accused of lapsing into abstract speculation during the Middle Ages. "Scholastic" theologies squelched trinitarian doctrine by pursuing increasingly speculative questions with technical concepts. The metaphysical approaches of Western philosophers prioritized the one "Unmoved Mover" who caused the universe. The Father, Son, and Holy Spirit played second fiddle to this monotheistic Most Perfect Being, because the history of salvation, in which the three persons' particularity is revealed, became an afterthought. The structure of Thomas Aquinas's *Summa theologica* is treated as emblematic: first, *De Deo Uno*, the one God, and only later *De Deo Trino*, the three-personed God.[15] A couple centuries later, the Protestant Reformers may have resisted scholastic speculation, but their emphasis on organic biblical theology did not foster a trinitarian renaissance, due to the doctrine's lack of explicit development in Scripture. Soon Protestant scholasticism reemerged, committed to the primacy of the one classical God.

Accordingly, the Enlightenment's quest for a universal, rational, and natural religion made the triunity of the Christian God embarrassing. Conservative theologians continued adhering to the doctrine, but they lacked confidence to develop its implications with verve. More liberal theologians hid the doctrine from public focus or deemed it to be inappropriate speculation. An oft-cited example is Friedrich Schleiermacher. Considering trinitarian theology to be unnecessary for the pious experience of redemption, he relegated the doctrine to thirteen pages at the end of his nearly eight-hundred-page dogmatic theology, while critiquing its orthodox formulation.[16]

Early in the twentieth century, however, Karl Barth embraced the revelatory scandal of trinitarian theology rather than cowering with embarrassment. Barth's christocentric focus on divine revelation brought trinitarian dogma

---

15. However, S. Holmes, *Quest for the Trinity*, 156n24, notes that the origin and meaning of these titles are problematic. A vigorous defense of beginning with the one God appears in Sonderegger, *Doctrine of God*, which is reviewed in Treier, "Theology on Fire."

16. See Schleiermacher, *Christian Faith*. The extent of Schleiermacher's orthodoxy is disputed, since his comments lean in a Sabellian direction—although the recent scholarly trend is to rehabilitate him (as in, e.g., S. Holmes, *Quest for the Trinity*, 190).

back to the forefront.[17] Barth was accused of modalism because he found the modern concept of "person" to be too individualistic; he preferred speaking of Father, Son, and Holy Spirit as three "modes of being" in God. Barth was not a modalist, but he maintained the Augustinian, Western emphasis on divine unity. He even developed a parallel to Augustine's Lover–Beloved–Love scheme, expounding divine revelation in terms of Revealer–Revelation–Revealedness. Simultaneously Barth developed a relational account of the image of God that, perhaps ironically, contributed to the later twentieth-century, more social, trinitarian emphasis on community.

This prominent narrative includes two Catholic contemporaries of Barth, Hans Urs von Balthasar (1905–88) and Karl Rahner (1904–84). Rahner famously insisted that "the economic Trinity is the immanent Trinity, and the immanent Trinity is the economic Trinity," which became known as *Rahner's Rule. This rule rightly claims that the God encountered in the economy of creation and redemption is the same as God is in God's own being: if divine self-revelation is really revelation, then there is not some other God hidden behind the mask of the economy. Yet stronger interpretations of Rahner's Rule are controversial: they seem to threaten God's freedom by making creation necessary—if the immanent and economic Trinities are so identical that somehow there must be an economic Trinity.

The next major protagonists in the renaissance narrative include Jürgen Moltmann (1926–) and Wolfhart Pannenberg (1928–2014). Along with Balthasar and others, they blended Barth's emphasis on trinitarian revelation with strong interpretations of Rahner's Rule. Indeed, Moltmann and Pannenberg embraced versions of *panentheism—the world somehow being "in" God. Hence they made the history of salvation—preeminently the cross (Moltmann) and the resurrection (Pannenberg)—integral to the unfolding realization of God's being. Moltmann has highlighted the cross as the ultimate site of the Triune God's identification with creation's suffering. Likewise, feminist and Global South theologians, such as Catholics Catherine Mowry LaCugna (1952–97) and Leonardo Boff (1938–), have explored the relational possibilities of a social trinitarian renaissance. Not all social trinitarianism is panentheistic, and not all proponents of the renaissance narrative promote strongly social trinitarian theologies. But *social trinitarianism typically embraces this narrative of a modern renaissance and emphasizes the mutuality of the three divine persons as a model for human community. Such healthy community is usually envisioned along democratic and egalitarian lines.

17. For an enduring version of this account, see Welch, *In This Name.*

Social trinitarianism became popular among evangelicals late in the twentieth century, as Western individualism came under intense criticism. The "postmodern" urge to seek community prodded pastoral accounts of divine fellowship as the motivation and model for human community. Forms of this social emphasis vary, but appeals to "relationality" have become almost ubiquitous. Unfortunately, the historical nuance of evangelical trinitarian theology has lagged behind the popular pastoral appeal of the social trinitarian renaissance.[18]

The renaissance narrative addresses not just community but also modern Deism and atheism. As noted above, modern people often rejected trinitarian faith because they could not reconcile the Christian God with universal reason: the revelation of a Triune God would be inescapably particular, tied to redemption in history. The renaissance narrative suggests, however, that modern thinkers may actually have been rejecting the lordly God of Western philosophical reason—the Most Perfect Being of medieval and Protestant scholasticism. This "God" seemed to hinder human autonomy while being unnecessary in light of scientific progress. By contrast, a more relational and less classically philosophical God would not have provoked that early modern backlash.[19]

Hence the development, not just the definition, of trinitarian theology has become disputed. If an eclipse of relational trinitarian theology fostered modern atheism, while its recovery fosters healthy human community, then this narrative of its fall and rise should be prominent indeed.

Revisionist History

Yet this prominent narrative now faces significant scholarly critique. Critics claim that there was no genuine twentieth-century "renewal" in the quality and novelty of trinitarian theology, even if its quantity increased.[20] The critics

---

18. Aspects of the present chapter are reworked from Treier and Lauber, introduction to *Trinitarian Theology for the Church*. Sincere thanks to InterVarsity Press and my coauthor for permission to reuse this material, which originated for a Wheaton Theology Conference.

An evangelical survey of the renaissance in trinitarian theology comes from Grenz, *Rediscovering the Triune God*. Among other evangelical contributions are Feenstra and Plantinga, *Trinity, Incarnation, and Atonement*, and Volf, *After Our Likeness*; both take a social approach. Letham, *Holy Trinity*, and several works by F. Sanders, including "The Trinity," are more traditional. Colin Gunton's trinitarian emphasis proved stimulating for many evangelicals, as evidenced in Metzger, *Trinitarian Soundings in Systematic Theology*. See also George, *God the Holy Trinity*.

19. See, e.g., Buckley, *At the Origins of Modern Atheism*; Gunton, *The One, The Three, and the Many*; Placher, *Domestication of Transcendence*.

20. See this argument more fully in B. Marshall, "Trinity." S. Holmes, *Quest for the Trinity*, xv, flatly insists "that the explosion of theological work claiming to recapture the doctrine of

emphasize first that Augustine discarded nearly all of his psychological analogies or at least qualified their strength.[21] West and East may have emphasized different analogies, but they did not do so exclusively; for instance, Augustine and Gregory of Nyssa each used both psychological and social analogies. Thinkers on both sides qualified the analogies as only analogies, primarily concerning themselves with rejecting heresies such as Arianism.[22] Next, critics tackle the charge of medieval abstraction. They suggest counterexamples such as Richard of St. Victor (d. 1173), although the renaissance narrative treats Richard's somewhat social model as an exception. The charge of medieval speculation elicits scholarly defenses of Thomas Aquinas, who has recently been recovered as a primarily biblical, not just philosophical, thinker.[23] As for the debated implications of the Protestant Reformation, critics emphasize that no straight line runs from the Reformers' relative biblicism to the philosophical rejection of trinitarian doctrine in figures such as Kant. At the same time, the Reformers preceded their scholastic successors in appropriating the medieval trinitarian heritage.

Admittedly, the *filioque* manifests a distinction between Eastern and Western trinitarian thought. But the textbook contrasts—East: threeness, monarchy, social analogies; West: oneness, equality, psychological analogies—stem largely from a nineteenth-century French Jesuit, Théodore de Régnon (1831–93).[24] According to critics, the claim that the Trinity is the most essential Christian doctrine is not particularly Eastern. Alternatively, novel versions of this claim could break the proper Christian connection to the one God of Israel. Similarly, critics hold that Rahner's Rule, identifying the immanent and the economic Trinities, may generate confusion rather than a novel contribution. Its basic interpretation is simply traditional, while its stronger interpretation raises questions about divine freedom. Anyway, stronger versions of the claim appeared in the nineteenth century, before the supposed twentieth-century renaissance. Whatever the debated degree of his orthodoxy, G. W. F. Hegel (1770–1831) is a key figure here: long before the twentieth century, he already shared Kant's critique of metaphysics. Hegel closely attached God's being to

---

the Trinity that we have witnessed in recent decades in fact misunderstands and distorts the traditional doctrine so badly that it is unrecognizable."

21. See, e.g., Augustine, *Trinity* 15.39 (p. 426).

22. The prominence of Exod. 3:14 and the "divine names" (involving not just proper names but all characteristics predicated of God) throughout the Christian tradition further minimizes East/West distinctions. See, e.g., Soskice, "Gift of the Name"; Soskice, "Naming God."

23. See, e.g., Levering, *Scripture and Metaphysics*.

24. See, e.g., Barnes, "Rereading Augustine on the Trinity"; Barnes, "Use of Augustine"; Barnes, "De Régnon Reconsidered"; although S. Holmes, *Quest for the Trinity*, 130n22, mentions a recent defense of de Régnon.

the world's historical becoming through formal concepts of incarnation and Trinity. Barth's dialectic of revelation, strong versions of Rahner's Rule, and Moltmann's theology of the cross all bear the marks of Hegel. Criticisms of the East-West contrast, then, are joined by criticisms of the contrast between the twentieth century and earlier in the West.

The individual definition and social emphasis in the renaissance narrative's concept of "person" adds another complication, departing from Barth and Rahner as early protagonists.[25] Criticisms of the premodern starting point—the one God, rather than the three persons or the economy of salvation—raise legitimate pedagogical questions. A doctrine's starting point, however, does not automatically determine its content or coherence. Much of the debate over the prominent renaissance narrative, therefore, really amounts to disagreement about whether to replace a classically "essentialist" (Aristotelian?!) account with a contemporary "personalist" (Hegelian?!) approach.

Several critics have challenged the personalist appeals to *perichōrēsis* as a divine model for human social orders.[26] One problem involves mystery: *perichōrēsis* signifies what we scarcely understand about the Triune God, so the concept sheds little light upon human relations. A second problem involves projecting human ideals onto God: we supplant the mystery of *perichōrēsis* with visions of human community that already seem preferable on other grounds. Sometimes those communal visions are progressive, championing egalitarian notions of social democracy. Others' communal visions are conservative, defending social hierarchies by showing that equal dignity coincides with differentiated authority. Such appeals to the Trinity are particularly visible in debates about gender and sex, but the danger of projecting human ideals onto God is even broader.

Critics insist that contemporary trinitarian theologies can be just as politically complicated as traditional alternatives. Appeals for "community" still depend on detailed application.[27] Similarly the recent focus on the economy of salvation can be rightly or wrongly pursued. According to the renaissance narrative's critics, the Bible does not use the trinitarian divine being as a structural model for human relationships. Instead, Scripture presents what the Father, Son, and Holy Spirit together do for our salvation. God's enacted love is what reshapes human relationships. Theology's relational focus should actually rest upon human participation in the fellowship of the Triune God so that we may be transformed for loving one another.[28]

25. B. Marshall, "Trinity," 188.
26. See, e.g., Otto, "Use and Abuse of Perichoresis"; Kilby, "Perichoresis and Projection."
27. Tanner, "Trinity," 323.
28. Tanner, "Trinity," esp. 328–29.

The critics' revisionist voices do not diminish the importance of trinitarian theology, but they challenge us to engage the doctrine carefully. The trinitarian "renaissance" may function like the stock market: even if there are elements of hype, perception influences reality. The profusion of trinitarian literature represents an opportunity to influence church life.[29] It would be wrong to treat the classical tradition as so comprehensively correct that fresh insight is impossible; the church must always be open to reform from God's Word. If nothing else, the renaissance narrative highlights John 17, since that passage somehow connects the fellowship of the Triune God with human life and love.

Contemporary Significance

Obviously, the contemporary significance of trinitarian theology will be affected by these ongoing debates. Even so, we should expect to find a trinitarian shape throughout the Christian faith—in responding to divine revelation, being amazed by divine love, and embracing our new humanity in Christ. The following are a few examples of the trinitarian perspective that implicitly shapes the rest of Christian doctrine in this book.

Revelation

To begin with, trinitarian revelation inextricably links love and knowledge, reflecting the perichoretic unity of the Word and Spirit. As Augustine saw while exploring "psychological" analogies, knowing truly is interwoven with desiring rightly. God personally initiates communion with us, speaking a loving Word and helping us to hear by the indwelling Holy Spirit. All things hold together in Jesus Christ, the very Son of God, including the truth into which the Spirit guides human inquiry.[30]

To think in trinitarian and christological terms, earlier Protestants spoke of "archetypal" and "ectypal" knowledge. *Archetypal knowledge is God's self-knowledge as Creator of everything; *ectypal knowledge involves creaturely correspondence to God's knowledge through revelation. The incarnation of the God-man brings archetypal and ectypal knowledge together—reassuring us that God condescends to reveal truth, and creaturely knowledge can be

---

29. F. Sanders, *Deep Things of God*, 11, suggests that evangelicalism has been tacitly trinitarian even in "low-church" sectors that do not emphasize formal liturgy, tradition, and sacraments. The contemporary task is to make explicit the gospel's trinitarian framework, including aspects expressed in popular phrases such as a "personal relationship with Jesus."

30. For a sophisticated example of relating trinitarian theology to epistemology, see B. Marshall, *Trinity and Truth*.

"justified true belief," corresponding to the reality God knows. Christians can make every thought obedient to Christ (2 Cor. 10:5) without typically rejecting the claims of others about the world he holds together—as long as those claims can be integrated within "the fear of the LORD" (Prov. 1:7) as framed by the gospel and informed by Scripture.

Providence

A trinitarian perspective illuminates God's providence as well. As *transcendent, the Lord is utterly blessed, beyond finite knowing. God's action does not compete with ours but operates on a different plane, sustaining our creaturely agency. Yet the Triune God is profoundly *immanent, near enough to be at home with us. The Son became radically immanent in the incarnation, incorporating human history within the divine life. The Spirit becomes radically immanent by empowering creaturely life and indwelling God's people. Transcendence and immanence are not pure opposites, despite what humans might suppose. God is so transcendent as to be immanent to anyone and everyone simultaneously. The Father relates to creatures through "two hands" (in the famous phrase of Irenaeus of Lyons [c. 130–202]), the Son and Spirit, who mediate divine action in deeply personal ways.[31]

The Son's incarnation and the Spirit's indwelling are unique operations, not just general principles of divine providence. In anchoring the economy of salvation, though, they fundamentally reveal the way the Triune God exercises lordship over history. Since God mediates fatherly care through the Son and Spirit, creaturely causes and human responses matter. God acts to establish creaturely freedom, engaging human beings in personal relationship. Creation and providence maintain a coherent form in the Word of the Son and dynamic life in the Spirit. Humans return grateful praise to a Triune Creator and Provider: prompted and enabled by the Holy Spirit, participating in the Son's self-offering back to the loving Father, who has initiated such grace.

Richard of St. Victor reminds us about the freedom of God's love for creation in the first place.[32] Since "God is love," some differentiation is required within God or else God, as love, would need the world as an object to love. Yet the Triune God is love first and foremost within the divine life: God did not need to create a world to love because the Father, Son, and Holy Spirit eternally enjoy loving communion. Creation was not a necessity but rather a free outpouring of the love that characterizes God's own being. Christians

31. Irenaeus, *Against Heresies*, 5.6.1 (ANF 1:531)—championed in numerous works by Colin Gunton.
32. See Richard of St. Victor, "Book Three of the Trinity."

"fear" the Triune God in faith, not as pagan cultures fear their gods, because the Father, Son, and Holy Spirit genuinely love (rather than manipulate or need) us.

Salvation

A trinitarian perspective is especially important for understanding Christ's work on the cross. The unity of divine action makes it wrong to pit the Son against the Father, as if "gentle Jesus meek and mild" simply takes our side to stem the tide of the Father's wrath. Instead, God the Father lovingly initiated the plan of salvation; the Son willingly accepted the mission of living, dying, and being resurrected as a human being to save us; the Spirit superintended and now spreads the Son's mission. On the cross, Christ sacrificially bore the weight of sin by virtue of his human nature. But that mysterious event ultimately involved God taking off judicial robes, so to speak, in order to assume human nature and take on our death. That sacrifice involved a trinitarian economy of personal missions and united divine action. The divine holiness expressed on the cross was the Son's and the Spirit's, not just the Father's; the divine love expressed there was the Father's as well.

A trinitarian account of the cross celebrates the saving importance of the rest of the Son's and the Spirit's work too. In particular, the Son's resurrection, ascension, and ongoing intercession for us provide crucial boldness in prayer. Not only is Christ an object of worship, but Jesus is also the faithful human being who mediates our worship back to God.[33] The Spirit fosters our participation in that self-offering; worship is not just a human responsibility but is also first and foremost a divine gift.

The trinitarian gospel has implications for engaging religious pluralism. Ontologically, there is only one God—a commitment that Christians share with people of other faiths, particularly Judaism and Islam. Epistemologically, though, there is ultimate divine self-revelation in Christ alone, while the Spirit is at work giving life throughout the created and cultural orders. How should Christians understand the Spirit's life-giving work in relation to people of other faiths? Given the religious elements of all cultures, and the globally interconnected nature of contemporary culture(s), such questions feel newly pressing.[34] Trinitarian theology does not determine all the answers, but it should influence the church's reflection upon these questions.

---

33. A. Torrance, "Being of One Substance," 59–61.
34. Appealing especially to the Spirit in this area is Yong, *Beyond the Impasse*. See also the extensive evangelical discussions in Kärkkäinen, *Constructive Christian*, esp. vol. 2, *Trinity and Revelation*; McDermott and Netland, *Trinitarian Theology of Religions*.

In particular, a trinitarian perspective reminds us not to treat salvation simply in terms of an eternal destination and a transactional means of getting there. Rather, salvation ultimately concerns personal communion with the Father, Son, and Holy Spirit.

Communion

Finally, in the context of trinitarian perspectives on revelation, providence, and salvation we return to contemporary debates regarding human personhood and Christian community. Here it is worth sketching the conceptual debates embedded in the earlier narrative, before seeking points of possible consensus.

DEBATES

For traditional trinitarianism, the Bible implied a "metaphysical" understanding of divine personhood: "the being that exists truly in itself, the reality that underlies the manifestation to others, the foundation of what appears in the action."[35] Each *hypostasis* "includes a special mode of action and a relational capacity, but . . . is defined foremost by its existence in itself and through itself," grounding and integrating psychological, moral, relational, and active features.[36] Ultimately, "the three divine *hypostases* are distinguished by eternal relations of origin—begetting and proceeding—and not otherwise."[37] A human person possesses a human nature as a singular existing individual, but for the Triune God essence and existence are not separable in that way. In *perichōrēsis* the divine persons exist as relationally distinct, but they are not separable from the divine essence.[38]

Orthodox metropolitan John Zizioulas (1931–) proposes a different understanding. He claims that classic trinitarians realigned *hypostasis* ("subsisting being") away from *ousia* ("being") and toward *prosōpon* (face and thus "person").[39] The crucial "ontological" word, *hypostasis*, now became "identified with a personal word. The basic nature of reality is now no longer about the 'stuff' from which things are made, but about the persons who made it, and their relatedness."[40] Zizioulas's emphasis on "being as communion" gained popularity during the trinitarian renaissance narrated above, casting Augustine as a culprit and the Cappadocians as heroes. On this account, the

---

35. Emery, *The Trinity*, 101.
36. Emery, *The Trinity*, 102, 104.
37. S. Holmes, *Quest for the Trinity*, 146.
38. Emery, *The Trinity*, 106.
39. Zizioulas, *Being as Communion*.
40. S. Holmes, *Quest for the Trinity*, 13.

West's psychological and philosophical myopia obscured the Cappadocians' personalist insight.

Debate over *divine personhood* now involves historical and theological facets. Historically, was Augustine a faithful exponent of the "pro-Nicene" tradition to which the Cappadocians contributed, or did he mislead Western trinitarianism? Was early modern atheism responding to abstract, scholastic, inadequately trinitarian theology, for which a twentieth-century renaissance provided correction? Or did nineteenth-century theologians already propose the key elements of the renaissance—balancing out antitrinitarian challenges on the one hand with unorthodox trinitarian speculation on the other?[41] Theologically, therefore, is the modern emphasis on "personality" illuminating or misleading within the trinitarian realm? How directly can we draw proper analogies between human and divine personhood?

A related debate concerns *social equality*. Does the equal personhood of Father, Son, and Holy Spirit support "egalitarian" social orders among humans—in broader society and/or specific relationships such as marriage? Or does the equal being yet differentiated economy of Father, Son, and Holy Spirit support "complementarian" social orders, at least regarding household and/or church authority? Or is the personhood of Father, Son, and Holy Spirit sufficiently unique that no analogies between trinitarian *perichōrēsis* and human social structures are appropriate?

Still another debate concerns *the gendered naming of God*. Does naming God as Father, Son, and Holy Spirit perpetuate stereotypes of God as male that hinder women from fully participating in the benefits of the gospel? Do substitute possibilities—such as Source, Wellspring, and Water of Life[42]—faithfully develop biblical metaphors for naming God? Or do substitute possibilities leave worshipers trying to address a coldly impersonal God? Does the Bible distinguish between using feminine *metaphors* for learning about God and using Father, Son, and Holy Spirit as *proper names* for praying to God? If the Christian tradition is correct to treat Father, Son, and Holy Spirit as proper names, does its emphasis on divine mystery adequately avoid the distortions of human gender categories? Finally, what about recovering the Jewish practice, which apparently Jesus followed but Christians abandoned, of not vocalizing the one God's proper name? Would that practice show proper reverence for God's transcendence, helpfully qualifying other "names," or would it fail to reflect the fullness of divine revelation in Christ?[43]

---

41. S. Holmes, *Quest for the Trinity*, 198.

42. E.g., Cunningham, *These Three Are One*.

43. This intriguing proposal of Soulen, *Distinguishing the Voices*, may underemphasize the distinction between proper names and other names or metaphors. See further Kimel, *Speaking*

CONSENSUS?

Despite interpreting personhood and community differently, Christians share faith in a uniquely relational God. Creedal teaching provides a grammar for worship, not a solution to intellectual problems. Honoring the Triune God together does not require knowing exactly how "person" applies to the mysterious *perichōrēsis* of Father, Son, and Holy Spirit. In light of biblical texts such as John 17, trinitarian theology ought to celebrate God's unique love and humans' related fellowship, even if we disagree over the precise connection.[44]

Modern social theories assume that difference entails conflict and produces violence that must be politically managed. These theories depict perennial realities of human society's fall into sin. Trinitarian theology offers an alternative hope: in God's own life, relational distinction is not just compatible with love; it is also integral to the fellowship of Father, Son, and Holy Spirit. Renewed humanity can enjoy communion with God by grace, thereby becoming a dim creaturely analogy of the divine communion. The life of the Triune God invites us to imagine an "ontology of peace"[45] in the very act of worship.

We become like what we worship, as the Bible teaches concerning idolatry.[46] Human beings ultimately orient their lives around either dangerous self-preoccupation or joyful self-giving. Worshiping a Triune God whose being is in communion—by whatever definition—orients Christians to expect that their joy will be made complete only in fellowship.[47] Of course, people can realize that humans are relational without embracing trinitarian theology; furthermore, biblical reconciliation hinges on embracing the "message" of God's love rather than corresponding to a "model" of trinitarian being. Excessive speculation about trinitarian relationality risks eclipsing the divine

---

the *Christian God*, and especially M. M. Thompson, *Promise of the Father*, 155–85. Thompson shows that the Old Testament treats God as Israel's Father, even if not by name; that the Jewish context of early Christianity may have been reticent to speak God's name, but "Father" is distinctive to the mode of addressing God in the New Testament; and that what it means to address God as Father depends ultimately upon eschatological hope in God's faithfulness, not human gender analogies.

44. Sexton, *Doctrine of the Trinity*, offers two versions of a "classical" view—Molnar as a Catholic and Holmes (cited above) as an evangelical—and two versions of a "relational" view. Both the "radical" (from Paul Fiddes) and the "creedal" (from Thomas H. McCall) versions of the relational view distinguish themselves from strongly "social" trinitarianism. Thus, specific arguments aside, they enhance the plausibility of seeking a basic consensus here—chastening social approaches historically and conceptually as needed, without automatically insisting on an altogether classical approach.

45. This paragraph very broadly appropriates the "radical orthodoxy" of Milbank, *Theology and Social Theory*.

46. Beale, *We Become What We Worship*.

47. McFadyen, *Bound to Sin*.

mystery: "Sooner or later analysis must cease, as we simply stand in awe, watching the unconsumed bush burn."[48] Despite those qualifications, however, in John 17:21 Jesus prays that his followers "may be one, Father, just as you are in me and I am in you. May they also be in us so that the world may believe that you have sent me." Even if human relationality is clear without biblical trinitarianism, truly enjoying human community means reflecting the love of the Triune God.

Much of human life deals with words—a relational reality that underscores the dependence of true community upon divine revelation. The blessed Trinity calls forgiven sinners into a new humanity by the Word and Spirit, so that Christian worship might reflect the fellowship of God's self-giving love. Actions speak louder than words, but our lives unfold in communicative action that—words included—should invite the world to embrace the Triune God's gift of *shalom*.

---

48. Humphrey, "Called to Be One," 225n6. On the contrast between the message and a model, see Adam, "Trinity and Human Community."

—5—

The Character of Providence

THESIS

From creation to consummation, providence reveals the Triune God's perfections of power, wisdom, love, and holiness; the drama of redemption is the setting in which the Bible addresses the mystery of divine sovereignty and human responsibility along with the meaning of evil.

LEARNING OBJECTIVES

After learning the material in this chapter, you should be able to:

1. *Define briefly* the key terms introduced here (marked with an asterisk and included in the glossary).
2. *List and recognize* the following: (a) various divine perfections or attributes; (b) three elements of divine providence.
3. *Describe and compare* the following: (a) traditional Christian theism, involving belief in creation *ex nihilo*, vis-à-vis Deism and panentheism; (b) models of divine providence.
4. *Identify and illustrate* the four preeminent divine perfections as presented in Scripture, especially in Isaiah 40.
5. *Explain* how the mystery of redemption in traditional Christian theism addresses the problem of evil biblically.

Providence involves God sustaining and governing all of creation. Many cultures attach some meaning to "god" in association with creative power. Yet the Nicene Creed introduces creation as the work of the Triune God, addressing our Creator not just generically as Almighty but also specifically as the Father of our Lord Jesus Christ. Christians understand who God is and how God acts in the light of trinitarian revelation.

101

Creation is a loving project, freely chosen in the Father's communion with the Son by the Holy Spirit. This chapter addresses providence first, before the next chapter addresses creation, to emphasize the Triune God's blessed character apart from the world and creation's loving purpose. God created as the inaugural movement of a larger project: displaying divine glory in a cosmic economy of communal delight. Providence preceded the act of creation in this sense: the Triune God eternally planned to provide for creatures' life—not only their existence but also their history. Hence the doctrine of providence can encompass two major tasks: first, characterizing God's perfection; second, addressing models of God's action.

God's Perfection

Trinitarian theology addresses God and how we know God: like Word and Spirit, "God" and "Word of God" are mutually informing concepts. Since God's self-communication unfolds in a history of creation and redemption, humans come to know *who God is* by hearing *what God says* in the context of *what God does*, and vice versa. God's actions may speak louder than words, but they are always interpreted by God's powerful Word. Therefore, our knowledge of God's *being* is determined by God's *act*.

Human Language and Divine Perfections

Ways of classifying God's attributes reflect inherent tensions in the human effort to speak of God.[1] Language is necessary to understand God at all, but human concepts are inherently limited. Such concepts combine appeals to *infinity (negating creaturely limits) and perfection (relating God to human ideals). Such concepts try to characterize God's being, apart from the world; yet humans depend upon the economy of divine action for any acquaintance with God in the first place. Given these tensions, most Christian theology maintains an *analogical view of language: concepts apply to God somewhat like they do to creatures. If language were *equivocal, then concepts would apply to God in an entirely different way from creatures, virtually nullifying divine revelation: for instance, human and divine "love" would differ so totally that we could not really speak of God's love at all. If language were *univocal, then concepts would apply to God and humans in the same way, jeopardizing

---

1. See the sketch in J. Feinberg, *No One Like Him*, 235–37. Classifications such as "incommunicable" versus "communicable" divine attributes eventually break down, for reasons that the treatment of analogical language below begins to clarify. To a degree, even the contrast between "finite" and "infinite" becomes relative rather than absolute in the light of divine revelation.

the distinction between Creator and creature: human "love" would somehow designate exactly the same reality as divine love.

A few theologians, including John Duns Scotus (c. 1266–1308), have periodically found a univocal view necessary to uphold the reality of divine revelation.[2] Scotus's univocal view is often criticized for putting God and creatures on the same plane of existence, thus competing as explanatory causes for events. Scotus was a *voluntarist, emphasizing divine freedom rather than any necessary or fitting relation between God's will and what is good. Critics of Scotus's voluntarism often oppose *nominalism as well. Associated with William of Ockham (c. 1287–1347), nominalism captured the modern West with the view that concepts lack real existence in the divine mind and are merely human names for things. Opponents blame univocal language, voluntarism, and nominalism for modern *disenchantment of the universe—for removing a sense of mystery from the world. Instead, these opponents claim, we need to recover the worldview of earlier "Christian Platonism," involving *sacramental participation in which created things are signs that mysteriously share in the Creator's life. Historically, however, many scholars object that blaming voluntarism and/or nominalism for modern disenchantment is grandiose and misleading. Theologically, others object that "Christian Platonist" accounts of participation in God are unclear and unnecessary, misapplying "sacramental" language beyond baptism and the Lord's Supper.[3]

These controversies aside, the overwhelming majority of the Christian tradition worries that a univocal view claims too much. With overinflated confidence in human concepts of God, a univocal view eventually generates skepticism about whether our language can really bear divine truth. If theological language is analogical instead, then human concepts overlap, but are not identical, with the divine characteristics they reveal. Human "love" can truly reveal aspects of divine love, despite immense differences between the two. Theologians can articulate some of those differences without ever fully identifying them.

Analogical approaches share a degree of *apophaticism: they agree that we cannot possess direct knowledge, using human concepts, of the divine

---

2. Modern proponents of a univocal view include Henry (e.g., *God Who Speaks and Shows*, 364). Gunton, *Act and Being*, 69–71, champions at least a univocal "element" within a concept of analogy.

3. The critique of Scotus is heavily associated with *radical orthodoxy, on which see J. Smith, *Introducing Radical Orthodoxy*. For a disenchantment critique that links these views to the Protestant Reformation, see B. Gregory, *Unintended Reformation*. For a call to recover sacramental participation, see Boersma, *Heavenly Participation*. It is impossible to survey the resulting historical and theological literature here; on Scotus's univocity, see Horan, *Postmodernity and Univocity*.

essence. We can, however, receive adequate knowledge of God by divine revelation. The incarnation signals God's commitment to communicate with us, rendering human language, although frail, an adequate vehicle for conveying what God is like. While apophaticism is often associated with a *via negativa*—approaching divine attributes by negating the application of human limitations to God—this moment of negation celebrates God's perfection.

Preeminent Divine Perfections

Naming God involves the one, the three, and the many. In the Old Testament God reveals an ineffable proper name: YHWH. In the New Testament YHWH is identified as Father and Son and Holy Spirit. The Bible applies many other "names" to YHWH: titles such as "El Shaddai," metaphors such as "rock," and confessions such as "compassionate and gracious, slow to anger, abounding in love" (e.g., Ps. 103:8). The classic tradition referred to God's perfections in terms of *divine names. Some are "proper names" while others are metaphors. Divine perfections are frequently called "attributes," characteristics that humans predicate of God. But these are the characteristics of no ordinary being; humans learn them only thanks to divine revelation. The language of "perfections" best conveys the unique blessedness of the Triune God, whose holiness is what makes these characteristics ideal.

The Bible names YHWH's perfections in the particular contexts of salvation history. Take "compassionate and gracious": God ineffably revealed the name YHWH in Exodus 3:14, indicating that the rest of the exodus event would disclose that name's meaning. Exodus delivers on God's promise in succeeding chapters: By Exodus 32–34 YHWH offers costly forgiveness for the redeemed people, who, by building and worshiping a golden calf, have idolatrously broken God's covenant. Moses asks to see God's glory; YHWH graciously hides him in a rock, providing a very partial glimpse. Again in that context, God's people encounter God's self-naming: "The LORD, the LORD, the compassionate and gracious God, slow to anger, abounding in love and faithfulness, maintaining love to thousands, and forgiving wickedness, rebellion and sin. Yet he does not leave the guilty unpunished" (Exod. 34:6–7). The exodus, followed by Israel's apostasy, clarifies what God's compassion and grace mean.

God's self-communication unfolds in saving acts, while God's saving acts are accompanied by speech—together providing the authoritative interpretation of the divine names. The blessedness of God's being authorizes many ways of naming God's perfections. The Psalms celebrate God as the Good, the gracious source and standard of creaturely goodness.[4] This Good One gives being, truth, and ordered beauty to everything else. These *transcendentals— being, oneness, goodness, truth, beauty—name perfections of the Creator in which creatures participate. In biblical theology four perfections are particularly crucial for relating God's unique blessedness to the human experience of goodness. These four—power, wisdom, love, and holiness—are prominent in Isaiah 40, the basis for the following exposition.

Isaiah 40

Isaiah 40 stands at the intersection of Old Testament hope and New Testament fulfillment: John the Baptist is the voice calling in the wilderness to prepare the way for the Lord, Jesus Christ (v. 3). John's call heralds the good news of rest in the wilderness of exile. Isaiah 40 heralds the book's "second half" turn toward future hope in the face of present judgment. Hence Isaiah 40 stands at the intersection of creation and redemption, addressing both human finitude (e.g., vv. 6–8, 15–17) and fallenness (vv. 2, 18–20).

This paradigmatic text anchors gospel hope in God's character. From the start, Isaiah 40 characterizes Israel's God in terms of *holy love*. The prophet is to comfort the people tenderly (vv. 1–2a); judgment (v. 2b) is coming to an end. God's glory is about to be revealed; this hope is sure because God's *powerful*, eternal Word has spoken a guarantee (vv. 3–8). God's power is underscored in another shouting of the good news (vv. 9–11). Still, this powerful God who is coming in holy judgment will tenderly gather and shepherd his flock (v. 11). Having appealed to God's holy love and power, the prophet turns to God's *wisdom* (vv. 12–14): The Lord needs no consultants, however obscure the divine plan may be.

In Isaiah's day, many assumed that whichever empire was reigning had the only or most powerful god(s). Israel's God, however, is the Creator of everything—not a tribal deity. Isaiah 40 shows all nations to be a drop in the bucket; comparison of YHWH with anything else is tantamount to idolatry, which is just silly (vv. 15–20). The Creator is sovereign over all nations and earthly history (vv. 21–24), as well as perfectly wise (vv. 25–26), attentively knowing every creature. The exiles should not conclude that God is either powerless or unaware of their plight (vv. 27–28); rather, this eternal Creator will empower weary and weak creatures (vv. 29–31).

Of course, other biblical passages characterize the divine perfections, and other divine perfections could be discerned from Isaiah 40. Yet power, wisdom,

---

4. To explore the Psalter's support for the Thomistic emphasis on divine goodness, see C. Holmes, *The Lord Is Good*.

love, and holiness are preeminent in this crucial passage's revelation of God's coming glory. These divine perfections offer a framework for integrating creation and redemption, Old Testament hope and New Testament fulfillment, and therefore the gospel's drama of judgment and grace with the identity of the Triune God.

POWER

The Creed follows the Bible—and joins many human cultures—in highlighting creation as the first and fundamental display of God's eternal power (Rom. 1:18–20). *Power is the capacity to act and to realize successfully one's intentions in so acting. For understanding God's power, though, this human definition is inadequate, because God is never inactive or vulnerable to unrealized potential; God is *pure act, albeit in a restful way. Exhibit A: God simply spoke the cosmos into being. Still, Christians could focus too strongly on natural knowledge of God as Creator. One danger is that of subordinating God's love to God's power, lopsidedly "conceived in terms of self-expansion, not self-emptying or self-limitation."[5] Another danger is that of linking God's will so tightly to God's power that world events seem necessary or God becomes directly responsible for evil. A biblical understanding neither makes God's power the only cause of everything nor leaves God out of any picture, just watching from a distance.

Two nuances place God's *omnipotence—being all-powerful—in the proper theological context. First, God's power must be understood in relation to other divine perfections, as revealed in Scripture's history of salvation. Philosophical paradoxes of omnipotence—for instance, Can God make a stone too heavy for God to lift? Can God sin?—are no worry for biblical faith, in which Almighty God is also wise, loving, and holy. God does have unlimited power, as Job testified: "I know that you can do all things; no purpose of yours can be thwarted" (Job 42:2). But this Sovereign is Lord of all causes, not the replacement of other causes. Indeed, God has chosen to give creatures a measure of freedom and responsibility; that purpose too cannot be thwarted.

Second, God's power must be understood in light of the New Testament's witness regarding Jesus Christ, not just the Old Testament's witness regarding creation. The Old Testament already nuances divine power in light of perfections like compassion. The New Testament goes dramatically further: Ephesians 1:19–23 emphasizes the resurrection, not creation, as the act that

---

5. Bloesch, *God the Almighty*, 104. The following account of the divine perfections has learned much from Bloesch.

quintessentially reveals God's power.[6] The God who spoke the cosmos into existence is the same God who "gives life to the dead" (Rom. 4:17) through redemption in Jesus Christ. The wider New Testament "paradox" is that God's power is made perfect in weakness (2 Cor. 12:9), while self-giving is integral to responsible agency—a Christlike exercise of true power.[7]

WISDOM

God's power is closely connected in Scripture to wisdom—the knowledge and skill to act in a way that realizes one's intentions. In God's case, this wisdom extends to interacting well with creatures, for the sake of God's glory and creation's good. The cosmos reflects purposeful design: "By wisdom the LORD laid the earth's foundations" (Prov. 3:19; cf. Jer. 10:12). Psalm 147:5, in context referring to creation, places divine power and wisdom in reinforcing parallelism: "Great is our Lord and mighty in power; his understanding has no limit." The New Testament chimes in: Jesus Christ is "the power of God and the wisdom of God" (1 Cor. 1:24). Given this connection with unlimited power, divine wisdom entails another "omni" attribute: *omniscience. God knows all things, past and present and future, divine and human and otherwise, because God made them and transcends any limitations of creaturely history. God's knowledge is immediate: God does not need to perceive and reason, because God eternally "knows his own mind," as it were.

Divine wisdom includes but transcends omniscience. In Scripture, wisdom indicates not only the manner of God's creative and providential activity but also God's commitment to communicate with creatures. God created a *cosmos, an orderly world, choosing to convey that order through both nature and history. Hence God's action is purposeful, promoting creaturely flourishing. Creation's fall did not catch God by surprise even if it complicates the human recognition of God's design. God wisely planned from the beginning to reclaim the cursed cosmos and to redeem fallen sinners. Whether or not its mysteries ever become transparent, the divine plan is eternally in place. In Christ, by the Spirit, God has executed its decisive element.

Wisdom can be associated with "the maternal face of God"[8] because God communicates a design for creaturely *shalom*—the flourishing that arises from abundant gifts and harmonious relationships. This divine commitment

---

6. Young, *God's Presence*, 94, notes a striking link between creation and resurrection in early Christian literature.

7. To encounter challenges on both sides—the dangers of glamorizing worldly notions of divine power or else dehumanizing notions of weakness—see, e.g., Rigby, *Power, Powerlessness, and the Divine.*

8. Bloesch, *God the Almighty*, 123.

to communication and communion appears not only in the covenantal gift of the Torah but also in Wisdom literature, which concretely addresses daily life. Fulfilling close connections between law and wisdom heading into the New Testament (e.g., in Sirach), Jesus Christ became the ultimate embodiment of God's self-communication and creaturely instruction. The incarnation fulfills Old Testament hints of Wisdom as God's self-expression in the created order (e.g., Prov. 8:22–36).

LOVE

God is both the benevolent Creator who communicates and the patient Redeemer who forgives. *Love is the giving of oneself to enhance fellowship with, and the good of, another. Creation and communication are loving enough. Yet "greater love has no one than this: to lay down one's life for one's friends" (John 15:13), and "God demonstrates his own love for us in this: While we were still sinners, Christ died for us" (Rom. 5:8). "This is love: not that we loved God, but that he loved us and sent his Son as an atoning sacrifice for our sins. . . . We love because he first loved us" (1 John 4:10, 19). In loving enemies, we imitate our heavenly Father (Matt. 5:43–48). The Christ-event shows God to be more than good in a philosophically satisfying sense: God is loving to a fault![9] Such love is not a New Testament change from the Old Testament, which constantly celebrates God's "compassionate and gracious" character. The *hesed—loyal love—of YHWH is so special that it can scarcely be translated into English. In Jesus Christ, God does not act differently but rather ultimately.

If "God is love" (1 John 4:8, 16), then is love God's quintessential attribute? God is also light, as a verse in the same biblical book insists (1 John 1:5). All divine names reflect different aspects of God without dividing God into parts. The perfections name the divine being in the multiple ways that are necessary for finite humans to know God at all. Saying that God is love simultaneously addresses God's power, wisdom, holiness, and so forth. Even so, emphasizing God's love is appropriate. God's self-revelation comes in the history of salvation, whose climactic event—the cross and resurrection—is scandalous to our concepts of God. Emphasizing God's love opposes pagan concepts that promote human greatness (Mark 10:41–45) rather than God's paradoxical glory. Emphasizing God's love also underscores that God is triune. God's identity as Father, Son, and Holy Spirit identifies loving communion as intrinsic to *who* God is; love is not just *what* God is like. Emphasizing

9. As I heard from my theology professor in seminary, Albert "Joe" Crawford.

God's love is fitting in light of the trinitarian economy of salvation: God the Father sending the Son, the Spirit sustaining the Son, the Son saving us via the cross, and all of these "persons" speaking to one another. God does not simply love by creating and then communicating wisdom; God patiently reclaims creatures from self-destructive folly.

HOLINESS

Divine patience and redemption do not overturn the order of creation and communication; instead, God's love restores the harmony of those relationships. *Holiness designates being sacred or set apart: for humans or other creatures, this means being devoted to God's service; for God, this means being the utterly unique and blessed Creator of everything else. Therefore, God's character and will constitute the standard of all truth, goodness, and beauty to which creatures are accountable.

Accordingly, God's love is holy and God's holiness is loving: "These two perfections coalesce in such a way that we may speak of the holy love of God . . . and of his merciful holiness. . . . The apex of God's holiness is the holiness of his love. The apex of God's love is the beauty of his holiness."[10] Wrath is not an immanent divine perfection like love and holiness; rather, wrath is an economic expression of God's holy love in response to sin. The Psalms' language suggests that wrath has an emotional element, being directed personally toward sinners and not just abstractly toward sin. Even so, God's wrath is not a fit of pique, a lack of self-control, or an expression of wounded pride.[11] *Wrath is God's just response to creatures' foolish, self-destructive refusal of love.

God's judgment actually expresses this love. First, God lovingly keeps promises, not letting patience run endlessly (e.g., 2 Pet. 3:9). Otherwise the martyrs at the heavenly altar would be betrayed when they ask, "How long, Sovereign Lord, holy and true?" (Rev. 6:9–11). Second, God lovingly responds to those who steadfastly refuse love by maintaining their God-given responsibility. Christian traditions explain human freedom differently, but all refuse to make God primarily responsible for sin.[12] Third, God's justice lovingly upholds creation's good purposes and addresses victims' claims. God's judgment expresses love, not just toward God's people or even unbelievers but actually toward all creation, by upholding a moral order.

---

10. Bloesch, *God the Almighty*, 141.
11. See Carson, "Wrath of God"; Carson, "God's Love and God's Wrath."
12. Lewis, *Problem of Pain*, 127, suggests famously that "the gates of hell are locked on the inside," as the damned persist in their rebellion to the end.

Divine holiness transcends its *ethical* aspect—God's righteousness or justice and its expression in loving judgment. God's character sets the moral standard for everything creaturely because of the *uniquely sacred* aspect of divine holiness—God's utterly unique glory as the Creator who alone is worthy of worship.

> Holy, holy, holy! Lord God Almighty!
> Early in the morning our song shall rise to Thee;
> Holy, holy, holy! Merciful and Mighty!
> God in Three Persons, blessed Trinity!
>
> Holy, holy, holy! All the saints adore Thee,
> Casting down their golden crowns around the glassy sea;
> Cherubim and seraphim falling down before thee,
> Which wert and art and evermore shalt be.

Those two verses, adoring the merciful and mighty, blessed Trinity, precede the beginning of the third: "Holy, holy, holy! though the darkness hide Thee, / Though the eye of sinful man, Thy glory may not see . . ." After this acknowledgment, Reginald Heber's magnificent hymn returns to adoring God's uniqueness: "Only Thou art holy, there is none beside Thee, / Perfect in pow'r, in love and purity." God's uniqueness is the context for adoring God's purity. In that larger context, "All Thy works shall praise Thy name in earth and sky and sea." We praise a Triune God who is holy, holy, holy—not a philosophers' god of religious awe or ethical righteousness or austere judgment.

The Bible reinforces that hymn's message by celebrating God as "the Holy One in your [Israel's] midst" (Hosea 11:9 NRSV).[13] Israel's sanctification—to obey God and represent God's character in the world—would flow from their worship. Israel's ritual practice was to express and deepen their identity as God's covenant people.[14] The same is true for the regathered Israel, the church, which prays for God's name to be hallowed on earth as in heaven. God's holiness confronts both idolatry and injustice because worship and ordinary life are interwoven in the calling of God's people (1 Pet. 1:15–16, quoting Lev. 11:44–45).[15]

Holiness undergirds a properly analogical account of theological language. God's holiness indicates the unique blessedness of this One we worship, whom

13. Webster, *Holiness*, esp. 45, draws attention to this passage. Webster rightly says that holiness is not primarily "legislative," but in suggesting that it is primarily "soteriological," he may neglect the liturgical or sacred aspect. In "Holiness and Love of God," though, Webster reminds us that holiness uniquely names an aspect of God's identity before it serves as a creaturely quality.

14. D. Peterson, *Possessed by God*, expounds the biblical focus of "sanctification": the status of being God's set-apart people.

15. Bloesch, *God the Almighty*, 137–39.

no human words could reveal fully. Yet the Holy One has come into our midst, calling us to be holy. This vocation communicates the hope that human words may somehow foster knowledge of God.

Other Perfections of the Holy One

Many other divine names specify entailments of the Triune God's power, wisdom, love, and holiness. Or, in other words, we can laud additional facets of God's infinite blessedness.

*Omnipresence, the third prominent "omni" attribute, runs in tandem with omnipotence and omniscience. As Spirit, strictly speaking, God is not localized anywhere in a physical sense; God is ontologically present with, not as, each point in space. Furthermore, the Bible distinguishes various kinds of divine presence. Thus, omnipresence involves not only ubiquity—God's presence everywhere—but also immensity: "God's immensity is the triune God himself in the boundless plenitude of his being, in which he is unhindered by any spatial constraint, and so is sovereignly free for creative and saving presence to all limited creaturely reality."[16] God's immensity makes space for us, to enjoy fellowship.[17]

God is omnipresent by virtue of being *Spirit, being personal in an infinite sense—not bound by a body in time and space. God can relate to anything and anyone anywhere at any time. God is so transcendent as to be profoundly immanent. God was free to work pedagogically with a particular people, Israel, at particular times and places through institutions such as the tabernacle; now God seeks a regathered Israel that will embrace all nations in true worship, which is not place-dependent (John 4:24).

In light of God's spiritual nature, additional perfections distinguish God as Infinite Creator from all finite beings, whose limits are divinely created.

A controversial perfection that infinity might entail is *necessity: the classic view that God cannot not exist. Once the classic "proofs" for God's existence fell into modern disfavor, divine necessity often faded from consideration; many people thought that they had no need of God to explain the world's existence. Yet necessity proclaims more than creation's need for a Creator. When Anselm of Canterbury (c. 1033–1109) spoke prayerfully of the Being "greater than which nothing can be thought,"[18] he celebrated the sheer plenitude of God's eternal life: if God can be thought, then there must be a God who enables us to think so.

16. Webster, "Immensity and Ubiquity of God," 92.
17. Webster, "Immensity and Ubiquity of God," 106–7.
18. Anselm, "Proslogion," 99.

Related to necessity, *aseity celebrates the sheer independence of God's life. God is utterly sufficient, *a se* ("from himself") in Latin. God has no need of involvement with any other being. Aseity undergirds divine freedom: God acts under no compulsion but in fitting correspondence with divine love.

Likewise related to necessity, *simplicity specifies the nature of God's unity as the one, holy Creator. As Spirit, God is not a composite being. Neither the three "persons" of the Trinity nor the divine "perfections" compose "parts" of God. There is no distinction between God's essence and God's existence (as divine necessity underscores); neither is there any ontological separation of God's various attributes. Divine simplicity has been difficult to define, subject to philosophical complexities and modern theological critique. For instance, while God may not have "spatial" parts, to lack "temporal" parts God must remain "outside of time" in a strong sense that many now reject. Defenders, however, find this doctrine to be an implication of Scripture's teaching (for instance, concerning God's spiritual character), not just a debated philosophical dogma.[19]

Another entailment of God's self-existent plenitude is *eternity, which can be understood in two main ways. "Timeless eternity," the classic view, holds that God exists endlessly outside of time (which God created as an aspect of the world). "Everlastingness," a modern view that some evangelicals have embraced, holds that God exists at all times, living "within" time even if temporality does not limit God. Standing behind these views are complex theories of time,[20] along with the challenge of relating the Bible's historical dynamism to God's transcendence.

Still another aspect of God's uniqueness is *immutability. Maximally, God's being is absolutely unchanging; only relations with creatures change. More modestly, God is constant, not changing in terms of personhood, perfections, and purposes. Because God's ways do not change, God's law does not change, although God's will operates variously in creaturely history—to accommodate human weakness and pedagogical needs (see, e.g., Jesus's teaching in Matt. 19:1–12).

Even more controversial today, God's *impassibility means that God does not "suffer," which would involve not only pain but even being acted upon from outside. (A "patient" is someone who is passive in relation to a healer's action.) Some of the modern controversy reflects the *Hellenization thesis,

---

19. See, e.g., discussion in J. Feinberg, *No One Like Him*, 325–37. For a defense of divine simplicity, see Duby, *Divine Simplicity*.

20. See Ganssle, *God and Time*.

which claims that Greco-Roman philosophical ideals substantially influenced early Christian theology. This Hellenistic influence went beyond terminology to involve ideas; notably, suspicion of the material world, including the body and its passions, frequently supplanted the earthiness of Jewish faith. Modern people also became newly sensitive to human, especially physical, suffering in a way that made divine impassibility seem cold.[21] Hence Jürgen Moltmann and others responded to events like the Holocaust by intensifying Dietrich Bonhoeffer's tantalizing aphorism: "Only the suffering God can help."[22] Abraham Heschel (1907–72) and other biblical scholars highlighted the dramatic divine emotions portrayed in prophetic writings.[23] Liberationist and other Majority World theologies emphasize God's identification with suffering.[24] Finally, still others worry that divine impassibility is inconsistent with the incarnation and the atonement.[25]

Divine impassibility may now be a minority view in evangelical circles. Traditionalists, however, have responded to the objections. They suggest that impassibility does not preclude God's emotional engagement with the world; impassibility simply denies that divine love operates like ours (involving bodies) or makes God dependent upon creatures. Hence Cyril of Alexandria (c. 376–444) said paradoxically that God's Son "impassibly suffered" in Jesus Christ.[26] The related christological complexities are precisely what Chalcedon's two-natures doctrine addresses (as we see in chap. 8): the *person* of the Son suffered *by virtue of* his *human nature*; the *divine nature as such* did not die. (After all, death involves the separation of body and soul, and the divine nature is only spiritual.)

Concepts of divine perfection do not offer easy philosophical answers. They offer language for seeking the coherent teaching of biblical revelation, reflecting its indirect character and narrative complexity in our feeble praise. Passages like Isaiah 40 celebrate the all-powerful, all-wise, everywhere-present and loving Creator as so holy that the *glory—the dazzling revelation and reputation—of this Triune God must be distinguished from everything created and finite. Thank goodness that, whether or not we use words like "impassibility," God's love is unlike ours!

21. On this historical contrast see, e.g., Taylor, *Sources of the Self.*
22. Inspired by Bonhoeffer, *Letters and Papers from Prison*; Moltmann (esp. in *Crucified God*) proposed a "social Trinitarian" account of the cross. For brief chronicles of such trends, see Bauckham, "Only the Suffering God Can Help?"; Goetz, "Suffering God."
23. Heschel, *Prophets*, vol. 1.
24. As evident throughout the figures surveyed by Kärkkäinen, *Doctrine of God.*
25. E.g., McCormack, "Actuality of God"; McCormack, "Only Mediator."
26. Here Cyril's *Scholia* 33–35 is cited in McGuckin, *Saint Cyril of Alexandria*, 185.

God's Providence

The biblical drama of salvation reveals how the almighty, wise, loving, holy Triune God unfolds an eternal plan and enacts providential care. First, creation *ex nihilo* ("out of nothing") distinguishes the Creator from all creatures while indicating their freedom for fellowship. Second, orthodox Christians disagree about biblical models of God's interaction with the world. But together they confess God's threefold providence in (1) preserving what has been created, (2) sustaining the creaturely causes of what happens, and (3) somehow willing all that happens. Third, a crucial mystery concerns how God addresses evil. Orthodox Christians agree that God did not directly cause evil but remains sovereign and will bring about a new creation where righteousness dwells. The answer to the problem of evil is eschatological: summing up all things in Christ (Eph. 1:10) so that God will be all in all (1 Cor. 15:28).

The Meaning of Creation

Creatio ex nihilo proclaims that the Triune Creator did not use preexisting materials, face threatening chaos or opposing forces, or have the cosmos emanate from the divine being. The next chapter expounds this Christian teaching about creation. Already, though, the doctrine has a twofold meaning for divine providence, ruling out "deistic" accounts that overemphasize God's transcendence and "panentheistic" accounts that overemphasize God's immanence.

Versions of *Deism suggest that after creating, God left the world to run on its own. God acts through laws of nature—alone. Prior to evolutionary science, God could thus be pictured as a brilliant watchmaker and/or a judge to whom humans are morally accountable—without intervening until history's end. After evolutionary science, in deistic accounts even creation might not require divine intervention.

Orthodox Christians likewise celebrate the world's natural order; some even treat God's action in "providentialist" terms that involve little interference with nature's laws.[27] Yet the Nicene Creed contains more than the first article: God the Father Almighty not only made heaven and earth but also sent the Son to become incarnate for us and our salvation, having sent the Spirit to give all creatures life and then to perfect the new humanity in Christ. Since creation *ex nihilo* commits God to a particular project in loving freedom, traditional Christians acknowledge the constant possibility and periodic reality of special divine intervention.

27. For a slightly more detailed set of categories, see Collins, *God of Miracles*, 19–21.

Alternatively, versions of panentheism (some known as "process theology") suggest that God created the world as an aspect of God's own being. The world is divine, existing "in" God, even if an aspect of God initially transcends the world (hence unlike *pantheism, which simply equates the world with divinity). A frequent metaphor for panentheism depicts the world as God's body. Because the world's constant change and evil exists "in" God, God's being "becomes" along with history, which God tries to redeem by "persuasion"— alone—thus coming oddly close to a form of Deism. For *process theology, the primary entities are actual occasions or dynamic events (e.g., involving bodily cells) rather than static substances (e.g., a particular human being). God acts only by persuading particulars to become what God wants them to be, but this persuasion is often subatomic and not necessarily personal.

Orthodox Christians likewise celebrate God's immanence in the world and the world's dependence upon God. Thus, some Christians have championed an "occasionalist" view of providence: God does not actually use creaturely causes but simply wills—directly—every event. On that account, moment by moment God sustains the world and everything in it by willing its history; creaturely "causes" are merely connections that humans see between items in the world.[28] Just as "providentialists" reflect deistic tendencies while remaining more orthodox, so the "occasionalist" minority reflects panentheistic tendencies while remaining more orthodox. The creedal confession that God is Almighty, along with the biblical confession that God spoke the world into being, resists making creation necessary for God to realize God's being in cosmic becoming. Since God made "all that is," everything "seen and unseen" must be distinct from God's own being. The distinction between Creator and creature upholds the integrity of the cosmos, a network of secondary causes that operates according to a divinely willed order.

Early Christian theologians did not seek a speculative theory about divine providence; they were too busy preaching the Bible in all its density and defending the faith in all its complexity. Eventually, Augustine's *City of God* offered a grand theological interpretation of history, contributing two key elements. First, Augustine denied that evil was a substance, instead defining *evil as the privation (the parasitic absence) of good. Everything that God created is good (1 Tim. 4:4), so evil must involve lack or misdirection of created being—not a substance that rivals God or detracts from the world's goodness. Second, Augustine recovered biblical teaching about divine predestination, whereas other Christian apologists and bishops staunchly championed human freedom. Augustine acknowledged the sheer mystery involved: sometimes

---

28. Again see Collins, *God of Miracles*, esp. chap. 3.

God will provide specially for us, yet other times God will lead us through suffering—perhaps to avoid the impression that people should serve God for worldly benefit.[29]

In the Middle Ages Thomas Aquinas developed a systematic account of classical theism using philosophical resources. The "transcendentals" of creaturely life—being, oneness, truth, goodness, and beauty—are grounded in God's own being. God is "pure act": there is no potentiality (associated with matter) in God, whose life is full of boundless delight. In a sense, God's interaction with the world is one continuous act involving many subplots. Although human actions (as both effects and secondary causes) are analogous to divine action (the primary cause), the analogy is weak and the dissimilarities are great. God's agency undergirds ours, operating on a different plane. God's chosen act includes upholding creation's meaningful history.

Classical Christian theism contains variety concerning the nature of human freedom and the operation of creaturely causes. Yet creation *ex nihilo* implies broadly "supernaturalist" providence.[30] God made everything to have original goodness and integrity of being. Simultaneously, God created human beings with a view to personal fellowship. The natural order is not a neutral machine but rather is lovingly upheld by God and open to divine intervention. God's intervention preserves creaturely causality and human freedom rather than threatening them, being necessary to move history toward its meaningful end.

Christian Models of Providence

Positively confessed in light of creation *ex nihilo*, God's providence has three primary aspects: *conservatio*, preserving what has been created; *concursus*, cooperating with all that happens (as the primary cause undergirding secondary causes); and *gubernatio*, directing all that happens. Various models have developed for how *gubernatio* works, especially for relating God's knowledge and will to human freedom. The first of these models, so-called Calvinism, comprehensively upholds Augustine's emphasis upon divine predestination. The rest of the models, loosely speaking, put decreasing emphasis upon God's sovereignty relative to human freedom. Eventually, one of these models is willing to speak radically of God taking "risk" by interacting with free creatures.

*Calvinism upholds the classical affirmation of God's timelessness and God's determination of everything. God foreknows everything by knowing

---

29. Augustine, *City of God* 1.8 (NPNF[1] 2:5).
30. Once more, the term is from Collins, *God of Miracles*, in contrast to what he calls "providentialism" and "occasionalism."

an all-embracing eternal decree. Creaturely *freedom is volitional: "Creatures do what they want to do but what they do is always within God's overall determination."[31] This "soft" form of "determinism" is not fatalistic because God decrees creaturely means along with ends, and those creaturely means include agents besides God.[32] God is not blameworthy for evil, which arose from creaturely misdirection of God-given goods; while God willed to permit evil, God did not directly cause creaturely rebellion. Calvinists emphasize divine sovereignty and do not speak of God "permitting" events in a merely passive sense. Yet mainstream Calvinists avoid suggesting that God "wills" evil in a directly causal sense. The epitome of evil, the crucifixion of Jesus Christ, vindicates God's righteousness because God and humans acted with different purposes: humans are guilty because of their murderous motives, while God is righteous because of loving self-sacrifice. Broadly speaking, Calvinists claim that prayer "changes things" within a divinely willed network of creaturely causes, but prayer primarily enhances fellowship with God. First and foremost, prayer changes us.

*Arminianism, named after Jacobus Arminius (1560–1609), reacted against Calvinism from within the Dutch Reformed tradition, focusing on God's "simple foreknowledge" of everything. Creaturely *freedom is libertarian, not merely volitional: people have "the power of contrary choice." Like determinism, libertarian freedom is subject to complex philosophical discussions with various meanings.[33] Typically, theological proponents of libertarian freedom deny the allegation that they exclude all factors besides the human will in shaping particular choices. They acknowledge that various factors make people more or less inclined toward certain decisions. Still, in principle, the power of contrary choice means that a genuinely free person could have done otherwise than what he or she chooses. God is not blameworthy for evil because God willed to permit evil for the sake of giving humans libertarian freedom. While knowing everything that will happen, God wills most events by permitting secondary causes to operate naturally rather than actively planning to intervene. Prayer "changes things" due to special providence that fits within the larger network of creaturely causes. Arminianism joins Calvinism in denying the idea that for God to know something causes it and precludes

31. Tiessen, *Providence and Prayer*, 232.

32. J. Feinberg, *No One Like Him*, esp. 635–39, provides the terminology of soft determinism, introducing the complex philosophical uses of "determinism" from which theologians often diverge.

33. Muller, *Divine Will and Human Choice*, argues that early Protestants used none of the relevant terms here—neither determinism nor libertarianism nor compatibilism—in their modern philosophical senses.

creaturely responsibility: the "necessity" of an event arises "contingently" because God foreknows the event *as* occurring due to creaturely causes.

*Molinism, named after Luis de Molina (1535–1600), arose as a Catholic variation upon Thomism and has become a philosophically popular version of Arminianism. Molinism champions "middle knowledge" as the means by which God's eternal plan developed. *Middle knowledge enables God to give creatures libertarian freedom while ensuring the accomplishment of divine purposes. God's "natural" knowledge involves self-knowledge, thus including what is necessary and what is past. God's "free" knowledge involves the history God knows by choosing to actualize it. Middle knowledge, in between, contains *counterfactuals of creaturely freedom: "things that God knows could happen if particular circumstances existed prior to and at the moment of the events in question."[34] God's decree involved choosing a combination of creaturely causes, a "possible world," to actualize. Like Calvinists and other Arminians, Molinists deny "backward causation," the idea that for God to know something will happen causes it to the exclusion of creaturely freedom. Likewise, Molinists affirm God's exhaustive foreknowledge based upon biblical texts such as Isaiah 41:21–24; 44:6–8; and 46:9–10. They further suggest that some biblical texts may support God's middle knowledge of counterfactuals, including 1 Samuel 23:6–13 and Matthew 11:20–24.[35]

Molinism faces the so-called *grounding objection, however: On what basis *could* God know counterfactuals of human freedom in advance if the humans and their circumstances are not actual? If creaturely freedom is libertarian, so that human choices are not *determined* by responses amid particular circumstances, then on what are counterfactuals based? Molinists may respond by challenging the assumed definition: libertarian freedom does not mean that humans could *just as easily* decide differently in particular circumstances— only that they *could choose otherwise*.[36] Nevertheless, the philosophical battle continues: Is middle knowledge viable if creatures' existence is potential in God's mind rather than actual in earthly history?

Another variation of Arminianism involves *open (or freewill) theism. Some nonevangelical proponents embrace panentheism in dialogue with contemporary science, and some evangelical proponents are in dialogue with process theology.[37] *Open theism denies that God has exhaustive foreknowledge, holding instead that God's foreknowledge is as comprehensive as possible

---

34. Tiessen, *Providence and Prayer*, 154.
35. Tiessen, *Providence and Prayer*, 162, 165.
36. Laing, "Compatibility of Calvinism and Middle Knowledge," 462.
37. Cobb and Pinnock, *Searching for an Adequate God*.

given the world God chose to create. Open theists maintain that for God to know something about the future renders it *necessary*, thereby causing it. Since the Bible portrays God entering into genuinely loving, give-and-take relationships with creatures, they must have libertarian freedom and God cannot know any future events that depend upon their choices. Biblical texts involve God learning, negotiating, and changing his mind,[38] as well as warring against Satan and other hostile powers.[39] Open theism claims to handle such narratives more faithfully than other views, while exempting God from much of the problem of evil. After all, God could not know about, let alone prevent, many evils without suppressing libertarian freedom.

Open theism initially gained a controversial hearing in evangelical circles through direct appeals to the Bible. Yet critics challenge open theism regarding the scriptural necessity of the cross, and numerous passages suggesting exhaustive divine foreknowledge. Notably, Isaiah 40–66 portrays God's uniqueness in terms of comprehensively knowing the future. Critics claim that open theism's crucial accusation against the classical view—dodging the plain meaning of Scripture passages by appealing to *anthropomorphism, nonliteral portrayals of God in human terms—ignores the analogical nature of theological language.[40] Finally, critics reject open theism's proposed solution to the problem of evil. Open theism suggests that limits on divine foreknowledge are not too risky, because God has promised to intervene as necessary for accomplishing certain ultimate ends. Open theism also suggests that God has the ability to make good predictions based upon past and present knowledge. At this point, however, critics notice that the problem of God's relationship to evil remains. For instance, the open theists' God could discern the intentions and likely success of terrorists before they actually strike, so their God is no less responsible for willing to permit such evils than the classical God. Thus, open theism helpfully sent traditional Christians back to the Bible, but in the eyes of most evangelicals it has not successfully addressed some fundamental criticisms.

A few variations on the preceding views need brief mention.[41] Karl Barth chastened a Calvinist account with a distinctive emphasis on Jesus Christ: creation is the external basis of God's covenant, but the covenant is the internal

---

38. For such arguments see, e.g., Pinnock et al., *Openness of God*; J. Sanders, *God Who Risks*.

39. E.g., Boyd, *God at War*.

40. See esp. Collins, *God of Miracles*, 42–47.

41. See further Tiessen, *Providence and Prayer*, who proposes middle knowledge Calvinism. Another survey appears in Beilby and Eddy, *Divine Foreknowledge*. Whether or not Thomism—or Thomas himself, anyway—advocates "libertarian" freedom is debated, so here it is treated as more generic rather than a particular model.

basis of creation.[42] God's providence is oriented toward reconciliation in Christ and should not be understood through a general analogy ("of being") between God and creatures. Some popular and non-Western Arminians emphasize church dominion, challenging fatalism and treating prayer as a primary means whereby the church establishes God's dominion over the earth. A few Calvinists have recently proposed their own version of middle knowledge, in which soft determinism solves the grounding objection: God could plan using creaturely counterfactuals because they existed in the divine mind. If middle knowledge precedes God's willing, however, then the grounding problem might remain, since God would not yet have determined the counterfactuals. So middle-knowledge Calvinism has not become widespread.

Traditional Christians agree that creation *ex nihilo* establishes *conservatio*, and for the most part *concursus*, while they understandably disagree over the workings of *gubernatio*. The biblical materials are numerous, diverse, and complex. Since humans ponder divine providence from within the very drama they seek to understand, mystery is no surprise. Evil is a crucial factor about which the various models disagree. For all of the disagreement, however, Christians share faith in God's past goodness, constant presence, and future promises.

The Mystery of Redemption

*Theodicy is the human attempt to defend God's existence, and to "justify" God's goodness and power, in response to the *problem of evil. Formally sketched, (1) evil exists on a considerable scale; (2) there is a God; (3) God is all-powerful; and (4) God is morally perfect. Granting the truth of (1), evil's considerable existence, makes (2), God's existence, false, or else it forces a choice between (3) and (4): God is either powerful or good but cannot be both. Difficulties over evil have always confronted the church, but the modern age newly perceived them as a barrier to faith.[43] Usually human freedom is a crucial component of modern theodicies: God permitted rebellion and its consequences in order to grant creaturely agency. Ultimately, though, a Christian *theological* response must involve the future: "waiting upon the Lord" of holy love to redeem the fallen creation. As the church waits, the following elements might contribute intellectual and pastoral help.

Addressing philosophical objections. Apologetics is complex and contextual. Theology cannot simply allow philosophy—itself full of contextual variety—to set the ground rules. Yet philosophy provokes theology to think

---

42. Barth, *CD* III/1, esp. 94 and 228.
43. For this sketch, see Surin, *Theology and the Problem of Evil.*

carefully, helping the church to care for vulnerable souls. Regarding evil, first, Christian philosophy has shown that the "problem" varies *depending on particular understandings of God.*[44] Christians are within their intellectual rights to address evil within a trinitarian theology of redemption. Second, the problem of evil poses *no simply intellectual "defeater" for faith.* While models of providence vary, creaturely freedom provides at least one possible justification for God's permission of evil. Despite obvious existential challenges, then, evil is not a technical defeater of Christian theism.[45] Accordingly, philosophical reflection sometimes helps more pastoral and theological apologetics to gain a hearing.

Advancing a theology of the cross. Martin Luther aggressively criticized medieval scholasticism for understanding God in terms of human ideals: a *theology of glory. Such a philosophical approach projects onto God a pagan notion of power (cf. Mark 10:35–45). By contrast, a *theology of the cross recognizes that God's power uniquely accomplishes its purposes through cruciform weakness (Phil. 2:5–11). Christ was ironically glorified on the cross (John 12:20–36). Theodicy must not simply address abstract problems using standard definitions of "power" and "goodness"; rather, the saving history of God's work in Jesus must redefine the problems. We should not expect God to confront evil with pagan forms of power. We also must beware projecting other contemporary ideals onto God: a God who "suffers with us" or "feels our pain" without overcoming evil could likewise replace the Triune God of the cross with a cultural construct. Substitute "glory" could contain either postmodern love or modern power.

Articulating biblical compatibilism. Philosophically, "compatibilism" has various definitions, and many who embrace "libertarian" freedom reject the term. But a modest biblical version seems necessary to embrace the cross: such modest *compatibilism

> simply means that God's unconditioned sovereignty and the responsibility of human beings are mutually compatible. It does not claim to show how they are compatible. It claims only that the evidence shows that they are not necessarily incompatible, and that it is therefore entirely reasonable to think they are compatible for there is good evidence for them. . . . When God addressed Assyria in Isaiah 10:5–19, He told them they were nothing more than tools in His hand to punish wicked Israel. However, because they thought they were doing all this by their own strength and power, the Lord would turn around and

---

44. See, briefly, J. Feinberg, "Evil, Problem of."
45. So A. Plantinga, *God, Freedom, and Evil.* For a recent survey of four typical responses to the philosophical problem, see Rae, *Christian Theology,* 124–28.

tear them to pieces to punish their hubris after He had finished using them as a tool. That is compatibilism. There are dozens and dozens of such passages in Scripture, scattered through both Testaments.[46]

Whatever model of providence they hold, Christians affirm mysterious "double agency"—divine and human—when affirming with Scripture the divinely willed necessity of the cross. Likewise, humans should not be able to *explain* providence any more than the incarnation—the singular event of the Word becoming flesh, which theology can only attempt to *describe* biblically and *celebrate* faithfully.

Praying biblical hope. God's providence is personal: we do not believe in fate. Simultaneously, God's providence involves design: we do not believe in chance.[47] Christians resist evil by appropriating biblical hope in prayer, crying out to God. Scripture does not theoretically resolve the problem of evil but rather communicates the hope of redemption in a drama involving various literary forms. Its stories celebrate God's saving intervention and anticipate an ultimate Deliverer. Wisdom texts express the complexity of earthly life and the perplexity of God's people. Psalms cry out from painful situations. Not only do lament Psalms authorize God's people to cry out "How long?" and "Why?"; Lamentations even authorizes God's people to decry exile with all the force they can muster. Although lament is perhaps the most neglected genre in Scripture, other biblical literature comes alongside. Consider Job: proving Satan wrong meant that God hid the cosmic wager to underscore Job's faithfulness. Plot develops characters through complexity. Christian faith *cannot* fully resolve the problem of evil right now without losing the tension ingredient in the biblical drama; full-scale theodicy risks denying human finitude and fallenness.

We learn Scripture's doctrine of providence primarily through praying its diverse literary forms. Many of us fail to lament when we personally suffer little or cannot admit our suffering publicly. Surely, however, brothers and sisters in Christ suffer constantly, even as martyrs. Jesus himself prayed the Psalms, and we must learn to lament "in Christ," in solidarity with fellow members of his body.[48] We are to "mourn with those who mourn" (Rom. 12:15). Beyond lament, other biblical forms such as apocalyptic can teach us to endure and to overcome evil with prayer. Learning to receive comfort from entrusting ourselves to God's providence is part of the unfolding drama of the Christian life:

---

46. Carson, "God's Love and God's Sovereignty," 263–64. For further illustrations, see Exod. 9:34; 4:21; 7:13 (as suggested by Bloesch, *God the Almighty*, 115–16); plus Acts 4:23–29.

47. Bloesch, *God the Almighty*, 114.

48. So Bonhoeffer, *Life Together*.

We must reach that comfort at the right pace—not too fast, lest we treat it lightly; not too slowly, lest we be overtaken by melancholy. We are instructed by the doctrine of providence to look to God for comfort; to cast ourselves in a tragic role, to allow ourselves to think that there is no comfort, is to fall prey to unbelief. But belief is learned, not given all at once. No small part of the office of dogma is to assist in that learning of the promises of God, describing them well and letting their goodness fill our sails.[49]

In sum, a doctrine of *creation* makes it impossible to explain evil fully at present while acknowledging the world's genuine goodness. A doctrine of *redemption* means that evil will someday be overcome, despite being inexplicable in the current act of the divine drama. A doctrine of *last things* maintains hope that in holy love God will fulfill every promise to make all things new. Providence involves God's project of bringing the whole creation to enjoy *shalom*—once all things are unified in Christ (Eph. 1:10). Until then, those who know God can rest and exult in Christ: "If God is for us, who can be against us?" (Rom. 8:31).[50]

49. Webster, "Providence," 164.
50. See the evangelical spiritual classic on this doctrine: Packer, *Knowing God*, esp. its final chapter, "The Adequacy of God."

— 6 —

The Goodness of Creation

THESIS	LEARNING OBJECTIVES
Creation out of nothing is an article of Christian faith according to which the Triune God has spoken the world into existence—granting dignified life, dependent freedom, and delightful fellowship to creatures in their materiality, sociality, and temporality.	After learning the material in this chapter, you should be able to: 1. *Define briefly* the key terms introduced here (marked with an asterisk and included in the glossary). 2. *List and recognize* the subcategories of larger views regarding Genesis and science (e.g., gap and day-age theories). 3. *Describe and compare* the following: (a) biblical and cultural notions of angels and hostile powers; (b) major views of the interpretation of Genesis, the history of Adam and Eve, and the effects of the fall. 4. *Identify and illustrate* the implications of creation *ex nihilo* for arts, history, science, and ecology. 5. *Explain* the following: (a) the "worldview" implications of the Christian doctrine of creation; (b) the trinitarian development of the Christian doctrine of creation.

As participants in salvation's drama, believers understand creation as the stage for God's mighty acts. Christian teaching does not focus on convincing pagan culture that a "creator" exists. Instead, we celebrate the Triune Creator's holy love. This love, definitively revealed in Jesus Christ, has been active from the beginning. So this chapter begins with the doctrine of creation out of nothing, emphasizing God's love for the

125

world and delight in its good design. Once those emphases are in place, we can engage modern science fruitfully.

The Classic Doctrine *Creatio ex Nihilo*

The beginning of revelation, Genesis 1–3, teaches that God created everything else ("the heavens and the earth") out of nothing but God's powerful Word. Eventually this divine Word became identified with Jesus Christ (John 1:1–18; Col. 1:15–23). The "spirit" ambiguously hovering in Genesis 1:2 grants divine power throughout the Old Testament; the New Testament identifies this breath of God with the Holy Spirit of Christ who dwells intimately with us. Christian faith links a trinitarian account of creation to the Old Testament—regarding not only the powerful presence of Word and Spirit but also the Creator's providential help. The Nicene Creed echoes Psalm 124:8 when identifying the "Maker of heaven and earth" as our Almighty Father.

Out of Nothing

The Creed makes creation a confession of faith—however much various cultures have myths or philosophies regarding divine makers. God created via the Word and the life-giving Spirit, so that the cosmos contingently depends upon the Creator's love. Rooted in biblical faith, this Christian doctrine contrasts with other "worldviews" by emphasizing fellowship with the Triune God.

Biblical Faith

The degree to which creation "out of nothing" appears directly in the Bible remains disputed. The doctrine became more explicit in the second century after Christ, when Christians contended—against prevailing Greek thought—that "matter both had a beginning and, for that reason, was not inferior but intended by a good creator."[1] This contrast with the Greco-Roman context reinforces a distinctive biblical emphasis: God's loving decision to speak the cosmos into being.

The material world's goodness was already clear in the Hebrew Scriptures. Genesis insists that the Creator deemed matter "good" (1:4, 10, 12, 18, 21, 25), and the cosmos was "very good" (1:31). God spoke personally in this cosmic beginning, even blessing creatures (1:22, 28) with encouragement to reproduce.

1. Gunton, *Triune Creator*, 8–9.

Despite the fall into sin and the resulting curse, physical things retained their good place in God's providence. Israel awaited a "land flowing with milk and honey" upon redemption from Egypt. As Deuteronomy reiterated, Israel's blessing for obedience and cursing for disobedience included material consequences. Wisdom literature routinely mines the nonhuman creation for positive examples. Poetry celebrates the praise that the physical creation renders to God. Prophetic literature anticipates redemption with material images, depicting a "new heavens and a new earth" containing creaturely delights.

Frequent denials that the Bible teaches creation *ex nihilo* highlight several factors to assess. First, the Hebrew *bārā'* ("created") is used exclusively of God's action, although the word itself does not demand a technical meaning. Second, in Genesis 1:1 "the heavens and the earth" encompasses the entire universe, although the phrase may introduce a narrative rather than narrating a specific act. Third, the creative activity in Genesis 1–2 emphasizes the functions of elements within a cosmic order, although the assignment of these functions could still relate to the elements' material origins. Fourth, Genesis 1 need not explicitly teach creation *ex nihilo* in order to support the doctrine; opposing philosophical theories scarcely existed when the text was composed. Other biblical texts (e.g., Isa. 40:26; Heb. 11:3; Rev. 4:11) likely build upon Genesis 1 and approximate the doctrine more closely.

Given such factors, some evangelical scholars affirm creation out of nothing as a logical, postbiblical development; others affirm it in light of various biblical texts; and many others already affirm it on the implicit or even explicit basis of Genesis 1.[2] The doctrine's basic claims—introduced in the previous chapter—have biblical warrant. First, the Creator did not use preexisting materials. "In the beginning" God made everything else, "the heavens and the earth"; in later language, "without him nothing was made that has been made" (John 1:3). Second, the Creator did not face threatening chaos or opposing forces. While Genesis 1:2 is complex, Old Testament allusions to

2. For brief but helpful discussion, see Collins, *God of Miracles*, esp. 88. For emphasis upon functional rather than material factors, see works by John H. Walton (most accessibly, *Lost World of Genesis One*, 43–44, where Walton affirms creation *ex nihilo* but does not find it in Gen. 1). For broader scholarly dialogue, see G. Anderson and Bockmuehl, *Creation* ex nihilo.

Bockmuehl presents a sophisticated version of the view that the "conceptual terminology" of creation out of "nothing" was a postbiblical, later development, yet the "substantive concern for God's free creation of the world without recourse to pre-existing matter" appears repeatedly in pre-Christian Jewish texts (quotation from the abstract of Bockmuehl, "Creatio ex nihilo"). For the stronger claim that the doctrine was assumed or explicit within the New Testament, see O'Neill, "How Early Is the Doctrine of *Creatio ex Nihilo*?"

The emphasis upon creative divine speech seemingly places the rudiments of *creatio ex nihilo* in Gen. 1. Indeed, Bockmuehl acknowledges that Scripture confirms "the central concern which that doctrine seeks to safeguard" (Bockmuehl, "*Creatio ex nihilo*," 268).

"chaos" minimize the actual threat.[3] Creaturely forces are drops in a bucket (Isa. 40:15) at which God laughs (Ps. 2:4). There is no biblical dualism that treats any cosmic element as God's rival. Third, the cosmos did not emanate from the divine being. The Logos and the Spirit structure and animate creation. Metaphors in Genesis neither incorporate the cosmos within God's being nor infuse it ontologically with divinity. Its account of divine presence in the cosmic temple associates God's image-bearers with physical dust; even spiritual life involves narrative distinction from the divine being. The rest of the Bible distinguishes between creatures and their Creator, even when celebrating God's omnipresence along with creatures' continual dependence (e.g., Ps. 139; Acts 17:24–31).

WORLDVIEWS

The original contexts of creation *ex nihilo* may seem strange to modern people. But this strangeness could reflect the doctrine's influence over Christian "worldview" formation and its "Western" influence, especially in confronting *dualism, a hierarchical split between two fundamental aspects of reality. Usually such dualism values spiritual or intellectual life over material things.[4] Greco-Roman dualism, which Christians tried to resist, left subtle traces in Western culture. Ancient *Platonism*, with its teaching about universal ideas behind earthly realities, may not have been altogether dualistic. But forms of *gnosticism* emerged from Platonic thought patterns: with special knowledge, spiritual people could escape the material world's downward pull. Against the dualism of "gnostic" religion, Christian theology championed creation's material goodness.[5] Modern Christians still frequently struggle with dualistic tendencies, treating material things as unimportant or evil. Broader Western culture can be dualistic too: celebrating the body as determining human life and personal identity, while trying to change the body—even drastically—for the sake of being true to oneself.

The modern West certainly contains other worldview influences that collide with Christian teaching. In *atheistic materialism*, *naturalism leaves

---

3. The "spirit" in Gen. 1:2 may initially suggest a wind ambiguously circulating over primordial waters. Yet the waters and darkness are not untamed chaos rivaling God. Instead, the verse prepares for God's subsequent ordering of the cosmos. For further discussion of the original context, see Hamilton, *Book of Genesis*, 108–17; Walton, *Genesis*, 72–78. Still, historically focused exegesis does not preclude relating the verse to the Holy Spirit given the later canonical context.

4. Popular "worldview" teaching often uses the term imprecisely, reflecting Western rationalism. For present purposes, to oppose cultural dualisms with creation's goodness, see Wolters, *Creation Regained*.

5. For an overview, see Perrin, "Gnosticism."

"nature" red in tooth and claw. Lacking ultimate accountability by denying a Creator, materialistic people find it easy to say, "Let us eat and drink, for tomorrow we die" (1 Cor. 15:32), rather than caring for creation as a good gift. Materialism's lingering predecessor, *Deism*, may retain some future judgment from a generic creator, but it presents nature as an impersonal, law-like machine, ripe for manipulation. Hence the "Christian West" commonly faces criticism for harming the material world. This criticism claims that treating humans as rational animals—the "image of God"—supports selfishly dominating nature.[6] Such critics champion a more spiritual or "sacred" view of the earth. Whereas *pantheism* simply treats everything as divine, denying the distinction between Creator and creature, *panentheism* is now more widespread, blurring this distinction by locating everything "in" God. According to the traditional Christian doctrine, though, locating everything within the divine being leaves nothing sacred. Biblical teaching encourages creation care because of God's love, and it resists locating evil within the divine being. In fact, early Christians opposed gnosticism for the sake of valuing material things—not just human reason or inwardness—without making the world divine.

Beyond the modern West, the East is loosely associated with monism and the South with animism. Those associations may be misleading, but such worldviews do contradict traditional Christian teaching. *Monism*, the idea that there is only one ultimate reality, does not celebrate creation's material integrity in terms of God's love. If ultimate reality is physical, then monism is simply materialism; if ultimate reality is spiritual, then matter is inferior, even illusory—hardly worth caring for unless it is divine. Here Christian doctrine disagrees with the diverse spiritual traditions that Westerners call the "religions" of Buddhism and Hinduism. Whereas Buddhism tends toward monism, relating suffering to illusive worldly desire, Christian doctrine celebrates the goodness of the cosmos as distinct from its Creator, acknowledging evil as a parasite upon that goodness. Whereas Hinduism tends toward polytheism or at least practical syncretism involving impersonal god-concepts, Christian doctrine worships one Creator definitively and personally revealed in Jesus Christ.[7]

Animism, "belief in a multiplicity of spirits" that attributes a ghostly "soul" to "animals, plants and even inanimate objects," is similarly problematic. By downplaying physical entities, animism can encourage fearing

---

6. Famously making such allegations is L. White, "Historical Roots," although White's historiography has been challenged.

7. See further Richter, *Religion*, esp. chap. 2, "Concepts of Ultimate Being."

spiritual powers besides the Creator.[8] Admittedly, these contrasts between Christian teaching and alternative worldviews are hastily drawn. The "middle tier" of many non-Western contexts—comprising local deities, ancestral spirits, demons, charms, and so forth—influences numerous lives. The Christian distinction between "seen" and "unseen" realms does not rule out their ambiguous intersections.[9] Even if we cannot fully understand unseen powers, however, the Bible acknowledges that they temporarily oppose God, not that they genuinely rival their Creator.

Trinitarian Fellowship

Given the communion of Father, Son, and Holy Spirit, creation was a loving act of divine freedom. The Triune God is free to interact with creatures personally rather than distantly, through the mediation of the Son and Spirit. Given the loving divine freedom involved in its creation, the world is good. Everything in the world is also dependent: the sovereign Creator has no ultimate rivals worth fearing. God lovingly made time and space for communion with embodied creatures. Creation is closely related to God, yet free to be itself.

Creation's original perfection did not require a static world with inability to change. The *eschaton, the final state to which redemption brings us, does more than return creation to its original state without sin.[10] Irenaeus's emphasis has been gaining contemporary favor: the initial creation was dynamically good, destined to grow into maturity. Creation's goodness involved a divine project: a future developing beyond what was initially present, yet arriving through God's providence, not merely natural or cultural causes. In other words, creation's original goodness incorporated the prospect of angelic and human history. Fostering fellowship is at the heart of how the Triune Creator acts in the world.

Hence *the Son holds together creation's structure and history.* John 1:1–18 relates creation to God's dwelling among us. The light of the Logos dispels

---

8. For this definition and a brief history (animism rightly or wrongly "continues to be used as an umbrella term covering tribal or primal religions, in contrast with the major world faiths"), see Hughes, "Animism," 34.

9. Paul G. Hiebert influentially wrote of "The Flaw of the Excluded Middle." As A. Scott Moreau, "Flaw of the Excluded Middle," 362, summarizes Hiebert's work, Westerners tend to distinguish simply between the seen world and an unseen, transempirical world, whereas many non-Westerners recognize a middle world containing unseen powers "that are very much a part of everyday human life (e.g., a person is ill because of a curse or a spirit attack)." Moreau comments about another flaw, an *expanded* middle (emphasis original) "in which every strange event is thought to have a middle domain explanation"; that would go beyond what Hiebert intended.

10. The nature of creation's original perfection and its relation to redemption is sketched in Gunton, *Triune Creator*, esp. 11–12, albeit with somewhat controversial categories and historical examples.

the darkness that hinders fellowship. Colossians 1:15–23 identifies Christ as God's fullest image who holds together creation and redemption, reconciling the alienation that results from sin. Hebrews 1:2–3, calling the Son the "heir of all things," identifies purification of sins as God's promised work in history. The incarnation discloses the Triune God's personal, sovereign interaction with creation: "On the one hand it is indeed a new and miraculous creative act of God, in continuity with those things promised as new creation in texts like that of Isaiah 43:19; while on the other, this new humanity is formed within the womb of Mary of earthly material in such a way that the creation is renewed from within."[11] The incarnation was an utterly unique miracle. Yet this miracle indicates how determined God is to be with us and to work in us, to redeem creatures and the cosmos itself.

The life of the Incarnate Son reflects the Holy Spirit's empowering presence. The Spirit now indwells the church as a foretaste of the new creation. Hence *the Spirit leads particular creatures to their God-given end(s)*. The Spirit gives life both by sustaining creatures' existence and by nurturing their service to God. The Spirit enables various creatures to realize God-given possibilities—especially fostering among humans the freedom to love God and neighbor.

Since the Triune God created for the sake of fellowship, the distinction between Creator and creature is vital to maintain—as creation out of nothing already suggests: God made others with whom to relate. This purpose—fellowship—resists turning the distinction between Creator and creature into problematic separation. Because humans are made for communion with God, delighted stewardship of the cosmos, and cultural engagement with one another, they have freedom as creatures distinct from God, even as this freedom is a gift from the Holy Spirit.

Of the Natural Order

A related distinction pertains between created things: between "heaven and earth" or, in creedal language, what is "seen" and what is "unseen"—the natural order and the spiritual realm. Such a distinction should not become a separation, but the God-given integrity of the natural order has several implications.

Arts

God made material things to be good within an ordered world, "according to their kinds": scientific details aside, "God is not a God of disorder"

11. Gunton, *Triune Creator*, 24.

(1 Cor. 14:33). Wisdom (e.g., Prov. 8–9) invites people to live according to the world's divine design, in close relationship with God. Wisdom literature frequently uses other animals and earthly rhythms for teaching people how to live well.[12] The cosmos relates material things to one another for the sake of *shalom*, thus constituting (in John Calvin's famous phrase) a theater for God's glory.[13] Encouragement for the *arts—creative, skilled acts expressing both internal states and external realities—lies just here: human arts, both practiced directly and applied within other activities, reflect ordered patterns and possibilities in praise of their Creator. Of course, to recognize patterns in "nature" will actualize possibilities in a "history," with a plot that now includes evil.

HISTORY

In light of creation's original goodness, evil is not God's ontological rival but merely a parasite. God preserves the *structure* of the cosmos; evil involves the (mis)*direction* of its good elements.[14] Leaving aside tragic "natural" evils for the moment, "moral" evil stems from willing rebellion against God. Evil emerges when created goods are desired too much, acquired unjustly, or used at others' expense—in other words, as idols. Evil is neither a substantive rival of God nor a matter of lower-class realities. God made everything—including bodies—good.

The Eternal God is the Living One, whose interaction with creation takes time. Fellowship, for which God made humans, involves action and response. In the fullness of God's kingdom, such fellowship will be unending and may not involve "time" as we know it, because there will be no sense of loss. In the meantime, God's unfolding work generates a history, which merits careful study. Historical study faces inherent limits, though, given both God's sovereignty and humans' location within history.

A Christian view of history is distinctively "linear": time moves forward, within God's providence, toward particular goals and an ultimate end.[15] Yet a Christian view incorporates "circular" elements: God has chosen not to realize history's goals instantly. As God works with creatures slowly and steadily, some patterns repeat themselves, almost endlessly. So Ecclesiastes suggests: Is

---

12. In addition to O'Donovan, *Resurrection and Moral Order*, see Brown, *Ethos of the Cosmos*. Regarding Lady Wisdom in Prov. 8, see Treier, *Proverbs and Ecclesiastes*.

13. E.g., Calvin, *Institutes* 1.6.2 (1:72); see further Schreiner, *Theater of His Glory*.

14. For a short presentation of this distinction between "structure" and "direction," see Wolters, *Creation Regained*.

15. Jaeger, *What the Heavens Declare*, 68, suggests that the Bible introduced the concept of linear historical development.

there really anything new under the sun? (1:9). The sun's daily rising reminds us to be thankful for repetition. Instead of complaining about monotony, we should celebrate the regularity of God's provision. As for redemption, the incarnation was the exceptional event that proves this rule about nothing new apart from God. When Jesus completed his earthly mission, he was not simply beamed up to heaven in ghostly fashion. Rather, even today as the ascended Lord, he retains his transformed body as the God-*man*. By sending the Spirit to raise Jesus and to renew humanity, God reaffirmed the commitment once expressed with a rainbow (Gen. 9): God is working out redemption within the patterns of creation's historical time until the Lord's return—a kind of upward spiral.

SCIENCE

Somewhat like historical study, the physical sciences were unleashed by the doctrine of creation out of nothing: "Only a theology which distinguishes God from the world ontologically justifies the practices of science," treating the cosmos as contingent.[16] This contingency means "that because the structures of reality happen to be what they are—and are not necessarily what they are—in order to understand the workings of the world one is bound to explore its actual material regularities rather than enquire into its underlying rational structures, as is the tendency of all Greek thought, Aristotle's included."[17] Empirical study honors the particularity of what God made. The doctrine of creation also limits such study, challenging any confusion of science with philosophical materialism. The universe's structures remain open to the Creator's involvement. Without undermining cosmic regularities, God providentially sustains them and periodically intervenes for redemptive purposes.

ECOLOGY

For a while history apparently spirals downward: salvation initially centers upon humans because we are at the heart of the problem.[18] Yet salvation incorporates the physical world in history's eventual upward movement: Adam and Eve were called to tend creation from the beginning; now, after the fall, the physical environment awaits redemption alongside the new humanity (Rom. 8:18–25). Whatever the precise interpretation of passages such as

16. Gunton, *Triune Creator*, 39. See further Jaeger, *What the Heavens Declare*, which suggests that Christian theism provides a distinctive definition and justification of "laws of nature."
17. Gunton, *Triune Creator*, 113.
18. Gunton, *Triune Creator*, 166–68.

2 Peter 3:10–13, God will not simply annihilate the present earth in favor of a totally new one. Such annihilation would contradict scriptural hopes; for example, Old Testament prophets frequently include present creatures in portrayals of the future. Furthermore, the renewal of creation has been inaugurated in Jesus's resurrection.[19] Somehow history's upward spiral will be completed when heaven comes down to earth—when the ascended Christ returns, fully reclaiming all that God has put under humanity's feet.

Hence proper care for God's creation integrates economic and environmental concerns. After all, an "economy" designates the administration of a "household," whether small or large. The physical cosmos comprises a fundamental set of economic resources, with poor stewardship and selfish misuse funding human poverty. But the physical environment is more than a set of raw materials, and economics ought to measure more than monetary transactions: "To seek to have an economy without ecology is to try and manage an environment with no knowledge or concern about how it works in itself—to try and formulate human laws in abstraction from or ignorance of the laws of nature."[20]

Contrary to a common assumption, God lovingly delights in the nonhuman creation for its own sake. The "creation mandate" of Genesis 1:28 does not subordinate the nonhuman creation to human interest. Already biblical evidence has highlighted God's ecological delight: the "goodness" of all that God made, Wisdom's appeals to creation order for teaching humans to flourish, the resurrection of Christ, prophetic hopes for a new creation that includes physical elements, and so forth. Biblical poetry and Jesus's parables too are replete with physical imagery. Some of this poetry, as in Job 38–41, celebrates God's fierce whimsy in creating strange creatures with no obviously "useful" functions. In poetry such as Psalm 19, God celebrates praise from the nonhuman creation. How can nonhuman creatures praise God without speaking? Their very existence and beauty speak volumes.

Of the Spiritual Realm

The visible cosmos is not all there is; God made invisible things too. As one theologian comments, though, "Among the guild of professional theologians

---

19. For emphasis on a transformed, not annihilated, heavens and earth, see several works by N. T. Wright; the popular treatment of Wittmer, *Heaven Is a Place on Earth*; and the more technical treatment of Middleton, *A New Heaven and a New Earth*. But note useful cautions about not overdoing this emphasis and losing the classical Christian critique of worldliness, in Jeffrey, "(Pre) Figuration," 377–82, 387–90.

20. The surrounding reflections are indebted to R. Williams, "Ecology and Economy," from which the quotation is taken.

in America today, serious talk about angels is roughly as common as serious talk about Santa Claus or the tooth fairy. If theologians bring up the subject at all, it is ordinarily not to debate whether or not angels actually exist, but to lament the prevalence of superstition among the rest of the population."[21] Yet the Bible is replete with accounts of angels and demons. Hence the Creed includes what is "unseen," not just what is physical, within what Almighty God has made.

ANGELS

Angels are rarely described at length in Scripture. For instance, Mary's encounter with Gabriel (Luke 1:26–38) turns upon whether or not she believes the angel. The message astonishes her, not primarily the visual appearance. Still, vivid appearances sometimes occur (e.g., Isa. 6; Ezek. 1; Revelation). Somehow the Bible distinguishes angels from human beings in terms of bodies; much of the theological tradition has held that angels have no bodies at all. For instance, since Hebrews 1:7 apparently labels them "spirits," angels have been treated as immaterial beings whose physical manifestations are occasional, only taking whatever form is necessary for a particular ministry. In that case, lacking bodies establishes a point of continuity with the God they serve. Others, however, think that view stretches the biblical evidence too far, creating philosophical problems; perhaps, they suggest, angels have bodies of a different kind.[22]

A related question concerns whether or not angels are "persons." If Boethius's famous definition is correct, that a person is "an individual substance of a rational nature,"[23] then traditionally it makes sense that angels are persons. However, if a person is a "someone" who can freely reflect upon their nature and enact that identity in a uniquely individual way,[24] then it is less clear that angels are persons. For the Bible does not emphasize their freedom but rather their faithful praise and service. True, *angels are messengers; that is what the Greek word *angelos* means. They communicate, they sometimes have names, and they can be narrative subjects, while demons apparently have enough sinful agency to rebel (2 Pet. 2:4). Yet they may lack freedom to obey God's will and advance God's kingdom as variously as humans do. Perhaps they have already been confirmed in either angelic righteousness or demonic rebellion, and that is why Scripture does not emphasize their individual freedom. Still,

---

21. B. Marshall, "Are There Angels?," 69. The following account is indebted to Marshall's.
22. E.g., P. Griffiths, *Decreation*, chap. 18.
23. Boethius, "Treatise against Eutyches and Nestorius," 91.
24. See the sophisticated treatment by Spaemann, *Persons*.

angels are not called the "image of God" as are human persons, who can be conformed to Christ.

Debatable details aside, the Bible clarifies what angels do: they advance God's praise and the world's salvation. Even when they help particular people, preeminently they advance God's kingdom, as in Peter's escape from prison (Acts 12:1–19). According to Revelation 4–5, angels' heavenly praise centers upon Jesus Christ—the Lion of Judah and the Lamb of God, who enacts God's decree in history. Understood in that light, angels' Old Testament missions prepare for Jesus's ministry. Their New Testament missions sustain him until his resurrection and support the church's subsequent witness. Bearing witness to God's work through heavenly praise, earthly announcements, and periodic warfare (Dan. 10:13; Jude 9) or rescues—that is the angelic vocation.

Accordingly, no philosophical speculations, cultural experiences, or scientific problems should determine how Christians understand angels. The fundamental factor should be the Bible's testimony concerning the resurrection—and angels' association with that history-making event. Angels appear "and are described as active, only when it is a matter of declaring the Word and work of God Himself as fulfilled in speech or action."[25] In Scripture, heaven is the boundary place of God's action in the world; from there angels "precede the revelation and doing of His will on earth as objective and authentic witnesses, . . . accompany it as faithful servants of God and man, and . . . victoriously ward off the opposing forms and forces of chaos."[26] God sends angels as accompanying messengers that foster creaturely attention to the Word, since humans must encounter God in creaturely and not merely divine form.[27] Their presence draws attention to God's.[28]

Hostile Powers

Of course, the biblical story contains hostile powers too. The Christian tradition usually treats the *devil or *Satan as a preeminent angel who pridefully rebelled and became God's chief adversary. *Demons constitute an angelic minority, albeit sizable, that joined the devil's rebellion. Traditionally,

---

25. Barth, CD III/3, 238. Barth's treatment of angels, like so much of his theology, is repetitive, long, and critical of seemingly everyone, yet it is periodically insightful and occasionally breathtaking. We can appreciate his biblical emphasis upon angels being *witnesses* (e.g., CD III/3, 461) without being as hesitant to consider angels' nature in passages like Heb. 1, and without leaving possible distance between the biblical proclamation and their reality (thus contra, e.g., CD III/3, 502).

26. Barth, CD III/3, 369.

27. Barth, CD III/3, 478.

28. Barth, CD III/3, 496.

certain biblical passages epitomize Satan's prideful fall (e.g., Isa. 14:12–27; Ezek. 28). Today these texts are widely interpreted in terms of historical kings. But it remains possible that they contain additional significance, since their language is quite grandiose and a fall from heaven likewise appears in key New Testament texts (Luke 10:18–20; Rev. 12).

Demonic phenomena are difficult to interpret, often having psychological dimensions. Possibilities such as satanic ritual abuse on the one hand, and the power of suggestion on the other, merit caution. Nonetheless, some Christian traditions, particularly Roman Catholicism, have carefully developed protocols for recognition and confrontation of possible demons. Among the relevant criteria are apparently superhuman powers or physical capacities like levitation, fierce aversion to holy things like a crucifix, knowledge of hidden things or unlearned languages, and the like.[29] The nature of "powers and principalities" (e.g., Eph. 6:11–12) remains debated, but they probably include or use human structures, such as cultural and political institutions. Even so, they should not be "demythologized" altogether—reduced to human institutions by denying that the devil and demons exist as distinct creaturely rebels.[30] Angels and demons are neither quasi-divine nor just mythical ciphers for something else.

Jesus has triumphed over every hostile power (Col. 2:8–15), and baptism incorporates people within that saving victory (1 Pet. 3:18–4:6). Still, Christians may be variously oppressed by demons (Eph. 6:10–20; 1 Pet. 5:8–9). Applying "possession" to such cases, even when attacks are dramatic, is controversial. It seems difficult to reconcile the Holy Spirit's indwelling, empowering presence with a person's will being totally dominated by hostile powers. Christ has claimed believers as his own, at great cost (1 Cor. 6:17–20), even if we must beware resisting the Holy Spirit (Eph. 4:30). The healing victory of the cross affects particular lives and contexts differently, however. Thus, discerning the spiritual realm requires both humility and courage. Pastoral engagement with unusual phenomena should explore human factors—family background, unconfessed sin, psychological states, and so on—without exaggerating or minimizing the relevance of spiritual powers.

The adversary and his demons work chiefly through deception and fear. The devil is the father of lies (John 8:44), masquerading as an angel of light

---

29. See Tennant, "In Need of Deliverance," 46–48, 50, 52, 56, 60, 62–63, which stand behind this paragraph.

30. Contra, e.g., the prominent work of Walter Wink (beginning with *Naming the Powers: The Language of Power in the New Testament* [Philadelphia: Fortress, 1984]) that treats the powers too exclusively in terms of violence, see Dawn, *Powers, Weakness*; more briefly, Dawn, "Powers and Principalities," although Dawn may distinguish the powers too sharply from the demonic.

(2 Cor. 11:14). If angels are fundamentally messengers, bearing witness to God's saving victory, then demons promote falsehood, which is ultimately unreal.[31] Dismissing the demonic altogether would leave us vulnerable to deception. "The devil prowls around like a roaring lion looking for someone to devour"; we need alertness to resist (1 Pet. 5:8–9). This metaphor suggests more than just danger, however; both the need to stand firm and the broader biblical context indicate that Satan uses fear as a prime weapon. Becoming obsessed with the demonic would leave us vulnerable to another kind of deception: forgetting that Christ has defeated all hostile powers, we might fear something besides God alone.

The spiritual realm is not totally separate from the natural realm or cultural history. Humans should neither expect to deal with demons everywhere nor deny their activity anywhere. Given their prominence in some contexts, hostile powers may be more or less visible, affecting cultural practices that generate religious effects and satisfy real needs. Yet given their primary work of deception, it would be inappropriate to think dualistically, as if demons actually rival God or always operate apart from other creaturely realities. Authentic exorcism appeals to Christ's authority as a gift, not a native capacity at which to marvel.

Contemporary Questions: The Genesis Story and Modern Science

Beyond the unseen spiritual realm, Christian teaching about creation faces questions concerning modern evolutionary science. Evangelical theology contains a range of disputed views about the Bible's creation narratives, the historicity of Adam and Eve, the effects of the fall, and accordingly the relation between Scripture and modern science.[32]

The Interpretation of Genesis

Hermeneutical strategies for engaging the Genesis creation narrative(s) have never been uniform. Nonliteral readings appeared as early as the patristic

---

31. Emphasizing demons' relation to falsehood is an insight of Barth, who treats demons very briefly, with the claim that they want to be considered theologically interesting but cannot be (CD III/3, 519–20). Barth goes further to apply his distinctive understandings of "myth" and "nothingness" to demons (CD III/3, 521–23). While he says that we can neither ignore nor absolutize demons (CD III/3, 526–27), his brevity does not reflect New Testament proportions. His statements that biblical demonology is simply a negative reflection of Christology and soteriology, and that demons merely act as if they came from heaven, are intriguing but perhaps problematic (CD III/3, 530–31).

32. With permission and modest revision, this section reuses material from Treier, "Creation and Evolution."

era, long before Charles Darwin's *Origin of Species* (1859). Augustine's opposition to Pelagianism stabilized the Christian teaching, especially in the West, about a historical *fall: from original goodness in fellowship with God, humans fell into willful rebellion, to which God responded by placing the cosmos under a curse. Many subsequent figures like Martin Luther have read Genesis historically and literally, yet they still differed over details and even read the text in multiple ways.

PHASES

To generalize, theological responses to Darwin's revolution have unfolded in three phases, which are reflected in the meaning of "theistic evolution" over time. Initially, in the late nineteenth and early twentieth centuries, theistic evolution could involve openness, even among conservative theologians, to God's superintending use of evolutionary processes.[33] Such thinkers insisted on distinguishing between evolutionary science per se and a materialistic worldview or denial of divine intervention.

In a second phase, the Scopes Trial of 1925 heightened emerging American controversy. The fundamentalist-modernist battle drove evangelicals away from mainstream academic and cultural engagement. Fundamentalists popularly embraced "literal" interpretation of Genesis, while modernists took theistic evolution into virtual Deism—God starting a process and leaving it alone. In the 1950s, "creation science" became the polar opposite of such deistic evolution. Mediating figures like Bernard Ramm (1916–92) acknowledged scientific evidence for an old earth, even for evolutionary processes, while retaining active divine involvement, especially in the creation of humans.[34] Often such mediating figures spoke of "progressive creation," which encompassed the "day-age" and "gap" theories. These theories tended to be "concordist," attempting to reconcile particular details in Genesis with modern scientific evidence.

In a third, recent phase, theistic evolution has encompassed various positions; among evangelicals, it is giving way to "evolutionary creation" as the preferred label.[35] This label more clearly emphasizes God's action, speaking of creation as the noun. As the adjective, evolution indicates a means of God's action.

---

33. E.g., Warfield, *Evolution, Science, and Scripture*, although the chronology and extent of Warfield's openness are debated; one of his most reliable interpreters, Bradley Gundlach, affirms the openness but notes that Warfield did not champion "theistic evolution" as such.

34. Ramm, *Christian View of Science and Scripture*.

35. Particularly represented by BioLogos (https://biologos.org).

APPROACHES

With this historical background, we can plot a spectrum of contemporary approaches. Different evangelical positions emphasize how authoritative or certain they take the biblical teaching, at one end, or the scientific evidence, at the other end, to be.

On the one hand, *young-earth creationists* interpret the Bible "literally" and only then evaluate scientific evidence. They correlate select scientific details with items in the Genesis account. The result is a "young" earth, a few thousand rather than millions or billions of years old. God directly created the earth in six twenty-four-hour days. Apparent conflict with modern science is attributed partly to a lack of faith in biblical revelation, for projecting post-fall conservation and deterioration processes back onto pre-fall creation. Conflict is also attributed to the Noahic flood, as a prime source of fossil evidence supporting an old earth. Other scientific evidence for surviving, species-level, genetic mutation (undergirding evolutionary explanations) is further challenged.

On the other hand, *theistic evolutionists* (in the strong, narrow sense, which others perceive as deistic) consult science for assured results first; where conflicts arise, Genesis is reinterpreted as "myth" (which can be a literary category, but in this debate often has the connotation of nonhistorical). Since modern science goes beyond observation to hypotheses about natural causes behind events, it pursues comprehensive pictures of the world's origins. Here science largely makes room for God as the first cause of natural processes, or a causal gap-filler in hypotheses.

As noted above, *earlier progressive (old-earth) creationist* theories arose when trying to correlate the Bible and science by privileging particular details. In the nineteenth century, geological evidence suggested an old earth, but evolutionary theory was not developed and knowledge of the Bible's ancient Near Eastern context was not as deep. Seeking middle ground hermeneutically, such concordist theories still interpreted the Bible as literally as possible, but with certain details slipped in or taken figuratively. The *gap theory* slipped in a time period between Genesis 1:1 and 1:2, where it placed the necessary history for old-earth evolution. The *day-age theory* took the days of Genesis 1 figuratively, since a "day" is to God like a thousand years (2 Pet. 3:8, quoting Ps. 90:4); each day could signal an indeterminate length of time, corresponding to geological processes. Progressive creation emphasizes that God personally superintended evolution, specifically intervening to create human beings.

More recent progressive or evolutionary creationist theories emphasize that young-earth creationism was not the church's only view prior to the rise of evolutionary theory. Like progressive creationists, they tend toward the middle of the spectrum between privileging certain biblical interpretations or scientific commitments. They emphasize that many evangelical Old Testament scholars today interpret Genesis in terms of its literary framework and historical background.

Scholars emphasizing the *literary framework* in Genesis 1–3 understand its historical and theological claims in that light. Surrounding nations had polytheistic cosmologies, which Genesis critiques.[36] Pagan myths focused on procreation rather than creation, on the genealogy of deities rather than natural origins. To counteract them, Genesis depicts God's loving creation of cosmic elements that surrounding peoples were inclined to worship (e.g., the sun). Days 1–3 are "days of preparation" to address the murkiness of Genesis 1:2: darkness, a watery abyss, and a formless earth. Days 4–6 are "days of population" to fill the realms prepared in the first three days. Such "days" are neither strictly literal twenty-four-hour periods (which would precede the sun!) nor indefinite ages allegorically correlated with specific scientific processes. They establish an analogy between God's creative activity and Israel's weekly work and worship.

Scholars emphasizing the *historical background* also locate Genesis in its initial context, focusing on the cognitive environment that surrounded Israel in the ancient Near East (ANE). One version claims that the ontology of Genesis is "functional" rather than "material" in Greek or later Western senses: for the ANE, coming into existence involved receiving a name, being separated from other things, and receiving a role in an ordered cosmos.[37] God's generous rather than selfish design is relatively unique in the ANE, but the text's functional focus is not. Only God is the subject of "create"; no use of materials is mentioned, because God was not making a substance (as we think of it) but rather was establishing existence by assigning functions (e.g., even the making of humans has a related reference to "male and female"). Even if this version of the historical background claims too much, many evangelical scholars agree broadly that the focus of ANE creation accounts was functional. Accordingly, the language of Genesis is phenomenological rather than scientifically precise.

Thus, recent evangelical scholarship alleges that both young-earth creationist "literalism" and altogether "mythical" interpretations risk falling prey to modern assumptions. In Genesis's original context, literary elements conveyed a theological message rather than a sequential, scientific description. Yet this

---

36. Behind the following account, see, e.g., Hamilton, *Book of Genesis.*
37. Most handily, see Walton, *Lost World of Genesis One.*

message concerns God and earthly history. For a key instance, Genesis uses the same formula when discussing the first humans ("This is the account of . . ." in 2:4) as it does later for the patriarchs: as with Adam, so with Abraham, and so on. Indeed, other canonical texts such as Romans treat the Genesis narrative as a history of the first humans. But the historicity of Adam and Eve as humanity's parents again generates a spectrum of major views—although discussion is heated enough that nuances are rapidly changing.[38]

The History of Adam and Eve

Young-earth creationists and many progressive creationists insist on *a historical Adam and Eve* (created de novo or via direct divine intervention) from whom all humans descend. Their reasoning sometimes involves "literal" interpretation of Genesis, but also it involves the rest of Scripture (e.g., Rom. 3–6), the overwhelming tendency of the Christian tradition, and the perceived consequences of alternatives. Among those perceived consequences is the weakening or loss of a traditional doctrine of original sin, tied to a historical human fall from created goodness.[39]

By contrast, many theistic evolutionists insist on *a mythical Adam and Eve* representing aspects of (evolved) human life.[40] Their reasoning involves genetic and paleoanthropological evidence for "common descent" of humans and other animals. This common descent incorporates intermediate "hominid" forms, as well as intrahuman diversity that contradicts an original human pair. (Theologically, "monogenesis" sometimes refers to all humans descending from this pair, Adam and Eve. Scientifically, this language works differently: polygenetic theories have multiple locations for evolving human life, but monogenetic theories—having not a single pair but a single interbreeding population in one location—currently dominate.) Such theistic evolutionists address biblical evidence and traditional Christian support for historical Adam and Eve by emphasizing historical contexts—with earlier notions of original sin preceding modern science.

Naming another group is complex.[41] Generally, evolutionary creationists and other progressive creationists propose *an archetypal or ancient Adam and Eve* representing all humans theologically. These first human representatives

---

38. The website for the Creation Project at Trinity Evangelical Divinity School (https://henrycenter.tiu.edu/section/creation-project/) has been hosting numerous symposia that keep these discussions ongoing and accessible.

39. See Madueme and Reeves, *Adam, the Fall, and Original Sin.*

40. E.g., Enns, *Evolution of Adam.*

41. The following categories come from Haarsma and Haarsma, *Origins.*

either evolved fully from animals (evolutionary creation) or evolved along with direct divine involvement (progressive creation).

One version of such a view, "recent representatives," has evolutionary creation of humans (tens or hundreds of thousands of years ago), with a representative human pair chosen about 10,000 years ago (matching the biblical Adam and Eve). This pair fell from created goodness into the original sin affecting all other humans. Another version, "pair of ancient ancestors," has evolutionary creation of prehuman hominids followed by miraculous creation of Adam and Eve (perhaps via the giving of "souls") roughly 150,000 years ago, from whom all humans subsequently descend. Still another version, "group of ancient representatives," has evolutionary creation of humans with God selecting a particular group to receive revelation. This group fell into sin. One difference from the "recent representatives" view lies in the timeline; here "Adam and Eve" archetypally represent this earlier group rather than a more recent selection. Another difference is that here all humans descend from the Adam and Eve group, whereas the "recent representatives" view does not treat "Adam and Eve" as the biological ancestors of most humans today.

Evidence of human genetic diversity still challenges the "recent representatives" and "pair of ancient ancestors" views.[42] As with young-earth creationism, according to which God created a cosmos with the appearance of age, theological questions arise: Notably, is it appropriate to believe that God would have modern scientific evidence point in a different direction than some interpretations of biblical revelation demand? Alternatively, how certain is the direction in which scientific evidence points? A third question follows from these, regarding the nature of the cosmic curse that followed humanity's fall.

The Effects of the Fall

For young-earth creationists and some progressive creationists, *neither animal nor human death preceded the fall*; both ensue from God's curse upon the cosmos.[43] This view appeals to Romans 3–6 and perhaps the Genesis narrative read literally. It may also appeal to a vision of the future—"the lion lying down with the lamb"[44]—as literally reflecting what Eden's paradise must have been like. The challenge for this view is not just the scope of modern science,

42. See the relatively readable sketch of genetic evidence in Venema and McKnight, *Adam and the Genome*.

43. See, e.g., the work of the Institute for Creation Research along with numerous publications from the likes of Henry Morris and John C. Whitcomb Jr.

44. No biblical passage actually contains this phrase, but it roughly corresponds to the peace among animals depicted in texts like Isa. 11:6; 65:25.

which assumes nature's metaphysical continuity from the beginning of creation onward, but also the essential goodness of creaturely finitude. The popular young-earth view instead affirms significant metaphysical and/or physical ruptures, including death, associating them with the curse and the Genesis flood.

For many theistic evolutionists, *both animal and human death preceded the fall*, which may be acknowledged as a historical event but more often is treated as a symbol.[45] Organic continuity is emphasized between the world at the beginning and the world experienced now. The challenge for this view is the Augustinian teaching from Romans about the historical relation of human death to sin. In response, either Romans is reinterpreted or else Paul is treated as sharing premodern assumptions (a literal Adam and Eve with a historical fall) that need not be affirmed.

In between, for many evolutionary creationists, *both animal and one kind of human death preceded the fall*.[46] The history within Genesis and Romans involved not "metaphysical" change in the very nature of things but rather "moral" or "relational" change in how the cosmos affects human lives. On this view, the Creator's gift of finitude, signaled by Old Testament depictions of a good death or passages like Psalm 90, gave way to spiritual alienation. The threat of annihilation made death deadly. The challenge for this view is still the Augustinian interpretation of Romans. While some have interpreted such texts in terms of spiritual and not biological death, that remains a minority view in evangelical circles.

For other evolutionary and progressive creationists, *animal but not human death preceded the fall*.[47] Such a view acknowledges scientific considerations supporting animal death from the beginning, while resisting widespread "metaphysical" change due to the curse. It maintains more easily a traditional interpretation of Romans about the historical origins of human death being due to the fall. One challenge for this view is the need to make a clear scientific or theological break between humans and other animals, whether or not Scripture's eschatological passages (again, of the "lion lying down with the lamb" type) pertain to creation. Furthermore, a distinction between metaphysical and moral or relational change is difficult to maintain clearly.

Biblical scholars widely agree that Scripture does not teach immortality of the soul per se, as Greek philosophy or other religions did. The eternity of either life or death is a conditional gift or punishment, not an automatic

---

45. E.g., Giberson, *Saving the Original Sinner*. For an attempt at defending the traditional doctrine of original sin without universal human descent from a historical Adam, see McFarland, *In Adam's Fall*.

46. E.g., Gunton, *Triune Creator*.

47. E.g., Munday, "Creature Mortality"; Faro, "Question of Evil and Animal Death."

result of a native property. Yet Christian tradition has interpreted Scripture as insisting that human death stems from the wages of sin—so, for example, Canon 1 of the Council of Carthage (418) when condemning Pelagianism. It remains possible that God originally offered conditional immortality to humans and then, without metaphysical change, left them subject to death only after the fall. Whether that is the right approach, however, will be a continuing debate, given the complexities just outlined. This sketch of possible views, admittedly, reflects a somewhat artificial attempt to bring order out of chaos.

The Relation of the Bible and Science

At stake in these debates is a challenging opportunity: integrating biblical faith with modern learning. Both Scripture and "nature" can serve as "books" of God's self-revelation, although it can be difficult to read them in harmony or to recognize the limits of their teaching and implications. The two-book metaphor is easily misunderstood, given how different the books' aims are. Scripture is God's final written authority and bears witness to the final Word, Jesus Christ. Yet it may not address scientific subjects very explicitly or extensively. The created world speaks about God in a rather metaphorical sense; even if it speaks volumes, it mostly puts on display the divine perfections about which we hear in Scripture. Yet scientific study does help humans to speak about creation; even if this human speech frequently changes, it can still inform the interpretation of Scripture. After all, Scripture's teaching does not change, but our theological understanding periodically does. Scientific and theological change makes correlations between biblical and scientific details seem vulnerable. Even so, as tempting as it becomes to focus on affirming a scriptural "worldview" while leaving scientific details alone, such a worldview would be lost if biblical interpretation provided no intellectual parameters at all. What it means to read the Bible "on its own terms" is a contested but necessary concept.

"Science" in Western culture is often confused with scientism, as if scientific practice were utterly factual or rational and nonideological. Science is also confused with philosophical naturalism, which ignores a long Western consensus (perhaps still the dominant popular intuition) acknowledging a Creator. Like theism, naturalistic materialism involves "faith," even when it waves the banner of reason. Although distinct in principle, boundaries blur for many between philosophical materialism and the "methodological naturalism" that seems integral to modern science—or even all academic inquiry.[48]

---

48. Defending a Christian version of methodological naturalism in science as distinct from metaphysical naturalism is Bishop, "God and Methodological Naturalism."

Recent appeals to *intelligent design (ID) initially tried to accept established evolutionary science while resisting smuggled-in philosophical materialism. ID highlighted gaps in current explanations for creatures' complexity.[49] If evidence suggested complexity so extraordinary that a natural explanation would be impossible apart from intentional design, then this evidence could authorize philosophical inquiry into the nature of the Designer—support for a Creator superintending evolution.

Ensuing debate became enmeshed in America's culture wars. Original ID claims and proponents involved scientific activity running alongside cultural and philosophical agendas. Nevertheless, many believing scientists worry that current ID falls into *"God of the gaps" thinking—using God to explain gaps in a scientific account of causes. God could be excluded as soon as an explanatory gap is filled. Another worry concerns whether "design" indicates miraculous intervention. These debates indicate the need to delimit clearer boundaries of science per se, and parameters for scientists addressing matters beyond their expertise. Christians further need to address how much knowledge to expect—from either Scripture or science—about cosmic and human origins, which inherently lie in the remotest past. Modern science by nature tries to fill every gap with exhaustive explanations. It is worth asking how much scientific observation, extrapolation, hypothesis formation, testing, and so forth are suited to inquiring about origins, along with how much God has actually told us in the Bible.

Reading Genesis in relation to modern science will continue to generate questions and tensions. Even so, *creatio ex nihilo* emphasizes that the Triune God lovingly spoke everything else into existence, fostering fellowship and creaturely delight in the Creator's glory. Although any analogy soon breaks down, God's creative action involves communication somewhat like a poet's, a composer's, or an author's.[50] Like an author's work with characters, the plot of God's creative and providential activity eternally encompasses everything while being dynamic and particular. God did not create an impersonal machine populated by robots but instead a garden temple full of harmony and wonder, cared for by creaturely images of God. Creation inaugurated a drama, in which—as the next chapter explores—humans play a unique role that includes study: "Great are the works of the LORD; they are pondered by all who delight in them" (Ps. 111:2).

---

49. See, e.g., Behe, *Darwin's Black Box*; Dembski, *Intelligent Design*. But see concerns expressed in, e.g., Haarsma and Haarsma, *Origins*.

50. See, e.g., Gunton, *Triune Creator*, 182; more extensively, Vanhoozer, *Remythologizing Theology*.

—7—

Human Beings

THESIS

Human beings are uniquely created to commune with God and to communicate what God is like; for this calling God has made them embodied souls and relational selves, with each person and culture having dignity rooted in God's love and their diversity being an occasion of divine delight.

LEARNING OBJECTIVES

After learning the material in this chapter, you should be able to:

1. *Define briefly* the key terms introduced here (marked with an asterisk and included in the glossary).
2. *List and recognize* the views of human constitution involving body, soul, and/or spirit.
3. *Describe and compare* the three major approaches to the image of God.
4. *Identify and illustrate* the complementarian and egalitarian ways of interpreting Scripture concerning gender and authority.
5. *Explain* the basic commitments of Christian anthropology concerning evil, ability, ethnicity, and sexuality.

In God's drama of redemption, humans take center stage: these are the creatures whose nature the Son of God assumed in the incarnation. These are the creatures who can know themselves truly in relation to God: "Nearly all the wisdom we possess, that is to say, true and sound wisdom, consists of two parts: the knowledge of God and of ourselves. But, while joined by many bonds, which one precedes and brings forth the other is not easy to discern."[1] A Christian account addresses human dignity in terms of imaging God.

---

1. Calvin, *Institutes* 1.1.1 (1:35).

Humans are also the creatures who can know one another, and themselves in relation to one another—forming families, neighborhoods, other small communities, and larger institutions such as businesses and governments. While all humans share a common dignity, each person is unique due to particular gifts in God's providence, and people group themselves in numerous ways. A Christian *anthropology—account of human being—addresses both the dignity and the cultural diversity of God's image-bearers.

Human Dignity

The *imago Dei, the image of God, has been the most fundamental concept of Christian theological anthropology for two millennia. But its precise meaning is mysterious. While the concept appears at the very beginning, in the Genesis creation narrative, it is not overtly crucial for the rest of the Old Testament. The New Testament applies this language in new ways, with a focus on Jesus Christ. After tracing three major approaches that emerge from biblical texts, we can sketch how the Christian tradition relates imaging God to the identity of the self and the nature of the human person. Finally, Christians also address the constitution of human beings—their bodies and "souls"—in light of their dignity in relation to God.

The Image of God

The first, classic, approach is "metaphysical" and/or "christological": loosely speaking, the image of God involves *reason* and/or *righteousness*. This approach focuses on a "substantive" reality that humans share with God and that animals lack. This inward intellectual or spiritual structure, often identified with the "soul" or "spirit," is like God's essence at the creaturely level: humans are "rational animals." Church fathers related the "image" of Genesis 1:26–27 to this metaphysical essence and the "likeness" to humanity's spiritual potential for conformity to Christ, the ultimate image of God (e.g., Col. 1:15–23). Later, more philosophical versions of this approach put less emphasis on the christological aspect and more on the metaphysical aspect involving rational capacities.

A second, modern, approach is "functional": loosely speaking, the image of God involves *royalty*. This approach focuses on the language of Genesis 1:26b, 28 in light of the context of the ANE. The image of God is explained by surrounding phrases about ruling over the animals and the rest of creation. Nations around Israel placed images of rulers in temples to represent their gods, supporting the rulers' authority.[2] Genesis tells the creation story in terms of a garden temple.[3] Extraordinarily, humans are placed in this temple with the privilege of naming and ruling over other creatures, and with the expectation of extending God's glorious rule through reproducing themselves. As embodied creatures, humans could represent within the created order what God's reign is like. While some theological traditions have spoken of humans as God's "vice-regents" or "vicegerents," classically they tied this function to a metaphysical essence. But many modern biblical scholars have been influenced by antimetaphysical tendencies in nineteenth-century Germany and by new insight into the ANE context. They now speak of imaging God, at least in Genesis, only in terms of this representative or ruling function. They also critique the metaphysical approach for defining the *imago Dei* apart from human embodiment.

A third, more "postmodern," approach is "relational": loosely speaking, the image of God involves *relationship*. This approach, popularized by Karl Barth, focuses on "male and female he created them" (Gen. 1:27) as the explanatory key.[4] The Jewish thinker Martin Buber (1878–1965) began emphasizing the uniqueness of persons as defined by "I-Thou" relationships. For Protestants who follow Barth on Buber's path, not to mention some Catholic and Orthodox theologians, marriage offers a creaturely analogy of the personal relations within God's triune life. More recently, those who take a "social" view of the Trinity emphasize relationality as the essence of human personhood and, hence, the divine image. Humans image God by living in relationship to God, one another, and the rest of creation.

Each approach contributes insight yet faces criticism. The metaphysical approach distinguishes humans from animals and relates them to God in terms of who they are—given the narrative context, "according to their kind" of being. But this approach struggles to demonstrate that the Israelites in their original context would have thought metaphysically, and to explain how human bodies relate to imaging God. Moreover, the language of "soul" in its original context referred to a living being, applying to animals as well (e.g., Gen. 2:19).

A functional approach apparently fits the original context better, while addressing human bodies: they are essential to representing, in this created order, what the invisible God's rule is like. But this approach struggles to demonstrate that image-of-God language is simply equivalent to creaturely

2. Middleton, *Liberating Image*.
3. See, e.g., Beale, *Temple and the Church's Mission*.
4. See Barth, *CD* III/1, 181–210.

rule, to address New Testament texts, and to embrace the distinct capacities that are necessary for humans to represent God.

A relational approach appeals to the nearby "male and female" language and an emphasis throughout other Scripture texts—including the mysterious relationship between human marriage and God's covenant love. But this approach struggles to demonstrate that human distinctiveness lies in relationality due to other animals' maleness and femaleness, and also to clarify how the *imago Dei* involves every individual person versus humanity as a whole. The dignity of individual persons obviously matters in contemporary bioethical debates, and in certain biblical texts (e.g., James 3:9–12).

Again, consider Israel's idolatry with the golden calf. Humans may not represent God according to their own ideas or initiative. No one can see God, as even Moses learned (Exod. 33:12–34:35). The problem was not that Israel treated the calf as another god, but that Israel used a forbidden image to present the true God. The image was forbidden because it was false: God is mysteriously Spirit, not something physically majestic or culturally useful. God is known in the Word of grace. The only physical image with which God is represented is the human being—the one who can hear, understand, speak, and embody the divine Word.

Identity in Christ

Therefore, the image of God involves an identity or a vocation—a calling that defines who we are.[5] In that way, the major approaches and biblical texts contribute to a unified narrative framework. Humans were *created* to be God's earthly representatives; it may even be better to translate that we are created "as" or "to be," rather than "in," the image of God (Gen. 1:26–27).[6] We are only an image, not an exact replica; yet only we bear God's image. We are now *fallen*, however, so the image is fundamentally distorted. The image of God remains the human identity after the fall (Gen. 5:1–3), the basis of our life and dignity (Gen. 9:6–7; James 3:9). Yet true representation of God has been lost; humans are now caricatures—grossly distorted images, all out of proportion—of what God is like.[7]

In Jesus Christ, the New Testament proclaims, *restoration* of God's image has begun—with that image already having been displayed not just accurately

5. R. Peterson, Imago Dei *as Human Identity*. Used more frequently than defined, "identity" can designate all significant aspects of human being, including biological, cultural, ethical, and socially constructed aspects (V. White, *Identity*, 44–45).

6. Blocher, *In the Beginning*, 85.

7. The notion of a caricature appears in Blocher, *In the Beginning*, 94.

but as fully as possible in one person. Numerous passages convey this idea, but the most direct "image" vocabulary appears in 2 Corinthians 4:4; Colossians 1:15; and Hebrews 1:3. In the first text, the light of the gospel displays Christ's glory as God's image. In the second text, Christ's reconciling work fulfills the divine purpose of creation, over which the Son is God's preeminent representative ("firstborn") and in which the Son is God's visible image. In the third text, again creation and redemption hold together in the Son, who sustains all things as the exact representation of God's being. Encountering God's glory in Christ transforms us into his image (2 Cor. 3:18–4:6).[8] Jesus Christ took humanity, including a body, into the divine life, so that he might enable us to see God's glory.

Since the *imago Dei* ultimately roots human identity in the calling to imitate Christ, Christians understand the human self and the human person distinctively. The "self" has a long theological history in Western culture, especially after Augustine's *Confessions* presented a new autobiographical sensitivity that emerged from deep engagement with the ancient psalms.[9] To speak of the *self is to look at human identity in individual and inward-looking terms, particularly once modernity equated this concept with the ego or personality. Yet the Augustinian heritage, which modern thinkers both appropriated and rejected, was also relational and upward-looking: the Christian self is identified in the pursuit of communion with God. Of course, it is important to acknowledge "postmodern" insights regarding the various "others" that shape human self-identities, often in overwhelming ways: nature, fellow persons, social systems, and even our own bodies and consciences. Still, theologically, a properly "hospitable" self will have a sense of "joyful obligation" shaped by worshiping the Triune God.[10]

We know ourselves more truly as we grow in knowing God and the others to whom God providentially relates us.[11] We characterize ourselves through patterns of communicative action and reaction over time, acknowledging that God knows us better than we can ever know ourselves. Being a human person does not mean being an autonomous individual, as the classic definition of "an individual substance of a rational nature" could mistakenly imply to modern people. Rather, human persons exercise freedom

---

8. See Grenz, *Social God and the Relational Self*, chap. 4, "From Structure to Destiny: The *Imago Dei* in Christian Theology."

9. On this history, see Taylor, *Sources of the Self*. On more recent developments, see Woodhead, "Theology and the Fragmentation of the Self."

10. See Ford, *Self and Salvation*; more popularly, Ford, *Shape of Living*.

11. Such is a more explicitly theological rendering of the narrative emphasis developed by Ricoeur, *Oneself as Another*; and Thiselton, *Interpreting God and the Postmodern Self*.

in relationships—being accountable for these responses and finding their self-identities in such opportunities. A person is "an irreducible ontological reality that cannot be defined in terms of something else. Perhaps the best way to render persons is to describe, in narrative rather than concept, how they typically relate and what they characteristically do. One of the primary ways in which humans relate is through language. Human being as communion is largely a matter of being in communication."[12] And "Jesus Christ is paradigmatic both of the divine communicative initiative and the human communicative response."[13]

A human *person, then, is a "someone," not just a "something"—a someone who engages his or her shared nature and individual identity with understanding and freedom.[14] Regardless of how "person" applies to angels, Christians address cautiously how the concept relates to the Triune God. Acknowledging both that God is one and that God exists in the three "persons" of the Father, Son, and Holy Spirit is to acknowledge a modestly analogical relationship between divine and human personhood. Divine personhood comes first in the order of being, while human personhood comes first in the order of knowing. The Father and Son and Holy Spirit know themselves as distinct communicative agents within the economy of their mysterious communion. The Triune God's communicative agency is utterly unique, being exercised in both internal relations and undivided external unity. The Father, Son, and Holy Spirit do not need to pursue understanding of their nature as a human "someone" does; they do not gain such understanding individually but rather enjoy it immediately in communion. They do not receive partial freedom as a relational gift, like humans do; already enjoying unique freedom, the Triune God bestows that relational gift on others. So humans learn the true meaning of their personhood as they participate in the fellowship of the Triune God. In thus realizing their communicative agency more fully, humans simultaneously recognize the wondrous mystery of the unique communion within God's own life.

Body, Soul, and Spirit

Until recently, the Christian tradition uniformly held that humans have both material and immaterial aspects. Bodies are crucial to the (dis)analogy between human and divine personhood: bodies are natural to human persons but are utterly unnatural to God as Spirit. God the Son became incarnate in

12. Vanhoozer, "Human Being," 174–75.
13. Vanhoozer, "Human Being," 184.
14. For an overview of this account, influenced by Spaemann, see Treier, "Person."

Jesus Christ because a body was crucial for revealing the divine nature and redeeming human nature. Thus, Christians have historically rejected "monistic" accounts that reduce humans to only one reality, either bodies (material) or spirits (immaterial). Instead, the chief debate concerned whether humans are constituted as two-part (a "dichotomist" view) or three-part (a "trichotomist" view) beings.

*Trichotomy distinguishes between body, soul, and spirit: the soul is the more psychological aspect (identity within the created order), the spirit is the religious aspect (relationship with God). A trichotomist view appeals to biblical passages that use the language of both soul and spirit (e.g., 1 Thess. 5:23). Hebrews 4:12 even speaks of God's Word piercing so inwardly as to divide soul and spirit. Some trichotomists treat the spirit as a part of human being whether or not a particular person serves the true God. Others treat the spirit as a dormant or even missing part until a person is redeemed and indwelt by the Holy Spirit.

*Dichotomy distinguishes only between body and soul, or a human's material and immaterial aspects. A dichotomist view appeals to biblical passages that use the language of the soul for a human's entire immaterial aspect (e.g., Matt. 10:28). Texts like Luke 10:27 pile up aspects of human life (all one's heart, soul, mind, and strength) without treating them as distinct parts. Such texts, according to contemporary scholarship, reflect a widespread biblical phenomenon: texts speak freely of the entire person in various terms rather than analyzing discrete parts. Even the language of the soul does not consistently designate a part of a person; often, including for animals, it simply designates a living being.

Today, given these scholarly developments, the trichotomist view is declining in the West, while even the dichotomist emphasis is changing. The primary views in the contemporary evangelical discussion are "nonreductive physicalism" and a more holistic version of dichotomy that goes by various names—"functional holism," "conditional unity," or most commonly "holistic dualism."

*Nonreductive physicalism holds that humans are essentially material; everything about us depends upon our bodies ("physicalism"). Yet not everything can be reduced ("nonreductive") to a material reality. Everything associated traditionally with "the soul"—language, feelings, and the like—relates to a physical substrate. But these phenomena cannot be explained solely in terms of sociobiological interactions; rather, these are "emergent" properties of what happens in the body.

Nonreductive physicalism emerged on philosophical and scientific grounds. Humans are biologically continuous with animals. Neuroscience can now assign mental functions to particular brain regions. Realities associated with the soul involve human language, which involves the brain. Consciousness may be inexplicable, but it involves brain activity. Attention to biological commonality may be liberating for historically oppressed groups, counteracting earlier attempts to justify slavery, gender bias, and the like.[15]

Of course, nonreductive physicalists must address the apparent scriptural teaching behind body-soul dualism.[16] They begin with method, criticizing simplistic word studies, contrasts between "Hebrew" and "Greek" thought, and speculative appeals to the afterlife. They suggest that apparent distinctions in the New Testament are rhetorical rather than ontological. They assert that a disembodied soul was "unthinkable" for Paul, as a crucial text (2 Cor. 5:1–10) indicates, and that such "problem" texts for the physicalist view should be read with narrative and rhetorical approaches rather than older conceptual assumptions. The very notion of an "intermediate state" between earthly death and eschatological resurrection is time-bound, yet we do not understand time and eternity very well.

*Holistic dualism responds by defending a traditional distinction between body and soul while emphasizing the biblical unity of the human person during earthly and resurrected life. The distinction between body and soul is prominent during the *intermediate state between physical death and bodily resurrection.[17] In earthly life prior to that, humans are sufficiently unified that body and soul seem inseparable, their functions indistinguishable. Still, "the soul"—the personal essence, by whatever definition—survives death and longs for resurrection, when it will be reunited with a transformed body.[18]

Holistic dualists acknowledge the propriety of reexamining biblical evidence in light of contemporary science and philosophy. Yet they find a "dualistic implication" alongside the "holistic emphasis" of the Old Testament. For instance, Saul's encounter with the medium at Endor (1 Sam. 28:3–25) suggests a postmortem soul; Saul's error lay in violating God's command, not necessarily in engaging something unreal. Admittedly, the Old Testament was cloudy enough regarding postmortem futures to generate intra-Jewish

15. For such arguments see, e.g., Murphy, Brown, and Malony, *Whatever Happened to the Soul?*

16. For the following, see Green, "Monism and the Nature of Humans in Scripture."

17. For the following, see Cooper, *Body, Soul, and Life Everlasting.*

18. As discussed in the final chapter, unbelievers may not be resurrected in exactly the same sense as those who are in Christ; the unredeemed will not enjoy the same bodily "life" that God gives to the redeemed. Rather, the second "death" involves torment; "immortality of the soul" is not a generic human reality but a divine gift.

debate over resurrection. But at least Isaiah 26:19 and probably Daniel 12:2 hint at bodily resurrection and an intermediate state after earthly death. The intertestamental Jewish views, with the possible exception of the Sadducees, who denied bodily resurrection, entailed some form of dualism related to the intermediate state. Whether Luke 16:19–31 is a story or a parable, it reflects such a view.

Next, holistic dualism maintains that New Testament passages like 2 Corinthians 5:1–10 are best interpreted in light of an intermediate state, especially given Christ's death, burial, and resurrection. The physicalist alternatives are unsatisfying. The "immediate resurrection" view would have our Lord receiving his transformed body on Good Friday, not Easter Sunday; this view would face added difficulties with Lazarus in John 11. The "extinction/re-creation" view would have an utter re-creation of the human Jesus, which does not fit well with the traditional emphasis on maintaining bodily personal identity or relating accounts like the transfiguration to what happened later.

Holistic dualists worry about aggressively reinterpreting biblical texts in order to accommodate modern science when some of its evidence remains disputed. Neuroscience has not *explained* consciousness or even the brain functions that it can *map*. Modern science helpfully provokes Christians to engage the Bible afresh, recognizing its holistic emphasis and resisting the confusion of Greek "immortality of the soul" with resurrection of the body. Still, according to most evangelical theology, disembodied survival of death as portrayed in the Bible entails a soft form of dualism. Human dignity lies in a mysterious capacity for personal relation to God that goes beyond what meets the eye.

Human Diversity

The previous chapter emphasized that God loves the physical creation. The present chapter must emphasize that God loves human individuality and cultural variety. The "creation mandate" names the human responsibility to care for the physical world and other creatures. Now the *cultural mandate names our calling to fill the earth and represent God's rule—a privilege that should generate healthy diversity, whereas after the fall we frequently become responsible for violence.[19]

---

19. Noting the typical failure of systematic theology to address gender, race, and class is Coakley, *God, Sexuality, and the Self*, 47. Liberation from poverty and oppression awaits discussion of Christ's ministry in chap. 9 below.

The Cultural Mandate

The grammar of this blessing in Genesis 1:28–29 is ambiguous: it could indicate a command or a gift. The rest of the Bible suggests both, while using this blessing of "being fruitful" to celebrate the gospel's work across human cultures. Acts 6:7, for instance, uses that vocabulary regarding the church's growth in Jerusalem; soon, in fulfillment of Acts 1:8, the gospel spread farther and farther, to the ends of the earth. Pentecost (Acts 2) signaled how the gospel would embrace these cultures: each hearing God's gracious Word in their own languages. Thereby the Old Testament hope of the "pilgrimage of the nations," bringing their various gifts to Israel's God, can become a reality (e.g., Isa. 2:1–5; Rev. 7:9–17; 21:26).

The cultural mandate is distinctively fulfilled in the church's mission to spread the gospel, but it embraces all of life. God kindly sends rain upon everyone (Acts 14:17) and providentially oversees their entire existence (Acts 17:25–28). God's people are called to seek the welfare of pagan places (Jer. 29:4–14), doing good to everyone, not just fellow believers (Gal. 6:9–10). Stewardship of God-given talent bears witness to the God of truth, goodness, and beauty, leading human cultures to join in creation's praise (e.g., Bezalel in Exod. 31:1–11).

Given this cultural mandate, human diversity ought to advance the Creator's glory, but often it fosters violence instead. Ethical conflict frequently hinges upon whether some human difference is understood as a gift to celebrate or a threat to resist. The following sections address some contested and theologically crucial aspects of human diversity.

Evil

All people have sinned and fall short of God's glory (Rom. 3:23). When God's people lament the prosperity of the wicked (e.g., Ps. 73), they do not claim that the righteous have intrinsic merit; rather, they lament that God's promises are not yet fulfilled. Any human righteousness depends upon divine grace. All people retain the calling to bear God's image, however distorted our representation may be. People do not lose this calling when they sin, even when they commit horrific evils. Being accountable for falling short of God's glory underscores the common dignity that remains despite humans' distorted representation of our Creator.

As an aspect of human diversity, evil goes beyond the distinctions between righteous and wicked people or particular acts they commit. Evil affects the different situations in which people find themselves responding to God and forming their character. What are called "natural evils" stemming from the curse give various individuals and groups certain advantages or disadvantages relative to others. As the doctrine of sin will address further, what are called "moral evils" go beyond idolatrous rebellion against God to create unjust oppression of others. Such evils go beyond harming personal relationships as they contribute to systemic injustice. Advantages and disadvantages stemming from such evils diversify human life by creating both opportunities and obstacles for moral excellence and cultural particularity.

Ability

The flip side of evil's effects upon human diversity is the panoply of natural talents and historical circumstances that God gives. As noted above, these providential gifts do not determine or undermine the shared human identity of bearing God's image. Instead, different kinds and levels of ability enable particular persons to fulfill that calling as they pursue its cultural mandate.

Likewise, the contemporary concerns associated with "bioethics" and "disability theology" underscore the common dignity of bearing God's image. Human persons are the beings who represent God in the world whether or not they demonstrate particular abilities. Their very lives express God's love, and they may enjoy spiritual communion with God in ways that others cannot see. However great the apparent need for physical or emotional, not just spiritual, redemption, humans can still uniquely communicate what God is like.

THE BEGINNING AND END OF LIFE

Acknowledging this human dignity along with the divine command not to kill, Christians traditionally have opposed abortion and infanticide.[20] It may be complicated to identify personhood in terms of a particular biological moment or state. Yet in opposing abortion, Christians have taken texts like Psalm 139 (especially vv. 13–16) to demand respect for human life as the object of God's love from the beginning. Likewise, Christians have opposed forms of euthanasia that prematurely end human life. It is the Lord's prerogative to give and to take away (Job 1:21), not ours. On a traditional Christian account, earthly *death is not the cessation of all existence but only the temporal separation of body and soul. This separation ends someone's earthly history, inaugurating an intermediate state of experiencing God's presence or absence while awaiting the final resurrection.

20. E.g., *Didache* 2.1–2 (ANF 7:377).

Modern technologies can "artificially" extend life beyond its previous norms, and medical intervention complicates the identification of physical death. Christians do not oppose medical care; they have promoted it, as when they pioneered hospitals. But proper medical care focuses on *healing* that relieves pain and restores created functioning after the curse, not on *enhancement* that takes life into our own hands. This focus may lead Christians to resist not only active euthanasia and "transhumanist" aspirations but also heroic medical interventions that practically deny the inevitability of death or the hope of resurrection.[21]

Life with Challenges

In between the beginning and end of earthly life, some people face special physical or emotional or intellectual challenges. Recent theological reflection on disability appeals to Christian traditions of giving hospitality to everyone.[22] A theology of disability goes further, though, seeking to change how we view ourselves and others. People are differently able, yet all people are spiritually broken and subject to effects of the curse. Disability should be a reminder for everyone, not a stigma for some. Of course, disability raises complex questions about what final redemption will accomplish. Special needs—like aspects of all human lives—so mark the self-identity of particular persons that it is hard to imagine simply having those realities removed or their memory erased. God will wipe every tear from our eyes (Rev. 21:4), however, and eternally facing certain challenges would seemingly leave the curse in place.[23]

Regrettably, Christian practice has not always been consistent with biblical commitment to human dignity. Beginning in the late nineteenth century, some Christians embraced *eugenics—attempts to improve human traits such as intelligence by genetic means, including selective breeding and population restriction. It is perennially tempting to view redemption as a technological project rather than a divine gift and to assess human dignity in terms of various abilities or assumptions about wholeness.[24] Similarly, Christians have failed to address ethnic diversity with a consistently biblical commitment to human dignity.

21. For intellectual and pastoral resources to address these questions, consult the Center for Bioethics and Human Dignity (www.cbhd.org).

22. On hospitality, see Pohl, *Making Room*.

23. Regarding memory see Volf, *End of Memory*, esp. 214. Regarding disability see Yong, *Bible, Disability, and the Church*.

24. See, e.g., Rosen, *Preaching Eugenics*. A. Hall, *Conceiving Parenthood*, offers poignant examples of the wider phenomenon.

Ethnicity

Addressing ethnic diversity requires careful definitions. *Ethnicity has a historical dimension, since it includes real or supposed ancestry alongside cultural factors such as language and nationality. Someone can claim more than one ethnic identity. The Bible does speak in ethnic terms—for instance, in narratives of Israel's history vis-à-vis surrounding nations, and in prophetic hopes for the unity of redeemed people "from every tribe and language and people and nation" (Rev. 5:9). *Race is not a biological category; rather, it is a modern social construct that separates ethnic groups along purportedly biological lines.[25] "Race" associates a particular person with one or more ethnic groups based on factors like skin color, self-designation, and family history; in short, the category of race presents an appearance of objectivity that it lacks.

Accordingly, *racism is a complicated term. Used narrowly to designate overt hatred for all persons of a particular race, the adjective "racist" would characterize some but not all people. Used more broadly to designate covert prejudices about certain persons or tendencies representing a particular race, the adjective would characterize the ideologies of many more people, at least in some moments. Used most extensively not just to designate personal hatred or prejudiced ideologies but also to encompass power structures, "racism" names a widespread phenomenon that applies to very particular people or groups in light of the unequal privileges that it generates. Debates about such loaded terminology make it tempting to dismiss racism as a narrow problem for earlier generations or other people. Yet most modern people somehow struggle with racial prejudice and are affected by resulting inequalities, to their social advantage or disadvantage or both. Hence, at the very least, we must acknowledge the reality of *racialization: "a racialized society is *a society wherein race matters profoundly for differences in life experiences, life opportunities, and social relationships.* A racialized society can also be said to be 'a society that allocates differential economic, political, social, and even psychological rewards to groups along racial lines; lines that are socially constructed.'"[26]

The most extreme manifestation of racism or racialization is genocide, an ongoing threat that reflects the global reach of ethnicity as a theological

25. Regarding the (early modern European) history of "race" as a category, and its relation to ethnicity, see Priest and Nieves, *This Side of Heaven*; West, *Prophetic Fragments*, esp. 100. The extent to which ethnicity has a biological background—tribes or nations having emerged from physical families over time—is disputed.
26. Emerson and Smith, *Divided by Faith*, 7 (emphasis original).

problem. In the United States, despite some desegregation, significant manifestations remain: racial profiling, criminal justice disparities, and immigration
debates, among others.[27] Most people now deny being racist, but racialization
means that "racial practices that reproduce racial division in the contemporary
United States '(1) are increasingly covert, (2) are embedded in normal operations of institutions, (3) avoid direct racial terminology, and (4) are invisible to
most Whites.'"[28] At minimum, evangelicals contribute to racialization through
apathy and inattention to structural evil, not to mention selfish overemphasis
on personal responsibility and downright prejudice.

Historically, Christians contributed to racial division through colonialism.[29] The centuries-long African slave trade involved Christian nations in
Europe.[30] Race-based slavery in America appealed selectively to the Bible.[31]
Slave owners discouraged a common language and literacy among their
slaves. As much as possible they prevented slaves from encountering Scripture
concerning liberation; they had preachers present obedience-oriented texts
instead. While churches and leaders like Martin Luther King Jr. (1929–68)
influenced the civil rights movement, they confronted substantial resistance
and outright racism among other Christians. The same division by faith
held true for South African apartheid: mainstream churches perpetuated
that segregated system, while only some Christians promoted justice and
eventually championed "truth and reconciliation" in the postapartheid
context.

Theologically, however, racialization violates the equal dignity of all humans as bearers of the divine image. Ethnic division, racial injustice, and the
resulting violence reflect the cursed pursuit of human autonomy. Since human
solidarity in bearing God's image includes a cultural mandate, human sinning
takes structural forms, systemically aggregating evil effects and reinforcing
prejudices. Even human cooperation has an idolatrous and unjust shadow
side. The restoration of harmony between God, humans, and the cosmos

27. Regarding genocide, see Power, *"Problem from Hell."* Regarding immigration, see on
the one hand, Carroll R., *Christians at the Border,* and on the other hand, Hoffmeier, *Immigration Crisis.*

28. Emerson and Smith, *Divided by Faith,* 9. Emerson and Smith provide extensive sociological evidence; theologically, see Felder, *Stony the Road We Trod.*

29. For an evangelical introduction to postcolonial theory, see briefly Treier, "Postcolonial
Theory"; more extensively K. Smith et al., *Evangelical Postcolonial Conversations.*

30. For a devastating description, see Kapuściński, *Shadow of the Sun,* 81–84.

31. As Martin, *"Haustafeln* (Household Codes)," 215n45, mentions, "Larry Morrison has
noted: 'Nearly every pro-slavery pamphlet, or article, or speaker made at least some reference
to a biblical sanction of slavery.'" See Morrison, "Religious Defense of American Slavery." See
further Noll, *Civil War as a Theological Crisis.*

requires Christ's reconciling work. In the incarnation God pursued universal reconciliation by assuming human particularity in Jesus of Nazareth—having a particular family and body and language and culture. The church's frequent failure to embrace Jesus's Jewishness helped to foster the modern ideology of race.[32]

In Christ God has inaugurated the promised liberation of the oppressed (see, e.g., Jesus's quotation of Isa. 61 in Luke 4:14–30). Jesus's followers learn compassion—not just pitying but suffering with others in a way that embodies God's love. Failing to pursue reconciliation means failing to realize the extent of God's forgiving grace (Matt. 18:15–35). Following Jesus, joy stems from reconciled relationships (e.g., Phil. 2:2; Heb. 12:2). Pursuing reconciliation involves more than speaking momentary words, as God demonstrates by loving sinners in Jesus Christ and indwelling redeemed people through the Holy Spirit.[33] The church is a community of forgiven sinners, not perfect people. As the earthly sign of God's coming kingdom, though, Jesus's followers anticipate a new humanity, which will involve people of every tribe and tongue bearing culturally distinctive witness to God's glory (Rev. 20–22). God's reconciliation of Jew and gentile in Christ already testifies concerning this glorious hope (Eph. 2:11–22). Accordingly, privileged Christians should humbly prioritize the interests of others (Phil. 2:3–4). In the American context, this principle challenges white Christians to take humble initiative in pursuing multiethnic ministries, characterized by genuine integration rather than minority assimilation into dominant cultures.[34]

Sexuality

Like the previous aspects of human diversity, sexuality requires accounting for creation, the fall, and redemption, plus attending to careful definitions. *Sex designates "the biological reality of bodies, the physical facts of maleness and femaleness," while *gender designates "the social reality of masculinity and femininity."[35] The following theological treatment begins with bodily integrity and identity, proceeds to gender identity and authority, addresses sexual orientation and activity, and concludes with comments on marriage and parenting.

---

32. As argued, e.g., in J. Carter, *Race*; Jennings, *Christian Imagination*.

33. On compassion see Davies, *Theology of Compassion*, reviewed in Treier, "I Feel Your Pain." On reconciliation more broadly, see L. Jones, *Embodying Forgiveness*.

34. See, e.g., C. DeYoung et al., *United by Faith*. Further theological help, especially for majority culture Christians, can be found in Harris and Schaupp, *Being White*; Sharp, *No Partiality*.

35. B. Jones, *Faithful*, 31–32.

BODILY INTEGRITY AND IDENTITY

The beginning of Christian sexual ethics is bodily integrity. People's bodies are their own, humanly speaking, for the sake of devotion to God (Rom. 12:1–2; 1 Cor. 6:18–20). During earthly life, the body is an inseparable part of personal identity. God regulated slavery, first in Israel's ANE context and later in the church's Roman imperial context, without ever indicating any permanent legitimacy of human ownership over others. God claims everything as Creator and Redeemer (1 Cor. 7:21–24). Bodily integrity also undergirds the immorality of *torture, inhumanely cruel treatment that uses physical pain and mental disorientation for breaking someone's will.

This Christian emphasis on bodily integrity before God counteracted the assumption of the Roman system that slaves were at their masters' sexual disposal.[36] Only the covenant of marriage allows another human to make any sexual claim upon someone, and before God this claim is strikingly mutual between male and female. Even this marital claim is limited, because biblical instruction about spouses not depriving each other assumes personal freedom regarding any particular sexual act (1 Cor. 7:2–5). Even marriage itself is limited; no one may properly force another person—their child, for instance—to marry, since that person may have discerned a different gift for which he or she is accountable to God (1 Cor. 7:6–9). In other words, the goodness of *chastity within marriage and *celibacy outside marriage rests in the bodily integrity that God gives to each person for the sake of his or her freely willed devotion.

"Masculinity" and "femininity" are cultural constructions. Technological changes, along with increased recognition of biological complexity, have raised new challenges regarding gender identity. Only a small percentage of people experience significant dissonance between their biological sex and cultural gender expression, but the prominence of such *gender dysphoria is rising. Some people experience dissonance early in life that resolves itself later. Western cultures, however, are decreasing the incentive to expect resolution, encouraging experimentation or sex change instead. Alongside such "transgender" and "inquiring" people, a tiny but real number of "intersex" people face a directly physical complication: being born with multiple, conflicting genitalia.

In response, biblical Christians understandably uphold the integrity of male/female biological differences rooted in the God-given order of creation. They interpret gender dysphoria as an aspect of brokenness stemming from

---

36. See K. Harper, *From Shame to Sin*, which highlights distinctive Christian teaching on free will in just this context.

the curse after the fall. Yet biblical Christians should embrace everyone with Christ's love, upholding their dignity as God's image-bearers. Scripture provides no direct prohibitions or explicit guidance about gender dysphoria, and many affected persons face profound social alienation. Hence Christians must exercise discernment about how to foster biblically welcoming communities for people who struggle with gender identity.[37]

GENDER IDENTITY AND AUTHORITY

Since the rise of second-wave feminism in the middle of the twentieth century, theological discussion of gender "roles" in the household and the church has revolved around "complementarian" and "egalitarian" positions. In broader feminist discussions, "complementarian" designates any position that honored biological distinctions between the sexes—in relation to child-bearing, for example.

In evangelical discussions, however, *complementarianism has a narrower meaning: men and women are equal in human dignity but have different God-given roles in the human family and/or the church. Although differing over applications of this principle, complementarians hold that men lead or have "authority" ("headship") over women. "Soft" complementarians restrict only certain aspects of female leadership, and only within the church and/or the home. Other complementarians restrict female leadership more comprehensively, perhaps even within broader society. While soft complementarians acknowledge insights from modern feminism, stricter complementarians essentially defend *patriarchy, the headship of the male as father figure. In the stricter view, there are biblical notions of masculinity and femininity that cohere with biological sex and transcend cultural gender constructions.

By contrast, in evangelical discussions *egalitarianism holds that men and women are equal in both human dignity and God-given leadership roles. Evangelical egalitarians are still complementarian in broader philosophical debates: they acknowledge God-given biological differences between the sexes. Yet they hold that such differences do not require traditional patriarchy or underwrite gender essences: patriarchy appears in biblical texts due to cultural backgrounds, not a divine mandate, as an aspect of the curse rather than creation or redemption. Evangelical egalitarians insist that theological complementarianism is not a traditional Christian view. Instead, earlier theologians operated in patriarchal contexts that encouraged them to view women as fundamentally inferior to men, perhaps not even fully bearing God's image.

---

37. The best evangelical resource, addressing both theological and psychological dimensions, is Yarhouse, *Understanding Gender Dysphoria*.

Accordingly, evangelical egalitarianism and complementarianism both wrestle with Scripture's teaching in modern contexts.[38] Both positions affirm that men and women alike are God's image-bearers. Both affirm that men and women are redeemed in Christ, the Mediator through whom men and women alike have priestly access to God. By and large, both affirm that men and women are equally affected by the fall, although some complementarians find 1 Timothy 2:13–14 depicting women as more susceptible to deception. The debate between the two positions regarding church leadership, then, centers upon 1 Timothy 2:9–15 and Galatians 3:27–28. Regarding the home, a crucial text is Ephesians 5:21–33.

Egalitarians appeal to Galatians 3:27–28 concerning the gospel's socially equalizing effects. Complementarians respond by limiting these effects to "spiritual" equality. Complementarians appeal to Ephesians 5:21–33 concerning the husband's headship, by analogy with Christ's headship over the church. Egalitarians respond by understanding "head" in terms of "source" or "prominent representative" rather than "authority over," by noting mutual "submission" in the passage, and by underscoring the countercultural command for husbands to love their wives as Christ loves the church. Complementarians appeal to 1 Timothy 2:9–15 concerning male teaching authority in the church. Egalitarians respond by limiting Paul's concern to improperly authoritative teaching, by limiting the text's application in light of the immediate context of false teaching, and by limiting the passage's appeal to Genesis—as an analogy with the situation in first-century Ephesus rather than a timeless principle about creation and/or the fall.

Other biblical texts affect these debates, including 1 Corinthians 11:2–16 and 14:34–35, as well as 1 Peter 3:1–7. Beyond particular Scriptures, however, the debates reflect different hermeneutical tendencies. Complementarians tend to be "maximalist" in applying biblical statements to contemporary contexts: they believe that churches should mirror the original forms reflected in the apostolic writings as closely as possible. Egalitarians tend to be more "minimalist," as do some soft complementarians. They believe that churches cannot mirror exactly the original forms; the initial contexts often limit the transferability of the apostles' direct statements. Since a passage concerning

---

38. The literature on this debate is massive. Representing complementarianism, see Piper and Grudem, *Recovering Biblical Manhood and Womanhood*, which spawned the Council on Biblical Manhood and Womanhood, and Köstenberger and Schreiner, *Women in the Church*. Representing egalitarianism, see Pierce and Groothuis, *Discovering Biblical Equality*, along with Johnson and Willard, *How I Changed My Mind about Women in Leadership*, and material from Christians for Biblical Equality. Representing attempts to transcend the polarization, see Husbands and Larsen, *Women, Ministry and the Gospel*.

Paul's cloak may be limited in its application, or Paul's greetings in the form of application, we must be cautious about assuming that church forms in other passages are biblically essential. Likewise, other ethical issues—notably slavery and homosexuality—are drawn into these hermeneutical debates.[39] Since evangelicals now read the New Testament in a way that opposes slavery, should they take a similarly contextual approach to gender roles? Or, since most evangelicals still read the New Testament in a way that restricts homosexual behavior, should they take a cautious approach toward contextual hermeneutics?

Sexual Orientation and Activity

The framework for an evangelical response to homosexuality has begun to emerge through these reflections. The bodily integrity of human beings orients God-given sexual activity around chastity within marriage between a man and a woman, requiring celibacy outside of that covenant relationship. A distinction is necessary, though, between cultural markers of gender identity and biblical entailments from the integrity of biological maleness and femaleness. Failure to observe this distinction contributes to the church's cultural stigmas against homosexual persons. Paul's claims about the unnatural character of certain sexual acts (Rom. 1:26–27) address paganism's social consequences rather than shaming a class of people. A surrounding litany of other sins encompasses everyone, including religious hypocrites (Rom. 1:28–32). Only once we acknowledge that sexual orientation does not fully define anyone's identity[40] and does not diminish human dignity can Christians properly engage the contemporary debates. Those debates involve several Scripture texts, of course, yet their interpretation unfolds in a fourfold theological context.

1. *Hermeneutics.* Do biblical texts condemning homosexual behavior condemn all homoerotic acts or only exploitative forms that characterized the ANE and the Greco-Roman world? Traditional Christian responses demonstrate exegetically that these biblical texts are not limited to condemning exploitation or promiscuity. Even some scholarly opponents concede that the traditional view is correct about what Scripture itself says.[41]

39. As epitomized by issues raised in Webb, *Slaves, Women and Homosexuals* and the ensuing debate.

40. Paris, *End of Sexual Identity.*

41. For multiple versions of the major views, see Sprinkle, *Homosexuality, the Bible, and the Church*; William Loader's chapter in that volume illustrates the concessions of many progressive biblical scholars to the traditional view. For an exhaustive exegetical defense of the traditional view, see Gagnon, *Bible and Homosexual Practice.* For a traditional perspective from a celibate gay Christian, see Hill, *Washed and Waiting.* Hill addresses celibacy and champions friendship in *Spiritual Friendship.*

2. *Modern science.* Are some people born with an "orientation" that indicates that homosexual relationships are permitted by their Creator? While noting that some scientific evidence remains ambiguous, traditional Christian responses often concede that sexual orientation may have a genetic component. Genetic components affect many sins, however, so human desires—even with biological backgrounds—do not guarantee divine permission. Accordingly, there is no fundamental divide between modern societies and ancient societies that lacked genetic knowledge or examples of monogamous homosexual marriage. The fluidity of sexual desires also complicates hermeneutical arguments about sexual orientation: pro-homosexuality (LGB) appeals to bodily integrity seem inconsistent with gender-dysphoria (TI) arguments.[42]

3. *Eschatological contrasts.* Since marriage will not continue in heaven, and its significance has already changed now that the messianic Child has come, might there be an eschatological reduction in the sexual normativity of Christian marriage? Traditional Christian responses often concede that modern churches have uncritically celebrated nuclear family life; debates over homosexuality offer an opportunity to recover the significance of both singleness and friendship. Yet the eschatological shift regarding marriage does not suddenly turn biblical celibacy into support for homoerotic activity. Humans remain embodied, finite, and subject to the curse. God's future kingdom is not yet fully present, and several passages (such as "household" texts) uphold the continuing importance of marriage and parenting.[43]

4. *Biblical theology.* If a traditional Christian understanding remains correct, though, how should we explain the biblical appearance of polygamy, divorce regulations, and the like? Traditional Christian responses note that Jesus himself provides a crucial answer in Matthew 19:1–12. God temporarily permitted deviations from permanent, monogamous marriage due to human hardness of heart. God regulated deviations such as divorce to reduce their social harm, particularly upon women. The Mosaic legislation must be read not merely in terms of surrounding patriarchal narratives, but more specifically in light of their implicit judgments. Polygamy is not primarily a sign of royal blessing but rather a source of household trouble, especially given its contrast with the Genesis creation narrative. Biblical

---

42. As Gunton, *Triune Creator*, 199n12, notes, "many of the things said in the modern world about 'sexual preference,' sex change and homosexuality are essentially gnostic in evading the respect in which we *are* our bodies."

43. A version of the eschatological argument appears in Song, *Covenant and Calling*. However, emphasizing the importance of embodied finitude, birth, and dying for this issue is Radner, *Time to Keep.*

ethics requires interpreting particular texts within the wider context of Scripture's salvation history.

In biblical theology, God-given sexuality is integrated with the shared human dignity yet biological differentiation of male and female, in their covenant union as husband and wife who may bear children. God blesses humans with life and freedom. As living beings, like animals they can reproduce—participating in God's creation of new life. As free beings, unlike animals they can reproduce responsibly—undertaking sexual activity as an aspect of human maturity, forming a new household. Given its evangelical focus, the present book lacks space to discuss how natural law addresses sexuality. Nor is there space to discuss how evangelical churches can uphold this traditional view in pastorally healthy ways. The biblical witness regarding God's will for human sexual complementarity, though, remains the underlying bedrock for traditional Christian accounts of marriage as a gracious pointer to God's covenant love.

Marriage and Parenting

Earlier discussion of the Decalogue introduced the sanctity of Christian *marriage, the covenantal union of one male and one female to form a distinct household that may welcome new children. Marriage is *unitive*: the two become one flesh (Gen. 2:24), a special embodiment of human sociality (Gen. 2:18). The unitive end of marriage underlies the evangelical tendency to view divorce as sinful except in cases when the covenantal bond has been fundamentally broken, as in sexual infidelity or physical abuse.[44]

Traditionally, marriage also has a *procreative* end: children are a blessing that initially fulfilled the mandate to fill the earth (Gen. 1:28) and then anticipated God's provision of a promised redeemer (Gen. 3:15). Children remain a rewarding heritage from the Lord (Ps. 127:3) who uniquely embody what it means to embrace Jesus (Matt. 18:1–5). Marriage is indeed a joyful occasion (e.g., Eccles. 9:9) of relational and physical delight, within the context of lifelong family commitment.

Any sexual activity may create psychological bonds. Yet by treating marriage as an analogy for the loyal love between God and God's people, Scripture privileges its lifelong covenantal bond as the exclusive context for proper sexual activity. Often, as in Hosea and Malachi, the marriage analogy confronts God's people regarding their infidelity while reminding them of God's faithfulness. Ultimately, this analogy confirms the sacrificial love of Jesus

---

44. To survey evangelical discussions of divorce and remarriage, see Atkinson, "Divorce."

Christ for the church (Eph. 5:21–33). When the church and the empire over-lapped in Western Christendom, the locus of the marriage covenant could be ambiguous. Outside that context, theological challenges arise for relating Christian marriage to the jurisdictions of church and state.

The procreative end of marriage faced new questions as certain forms of *contraception—"birth control"—became available in the twentieth century. The official Catholic position, held among earlier Protestants as well, has maintained the intrinsically procreative nature of each sexual act in a way that prohibits artificial contraception. "Natural family planning" allows married couples to refrain from sexual activity at times that help to avoid conception, but any sexual act properly remains open to childbearing. Most modern Protestants gradually rejected such a view, and some have denied the intrinsically procreative aspect of legitimate sexual activity. Others have maintained this aspect while reinterpreting openness to childbearing and thus permitting nonabortive forms of artificial contraception. On that account, married couples must remain open to the possibility that any sexual inter-course may conceive a child; after all, no artificial contraception is absolutely effective. Whatever view an evangelical couple takes regarding contraception, generally the Christian tradition still understands their sexual union in terms of a procreative end, in addition to its unitive joys.

Reconciliation

A theology of reconciliation addresses not only ethnicity but other aspects of human diversity as well, including sexuality. Human beings were created to enjoy and communicate the love of the Triune God. Creation has a God-given order with which humans should live in harmony. Yet we have fallen from created grace, and our pursuit of moral autonomy resulted in a cosmic curse. Even so, God has preserved the cosmos for redemption. Despite hu-mans' gross distortion of the divine image, God's liberating and reconciling grace in Christ has begun to make all things new, including humans and their bodies. Until we enjoy the fullness of God's redemptive rule, all cultures and every aspect of human culture will reflect personal, social, and institutional brokenness alongside hints of God-given beauty and creativity. This fragile goodness, present in all of creation and culture, will characterize human sexuality too. Sexuality offers a mysterious interface with human devotion to God, and marriage offers a vital analogy for the mystery of God's covenant communion with people.

Humans are the creaturely beings whose relationships bear embodied tes-timony concerning what God is like. In light of the gospel of God's love, we love the world of God's creation, the world of nations and cultures, and thus the world's poor and suffering in particular. In short, we love God by loving our neighbors as ourselves.[45] Too often we confuse gospel-prompted, creation-embracing love with idolatrous love of "the world," fostering the very injustice over which God triumphs in Jesus Christ.

45. See the helpful exposition in *Cape Town Commitment*, 19–22, 39–46, concerning social implications of Christ's peace.

PART 3

*S*on,
THE
THE MEDIATING
LOGOS

── 8 ──

The Identity of Jesus Christ

THESIS	LEARNING OBJECTIVES
The orthodox identity of Jesus Christ involves the hypostatic union: in the incarnation the fully divine Son of God has assumed a fully human nature, to serve as the one Mediator of revelation and redemption.	After learning the material in this chapter, you should be able to: 1. *Define briefly* the key terms introduced here (marked with an asterisk and included in the glossary). 2. *List and recognize* the following: (a) Alexandrian "Word-flesh" and Antiochene "Word-man" frameworks; (b) historical details (e.g., particular creeds) related to the major christological heresies. 3. *Describe and compare* the major christological heresies. 4. *Identify and illustrate* key biblical arguments for the hypostatic union and against the major christological heresies. 5. *Explain* the three major elements of conciliar Christology.

The gospel involves drama—what the Triune God says and does to redeem fallen humans and establish cosmic *shalom*. The climax is the incarnation of God in Jesus Christ, which altered the very way we mark time. But the incarnation itself does not exhaust the drama. Even for Jesus's immediate followers to recognize his true identity involved plenty of twists and turns. Soon the early Christians labored to understand the full significance of what the apostles said about the risen Lord.[1] So the intellectual story told in this chapter has a moral: how the church identifies Jesus Christ

1. With permission, portions of this chapter draw upon previously published materials from Baker Academic, including Treier, "Jesus Christ, Doctrine of"; Treier, "Incarnation."

is crucial to worshiping faithfully and embracing salvation fully. The heart of the gospel—what God has done for fallen humanity in Christ, and how we celebrate this gift—is at stake.

In the Nicene Creed's second article, the church's confession of Jesus Christ as its one Lord begins with a series of clarifications: "the only Son of God, eternally begotten of the Father," and so forth. Then the Creed confesses, "Through him all things were made," identifying the Lord Jesus Christ with the Almighty "maker of heaven and earth." Next the article narrates the Incarnate One's redeeming work: "For us and for our salvation he came down from heaven." In line with this movement, dogmatic theology distinguishes between the Son's "person" and his "work," as in the next two chapter titles: "The Identity of Jesus Christ" and "The Ministry of Reconciliation."

This chapter addresses the person of Christ, the traditional focus of *Christology. Yet although Christ's person and work can be distinguished, they must not be separated. The ministry of reconciliation depends upon the identity of Jesus Christ as both the divine Son and God's faithful human servant. This chapter's first focus, the *history* of the church's wrestling with potential heresies, helps to clarify the dual identity of the Incarnate Lord. The chapter's second focus, the biblical *grammar* of orthodox Christology, both supports and helps to specify that dual identity of the God-man.

The History of Christology

The history of orthodox Christology is initially a tale of four cities. Then the story unfolds in terms of six heresies that provoked the creedal definitions of orthodox, or "conciliar," Christology. With conciliar definitions in place, the church's christological odyssey continued—traversing medieval philosophy and piety, Protestant controversy and reform, and modern historicizing.

A Tale of Four Cities

Conciliar Christology affirms that Jesus Christ is fully divine, fully human, and one person. The hypostatic union means that two "natures," divine and human, are fully united in this one Mediator between God and humanity. The two "terms"—divine and human—are asymmetrical in this one "relationship":[2] God's Son was already, eternally, divine "before" assuming human nature in time. The union therefore privileges the eternal divinity of the one person even while insisting on the full humanity of the Incarnate One.

2. Hunsinger, "Karl Barth's Christology."

Four cities—Jerusalem, Athens, Alexandria, and Antioch—provided the chief contexts that eventually provoked these affirmations.

Jerusalem and Athens. The first and second centuries contained relatively little abstract reflection about the incarnation. Jerusalem and Athens symbolize the complex relation between the biblical faith of Christianity's Jewish origins and the ontological focus of Greco-Roman philosophy. By the third century, criticizing apologetic engagement with philosophy, Tertullian asked, "What has Jerusalem to do with Athens?" Highlighting this contrast, early modern scholarship, especially in Germany, developed the so-called Hellenization thesis, often associated with Adolf von Harnack's (1851–1930) immense history of dogma. Christologically, this thesis contrasts a simpler Hebrew focus on *functions* with a Greek focus on *ontology, the *natures* of things: such "Hellenization" gradually heightened christological affirmations about the Messiah fulfilling divine functions into a philosophical decision about the Son having a fully divine nature.

Patristic scholarship, however, increasingly critiques the Hellenization thesis.[3] Of course, Christian theology reflects a largely gentile context from the first century onward. Yet the church fathers' engagement with this context was not naive. For instance, in one controversy described below, the Arian party was more committed to Greek philosophical assumptions than was the orthodox party. As for Tertullian's contrast between Jerusalem and Athens, it concerned rival bases for making theological claims. While criticizing apologetic appeals to philosophy, Tertullian himself developed concepts for trinitarian theology. In biblical studies, the Hellenization thesis remains influential, but notable scholars are now finding ontological interests or implications in scriptural texts. For the moment, Hellenization aside, Jerusalem and Athens form the backdrop for the first two heresies profiled below.

Alexandria and Antioch. In the third century, Origen's school emerged at Alexandria and began to advance Christian thinking. Although the contrast is oversimplified, it became common to contrast "Alexandrian" with later "Antiochene" concerns. The "Alexandrian" environment had a "Word-flesh" orientation: focusing on how the divine Logos could unite with human flesh, which is subject to weakness and change. Of course, these terms—*logos* and *sarx*—appear in Scripture texts such as John 1:1–18, but the Alexandrian anthropology also shaped the ensuing questions.

The "Antiochene" environment gained prominence in the fourth and fifth centuries. Antioch had a "Word-man" orientation: focusing on how the divine

---

3. See, e.g., Ayres, *Nicaea and Its Legacy*—both panoramic comments about this issue on 31–32 and the book's larger contribution.

Logos united with a fully human being. By that point, orthodox Christology insisted on the humanity and full divinity of the Incarnate One. The ongoing questions concerned the nature of that humanity and its union with the Logos. Beyond physical existence, did the Logos assume humanity fully, including a human personality, or did the Logos fill that psychological space in the Incarnate One? The Alexandrian anthropology treated the soul as the body's animating principle, so it had been natural to imagine the Logos inhabiting human flesh without affirming a distinct human soul. By contrast, in the history of heresies below, Antioch's increasing prominence reflected the increasing prominence of the Son's full humanity after the defeat of Arianism.

To summarize the conceptual contrasts, then, Alexandria tended to begin "from above": the historical Jesus was not as important as the mystical Christ. This Alexandrian tendency still characterizes "Eastern" theology, as evidenced in Orthodox art, architecture, and ritual. Alexandria embraced allegorical interpretation of Scripture, sometimes reflecting the influence of "Platonic" dualism contrasting the material and spiritual realms. Because the divine Word tended to take the human soul's place, at its extreme Alexandria spoke of a single divinized person.

Antioch tended to begin more "from below": the human Jesus was the starting point, although not "historically" in the modern sense. Antiochene Christology was more Aristotelian: a necessary connection exists between body and soul; God is understood through the world, not apart from it. Indeed, the divine Word is known only through the human Jesus, not apart from him. Antioch focused more on Scripture's literal sense, critiquing allegorical interpretation in theory although not consistently avoiding it in practice. The Word took a human soul that accounts for many of his actions and emotions recorded in the Gospels. At its extreme, though, Antioch tended to speak of the union of the two natures in the Incarnate One as only moral or relational, not fully personal—implying that a human personality, already established, was adopted into union with the Logos.

The New Testament depicts Jesus Christ as both the Word becoming flesh and a fully human being who communicates that Word in what he says and does. John's Gospel focuses on the former, the Synoptic Gospels on the latter. These Word-flesh versus Word-man frameworks offer loose generalizations that obscure historical nuances.[4] But they indicate how certain intellectual contexts shaped the church's questions and answers regarding the incarnation.

---

4. The Alexandria/Antioch contrast remains widespread in textbooks, and specific disputes arose between figures from the two. Yet the scholarly trend is to minimize the contrast. For introductory articles on these schools and other parts of the history, see Treier and Elwell, *Evangelical Dictionary of Theology*.

A History of Heresies

The church clarified orthodox boundaries by evaluating possibilities that eventually were deemed heresies. Within God's providence these heresies prompted faith seeking biblical understanding. Each episode of the following narrative highlights a question raised by an eventual heresy. In response, key figures or texts clarified biblical teaching. The resulting creeds do not exhaust the identity of Jesus Christ, but they establish orthodox boundaries within which the church faithfully worships and fully proclaims the good news. These boundaries make space within which theological exploration may freely and safely occur.

The early rejection of Ebionism and "docetism" established two essential commitments: Jesus's divinity and Christ's humanity. The eventual rejection of Arianism at Nicaea (325) and ultimately at Constantinople (381), along with the rejection of Apollinarianism, clarified those essential commitments: Jesus's full divinity and Christ's full humanity. Then the rejection of Nestorianism and Eutychianism at Chalcedon (451) secured the integrity of those two commitments by adding a third: the "hypostatic union" of these fully divine and fully human natures in the one person of God the Son, Jesus Christ our Lord.

EBIONISM

*Ebionism forced the church to answer this question: *Is Jesus the Christ in the sense of being the preexistent divine Logos?* The orthodox answer is yes. Ebionism (or Ebionites) probably emerged from Jewish Christianity, perhaps the "Judaizers" whom Paul opposed. The Ebionite Jesus was a unique human, the "Christ" (at least for a time) but not fully divine. Ebionism was an early form of a recurring tendency known as *adoptionism. "Adoptionist" Christologies treat Jesus as only a human being with a unique role in God's plan. The Ebionite Jesus was Israel's Messiah; in a heightened sense, God's election of Jesus paralleled the election of other humans by grace. This early Jewish Christology, to which historians lack direct access, arose in the late first or early second century and scarcely outlasted the third. For all of the half-truths it recognized about Jesus's humanity and identification with Israel, it did not meaningfully acknowledge his divinity.

DOCETISM

At the opposite end of the spectrum, *docetism raised this question: *Did the Logos really assume humanity in Jesus Christ?* The orthodox answer is yes. "Docetism" labels a family of early heresies that would not meaningfully acknowledge Christ's humanity. The label comes from modern scholars, who recognize a shared tendency among these heretics to say that Jesus only "appeared" to be human. "Platonic" dualism influenced the surrounding context: matter seemed to be evil or deficient in being, subject to change, whereas a truly divine being would be unable to change or suffer. Holding to Christ's divinity, docetists denied that he was really human, since that would require a body.

Some "gnostic" versions of docetism related Jesus to a mythological redeemer figure because they wanted to break free of the present world through a spark of illumination. If a redeemer walked on earth, his body could be only phantom, whereas for orthodox Christianity "redemption is primarily a freeing from sin and its consequences. It includes the body along with the rest of the physical world."[5] Thus, gnostics like Cerinthus (first century AD) sharply distinguished between Jesus and the "Christ"; for them, the divine aspect or Christ-figure came upon Jesus at baptism, using him to appear until the crucifixion, when it left—never having been genuinely united to the human. Other gnostics like Marcion (c. 85–160) suggested that Christ only appeared to be human; for them, Jesus's body was ghostly.

Tertullian and Irenaeus were heroic opponents of docetism and gnosticism. Tertullian opposed patripassianism, the idea that God directly (as the Father only) suffered on the cross. Since the divine being could not die on the cross, distinct divine persons and the Son's real humanity had to be affirmed—for God to remain alive, so to speak. Related to patripassianism was *monarchianism, which treated God in terms of one monarch (the Father). In heretical forms, monarchianism treated the Son and the Spirit as mere appearances (so Sabellius's modalism) or at least denied them equality with God.

Irenaeus also played a key role in emerging orthodoxy. Against gnostic redeemer myths, Irenaeus emphasized a "Rule of Faith" tied to salvation history, passed down from the apostles. This *regula fidei* told the church to read the Old and New Testaments together as Scripture, telling one story of one God, the God of Israel. For Irenaeus, this one story involved *recapitulation: Jesus faithfully reliving the fallen human story in his own redemptive life history. Rather than providing an escape from the drama of earthly life, the divine Redeemer completed the story by rewriting a second human act himself. Docetic heresies therefore represent extreme pathologies of Word-flesh Christology early on, in the second and third centuries, before the Christian canon—read in terms of one unified salvation history—firmly took hold.

---

5. Grillmeier, *From the Apostolic Age to Chalcedon*, 83.

ARIANISM

"Arianism" is perhaps the archetypal heresy—certainly the most influential of its time—raising this question: *Is Jesus Christ the Logos fully divine, in the sense of being uncreated and of the same essence with the Father?* The quotation marks surrounding "Arianism" (not used hereafter) indicate that this heresy had a life of its own beyond its key figure, whose exact views are difficult to discern. Historical access to Arius is largely indirect, through his opponents.

*Arianism denied the Son's self-existence and, accordingly, his eternity: instead, he was "begotten timelessly" as the first creature, the one through whom God initiated the rest of creation and its history. Arianism treated the Son as a mediating, semi- or quasi-divine creature—somewhat parallel to gnostic views. Arianism was willing to call Jesus Christ the Son of God but not to associate full divinity with that name. A particular (mis)reading of Colossians 1:15 can epitomize the Arian position, relegating the Son to being "the firstborn over all creation" in a chronological sense.

The heroes of this episode took long years to win a decisive victory. The First Council of Nicaea in 325 created a brief creed that rejected the Arian position. Debate centered on the term *homoousios, saying that the Son is of the same being or essence as the Father. Arianism was willing to say that the Son is *homoiousios*, similar to the Father but still created and subordinate. Apparently, Arianism shared the wider Greek commitment to protect God's transcendence, keeping the divine from getting hands dirty with the world. By treating the Son as a mediating creature, Arianism could keep God indirectly related to creation. Although this position was initially rejected in 325, its defense of one transcendent God, the ebb and flow of emperors' allegiances, and nasty church politics periodically favored Arianism throughout the fourth century. Athanasius (c. 296–373), a young observer at the Nicene council in 325, soon became bishop of Alexandria and Arianism's chief opponent, but he was exiled from his bishopric on five occasions.

Like much of early Christianity, Athanasius championed *theosis, in which salvation involves "deification" or "divinization"—human participation in the divine nature (2 Pet. 1:4). "For he was incarnate that we might be made gods."[6] God must communicate the divine nature in a way that makes human participation possible. If Jesus Christ is not God incarnate, then humans cannot receive the essence of salvation: communion with God. If salvation means knowing the true God (John 17:3), becoming conformed by the Spirit to the true divine image in the Son (Rom. 8:28–30), then salvation must involve

---

6. See, e.g., Athanasius, *On the Incarnation*, 167 (25.192b in *Patrologia Graeca*).

direct communion with God. A truly divine Mediator must reach down, not a quasi-divine intermediary who could lead humans only on a self-saving ascent toward God. Athanasius also underscored life: if humans became subject to death by virtue of the fall, then salvation must involve the divine life triumphing over death in the Son's resurrection.

Athanasius distinguished between the *agennētos* ("unbegotten") Father and the *agenētos* ("uncreated") Son.[7] The Father and the Son are distinct persons within the Triune God: the Father generates the Son, and the Son is generated. But this generation is "eternal," contra the Arian view that "there was a time when he [the Son] was not." In the trinitarian economy the Father initiates and the Son implements in response. Yet the Son is of the same essence as the Father, sharing in divine eternity and self-existence by the Father's good pleasure. The Logos is the Son of God in a vitally different way than redeemed humans, who are adopted as God's children: the Logos is the Son of God by nature, whereas humans become God's children only by grace. According to Athanasius, "the distinction between the coming forth of the Son and our createdness is made by the Son's 'being from the substance of the Father.'"[8]

If Arianism were true, then humans could not know that the love revealed in Jesus Christ is really God's; there could be a hidden God to whom we lack saving access. Arianism would have humanity reaching toward God, finding a quasi-divine intermediary rather than a gracious God taking personal saving initiative.[9] Admittedly, the church sometimes was nervous about connecting the Logos directly to the change and suffering associated with human flesh. In the end, however, the necessity of acknowledging the Son's full divinity became clear. Salvation is at stake, if fallen humanity is to participate in the communion of the divine life. Furthermore, worship is at stake: if, with Arianism, the church honored the Son as quasi-divine but not fully divine, then that worship would violate the distinction between Creator and creature. The Bible allows for no third kind of being. Ironically, by attempting to protect divine transcendence, Arianism promotes idolatry instead.

APOLLINARIANISM

At long last, in 381 the Council of Constantinople reaffirmed the decision of Nicaea from 325, officially vanquishing Arianism. The Niceno-Constantinopolitan Creed insisted on the Son's full divinity. Protecting this

---

7. Grillmeier, *From the Apostolic Age to Chalcedon*, 267.
8. Grillmeier, *From the Apostolic Age to Chalcedon*, 268n68.
9. This point is made well in Gunton, "And in One Lord," and A. Torrance, "Being of One Substance."

commitment, however, led some to deny the fullness of the Son's humanity. This question arose: *Did Jesus Christ the Logos possess a human mind?* Docetism was already heretical, so Apollinarians acknowledged the Son's humanity. But they focused upon the union of the Logos with human flesh. They denied the Son's full humanity by having the Logos replace what would otherwise have been the human spirit.

Broadly speaking, then, *Apollinarianism was a form of *monophysitism, a one-nature (*physis*) Christology opposite adoptionism. In Alexandrian anthropology, the divine Logos could naturally become the life-giving principle normally provided by the *nous*, the rational soul. Emphasizing the Logos's intimate union with the human body would protect the Son's personal unity. Yet Apollinarians did not merely promote *mia physis*—one nature—in this largely orthodox way. Apollinarianism reflected concerns (especially in the East) about an emerging focus on Christ's full humanity. A monophysite Christology would avoid not only a division of the Son's person but also corruption from a sinful human spirit. Like the Arians, the Apollinarians protected divinity from direct contact with a defective aspect of creation; unlike the Arians, they denied the full humanity, rather than the full divinity, of the Son.

The anti-Apollinarian heroes were the Cappadocian fathers. Their formula, "What is not assumed is not healed" (*quod non est assumptum non est sanatum*), had roots as early as Origen and Tertullian. But the Cappadocians emphasized this point, as did the Antiochene Theodore of Mopsuestia (c. 350–428), although he was controversial and came into posthumous disrepute. The point is that the Redeemer must take up all aspects of humanity; any aspect not assumed by the Mediator is irredeemable, being treated as essentially corrupt. Hence Apollinarianism was condemned, beginning in 362 at Alexandria and decisively in 381 at Constantinople. Somewhat similar tendencies had been widespread among the orthodox, helping to preserve the Son's divinity and personal unity, and Apollinarius made helpful contributions.[10] Yet salvation is at stake not only in the Son's full divinity but also in his full humanity: any aspect exempted from the Incarnate Lord would remain unhealed.

10. "The successful use of *hypostasis* to interpret the unity of person in Christ does, however, seem to have been the work of Apollinarius, though we were able to see a first appearance of the root of this very significant word as early as Hippolytus" (Grillmeier, *From the Apostolic Age to Chalcedon*, 337). "Apollinarius, therefore, at first had the initiative. As far as we can still see from the tradition, he must be credited with having introduced into christology, or having brought to bear on the discussion, the three most important concepts which occur in the Chalcedonian Definition"—namely, *physis*, *hypostasis*, and *prosōpon* (347).

NESTORIANISM AND EUTYCHIANISM

Although the church confessed the Son's full divinity and full humanity, a question remained: *How are the divine and human natures related in Christ?* Alexandria, focused on a single divine person assuming human flesh, was waning in influence. Antioch, focused on the full humanity assumed by the Logos, was gaining influence. The new focus on two distinct natures raised fresh challenges in articulating their relationship, while lingering misunderstandings still jeopardized the genuine affirmation of one nature or the other.

Imagine Christologies being poured into a funnel. The widest denial of the Son's divinity was Ebionism, the narrower denial Arianism. The widest denial of the Son's humanity was docetism, the narrower denial Apollinarianism. In 381, Constantinople reduced the width of potential errors considerably. Yet subtle errors continued to flow on each side. On the adoptionist side, Arianism's successor was *Nestorianism; on the monophysite side, Apollinarianism's successor was *Eutychianism.

The heresy known as "Nestorianism" implicitly denied the Son's full divinity by distinguishing the two natures too sharply, falling into a form of adoptionism. Nestorianism took an Antiochene approach to an extreme, although Nestorius (c. 386–450) may not have held the teachings of some of his followers. As archbishop of Constantinople, he was asked to rule about calling Mary the *Theotokos (God-bearer, the mother of God), a title widely accepted in the Alexandrian school. Nestorius rejected the title, worrying that it led to Arianism (treating the Son only as Mary's child, a creature) or else Apollinarianism (treating the Son as not completely human). Nestorianism was thereby perceived as teaching that Mary gave birth to a man who became an instrument of the divine.

The *Theotokos* title has biblical support: Elizabeth, Mary's cousin, cried out, "Blessed are you among women, and blessed is the child you will bear! But why am I so favored, that *the mother of my Lord* should come to me?" (Luke 1:42–43 [emphasis added]). The title is especially pertinent since the Greek *Kyrios* ("my Lord") renders the Hebrew and Aramaic *Adonai* ("my Lord"), which substituted among Jews for the divine name YHWH. In denying this title to Mary, Nestorianism lost the Son's personal unity by overemphasizing the distinction between the two natures. Refusing to identify the one born of Mary as "God" made the two natures seem to be two persons: the *Logos* coming upon the human Jesus and "adopting" him. Put differently, the union of the natures would be only "moral," not essential—as if God is in Christ, but Christ is not God.

Cyril of Alexandria vigorously opposed Nestorius, who was condemned at Ephesus in 431. Afterward, some of Cyril's supporters still thought that he conceded too much to the principle "What is not assumed is not redeemed." Hence another form of monophysitism arose from Eutyches (c. 380–456). Now the Son's one "nature" had to be both divine and human, since Apollinarianism had been ruled heretical. So the Eutychian solution involved one hybrid nature, a *tertium quid* (third thing) fusing divinity and humanity.

Facing condemnation, Eutyches pleaded his case to Leo I (the Great), bishop of Rome (c. 400–461). In response, Leo's "Tome" drew on both Cyril of Alexandria and Tertullian to frame a consensus position. The result influenced the Definition at the Council of Chalcedon (451), where Eutyches was condemned. According to Chalcedon, the two natures are united in the one person (*hypostasis*)—the "hypostatic union"—yet they remain distinct: divinity and humanity may not be confused, even when they come into intimate personal union in the Son.

The Chalcedonian Definition describes the hypostatic union by providing boundaries: "[We also teach] that we apprehend [*gnōridzomenon*] this one and only Christ—Son, Lord, only-begotten—in two natures [*duo physesin*]; [and we do this] without confusing the two natures [*asynkytōs*], without transmuting one nature into the other [*atreptōs*], without dividing them into two separate categories [*adiairetōs*], without contrasting them according to area or function [*achōristōs*]. . . . Instead, the 'properties' [*idiotētos*] of each nature are conserved and both natures concur [*syntrechousēs*] in one 'person' [*prosōpon*] and in one *hypostasis*."[11]

Chalcedon therefore ruled out both Nestorianism ("one and only Christ . . . without dividing them . . . without contrasting them") and the Eutychian overreaction ("in two natures . . . without confusing the two . . . without transmuting one nature into the other") against it. By the middle of the fifth century, then, conciliar Christology had three essential points: the Son's full divinity, full humanity, and personal unity. Chalcedon's theoretical modesty left a partial vacuum, though: reticence about trying to explain the mystery of the incarnation left space for competing descriptions and periodic controversy.

An Ongoing Odyssey . . .

Periodic controversy stemmed first from the largely Eastern tendency to discount Cyril's influence over Chalcedon. The Second Council of Constantinople in 553 upheld Chalcedon, although it was friendlier to monophysites

---

11. "The Definition of Chalcedon (451)."

in its ardent opposition to Nestorianism. Feeling that Chalcedon did not adequately preserve the single Subject of the Incarnation, some monophysites rejected the orthodox position. Other champions of Christ's single subjectivity, avoiding monophysitism, still refused to speak of distinct divine and human wills. Their *monothelitism ("one will," *thelēma*) held that Christ had only one will or principle of operation, but it was condemned in 680 at the Third Council of Constantinople. Among other arguments, Jesus's prayer in Gethsemane (Matt. 26:36–46) was crucial: unless both the divine will and the obedient submission of the human Messiah were involved, the resulting passion could not accomplish our salvation. Yet christological variety lingered in the Middle Ages and beyond.

MEDIEVAL PIETY AND PHILOSOPHY

In 787 the Second Council of Nicaea, the last of the seven ecumenical councils recognized by both East and West, addressed an important practical implication of Christology: the iconoclast controversy. Iconoclasts criticized the use of icons, visible representations of divine or angelic or saintly beings, as a form of idolatry. Iconodules victoriously defended the use of icons by appealing to the incarnation. In Jesus Christ God sanctified human flesh. Icons may not be worshiped, but they may be venerated as vehicles for worshiping the true God. Users of icons do not worship the human nature of Christ per se; they worship the divine person of the Son of God. Icons do not reduce the Triune God to a visible, material level, but they honor God's self-revelation via the Son's flesh. While icons became especially important within Eastern Christianity, they also influenced the piety of the Catholic West. Both East and West sometimes underscored Christ's divinity so strongly that they seemingly neglected his full humanity; accordingly, appeals to Mary and the saints for intercession became more prominent. In one respect, though, Jesus's humanity remained prominent: medieval Roman Christianity often gave mystical attention to Christ's suffering, sometimes in gory detail.[12]

In the Middle Ages, while learning initially stagnated, monastic communities preserved classic texts and traditional wisdom. Soon enough, Aristotle's writings were recovered and fresh philosophizing ensued. The university was born, becoming prominent at Paris, Cambridge, and Oxford. "Scholasticism" developed a particular method of study, using disputed questions and thorough answers. Its epitome is the *Summa theologica* of Thomas Aquinas,

---

12. On Mary and the saints increasing as intercessors when Jesus's humanity is neglected, see Farrow, *Ascension and Ecclesia.* For an overview of medieval christological piety, see R. Williams, "History of Faith in Jesus."

which systematized christological orthodoxy within the language of Aristotelian metaphysics. Later medieval thinkers are frequently accused of abstract speculation, which may appear in isolated cases. But Thomas was a deeply biblical thinker, and scholastic thinkers provided vital concepts for many Christians after them.

PROTESTANT CONTROVERSY AND REFORM

Protestants are often credited with reemphasizing the biblical narrative of salvation history. Early Reformers criticized abstract speculation, paying less attention to metaphysical disputes. Before overemphasizing the contrast between medieval Catholicism and the Reformation, however, it is worth noting that the Protestants assumed christological concepts from their Catholic heritage. Soon they generated their own "scholastic" thinkers and texts. If Protestants modestly reformed Christology, they did so by reemphasizing the biblical good news that Jesus Christ is the one Mediator between God and humanity (1 Tim. 2:5).

Much earlier, in Chalcedon's wake, the *communicatio idiomatum*—the communication of divine and human attributes in the Incarnate Son—became a standard orthodox category. Acts 20:28 can illustrate the basic principle by referring to "the church of God, which he bought with his own blood": redemption is attributed to God, in the person of the Son, while, properly speaking, the blood is attributed to him by virtue of his human nature. Granted this need to speak of a communication of attributes, however, its entailments generated dispute among Protestants. Lutherans uniquely promoted communication *between the natures*, to the extent that the Son's human nature came to share in divine properties such as omnipresence. The underlying issue was the Lord's Supper: Luther held that Jesus Christ could become really present—physically, though not locally—in any and every eucharistic celebration. If the whole Christ, undivided, were present in each celebration, then his presence must be human, not just divine; hence the human nature must share in the divine ubiquity.

By contrast, the Reformed focus was the ascended Son's human body. Calvinists feared that Lutherans violated Chalcedon by mixing together the two natures, that they lost the integrity of the Son's humanity, and that they minimized the Holy Spirit's mediation of Christ's presence. Calvinists held that Christ's eucharistic presence is real (agreeing with Lutherans against Zwinglians and Anabaptists) but spiritual (since, contra Lutherans, the Son's human nature remains specifically located in heaven). In return, Lutherans feared that Calvinists not only minimized Christ's presence but also fell into

Nestorianism; Lutherans insisted that the whole Christ, human and not just divine, must be present in the Lord's Supper. Calvinists instead saw the Lord's Supper as a meal at which Jesus presides and feeds his people by faith, with the Holy Spirit helping believers to ascend into his presence. So Reformed theology strictly located the communication of attributes *at the level of the person*, rather than between the natures. The person of Christ is wholly present in the Lord's Supper—and everywhere else for that matter—by virtue of divinity; by virtue of humanity, however, he is particularly located in heaven. Whereas Luther would say that Christ's human nature shared in omnipresence, Calvin would say only that Christ himself was omnipresent, according to divinity—with such an attribute applying to the human nature by a kind of rhetorical license when speaking about the person.

The church classically maintained that the Son was omnipresent during his earthly ministry: by virtue of his divine nature Jesus Christ shared in ruling the universe even while incarnate in Judea. Eventually Lutheran opponents dubbed the Calvinist version of this affirmation the "extra" for holding that Christ's divine lordship extended beyond or outside of his embodied human locale. Lutherans worried that this *extra Calvinisticum* threatened the Incarnate One's personal integrity. For Calvinists, the human nature never restricted the omnipresence that the Son has by virtue of his divine nature; he always filled the whole earth, participating in the Triune God's cosmic reign, or else the incarnation would threaten his genuine divinity. Early Lutherans agreed that the Incarnate Son continued to share divine rule even on earth. But they did not speak of his omnipresence being beyond the human nature; rather, they saw the human nature as participating ubiquitously in the Son's cosmic rule, albeit in hidden form. If the primary concern of classic Lutherans was maintaining the Son's personal unity, eventually opposition to the *extra* arose from another concern: maintaining his genuine humanity.

Modern History and Humanity

In that vein, modernity introduced a series of christological debates. First, so-called *quests for the "historical Jesus" in contrast with the "Christ of faith" were animated by a contrast between studying Jesus historically, "from below," and affirming conciliar Christology "from above" as biblical dogma. The quests began among Enlightenment figures in the eighteenth century; their nineteenth- and twentieth-century histories are narrated in various ways. The most important pattern of the eighteenth- and nineteenth-century versions was the striking reflection of the questers' own commitments in their biographies of Jesus, whether positively or negatively. The most important pattern for much of the twentieth century was a lack of confidence about finding Jesus himself in contrast with high confidence about reconstructing the early church's constructions of Jesus. As the twenty-first century dawns, the quests' most promising contribution is the provocation to understand the Jesus of the Gospels within the context of Second Temple Judaism.

Second, controversy arose within Lutheran circles over "kenotic" Christologies. In Philippians 2:7, *kenōsis* describes the incarnation: Christ Jesus "emptied himself" or "made himself nothing." Some Lutherans feared that the church had been minimizing the Son's full humanity. Given increasing modern attention to human history and psychology, kenosis vocabulary suggested a theological paradigm. Such *kenotic Christology retained Chalcedon's commitment to the eternal Son's full divinity while suggesting that in the incarnation he gave up or restricted the use of certain divine attributes. Early and more radical kenoticists—German Lutherans, then some Anglicans and Scots—held that in the incarnation's earthly phase the Son actually emptied himself of divinity or at least particular attributes. After the nineteenth-century controversy died down, more restrained or "modified" kenotic approaches became common in certain evangelical and philosophical circles.[13] In modified kenotic accounts, the Son temporarily restricts the use of certain attributes while remaining fully divine in principle. Sometimes overlapping with kenotic accounts are *Spirit Christologies, which emphasize that Jesus performed his earthly wonders as a faithful human being empowered by the Holy Spirit. That is a perfectly orthodox affirmation, but some Spirit Christologies go further, rejecting conciliar "Logos Christology" as incompatible with Jesus's full humanity.

As modern Christologies generally became more interested in the Son's humanity (the first development), they wondered especially about the self-consciousness of Jesus Christ (the second): How could he have known himself as both God and man while remaining a unified person? Such an experience seemed unimaginable as Western culture became newly preoccupied with human subjectivity and historical location. Today, three basic approaches to this question are dominant among evangelicals. Many affirm a *modified kenotic* account, perhaps with some influence from quests for the historical Jesus and/or an appeal to Spirit Christology. Others retain traditional affirmations by appealing to *paradox*: if the Incarnate Son is the only two-natured person ever, then we should expect his subjectivity to be mysterious. Still others retain traditional affirmations in a more philosophical mode, appealing to *two "minds"* as the next appropriate step beyond two wills. The two-minds

---

13. See especially C. S. Evans, *Exploring Kenotic Christology*.

approach seeks psychological analogies for the Son's self-consciousness. Such analogies have included disorders in which the subject is seemingly divided into multiple personalities.

Traditional theologians find it unhelpful to use analogies involving abnormal or unhealthy human subjectivity. Should finite thinkers expect to find analogies for the union of finite and infinite self-consciousness? "Paradox" may not indicate logical impossibility, just the limits of human understanding. Since self-consciousness is a modern, Western preoccupation, any pursuit of explanations should be cautious. Traditional accounts, then, ascribe all of the Son's actions to the one person. When addressing the principle of agency by virtue of which the Son performs particular actions, certain biblical texts focus on divinity while others focus on humanity. Some traditionalists acknowledge an element of *krypsis, a level of hiddenness regarding the Son's divinity, without ontological or functional kenosis.[14] By contrast, of course, the modified kenotic and two-minds accounts worry that lacking an account of the Incarnate One's self-consciousness jeopardizes his full humanity.

Nevertheless, all three approaches can say, shockingly enough, that God died for our sins, that Mary is the mother of God, and that a human being participates in ruling the world with truth and grace. Jesus Christ died for our sins by virtue of his human nature; Mary is the mother of God by virtue of the Son's divine nature; and Jesus Christ rules the world with truth and grace as the divine Son in whom human life comes to its ultimate fulfillment. That is the glorious meaning of the communication of attributes!

Third, though, another modern debate concerns the Son's *impeccability, his inability to sin. The divine nature suggests that ultimately Christ was unable to sin (*non posse peccare*)—as humans will someday become when they are glorified in him. To some, however, the human nature suggests that Jesus must have been able to sin (in order to be tempted), even if he was also able to resist temptation and avoid sin (*posse non peccare*)—as Adam and Eve were originally. Traditionally, focus rests not on one nature or the other but on the *person*, Jesus Christ the Son of God. Asymmetry is involved: divinity rendered the Son incapable of sinning, while humanity rendered him capable of being tested yet resisting temptation in the Spirit's power. It is not entirely true that "to err is human": the fall meant inexplicably turning away from God's goodness. Eschatological glory will unite us to Christ so that we no longer sin. If that is true of our future, and Jesus brought God's kingdom

---

14. Regarding *krypsis*, see Crisp, *Divinity and Humanity*, esp. 121, 150–53. The best recent traditional evangelical Christologies are Horton, *Lord and Servant*, and Wellum, *God the Son Incarnate*.

into the present, then he could be fully human despite being gloriously unable to sin. Indeed, he could know temptation's full power precisely because he could fully resist it.[15]

Some modern Protestants such as Karl Barth, however, began suggesting that Christ—whether or not he was impeccable in principle—assumed a *fallen human nature: not actively sinful himself, but embracing humanity's "fallen" condition in spiritual solidarity. Like modified kenoticism, this view has attracted some evangelicals. By contrast, according to classic Protestants, any aspect of the human will that does not wholeheartedly embrace God's will is already sinful, even before someone commits a particular sin. Hence this debate largely concerns what is involved in a fallen human will and whether it already counts as sinful.[16] The classic Protestant view recognizes the importance of saying that "God made him who had no sin to be sin for us" (2 Cor. 5:21), but ties this identification with our sin ultimately to the cross.

Fourth, another modern christological concern involves liberation in various contexts. The largest contextual concern is the feminist question of whether Jesus Christ can bring liberation to women as a human male. Most pointedly, the worry is that "if God is male, then male is God."[17] Granted that the Christian tradition has not always addressed this concern well, orthodoxy offers an answer. God is Spirit, so biological maleness is not essential to the divine identity of God the Son or to human communion with God. The proper direction of the analogy in the names "Father" and "Son" runs from divine paternity toward human life, not from human paternity toward God.[18] Jesus's maleness was contingent upon the incarnation's place in Israel's covenant history. His maleness was essential to the incarnation only like other aspects of his particularity: his liberating mission had universal reach precisely by embracing a particular human condition—as a Jewish man in first-century Palestine—not by privileging male over female.

Eventually modern Christology began to reflect cultural locations beyond European and American domination. Liberation-oriented theologies arose first from Latin America and then from Asia, Africa, and marginalized groups in the West. Like modern Christologies generally, these emphasize the human Jesus proclaiming God's kingdom in word and deed. They critique traditional

15. Lewis, *Mere Christianity*, 142, observes, "Christ, because He was the only man who never yielded to temptation, is also the only man who knows to the full what temptation means."

16. To survey the issue, see Kapic, "The Son's Assumption of a Human Nature."

17. The quotation famously stems from Mary Daly. For helpful analysis of how masculine condescension has shaped discussions of *kenōsis* in Phil. 2, see Coakley, "*Kenōsis* and Subversion."

18. Again, see M. M. Thompson, *Promise of the Father*, as discussed in chap. 4.

Christologies for a perceived tendency to treat the person of Christ in abstraction from his work. The liberationist understanding of God's kingdom addresses human brokenness in strongly structural terms and emphasizes God's embrace of the poor. Contextual concerns now proliferate, as theologians recognize that the entire christological tradition, from the first four cities onward, was itself culturally shaped. Thus, beyond clarifying orthodoxy, this christological odyssey offers the following "moral": seeking to understand Jesus requires constantly returning to the Bible—even to help us reexamine the lenses with which we read.

The Biblical Grammar of Orthodox Christology

God providentially used Greek ontological language for helping the church to articulate the identity of its Lord. The resulting grammar—"the hypostatic union"—guides Christian worship to proclaim the good news of salvation. As with any language, though, the conciliar rules reflect a particular context. Modern criticisms include the lack of a full explanation for the incarnation, alongside a supposed inability to convey the dynamism and fullness of the gospel narrative. Critics, however, have not been successful at simply replacing conciliar "metaphysics" with history: sooner or later a narrative raises questions about the character of its key agent(s). The creedal grammar helps the church's proclamation to answer those questions as faithfully as possible—even if critics helpfully highlight the broader context of Israel's history, the incarnation's dynamic character, and the Protagonist's human identity.

To demonstrate that conciliar orthodoxy is truly biblical, the following sections explore the Son's divine identity in Scripture. While Chalcedon's minimalism grants considerable freedom for christological exposition, its grammar also governs our fidelity to the full divinity and humanity of Jesus Christ as our One Mediator.[19]

The "Son" in Scripture

Scripture names Jesus Christ in numerous ways that are rich in significance. Most noteworthy, to begin with, are the two names that became his foundational human identity among his earliest followers: (1) *"Jesus," his given name, told Israel that he was their Savior (Matt. 1:21); (2) *"Christ," the Greek equivalent of the Hebrew *"Messiah," told Israel that he was divinely

---

19. For a critique of merely metaphorical and overly literal views, see Coakley, "What Does Chalcedon Solve?"

anointed. Then "Christ" gave Jesus followers their name, "Christians," in the wider Greco-Roman context (Acts 11:26). Like prophets, priests, and kings of old, this Anointed One had a divinely ordained office in God's kingdom. Jesus rarely spoke of himself in this way (e.g., Mark 14:61–65), to avoid confusing potential followers about aspirations to overthrow the Romans and establish immediate Davidic kingship. Yet "Messiah" crucially captures his ultimate fulfillment of various Old Testament offices.

Being Israel's Savior and God's anointed Mediator already hints at the Son's divinity, not just humanity. Two other titles point further in this direction. (3) *Lord, which like "Messiah" is not dominant in the Gospels, typically was a form of respectful address (something like "sir"). Initially it may have meant little more when applied to Jesus. After his resurrection and ascension, however, its use as the Greek equivalent of YHWH in the Old Testament certainly became significant. As explored below, for passages like Philippians 2:9–11 to identify Jesus so strongly with Israel's God reveals his divinity. Gospel writers probably expected that their readers would understand some earlier appearances of "Lord" in light of the resurrection. (4) "I AM" sayings in the Gospel of John also identify Jesus with YHWH, hearkening back to the revelatory trajectory from Exodus 3:14 to Exodus 32–34 that was traced earlier in trinitarian theology. Jesus takes "I AM" to his own lips in John, often following it with images reflecting Israel's God—light, shepherd, and so on.

Above all, the Bible identifies Jesus Christ through sonship. (5) *Son of Man apparently was Jesus's favorite earthly self-designation. In the Old Testament, this title primarily designates humanity. The Gospels associate "Son of Man" with their entire narrative: his ministering, suffering and dying, and being exalted to eschatological glory. By naming himself "Son of Man," Jesus avoided the political hazards associated with "Messiah" while acknowledging his mission's supernatural origin. In Daniel 7:13, somehow the Son of Man participates in God's eternal reign. Given this background, New Testament texts take the honorific language of Psalms 2 and 110, "whereby Israel's anointed king was thought of as God's son seated at God's right hand," to new heights regarding Jesus's relation to God.[20]

Correspondingly, (6) *Son of God does not assert Christ's divinity in every case, but it gradually points in that direction. Whereas "Son of God" is not recorded as Jesus's own term, it is a favorite of the New Testament Epistles. In the Gospels, it emphasizes Jesus's supernatural power over the spirit world (e.g., Mark 3:11; 5:7). In Hebrews, Christ's divine sonship establishes his

---

20. Further reasons for this view may be found in C. A. Evans, "Jesus' Self-Designation 'The Son of Man,'" esp. 32.

uniqueness as Mediator in contrast with earlier prophets, angels, and leaders like Moses. In Paul's Epistles, some passages suggest the Son's divine *preexistence, at least prior to the incarnation and even eternally (e.g., Rom. 8:3; 1 Cor. 10:4; Gal. 4:4; Phil. 2:6–11; Col. 1:15–17; 1 Tim. 3:16). Whereas some have worried that Romans 1:4 supports adoptionism, there are good reasons to think otherwise. "Son of God" is not an adoptionist category elsewhere in Romans, let alone elsewhere in Paul's other writings. Yet the resurrection of Christ has strong associations with divine sonship, as in Acts 2:24. Thus Romans 1:4 attaches *en dynamei*, "with power," to the verbal action: "The contrast is not between a time when he was Son and a time when he was not Son, but between a time when he was Son in weakness and a time when he became Son with power."[21]

The church therefore teaches the *eternal generation of the Son, who is eternally "begotten," not "made," of the Father. This eternal begetting is metaphorical, not physical, and it does not subordinate the Son to the Father in being. Any "subordination" that appears in John's Gospel, for example, is not ontological, as if the Son were second-class. Instead, any subordination is "functional," arguably economic and temporary, the appropriate way for the one sent to respond to the one who sends—the Word in flesh obeying the speaker, the Son as the Father's apprentice (John 5:19–27). Indeed, being the divine Son by nature establishes that the Logos is of the same essence as the Father, uniquely able to reveal God (John 1:14–18). Such internal ordering of the persons of the Blessed Trinity makes it fitting for the Son to be the Incarnate One, who renders faithful obedience to God on behalf of the covenant people. Such internal trinitarian relationships leave room for shared exaltation: the Father will be glorified not apart from the Son but rather *through* the Son's exaltation in the Spirit. The larger New Testament pattern is fitting: the Son's glorified existence after the resurrection and by virtue of the ascension fostered the church's recognition of his preexistence as Creator. Hence Christian theology shockingly confesses the humiliation of the Son of God as Jesus of Nazareth, and the exaltation of the Son of Man, Jesus of Nazareth, as the Son of God.[22]

The Son's Divine Identity as Good News

The person of Jesus Christ and his ministry of reconciliation are inseparable. At stake are the faithfulness of Christian worship and the fullness of human salvation. Two traditional principles underscore these claims. First,

21. Macleod, *Person of Christ*, 90–92.
22. Hunsinger, "Karl Barth's Christology," 143.

lex orandi lex credendi, "the law of prayer is the law of faith": we either worship the Triune God faithfully or else commit idolatry when we identify Jesus Christ as the Son of God. Second, as mentioned earlier, "What is not assumed is not healed": the fullness of salvation hinges on the Son's genuine humanity. Indeed, the reality of salvation hinges on the personal unity of the divine Son as our Mediator; otherwise, salvation gets defined as something besides knowing God—maybe just a benefit like forgiveness, obtained by an intermediary. Then no one can be sure that the benefit has really been obtained, being unsure whether the kindness is truly God's.

Against these principles, many modern biblical scholars divide "functional" and "ontological" categories, limiting Scripture's christological claims to the former. On this view, starting "from below," most of the New Testament reflects the earliest Christians' simpler Jewish concepts—at most portraying Christ as a divine representative. The supposed path from Jesus's divine role to the Son's divine nature in the later creeds involved evolutionary development (a rather modern philosophical principle!). Such ontological development is criticized for preventing the church from following the human being portrayed in the Synoptic Gospels.

According to this common story, Jesus climbed from functional to ontological divinity between the middle of the first century and the middle of the fourth because divine functions gradually connected him to intermediate, quasi-divine figures. Various intermediate beings have been proposed—principal angels like Michael; exalted patriarchs like Abraham; emanating figures like Word and Wisdom—who gained quasi-divine status as God's representatives. Through association with these Jewish figures, the story goes, Jesus gradually climbed the Greek philosophical ladder to God's throne.

Under the banner of *early high Christology, however, other scholars have challenged that adoptionist "evolutionary" view; they demonstrate that divine Christology is present in the New Testament beyond John's Gospel, including early texts and the Synoptic Gospels. To start with, biblical faith acknowledges only two kinds of beings: the Creator, who must be worshiped, and creatures, who may not be worshiped.[23] Principal angels and exalted patriarchs may not be worshiped, since they are only creatures. By contrast, Word and Wisdom must be worshiped when they reflect the Creator's self-expression in the created order. Second Temple Jewish literature usually reflects this biblical pattern, in which angels and patriarchs are not worshiped. Jesus did

---

23. The following paragraphs expound the key ideas of Bauckham, *Jesus and the God of Israel*, supplemented by Yeago, "New Testament and the Nicene Dogma." See also Hurtado, *Lord Jesus Christ*.

not ascend to the creedal status of full divinity by becoming identified with such beings. To the contrary, the New Testament's identification of Jesus with God's Word and Wisdom reflects an already early high Christology, in surprising fulfillment of Old Testament hopes.

Attached to the distinction between Creator and creature are three unique aspects of the divine identity: not only receiving worship as the Creator, but also exercising sovereignty and accomplishing redemption. "Identity" is a helpful term because the Bible focuses upon the mighty acts that reveal the True God, not a "nature" itemized via static traits. The God of Israel is the Creator who remains sovereign over the cosmos, and who is currently reestablishing the submission of all things to that divine rule through redemption. Every knee will ultimately bow at the final judgment, but redemption invites every tongue to acknowledge the God of Israel joyfully.

In Philippians 2:9–11 the exalted Jesus shares in God's sovereignty, returning to the Son's former glory. Accordingly, the church recognized that Christ must have shared in the work of creation at the beginning. The new element of exaltation involves Christ's identity as the God-man, having accomplished the work of redemption that will reestablish comprehensive divine sovereignty. Paul cites Isaiah 45:20–23, one of the strongest monotheistic passages in the Old Testament, identifying Jesus with YHWH, of whom the Greek *Kyrios* ("Lord"—the "name above every name" in Phil. 2:9) spoke. The surrounding section of Isaiah anticipates that God will be more fully known—"then they will know" is the familiar prophetic refrain—when the Servant comes to reveal the sovereign Creator as the Redeemer of the covenant people. What Isaiah anticipated, Paul saw fulfilled. Although the form of that fulfillment could not have been clearly anticipated in advance, the definitive revelation of Israel's God happened *through* his Son's assumption of humanity as the redemptive Servant.

Focusing on divine identity integrates being and action, ontology and function. Among key Old Testament texts repeatedly applied to Christ, Psalm 110 places Jesus on the divine throne itself, linking this exaltation with divine preexistence already at creation. Isaiah 40–55, in which the redemption of a new exodus would definitively reveal God, anticipates the Servant fulfilling Israel's calling toward the nations (see Isa. 40:1–5, 27–31; 42:1–9, 18–25; 43:10; 44:1–5, 21–22; 49:5–6; 50:4–11; 52:13–53:12). Not only, then, does the New Testament apply all three aspects of the divine identity—sovereignty, creation, redemption—to the Son; this divine identity is also integrated with his human vocation. For he identified with humanity by identifying himself with Israel. Philippians 2:6–11 parallels the creedal grammar by identifying the one person "Christ Jesus" with "the form of God" and "the form of a servant," while appealing to Old Testament Scripture. Even before alluding to Isaiah 45 in Philippians 2:9–11, in Philippians 2:6–8 Paul echoes Isaiah 52–53 when speaking of the Son's obedience unto death.

The Son has fulfilled the promise of YHWH's final self-revelation, bringing a new exodus as both Passover Lamb and Mediator. The divine identity of the Incarnate One is good news: YHWH has reclaimed the joyful allegiance of the covenant people by coming in person to bear our curse. The Creator's Word and Wisdom have reestablished a sovereign claim over the cosmos whose redemption is promised. Thanks to the Son of God fulfilling Isaiah's vision of the Servant, "the law of prayer is the law of faith" has been integrated with "what is not assumed is not redeemed." We worship our Savior Jesus because only God could save us. At the same time, hard as it is to believe, God saved us by becoming one of us. The next chapter narrates this ministry of reconciliation.

— 9 —

The Ministry of Reconciliation

THESIS

Jesus Christ's ministry of reconciliation as the Mediator between God and humanity is signaled by his virginal conception; continues throughout his earthly ministry as messianic prophet, priest, and king; climaxes in his atoning passion; and commences a newly exalted phase in his resurrection and ascension.

LEARNING OBJECTIVES

After learning the material in this chapter, you should be able to:

1. *Define briefly* the key terms introduced here (marked with an asterisk and included in the glossary).
2. *List and recognize* the following: (a) the two states of Jesus; (b) the three offices of Christ.
3. *Describe and compare* the major terms and models for the atonement.
4. *Identify and illustrate* the contemporary concerns about traditional Protestant atonement theology and biblical responses to them.
5. *Explain* the significance of Jesus's incarnation (including the virginal conception), mission (including healing and liberation), passion (including the descent into hell), and exaltation (including the resurrection and ascension).

Accowding to conciliar Christology, true worship and full gospel proclamation acknowledge Jesus Christ as the church's Incarnate Lord. The traditional distinction between Christ's "person" and "work" should reflect an integral relationship rather than separating what Scripture joins together. Speaking of the Son's "identity" and vocation or "ministry"—a term that identifies him as God's Servant—promotes this integral relationship.

The gospel reveals what is eternally true of the Son's identity and essential to his earthly ministry: he is the unique Mediator of divine action, the

197

One in whom God and humans relate. This relational history plays out in a redemptive drama of descent and ascent, from the Son's initial humiliation in the incarnation to Jesus's exaltation upon the completion of his earthly mission. The climax of his reconciling ministry was his passion on the cross and his victorious resurrection.

The Incarnation

The major events in this redemptive drama reveal their protagonist as the "one mediator between God and mankind" (1 Tim. 2:5). For the Son's ministry of ransoming sinners from bondage and condemnation, "reconciliation" or "atonement" is the proper term. Yet the Son is the very Word who reveals God (John 1:18), the Mediator of revelation from creation onward. Creation and redemption hold together in Christ (Col. 1:17), because their common end lies in realizing the fellowship for which humans were made. Therefore, the incarnation is the redemptive pinnacle of God's self-communication, fulfilling a hope at which the Old Testament hints from the beginning, ever since God walked and talked with the first humans.

A Unique Event

*Incarnation means becoming embodied, referring theologically to the Son of God becoming fully human in Jesus Christ. The root metaphor of being in flesh generates the regular christological concept of assuming full humanity: if God assumed even our embodiment, then this act of divine self-revelation embraced all aspects of human life. The beginning—the initial becoming—of this incarnate state was the event of the Holy Spirit accomplishing Christ's virginal conception in Mary.[1]

John 1:14 provides the root metaphor: "The Word became flesh and made his dwelling among us." Jesus's body became the new temple through which God made a home with humans. The incarnation is an event with a beginning: "became." The incarnation is an event with a human body: "flesh." The incarnation is an event with a subsequent history, an enduring life: "made his dwelling among us." The incarnation is an event with revelatory significance: "the Word," whose glory the first disciples saw, overflowing with the "grace and truth" glimpsed by Moses. The incarnation is therefore a singular event, having no earthly analogies that could sustain full explanation. The incarnation is a reality with its own mysterious rationality,

---

1. Portions of this chapter appear in Treier, "Incarnation," used here with permission.

having its cogency in the Logos, through whom all creation came to exist and comes to light.

Incarnation is a metaphor that became a concept. All language originates in metaphor, thinking of something in terms that suggest something else. Concepts are dead metaphors—somewhat language-independent habits that associate particular ideas or objects with words. Various concepts can express similar or shared theological judgments, while the same concept could inform various judgments. The root metaphor of Word becoming flesh primarily appears in John's Gospel, yet related judgments in other biblical texts are conceptually similar. "Incarnation" understandably became the most central, regular way for Christians to name the advent of Jesus Christ.

The canonical biographies of the Incarnate One begin variously, but Isaiah stands prominently in the background. Whether the Gospel narratives begin with a genealogy drawn from Israel's covenant history (Matthew), or with John the Baptist preparing the way (Mark), or with extraordinary births (Luke), or even with eternity before creation (John), the Gospels identify Jesus as God's Spirit-anointed Servant—as anticipated in Isaiah 49; 52–53; 61. This Servant is ultimately God's Son—God coming personally to redeem Israel, the people called to be God's servant to the nations. In that context Jesus's virginal conception in Mary is fitting as a sign of "God with us"—God returning to the covenant people (Isa. 7:14).

The Virginal Conception

Modern objections to the "virgin birth" are common, however, resting on two major claims.[2] First, the New Testament supposedly contains multiple, contradictory depictions of Jesus's origins, while the virginal conception in Matthew and Luke is a "minority report" among them.[3] The minority report, it is argued, involves literary creations, not straightforward historical claims. Second, modern genetics supposedly requires a male Y chromosome for Jesus to be fully human. Ancient anthropologies had Mary providing the fullness of Jesus's humanity; virginal conception actually helped to resist "docetic" tendencies. But today, some say, those who would maintain Jesus's full humanity must account for deeper genetic understanding by rejecting the virginal conception.

It is important to identify the problematic assumptions behind these two claims. The first claim, about biblical diversity, rests on a tradition-historical approach that denies the trustworthy unity of Scripture, splitting

---

2. See, e.g., Lincoln, *Born of a Virgin?*, with counterarguments in Treier, "Virgin Territory?"
3. Lincoln, *Born of a Virgin?*, 39.

the Gospels apart from one another and from Pauline Epistles. The second claim, about theological difficulty, rests on assumptions about full humanity. To focus on this theological challenge: precisely because of differences between ancient anthropologies and modern genetics, no one should assume that a divinely provided Y chromosome precludes the Son *becoming* fully human. After all, the "Adam" of Genesis, God's first image-bearer, was fully human without having the same origins as his progeny. Moreover, orthodoxy has consistently maintained that the Son's humanity is fully personal only in the Logos who assumed it, not independently—another claim that resists tying the Son's full humanity to the nature of its origin.[4] The Son's personal assumption of humanity gave life to *this* individual; before the incarnation, there was no preexisting human being named "Jesus." For the theological objection here (that the virgin birth precludes Christ's full humanity) to stick, its alternative proposal (involving a complete human person from the very genetic beginning) would have to show how it could avoid heretical adoptionism.

The Son assumed a fully human *nature* to identify sinlessly with our helpless condition. As a sign, the virginal conception bears eloquent witness to this creative divine act of the Word becoming flesh. Yet the *origin* of Jesus's humanity must be distinct from ours. Virginal conception may not have been necessary to preserve the Son's sinlessness; no account of sin's transmission attained creedal consensus as a rationale for this miracle. Merely removing Joseph from the scene would not have preserved Jesus's sinlessness without addressing Mary. Even if the Catholic doctrine of Mary's "immaculate conception" were true, that would simply move the mystery one step backward regarding how divine intervention preserved the Son's sinlessness. So, rather than a mechanism for sinlessness, the virginal conception was a theological "sign": announcing God's fresh visitation of the covenant people, via the Father's initiative and the Spirit's overshadowing (Isa. 7:14; 59:21; 61:1–3). Such divine initiative further signals the preservation of the Son's sinlessness, by whatever means necessary—including the Spirit's presence from beginning to end.

With God nothing is impossible (Luke 1:37)—not even a virginal conception that joins together the Spirit's creative power, Mary's faithful response, and the Son's full identification with broken humanity. As a sign, the virginal conception indicates Christ's ultimate impeccability, overshadowed by the

---

4. The technical terms frequently used for this point are *anhypostatic Christology and *enhypostatic Christology: the Son's humanity was anhypostatic, without a personal *hypostasis* until being united to the Incarnate Son; the Son's humanity is then enhypostatic, having become a *hypostasis* in the person of the Incarnate Son.

Holy Spirit. Inability to sin did not make the Son less authentically human, for someday our humanity will become sinless like his (1 John 3:1–3). Meanwhile he suffered the panoply of temptations that we face (Heb. 4:14–16). His obedience, although inevitable, was genuinely voluntary, an expression of deepening moral formation (Heb. 5:8).

As a sign, the virginal conception indicates still another reality, which has been pervasively neglected in modern scholarship. Whatever the Incarnate One heard directly from Joseph or Mary or John the Baptist, or discerned indirectly from scandalous rumors, or simply perceived in communion with the Father, such an extraordinary birth would have profoundly influenced his self-understanding. Isaiah's widespread influence upon New Testament Christology suggests that it was hardly astonishing for the God-man to recognize himself as the embodied Servant of YHWH, to expect rejection and atoning death, to hope for resurrection by which he would renew Israel and reach the gentiles. Once he understood his strange beginning in light of Isaiah 7:14, the hope of Isaiah 40–66—that as God's Servant he would attain the redemption of God's people in person—could organically follow.

The incarnation is an utterly unique event, having no exact parallel with any precursor, analogue, or successor. By its very nature, although mysterious enough to transcend human logic—even to render any full explanation heretical—the incarnation relates God to earthly history. Yet we cannot talk about the incarnation through natural analogies, but only through God's historical self-communication that provides scriptural words to contemplate. The extraordinary truth signaled by the virginal conception is that "Jesus is himself *as God*, and without God he is not himself."[5]

Revelation and Reconciliation

The incarnation initiates the ultimate redemption of God's covenant people. Though not atoning in itself, the incarnation inaugurates, embodies, enables, and thereby participates in God's reconciling action. Atonement as a distinctive area of Christian teaching is treated below in relation to Christ's passion. While increasing numbers of theologians treat the incarnation itself as atoning,[6] it is better to speak of the incarnation as the beginning and underlying condition of the Mediator's reconciling ministry, to honor the divinely willed necessity of the cross portrayed in the New Testament (e.g., Luke 24:26, 46). It is true that the church discerned the identity of Jesus Christ

---

5. Webster, "Jesus—God for Us," 90.

6. For an evangelical representative of this tendency, see T. Torrance, *Incarnation*; T. Torrance, *Atonement*.

partly from his saving mission—both its divine initiative and its full identification with humanity. Hence it is impossible to understand the incarnation apart from atonement. Yet that is not the same as saying that the incarnation itself is atoning.

Recognizing the linkage between Christ's "person" and "work," modern theology has intently pondered the incarnation's necessity: Would the incarnation have occurred without the fall, or is it inherently redemptive? Traditional theologians have been leery of the minority view that the incarnation would have happened regardless of the fall. That minority view is speculative, risking movement behind God's revelatory history of redemption. Still, the question presses how the incarnation relates to God's self-revelation: If revelation is meaningfully personal, then could humans have come to know the *Triune* God in some other way than Jesus Christ? Did the divine fellowship with the first humans in the garden temple anticipate an ultimate happening of "God with us," even more directly in person? The traditional view rightly highlights explicit biblical statements indicating that God's Son became fully human in order to make atonement (e.g., Heb. 2:17–18). By contrast, the "incarnation anyway" view rightly highlights the Triune God's self-revelation happening through the incarnation. Depending on what atonement model(s) we adopt, as discussed below, the incarnation inaugurated "reconciliation" in the broad sense of God's triune self-communication, yet it did not accomplish "atonement" in some specific senses that awaited the cross.

*Reconciliation can speak broadly of all that God does in Christ to restore covenant fellowship with and among sinful humans. The incarnation initiated this ministry, thus enabling Christ's active obedience, his kingdom proclamation, his passion, his resurrection, and his ascension and outpouring of the Holy Spirit to work comprehensively for us and for our salvation. Indeed, this ministry of reconciliation addresses not just the sins and status of particular persons but also the state of humanity as a whole. Moreover, this ministry goes beyond reconciling humans to God and to one another, initiating the renewal of the entire cosmos.

Mission

The ecumenical creeds do not linger over the Son's earthly ministry. "For us and our salvation he came down from heaven" and became incarnate, they tell us; next they narrate his crucifixion. Today some criticize the Nicene Creed for focusing on the incarnation and the passion. The twofold risk of this focus is to neglect the larger story of Israel and to diminish the fullness of Jesus's humanity. Sometimes, admittedly, the church has failed to proclaim the kingdom of God as integral to Christ's reconciling ministry.

Nevertheless, the creedal focus remains appropriate. First, the creeds addressed the controversies of their contexts, and in so doing confronted perennial heresies. The incarnation raised the crucial issues of the Son's full divinity and humanity, while the passion brought the Christ narrative to its climax. The creeds never claimed to offer a comprehensive Christology as they established boundaries for Christian worship. Second, the creeds assume a liturgical context in which the public reading of Scripture incorporates the Old Testament and the Gospels.[7] Orthodox churches should regularly hear the Savior's proclamation of God's kingdom, in word and deed, within the context of Israel's Scriptures. Third, the Gospels themselves are often called "passion narratives with extended introductions," and thus the creeds reflect an emphasis from Scripture, in which the cross is the climax of the covenant, the "one righteous act" that brought life for all (Rom. 5:18).

Given the creedal focus, the church has developed other biblical concepts with which to proclaim the Son's earthly ministry. First, the drama of his mission involved two states: suffering and glory, humiliation and exaltation. Second, the Son's mission fulfilled three offices: prophet, priest, and king. Third, the Son's mission fulfilled Old Testament hopes that God would heal and liberate the oppressed.

Humiliation and Exaltation

The Incarnate One's earthly ministry involved the *status duplex, the two states of humiliation and exaltation. On the one hand, Christ exercises all his offices in both states. For instance, God's kingdom has been in our midst from the incarnation onward, not just from the resurrection onward; Jesus's prophetic preparation of his disciples intensified between his resurrection and ascension, not ending with his crucifixion; our Lord's priestly self-offering incorporates his exalted return to the Father and ongoing intercession for us, not just his crucifixion.

On the other hand, while the two states are not merely sequential, Christ's earthly ministry had narrative movement. A descent/ascent pattern commenced in the Son's birth, culminating in the resurrection and its aftermath (besides Phil. 2:5–11, see Eph. 4:8–10). Humility pervaded Jesus's earthly life—having no place to lay his head (Luke 9:58)—in solidarity with cursed humanity, culminating in sacrificial obedience upon the cross. Exaltation

---

7. As helpfully noted by S. Holmes, "Of a Troublesome Comma."

vindicated this humble completion of the earthly mission: although the Son remains incarnate in his heavenly session, his glory is no longer hidden, but now is shared.

Accordingly, the two states both surprise us and tell a story. They surprise us: the ironic reversals in John's Gospel reflect broader biblical patterns. Jesus's suffering reflected God's greatest glory, as he was "lifted up" in multiple senses.[8] They tell a story: these ironic reversals still compose a sequence—first suffering and unexpected glory (Luke 24:25–27), then ultimate glory with no more suffering.

Prophet, Priest, and King

In assuming full humanity, the Son of God fulfilled three primary offices in an ultimate way that previously were filled by many humans in partial ways. Christ's *munus triplex, or "threefold office," emerges from the anointing associated with prophets, priests, and kings in the Old Testament.[9] This framework not only emerges from Scripture and ties together the two Testaments; the threefold office also helps those who are "in Christ" to understand their identity. The church is the new community that bears witness to the work of the one Mediator: we are a royal priesthood that declares his praises (1 Pet. 2:9).

As "Messiah," God's Anointed One, Jesus addressed the fundamental needs of sinners in fulfilling all three of these offices:

> Among the Jews, anointing was the ceremony whereby prophets, priests, and kings were initiated into those offices. And if we look into ourselves, we shall find a want of Christ in all these respects. We are by nature at a distance from God, alienated from him, and incapable of a free access to him. Hence we want a Mediator, and Intercessor; in a word, a Christ in his priestly office. This regards our state with respect to God. And with respect to ourselves, we find a total darkness, blindness, ignorance of God and the things of God. Now here we want Christ in his prophetic office, to enlighten our minds, and teach us the

---

8. Karl Barth, in his daring *Church Dogmatics* volume IV, advocates a nonsequential account of the *status duplex*. Barth also generally champions the *history* of Jesus Christ. Yet such "actualism" actually requires maintaining sequential aspects of the two states; otherwise the dynamic "movement" that Barth prefers (to the "calm" of the classic doctrine; see *CD* IV.2, 105–10) gets lost. Without sequence being dialectically included, Barth's treatment of the entire history of Jesus Christ as one "act" can supplant the internal dynamism of the narrative with paradoxical abstraction about obedient divinity and exalted humanity.

9. Much of the following account is indebted to G. Wainwright, *For Our Salvation*. As a Methodist, Wainwright shows that the *munus triplex* predates the Reformed tradition (e.g., in Thomas Aquinas) and appears widely outside it (e.g., in John Wesley).

whole will of God. We find also within us a strange misrule of appetites and passions. For these we want Christ in his royal character, to reign in our hearts, and subdue all things to himself.[10]

The Holy Spirit is the gift of this anointing. Thanks to the Spirit, this threefold office fits "the church's liturgical experience of Christ as 'object of worship,' 'mediator in worship,' and 'pattern for worship.'"[11] Indeed, the Spirit not only anointed Christ in an ultimate sense; he also anoints us in a participatory sense, as we share in these ministries by being the body of Christ.

As prophet, Christ is the revelatory Mediator, representing God to humanity, addressing our ignorance. Primary passages signaling this truth include Isaiah 61:1–2, with Jesus unveiling its fulfillment in Luke 4:18; Hebrews 1:1–2, with the Son as the climactic divine speech in a long series of prophetic words; Matthew 17:5, with the beloved Son of Matthew 3:17 being gloriously transfigured; and John 4:25, with the Samaritan woman expecting the Messiah's clear teaching. The church received a prophetic ministry (Joel 2:28; Acts 2:17–21) from its encounter with the Messiah. Accordingly, "the messengers of Christ find themselves anticipated by the One who sends them, not in such a way as to render their mission unnecessary but rather to make it awaited."[12] Yet the church can overemphasize this prophetic office; when it does so, the focus on teaching leads toward moralism and/or rationalism.[13]

As priest, Jesus is the redemptive Mediator, representing humanity before God by offering himself as a once-for-all sacrifice, addressing our enmity. Primary passages signaling this truth include Psalm 110:4, with its appeal to Melchizedek typifying an eternal priesthood in Hebrews 5:6 and 7:15. Other texts in Hebrews, such as 4:14–16 and 7:28–8:2, address aspects of Christ's priestly ministry, as does John 1:29 by depicting Jesus as the Lamb of God. Baptism anoints believers into royal priesthood, with several texts such as Revelation 1:6; 1 Peter 2:5, 9–10; Hebrews 10:19–25; and 2 Corinthians 5:17–21 applying priestly concepts to the church's identity. The church mysteriously participates in Christ's suffering (Col. 1:24). The church's ministry is not redemptive like the once-for-all sacrifice of the Mediator, so overemphasizing this office leads toward pietism and/or mysticism—focusing too much on the church's spiritual sacrifices.

---

10. John Wesley relates the offices to our respective wants in this way, as quoted in G. Wainwright, *For Our Salvation*, 108, from Wesley's *Explanatory Notes on the New Testament*, regarding Matt. 1:16.

11. G. Wainwright, *For Our Salvation*, 118–19.

12. G. Wainwright, *For Our Salvation*, 132.

13. So G. Wainwright, *For Our Salvation*, 174–75, suggests from W. A. Visser 't Hooft, *The Kingship of Christ*, 17.

As king, Jesus Christ mediates divine rule as both God and man, addressing our bondage.[14] The Mediator initiates our priestly participation in God's
reign over the entire cosmos (e.g., Ps. 89:35–37; Eph. 1:22–23; Phil. 2:9–11).
Accordingly, overemphasizing this office leads the church toward utopianism
and/or apocalypticism, whereby Christians think that they must either passively wait for, or heroically usher in, the fullness of God's kingdom. Far from
being triumphalist, the Son's revelation of his glory in exercising these three
offices involved earthly suffering: no crown before or without the cross. The
cross brings freedom from sin and a paradoxical new form of "slavery" to
God through serving our neighbors—the true freedom of love.[15]

Broadly speaking, then, the prophetic office highlights that Christ is the
truth, eliciting faith. The priestly office highlights that Christ is our life, eliciting love. The kingly office highlights that Christ is the way, eliciting hope.[16]
Modern people may not be as familiar with prophets, priests, and kings, but
they still seek gurus, honor experts (even if doctors have replaced priests), and
find rulers and celebrities fascinating.[17] Jesus Christ exercises these offices in
both humiliation and exaltation. Prophet and priest continue to characterize
his ministry after the resurrection, as our ascended Lord. King already began
to characterize his ministry prior to the resurrection, as the personal bearer
of God's Spirit returning to the covenant people.

Healing and Liberation

Christ's kingship is unlike what people expect. Earthly kings lord it over
people, accumulating wealth and enjoying privileges at others' expense. Bureau-
cracies get preoccupied with status and systems rather than service. By contrast,
in proclaiming God's reign Jesus emphasized his lowly status as a slave, his
mission of service, and his ultimate self-sacrifice (Mark 10:35–45). Thus, the
Gospels narrate Jesus's ministry addressing the full range of human needs—
not just forgiveness, which traditional atonement theologies emphasize, but
also healing and liberation that will restore justice. *Justice, very much related
to *shalom*, is "the flourishing that results from the right ordering of power."[18]

14. For further reflection on royal priesthood, see Anizor and Voss, *Representing Christ*,
plus the more technical works that Anizor and Voss have authored.

15. G. Wainwright, *For Our Salvation*, 158–59, cites Luther, *Freedom of a Christian*, from
LW 31:344, in relation to 1 Cor. 9:19 and Rom. 13:8.

16. G. Wainwright suggests these correlations in *For Our Salvation*, 175–78.

17. G. Wainwright, *For Our Salvation*, 172.

18. Hoang and Johnson, *Justice Calling*, 40. This helpful book highlights the link between
justice and Sabbath, recognizing that our calling is to participate in God's loving promotion of
justice rather than expecting our own efforts to produce it.

*Healing—"restoration of wholeness (Ps. 41:3), making well whether physically, mentally, or spiritually"[19]—is integral to Jesus's mission, as announced from Isaiah 61:1–2: "The Spirit of the Lord is on me, because he has anointed me to proclaim good news to the poor. He has sent me to proclaim freedom for the prisoners and recovery of sight for the blind, to set the oppressed free, to proclaim the year of the Lord's favor" (Luke 4:18–19). When John the Baptist sent messengers from prison, asking if Jesus really was the one he hoped for, Jesus responded with more references to Isaiah. He told the messengers to report the healings and exorcisms they had seen (Luke 7:18–23), using the language of Isaiah 29:18–19 and 35:5–6 as well as 61:1–2. These healings meant preliminary liberation from death's power, signaling the ultimate liberation to come in the fullness of God's kingdom. Healing and salvation are intertwined, at least metaphorically: "By his wounds we are healed" (Isa. 53:5).

Jesus's mission charter from Isaiah 61 speaks of healing in the context of *liberation—release from bondage, restoration of justice and freedom—for prisoners and the oppressed. Such prophetic and thus poetic passages do not strictly identify these beneficiaries so much as celebrate widespread future hope. The announcement of Isaiah's fulfillment in Luke 4 is followed by an exorcism (4:31–37) and numerous healings (4:38–44). These forms of liberation are surrounded by others: healing and forgiving a paralyzed man (5:17–26), liberating him from sin and guilt; eating with tax collectors and sinners, liberating them from social rejection (5:27–32); and challenging expectations about fasting, liberating people from merely external religious restrictions (5:33–39). Jesus's coming liberated women from being utterly marginalized, establishing Mary and others as trustworthy witnesses to his liberating work (1:46–56; 24:1–12). Occasionally Jesus even liberated followers from physical threats, suggesting that someday he will reconcile human relationships not only with God and one another but even with the cosmos. Of course, Jesus did not lead a political revolution against the Romans, as some expected. Yet his followers shook up the entire world (Acts 17:6), precisely by challenging social and religious norms with God's grace in Christ.

Hence Christ's ministry of reconciliation addressed social sin and systemic evil as well as personal sin. A controversial recent approach highlights this broader ministry by appealing sociologically to "scapegoat" mechanisms.[20] On this account, Jesus endured being the scapegoat for the Jewish people's oppression at the hands of the Roman Empire. His endurance of this social

19. Chappell, "Heal, Healing."
20. See the work of René Girard; notably, *I See Satan Fall Like Lightning*.

mechanism exposed and subverted the entire system. Another approach highlights social liberation by focusing on race. On this account, Jesus endured a "lynching" like black people faced in the American South.[21] He faced mob violence that relied on the tacit support and overt misuse of government power. This mob violence substituted prejudice for truth in a frenzy of scapegoating. Christ's willingness to undergo such injustice reflects God's solidarity with the oppressed, who face constant vulnerability to oppression and have their sense of dignity diminished by pervasive fear in the face of such a system. These proposals may not account for the fullness of biblical material on atonement, as we will see, and they may not champion aspects of conciliar Christology, but they do highlight aspects of Jesus Christ's suffering that we easily neglect.

Christian traditions understand the current parameters for seeking physical healing and political liberation in various ways. They differ especially over the nature of the Holy Spirit's ministry and the inauguration of the last days. The biblical passages above, and others, emphasize Jesus's proclamation of God's kingdom—with his very presence, with powerful deeds, and with authoritative words. How and when his followers should expect to enjoy healing and liberation is naturally debatable in light of the ascension and the uncertain timing of the second advent of Christ. But it is undebatable that Christ proclaimed holistic good news, relating the forgiveness of sins and the reconciliation of relationships to the healing of bodies and the liberation of oppressed lives and marginal communities.

The Passion

The Son's earthly ministry involved being the faithful covenant partner that Israel was called to be on the world's behalf. His obedience, according to Philippians 2:8, reached its uttermost with death on the cross. Theologians call this cruciform obedience *passive obedience—not as if Christ was inactive, but because he lovingly chose to suffer (to be a "patient," to feel "passion") at human hands. Jesus's obedience throughout earthly life was *active obedience, because he submitted constantly to the Father's will, acting as our righteous representative. The "passive" obedience on the cross was the climax of this "active" obedience, for no one took Jesus's life from him; he laid it down of his own accord (John 10:18), willingly accepting the cup that the Father gave him to drink (Matt. 26:39).

---

21. Cone, *The Cross and the Lynching Tree.*

The ecumenical creeds tell the story of Christ's suffering, death, and burial on our behalf, without specifying a theory of what the passion accomplishes. No theory could exhaust the kaleidoscope of biblical images for atonement or the surplus of love God poured out. Gratefully telling the story of the cross and marveling at Christ's sacrifice "for us and for our salvation" are the fundamental tasks of atonement theology. Nevertheless, it is worth pondering whether the Bible prioritizes certain concepts; if so, they help us to embrace the very heart of the good news.

Atonement

Evangelicals have emphasized *sacrifice for our sins as the heart of Jesus's saving work. To what degree can a particular model explain the workings of this sacrifice? Modern evangelical models typically involve *substitution, most commonly *penal substitution—Jesus undergoing our penalty, God's wrath against sinners. To placate God's wrath in this active sense is *propitiation. A more passive concept of bearing away sin and its penalty is *expiation. Broadly speaking, *atonement means reconciliation—restoring peace between offended parties. That raises the question of who has been offended or become an enemy of the other: God, humans, or both? Additional atonement metaphors include *redemption, buying us back, and *ransom, freeing us from captivity under sin, Satan, or other hostile powers. The apparent paradox is that God handed us over to these enemies in response to our sin, yet God lovingly initiated our rescue. How then should we understand Christ's ministry of reconciliation?

HISTORICAL MODELS

A threefold typology of atonement models emerged early in the twentieth century from Gustaf Aulén (1879–1977). Aulén associated the early church with "classical" models involving victory, which he wanted to recover in a modern *Christus Victor* model. Through paying the devil, tricking the devil, or (for Aulén) defeating sin, death, and the devil in battle, God ransomed us from these hostile powers. According to Aulén, there was no classical emphasis upon God being offended by our sin.

On this account, "objective" models emphasizing *satisfaction of an offended God arose in the Middle Ages. Notably, Anselm compared God to a feudal lord whose honor we shamed. When Luther, Calvin, and other Protestants developed penal substitution models, they reflected the influence of Anselm's objective focus. Luther retained some of the classical emphasis upon victory, according to Aulén, while Calvin and other Protestants did not.

By contrast, "subjective" models involve moral influence upon humanity. From a century or so after Anselm, Peter Abelard (1079–1142) has often been associated with a subjective view: God reconciles people by overwhelming them with the extent and example of Christ's love. Whether or not that was Abelard's primary view, subjective models largely awaited the heretical Socinianism of the sixteenth and seventeenth centuries, which rejected a trinitarian view of God and the need for saving grace in Christ; subjective models then reappeared within modern theological liberalism. Some of these models, like Abelard's, emphasize the moral "influence" of God's love upon us; others emphasize the moral "example" of Christ's love for us to follow.

Other atonement models have maintained an "objective" element outside of humans and related to God, without treating Jesus Christ as the substitute for each forgiven sinner. Among others, early on Irenaeus emphasized recapitulation: Jesus reliving faithfully the human story that went wrong with Adam and Eve. More recently, the *governmental model of atonement associated with Hugo Grotius (1583–1645) has influenced Wesleyans in particular. On this account, rather than suffering the penalty for particular sinners, Christ died to set right the world's moral order—enabling God to forgive while remaining a just ruler who confronts sin.

CONTEMPORARY CONCERNS

Four concerns have become especially prominent within contemporary atonement theology. Their advocates often favor the rhetoric of "reconciliation" over "atonement" and criticize or reject the penal substitution model that has been prominent among evangelicals.

The first concern involves *biblical metaphors*. At minimum, penal substitution reflects one cluster among many biblical metaphors, yet its advocates usually treat it as the primary if not exclusive model. At maximum, penal substitution is unbiblical because it rests on misunderstanding sacrifice. According to some critics, sacrifice is an image or analogy, not a literal reality, regarding how God saves us. According to others, sacrifice does not actually involve self-giving or personal substitution; the various biblical sacrifices reflect a range of gift-giving, ritual, and relational practices, not a mechanism for addressing sin's legal consequences.

A second, related concern involves the Bible's *relational, rather than legal or contractual, emphasis*. On this account, penal substitutionary views filter biblical material through Western feudal or judicial concepts that were not part of the ancient Near Eastern or Greco-Roman contexts. Thus, the penal substitutionary model overemphasizes legal minutiae and diminishes the irrational abundance of God's love. As a result people still treat "faith" as a condition that they must fulfill, simply replacing "works" with a different human part of salvation's bargain.

A third concern involves *immoral consequences*. At minimum, some assert, a penal substitution model metaphorically depicts divine child abuse. Abraham's near-sacrifice of Isaac in Genesis 22, which would have been morally reprehensible according to God's law, becomes an unhealthy model of what God actually does in penal substitutionary atonement. At maximum, others allege, such a model promotes actual violence among believers—notably, by men against women—because it tacitly requires violence in order for God to save us. Jesus's self-sacrifice becomes a model of passive victimization that is easily and disproportionately imposed upon women.

A fourth concern over *popular misunderstandings* arises even among advocates of a penal substitution model. Prayers and gospel explanations often imply that God the Father is implacably angry whereas "gentle Jesus meek and mild" is a loving advocate for sinners. This picture has a trinitarian problem, losing the unity of God's external actions: the Father, Son, and Holy Spirit always participate together in our redemption. This picture also has a christological problem, losing the personal unity of Jesus Christ: he is our Mediator as both sacrifice and priest, both human and divine. This picture has further biblical problems, losing scriptural emphases: the Father lovingly initiated our salvation and the Son willingly embraced that mission. This picture finally has a pneumatological problem, marginalizing the Holy Spirit. However mysterious the crucifixion was, the Spirit's constant presence from the conception to the ascension indicates that the Son's passion was a united expression of the Triune God's holy love.

Biblical Holism

Given these important concerns, how should evangelicals speak of atonement today? Despite all the complexities, a careful account of penal substitution continues to claim a proper theological place alongside other scriptural atonement metaphors.[22] For evangelicals to make that claim requires integrating historical, biblical, ethical, and theological responses to the preceding concerns.

First, *historically*: Aulén's recovery of a "classical" approach is important but selective. He prompted many to retrieve a neglected part of the church's

---

22. For an evangelical version of some of the preceding concerns, see Baker and Green, *Recovering the Scandal of the Cross*. Some of the following comments reflect Henri Blocher's influence from various articles, such as "Atonement." See also Gathercole, *Defending Substitution*.

heritage. The classical emphasis upon victory connects well with non-Western contexts, where victory over hostile powers is a treasured biblical and pastoral theme. Historians have criticized Aulén's historical work, however. For instance, he read Luther as less "objective" than he probably was, and it is questionable whether the patristic focus on victory should be contrasted with an "objective" orientation. For example, the church fathers frequently cited Isaiah 53 when dealing with Christ's work, and that text involves punishment (e.g., vv. 4–6). Objective elements apparently coincided with or even explained the victory that the classical approach celebrated.

Second, *biblically*: Even a revised understanding of sacrifice must acknowledge that numerous passages contain "for us" or "on our behalf" logic. At least some passages contain the concept of punishment. It is true that the Bible's metaphors for atonement deal with more than just sin, and its treatments of sin deal with more than just guilt. It is also true that the cross's necessity stemmed from God's freely willed love. Yet the Bible takes pains to portray God as both being righteous and lovingly justifying believers in Jesus apart from their works—with Christ's sacrifice making such forgiveness possible (Rom. 3:25–26).

Third, *ethically*: All theological models require distinguishing genuine versions from popular misunderstandings and then graciously but firmly addressing pastoral dangers. If someone presents penal substitution as implying divine child abuse, then that version is inaccurate, heretically nontrinitarian, and unethical. God the Father did not ultimately sacrifice God the Son because our Lord did not "die" in his divine nature. As for the separation of body and soul by virtue of his human nature, this death highlights the usual mysteries of God's providence in relation to evil: it was willed by Father, Son, and Holy Spirit in eternal communion. But it was also sinfully willed by Roman and Jewish leaders, as well as crowds that simply represented the hatred that all humans have shown toward God's surprising love. Furthermore, this death was heroically willed by Jesus Christ in his human nature, as he accepted the cup of martyrdom once there was no way to fulfill his loving mission apart from the cross.

At the same time, Jesus's martyrdom is *not* a model for everyone in every situation. No other human self-sacrifice contributes to the redemption that Christ's sacrifice accomplished once for all (see Hebrews, especially 9:26–28). Scripture highlights the incredible, unique value of Jesus's sacrifice (1 Pet. 1:18–19), calling for grateful obedience to God on that basis (1 Cor. 6:19–20). When highlighting Jesus's sacrifice as an example, Scripture limits its exhortations to ensuring that suffering involves good rather than evil, to responding nonviolently, and to entrusting oneself to God (1 Pet. 2:20–23). Scripture is clear that *his* wounds, and no others, heal us (1 Pet. 2:24). The dangers of misapplying Christ's example to slaves, women, and other marginalized groups are real. First Peter does not call for immediate revolution against the unjust system of slavery, which was so entrenched in the Roman Empire that any such revolution would have quickly failed. When the text carefully encourages submission, God is clearly identified as the true Master (1 Pet. 2:18–19). In the long run, this truth would encourage slaves that properly following Jesus's example promised eventual justice and eternal reward. Jesus's ministry of reconciliation would not preclude gaining freedom but could authorize it (1 Cor. 7:21–24).

Fourth, then, *theologically*: The need for faithfully trinitarian presentations of penal substitution should now be obvious. God the Father lovingly sent the Son to redeem us. The Son lovingly embraced this mission as not just a human sacrifice but also the divine Mediator. Rather than the Father being an angry judge while Jesus stands on our side, God lovingly left the judicial bench to take our place. In the loving bond of the Holy Spirit, the Father and the Son undertook this mission together, even if the Son undertook unique forms of suffering by virtue of his humanity. All three persons of the Triune God are loving and holy alike. No human violence serves a redemptive purpose. Rightly viewed, the story of the cross does not even involve divine violence. Instead, God willed to overcome human violence by bringing good out of the evil for which we are responsible.

Fifth, *relationally*: In light of this trinitarian theology, penal substitution belongs in a properly covenantal perspective. On the one hand, some biblical metaphors appear so frequently that they become concepts—stable habits for thinking and speaking. Of the five most significant biblical atonement metaphors, sacrifice is particularly prominent. At least sometimes it seems impossible to understand sacrifice in nonsubstitutionary terms. Accordingly, penal substitution is a biblical model, even an important one. Substitution is more than just an image; the reality behind various biblical images is that God satisfies justice by substituting for us.[23]

On the other hand, it is important to keep the penal substitution model in its proper place. For starters, penal substitution is more specific than the broader reality of substitution. Penal substitution should not minimize the significance of other metaphors and complementary models. The God-man substituted for more than just our penalty. God won the victory over hostile powers that took advantage of our sin, and God transforms us so that we may follow the example of Christ's love. There is also danger of understanding

23. Stott, *The Cross of Christ*, esp. chap. 6.

penal substitution too contractually. God's reconciling love pours out in abundance that we could never imagine, overwhelming any human category or model. The point of penal substitution is not to focus on legal categories, but rather to acknowledge the biblical claim that God reestablishes relationship with us justly. Humans constantly use legal categories to serve the real priority: relationships. Marriage is a notable analogy, especially since our reconciliation to God happens through union with Christ. Hence penal substitution is a biblical atonement model because God relates to us in a *covenant* like marriage, not because any human could fulfill the conditions of a contract with God.

Descent into Hell

Christ's descent into hell underscores the amazing extent of God's covenant love. At its earthly climax, the incarnation led to the cross. Resurrection and ascension followed, indicating that the incarnation continues forever. In between, the Apostles' Creed narrates an additional phase of the Son's earthly career: descent into hell. Some evangelical thinkers reject the phrase, pointing to complexities in key biblical passages. In particular, sometimes the referent is "Hades," involving the realm of the dead, not "hell" anticipating final judgment. A crucial passage, 1 Peter 3:18–22, probably concerns Christ's proclamation of victory over all hostile spirits during the ascension, not preaching the gospel in hell.[24]

Such biblical complexities, however, do not call for rejecting the creedal phrase. Instead, per the Protestant Reformers, its location is the key: at the extreme point of Christ's humiliation unto death, prior to the resurrection and exaltation. The *descent into hell underscores the Son's full identification with sinful humanity's plight—even, mysteriously, suffering our alienation from God. This descent completes the humble obedience that began in the manger. Its dogmatic function is captured by Romans 8:38–39: "neither death nor life, neither angels nor demons, neither the present nor the future, nor any powers, neither height nor depth, nor anything else in all creation, will be able to separate us from the love of God that is in Christ Jesus our Lord."

Exaltation

The incarnation endures forever as the Son retains full, now glorified, humanity. When he returned to divine glory after descending into hell, he ascended as the God-man. In union with him the church begins to enjoy God's fellowship

---

24. The classic study remains Dalton, *Christ's Proclamation to the Spirits.*

on earth. We prayerfully depend on his intercession, we obediently listen to his Word, and we celebrate his presence at the Lord's Supper as we anticipate the complete restoration of God's reign over creation.

The *transfiguration anticipated this exaltation, the revelation of Christ's glory to and through his disciples.[25] In all three Synoptic Gospels the transfiguration follows Peter's confession of Christ's identity and Jesus's prediction of his passion. Immediately beforehand, Jesus told the disciples that they would not taste death until they saw God's kingdom. Like Moses, they received a tiny glimpse of the divine glory in the radiance of Christ's face and clothes; they also received notice that, like Elijah, Jesus would not ascend to God's presence via normal earthly death. The transfiguration further signaled the essence of the church's discipleship: bearing witness. Certain disciples were called to ascend the mountain, and they did as they were told; they glimpsed Christ's glory with fear and misunderstanding; after the resurrection they began to understand, did as they were told, and told what they saw. Their testimony gives the rest of us our only access to this event of divine revelation.

Therefore the resurrection and ascension, not just the passion, are crucial events for our salvation. They vindicate Jesus's covenant obedience and representation in his passion. They actualize God's victory over sin, death, and the devil. They initiate Christ's heavenly lordship over the church, his earthly outpouring of the Holy Spirit, and his sending of witnesses throughout the world.

Resurrection

It is easy to fall into the idea that if the cross is God's central act of atonement, then it is the exclusive event of our salvation. Yet Romans 4:25 indicates otherwise: Christ "was delivered over to death for our sins and was raised to life for our justification." The vindication and application of his atoning work unfold in the resurrection. While the cross spares sinners from death, the resurrection actually rescues them, inaugurating abundant life in the Holy Spirit. We participate in the life of the risen Christ by virtue of the same powerful Spirit who raised him from the dead. For the new humanity, to live is Christ (Phil. 1:21): union with him now defines us.

*Resurrection did not simply mean "life after death" in Jesus's context. It meant dead people returning to new bodily life, a strange possibility about which ancient people were no more gullible than modern people. Daniel 12 and possibly a few other Old Testament texts began to hint at the possibility.

---

25. For helpful comments on the transfiguration, albeit with a hermeneutical focus, see Vanhoozer, "Ascending the Mountain."

These hints were consistent with belief in YHWH as Creator and Judge of a good cosmos. The Pharisees, devoted to the Torah, embraced belief in resurrection, while the Sadducees, perhaps more devoted to their aristocratic position, did not. In Jesus's context, resurrection was a disputed and unclear possibility. The disciples did not understand Jesus's prediction of his crucifixion or promise of his resurrection. They became convinced of his resurrection only once they encountered two realities: the empty tomb and tangible appearances of the risen Christ (e.g., John 20; 1 Cor. 15:4–8). Downtrodden disciples quickly turning the world upside down adds historical support for the Lord's bodily resurrection. What else explains their sudden communal courage?

Jesus's resurrection was the initial fulfillment of Israel's resurrection as anticipated in Ezekiel's vision of the dry bones (Ezek. 37). Jesus's resurrection clarified that resurrection would be a personal and not just communal reality, and that human "immortality" would not leave us disembodied. Resurrection would involve a historical event, "bringing to birth God's future world in advance of its full appearing."[26] Given its anticipation of cosmic redemption (Rom. 8:18–25), "resurrection itself challenges the very split between faith and reality that has been endemic in post-Enlightenment worldviews, including those of much Western Christianity." Resurrection means "life after 'life after death,'" as we usually think of it, in which the present human body will be transformed into "a new type of physicality, incapable of corruption" and on that basis immortal. Such is Paul's teaching in 1 Corinthians 15.

Therefore, the resurrection goes beyond demonstrating God's approval of Christ's atoning work and the gospel's credibility. It initiates Christ's triumphant, bodily ascent to enjoy the glory of God's kingdom—and our ascent with him. If Christ has not been raised as the firstfruits of our resurrection, then Christian faith is futile and we remain in sin (1 Cor. 15:17–20). Since Christ has been raised, God has given us victory in him and our labor is not in vain (1 Cor. 15:54–58). In the meantime, another way in which Jesus's resurrection is essential to our salvation involves the Holy Spirit, whom the living Christ poured out upon his people. The Spirit abides with us in Christ's bodily absence and empowers us to live as Christ's body in the world. It is important to remember that the risen Lord, in his glorified body, spent forty days on earth after his resurrection and before his ascension—preparing his followers to live as his body in the powerful presence of his Spirit.

---

26. These paragraphs are largely summaries of a summary, from which the quotations are taken: N. T. Wright, "Resurrection of the Dead." This article distills key aspects of Wright's massive *The Resurrection of the Son of God*.

Ascension

In the *ascension Jesus visibly—even liturgically—marked the end of his earthly descent and announced his future return. Upon his resurrection, he began this ascending trajectory of his divinely vindicated mission—what we often mean by his *exaltation. The Triune God was so committed to the incarnation that by the Spirit the Father restored the Son to embodied, albeit glorified, human life. Since the Son is eternally glorious, the new element of exaltation involved his identity as the God-man. For *Jesus* to share in the name above every name (Phil. 2:9) exalted a human life to initiate our promised participation in God's reign. Now the Son of Man anticipated in Daniel 7 has received authority in God the Father's presence, inaugurating everlasting dominion in which the church will participate.[27]

The ascension began Christ's heavenly *session, ruling over his regathered form of Israel called "church," thereby advancing his earthly reign. As a royal priesthood, the church experiences his presence and absence dialectically. Remaining incarnate, the Son is physically absent from earth; indeed, the church does not know where "heaven" is. God apparently has delayed Christ's return in order to magnify opportunities for unbelievers' repentance and believers' sanctification (2 Pet. 3:9–15). When the church fails to acknowledge Jesus's absence adequately, it becomes too triumphant about being an earthly mediator. God has poured out a new form of Christ's presence through the Holy Spirit, who offers a guarantee of our salvation yet thereby teaches us to wait for its fullness (Eph. 1:13–14). This new form of God's presence is less tangible—apart from the Lord's Supper—but more universally immediate and intimate. The Spirit can make the risen Christ present to anyone, whereas if the Son remained on earth, that form of presence would be locally limited.

The ascension actively reiterated God's approval of the Son's reconciling mission. A new phase can unfold: a heavenly presentation of Christ's once-for-all sacrifice, a ministry of intercession on behalf of his people. Now they draw near boldly, confident of God's welcome, in Jesus's name. When the church fails to acknowledge adequately Jesus's human presence with God the Father, it fears the Son as if he were too divine to be of earthly, saving good. Then the church threatens to displace the one Mediator between God and humanity with additional intermediaries—Mary, the saints, and the like. Since Christ already presents a faithful covenant response in heaven, though, believers can confidently approach God in him. After his second advent, when all things will finally be under his feet (Heb. 2:8) so that God will be all in

---

27. Influential here is Farrow, *Ascension and Ecclesia*.

all (1 Cor. 15:26–28), then we will enjoy full communion face-to-face (1 Cor. 13:12) as we see the marks of God's wounds for us in Jesus.

Conclusion—and Beginning

The incarnation invites followers of Jesus to share in costly love as forgiven sinners. Given Christ's identification with all humanity, God loves without any partiality based on sex or gender, race or ethnicity, wealth or status, abilities or challenges. Imitating the love we encounter in Jesus Christ, the church bears witness to God's redemptive self-revelation. Reconciliation with God calls us to be reconciled with fellow humans and the entire creation.

Thus we hear a call to find new life in following the Incarnate One. The New Testament does not reduce "incarnation" to a principle of philosophy or piety or even, more fashionably these days, a church practice of emphasizing embodiment, contextualization, and vulnerability.[28] The incarnation is a singular and enduring, revelatory and redemptive, event: God coming to dwell with us. Strictly speaking, there can be no parallel, least of all in the failed humanity from which the Incarnate One came to rescue us. Far too often in Christendom "Christ" became identified with a prized principle of a dominant culture, while more recently "incarnation" has generated a broad principle of inclusion. The incarnation surely has implications for how the church should live. Yet the incarnation is the event of God becoming a Jewish man in Jesus, to fulfill Israel's covenant history and thereby redeem a lost world. Since the Creator redemptively embraced all humanity in a particular person, sexism, racism, classism, and the like should have no place—to the church's frequent shame.[29] God lovingly addresses all persons in their created particularity, while addressing redemption as a universal need. The incarnation offers no general hope rooted in the histories or loves of earthly cultures, revealing instead that they need divine reconciliation.

Extraordinarily, though, the humiliation-exaltation pattern of the incarnation both welcomes and obligates those who would be rescued: "have the same mindset as Christ Jesus" (Phil. 2:5)—namely, "in humility value others above yourselves, not looking to your own interests but each of you to the interests of the others" (Phil. 2:3–4). In light of God highly exalting this Incarnate One,

---

28. On this concern, see Billings, *Union with Christ.*

29. Recall the previous discussion in chap. 7, including the correlation between European development of "race" as a concept and more "gnostic" notions of "Christ" supplanting Jesus's Jewishness. Further illustrating the doctrinal challenges of addressing the incarnation's social implications is Mouw and Sweeney, *The Suffering and Victorious Christ.*

"continue to work out your salvation with fear and trembling, for it is God who works in you" (Phil. 2:12–13), and he "will carry it on to completion until the day of Christ Jesus" (Phil. 1:6). "Jesus Christ is the same yesterday and today and forever" (Heb. 13:8). The conclusion of Jesus's earthly story is a new beginning—the beginning of a new humanity in the church, which extends what Jesus began to do and to teach through time and space in its apostolic ministry on earth (see Acts 1). The Son whom the Father sent now sends the Spirit, sending his people into the world. The application of Christ's reconciling work, to unite rescued sinners in a redeemed humanity, is the subject of our next chapter, on sin and salvation.

—— *10* ——

Sin and Salvation

THESIS

All of Adam and Eve's descendants are born dead in sin, which is rooted in idolatry and inevitably results in injustice. The Spirit's application of Jesus's reconciling work brings salvation from sin's past, present, and future effects; justification removes sin's penalty, regeneration removes sin's power, and glorification removes sin's presence from those who are united with Christ.

LEARNING OBJECTIVES

After learning the material in this chapter, you should be able to:

1. *Define briefly* the key terms introduced here (marked with an asterisk and included in the glossary).
2. *List and recognize* the following: (a) seven deadly sins; (b) views of original sin.
3. *Describe and compare* elements within and views of the order of salvation.
4. *Identify and illustrate* key aspects of the biblical doctrine of sin.
5. *Explain* the following: (a) the distinction between Protestant and Catholic views of justification by faith; (b) the holistic nature of the *ordo salutis*.

The Son's ministry of reconciliation ultimately renews all of creation. At its heart, though, is the redemption of human beings, for our brokenness occasioned the cosmic curse. The doctrines of sin and salvation address the world as it is from Genesis 3 onward. In Genesis 4, 6, 11, and beyond, sin fractures communion with God, community among humans, and cosmic *shalom*. Sin is a very personal, but also public and not merely private, matter. Yet salvation heals sinners' past, present, and future—removing sin's penalty, its power, and eventually its presence.

Sin

It is important to give proper attention to *hamartiology, the doctrine of sin (from the Greek *hamartia*, "missing the mark")—no more and no less. Without understanding sin's nature and depth, we do not fully appreciate salvation. Yet focusing too much on sin obscures the gospel, either overwhelming us with guilt and despair or leaving us obsessed with self-improvement. Christ has triumphed over sin and its consequences, exposing evil's parasitical nothingness. Contemporary culture, however, does not know what to think about sin; modernity has tried to maximize human goodness by minimizing this category. But after countless wars, genocide, terrorist strikes, and school shootings, tides of suspicion from Marx, Nietzsche, and Freud—frequently labeled "postmodernism"—have overwhelmed us. People feel hopeless about overcoming certain weaknesses. Small "sins" are mocked, while large "evils" are bureaucratically prevented—if possible. This cultural situation highlights the problems of thinking about sin apart from the biblical gospel.

Biblical Emphases

As the initial human fall displays, sin involves doubting and disobeying God's Word, which inevitably harms other humans and the rest of creation. Eve and Adam took "knowledge of good and evil" into their own hands—that is, they sought moral responsibility and creaturely delight apart from God. God exiled them from the garden temple, graciously preventing them from living forever with their deadly declaration of independence. They could reenter God's presence only by means of grace that addressed divine judgment: elements at the end of Genesis 3 anticipated Israel's tabernacle with its sacrifices. Sin is first and foremost the self-centered pursuit of autonomy from God.

Yet this Godward dimension is not sin's only feature. Genesis 4 immediately follows with the first murder: Cain enviously slew his brother Abel. He instantly feared both isolation and predation from others. By Genesis 6 the earth was so full of violence that God brought the drastic judgment of the flood. At Babel (Gen. 11) God rejected the idolatry of human politics: to stop the tower builders from self-destruction, God confused languages and dispersed people across the earth. The idolatrous pursuit of autonomy fractures community.

God graciously initiated redemption by making a covenant with a particular group of people: Israel's history with God dramatizes humanity's rebellion. So Deuteronomy opposes apostasy, God's covenant people falling into fundamental idolatry.[1] Judges cycles through covenant violation: the people commit apostasy; they become subject to foreign powers; they cry out amid such judgment; God delivers them through flawed leaders; repeat—since "everyone did as they saw fit" (Judg. 21:25). Eventually Israel asks for a king, rejecting God's kingship while unknowingly anticipating their Redeemer. As the king goes, so go the people: Saul, with everything in his favor, disobeys the divine Word and is rejected; David, initially obscure, treasures the divine Word and flourishes until he becomes complacent; Solomon, beginning with promise by asking for wisdom, soon turns that "wisdom" toward worldly apostasy.

Within this covenant history, two penitential Psalms, 32 and 51, offer lasting models for confession. Likewise associated with the monarchy, Wisdom literature fleshes out sin's relation to creation's design: sin is folly, refusing to align with the natural and social orders through which God restrains chaos. Sin damages relationships not only with God and among persons but also with the rest of creation. The prophets do not excuse the idolatry and violence of surrounding nations, but they confront the self-serving religion of God's own people, even (in Jonah's case) the refusal to share God's mercy with others. Israel's apostasy brings exile, representing the rebellion of all humanity while exposing the linkage between idolatry, insincere worship, and social injustice. The prophets also confront individuals and not just people groups (Ezek. 18:20).

The New Testament continues to address sin in terms of idolatrous enmity toward God and injustice toward neighbors. The link between selfish desire and violence is evident throughout James, which reflects both wisdom and prophetic backgrounds. Catalogs of vices express internal character in patterns of external action (e.g., 1 Cor. 6:9–10; Gal. 5:19–21), actions that violate God's law (1 John 3:4). Within these catalogs, as well as depictions of the "last days" (e.g., 2 Tim. 3:1–9), injustice and immorality emerge from underlying idolatry. Romans 1:18–32 fits this pattern writ large. The vice catalogs make a "lesser to greater" argument: if even pagans oppose certain sins in principle, how much more should God's people avoid them in practice? Judgment begins with God's household (1 Pet. 4:17), and those who do not abide in Christ even risk apostasy as their love runs cold. Love for God and neighbor is the heart of God's law (Matt. 22:37–40); correspondingly, sin is rooted in idolatrous self-love and results in unjust treatment of others.

1. D. Smith, *With Willful Intent*, informs this brief biblical theology of sin. For helpful comments on the pairing of idolatry and injustice, see González, *Gospel of Faith*, esp. 23–27.

Theological Implications

As a rejection of the Creator's goodness, sin is difficult to explain. The Bible does not provide technical definitions but instead depicts sin with an array of images and stories, set within the larger history of redemption.[2] Nevertheless, this biblical material has some theological implications.

SIN'S DEFINITION

Sin breaks relationship with God through unbelief and idolatry. Pagan gods have always represented punishments to fear and possibilities to manipulate; idols of whatever kind still appeal to self-promotion or self-protection. Unlike false gods, the Triune God simultaneously claims our entire lives and offers genuine freedom. God's Word tells people what is good, inviting communion with God.

Therefore, *sin is "any act—any thought, desire, emotion, word, or deed—or its particular absence, that displeases God and deserves blame"; breaking relationship with God, sin disturbs *shalom*, creation's harmony.[3] Sin must not be confused with error or finitude: humans are not divine, and the limitations of embodied creatures in time and space are gifts that foster dependence upon God. Sin is both objective and subjective, even if some sins are primarily one or the other.[4] Sin breaks divine law and expresses broken relationship; in that sense all sins are equally heinous. Yet sins involve degrees, at least in terms of intentional rebellion against God and consequences for neighbors.[5] For instance, while inner hatred and verbal violence rebel against God just like actual murder, they obviously do not harm neighbors in the same way. In confronting hateful impulses or words (Matt. 5:21–26), Jesus does not suggest that the person who commits them may as well go ahead with murder.

SIN'S DYNAMICS

Broken relationships with God and others include both attack and flight.[6] Accordingly, theologians now debate sin's root: pride, which tended to be the classical emphasis, or despair. Confronting pride reflects the patriarchal

---

2. See especially C. Plantinga, *Not the Way*, 5.

3. C. Plantinga, *Not the Way*, 13.

4. C. Plantinga, *Not the Way*, 20–21.

5. See further Packer, "All Sins Are Not Equal," 65. Among additional issues: the extent to which sinners know better; the entity who is offended; the extent to which action is deliberately against conscience; the circumstances of time and place; and the unforgivable sin.

6. On forms of flight, see C. Plantinga, *Not the Way*, 153–57, 173–97. See also Volf, *Exclusion and Embrace*.

world in which classic doctrine emerged: the men who blamed pride knew well the prospects of shaking fists at God while succeeding in the world. Simply treating pride as sin's root, though, may neglect the struggle of many women and other marginalized persons with despairing self-appraisals.[7] The interconnected nature of sin's roots is evidenced by the "seven deadly sins," and it is better to focus on unbelief and idolatry rather than pride as such. In the end, sin displaces God and God's Word with the self—whether overrated or undervalued—and the world, to the inevitable distress of others. Rooting sin in self-preoccupation should not damage marginalized persons if human beings find true life in loving communion with the Triune God.

Sin involves both responsible persons and involuntary acts. Sinful dispositions can be inherited, and certain sins can become almost inevitable; persons remain responsible, though, for how they acquire or enhance dispositions behind sinful acts.[8] Beyond a special form of brokenness, addiction dramatizes sin's dynamics: desire or distress gets someone to indulge; the tolerance level slowly increases; efforts at self-management eventually fail; shame intensifies the addiction, which damages relationships. Apart from radical intervention, these situations end tragically, yet addicts are still culpable even when acts become virtually involuntary.[9]

Hence sin generates not just addictive behavior but also, unfortunately, horrendous evils. Sin's idolatrous roots explain what other societal categories cannot fully grasp: humans become what they worship.[10] Worship expresses and reinforces absolute and actual loyalties: "To worship is actively to orient and order one's life, whether more or less explicitly, around a reality as primary to and constitutive of meaning, worth, truth and value."[11] Worshiping the wrong "god" reinforces self-projection, being—in classic terms—curved in upon ourselves.[12] We are made for communion with the Triune God that flows into joy with others. Horrendous evils arise when warped self-obsession becomes pathologically harmful, overwhelming moral and social boundaries. These pathologies may even manifest themselves in warped notions of serving

7. Note, e.g., Moltmann-Wendel, *Women around Jesus*, 72: "The 'sin' of women is not pride, but persistence." The issue was raised earlier in a poignant, although conceptually freighted, way by Goldstein, "The Human Situation." The basic worry concerns Augustine's influential claim that pride is the beginning of all sin (*City of God* 12.6 [NPNF¹ 2:229]).

8. C. Plantinga, *Not the Way*, 23.

9. C. Plantinga, *Not the Way*, esp. 131–37, 145–48.

10. Beale, *We Become What We Worship*.

11. McFadyen, *Bound to Sin*, 227. This paragraph summarizes implications of McFadyen's larger account, which expounds Christian doctrine by exploring concrete psychological pathologies such as child abuse and the Holocaust.

12. See Jenson, *Gravity of Sin*.

others through changing society or making history—which can still be a way of worshiping oneself rather than joyfully communing with the Triune God.

SEVEN DEADLY SINS

Sin goes beyond inward rebellion and broken relationships, into narrative contexts and cultural effects. Beyond individual acts of will—"sins"—people accumulate sinful patterns; institutions aggregate evil powers and reinforce wicked practices. Since *love* for God and neighbor lies at the heart of the law, sin frequently goes beyond breaking a behavioral command. For instance, what counts as not forsaking the assembly of believers (Heb. 10:24–25)? Is it simply attending every Sunday service? When considering whether skipping church to attend a football game would be sinful, the context of a single Sunday or an entire season makes a difference. Humans understand their character within narratives: ascribing actions to themselves, recognizing patterns of action, and fitting events into those patterns. Such narrative self-interpretation affects how we identify whether particular acts would count as obedience or disobedience, fostering virtue or vice.

Sinful desire responds to three classic tempters: the world, the flesh, and the devil. All three tempters involve God's originally good creation. (1) The "world" designates both the totality of God's creation and more specifically human cultures. Rather than loving the world as a way of loving God, though, sinners love creaturely things for their own sake and embrace cultural interests that oppose God. (2) Embodiment in "flesh" is an essential feature of natural humanity. Yet sinners are wrongly obsessed with material things: resentful of bodily limitations, enslaved to physical appetites, and fearful of earthly death as an absolute end. (3) Apparently some kind of spirit, the "devil" is not a rival on equal footing with God. His rebellion is doomed; he simply wants to take other creatures down with him. He deceives sinners into misusing God-given freedom to oppose the purpose of created things—replacing grateful delight in the Creator's gifts with unhealthy, unjust selfishness.

The so-called *seven deadly sins detail how the devil uses "the lust of the flesh, the lust of the eyes, and the pride of life" (1 John 2:16) for tempting people to love the world rather than God. More precisely, the "deadly sins" are capital vices: "capital" because they are chief or primary, and "vices" because they are internal dispositions from which sinful acts arise. The Christian tradition varies slightly in naming the capital vices, but the following have become fairly standard: lust (warped desire, especially regarding sex); gluttony (excessive preoccupation with food and drink); avarice (greed, which is equated with idolatry in Col. 3:5); sloth (which is not simply laziness, but despair over the difficulty of spiritual transformation); wrath (unrighteous anger, expressed in verbal as well as physical violence); envy (which is not simply jealousy in wanting what someone else has, but hatefully wanting them not to have it); and pride and vainglory (with pride perhaps being more inwardly oriented, vainglory more outwardly oriented toward status).[13]

SIN'S STRUCTURAL DIMENSIONS

After the fall, sin emerges from disordered desire, but desire becomes disordered within relational contexts. Systemic sin and *structural evil name these relational dimensions: the ways in which sin aggregates in social groups, and the ways in which societal institutions oppress particular persons or foster communal evils. Cultural contexts do not fatalistically determine individual responses, but they influence personal agency. Corporate solidarity and communal responsibility are prominent in the Old Testament—for example, when Achan's sin affected first Israel and then his own family (Josh. 7). The prophets and the New Testament may intensify personal responsibility, but they do not deny communal solidarity.

When dealing with society, the language of "evil" may transcend sin in the usual sense. For some wrongs, no person or group can be held directly responsible, even if particular people remain responsible for contributing to social dynamics. Giving more definition to systemic sin or structural evil are "principalities and powers" (Eph. 6:12). These authorities may transcend the angelic or demonic regimes of the spiritual realm, incorporating cultural institutions. Their societal effects accumulate not only beyond particular persons but also across time and place. Hence the preceding efforts to understand sin highlight the complex, personal and social and spiritual, nature of human responsibility—complexity that unfolds further in the doctrine of original sin.

Original Sin

Original sin, people quip, is the only Christian doctrine that can be verified empirically. Despite constant evidence of human wickedness, though, modern people continue to champion optimistic anthropologies. Correspondingly, they reject traditional accounts of original sin that have everyone sharing ancestral guilt and moral bondage.[14] These aspects of *original sin are distinct

---

13. For a brief overview specifically related to Proverbs, see Treier, *Proverbs and Ecclesiastes*, 82–101. See further R. DeYoung, *Glittering Vices*.

14. See further Jacobs, *Original Sin*.

but related: our relationship to the original guilt of Adam and Eve, and the relation between their sin and our moral bondage.

ORIGINAL GUILT

The earliest Christian theology after the New Testament emphasized virtue and vice and may not have taught original guilt: instead, its focus was Christ's medicine healing God's image-bearers. Soon enough, political developments generated concerns over moral laziness. Under persecution, some believers—even priests—fell away to avoid martyrdom. Then, under "Christendom," nearly all citizens were being baptized. In this context the ascetic Pelagius (c. 360–418) urged people to redouble their moral effort. The exact nature of Pelagius's own teaching remains disputed because most of our access depends upon his chief opponent Augustine. *Pelagianism stressed that by virtue of creation, apart from redeeming grace, humans can freely choose to obey God's commands rather than sinning.[15] Regarding original sin, the enduring crux concerns whether humans freely *imitate* Adam's sin (the Pelagian view) or have Adam's sin somehow *imputed* to them (the Augustinian view).

Pelagianism viewed grace as a general, creational category, not a redemptive necessity. While Orthodoxy in the East never opposed Pelagianism as decisively as Augustine in the Catholic West, Pelagius was condemned at the Council of Carthage (418) and again at the Council of Ephesus (431). Then the Second Council of Orange (529) opposed what was later termed Semi-Pelagianism in the West: the view that initial faith is a free human act, only later increased (rather than previently enabled) by divine grace.

Biblically, the debate centers on Romans 5:12–21, in which most evangelicals find support for a broadly Augustinian position. First, Romans 5:14 speaks of guilt for some who did not sin after Adam's likeness. Second, there is repeatedly a fairly tight link between Adam and Christ: people are not saved by imitating Christ, which suggests that the passage does not relate sinners to Adam merely as imitators. Third, the passage repeatedly links one person's disobedience and the many being made sinners. The exact nature of these two links—between Adam and Christ, and between each one and the many they affect—remains debated. But their existence indicates a stronger connection with Adam than mere imitation: somehow all of us are guilty before God by virtue of Adam's disobedience. Accordingly, orthodox Christians acknowledge the necessity of redeeming grace for any human righteousness.

---

15. The more positive appraisal of Pelagius among recent historians is represented briefly by Yates, "Pelagius, Pelagianism."

THE BONDAGE OF THE WILL

Regarding the nature of original guilt and the resulting bondage of our wills, though, "Augustinian" approaches vary. Does guilt arise solely through sinful acts of our own volition, or does everyone share in Adam's guilt by somehow sharing in Adam's act? A threefold rubric helps with detailing the alternatives: Sin affects a person's *status*, or standing before God; the related *actus*, or the particular act that counts for a person's status; and a person's *habitus*, or the internal disposition behind particular acts.

The oldest Augustinian position has shaped the *Roman Catholic* tradition. On the Catholic account (notwithstanding its internal variety), all humans are guilty in principle because they share in Adam's sinful act. Augustine himself related this participation to sexual propagation,[16] but Catholic teaching affirms that we became implicated in Adam's act regardless of the precise mechanism. Yet this universal participation in the original human sin was mitigated by Christendom: nearly every infant was baptized, and at baptism the share in Adam's act is removed. With Adam's *actus* removed, a person's *status* is restored to graced innocence. Some corruption lingers in the *habitus*, so that freely willed righteousness remains impossible. This remaining corruption, *concupiscence, does not make a person guilty, though. *Baptismal regeneration renews the will to begin cooperating with grace, especially through the sacraments. A baptized child eventually undergoes *confirmation, personally affirming faith and then partaking of the Mass and other sacraments as appropriate. Since concupiscence brings no guilt, Catholicism rejects Martin Luther's claim that baptized humans are *simul iustus et peccator*—simultaneously justified before God yet still sinful. Catholicism holds that baptized humans are not guilty of sin until they express concupiscence by willing a sinful act.

The *Lutheran* tradition moderately reforms the Catholic approach. Adam's *actus* belongs to each human, and therefore his guilty *status* does too, until its removal in baptism. In Lutheranism's original Christendom contexts, most infants were baptized. Baptismal regeneration renews the human *habitus* in grace. Yet the Lutheran construal of grace focuses less upon a sacramental system and more upon the preached Word of justification by faith alone. For present purposes, the crucial difference with Catholicism concerns the lingering corruption of the regenerate will. On Luther's account, wayward desire is sinful. Humans are guilty for concupiscence itself, which is not merely potential but already actual. Hence Luther championed *simul iustus et peccator*: a baptized sinner is justified by faith yet remains not merely a potential but already an actual sinner. Concupiscence is not eliminated by forgiveness.

---

16. See Augustine, "The Punishment and Forgiveness of Sins," 1.9.9 (pp. 38–39).

A different set of positions, in the *Arminian and Wesleyan* traditions, arose in the centuries after the Reformation. Though many of them retain infant baptism, not all do, and today post-Christendom contexts limit the practice to a minority of the population. Some retain baptismal regeneration, but most do not. Generally speaking, a Wesleyan approach gives all humans an initial share in Adam's guilty *status*, whether the underlying *actus* was Adam's or ours. Then this initial share in Adam's guilt is removed, reestablishing personal innocence—through either infant baptism or, more commonly, a universal benefit of Christ's crucifixion. On this account, "the many" in Romans 5 relates all humans to Christ. Everyone's *habitus* is affected: all humans have enough free will restored that they can believe the gospel. Some, especially earlier "Arminian," accounts of this freedom appeal to humans' created moral responsibility. But most accounts set this free will in the context of redemption, distributing some restorative benefits to everyone by the Holy Spirit's *prevenient grace that comes before faith. Although the will's lingering corruption counts as sinful—as in the Lutheran account—the Wesleyan doctrine of Christian perfection emphasizes intentional acts (as we will see in later chapters), like the Catholic account.

The *Reformed* tradition, arising soon after Lutheranism, emphasizes God's salvation of particular sinners. The original Reformed account retained infant baptism in a Christendom context, yet without baptismal regeneration: baptism was a gracious sign but not, in itself, a saving act. Everyone's *status* involved Adam's guilt, based on Adam's *actus*. Some held a *realist view of how everyone related to Adam's act: sinners were somehow present, biologically or otherwise, as participants in Adam's sin. Yet most Reformed theology has embraced a *representative (or "federalist") view: just as God imputes Christ's righteousness to people for whom he is the "federal head"—counting it as theirs in union with him—so God imputed Adam's sin to all people for whom he was the federal head by being the ancestor of the human race. Because baptism is not regenerating, everyone's *habitus* in Adam continues to involve *total depravity: not being as wicked as possible, but being sinful in every aspect of life. In this respect the Reformed view is resolutely Augustinian: no one in Adam produces an untainted act of righteousness; no one even seeks the true God, let alone believes the gospel, apart from regenerating grace. Even when someone is made new by the Holy Spirit, a corrupted will remains; even good deeds contain mixed motives. Remaining sinfulness means that even regenerate people can be righteous only in union with Christ.

In wider evangelical discussions, some advocate a realist view of biological or metaphysical presence in Adam. Realists appeal to Hebrews 7:9–10 as a biblical example of ancestral participation, along with the apparent justice involved: sin should be imputed only to those who somehow participated in Adam's act. Yet a representative view is more common. If biological generation were the ground for imputation, why would the Bible emphasize Adam, not Eve? For that matter, why is just Adam's first sin the focus, not all his and all ancestors' sins? Does a realist view make imputation personal enough to improve justice? Most of all, does not the Adam-Christ link in Romans 5 work poorly with a realist view (since we relate to Christ by imputation without biological ancestry)?[17]

Admittedly, Romans 5 is complex, and Augustine did not know Greek. He read the end of Romans 5:12 in Latin as saying that all sinned "in" Adam, which is grammatically dubious. The text probably says that death came to all *in this way* (involving sin's entry through Adam), not that all sinned *in* Adam. The point is that Adam's sin brought death *because thereby all sinned*. Against Pelagianism, Adam's effect is causal and necessary, but Augustine's realist notion of our participation in Adam is not the teaching of Romans. The parenthesis in 5:13–14 addresses an ensuing Jewish question: What about humans outside of Israel's covenant connection to Adam—how would the death penalty apply to them? Paul answers that they bore the *consequences* of Adam's death in their sin, even if they did not directly choose to disobey the Torah. After receiving God's law, Israelites died because of breaking covenant commands. Outside that context, Adam fills the explanatory gap: people bear the deadly consequences of the first human's representative action, with the result that "all have sinned and fall short of the glory of God" (Rom. 3:23). Due to Adam's sin and death, we are born as sinners subject to death: against Pelagianism, Augustinians together claim at least that much, even if they differ about whether we directly share Adam's guilt or become personally sinful due to his corruption.[18]

Salvation

As with sin, Christian teaching about salvation—*soteriology—involves both broad consensus and much variety. *Salvation denotes deliverance from danger or bondage, healing from a deadly illness or wound. As an action of the

---

17. Crisp, "Original Sin and Atonement," traces philosophical challenges for views of atonement sketched in chap. 9 and original sin sketched here. But in this paragraph "representative" does not preclude the kind of "realist" view that Crisp champions: a metaphysically unified "fallen humanity" that Adam headed, with Christ heading a "redeemed humanity." Crisp, however, associates representation with a kind of "imputation" that he dismisses as a "forensic fiction" (perhaps by neglecting covenantal union).

18. This treatment of Rom. 5 reflects the reworked representative view of Blocher, *Original Sin*. On its difference from earlier proposals of "mediate imputation," see Treier, "Review of *Original Sin*."

Triune God, salvation depends upon the Father's loving initiative, the Son's ministry of reconciliation, and the Spirit's application of the Son's atoning work. An *ordo salutis*, or "order of salvation," describes in sequence how the Spirit unites people to Christ. "To know Christ is to know his benefits," said Luther's sidekick Philipp Melanchthon (1497–1560).[19]

The corollary truth is vitally important: to know Christ's benefits is to know Christ, or, even more forcefully, *knowing Christ is the crucial benefit* that defines salvation (e.g., John 17:3; Phil. 3:10–11). *Union with Christ is the central, overarching category in Paul's theology, naming the covenant relationship in which we receive the benefits of salvation. Numerous prepositions in the New Testament Epistles relate us to Christ: we participate "together with" him in the saving events of his life, so we receive God's grace "through" him, we have our identity "in" him, and we live "for" him. This union is therefore preeminently a covenant relationship, while this relationship has intimate and mystical aspects. Marriage is the most prominent human analogy, but adoption is another: in union with Christ we become God's children, joint heirs of a glorious inheritance that his indwelling Spirit guarantees.[20]

The Bible may not use enough consistent vocabulary and technical concepts to convey one clear, systematic *ordo salutis*. Nevertheless, the application of salvation involves a basic series of divine actions and human responses. God's actions involve *election* to redeem humans, which is accomplished by *calling* them into *union* with Jesus Christ, so that they may receive *justification*, which addresses their *status* (removing sin's penalty); *regeneration*, which addresses their *habitus* (removing sin's power over them); and *glorification*, which applies salvation fully (removing sin's presence entirely). Along the way, regeneration involves *baptism with the Holy Spirit* and *sanctification*; humans respond with *conversion, consecration, assurance,* and *perseverance*. Those aspects of the Spirit's application of salvation will be treated later, in chapter 12. The current chapter focuses on how the Spirit unites people to Jesus Christ and what that means for their past, their present, and their future.

The Order of Salvation

Divine action	Human response
Election[†]	
Calling[†]	
Union with Christ[†]	

---

19. Melanchthon, *Loci Communes*, 68.

20. On the neglected significance of adoption for contemporary debates, see Vanhoozer, "Wrighting the Wrongs."

Divine action	Human response
Justification[†]	Conversion
Regeneration[†]	Consecration (or "sanctification")
Baptism with the Holy Spirit	
Sanctification	Assurance and perseverance
Glorification[†]	

[†] treated in this chapter (other elements treated in chap. 12)

Of course, this soteriological framework is Protestant. Chapter 11, which examines several traditions of embodying the gospel in culture, will clarify the Orthodox and Catholic alternatives. Meanwhile, amid all the Protestant variety, "justification by faith alone" typically supports a basic consensus. Where Protestants differ, they struggle over which of two principles to emphasize. Lutherans and Calvinists emphasize that *God alone saves*, the "evangelical principle"[21] within which they address human responsibility. Conversely, Arminians and Wesleyans emphasize *how grace works* to restore human freedom.[22] In both cases, a holistic soteriology addresses past, present, and future: salvation initially removes sin's penalty and confronts sin's power, it progressively removes sin's power altogether, and it ultimately removes sin's presence.[23] As precious as God's forgiveness is, salvation heals more than our personal destinies: God is creating a new humanity as part of redeeming the entire cosmos.

United with Christ: Election and Calling

First in the order of salvation, *election designates God's eternal decision to redeem sinners. *Calling designates God's invitations in history for people to receive salvation. Election may be either "conditional" or "unconditional," and either "corporate" alone or "individual" as well. Correspondingly, calling may be only "general," involving gospel proclamation to which people respond in faith, or it may also be "effectual," involving the Spirit's internal persuasion that enables specific people whom God has elected to respond in faith.

The *Calvinist* position teaches *unconditional* and *individual* election: God eternally chooses to save particular sinners. God calls people generally to believe the gospel they hear proclaimed, and God's Spirit calls the elect

---

21. See Warfield, *Plan of Salvation*, 23, 87.
22. See Langford, *Practical Divinity*, chap. 2.
23. On the Bible's three-tense use of salvation vocabulary, see Thiselton, *Systematic Theology*, 190.

effectually, convincing them that "Jesus is your saving Lord!"[24] For the strictest Calvinists, predestination is "double": God both elects some to salvation and consigns others to damnation. Other Calvinists treat predestination as "single": God elects some to salvation while leaving aside others to the damnation they have sinfully chosen. The acronym "TULIP" famously summarizes the Calvinist tenets: *T*otal depravity (sinful humans cannot seek God or believe the gospel without regenerating grace); **U*nconditional election; **L*imited atonement (Christ's death is effective only for the elect); **I*rresistible grace (an internal call to salvation is effectual for the elect); **P*erseverance of the saints (the indwelling Holy Spirit preserves the elect so that they persevere in faith). Election is unconditional because no one can respond apart from God's grace (Rom. 3:10–18). Human freedom is "volitional," not libertarian: a person is not equally able to choose between options, but simply chooses according to her or his nature. Totally depraved sinners may perform outwardly good acts, but they do not worship the true God and they cannot believe the gospel unless God regenerates them. God chose Jacob and not Esau before they were born, without regard for their character or actions (Rom. 9:10–13).

By contrast, the *classical Arminian* position interprets biblical election passages in *conditional* terms: God chooses people for salvation based on "foreknowledge" of who will believe the gospel. God's only saving "call" is the *general* gospel invitation. The human will has "libertarian" freedom: ability to choose between options. At minimum, prevenient grace restores enough freedom that sinners can seek God and believe the gospel, even if they cannot live righteously. A *Molinist* position, introduced earlier regarding divine providence, adds "middle knowledge" to this mix: God looks ahead to see who will believe based on knowing how people would respond in particular situations.

Some *contemporary Arminians* interpret biblical election passages in *corporate* terms: they address God's choice to redeem the world through a particular covenant people.[25] Responding in faith to a *general* gospel invitation joins a particular person to that covenant people. Election is not really about which individuals are saved and which are not; election is about servanthood, not salvation—about God's people being chosen as the instrument of blessing for a needy world.

The *Barthian* position emphasizes election's *christological* focus in a way that resonates with contemporary Arminian, more corporate accounts. Barth

---

24. For a contemporary Reformed account that avoids being overly deterministic and argues for this content in the effectual call, see Hoglund, *Called by Triune Grace*.

25. See, e.g., Abasciano, "Misconceptions about Corporate Election"; Klein, *The New Chosen People*.

read Ephesians 1:3–14 in terms of election "in Christ," who, as fully divine and fully human, is both the electing God and the elected human. Election is fundamentally about God choosing to be for humanity in the incarnation. Election is so christocentric that it deals with both redemption and reprobation: Christ is both the elected and the rejected human, the Mediator who suffered our judgment on the cross. Barth's exegesis of Romans 9 anticipated trends in contemporary Pauline scholarship with his corporate focus on Israel. Israel typifies God's people in their rejection; the church, true Israel, typifies God's people in their election unto salvation. The church is the people that, having come to realize their election, can bear witness as God's servant to the world. Barth's account so focused on universal election in Christ that many assumed that he had to embrace universal salvation. Yet Barth himself denied this implication, since assuming universal salvation would deny God's freedom.[26] We may hope and should pray for God's reconciliation of all things, but we cannot dogmatically assert that such reconciliation will include the final salvation of all humans.

Beyond these four accounts of election—as unconditional, conditional, corporate, and/or christocentric—others make slight alterations. The Catholic and Lutheran traditions tend to be more generically Augustinian. Some early Lutherans shaded toward the Calvinistic emphasis on divine sovereignty, many Catholics toward emphasizing human responsibility. Moderate Calvinists, who are widespread among Baptists and other groups, embrace four of the five TULIP petals while affirming unlimited rather than limited atonement. On this modified Calvinist account, offering the general gospel call implies that Christ somehow died for everyone, as certain biblical texts suggest (e.g., 1 John 2:2). At minimum, even if Jesus's death is effective only for the elect, its benefits still are sufficient in principle for anyone.

Beyond the most crucial passages, Romans 9–11 and Ephesians 1, numerous other Scriptures affect these debates: prayers that mention election (e.g., 2 Thess. 2:13–14), human "resistance" texts vis-à-vis divine calling (e.g., Acts 7:51), texts that may suggest universal prevenient grace (e.g., John 12:32), and narratives that seem to hinge on human freedom (e.g., God's "wager" with Satan over Job). Trinitarian implications—the unity of the Father's love with the ministry of Word and Spirit—are also at stake. Furthermore, we have to discern the extent of biblical revelation: at some point, the interface between divine sovereignty and human responsibility lies beyond our understanding. For all its mystery, though, the doctrine of election celebrates that God has chosen to be for humanity, and indeed with us, in Christ.

26. Barth, CD II/2, 417–18.

Delivered from Sin's Penalty: Justification

Those who respond to God's call in faith are united with Christ by the Holy Spirit. Participating by grace in Jesus's death and resurrection, they are forgiven and become God's friends: *justification by faith alone delivers them from sin's penalty, changing their status from unrighteous to righteous. This legal metaphor goes beyond initial entry into salvation, affecting how people journey toward its ultimate end.

THE CATHOLIC BACKGROUND

The legal metaphor of justification extended the influence of Pauline theology over medieval Western Christianity. Yet Augustine did not know Greek, and he related justification to regeneration. Based on a Latin translation, he related the concept to *iustus* plus *facere*, meaning "to make righteous." This meaning misses the Hebrew background to Paul's Greek term, which means "to declare righteous." As the medieval church pondered salvation in increasingly legal terms, the process of being made righteous became the normative Catholic understanding of justification. Justification became connected to the sacramental system—baptism with its cooperating grace, penance, the Mass, increases of merit, and so forth. Regeneration was focused ontologically, on renewing the actual nature of human persons. In the East and the earlier Middle Ages, this ontological orientation was relational, focused on God's presence; in the later Middle Ages within the West, this ontological orientation became more philosophical, focused on transformation of human nature itself. Thus, justification involved the *process* of Christ's righteousness being *infused* within believers, *making* them righteous via sacramental grace.

No one was qualified to enjoy the beatific vision of God, and therefore entitled to assurance of salvation, until that renewal in righteousness was complete. At death, unless someone was a saint, time would be spent in purgatory to complete the renewal. So, when consciences like Martin Luther's were troubled, it was not enough merely to do penance and depend upon the sacraments. Luther was even concerned about whether he cooperated sufficiently with prevenient grace. He worried about nullifying sacramental grace with mixed motives, even simply the desire for forgiveness. Medieval Catholic theology became preoccupied with various types of grace corresponding to levels of merit. Even when Thomas Aquinas used "justification" to address forgiveness, he presupposed the process of cooperation with divine grace that fostered the Lutheran problem of anxiety.[27]

---

27. On the divisions of grace, see Thomas Aquinas, *Summa theologica* I-II, q. 111, a. 1–5; on justification, see q. 113.

THE LUTHERAN DIFFERENCE

Luther's Catholic confessor urged him to read Romans, which initially made the situation worse. When Luther read of God's righteousness, he could only imagine God condemning sinners. Eventually, however, he came to see Romans 1:17 in terms of gracious righteousness *from* God rather than the terrifying righteousness *of* God. Luther's breakthrough reading is debatable in some details, but its basic thrust recaptured Paul's gracious message: God's righteousness is revealed in the gospel, which is good news from beginning to end even though judgment is involved. Of course, sinners in themselves are not righteous: God does not *make* them so instantly, and it would be a "legal fiction" for God simply to *declare* them so. Yet God declares sinners righteous *in Christ*, to whom God imputed our sin on the cross and in whose human righteousness we participate by faith.[28] Like a marriage, so the believer's union with Christ involves a new status based on a transfer of properties.

Famous post-Reformation slogans unfold the logic of a Protestant account. Salvation is *sola gratia, by grace alone. But what kind of grace? Catholic teaching affirms grace alone, but the key question is how grace works: Does prevenient grace prepare the human will, in relation to baptism, for cooperation with God in sanctification? No, such cooperating grace rests too much on a human basis. Salvation is also *solus Christus, by Christ alone. But what kind of righteousness do believers receive in Christ? Catholic teaching affirms Christ's righteousness alone, but the key question is how it becomes ours: Does ontological renewal, treating grace almost like a substance, happen through a churchly system of saints, sacraments, and so on? No, such infused righteousness again rests too much on a human basis, introducing other mediators alongside the one Mediator. Salvation is accordingly *sola fide, by faith alone. But what kind of relationship between faith and works? Perhaps Catholic teaching could affirm faith alone, but instead it spoke of faith formed by love (appealing to Gal. 5:6). No, such faith formed by love rests too much on a human basis because faith turns into a virtue that someone must acquire.

Faith alone implies that Christ's righteousness remains *extra nos, ontologically outside of believers, becoming ours only in covenant union with Christ. Love does not coinhere with grace as a creative power; faith is not cooperation with grace as an ontological gift that comes via the sacraments.

---

28. Internal Protestant disagreement has arisen over the positive imputation of Christ's righteousness. For an argument that this doctrine goes beyond what the Bible demands (which is only the negative imputation of our sin to Christ), see R. Gundry, "The Nonimputation of Christ's Righteousness"; for an argument that the doctrine is implicit in Rom. 4 and elsewhere, see Carson, "Vindication of Imputation."

Faith is not an instrument of justification by gradually *infusing* Christ's righteousness within us so that we are no longer sinners. Rather, justification is a divine declaration that already *imputes* Christ's righteousness to those who remain—in and of themselves—sinners. God's Word creates faith, eliciting the Reformation cries of *solo verbo (the Word alone) and *sola scriptura* (Scripture alone). Justification is the *event* of God *declaring* us righteous, not the process of making us righteous. Emphasizing the preached Word of forgiveness, with justification as the Reformation's "material principle," complements the Protestant "formal principle": Scripture alone has ultimate theological authority, proclaiming Jesus Christ as our one Mediator.

To be sure, Roman Catholicism does not teach "salvation by works"! Luther saw parallels between the Judaizers of Paul's day and medieval Catholics, but those parallels depended upon subtleties regarding grace, righteousness, and faith formed by love. If assurance rests on loving cooperation with God, salvation easily shifts toward a human and subjective basis rather than a divine and objective basis. To illustrate: In conversation between Dietrich Bonhoeffer and a young Catholic priest, they asked about each other's purposes in life. The priest answered, "I would like to become a saint." Bonhoeffer answered, "I should like to learn to have faith." As one Lutheran theologian comments, "Only later did he [Bonhoeffer] become aware of the deep divide between the two answers. He had first to understand that 'learning to have faith' means completely renouncing 'any attempt to make something of oneself, whether it be a saint or a converted sinner' . . . believers [according to the New Testament] are already hagioi [saints]. Thus, to say 'I would like to learn faith' is to be a saint."[29]

BIBLICAL TEACHING

The doctrine of justification has remained controversial since Luther's breakthrough and the Council of Trent's (1545–63) reaction against Protestantism. Yet contemporary biblical scholarship contains fairly widespread agreement among Catholics and Protestants that Paul's "justification" language is forensic, at least including an initial declaration of forgiveness.[30] Rather than focusing on key Pauline terminology, ongoing debates usually

29. Jüngel, "On the Doctrine of Justification," 49–50.
30. Admittedly, justification by faith alone faces criticism within Pauline scholarship. This claim about Paul's justification *terminology*, however, is acknowledged by critics such as N. T. Wright, who actually does not deny the doctrine but criticizes its prominence and misuse (see, e.g., *Justification*, 87; *What Saint Paul Really Said*, 113). Similarly, Peter Leithart does not deny the doctrine, despite treating Pauline justification as a "deliverdict" with transforming power (*Delivered from the Elements*, esp. 180–92). Leithart does blur Paul's *dikaioō* terminology (the

concern the relation between this initial forgiveness and the remaining order of salvation, as well as the rest of the New Testament.

"Justification" language with this Pauline sense appears elsewhere only in Luke 18:9–14, where the sinner begging for God's mercy goes home justified while the self-righteous Pharisee does not. Still, initial forgiveness appears elsewhere in other words; the core truth of justification by faith alone is not idiosyncratically Pauline. Indeed, the Pauline language usually appears in a particular context: Paul defends including gentile believers in the church without circumcision, which had been Israel's gateway into an ongoing commitment to keep Mosaic law. Paul's opponents worried that his gospel promoted lawless living. When the nature of faithfully "staying in" the community of salvation was disputed, Paul clarified that covenant life for both Jews and gentiles must reflect "getting in" by the Messiah's justifying grace.[31] If circumcision and law-keeping were required to stay in God's good graces, that would replace the freedom brought by the gospel with a human basis for getting right with God.

Paul's concept of justification by faith alone, notably in Romans 4, appears to be in tension with other New Testament texts, notably James 2. Despite the surface tension, though, the texts can complement one another. James confronts a faulty notion of "faith"—merely mental belief—that is different from Paul's positive concept of personal trust. Hence James provides a healthy pastoral warning with which Paul would agree. James may also speak of "justification" differently: as the demonstration of righteousness before other humans rather than before God. People who profess faith but live disobediently give others no evidence of their salvation. The presence or absence of good works is not the basis of salvation, however, even if genuine faith will eventually produce spiritual fruit.

Admittedly, evangelicals today have less clear consensus about justification by faith alone. Biblical scholars multiply disagreements about nuances in Paul's teaching. Some Lutherans, among others, have undertaken substantial dialogue with Catholics and revised earlier interpretations of Luther. Some Anabaptists and Arminians have always worried that justification by faith

---

issue here) with transformation themes from the surrounding contexts, as shown by Allen and Treier, "Justification: A Reply to Leithart."

A louder critic, Douglas A. Campbell, raises important questions about the "apocalyptic" nature of Pauline theology and the "contractual" nature of popular Protestant soteriologies (*Deliverance of God*). But Campbell's reading of Romans unconvincingly relies on the idea that Paul significantly quotes opponents rather than saying what he means. Campbell also misconstrues the traditional Protestant doctrine (as shown aggressively by Allen, *Justification and the Gospel*, 42–43, esp. n. 29).

31. R. Gundry, "Grace, Works, and Staying Saved."

alone involves a "legal fiction," promoting lawless living and a lack of social concern. By contrast, some "free grace" advocates have interpreted justification by faith alone, combined with appeals to "eternal security," as suggesting that persons may be saved without ever bearing spiritual fruit. Such a position departs from Luther's own insistence that while we are justified by faith alone, the faith that justifies is never alone.[32]

Today some Catholics construe their church's teaching in ways that are friendlier to Protestant commitments. In the unofficial "Evangelicals and Catholics Together" dialogue, Catholics embraced justification by faith, albeit without the key word "alone"; in the semiofficial "Joint Declaration on the Doctrine of Justification," Lutherans and Catholics found enough "basic consensus" to remove their mutual Reformation-era condemnations while accepting continued differences of emphasis.[33] Such ecumenical efforts have intensified disagreements among evangelicals. Simultaneously, they have advanced the basic recognition of justification by faith: God assures sinners of forgiveness when they enter the Christian life. Christians will continue debating about how forgiven sinners are subsequently renewed in Christ's image; from a classic Protestant perspective, that renewal is vitally connected to justification by faith alone. But amid such debates we can celebrate some wider clarity about the grace involved in our initial forgiveness.

Delivered from Sin's Power: Regeneration

The good news does not stop with salvation from sin's penalty. If anyone is in Christ, behold—a new creation (2 Cor. 5:17)! The term "regeneration" is rare in the New Testament. It evokes Israel's future (Matt. 19:28), suggesting that the regeneration of particular Christ-followers (Titus 3:5) initiates the renewal of God's people. Despite the term's rarity, though, the basic concept of *regeneration—God making new those who belong to Christ, releasing them from sin's power—is widespread. Two key questions arise: (1) Is regeneration primarily an event or a process? (2) How does regeneration relate to baptism or the moment of initial faith? Answers to these questions generate four basic approaches.

The classic Orthodox, Catholic, and Lutheran position, held by many Anglicans too, affirms *baptismal regeneration* (logically *before or at* initial faith),

---

32. The gist of this sentiment appears, e.g., in *LW* 34:124 ("Theses Concerning Faith and Law"); 34:176 ("Disputation Concerning Justification"); 44:298 ("Judgment of Martin Luther on Monastic Vows").

33. See Evangelicals and Catholics Together, "The Gift of Salvation"; The Lutheran World Federation and the Roman Catholic Church, *Joint Declaration on the Doctrine of Justification*.

tied when possible to *paedobaptism (baptism of infants). Beyond appeals to the New Testament, this position reflects the context of Christendom, where infant baptism was widespread. As the initial sacrament, baptism removes original guilt and makes growth in grace possible. As explained earlier, these traditions relate regeneration differently to initial justification and subsequent Christian life. Orthodoxy and Catholicism emphasize the subsequent *process* of ontological renewal that baptism initiates; Lutheranism emphasizes the initial *event* of justifying faith.

Traditional *Calvinism* also locates regeneration logically *before or at* the *event* of initial faith. Regeneration is virtually equivalent to the effectual call: God's gift of a new nature, which removes total depravity and enables someone to believe the gospel. Upon receiving the indwelling Holy Spirit, a believer can respond to God's grace with progressive sanctification.

Modified Calvinists and some Arminians likewise see regeneration as an *event*, but they place it logically *after* initial faith. For modified Calvinists, God's gift of a new nature removes total depravity to foster ongoing sanctification, with effectual calling as a previous work that enables belief in the gospel. For Arminians, total depravity has already been removed by universal prevenient grace. There is only a general gospel call, with no effectual call. So, when someone freely believes the gospel, God gives a new nature through the indwelling Holy Spirit to enable sanctification.

Other Arminians treat regeneration in terms of a *process*, as a synonym for sanctification *after* initial faith. This approach may coincide with treating conversion as a process rather than trying to identify a particular moment when a person initially responds in faith. This approach may also coincide with baptismal regeneration to a degree, yet it typically operates without the same ontological emphasis. Thus, instead of baptismal regeneration inaugurating the sacramental life of faith, here the process of sanctification follows the initial, personal act of faith.

Biblical debates over infant baptism and baptismal regeneration involve particular texts like Acts 2:38. Understandings of regeneration further reflect different emphases when synthesizing scriptural teaching. Some passages focus on the beginning of a person's spiritual renewal, others on the continuing process. Most Protestants emphasize that regeneration does not involve receiving "the divine nature" in a way that blurs the distinction between Creator and creature. Regeneration is not the addition of a God-related "spirit" as a missing "part" of humanity.[34] Regeneration is not simply the addition of a "new"

---

34. Admittedly, there are evangelical exceptions to almost any rule; in this case, trichotomists like the Chinese leader Watchman Nee (1903–72) hold such a view.

nature alongside the old "sinful" nature.[35] Before regeneration, someone is dead in sin; regeneration makes a person newly alive in Christ, even if sinful habits linger due to the "flesh," our earthbound spiritual weakness after the fall. Regeneration is a relational change, with the Holy Spirit indwelling us and empowering us to overcome sin's former mastery.[36]

Delivered from Sin's Presence: Glorification

God ultimately will deliver us not only from sin's penalty and sin's power but also even from sin's presence, so that we no longer suffer evil or commit sin. *Glorification is a term many Protestants use to describe this removal of sin's presence, through resurrected bodies, fully reconciled hearts, and a redeemed cosmos. Romans 8 promises that nothing will separate us from God's love in Christ, although currently we groan with creation as we await redemption. Second Peter 3 anticipates a cosmic purification that ought to reshape our present living. Second Corinthians 3:18–4:6 ties the glory we anticipate to the face of Christ: the community of the new covenant encounters God personally in Jesus, awaiting full transformation into his image. The New Testament speaks of "glorification" as already beginning with conversion, but not being complete until we see Christ face-to-face (1 John 3:2–3). Then, as John Wesley celebrated, happiness and holiness coalesce.[37]

Catholicism presents *purgatory (and Orthodoxy believes in a similar concept, usually by another name) as an interim phase of purification between a person's death and glorified enjoyment of the beatific vision. Popular perception often associates purgatory with suffering punishment in an undesirable place for an extended time. Accordingly, most Protestants have rejected purgatory as unwarranted in Scripture and inconsistent with Christ's once-for-all suffering on our behalf. Whatever the strange text regarding baptism for the dead means (1 Cor. 15:29), it hardly provides a strong basis for the contested doctrine. The fire of passages like 1 Corinthians 3:10–15 metaphorically represents divine judgment of human ministries, not postmortem purgation. Other support for purgatory appeals to the Apocrypha, not the Scriptures accepted by Protestants as canonical. Instead, Protestants emphasize passages

---

35. When editions of the New International Version translate *sarx* with "sinful nature" rather than the more "literal" term "flesh," the point is not that believers fundamentally have two natures, retaining the old self unchanged. Instead, the translators wanted to avoid conveying the gnostic idea that bodies are inherently evil or secondary in value.

36. See Fee, *God's Empowering Presence*.

37. B. Jones, *Practicing Christian Doctrine*, 230.

like 1 Corinthians 15:51–52, suggesting that the believer's transformation at the resurrection will be instantaneous, "in the twinkling of an eye."[38]

As the next chapter explores further, Orthodoxy and Catholicism speak of *theosis* rather than glorification. This end of salvation conveys not just the removal of sin's presence but also full reflection of God's image, partaking in the divine nature as humans were made to do. The ontological focus of *theosis* is consistent with the Orthodox de-emphasis on justification and the Catholic doctrine of justification as a process, as well as the doctrine of purgatory. While some Protestants speak of *theosis*, doing so neither affirms purgatory nor denies justification by faith alone.

In glorification, those who have begun to participate in Jesus's resurrection participate in his ascension, being completely transformed and finally exalted to enjoy the new creation. Far from taking more time, this exaltation will end earthly history as we presently know it.

---

38. A few Protestants, notably Jerry L. Walls (*Purgatory*), have recently become sympathetic to a doctrine of purgatory (likewise Stackhouse, "Hard Work of Holiness"). They contend that instantaneous transformation is inconsistent with human sanctification, which involves bodily, social, and temporal life.

A crucial rejoinder, however, is that final glorification cannot remain just more of the same, for its transformation involves kind and not just degree—the entire removal of sin's presence, making sin impossible. As for bodily life, glorification should be different than historical sanctification, because resurrected bodies are transformed. As for social life, purgatory largely addresses individual persons without social relations. As for temporal life, purgatory operates outside of earthly experience. Merely extending the same process would not accomplish the full transformation needed—and purgatory does not continue the same process. In glorification, God graciously provides the necessary transformation.

$$—11—$$

The Gospel in Christian Traditions

THESIS

The gospel takes cultural form in Orthodox Christianity, emphasizing a tradition of *theosis*; in Catholic Christianity, emphasizing the sacramental renewal of creaturely being; and in seven major traditions of Protestant Christianity, emphasizing the gospel's freedom for biblical reform.

LEARNING OBJECTIVES

After learning the material in this chapter, you should be able to:

1. *Define briefly* the key terms introduced here (marked with an asterisk and included in the glossary).
2. *List and recognize* the fundamental concepts of the major Christian traditions.
3. *Describe and compare* the major Christian traditions.
4. *Identify and illustrate* the significance of traditions' fundamental concepts vis-à-vis cultural engagement.
5. *Explain* the gospel.

The preceding chapter focused on how the good news affects particular people. Yet sin has systemic dimensions and redemption has a cosmic scope. Hence the Holy Spirit is creating a new community that heralds the gospel in word and deed, even in its cultural presence. Accordingly, the present chapter explores major church traditions, beginning with Orthodoxy and Catholicism before examining seven Protestant groups. For each tradition, the chapter briefly chronicles its history and outlines its theology, especially its account of the gospel and approach to culture. Of course, it is impossible to tell the entire story of any tradition or to be truly global in this chapter's scope. It is necessary to choose the most enduring traditions, influential figures, and widespread tendencies.

These traditions have distinct ideas, but often they vary more modestly, over relative emphases. Ideas and emphases have tangible consequences, but their institutional embodiment is always local. "Church" is both a theological reality and an intellectual abstraction from cultural particulars, so we cannot automatically reason backward from apparent effects to doctrinal causes. While theological emphases influence church practice, the reverse is also true, in the context of numerous contingencies. For all their differences, these traditions ultimately constitute a singular Christian tradition—celebrating that Jesus Christ came down from heaven "for us and for our salvation," while longing to be "one holy, catholic, and apostolic church," with "one baptism for the forgiveness of sins."

Orthodox Christianity: A Tradition of *Theosis*

(Eastern) Orthodox Christianity champions two fundamental concepts: *theosis* and Tradition. *Theosis* is the process of deification whereby God overcomes the mortal corruption of humanity. This salvation occurs in the context of the church's liturgical Tradition. Orthodoxy contains a family of churches, self-governing yet in communion with one another. Each church has its own leader: a patriarch, archbishop, or metropolitan. The first four patriarchates—Constantinople, Alexandria, Antioch, Jerusalem—receive particular historical honor. Whereas Rome was once a fifth honored patriarchate, now this distinction belongs to Moscow. Constantinople is the ecumenical patriarchate through which Orthodox unity is channeled, but does not have papal, potentially infallible, authority. Some Eastern churches have not officially acknowledged Chalcedonian Christology, remaining "monophysite" although now they are called "Oriental Orthodox."[1]

History

Orthodox history falls broadly into three periods. First, a classical period runs until 787, when iconoclasm was defeated at the Seventh Ecumenical Council at Nicaea. Creedal theologians and subsequently John Chrysostom were most influential early on. By defending Christ's two wills, Maximus the

---

1. For overviews that inform this summary, see Galli, "The Great Divorce," and Nassif, "Kissers and Smashers," as well as Clendenin, *Eastern Orthodox Christianity*. For specific churches, see Bouteneff, "Oriental Orthodox." Also note that the overviews in Treier and Elwell, *Evangelical Dictionary of Theology*, inform this chapter throughout.

Confessor (580–662) became prominent in the Byzantine context that later became Constantinople. John Climacus (579–649) produced the *Ladder of Divine Ascent*, an important manual of mystic spirituality. In the eighth century, amid the iconoclast controversy, John of Damascus (675–754) wrote Orthodoxy's first and most important systematic theology, *The Orthodox Faith*.

Second, a middle period runs from 787 to 1453, with three primary elements: conversion of the Slavs (c. 988); deepening and then formal schism with Western or "Roman" Christianity (official in 1054); and Constantinople's fall.

Third, a modern period runs from Constantinople's fall onward. Orthodox engagement with the West has been sporadic, although several intellectuals— particularly Russians like Sergei Bulgakov (1871–1944)—have intrigued the West with their concepts of Sophia (Wisdom) and celebration of mysterious trinitarian union. Arguably, there has been a twentieth-century revival of Orthodox theology, although some leading figures have been controversial. In any case, encounters with Islam and Marxist atheism have shaped Orthodoxy more than dialogue with Western thought. Islam's late medieval surge took Orthodox Christianity from peace or at least possible coexistence into frequent, sometimes devastating conflict. Marxist atheism in Eastern bloc countries challenged the church's very right to exist or at least its missionary integrity. In both cases, national or geographically defined churches struggled to engage political power responsibly without falling into ethnocentrism or other cultural compromises.

Theology[2]

Generalizing about Orthodoxy's *ordo salutis* is difficult due to its historical breadth and theological ethos. Beginning with creation, though, Eastern Christianity tends to understand humans trichotomously. The spirit, which apprehends the Holy Spirit, establishes moral freedom. Humans were created in God's "image" and called to attain God's "likeness"; they fell by misusing their freedom. They are guilty for their own sins but share the deadly consequences of Adam's sin.[3] For mortal beings, bodily needs like food and drink become excessive "passions" that foster sin. The fall's direct inheritance is mortality; sin is inherited indirectly.

Salvation as *deification means "participation in the divine nature" (2 Pet. 1:4). *Theosis* does not fuse or confuse human beings with the divine essence, but it blurs rhetorical lines between the two. In the incarnation, the Son became

---

2. This section reflects earlier research help from Darren Sarisky. These traditions are also profiled briefly in Treier, "New Covenant and New Creation."

3. An Eastern patriarch, Photius, went so far as to call the idea of a sin nature "heresy" (Meyendorff, *Byzantine Theology*, 143).

what we are, so that we might become what he is.[4] Whereas Christ is the Son of God by nature, we become children of God by grace. Here the *Philokalia*, an anthology written from the fourth to the fifteenth centuries, exerts Orthodox spiritual influence second only to the Bible, by emphasizing cooperation with divine grace.[5]

For Orthodoxy, Christ's passion was primarily a divine victory over sin, death, and the devil—every hostile power. The incarnation inaugurated Christ's triumph over mortal corruption. Participation in this triumph comes sacramentally, through Christ's assumption of a particular human nature becoming definitive for ours. The two chief sacraments—creaturely means of receiving the Holy Spirit's grace—are baptism and the Holy Eucharist. Baptism is the initiatory rite for church members' pilgrimage toward full union with Christ. The Eucharist advances this pilgrimage, uniting people with Jesus's divinizing flesh. *Theosis* is a progressive reality, not completely fulfilled until death and resurrection. In the meantime, Orthodoxy has an ascetic ethos, encouraging some to withdraw from worldly engagement and everyone to resist corrupting passions in pursuit of virtue.

In light of this gospel, the ethos of both Orthodoxy and Catholicism begins with a claim of comprehensive institutional unity—of being the *one* "orthodox" and "catholic" church. The adjectives "Eastern" and "Roman" reflect outside perspectives, clarifying when a particular institution rather than a theological concept is in view. But the respective claims of Orthodoxy and Catholicism are mutually exclusive. By comparison, Orthodox theology is more apophatic, producing few "systematic" accounts: humans cannot know God's "essence" but can only encounter the "energies" with which God relates to the world. Accordingly, the Orthodox ethos is aesthetic, an integrated Tradition of liturgical practices and icons: theology clears space for encountering the divine mystery. By excluding error, as in the Chalcedonian Definition, the church fosters participation in God through the sanctification of material realities and liturgical repetition, rather than intellectual explanation. Thus, Orthodoxy is unapologetically traditional:[6] Tradition preeminently includes the Scriptures, but Eastern churches expressly deny *sola scriptura*. They honor as infallible the seven "ecumenical" councils that preceded the schism with Rome. While

---

4. E.g., Ware, *The Orthodox Way*, 97.

5. Nikodimos of the Holy Mountain and Makarios of Corinth, *The Philokalia*.

6. The distinction between church teachings from written sources and others from oral apostolic Tradition is often represented with a quotation from Basil the Great, *On the Holy Spirit* 27.66 (pp. 104–6). However, Sarisky, *Scriptural Interpretation*, 111–28, shows that the Basil quotation is widely misunderstood. Basil did not hold a "two-source" theory of revelation in which tradition adds material content; rather, liturgical participation and personal apprenticeship are among the church practices that tacitly orient readers to Scripture.

"dogma" (requiring universal assent) is distinct from "theological speculation" (*theologoumena*), in practice these can be difficult to distinguish.

Several Orthodox practices have affinities with Catholicism while being rare among Protestants. Orthodoxy canonizes some believers as *saints, who have attained a level of sanctification through which others may be specially blessed. Orthodox Christians pray for the dead, holding that ordinary believers face purgatory whereas someone's ultimate fate is not determined until the final judgment. Orthodoxy maintains the Marian doctrines of her perpetual virginity, freedom from actual sin, bodily assumption to heaven, veneration as the most holy saint, and intercession on our behalf.

Finally, Orthodoxy contains strong ethnic identities and political ties. Catholic and Protestant Christianity likewise have complex histories of cultural entanglement, but Orthodox Christianity can loosely be called "caesaropapist": imperial or temporal rulers having authority integrated with, or even over, the church hierarchy. This tendency primarily reflects historical circumstances, not dogma: other than the distinction between divine essence and energies mentioned above, Orthodoxy does not have a systematic approach to nature and grace like some that will be profiled below. Often, however, Orthodoxy continues to reflect Christendom-like aspirations for a synthesis between church and state. This synthetic tendency is consistent with the larger theme: a holistic Tradition of *theosis*.

Catholic Christianity: The Sacramental Renewal of Creaturely Being

The (Roman) Catholic tradition champions three fundamental concepts: the analogy of being between the Creator and creatures, the church's mediation of grace through the sacraments, and the pope's authority. As the Eastern churches claim to comprise the "Orthodox" church, so the Roman church claims to be the "Catholic" church, "outside which there is no salvation."[7] After Vatican II (1962–65), the Catholic Church has acknowledged the Holy Spirit's active presence among other brothers and sisters in Christ, who remain in "imperfect" forms of communion.[8]

History

Catholicism shares an ecumenical heritage with Orthodoxy. Gradually the *pope, the bishop of Rome, gained prominence by association with Peter. The

---

7. Cyprian, "Epistle LXXII: To Jubaianus" (*ANF* 5:384).
8. See Vatican Council II, "Decree on Ecumenism," 1.3 (p. 502). See further 3.19–24 (pp. 518–22).

church entered into a new synthesis with the empire after Constantine's conversion to Christianity in 313 birthed this *Constantinian paradigm (or "Christendom"). Papal power increased with Pope Leo I's *Tome*, which influenced the Chalcedonian Definition, the skillful ministry of Pope Gregory I ("the Great") from 590 to 604, and the decline of the emperor's influence from Constantinople. Aspects of the Christendom synthesis—such as the *historic episcopate, whereby bishops lead the church as the apostles' successors—ground continuing affinities between Catholicism and Orthodoxy. Key differences during their shared history reflect the Western influence of Augustine and of Roman law, as well as the medieval learning cultivated by the reign of Charlemagne (742–814), the role of monasteries, and the recovery of Aristotle's writings.

After the Great Schism with the East, during the Reformation the Council of Trent specified Catholic teaching beyond the earlier ecumenical councils, excluding alternatives that were perceived as Protestant. The Counter-Reformation, now called the "Catholic Reformation," reformed church life. Vatican Council I, the nineteenth-century conciliar response to modernity, presented a stiff counterattack. At this council, papal infallibility—an increasingly de facto reality—was formally adopted, hardening church authority against the Enlightenment's attack on tradition. The doctrine insists that a solemn declaration on faith and morals will be infallible when the pope speaks *ex cathedra* (from his cathedral chair, his seat of office). Catholic accounts of doctrinal development now reflect the influence of John Henry Cardinal Newman (1801–90), a convert from Anglicanism who emphasized organic continuity between biblical seeds and later formulations.

The twentieth century brought new engagement with modernity, as in the Catholic Workers' Movement. Vatican II embraced such engagement, although it remains subject to more and less progressive interpretations. Vatican II reflected the influence of the *nouvelle théologie*, the new theology of figures like Henri de Lubac (1896–1991). They encouraged *ressourcement*, a creative retrieval of tradition through fresh historical study. *Ressourcement* figures critiqued neoscholastic—rigid and philosophical—versions of Thomism. They particularly opposed the concept of "pure nature"—considering creatures without reference to God's grace in Christ.

In the aftermath of Vatican II, liberation theology controversially emerged. Pope Paul VI (1897–1978) galvanized liberal opposition in 1968 when he rejected (in *Humanae Vitae*) a theological commission's recommendation to approve forms of artificial conception. In 1978, however, Pope John Paul II (1920–2005) became the first non-Italian pope in several centuries. He enhanced the church's appeal among Protestants, championing a "culture of life" while encouraging additional forms of dialogue. The church continues to exert wide influence but also to endure great challenges in the wake of modernity.

Theology

The *Catechism of the Catholic Church* is structured around the Creed, the Sacred Liturgy (expounding the sacraments), the Christian way of life (expounding the Decalogue), and prayer (expounding the Lord's Prayer).[9] Catholic gospel teaching retains a historical fall from created justice. Destined for *theosis*, humans fell by seeking glorification independently. The resulting original sin is a wound in human nature, whose powers are restored in baptismal regeneration. Ideally, infant baptism grants remission of sins early and widely.

The Trinity is "the most fundamental and essential teaching in the 'hierarchy of the truths of faith'" (p. 62, §234). The gospel focuses on the incarnation, which lovingly embraces everyone with the invitation to *theosis* through Jesus's sacramental humanity. Union with Christ frames human life: "On the threshold of the public life: the baptism; on the threshold of the Passover: the Transfiguration. Jesus' baptism proclaimed 'the mystery of the first regeneration,' namely, our Baptism; the Transfiguration 'is the sacrament of the second regeneration': our own Resurrection" (p. 143, §556). Jesus's death made sacrificial satisfaction for sins, and he descended into the realm of the dead to free those who were deprived of the vision of God. This end, the *beatific vision ("Blessed are the pure in heart, for they will see God" [Matt. 5:8]), transcends human cognition but incorporates the knower into mystical union with God.

Faith is a gift, but it can be lost: "it must be 'working through charity,' abounding in hope, and rooted in the faith of the Church" (p. 44, §162). The Catholic gospel emphasizes cooperation with God, not just the Son's but also Mary's and ours. Mary reverses Eve's failure: "At once virgin and mother, Mary is the symbol and the most perfect realization of the Church" (p. 128, §507). Predestination evokes free responses to grace. At the judgment, culpable unbelief will be punished, while our "attitude about our neighbor will disclose acceptance or refusal of grace and divine love" (p. 177, §678).

Like Orthodoxy, Catholicism canonizes saints. Other believers must experience purgatory in order to complete their transformation by grace. Whatever its popular resonances, purgatory may be existential rather than temporal and spatial, given the differences between time and eternity. The associated practice of *indulgences—gifts through which purification is eased after death and penitential time is shortened on earth—remains distinctive and controversial. Like Orthodoxy, Catholicism venerates Mary as the most holy saint, given

---

9. *Catechism of the Catholic Church*, 5. For subsequent quotations throughout this summary, page and paragraph references appear parenthetically in the main text.

her perpetual virginity, immaculate conception, bodily assumption to heaven, and intercession for the church that she mothers. This institutional context of sacramental grace generated the Protestant perception that the Roman church did not clearly uphold Christ as our one Mediator.

As profiled in chapter 1,[10] earlier interpretations of the Council of Trent involved a "two-source" theory: Scripture as one source of revelation, Tradition another. Vatican II's final draft of *Dei Verbum* shifted toward a "one-source" theory: revelation is ultimately Jesus Christ; Scripture is the definitive source for learning of Christ; Tradition is its authoritative interpreter. This account moves closer to Protestant, particularly Barthian, emphases. Yet at least from Trent onward, Catholicism rests human certainty about Scripture's authority upon the church's teaching, not upon Scripture's own claims or the Holy Spirit's internal testimony. Relatedly, the magisterium identifies the authentic Tradition that authoritatively interprets Scripture.

Scripture is infallible as God's Word, although Catholic scholarship after Vatican II responds variously to biblical criticism. Like Orthodoxy, Catholicism treats decrees from the early ecumenical councils as infallible. Then Catholicism goes further to include the possibility of papal infallibility. Papal primacy is less formal but has a longer pedigree and a wider reach; because infallibility pertains only when the pope speaks *ex cathedra*, its application is rare. Since the doctrine became official in 1870, only the dogma of the assumption of Mary (1950) has garnered this status. Papal primacy, however, gives other Vatican documents considerable, albeit varying, influence. Catholic doctrines rarely change except through the ways in which they are stated or interpreted.

Like Orthodoxy, Catholicism incorporates mystical and aesthetic aspects of tradition, refusing to claim direct knowledge of God's essence. Even so, the West has produced more systematic theology, while defending natural law and developing natural theology more "philosophically" than has the East. Through the Middle Ages in the West, philosophy and theology were essentially the same enterprise, although an apophatic element chastened the philosophical pretensions of Catholic theology.

In the famous Christ/culture typology of H. Richard Niebuhr (1894–1962), Catholicism promotes a "synthetic" relation between nature and grace: Christ's ultimate authority operates mutually with culture's derived authority.[11]

---

10. This discussion is informed by McBrien, *Catholicism*, despite its American, moderate-to-liberal, tendency.

11. Niebuhr, *Christ and Culture*, created a fivefold typology of how Christians relate Christ's authority to culture's authority. Although qualified by Niebuhr himself and criticized by others (see especially the Anabaptist critique by C. Carter, *Rethinking Christ and Culture*, and

In this synthesis, grace perfects nature: *gratia supra naturam*. The synthesis reflects the three emphases with which this section began: the analogy of being promotes a nature/grace synthesis; the sacramental mediation of grace promotes churchly authority; and centralized, papal, churchly authority promotes integration with political authority. Sometimes, Protestant critics and *nouvelle théologie* Catholics worry, the traditional scholastic account has grace merely supplementing "pure" nature. That is, social institutions such as government retain too much natural integrity apart from the gospel. Given created integrity, people of conscience—believers or unbelievers—can function fairly well in cultural spheres and institutional vocations. But the synthetic approach, aligning with natural realities as they are after the fall, may foster social conservatism and ecclesiastical corruption rather than gospel transformation. So Protestant critics emphasize fallen humanity's fundamental antithesis toward God's purposes, while conversely the *nouvelle théologie* emphasizes a graced desire for God that is latent outside the church as well.[12]

Modern Catholic social teaching acknowledges that human dignity incorporates a right against religious coercion, even if this personal right does not require full disestablishment of religion by the state. An orienting concept is *subsidiarity: "a community of a higher order [e.g., national government] should not interfere in the internal life of a community of a lower order [e.g., nuclear family], . . . but rather should support it in case of need and help to co-ordinate its activity with the activities of the rest of society" (p. 460, §1883). Thus, while engaging a post-Christendom world, Catholic social teaching still champions the sacramental renewal of creaturely being in a way that integrates with centralized church authority.

Protestant Christianity: The Gospel's Freedom for Biblical Reform[13]

"Protestant" churches share no obvious consensus or official definition. Beyond denying Catholic and Orthodox claims, Protestant identity needs additional

---

the biblical critique by Carson, *Christ and Culture Revisited*), the typology reflects enduring biblical motifs that undergird the tendencies of several traditions.

12. For a Protestant critique of the Catholic tendency toward a "supplemental" view of grace (involving humanity's need for a *donum superadditum*—a "superadded gift" above and beyond created nature yet independent of the fall), see Bavinck, *God and Creation*, esp. chap. 12. The characterization of Thomas's position as *gratia supra naturam* comes from Wolters, "No Longer Queen," which informs this chapter's nature/grace summaries.

13. This section reflects earlier research help from Barry Jones and from K. Long and Noll, "What Are the Varieties of Classical Protestantism?" The profiles of these traditions focus on original tendencies rather than later "liberal" versions, and largely overlap with Buschart, *Exploring Protestant Traditions*: Lutheran (A Gospel of Grace), Anabaptist (Faith

narrowing, at least to exclude trinitarian and christological heresies. While many Protestant churches are noncreedal, most affirm the content of ecumenical orthodoxy, often in confessional statements. Accordingly, other modern religious movements—notably *Jehovah's Witnesses and *Mormonism—should be excluded, despite functioning somewhat like Christian churches.[14] Awkwardly, boundary cases remain: some qualify without claiming the label, while others may claim the label but do not qualify.[15]

Magisterial Reformers such as Martin Luther and John Calvin sought to reform the one church—until the Catholic Church excommunicated them, anyway—while Radical Reformers deemed it apostate. These Reformers sometimes differed over which "*solas*" to prioritize. Affirming *sola scriptura* yet differing over its interpretation, they unleashed appeals to freedom of conscience that fostered tens of thousands of new movements. Amid such diversity, it may seem impossible for seven theological profiles to encompass the main alternatives. Patterns have been emerging, however, in other chapters' coverage of key concepts. The purpose of covering these conceptual patterns here is to show that church traditions comprise historically developing and theologically integrated systems rather than isolated menu choices. Some traditions have longer histories, more formal confessions, or more distinct concepts than others, as the following expositions reflect. For all their diversity, "Protestant" churches share a commitment to ongoing freedom for reform according to the biblical gospel.

Lutheran: Justification by Faith Alone

The fundamental Lutheran concept is justification by faith alone, "the doctrine by which the church stands or falls."[16] An ensuing cultural stance sharply distinguishes between two kingdoms: the eternal, spiritual, inward rule of Christ in the gospel; and the temporal, earthly, external rule of law.

---

for Radical Community), Reformed (To the Glory of God, and God Alone), Anglican (The Spirit of a *Via Media*), Baptist (Freedom for Immediacy), Wesleyan (Grace-Full Holiness and Holy Wholeness), Dispensationalist (Rightly Dividing the Scriptures), and Pentecostal (The Spirit of Continuity). Whereas Buschart includes dispensationalism, the focus here is upon church traditions.

Kevin Hector dares me to admit that nobody still adheres to these traditions in pure form. To that I can only say: he must not have met some Calvinists I know!

14. For brief overviews, see Hexham, "Jehovah's Witnesses" and "Mormonism." Jehovah's Witnesses reject the incarnation and trinitarian theology in favor of an Arian-like Christology. Mormonism historically teaches that God the Father has a body, the human fall into sin was necessary, and evolutionary eternal progression involves deified humanity.

15. Notably, Oneness Pentecostalism, discussed earlier in chap. 4.

16. See, e.g., Luther, "Smalcald Articles," 301.

Thus, *gratia iuxta naturam*: grace dialectically flanks—runs distinct but parallel to—nature.

HISTORY

Luther was educated in the "Ockhamist axiom" that "to those who do what is in them, God does not deny grace."[17] Luther was anxious, however, that he could not live up to this gospel's demands for cooperation with God's grace. His confessor, Johann von Staupitz (c. 1460–1524), convinced him to abandon Ockhamism for a more Augustinian theology. A "tower experience" brought sudden insight into Romans 1:16–17: the righteousness revealed in the gospel, as Luther came to understand it, is not the active righteousness with which God judges unrighteous sinners; rather, it is the passive righteousness with which God justifies sinners by faith alone—not what God *is* but what God *gives*.

According to tradition, Luther nailed his Ninety-Five Theses to the church door in Wittenberg on October 31, 1517, igniting the Protestant Reformation. Luther challenged the practice of selling indulgences as well as the common conception of penance. Within weeks Luther's theses were translated into German, published via newly invented printing presses, and circulated widely. In 1520, Luther published three treatises that marked a decisive break with Rome. *Address to the Christian Nobility of the German Nation* called upon German princes to take church reform into their own hands. *The Babylonian Captivity of the Church* rejected the doctrine of transubstantiation and the sacrificial conception of the Mass. *The Freedom of a Christian* delineated Luther's teaching on justification by faith.

In December 1520, Luther publicly burned a papal bull of excommunication set for January 1521 if he did not recant. Called before the emperor at the Diet of Worms in April 1521, he again refused to recant, appealing to a conscience held captive by God's Word. Forced into hiding, he began his German translation of the Bible, only returning to Wittenberg in 1522 to thwart chaos among his followers. In 1529, he traveled to Marburg to address conflict over the Lord's Supper with the Swiss Reformer Ulrich Zwingli (1484–1531), but the two failed to agree; Luther adamantly defended Christ's real presence against Zwingli's memorial interpretation. In 1525, Luther married Katharina von Bora (1499–1552), a former nun, with whom he had six children and lived at Wittenberg for the rest of his life.

Philipp Melanchthon joined him and composed the Augsburg Confession in 1530, although his more moderate theology generated later controversy.

---

17. Walker et al., *History of the Christian Church*, 354.

In 1577, the Formula of Concord, composed primarily by Martin Chemnitz (1522–86), sought to establish a common Lutheran confession. Today, the Book of Concord, a Lutheran compilation of confessional documents, contains ecumenical creeds, the Augsburg Confession, Melanchthon's *Apology of the Augsburg Confession*, the Smalcald Articles, Luther's Smaller and Larger Catechisms, *A Treatise on the Power and Primacy of the Pope*, and the Formula of Concord.

Lutheran orthodoxy elicited a seventeenth-century pietist movement. With *Pia Desideria*, Philipp Jakob Spener (1635–1705) provided pietism's impetus: he criticized theologians for pursuing philosophical speculation, nobles and princes for exercising undue control over the church, clergy for replacing active faith with arid doctrine, and laypeople for neglecting holiness. Inspired by Spener and his successor August Hermann Francke (1663–1727), the pietist movement continued into the nineteenth century, transcended German Lutheranism, and influenced later evangelicalism.

THEOLOGY

The Lutheran gospel champions Scripture's proclamation of forgiveness in Christ alone (*solus Christus*; *sola scriptura*). Against Erasmus, Luther insisted that apart from grace the human will is in bondage to sin (*sola gratia*). Christ's righteousness is imputed to unworthy sinners through faith alone (*sola fide*). Good works flow from grateful faith but do not merit salvation; justification frees sinners to love God and their neighbors. While Luther rejected the medieval Catholic system, he retained a sacramental theology, including baptismal regeneration and Christ's real presence in the Eucharist.[18]

Given Luther's tendency to retain Catholic teaching unless biblical reform seemed necessary, he maintained a version of Christendom in which "church" and "state" had overlapping authority. His two-kingdoms doctrine remained within the Augustinian tradition of two cities—the city of God and the city of man. He affirmed a form of natural law focused on the Ten Commandments. Yet Luther prioritized the eternal kingdom of the gospel over the temporal kingdom of societal institutions. In principle, true Christians are governed solely by the gospel, all others by earthly law. Christians should appeal to civil law or use temporal power only out of love for neighbors, not on their own behalf; Christians exercise and are subject to earthly rule for others' sake. In practice, Luther attempted to gain political freedom for Protestant

---

18. On the complex relation between Lutheran sacramentalism and other evangelical traditions, see Cary, "Why Luther Is Not Quite Protestant."

reform while avoiding anarchic revolts. His two-kingdoms model has influenced modern political theology both overtly and covertly.[19]

Later Lutheranism has been accused of making the church socially complacent, notably in the German capitulation to Nazism. Its "dialectical" approach to nature and grace has freed Lutheran culture to make distinctive contributions—in music, for example. Others worry, however, that this dialectical approach allows natural reason or cultural realities to operate without gospel transformation. Even so, the Lutheran dynamic of "law and gospel" has kept Pauline soteriology prominent in Protestant life.

Reformed: God's Sovereign Glory as Creator and Redeemer

Naming the next tradition is complex: "Reformed" designates a theological perspective, "Presbyterian" a church polity. Reformed theology is broader than Calvinism, given the influence of Zwingli, of Martin Bucer (1491–1551) over ecclesiology, of John Knox in Scotland (c. 1513–72), and so forth. Despite such complexities, the Reformed tradition shares the fundamental concept of God's sovereign glory as Creator and Redeemer.

HISTORY

After an evangelical awakening, Zwingli went to Zurich in 1519 as the reforming "People's Priest." Some early followers, including Conrad Grebel (1498–1526), were unconvinced by his support of infant baptism; they rebaptized one another in January 1525. Zwingli defended the traditional practice by appealing to the unity of God's covenants, arguing that baptism, as the sign of the new covenant, corresponds to circumcision.

Though not the earliest, Calvin undoubtedly was the most influential Reformed theologian. After a sudden conversion and subsequent flight from France as a Protestant, Calvin published the first edition of *Institutes of Christian Religion* in 1536 at Basel. Originally a pocket-sized handbook on Protestant belief, it was expanded several times before its final Latin edition appeared in 1559. Calvin ended up in Geneva for most of his last twenty-five years, serving as a dedicated pastor and political leader. Alongside the *Institutes*, he wrote commentaries on most books of the Bible and left behind a large collection of sermons, polemical tracts, and catechetical materials.

In parallel with Lutheranism, a period of Reformed "orthodoxy" ran from the mid-sixteenth century into the eighteenth. Important confessional documents include the Gallican Confession (1559), the Scots Confession (1560),

---

19. As traced in Crouse, *Two Kingdoms and Two Cities.*

the Belgic Confession (1561), the Thirty-Nine Articles of the Church of England (1563), the Heidelberg Catechism (1563), the Second Helvetic Confession (1566), the Canons of Dort (1618), and the Westminster Standards (1647–48). "Scholastic" theologians explicated this orthodox teaching with academic methods.

In the seventeenth century, Dutch theologian Jacobus Arminius (1560–1609) challenged Calvinist teaching on predestination. According to Arminius, election is based on God's foreknowledge of who will exercise faith. In 1610, Arminius's followers presented their beliefs to the Dutch Reformed Church, sparking a debate that led to the Synod of Dort (Dortrecht) in 1618. Responding to the Arminian *Remonstrance*, Dort affirmed pervasive original sinfulness, entirely gracious election to salvation, the elect's perseverance in faith, and the particular application of Christ's all-sufficient atonement to the elect. Dort's decisions became definitive for much of the Reformed tradition.

The late nineteenth century saw a revival of Calvinism in the Netherlands, led by Abraham Kuyper (1837–1920) and Herman Bavinck (1854–1921). Kuyper, who founded the Free University of Amsterdam and served as prime minister, elaborated the notion of common grace and emphasized a Christian worldview. He also contributed to the theory of *sphere sovereignty, which holds—somewhat like the Catholic concept of subsidiarity—that God's common grace authorizes the integrity of distinct areas of life within the created order.

The Westminster Assembly, called by Parliament to advise on restructuring the Church of England, produced a staunchly Calvinist confession (1646) that remains the best known in the English-speaking world. Many North American colonists were English Puritans. The First Great Awakening involved Calvinist ministers such as Jonathan Edwards and George Whitefield (1714–70). Until 1929, Princeton Seminary was guided by committed Calvinists, including Charles Hodge (1797–1878), B. B. Warfield (1851–1921), and J. Gresham Machen (1881–1937). These Princeton theologians, following Westminster more than the Dutch stream, influenced the modern evangelical doctrine of Scripture.

THEOLOGY

Reformed theology emphasizes God's comprehensive sovereignty while celebrating creation as "the theater of God's glory." After the fall, the seed of divinity in human hearts generates idolatrous religion. Special revelation by Word and Spirit is necessary for saving knowledge of the Triune God. The Scriptures are "spectacles" through which to view all of life. At its best, the Reformed tradition thinks deeply, with a lively sense of divine greatness and human sinfulness that magnifies God's love. At its worst, Reformed thought minimizes human dignity and freedom. Through the "double grace" of covenantal union with Christ, justification comes by faith alone; sanctification progressively follows as God's law instructs believers in good works. Unconditional election is not part of gospel proclamation but rather is a background doctrine that comforts believers and promotes gratitude. "Covenant" or "federal" theology, which is explained in chapter 15, arose after Calvin to clarify the biblical history of redemption that undergirds these doctrines.

Reformed theology identifies two sacraments, baptism and the Lord's Supper. Calvin's understanding of the Lord's Supper stood between Luther and Zwingli, maintaining Christ's real yet spiritual presence. The Reformed tradition retained infant baptism but discarded baptismal regeneration; baptism serves as a sign and seal of God's covenant promises.

The Reformed approach to culture is "transformationist": *gratia intra naturam*, grace restoring nature. The fall's cursed effects are tragically deep and wide, but common grace preserves the created order and redeeming grace has a cosmic reach. The Westminster and Puritan streams emphasize the need for post-fall transformation; Dutch neo-Calvinist streams emphasize the hope of restoration—creation's originally intended progress and redemption's comprehensiveness. Divergent emphases notwithstanding, a Reformed framework of creation, fall, redemption, and consummation has galvanized broader Christian "worldview" formation.

Anabaptist: Radical, Communal Discipleship

The fundamental Anabaptist concept is the church's calling to follow Jesus: the gospel creates a community that radically practices Christian nonviolence here and now. Anabaptists are radical in seeking a return to Christianity's *radix*, or root: rejecting the Christendom synthesis underlies their rejection of paedobaptism. Since they demanded that people baptized as infants be "re" (*ana* in Greek) baptized (again for the first time, as it were), various individuals and groups were dubbed Anabaptists even if "Radical" Reformers might be more accurate. Their theology typically reflects *gratia contra naturam*: grace incompatible with, or at least judging, nature.

History

Radical Reformers varied by geographic region and local leadership. Grebel and others became critical of Zwingli for allowing Zurich's city council to determine the speed of reformation, particularly abolition of the Mass. Grebel allied with rural leaders who established self-governing churches; then he broke with Zwingli over believer's baptism. The rebaptizing movement spread quickly while meeting severe persecution from both Protestants and Catholics. Grebel was imprisoned before dying of plague in summer 1526, just a year and a half after igniting the Anabaptist movement.

In 1527, a group led by Michael Sattler (1490–1527) composed the Schleit-heim Articles to consolidate the movement: (1) Baptism would be administered only to believers. (2) Based on Matthew 18, the ban would discipline believers who persisted in sin. (3) Participation in the Lord's Supper was limited to baptized believers. (4) Believers must separate from the sinful world. (5) Every church should be led by a pastor who met New Testament qualifications. (6) The government is ordained by God to punish the wicked and protect the good; however, the sword's power is "outside the perfection of Christ," so believers should not wield it. (7) Believers must not swear oaths.

Magisterial Reformers sought to discredit the radical movement based on a revolutionary stronghold that developed at Münster. Münster Anabaptists were characterized by grandiose eschatological claims (such as reestablishment of the Davidic kingdom, with Jan van Leiden [1509–36] ruling), plus outbursts of violence and debauchery (such as Leiden's royal harem of sixteen concubines). Anabaptist control of Münster came to a violent end in June 1535 at the hands of mercenaries.

Menno Simmons (c. 1496–1561), a former Catholic priest, joined the Anabaptist movement in 1536. In Münster's wake, Menno nurtured surviving members of the movement in the Low Countries. Menno was committed to nonviolence and to disciplined, visible yet separate, communities, similar to the Swiss vision. Menno was a capable leader whose name attaches to one of the movement's most enduring branches, the Mennonites.

Contemporary Anabaptist heirs consist mainly of Brethren, Hutterites, Mennonites, and the Amish. The Amish and the Hutterites live primarily in the United States and Canada, continuing a tradition of radical separation from society; they maintain agrarian and communal lifestyles, rejecting modern dress and technology. Mennonites have adherents worldwide, many of whom maintain traditional convictions without withdrawing as radically from society; they actively promote peace and human relief.

Theology

Radical Reformers were committed to *sola scriptura*; unlike the Magisterial Reformers, they were less inclined to attach biblical interpretation specially to learned theologians. Gatherings of committed disciples were the locus of discernment, which contemporary scholars call "the hermeneutic community." Whereas the Magisterial Reformation focused on Paul's Epistles, Anabaptists favor the Gospels, particularly Jesus's Sermon on the Mount. They also favor the Epistles of James and Peter to emphasize discipleship. Anabaptist theology highlights discontinuity between the Old and New Testaments, with the ethic of the New tending to supplant the Old.

With prominent exceptions, Anabaptists were trinitarian. But they traditionally gave little attention to the doctrines of God and Christ, which were considered abstract and speculative, disconnected from active discipleship. Anabaptist theology has been less influenced by Augustine, particularly his emphasis on the bondage of the will, than Magisterial Reformation traditions have been. While stressing the corruption of societal structures, Anabaptists are voluntaristic—centered on human responsibility. Early Anabaptists feared that highlighting original sin and forensic justification led to moral laxity rather than committed discipleship. The Anabaptist focus lies upon the *imitatio Christi*, the imitation of Christ in all areas of life.

In their efforts to embody God's kingdom on earth, early Anabaptists took the Great Commission (Matt. 28:18–20) very seriously. Disciples were called to imitate Jesus radically, even to the point of martyrdom. Anabaptists believed that persecution confirmed their authenticity, for the true church shares in Christ's suffering. Through baptism, believers form a voluntary association of those willing to "take up the cross" and follow Jesus. Strict discipline marks the true church. For early Anabaptists, renouncing the world often meant agrarian life outside the city, simple even to the point of abandoning private property.

Radical Reformers believed that the church was radically fallen. Magisterial Reformers certainly were critical of the Catholic Church, but they remained confident about "vestiges of the church under the papacy,"[20] whereas early Anabaptists viewed the Church of Rome as "the Babylonian whore."[21] There was no clear consensus regarding when the church became apostate, but all agreed that the corruption came early. Some suggested that it came almost immediately after the apostles' death, with the rise of clericalism. Others identified the decisive turn with Constantine's alliance between church and empire. Still others maintained that the final corruption was the official establishment of paedobaptism. In any case, with the Roman church beyond hope of renewal, the primitive church became essential to recover.

20. Calvin, *Institutes* 4.2.11 (2:1051–52).
21. E.g., Marpeck, "Exposé of the Babylonian Whore."

Accordingly, even if "withdrawal" unfairly characterizes their cultural stance, Anabaptists emphasize that grace judges nature—not least because of the overlap between nature and the church in Christendom. Any violence, even in self-defense, would contradict Jesus concerning the voluntary surrender of power. Anabaptists cannot serve in positions of civil authority, as either soldiers or magistrates. Their focus rests upon the fall and redemption. When neo-Anabaptists such as John Howard Yoder expand their account of creation, they still treat its present structures as "principalities and powers"—originally good, yes, but now systemically cursed. Conversely, the new community of Jesus followers must not delay its own transformation until the future coming of God's kingdom; God's jubilee should begin to appear here and now.[22]

Anglican: A Middle Way via Common Prayer

Characterizing a final Reformation-era communion, Anglicanism, is again complex. The Church of England embodied the Christendom to which Anabaptists and later Baptists objected. The English church borrowed Lutheran and Reformed elements to reshape its Catholic and Orthodox heritage. The English church gave an unwilling birth to the Wesleyan tradition, while Pentecostal Christianity now makes its presence felt within the Anglican Communion. Given such intersections, the fundamental Anglican concept is often summarized as a *via media* or "middle way," especially between Catholic and Protestant Christianity—even though, by historical definition, Anglicanism is Protestant.

HISTORY

The Church of England's break with Rome stemmed from King Henry VIII (1491–1547) desiring a different wife in order to produce a male heir. When the pope refused to annul his marriage, the king severed ties with Rome and became the sovereign head of the church. The archbishop of Canterbury, Thomas Cranmer (1489–1556), took this opportunity to pursue a reformist agenda. The resulting Book of Common Prayer retained Catholic rituals with Protestant alterations. The Thirty-Nine Articles of Religion borrowed heavily from the Continental Reformers.

Expansion of the British Empire extended Anglican influence through colonial churches. The archbishop of Canterbury does not have papal power but is a first ecumenical patriarch among equals. Other instruments of Anglican

---

22. See Yoder, *Politics of Jesus*, which has influenced Stanley Hauerwas and others.

unity include the Thirty-Nine Articles, which offer a nonbinding doctrinal standard; Lambeth Conferences, which have convened global leaders approximately once per decade since the nineteenth century; the Anglican Consultative Council, which hosts the Lambeth meetings and provides a bureaucratic apparatus; and, preeminently, the prayer book, which remains "common" despite increasing local modifications.

THEOLOGY

The Anglican doctrinal genius—or flaw—lies in sharing a prayer book yet producing few systematic theologies.[23] Anglican theology is even more difficult to characterize in light of distinctions between British theology and Anglican churches elsewhere. To highlight one example, British (and sometimes American) Anglicanism often champions a "sacramental" account of reality, appealing to the incarnation and the dignity of creaturely embodiment. British academic theology likewise prioritizes historical inquiry, consistent with English empiricism. Yet Anglicans elsewhere may share neither English historicism nor broad sacramentalism.

Richard Hooker developed an early Anglican account of theological authority, speaking of a three-legged stool: Scripture, tradition, and reason. Scripture is preeminent but cannot be read without tradition and reason. The Thirty-Nine Articles, like other Magisterial Reformation documents, underscore freedom: the church may not bind the conscience for salvation beyond the biblical gospel. This gospel initially reflected Magisterial Reformation themes, especially justification by faith alone and sacramental grace, with liturgical language remaining open to different theological explanations.

Alongside gospel freedom, the Anglican ethos emphasized ecclesiastical freedom for prudential traditions beyond Scripture's explicit commands. The church need not maximally imitate primitive Christianity (contra Anabaptists, along with some Lutherans and Calvinists); instead, the church may discern appropriate forms for fulfilling essential functions in new contexts. Rather than being a middle way, the Anglican essence arguably lies in distinguishing essential elements of faith and order from *adiaphora*.[24]

23. For indications that this tide may be turning, albeit while challenging some concepts of systematic theology, see McMichael, *Vocation of Anglican Theology*. O'Donovan, *Thirty-Nine Articles*, 6, opines that "it was not then, and has never been to this day, the genius of the Church of England to grow its own theological nourishment, but only to prepare what was provided from elsewhere and to set it decently upon the table."

24. O'Donovan, *Thirty-Nine Articles*, 8–9.

The modern Anglican Communion is frequently depicted with three "wings": Anglo-Catholic, broad church (sometimes called "liberal"), and evangelical. The first, Anglo-Catholic wing rues the breach with Rome, remaining as Catholic in thought and practice as possible. The second, broad-church wing has been dominant in the Church of England, not least because its "establishment" as the state church naturally gives weight to public consensus, which has theologically minimalist tendencies. The third, evangelical wing ebbs and flows in influence, tending to be a minority in England because it competes with "dissenting" or free-church groups for adherents. Both the three-wing depiction and the appeal to a *via media* are oversimplifications, yet these notions exert lingering influence. On particular doctrines, Anglican believers or groups may hold very divergent views; in principle, the distinctive glue holding them together is common prayer.

Baptist: The Church's Spiritual Nature

As the names imply, Baptists have points of overlap with Anabaptists. Yet their history is distinct, they do not share a commitment to Christian nonviolence, and their modern numbers are much larger. Despite the name, Baptists are not primarily concerned about the administration of baptism; rather, their fundamental concept is the spiritual nature of the church, from which believers' baptism arises.[25]

HISTORY

Baptist history is contested. A fringe minority attempts to trace Baptist origins through reformist groups across the ages—a "trail of blood" (a term from Landmark Baptist ecclesiology)—all the way back to John the Baptist. A more prominent alternative traces the Baptist tradition back to sixteenth-century Anabaptists. Now, though, scholarly consensus roots Baptist origins primarily among English Puritans and separatist groups. Of course, there was traffic between English dissenters and Continental Reformers, both Magisterial and Radical.

John Smyth (c. 1570–1612), an ordained priest, withdrew from the Church of England in 1606, heading to Amsterdam to avoid persecution. There he and others, including Thomas Helwys (c. 1570–1616), formed a simple New Testament church and (re)baptized themselves in 1609. In 1611 Helwys led

---

25. So Kevan, "Baptist Tradition." Given similar roots among English dissenters, the Quaker tradition probably best fits here as well, albeit with a distinctive emphasis upon an "inner light" rather than biblicism.

a group back to England, where he established a church near London. This Baptist church synthesized Mennonite and Puritan elements, promoting a regenerate church membership and religious freedom. Numerous congregations soon followed; eventually, in 1689, the Act of Toleration granted English religious freedom. Yet many Baptists also emigrated to the American colonies. Colonies favored particular churches, but Baptists like Roger Williams (c. 1603–84) led the fight for freedom of worship. The American frontier proved quite hospitable to Baptist initiatives. Baptists grew from the First and Second Great Awakenings around the 1730s and the 1790s, as well as black congregations and other marginal groups.

Unfortunately, like other groups, American Baptists endured two splits. The first ran between North and South around the Civil War. The second ran between fundamentalists and modernists in the early twentieth century, especially in the North. While the Southern Baptist Convention held fundamentalists and modernists together for several decades, toward the end of the twentieth century "conservatives" were able to enforce their theological standards throughout the denomination, leading "moderates" to break away. America's best-known Baptist theologians have been Augustus Strong (1836–1921) in the North and E. Y. Mullins (1860–1928) in the South. While Baptists are often anticreedal, they have produced numerous confessional statements, including the Second London Confession of 1677 and the New Hampshire Confession of 1833.

THEOLOGY

Baptist theology borrows and blends other traditions. Concerning salvation, many are Arminian ("General") while some are Reformed ("Particular"). Concerning sanctification, Baptists may sound Lutheran in emphasizing assurance of justification by faith alone, Reformed in emphasizing progressive sanctification, or Keswick in emphasizing the Spirit's regular filling. Concerning public life, they sharply distinguish between temporal and eternal kingdoms, yet sometimes they promote "civil religion" when possible (as recently in the United States). Such complexities aside, a well-known acrostic captures distinctive Baptist views.

(B) Baptists classically emphasize *biblical authority*, appealing radically to *sola scriptura*. They have been suspicious of creeds and other aspects of tradition, as well as appeals to public reason.

(A) Baptists celebrate the *autonomy of the local church*. No connecting structure may impinge upon congregational authority. Many will not even speak of "denominations" but advocate fellowships of churches instead.

Congregations call their own pastors and deacons. All members should participate in decision-making (although large congregations implement this provision variously).

(P) Baptists champion the *priesthood of every believer*. Each Christian may directly pray to God and hear from God in Scripture. Whereas Lutheran and Reformed versions of this doctrine emphasize the priesthood of all believers in a more communal context, the Baptist emphasis is more individual.

(T) Baptists acknowledge *two church offices*, pastor and deacon. "Bishop," "elder," and "pastor" are treated as equivalent biblical terms. In congregations with multiple pastors, all serve as teaching elders. Congregations have spiritual leaders devoted to teaching and prayer, and temporal leaders devoted to administration and service. Deacons usually have the latter responsibility, but sometimes function like the former.

(I) Underlying these concepts is *individual soul liberty*. "God doesn't have grandchildren," the saying goes. Each person is responsible before God to believe the gospel, join the church in baptism, and grow in faith.

(S) A corollary emphasis is *separation of church and state*. Baptists oppose church establishment and infant baptism as restrictions upon individual soul liberty and hindrances to biblical authority, congregational autonomy, and the priesthood of the believer.

(T) Baptists acknowledge *two church ordinances*: baptism and the Lord's Supper. *Ordinances are not sacraments, but rather are commanded practices for symbolically remembering Christ.[26] Baptism involves full immersion, not sprinkling or pouring as in paedobaptist traditions; only immersion symbolizes Christ's death, burial, and resurrection as in Romans 6:3–5.

(S) Finally, the church's spiritual nature requires a *saved church membership*. All who profess faith, are baptized, and are not under discipline should be members; only disciples who so qualify may be members. Hence Baptist ecclesiology has obvious affinities with reforming and pietist impulses that are widespread among evangelicals.

Wesleyan: The Pursuit of Perfect Love

Wesleyan theology emerged from pietist roots in the early eighteenth century through John Wesley's ministry, to which both Methodists and later Holiness groups appeal. Wesley was foremost a biblical preacher, but he engaged the catholic tradition considerably. He blended various elements: from Arminianism, aspects of the Reformed tradition; from Anglicanism,

---

26. A caveat: As chap. 14 addresses, the "new Baptist sacramentalism" has been recovering sacramental language from earlier Baptists.

moral and sacramental emphases; from Moravian pietism, justification by faith; and from Puritanism, spiritual zeal. Yet Wesley opposed Anglican formalism, Moravian "stillness," and Calvinist passivity. The fundamental concept of perfect love ensued—love, focusing religion on the heart; perfect, seeking a second blessing that would fill the heart completely with love for God.

History

From 1729 to 1735 Wesley led a small group (including his younger brother Charles [1707–88] and his friend George Whitefield), known among other Oxford students as the "Holy Club." Later this group became known as "Methodists," reflecting their rigorous approach to discipleship. In 1735, the Wesleys traveled to Georgia as missionaries. Three years later, John returned to England with an abiding sense of failure and a lack of assurance.

Wesley's journey connected him with Moravian missionaries. On May 24, 1738, he attended a Moravian Bible study at Aldersgate Street in London. While an unknown layman was reading Luther's commentary on Romans, Wesley experienced some kind of evangelical conversion, although its precise nature remains debated. In Wesley's words, "I felt my heart strangely warmed. I felt I did trust Christ, Christ alone for salvation; and an assurance was given me that He had taken away my sins."[27] The Aldersgate experience assured Wesley of his salvation and gave his ministry new vitality.

Soon, along with Whitefield, he began calling for evangelical conversion. The Church of England closed its doors to these "Methodist" preachers, believing that their doctrine was new and unnecessary. Wesley and Whitefield were forced to preach in the open air, wherever they could gather a crowd. Despite church opposition, they went to Bristol in 1739, where revival broke out among coal miners. Perhaps Wesley's greatest contribution was organizing converts into "societies" or "bands" for discipleship. These small groups spread revival's momentum throughout England, Ireland, Scotland, and Wales, and even across the Atlantic.

Wesley provided leadership to the revival for over fifty years, traveling as many as 250,000 miles and preaching some 40,000 sermons yet remaining loyal to the Church of England. However, when the bishop of London refused in 1780 to ordain any Methodist preachers serving in the American colonies, Wesley himself ordained three—the first step toward an independent Methodist body. In 1784 the Methodist Episcopal Church organized in

27. Wesley, *Journal*, 35.

Baltimore under the leadership of Thomas Coke (1747–1814) and Francis Asbury (1745–1816). Methodists in England did not officially separate from the established Anglican Church until after Wesley's death.

Due to a growing sense that American Methodism was straying from Wesley's teaching of "Christian perfection," a new Holiness movement emerged in the mid-nineteenth century, stressing a two-stage process. First, someone experiences conversion or justification in which sins are forgiven. Second, entire sanctification comes at a later crisis in which sin as an abiding disposition is removed. The Holiness movement emerged from camp-meeting revivals throughout rural America, the Christian perfectionism of popular preachers such as Charles Finney (1792–1875), and the ministry of Phoebe Palmer (1807–74), including her "Tuesday Meeting for the Promotion of Holiness." While the Holiness movement began with strong ties to Wesleyan theology, it quickly transcended denominational lines. Along with independent Holiness congregations, new denominations formed, including the Church of God (Anderson, Indiana), the Church of the Nazarene, the Salvation Army, and the Christian and Missionary Alliance. Beginning in 1875, a "higher life" variety of Holiness teaching spawned the annual Keswick Convention in northern England. Although today's Keswick Convention no longer exclusively represents this earlier teaching, the label "Keswick" is still associated with a higher-life view.

THEOLOGY

Wesley taught justification by faith alone in basic agreement with the sixteenth-century Reformers. Yet he followed Arminius in holding that prevenient grace enables all humans to respond freely to the gospel. This universal work of the Spirit overcomes the dire effects of original sin. Thus, Wesleyan theology rejects the Calvinist doctrine of unconditional election and its account of total depravity, holding instead that election involves God's foreknowledge of human faith and that total depravity is addressed by prevenient grace so as to enable freely willed faith. For personal assurance of salvation, Wesley emphasized both the Holy Spirit's testimony and the human spirit, as described in Romans 8:16. External evidence enables a believer's spirit to confirm the Spirit's inner persuasion. Such assurance, though, does not provide certainty that someone will persevere in faith to the end of life.

Wesleyan theology generally understands sanctification as beginning at conversion but experienced more fully after a *second blessing. This "second work of grace" removes the inclination to sin and fills the heart with perfect love of God and neighbor. The believer moves into the sphere of *Christian perfection or "perfect love," in which the Spirit makes it possible to live without committing voluntary sin. Influenced by Wesleyan thought, Keswick teaching specifies that a second blessing does not eradicate sin but involves being filled with the Spirit for victory in an ongoing struggle (thus, likely, more than once). A single act of self-surrender in faith brings the blessing (automatically, many would say); direct moral struggle will end in defeat, whereas "letting go and letting God" will make someone properly reliant on Christ.[28]

Wesleyan influence has been pervasive upon evangelical piety and substantial upon evangelical theology. Whereas some Holiness offshoots have largely focused on personal spirituality, many Wesleyans have been pioneers in the pursuit of social justice. If Calvinists and Lutherans championed Romans, even to the point of Lutherans marginalizing James, then Wesleyans renewed interest in 1 John. Accordingly, Holiness groups practiced active love in promoting abolitionist, temperance, and women's suffrage causes. What the Wesleyan tradition may lack in a formal consensus for relating nature and grace has been balanced out by energetic cultural and political populism that is consistent with its religion of the heart. Evangelicals today reflect substantial Wesleyan influence as they take for granted small groups, lively songs, popular experience, missionary activism, and parachurch ministries.

Pentecostal: The Holy Spirit's Empowerment

Christian faith around the globe is increasingly Pentecostal. Burgeoning movements in the Global South or Majority World are widely labeled "Pentecostal" even when they operate within other established churches, whether Orthodox or Catholic or Protestant. The sketch here highlights specifically Pentecostal and charismatic movements that began in the West. Although some non-Western Pentecostal movements overlap with this Anglo-American history, others reflect indigenous leadership that arose independently. Global Pentecostalism may contain more emphasis upon supernatural activity in some contexts, while reflecting less primacy for *glossolalia (speaking in tongues) in others, than historic American Pentecostalism. Despite such variety, Pentecostals share a fundamental concept of the Holy Spirit's empowerment: expecting the full range of the Spirit's baptizing and gift-giving work in the New Testament, especially from Acts, to be repeated among Christians today.

---

28. Packer, "Holiness Movement." See further Kostlevy, *Historical Dictionary of the Holiness Movement.*

History

On January 1, 1901, during a prayer vigil, Agnes Ozman (1870–1937), a student at Bethel Bible School in Topeka, Kansas, spoke in tongues after Charles Fox Parham (1873–1929) laid hands on her and prayed for her to receive the baptism of the Holy Spirit. This event usually marks the beginning of modern Pentecostalism. Parham, a former Methodist minister and a Holiness preacher, introduced the basic Pentecostal doctrine of tongues as the *initial evidence of Spirit baptism. When Ozman received glossolalia, Parham had been teaching on the "latter rain," the Spirit's outpouring at the end of the current age.

Beginning in 1906, one of Parham's students, William Seymour (1870–1922), an African American Holiness preacher, led a revival at an abandoned church on Azusa Street in Los Angeles. The Azusa Street revival gained notoriety via newspaper reports. Thousands flocked to the meetings, which launched a worldwide phenomenon. Pentecostal denominations sprang up, including the Church of God (Cleveland, Tennessee), the Pentecostal Church of God, the International Church of the Foursquare Gospel, and the largest, the Assemblies of God. Through missionary zeal, the Pentecostal movement experienced remarkable growth in its first century.[29]

Pentecostalism's second wave, the "charismatic" movement, arose in the 1950s through the 1970s within mainline denominations and some evangelical churches. People in these other traditions experienced special gifts of the Holy Spirit; so, for instance, some Episcopalians began speaking in tongues and then some formed charismatic congregations.[30] Pentecostalism's third wave began with the "Vineyard" movement, which had its peak influence in the 1980s and 1990s within the United States. Vineyard churches placed less emphasis on glossolalia and Spirit baptism, with more on "power encounters" confronting Satan's forces via signs and wonders. Of course, much Vineyard worship music became mainstream throughout evangelical churches.

Theology

Pentecostal theology springs from the Holiness "second blessing" tradition. For classic Pentecostals, this second blessing involves *baptism in the

29. A. Anderson documents this growth in what has become a standard work: *Introduction to Pentecostalism*. Anderson counteracts the "made in America" narrative traced here, locating Pentecostal origins half a century earlier in Britain and India (*Introduction to Pentecostalism*, 19–39). See also Burgess and van der Maas, *Dictionary of Pentecostal and Charismatic Movements*.

30. Some now use "neo-charismatic" to designate those outside mainline institutions (Sweeney, *American Evangelical Story*, 195n22).

Holy Spirit after conversion. This baptism is ideally for all but becomes actual only for some Christians. Spirit baptism is manifest in speaking in tongues as its initial evidence, and subsequently in greater joy and power for ministry.

The charismatic renewal retained Spirit baptism, but not always manifest in glossolalia. Vineyard churches tend toward a more progressive, less "crisis" oriented, view of sanctification. They acknowledge that the Holy Spirit indwells every believer—which some earlier Pentecostals denied—not just those baptized with the Spirit. Vineyard churches maintain the continuing pertinence of all spiritual gifts, but the special gifts descend upon some believers without receiving normative emphasis for all. Vineyard groups distinguish more clearly between prophecy as a spiritual gift and the revelation finally settled in Scripture. They often hold that prophecy may be fallible and is not ongoing "revelation" in the same sense that earlier Pentecostals anticipated.[31]

Pentecostal diversity reflects rapid cross-denominational growth and inherent openness toward new developments that challenge formal definitions. Like Anabaptist, Holiness, and Baptist groups, Pentecostal groups are sometimes seen as world-denying; they lack a formal framework for relating nature and grace or articulating political theology. Although "health and wealth gospel" and "word of faith" approaches have been prominent, they do not characterize the entire tradition. Indeed, it is worth repeating the widespread canard that liberation theologies articulate a preferential option for the poor yet the poor choose Pentecostalism. Thus, an implicit Pentecostal theology of culture might celebrate the Spirit's diverse work in practically empowering the marginalized.[32]

The preceding traditions do not exhaust the theological possibilities for enculturating the gospel. The late modern world weaves their strands together in new fashions: the internal variety of Orthodox and Catholic Christianity, increasing interaction between them and Protestants, plus tens of thousands of Protestant groups—all this complexity can make Christian doctrine appear to be incoherent and divisive. Yet certain paths are taken repeatedly, even if they eventually branch off into new territory. Amid the variety, the Triune God's self-revelation still reverberates through the good news of reconciliation in Christ.

Having addressed Christ's identity and ministry of reconciliation, sin and salvation, and major church traditions, it is appropriate to conclude this set of chapters with a summary of the *gospel. "Gospel" is not just a literary

---

31. On fallible prophecy, they followed Grudem, *Gift of Prophecy*.
32. See Yong, *Days of Caesar*.

genre in the Bible, a means of atonement, an invitation to accept personal salvation, or a program to promote social justice. "Gospel" is both a word that appears in particular biblical texts and a concept that is present more widely. In the context of Israel's story and Christ's proclamation of God's kingdom, "gospel" is an announcement of promises fulfilled in the arrival of King Jesus. Indeed, "gospel" is what the creedal Rule of Faith conveys as a normative summary of Scripture's message; in that Rule "gospel" is trinitarian in structure and narrative in content. The gospel, then, is the joyful *announcement* that the Triune Creator has returned to redeem Israel in Christ, who bore human sin on the cross and was raised from the dead as the firstfruits of our new life; the Holy Spirit is regathering the covenant people around Jesus as Lord and is welcoming gentiles into this redeemed community; ultimately Christ will return to establish the *shalom* of God's comprehensive reign.[33] *Evangelism heralds this good news in essential words and accompanying deeds. The church's announcement of the Triune God's royal grace carries an implicit *exhortation* that evangelism turns into an explicit *invitation*: be reconciled to God (2 Cor. 5:20)!

This good news inevitably takes cultural shape in church traditions. Since the church is composed of forgiven sinners who seek understanding of their faith while still being reconciled with one another, evangelical theology must reflect both biblical conviction and patient openness to reform.[34] The gospel reassures us that someday God will make all things new—even the human community. Until then, we believe in one holy, catholic, and apostolic church without seeing its fullness—which doctrinal traditions are necessary to anticipate.

---

33. See further the biblical-theological overview in Bird, *Evangelical Theology*, 47–54.

34. For a biblical ecclesiology that attempts to address intra-evangelical theological diversity, see Vanhoozer and Treier, *Theology and the Mirror of Scripture*, chap. 5.

PART 4

THE
Holy Spirit,
THE LIFE GIVER

—— *12* ——

God's Empowering Presence

THESIS

The Holy Spirit is the divine Giver of creaturely life, pouring out common grace, and the divine Giver of new life, applying Christ's redeeming grace as God's empowering presence—fostering conversion, consecration, assurance and perseverance, and shared ministry.

LEARNING OBJECTIVES

After learning the material in this chapter, you should be able to:

1. *Define briefly* the key terms introduced here (marked with an asterisk and included in the glossary).
2. *List and recognize* the following: (a) views of how the Holy Spirit works in conversion; (b) views of assurance and perseverance.
3. *Describe and compare* six major models of sanctification.
4. *Identify and illustrate* key biblical themes regarding the Holy Spirit.
5. *Explain* the following: (a) the significance of the Holy Spirit for addressing common grace and the cultural mandate; (b) biblical approaches to spiritual gifts.

S ometimes *pneumatology, the doctrine of the Holy Spirit, appears to get little attention.[1] Talking about the Holy Spirit focuses on our experience of God;[2] perhaps that is why pneumatology leaves many of us feeling lost for words. Pneumatology also raises the question of betrayal: Has Christianity domesticated, even fatally quenched, the genuine experience of God in the Spirit?[3] Various branches of the church press these charges

1. Kärkkäinen, *Pneumatology*, 176.
2. Badcock, *Light of Truth*, 1.
3. McIntyre, *Shape of Pneumatology*, esp. chap. 1. See also Radner, *End of the Church*.

against one another. Orthodox Christianity charges Western Christianity with failing to celebrate the Spirit's full personhood and mysterious work as a result of the *filioque* clause. Catholic Christianity charges Orthodox and Protestant Christians alike with resisting the Spirit's institutional work by failing to be in full, sacramental communion with the bishop of Rome. Pentecostal Christians charge the rest of Western Christianity with failing to embrace the Spirit's personally empowering presence by resisting the full pursuit of supernatural experiences and gifts. Given such charges of domesticating the Spirit, contemporary theologians have heightened the prominence of pneumatology in various ways: rejecting or questioning the *filioque*; appealing to social accounts of the Trinity that emphasize the Spirit's distinct personhood; celebrating the Spirit's distinct life-giving presence throughout creation; advocating "Spirit Christology" that emphasizes the Spirit working in the Son's humanity; affirming the full range of *charismata*; and appealing for all Christians to seek the baptism of the Holy Spirit after conversion.

Evaluating these proposals is difficult because evangelical traditions understand the Bible's teaching quite differently. In some cases, what counts as domesticating the Spirit on one interpretation counts as rightly dividing God's Word on another. In other cases, what counts as domesticating the Spirit is a matter of differing emphases rather than direct disagreements. Of course, nearly all Christians periodically "quench the Spirit" (1 Thess. 5:19) on their own theological terms. Furthermore, alongside traditional differences and the experiential effects of obedience or disobedience, pneumatology wrestles with the intellectual effects of the Spirit's mysterious character and Christ-glorifying focus (e.g., John 16:12–15). Thus, the modesty of biblical revelation may legitimately foster pneumatological modesty.

The Bible depicts the Spirit in terms of air in motion: intangible, yet powerful.[4] Like the wind, the Spirit is invisible, yet present and powerful in ways that we can feel and hear and recognize (John 3:8). The very name "Spirit" is an important reminder that the Triune God transcends human gender.[5] The Holy Spirit is more than an impersonal power, though: as God's presence with the covenant people, the Spirit anticipates the ultimate fulfillment of the following promise: "My dwelling place will be with them; I will be their

---

4. Fee, *God's Empowering Presence*, 906.

5. Migliore, *Faith Seeking Understanding*, 174. The grammatical gender of *pneuma* is neuter, not masculine. Accordingly, some use feminine pronouns for the Spirit to counterbalance masculine pronouns for the Father and Son and to clarify that God is not culturally masculine. But grammatical gender is not biological, and "spirit" designates that which transcends embodiment. John's Gospel personalizes the Spirit with a masculine pronoun (B. Jones, *Practicing Christian Doctrine*, 175). The Holy Spirit is also called the "Spirit of Christ," so feminine pronouns might not convey the unity of the Trinity.

God, and they will be my people" (Ezek. 37:27). Paul's Epistles emphasize that the Spirit is God personally dwelling in and among the covenant people, bringing the eschatological fulfillment of their salvation forward into their present experience. While Old Testament precursors specially associated the Spirit with leadership and prophecy, the new covenant's initial fulfillment brought a democratic outpouring: the Spirit's ministry broadened to include all those who are believer-priests in Christ.

It is no accident that the Nicene Creed describes the Holy Spirit as the "giver of life," since *life* is the Spirit's particular grace in both Testaments. The Spirit is life's *giver* in effecting creation and applying redemption: by the Spirit God breathed into us, as it were, creaturely life (e.g., Gen. 1:1–2; 2:7; Ps. 33:6; 104:30). Now, by that same Spirit, God is making all things new in Christ (e.g., Rom. 8:18–25). Other important associations with the Spirit's ministry include *fullness*.[6] The Spirit brings creatures to the fullness of their divinely designed end. Crucial to that design for human life are *freedom* and *love*: God made us for the freedom to love God and others. Love will characterize us when we are truly free to be ourselves (see Rom. 6–8; 12–15; 1 Cor. 12–14).

Such freedom comes to those who embrace the gospel of Christ. Therefore, as a bridge between the doctrine of salvation and the rest of the creedal teaching about the Holy Spirit—in subsequent chapters—here we consider the human responses involved in the "order of salvation." This *ordo salutis* analyzes how people participate in salvation through conversion, consecration, and perseverance in faith as they respond to the Spirit's invitation and assurance regarding life in Christ. Put differently, these human responses fit within the "application" of salvation: how the Spirit makes the work of Christ effective in particular human lives.

The people to whom the Holy Spirit applies the Son's work are members of communities, not isolated individuals. Three doctrines, therefore, have developed under the Creed's third article to address the Spirit's work of creating a *new humanity* in Jesus Christ: (1) *Scripture*, God's speaking the Word to (2) *the church*, God's calling together a people to be Christ's body, and (3) *last things*, God's consummation of the new creation through Jesus's return. Before the following three chapters address those three doctrines, here we address the Spirit's work in creation and in personal responses to redemption. The wind of God's Spirit mysteriously attaches people to the Father through fostering childlike faith in Jesus. Christians do not fully agree about how to describe this unseen work. Yet they do agree that the Spirit is

---

6. Especially in Acts. See Pelikan, *Acts*, 49.

not just a divine power but is a person of the Trinity whose life-giving work is both ultimately cosmic and intimately personal.

The Giver of Life: Pouring Out Common Grace

The first major dimension of the Spirit's work, then, lies in the creedal designation "giver of life": before applying redemptive grace in Christ, the Spirit has already been pouring out "common grace" upon all creatures and particularly upon humans as bearers of the divine image. This common grace addresses both nature and culture.

The Creator Spiritus

The Holy Spirit is the Giver of life in "nature," the physical creation: the *Creator Spiritus, the Spirit of creation. The Creator Spirit brooded over the initial creation (Gen. 1:2). Traditionally, Psalm 33:6 has applied to the trinitarian work of Word and Spirit in creation: "By the *word* of the LORD the heavens were made, their starry host by the *breath* of his mouth" (emphasis added). Psalm 104 develops a litany of God's gifts in creation: light, clouds, winds, waters, mountains, valleys, beasts, birds, grass, plants, wine, oil, bread, trees, seasons, food, work, and so forth. The earth is full of God's creatures (v. 24), all of which look to God for their food at the proper time (vv. 27–28). Toward the end, this litany highlights that creatures depend on God for the breath of life (v. 29), associated with the Spirit: "When you send your Spirit, they are created, and you renew the face of the ground" (v. 30). God sends rain on the righteous and the unrighteous (Matt. 5:45), and the Spirit intimately ministers this comprehensive providence: the Spirit not only gives but also upholds creaturely life.

The Spirit's work in the physical creation does not entail pantheism or panentheism. Ontological distinctions remain between God and the cosmos. Creatures "live and move and have [their] being" in God (Acts 17:28) by virtue of the Creator Spirit, but this participation in God's life does not make creatures divine. Creatures are sacred because they share in God's love, not God's essential being; creaturely life is sacred in a secondary sense. The Spirit's work in the physical creation must also be distinguished from the unfolding of earthly and human history. While God providentially sustains and ultimately directs all history, the Creator Spirit's work does not remove distinctions between good and evil. After the fall, we cannot directly appeal to what "is" for determining what "ought to be"; the Creator Spirit upholds the goodness of creaturely life but does not guarantee intrinsic goodness for every event.

The Spirit is not known in quite the same way as the Father and Son are—by a history of their distinctive works. As noted above, the Spirit is self-effacing by pointing to Christ. The Spirit's ministry involves perfecting what is creaturely, thus remaining eschatologically oriented and temporally unfinished. The Spirit's transcendence involves distinctive immanence, in particular being intimately close to each member of God's covenant people. Whereas in Christ the Logos all things hold together, in the Spirit creatures receive the energy to become what they are particularly designed to be.[7] Almost paradoxically, the Spirit is the divine person most generally related to all of creation precisely as the one who is most intimately related to each of its particulars. Yet the Spirit is most specifically related to the church, personally indwelling and empowering the new humanity in Christ. Because of these factors that enhance its mysterious character, recognizing the Spirit's work requires biblical discernment. History shows how tempting it is to understand the Spirit's ministry primarily in terms of some aspect(s) that a particular individual or group prioritizes—within the church, spiritual gifts or sacraments or sanctification; outside the church, cosmic energy or political liberation or human creativity. Hence, to honor the *Creator Spiritus* requires further examination of what the Bible teaches about God's work in human culture.

The "Cultural Mandate"

The concept of common grace appears especially in the Reformed tradition and others that maintain more "catholic" sensibilities. *Common grace designates provision from the Creator Spirit of God throughout human culture(s), among both Christians and non-Christians. The Spirit not only sustains physical life but also restrains wickedness and manifests God's glory, generously making society possible and realizing more justice than otherwise. The concept of common grace is misused when culture is entirely detached from the Spirit's ministry of the Word and treated as an independent source of authority or blessing. Yet common grace is vital for our lives as citizens and as students of God's world. Christian mission includes pursuit of the common good, even if its ultimate focus is to bear witness to redemption in Jesus Christ.

As a previous chapter mentioned, many theologians see a "cultural mandate" appearing just after Genesis introduces human beings as the image of God: "God blessed them and said to them, 'Be fruitful and increase in number; fill the earth and subdue it'" (Gen. 1:28). The following sentences in Genesis 1

---

7. A particular emphasis of Gunton in, e.g., *Christ and Creation*.

detail human rule over a series of other creatures. Unfortunately, sometimes Christians have celebrated this human rule in a way that overemphasized reason and promoted domination over the rest of creation. Culture, however, involves more than intellectual superiority. As complicated as culture is to define, it trades on an agricultural metaphor: humans cultivating freedom for making meaning and creating institutions. Culture involves self-expression and social life unfolding in the context and using the resources of the physical creation.[8] Once humans have expressed themselves, though, the resulting institutions create a feedback loop that affects others—present and future. The fruit harvested from cultivating human freedom provides new seeds that influence the future use of freedom.

Given God's delight in the physical creation, as depicted throughout Scripture, "stewardship" and "care" are more appropriate concepts than "use" for speaking of human cultural engagement with the natural world. If humans are to reflect the Triune God's self-giving love, then they cannot use the rest of creation simply for their own interests. The Spirit leads us to delight in and care for fellow creatures as gifts rather than possessions or mere commodities. The implications for concrete questions of stewardship—whether vegetarianism, animal research, use of natural resources, or myriad other concerns—remain debated. But the call to creation care is clear.

Culture emerges in the context of physical creation, but it expresses personal meaning and fosters social life. How do human beings recognize the Spirit's truly life-giving work within a messy unfolding history? The sheer variety of the Spirit's activity is astonishing: personal transformation, deep joy, persevering hope, empowered prayer, bold witness, courageous struggles for justice, and so forth.[9] Regarding the Spirit's cultural work beyond the church, currently ecology, the artistic imagination, and religious pluralism generate prominent debates. The first two were addressed briefly in an earlier chapter on creation (chap. 6). The third will be addressed once again in the final chapter (chap. 15), on last things. Here it is worth noting that Christian theologians increasingly appeal to pneumatology for maintaining a trinitarian view of God while engaging other religions charitably. Explicit biblical evidence for the Spirit's work among other religions is relatively scant, and

8. For a primer on theories of culture that advocates a "postmodern" perspective (while introducing other perspectives too), see Tanner, *Theories of Culture*. For a primer that emphasizes the agricultural metaphor, see D. Long, *Theology and Culture*.

9. Kärkkäinen, *Pneumatology*, 177. Plurality is also a major theme of Welker, *God the Spirit*, which attempts one of the first comprehensive biblical theologies of the Spirit but also champions its proposal as "realistic" and even "postmodern"—precisely because of its attempt to account for pneumatological variety.

that concept could create tension with the distinctive Christ-centeredness of biblical revelation and redemption. Yet the Spirit's life-giving work in creation, sustaining work in providence, and perfecting work in moving history toward eschatological consummation do suggest thinking about other religions in light of pneumatology. At minimum, the Spirit works providentially among adherents of other religions and within cultures to prepare the way for the gospel—whether or not the Spirit works particularly in and through non-Christian religions themselves. Trinitarian theology both celebrates the Spirit's life-giving activities throughout creation and remembers that all of creation holds together in Christ, the Redeemer.

The Giver of New Life: Applying Christ's Redeeming Grace

Hence we celebrate the Holy Spirit as not only the Giver of creaturely life but also ultimately as the Giver of new life in Christ. Debates about an *ordo salutis* aside, God the Spirit fosters a series of human responses to God the Son's saving work: being converted, consecrating ourselves to God, and receiving assurance as we persevere in faith.

Conversion

First in the Spirit's application of salvation is *conversion, turning people away from sin's mastery so that they turn to God. Embracing the good news involves conversion's two elements of turning away from and turning toward— repentance and faith. *Repentance, *metanoia*, involves a change of mind and heart, especially turning away from sin's mastery. Repentance is a more biblical way to name converts' initial disposition toward life change than "making Jesus Lord" of their lives, which Scripture does not treat as a separate, one-time step after believing the gospel.[10] In the Greco-Roman context, the imperial lord was the self-designated savior of the people; turning toward Jesus Christ in repentance and faith does not make him Lord but simply acknowledges his authority. As conversion's positive turn to God, faith is closely linked with baptism in the New Testament. Baptism is the public way of confessing faith, attaching the convert not only to Christ but also to his church.[11]

The initial repentance and faith involved in conversion have a three-part structure. Traditionally, the intellect, the emotions, and the will composed

---

10. Some adherents of Keswick theology, and a minority of evangelical scholars, would disagree, but this claim represents the overwhelming majority of evangelical scholarship.

11. See how closely these are related in, e.g., Acts 2:38, with biblical-theological treatment in Dunn, *Baptism in the Holy Spirit*.

this structure. The intellectual element contained recognition of sin (repentance) and knowledge of the gospel (faith). The emotional element contained sorrow for sin (repentance) and trust in Christ's sufficiency (faith). The volitional element contained abandonment of sin (repentance) and allegiance to Christ as Savior and Lord (faith).[12] A more recent proposal arises more directly from the language of certain New Testament passages, suggesting that conversion involves a moment of insight, a process of turning, and the resulting transformation.[13]

This proposal raises the related question of conversion's timing. Biblical depictions of Paul's conversion focus on an event (e.g., Acts 26:18; 1 Thess. 1:9). These event-oriented depictions have become tremendously influential among modern evangelicals. They focus on Paul's theology and on discrete acts of voluntary heart religion. Yet the Bible contains process-oriented depictions too, such as the narratives of Jesus's twelve disciples in the Gospel of Mark. So some contemporary scholars suggest that communally oriented cultures and seeker-oriented ministry approaches may legitimately treat conversion as a process. Furthermore, some now find it helpful to speak of the church's need for "continuing conversion."[14]

Conversion's timing involves two dimensions in Scripture. On the one hand, we should not extrapolate too quickly from the disciples' pre-resurrection experience to a perennial model. Christ's resurrection and the Spirit's outpouring were eventually decisive for those disciples. At the transition between the old and new ages of redemptive history, conversion was more likely to require processes of recognition, making precise moments difficult if not impossible to identify. On the other hand, we should not extrapolate too quickly from Paul's dramatic conversion to a model for everyone else. First-century Jews faced distinctive challenges for becoming convinced of Jesus's messianic identity; once they were convinced, though, a conversion event could readily follow. For gentiles lacking acquaintance with Old Testament faith, by contrast, a more extensive process of seeking and learning might be necessary. Moreover, the decisive nature of initial regeneration as a divine action must be balanced with the difficulty of pinpointing how or when the Spirit is working. If regeneration's decisive nature suggests an event, then human recognition of the Spirit's mysterious work allows for a process of conversion—at least from a pastoral perspective.[15]

12. See, e.g., Demarest, *Cross and Salvation*, 249.
13. Peace, *Conversion in the New Testament*.
14. Beyond Peace's argument, see Guder, *Continuing Conversion of the Church*.
15. Pelikan, *Acts*, 122, notes (with Lydia as a test case) that "one popular way of differentiating between them [event or process], by ascribing the first to divine action and the second

Biblical portrayals of conversion surely have implications for contemporary evangelism, but contextual differences will require discerning application. The modern dominance of "encounter evangelism" appears to be problematic, even if Scripture certainly contains examples of immediate mass conversion. Biblical precedent suggests, at minimum, that even dramatic and momentary conversions should be followed by baptism and catechesis. Converts need initiation into the church as not only a necessary context but even a primary goal of sanctification: the new humanity whose growth is measured in relation to Christ's fullness is the body of Christ, not just an individual part (Eph. 4:11–13). While faith may initially arise in a particular moment, corresponding to an event of regeneration, genuine faith does not remain just a mental or experiential moment of personal initiation. Biblical faith becomes an enduring and increasing virtue, not in the sense of a human achievement or possession but as the trust and loyalty that deepen during a covenant relationship with God. This covenant relationship binds particular persons together as a community of faith.

Sanctification and Consecration

God calls the covenant people to "be holy, because I am holy" (1 Pet. 1:16, quoting Lev. 11:44–45), to "live a life worthy of the calling you have received" (Eph. 4:1), to "work out your salvation with fear and trembling" (Phil. 2:12–13). To produce this second fruit, the Spirit sets us apart initially as members of God's holy people. Then, ultimately, God transforms us into people whose lives conform to the pattern of Jesus Christ. *Sanctification is the most common Protestant term for this process of becoming holy. It is helpful, though, to highlight the divine initiative emphasized in the New Testament with this term "sanctification," while speaking distinctly of the appropriate human response: "consecrating" ourselves. Although most people do not carefully observe this distinction, *consecration can specifically designate human responses to God's sanctifying work. In initially setting us apart as members of the covenant people, God promises to sanctify us entirely. In responses of consecration, we set ourselves apart, moment by moment, to serve the living Christ in the power of the Holy Spirit.

Of course, Christians understand the work of God's sanctifying grace in various ways. Some of these models assume that one or more special encounters with God move converts to a fundamentally "higher" state of spiritual life.

---

to human, does not find support in the text of the book of Acts, for conversion by a gradual process of persuasion is seen here to be fully as much the work of God as is conversion by an instantaneous and dramatic intervention."

Others focus on slow but steady growth, using ordinary "means of grace," as the biblical norm. These models also vary about measuring spiritual progress in ourselves and in others.

TRADITIONAL MODELS

In addressing such issues, six models have become primary among evangelicals. Several of them already surfaced within the previous chapter, since they reflect broader themes that distinguish certain theological traditions. So the present summaries can be brief; yet the final two models focus uniquely on sanctification and run more freely across church traditions.

The first Protestant model of spiritual life is *Lutheran*, in which sanctification is "the art of getting used to justification."[16] The Lutheran tradition eventually generated its own brand of pietism reacting against "dead" orthodoxy. Overall, though, the Lutheran model emphasizes justification by faith as the article upon which the church stands or falls. Accordingly, Lutherans remain hesitant concerning the language of cooperation with God. They fear that trying to assess or achieve consecration moves the focus away from Christ and onto ourselves. The result is repeating the Judaizers' error that Paul opposed: trying to achieve some kind of standing with God through good works, even after initial justification.

The second model is broadly *Reformed*, focusing on union with Christ (expounded especially in terms of Rom. 6). This union involves justification and sanctification as inseparable blessings of God's personal saving grace. On this account, sanctification is *progressive: not that believers always grow without moving sideways or sometimes backward, but no postconversion "crisis" experiences are necessary or normative. Instead, growth normally occurs via *means of grace: classically, these ways by which God helps believers to grow include the Word (hearing it preached, and reading it oneself), the sacraments, providence (God-given joys and trials), and prayer. Believers are called not only to appropriate the means of grace but also to undertake the *mortification of sin—actively resisting the devil by putting sin to death.

The third model emerged from the *Wesleyan* tradition. The various Holiness movements urge believers to appropriate the means of grace and to mortify sin. Their account of sanctification is not entirely progressive, however, for they advocate a postconversion second blessing, a special "crisis" experience of the Holy Spirit. Not all believers will experience this second work of grace, but it is normative—ideally to be sought by everyone. The

---

16. The following sketch, including key phrases such as the one quoted above, depends upon Alexander, *Christian Spirituality*, plus S. Gundry, *Five Views on Sanctification*.

second blessing produces a state of Christian perfection: with such "perfect love" (1 John 4:18), a person commits no voluntary, known sin. The heart is flooded completely with love for God. In some versions, the second blessing is not endless; one might fall out of perfect love and need renewal. Generally, though, the second blessing is a *crisis experience, a decisive life event.

The fourth model emerged later from the various *Pentecostal* movements. Versions of this model treat the "baptism with the Holy Spirit" as some kind of second blessing. For Pentecostals, the baptism with the Holy Spirit is normative for all Christians after conversion. Temporally, it may be experienced by some at conversion, but it is a distinct event, and other converts may never experience it. For classic Pentecostals, speaking in tongues is "initial evidence" of Spirit baptism, whereas charismatic Christians and some current Pentecostals do not insist on speaking in tongues. "Vineyard" or "third wave" churches tend not to fit this model of sanctification; instead, they affirm charismatic gifts while maintaining a more Reformed, progressive view of sanctification. At the very least, they affirm more clearly than some classic Pentecostals that the Holy Spirit indwells every believer, and they put less or no emphasis upon a distinct Spirit baptism.

Fifth, the *Keswick* model presents a third version of two-stage sanctification. As noted previously, the Keswick Convention no longer exclusively maintains this model. Many Baptist and dispensationalist groups, though, especially through camping and Bible conference ministries, reflect ongoing Keswick influence. This model distinguishes sharply between "carnal" and "spiritual" Christians, appealing to 1 Corinthians 1–3. Instead of correlating this distinction with Spirit baptism or its absence, Keswick views distinguish between believers who are fully consecrated to God and those who are not— often, between those who have made Jesus their Lord and those who treat him only as Savior. Keswick preaching urges carnal believers to seek consecration, often in terms of intensified or daily "filling" by the Holy Spirit. Typically, such preaching presents a series of stages (sometimes correlated with camping or conference programming) for cooperating with God or emptying oneself to be filled entirely by God. The former, cooperation emphasis is more active; the latter, passive emphasis on "letting go and letting God" has been more widespread. Either way, the process generally starts with confession of known sin and proceeds through other steps. These steps have parallels with Holiness and Pentecostal approaches toward seeking the baptism with the Holy Spirit. They also have parallels with the stages in some "Contemplative" approaches.

The sixth, *Contemplative*, model is simultaneously the oldest and the most recent to exert distinct influence among evangelicals. "Contemplation" has early Protestant antecedents, notably among Puritans. Its affinities with *theosis* indicate its classic pedigree, with evangelical versions of the *Contemplative model of sanctification appropriating ascetic and mystical strands of Orthodox and Catholic spirituality. Contemplative spirituality promotes "union with Christ" in a more mystical, transrational sense than the Reformed model. Such mystical union can be temporarily attained or experienced in this life as preparation for the hereafter. Pursuing this union with Christ may involve a series of steps containing self-denial, stages of prayer, or the like, although the details vary. Classically, contemplation was oriented to the *visio Dei*, the transrational "beatific vision" of God for which the human intellect was made. Evangelical appropriations of this tradition—by figures such as Richard Foster (1942–) and Dallas Willard (1935–2013)—do not necessarily assume the classic ontology of the beatific vision with hierarchical levels of reality. But the Contemplative tradition has been a fertile resource for evangelical recovery of spiritual disciplines.

BIBLICAL-THEOLOGICAL SYNTHESIS

Each of these models has abiding strengths and weaknesses. Many of their differences involve emphases and norms, so they are not altogether mutually exclusive. For instance, the Lutheran: others typically affirm justification by faith alone even if they give the doctrine less emphasis. The Reformed: others typically affirm means of grace and progressive aspects of sanctification, even if they understand union with Christ differently. As for the Wesleyan, Pentecostal, and Keswick: others do not normalize any postconversion "crisis" experiences; yet, with the possible exception of Lutherans, the others can acknowledge that such experiences are possible, even sometimes helpful given the biblical emphasis upon pursuing holiness. The Contemplative: others typically affirm mystical communion with God in prayer and value disciplined practices for deepening personal holiness, even if they construe union with Christ less ontologically than does the classic tradition.

To itemize the fundamental disagreements, first, whose action should we emphasize: intentional human effort, or prior divine initiative? Second, what kind of action is basic: human ontological renewal, or divine covenantal forgiveness? Third, what is the normative focus of sanctification: all believers' union with Christ and ordinary growth in grace, or distinctive postconversion experiences to seek? Fourth, what are the primary means of grace, and in particular do they include sacraments?

Of course, each model has potential weaknesses. The Lutheran model risks underemphasizing the Holy Spirit's transforming power in the new covenant, despite its insight regarding Christ-centered assurance of forgiveness.

The Reformed model risks overemphasizing either divine grace or personal struggle against sin, despite its insight regarding progressive sanctification. The Wesleyan model risks overemphasizing either Romantic heart religion or legalistic external religion, despite its insight regarding the fullness of divine love. The Pentecostal model risks dividing Christians into fundamentally separate levels of spiritual life and access to God's blessing, despite its insight regarding the fullness of the Holy Spirit. The Keswick model of sanctification risks overemphasizing personal introspection or extraordinary experiences, despite its insight regarding the Spirit's work through moments of intentional consecration. The Contemplative model risks overemphasizing individualistic or disembodied aspects of union with Christ, despite its insight regarding spiritual disciplines and mystical knowledge of God.

Biblical teaching calls evangelicals of various traditions to understand consecration as a *grateful response to God's action in Christ*—hence the "crucicentrism" for which evangelicals are known. Consecration is *the persistent embrace of the indwelling Holy Spirit's renewing power*, enjoying the initial fulfillment of God's promise in the new covenant—hence the "conversionism" for which evangelicals are known. Undergirding such consecration is *holistic transformation of a believer's "worldview,"* involving dispositions and habits that emerge from having the mind of Christ—hence the "biblicism" for which evangelicals are known. The measure of consecration is *the fullness of the image of God in Christ*, so that the goal of our transformation is *the preeminent virtue, love*—hence the "activism" for which evangelicals are known. Therefore, genuine transformation occurs in, depends upon, and builds up *the church*, whose mature reflection of Christ is the Spirit's ultimate goal in personal consecration (e.g., 1 Cor. 13; Eph. 4:11–16).[17] Consecration is about keeping in step with the Spirit (Gal. 5:13–26) so that believers may bear God- and other-centered fruit. Accordingly, consecration fits in "between the times" of Christ's first and second advents, between believers' status of *already* being "in Christ" and the glory of being "like Christ" that they do *not yet* fully experience.

Assurance and Perseverance

As the Spirit applies Christ's work by converting and sanctifying, the Spirit assures believers that they are God's children (Rom. 8:14–17), empowering them to persevere in their allegiance to their new family. While various

---

17. On the countercultural importance of Eph. 4:11–16, which confronts the evangelical tendency to turn spiritual formation into a self-absorbed form of therapy, I am indebted to one of my seminary teachers, John R. Lillis.

traditions understand assurance and perseverance differently, they all agree that the indwelling Holy Spirit promotes them in believers.

Major Views

Some of the six models of consecration overlap regarding assurance and perseverance, with the result being four major views on the latter. The first three of these four views correlate with the approaches to election and calling detailed in a previous chapter.

Arminianism, which includes the Wesleyan and Pentecostal traditions as well as many Keswick believers, denies that the Spirit ensures perseverance. Arminians hold that the Spirit enables perseverance, but believers may commit apostasy and lose their salvation. What counts as apostasy varies both in principle and in pastoral practice. Some hold that only decisive and permanent rejection of one's faith constitutes apostasy (see Heb. 6:4–6). Others hold that apostasy may occur within severe kinds or degrees of sin (e.g., 1 Cor. 6:9–11), even without overtly rejecting the confession of faith.

By contrast, *Calvinism*, which includes the Reformed tradition as well as some believers from Baptist and other groups, denies that true believers can commit apostasy and lose salvation. Calvinists hold to the divine preservation and human perseverance of the saints as one of salvation's gifts. The Holy Spirit effectually calls and seals those who are divinely chosen for salvation. In sealing them, the Spirit ensures that they will persevere. When people who make a confession of faith and affiliate with the church later commit apostasy, they do not lose salvation that they genuinely possessed. Instead, they lose certain benefits of contact with the gospel and the church that unregenerate people may enjoy for a time. On this view, such benefits are depicted not only in Hebrews 6:4–6 but also in Jesus's parable of the soils (Matt. 13:1–23) and other texts: "They went out from us, because they did not really belong to us" (1 John 2:19).

Lutheranism has a complex relation to assurance and perseverance. Martin Luther apparently held an Augustinian- and Calvinist-like account of predestination, although less staunchly than did John Calvin. Lutherans do not hold that apostasy is possible simply through grievous sin, for that view would contradict their emphasis upon objective assurance of justification by faith alone. Still, Luther spoke strongly against apostasy in pastoral contexts. Later Lutherans moved toward a more Arminian view, at least regarding the danger of apostasy through overtly rejecting the faith. To oversimplify, Lutheranism champions objective assurance along with the subjective necessity of persevering in faith. Such perseverance in faith reflects a strongly sacramental orientation: faith clings to hearing God's Word of forgiveness in Christ rather than operating primarily as an internal human act.

A fourth evangelical view of assurance and perseverance largely operates at the popular level. The concept of the *eternal security of the believer is widespread, accompanied by the phrase "once saved, always saved." This phrase appears among some Arminians who believe that God prevents apostasy, and among "free grace" dispensationalists who believe that salvation can never be lost after a genuine confession of faith, regardless of severe sin or even apostasy. In both principle and pastoral practice, this popular phrase differs from the Calvinist view of perseverance of the saints. The Calvinist view maintains that genuine faith endures, thanks to God's preserving grace. This popular phrase conveys that no human condition circumvents unconditional forgiveness. Popular versions of eternal security are marginal in theological scholarship because they misconstrue faith as a momentary, largely mental act. Initially praying a sinner's prayer or responding at a revival meeting may not attach someone to Christ in biblical faith. These may be legitimate preliminary steps or public expressions of conversion, but biblical faith grows over time and beyond the mind. Popular versions of eternal security often reflect the dead faith that James 2:14–26 opposes, rather than the good news that Paul proclaims (e.g., in Rom. 4).

THEOLOGICAL TENSIONS

Thus, the human side of the *ordo salutis* unfolds a biblical tension between divine grace and human responsibility that the divine side introduced. As with election and calling, so with assurance and perseverance: evangelical theology affirms both that salvation depends upon God's grace alone through faith alone and that grace transforms those who enjoy the benefits of being in Christ. Final justification is "not by works," just like the initial declaration of forgiveness at conversion. Yet the believer who has been forgiven much learns to love much. On the one hand, if believers lack assurance that they share in Christ's victory from conversion all the way till final consummation, then the gracious emphasis of justification by faith alone is lost. Unfortunately, Protestants often say that justification has nothing to do with works but then treat sanctification as a form of righteousness that has nothing to do with justification.[18] On the other hand, some forms of assurance may involve the believer's conduct without conditionally basing salvation on human works.[19]

---

18. O'Donovan, *Resurrection and Moral Order*, esp. 253–56.
19. Carson, "Reflections on Christian Assurance."

The resulting tension from a human perspective does not reflect a tension in God's perspective. Instead, human tension arises from trying to reflect biblical teaching about the inaugurated community of the new covenant. Unlike the community of the old covenant, the community of the new covenant is constituted by the remnant of those who are truly in Christ through the Spirit: genuine faith will produce a harvest. Still, the New Testament acknowledges the unfortunate possibility of spurious or transitory faith: tares grow alongside the wheat, and we cannot immediately tell the difference (see Matt. 13:24–30). By God's design, "warning passages" like Hebrews 10:24–31 promote perseverance when their rhetoric is not prematurely blunted by false promises of "eternal security." At the same time, such rhetoric is negatively rather than positively framed: perseverance is not the primary ground of assurance, even if failing to persevere undermines assurance. Classic Protestants rightly championed an objective basis of assurance in Christ while keeping subjective assessment of perseverance secondary. *Assurance of salvation—a person's confidence in being God's beloved child, awaiting a heavenly inheritance—ultimately comes from clinging to Christ by the Spirit, not from assessing evidence about how tightly we cling.

This distinction confronts unhealthy pastoral practices that are rooted in judging others, as well as personal spirituality that is rooted in unhealthy introspection.[20] Spiritual progress is a benefit of the gospel, not a result of struggle apart from grace. Even Luther, who staunchly championed justification by faith alone, recognized the New Testament teaching that "the faith that justifies is never alone." The truth that "without holiness no one will see the Lord" (Heb. 12:14), that we are "created in Christ Jesus to do good works" (Eph. 2:10), does not make holy work the primary basis for positive assurance of salvation. Assurance rests objectively upon Christ and subjectively depends upon the Spirit's inner testimony. When the New Testament calls for believers to examine their spiritual fruitfulness, the contexts usually involve spurious or transitory faith—requiring confrontational rhetoric rather than offering a works-oriented basis of assurance.[21]

Much tension over assurance and perseverance arises from the need to understand what "faith" is. Regarding its *character*, biblical faith is trust in the divine Word, which generates loyalty to the God of covenant promises.

20. Here a seminal article is Stendahl, "Paul and the Introspective Conscience," which is one-sided but raises a concern that is sometimes valid.

21. Such passages include Jesus's challenges of contemporary religious leaders as bad trees producing bad fruit (Matt. 7:15–23), the call to genuine virtue in 2 Pet. 1:3–11 (which works by an implicit lesser-to-greater argument: if even pagans can pursue certain virtues, then how much more . . .), and Paul's confrontation of the Corinthians for embracing false apostles (2 Cor. 13:5).

Regarding its *timing*, biblical faith deals not only with entering the covenant but also with enduring—with whether God will find faith among the people when Christ returns (Luke 18:8). Regarding its relationship with *love*, then, biblical faith is fulfilled, displayed, and energized by that ultimate virtue. But faith's reality is not measured by some particular amount of human love, as if that virtue functioned as an initial or final condition for being worthy to receive Christ's love. Love for God and neighbor transcends the kind of discrete actions that could be used to calculate meeting a quota. Faith expressed in love is not a substitute form of "justification by works," but rather an empty hand, open to receive God's gift.[22]

As to its *posture* or characteristic *practice*, biblical faith calls out to God in prayer, begging initially for forgiving mercy and subsequently for continued grace. Biblical faith learns gradually to seek first God's kingdom and righteousness, praying for God's kingdom to come. On the one hand, we are invited to call on the Lord's name for salvation, being reassured that God will never despise a broken and contrite heart (Ps. 51:17). On the other hand, we are warned not to call on the Lord's name frivolously or selfishly, with bloodstained hands or unrepentant hearts (Isa. 1:10–20). The Old Testament prophets, on whose notions of faith and righteousness Paul's teaching depends, vigorously confront the hypocrisy of God's people: we may never claim to love God adequately in our own strength, yet we are encouraged to cry out for mercy rather than trivializing our sin. Cries for mercy ring hollow, however, if we harbor no intention of repenting and every intention of continuing to harm our neighbors. It is no accident, then, that believers can grieve the Holy Spirit (Eph. 4:30–5:2), hindering the gift of subjective assurance with a refusal to confess sin. While assurance is objectively based in Christ, the Spirit uses occasions of repentance for leading us boldly toward God our Father: acknowledging our sin, especially our failure to love our neighbors as God has loved us, reassures us of salvation by reminding us of how much we have been forgiven. In dealing with such theological tensions, all evangelical models of sanctification have insight to contribute, despite their tendencies to overemphasize aspects of the truth.

Giver of the Church: Extending Love's Reach

A final dimension of the Spirit's life-giving love involves *charismata*, lavishing spiritual gifts upon the church. All Christians acknowledge that the spiritual

---

22. The "empty hand" sometimes associated with Calvin is not his, but for a very similar emphasis, see, e.g., Calvin, *Institutes* 3.11.7 (1:733).

gifts listed by Paul and Peter (esp. in Rom. 12:6–8; 1 Cor. 12; Eph. 4:7–16; 1 Pet. 4:10–11) constitute a significant, enduring ministry of the Spirit within the church. But a few of the gifts are disputed.

*Cessationist Christians distinguish certain sign gifts, notably glossolalia, from others, treating these sign gifts as special aspects of the old covenant and/or apostolic eras. On this account, because particular gifts signaled and accredited the new "revelation" of Christ, they have ceased, roughly when the initial apostles passed from the scene. Once the canon of Scripture was complete and began to be recognized as such, it provided a unique and enduring witness to the apostolic revelation (Eph. 2:20; Heb. 2:3–4).[23] By contrast, Pentecostal Christians reject cessationism. Strong *continuationists urge the contemporary church to pursue actively the full range of *charismata* in correspondence with the early Christian experience recorded in Scripture. On their account, the apostolic era is paradigmatic for ideal Christian ministry throughout the ages.

The twentieth-century explosion of charismatic phenomena throughout global Christianity and across various church traditions has made strict cessationism difficult to maintain. At the very least, it is fairly marginal among evangelical scholars. Yet the Pentecostal assertion of paradigmatic continuity between the apostolic and subsequent Christian eras, while widespread, is by no means universal. Many noncharismatic scholars, while open to episodic appearances or even pursuit of special sign gifts today, remain cautious about certain claims regarding them. These noncharismatic, noncessationist scholars—who might be characterized as weak continuationists, or open but cautious—acknowledge the potential legitimacy of all *charismata*; still, they resist normatively urging all Christians in all times and places to seek them. On their account, the New Testament stories and portrayals of the early church are often but not always paradigmatic. In some ways the apostolic era was unique. Even some Pentecostal scholars have recast the baptism with the Holy Spirit in ways that more clearly acknowledge the Spirit's ministry within all believers and the element of apostolic uniqueness in the New Testament. Although debates over the *charismata* and Spirit baptism have not completely abated, it seems that the distances between many adherents of these three approaches—continuationist, cessationist, and cautious—may be growing smaller.

Debates about *charismata* aside, Scripture, particularly 1 Corinthians, emphasizes their primary purpose: building up Christ's body in love (1 Cor. 13).

---

23. For a while, many cessationists appealed to 1 Cor. 13:10, interpreting "that which is perfect" (KJV) in terms of the completed canon of the Scriptures. That interpretation is largely discredited now, however; as the recent translation "completeness" (NIV) suggests, contemporary scholars understand this verse as referring to spiritual maturity in Christ.

The New Testament lists of spiritual gifts are not strict frameworks that exhaustively detail and carefully regulate them. Instead, these situation-specific lists of broad categories indicate that God will provide whatever and whomever the church needs for healthy ministry. The *charismata* may involve natural talents, but special grace can also go beyond or work apart from talents alone. The contemporary use of spiritual gift inventory tests can confuse people regarding this potential overlap between talents or personal interests and *charismata*; such reflection can be helpful, but it can convey the misleading impression that we wait to decide upon serving in the church until we find opportunities we like or ministries we are good at. The more biblical approach is to begin serving with all fellow believers in various ways, and then perhaps to identify gifts for focused service when the particular blessing of God's Spirit in certain areas is recognized by other believers and/or church leaders.

Nor is the Spirit's empowerment merely for the church's internal good: the proper use of tongues-speaking and prophecy affects Christian ministry to unbelievers as well, minimally by affecting the church's worship (1 Cor. 14). Spiritual gifts build up Christ's body for bearing witness to God and the gospel. The Spirit of power is extending the apostolic witness from Jerusalem through Judea and Samaria to the uttermost parts of the earth (Acts 1:8). As numerous stories in Acts testify, the Spirit not only pours out spiritual gifts but also sends out spiritual leaders to advance Christ's name in the world. Furthermore, the Spirit consoles and sustains those who suffer for the sake of Christ's name (see, e.g., 2 Cor. 1 in the context of vv. 21–22, along with 4:7–18 and other passages in the book). The Spirit ministers the presence of Christ to empower the church's participation in the mission of Christ.

As Ephesians 4:7–16 indicates, the Spirit is creating a new humanity that should increasingly correspond to the fullness of Christ. Spiritual gifts are not just impersonal means to an end; Paul speaks of people—apostles, prophets, and so on—*as* such gifts, within the church's unfolding history. Gifts to people and people as gifts—their ultimate end is love: God's Spirit personally poured into the hearts of members in Christ's body. The Spirit pours into the church people who will receive and share the love of Jesus. The Spirit is not just the Giver of created life, the Giver of new life in Christ, or even an external Giver to the church. As the internal Giver of God's presence and power to Christ's body, the Spirit is the Giver of the church to a world in desperate need of reconciling love.[24]

24. The way in which eternal procession identifies the Spirit with the love between the Father and the Son and, correspondingly, a mission of fostering contemplative love of God within the church is the emphasis of C. Holmes, *The Holy Spirit*. Holmes believes that in this way Augustine, Thomas Aquinas, and Karl Barth have been faithful to the biblical emphasis upon the Spirit directing people to the Father through Jesus Christ.

—*13*—

Scripture

THESIS

The authority of Holy Scripture emerges from God's final Word having been spoken in Jesus Christ; by the Holy Spirit, the written words and message of the prophets and apostles faithfully proclaim divine truth and powerfully rule over the church—even, with appropriate nuance, through various translations and the process of interpretation.

LEARNING OBJECTIVES

After learning the material in this chapter, you should be able to:

1. *Define briefly* the key terms introduced here (marked with an asterisk and included in the glossary).
2. *List and recognize* major elements of biblical authorship and approaches to canon formation.
3. *Describe and compare* the following: (a) Protestant and Catholic approaches to the authority of Scripture; (b) Christian and Islamic approaches to the authority of translations of Scripture; (c) evangelical approaches to the inerrancy of Scripture.
4. *Identify and illustrate* key biblical attributes of Scripture as God's Word.
5. *Explain* key Protestant commitments regarding the unified, authoritative ministry of the Word and the Spirit.

The Nicene Creed's third article addresses the Holy Spirit as the Lord who gives life. When God first spoke the Word to create, the Spirit breathed the cosmos to life; when God spoke the final Word to redeem creation, the Spirit breathed new life into humanity. In communion with the Father who speaks and the Son who is spoken, the Spirit empowers the Word and enlivens our hearing. *Scripture*, the first of three additional doctrines to consider under the Creed's third article, is the primary means by which God calls into existence *the church*, the new humanity in Christ, as the communal sign of the *last things*, which God has inaugurated by raising Jesus from the dead.

The Authority of the Bible as Scripture

The Bible's authority lies in divine speaking: the Holy Spirit "has spoken through the prophets." As the written testimony of the prophets and apostles, the Scriptures anticipate and proclaim Jesus Christ as God's final Word. The Scriptures are the Spirit's vehicle for preserving human testimony and making it available across time and place. Therefore, *authority* is the first aspect of the Christian doctrine of Scripture, unfolding the texts' collective identity as the canonical Word by which God directs the covenant people. A second aspect, Scripture's additional *attributes*, stem from the authority involved in its inspiration: these attributes unfold further the Bible's identity as God's Word in human words. A third aspect involves the Spirit as the Word's divine *accompaniment*, whose illumination shapes the human activities involved in fruitful interpretation.

Authorship: Divine and Human

Beginning with canonical authority acknowledges the fundamental claim of the Bible itself and affirms the church's ecumenical response: identifying Scripture as God's Word. As the overlapping terminology suggests, the Bible's authority rests in divine *authorship, God's self-identification with the textual words as the "voice" who is their ultimate source, speaking in and through them. Next, the concept of *canon, as both list and rule, identifies which texts share divine authorship and what their authority involves. Finally, the propriety of translation addresses how these texts may be heard as God's Word beyond the originally penned manuscripts—in other times, places, cultures, and therefore languages. *Translation is both a literal, linguistic process and a metaphorical, mental aspect of hearing with understanding. Still, although human agents participate at every stage—authorship, canon, translation—the Bible's authority begins and ends with presenting the speech of the divine Author.

The Bible's self-attestation as God's Word is widespread. The *locus classicus* is 2 Timothy 3:16–17: "All Scripture is God-breathed [*theopneustos*] and is useful for teaching, rebuking, correcting and training in righteousness, so that the servant of God may be thoroughly equipped for every good work." Modern scholars have spilled much ink about the precise meaning of *theopneustos*, about whether "Scripture" designates a broad category of "sacred writings" or a more specific set of canonical texts known as the Old Testament, and about how a category applied to the Old Testament extends to the New. But these subtleties do not obscure the main point: certain writings are associated with the wind or breath or spirit of God. Those writings are not peripheral; they have been central to Timothy's upbringing, and they convey saving wisdom that points to Jesus Christ.

The church's orthodox tradition has consistently recognized that the biblical texts together constitute one unified (form of the) Word of God: "He has spoken through the prophets." Given so much division in the church, especially over questions of authority, the nearly unanimous identification of Scripture as God's Word is striking. The crucial consensus existed early, in the Rule of Faith: the Old Testament would be read as Christian Scripture; the God of Israel is its speaker, the same One revealed in Jesus Christ. The authoritative apostolic writings of the eventual New Testament would include the Pauline and Catholic Epistles, along with four Gospels, but not their "gnostic" alternatives.[1]

Subsequently Scripture has regulated, and had its interpretation regulated by, Christian faith and love. Like 2 Timothy, this Rule of Faith and love emphasizes that Scripture equips God's people for good works. Together these texts present a complex, Christ-centered unity; the church has defined their literal sense variously, given the interplay between divine and human authorship. Beyond its basic identification as God's Word, Christians have developed various notions of Scripture's authority, exact canonical boundaries, and interpretive approaches. The doctrine of Scripture per se did not garner significant attention between the conclusion of the Christian canon and the beginning of the Protestant Reformation. From then on, the doctrine has frequently come under a searchlight, an occasion for polemical heat as much as illuminating insight. Whereas a dogmatic account of Scripture should focus on authoritative consensus regarding God's action, instead polemics arise because the church no longer hears the Word as one body. Parts of the church each claim to be its true heart, uniquely indwelt by the Word's Spirit. But none of those disagreements threaten the consensus that the various churches express in worship: when Scripture is read, "This is the Word of the Lord"; "Thanks be to God."

Second Peter 1:21, a companion to 2 Timothy 3:16–17, rules out merely human origins for God's revealed message. The human prophets have the

---

1. Small portions of this paragraph and the next appear in Treier, "Freedom of God's Word," and are used here with permission. Further discussion of some contemporary challenges to Scripture's divine inspiration can be found there.

Spirit's wind blowing in their sails; the relevant term, *pherō*, also appears in Acts 27:15 to describe a ship being driven along. Second Peter addresses the prophetic ministry of the apostles who were sent to bear witness concerning Jesus. Strictly speaking, 2 Timothy 3 and like passages address the sacred status of "Old Testament" writings among the early Christians. Naturally the "New Testament" cannot contain a full account of its own authority or its table of contents. Even so, the 2 Peter passage starts to address the New Testament's authority by identifying the apostolic message with the Spirit's revealing work.

Several other texts strengthen this identification of the apostolic writings with the Spirit's revelation of Christ. In 2 Peter 3:16, Peter identifies Paul's writings as "Scripture," even if (as we know all too well!) they are hard to understand and easy to distort. A complementary text is 1 Corinthians 2:9–13, where Paul attributes his proclamation of God's eschatological mystery to the Spirit's revelation. Jesus himself treated Old Testament texts as God's Word, not least in resisting the devil's temptation (Matt. 4:1–11; Luke 4:1–13). He anticipated the apostles remembering his teaching and revealing its significance by the Holy Spirit (John 14:26; 16:12–15). Their unique prophetic role, confirmed by passages like Hebrews 2:3–4, authorizes preserving their writings as God's Word. This litany of biblical texts could continue, but the pattern of these examples should suffice.

Scripture's divine authorship accounts for its overall unity, yet this unity involves an internal history of salvation that begins to account for apparent theological diversity. Jesus Christ is God's final Word (John 1:1–18; Heb. 1:1–4). This ultimate, personal divine speech enables fuller understanding of the earlier revelation preserved in the Old Testament. There will be no fundamentally new revelation after the incarnation of God's Son; now divine "speaking" illuminates what God has already said in the apostolic testimony regarding the Son. The church's understanding of that final revelation may increase, but the Triune God has already said enough.

Given Scripture's divine authorship, the meaning of any particular text comes fully to light within the Bible's overall message and the particular contexts of salvation history. Hearing God's Word is the ultimate priority in biblical interpretation. God's speaking is a redemptive event, requiring a response (Heb. 3:7–4:13). It is as if hearing Scripture read and proclaimed were like Israel's encounter with God in the thunderous theophany at Mount Sinai. As God's people who now draw near in Jesus Christ, we should not be fearful in quite the same way as the Sinai generation was (Heb. 12:18–29). But the life-changing consequences of hearing God's voice remain every bit as dramatic.

Scripture presents God's Word in and through human words. The biblical writers were not just impersonal, passive instruments of God's self-communication but also active secondary sources of the primary "voice" heard in Scripture. Luke 1:1–4 confirms and illustrates this human agency: Luke mentions the careful investigation that he undertook in producing his Gospel. John 14:26 and 16:12–15, already mentioned, relate human authorship to the divine Word: Jesus indicates that the Spirit will guide the church into all truth through the apostles' testimony. Additionally, the phenomena of human authorship are pervasive: biblical texts reflect diverse times, places, languages, genres, voices in relation to God, and so forth. For all this variety, the texts' human communication remains the basic vehicle for the divine Word. The *literal sense may be impossible to define theoretically, but the church has always held in principle that following "the way the words run" is basic to hearing God speak in Scripture. The Protestant Reformation championed a recovery of this literal sense in practice. Hence the basic biblical truths necessary for salvation are clear enough for even unlearned people to understand them with "a due use of ordinary means" (Westminster Confession of Faith 1.7). Since salvation history periodically reconfigured the relationships between parts of Scripture in light of new revelation reshaping its overall unity, God may say "more" than a particular human author does. Still, although the canonical context shapes the application of any particular text, God does not speak against or apart from the human witnesses.

Canon

"Canon" further unfolds the meaning of Scripture's authority. One sense of "canon" involves a *list* of which texts are identified with Scripture's divine authority. Scripture does not contain its own table of contents, which solidified over time. Orthodox and Catholic theology sometimes speak of the church *determining* the canon, an emphasis that (Protestants worry) gives the church some theological precedence over the Bible. By contrast, Protestant theology speaks of the church *recognizing* the canonical books, an emphasis that (Protestants hope) gives the Bible as God's Word some theological preeminence over the church. Of course, both divine and human agencies are involved in the church's reception of the canon; at stake is where to put the relative emphasis.

A second sense of "canon" involves a *rule*, the standard by which the living Christ regulates faith and practice. Here the focus rests upon how Scripture's authority operates, not which books share that authority. Speaking of a canonical rule does not mean applying an external standard for determining which books are canonical; rather, speaking of a canonical rule means recognizing the scriptural texts as the church's internal standard. In Protestant perspective, *sola scriptura* designates Scripture's supreme authority as the final arbiter over all secondary authorities. Scripture is the norming norm (*norma normans*) over normed norms (*norma normata*) such as church confessions. With Scripture as our canonical rule in this way, the fact that different churches have different lists of canonical books requires identifying a table of contents.

THE OLD TESTAMENT

The New Testament reflects basic agreement between Christians and Jews regarding "the Scriptures" (e.g., Acts 18:28) that we call the Old Testament. "Old Testament" reflects the overlap between "testament" and "covenant," combined with the distinction between "former" and "new," as reflected in Hebrews. We lack evidence of formal councils or processes by which Israel defined official parameters of this canon. Yet the basic parameters of the *Tanakh*, the Jewish Scriptures, were in place by the early Christian era.[2] The Torah, the Prophets, and the Writings gave the *Tanakh* a threefold shape. The Pentateuch provides the heart of Israel's covenant relationship with YHWH. The Prophets call Israel back toward faithfulness at the heart, rather than just the surface, of that relationship; they issue that call by looking forward, anticipating God's final restoration of the people. The Writings sketch the rest of Israel's history while sustaining Israel's ordinary life through regular worship and mundane wisdom that applies the Torah.

Questions concerning the canonical authority of Old Testament texts have chiefly concerned Ecclesiastes, Song of Songs, and Esther. Ecclesiastes can be treated as skeptical or at least challenging to mainstream Israelite wisdom, but from a canonical perspective it celebrates ordinary human life honestly and calls people to remember their Creator. Song of Songs can be treated as merely earthy love poetry, but from a canonical perspective it celebrates God's love for the covenant people and appropriate human desire. Esther does not include the divine name anywhere at the surface of its story, which presents a rather mixed legacy on the part of God's people, but from a canonical

---

2. For earlier but important accounts, see Beckwith, *The Old Testament Canon*; Bruce, *The Canon of Scripture*; Dunbar, "The Biblical Canon." For broader perspectives, see MacDonald and Sanders, *The Canon Debate*. More recently, see C. A. Evans and Tov, *Origins of the Bible*. In the comprehensive volume edited by Carson, *Enduring Authority of the Christian Scriptures*, see particularly Dempster, "The Old Testament Canon." Dempster parses out a canonical list, a canonical epoch, and canonical organization, finding that Josephus attests early to a narrow (eventually Protestant) list of Old Testament Scriptures. Eventual widening of that list in Orthodox and Catholic circles stemmed from excessive Hellenization, leading the church to depart from its Hebrew roots.

perspective Esther too celebrates God's love for the covenant people and calls them to courageous wisdom.

The New Testament reflects an early Christian focus upon Genesis, Deuteronomy, Psalms, and Isaiah. Genesis established the framework of salvation history: creation, fall, and redemptive covenants that anticipate the Messiah. Deuteronomy established the covenant framework of blessings and curses along with an anticipated history of Israelite failure, gentile inclusion, and redeemed hearts. Psalms established the prayer book for God's people, testifying of Yhwh's character and anticipating ultimate victory through the messianic Son of David. Isaiah established the hope of a definitive return from Israel's exile through a new exodus, even a new heavens and earth. The promise of God's ultimate Servant again anticipated the coming of Jesus Christ.

THE APOCRYPHA?

By the fourth and fifth centuries, the sixty-six books later recognized in the Protestant canon were generally recognized throughout Christendom due to usage in the churches. Others, especially rival gnostic texts, were excluded; notably, the Council of Carthage in 397 formalized decisions that were already evident from the early church fathers and widespread practice.

Debate continued at points, though, and usage of certain texts remained fluid. Eventually, at the Council of Trent in 1546, the Roman Catholic Church accepted the additional books of "the Apocrypha" as canonical. Eastern Orthodox churches do likewise, with some variation. These books are called "apocryphal" by Protestants because they are associated with "hidden things" and not regarded as Scripture. They are called "deuterocanonical" by Catholics as a "second canon," and *anagignoskomena* ("worthy to be read") by some Orthodox, who treat the Greek Old Testament (Septuagint [LXX]) as authoritative, including books that it contains alongside the *Tanakh*. The books of the Apocrypha stem from the period between the Old and New Testaments, focusing on the Jews' engagement with surrounding empires. While most Protestants ignore the Apocrypha, Luther and others acknowledged the deuterocanonical books as worthy to be read. For these Protestants, doctrine should not be based on the Apocrypha, but such books should not be totally neglected either.

THE NEW TESTAMENT

Despite variety regarding the deuterocanonical books, all three major branches of Christianity acknowledge the New Testament in common. The criteria by which the church recognized these twenty-seven canonical books are basically three, although they overlap and operate cumulatively.

First, *apostolicity* involved conformity to apostolic doctrine and association with an apostle. Some New Testament books were written directly by the original twelve apostles, at least according to tradition: Matthew's and John's Gospels; the Epistles of 1–2 Peter and 1–3 John; and Revelation. Later Paul became an apostle, and thirteen epistles are attributed to him. The remaining six books were written by close associates of an apostle: Mark, associated with Peter; Luke-Acts, associated with Paul; James and Jude, associated with Jesus's family and leadership of the earliest church. Hebrews was associated with Paul, although most modern scholars doubt Pauline authorship. Hebrews still conforms to apostolic doctrine, however; its theological contributions are distinctive but amenable to Pauline teaching. Ancient writing practices allow for maintaining traditional attributions of apostolic authorship even as others may have assisted in the writing—for instance, as amanuenses or secretaries through whom Paul may have written during imprisonment.

Second, the canonical New Testament reflects *orthodox Christ-centeredness.* Lots of other, often "gnostic," texts talk about Jesus; Christ-centeredness means more than that. Scriptural texts promote an early Christian "kerygma" or specific, Christ-centered, gospel message. For instance, 1 Corinthians 12:3 proclaims "Jesus is Lord" in a way that mirrors the baptismal confession of Romans 10:9–10. First Corinthians 15:3–4 narrates Christ's passion according to the Scriptures in a context that emphasizes his resurrection. Philippians 2:5–11 and 1 Timothy 3:16 possibly offer examples of early Christian hymns or creeds. Other texts define the boundaries of the early kerygma by opposing false teachers. So, for instance, 1 John insists on Christ's full divinity and genuine human flesh, confronting proto-gnostic spiritual errors: believers must acknowledge that they are sinners, not claiming to be without sin; yet they must pursue holiness, not acting as if sin does not matter. Orthodox Christ-centeredness grounds Christian living in the biblical gospel—the good news that in Jesus *God* graciously took on *full humanity* to triumph over sin and death.

Third, the reception of the canonical New Testament reflected the church's secondary authority, exercised in recognizing *the Spirit's testimony that operated through the books' usage.* The church made primary use of texts that conveyed the apostolic circle's orthodox, Christ-centered gospel. Texts that did not minister this gospel were gradually excluded. These patterns of primary usage and exclusion—in public reading, preaching, catechesis, and so forth—eventually reflected "the witness of the Holy Spirit given corporately to God's people and made manifest by a nearly unanimous acceptance of the NT canon in Christian churches."[3]

---

3. Nicole, "The Canon of the New Testament," 204.

To be sure, challenges have periodically surfaced. Anonymous authorship made Hebrews susceptible to challenge. Jude and 1–2 Peter faced suspicions of being *pseudepigrapha, or falsely named writings, with apparent literary dependence between 2 Peter and Jude raising questions as well. Yet plausible scholarly answers are available for addressing these challenges. Other challenges have focused less on authorship and more on content. The book of Revelation has been vulnerable to misuse and thus, in Orthodox circles, to canonical uncertainty. Among Protestants, Luther famously doubted the canonical consistency of James (which he dubbed an "epistle of straw")[4] with the Pauline gospel of justification by faith alone. Yet such cases understandably reflect the somewhat informal nature of canonical recognition. Apart from formal mechanisms of institutional reinforcement, the typical witness of various churches across time and place has supported the canonical authority of all twenty-seven New Testament books. These challenges, then, are best viewed as periodic issues of interpretation rather than indicators of significant canonical confusion.

Translation

God's Word addresses us through humanly authored texts that together rule faith and practice. Like other texts, these Scriptures accumulate versions across time and place. Islam understands the Qur'an as verbally revealed to the prophet Muhammad through the angel Gabriel in such a way that translations do not share the authority of the Arabic original. Hence Muslims usually recite only the Arabic—not translations—in prayer. By contrast, Christians more willingly say that people hear God's Word in and through translations, with modest qualifications. Of course, we do not possess the *autographa*, the initially authored manuscripts of the Scriptures. Scholars can only approximate their contents through the practice of *textual criticism. Yet Christians celebrate God's preservation of reliable manuscript traditions even as they remain open to human ambiguities and historical complexities involved in textual criticism and translation. This openness to translation is consistent with the incarnation, in which the Logos has taken up human flesh for the sake of divine self-revelation. God communicates to humanity through humanity. And Jesus himself anticipated the Holy Spirit's ministry to and through human understanding. Pentecost, when

4. Luther, "Preface to the New Testament," 362. But see also Luther's "Preface to the Epistles of St. James and St. Jude," where he considers James a "good book" that "vigorously promulgates the law of God."

the Spirit helped people to hear the Word in their own languages, speaks volumes.[5]

Reconstructing the original texts already requires translation and interpretation. Scholars can reconstruct these with high probability—beyond the usual reliability for ancient texts—and lingering complexities have relatively minor significance. By not preserving the actual *autographa*, God has given opportunities for meaningful human participation in the understanding of divine revelation. Moreover, God has thereby protected the church from two temptations. One temptation would be "bibliolatry," treating the manuscripts as fetishes with magical powers. Another temptation would be prideful rigor, treating the manuscripts as a guarantee of proper interpretation. In either case, humans would be tempted to put secondary authorities in a position to control the hearing of God's Word.

Lacking the actual manuscripts, we certainly cannot insist that everyone access the texts in their original languages. Reconstructed, composite texts may be translated; indeed, given Protestant commitment to the priesthood of all believers, they must be. In preserving the texts through traditions of manuscript copying, God has provided reliable access to the Word along with occasion for humility. Similarly, vernacular translations provide reliable access to the basic message of God's Word along with realism about human understanding. Like textual criticism, translation generates a measure of plurality. Translations accomplish various goods, excelling at some more than others. Engaging multiple translations together, recognizing the limits of any one translation, enables Christian believers to make a "due use of ordinary means" in understanding the Bible.

A composite Latin translation, the *Vulgate, dominated Western engagement with Scripture for over a thousand years, while Eastern and monastic Christianity (among other factors) still provided several families of manuscripts. Protestant Reformers took initiative in encouraging lay Bible reading through vernacular translations. But they also expected that Bible reading would occur within a twofold churchly context: catechetical instruction and a trained clergy. The clergy would not have special access to God that other baptized believer-priests lacked, but their training in the biblical languages would provide congregational access to the Hebrew and Greek texts. Modern textual criticism follows no particular manuscript tradition exclusively. Sometimes textual criticism has been controversially associated with "higher criticism," by which some scholars reject the authority and truth of all or part

---

5. On relating the incarnation to translation and the expansion of mission, see A. Walls, "Christianity in the Non-Western World."

of Scripture. But, like other "historical-critical" methods, textual criticism is a helpful scholarly discipline, as long as its presuppositions and practices incorporate theological discernment. Indeed, some of its leading practitioners have been faithful Christians, honoring Scripture as God's Word.

For English readers, textual criticism has generated controversy in the realm of translations—particularly concerning the *Textus Receptus, the "Received Text" that stands behind the Authorized (King James) Version of 1611. In the middle of the twentieth century, "King James–only" advocates had understandable concerns about certain translations and about loss of cultural reference to a common English translation. But they failed to put such concerns in a proper theological context: it was naive and ethnocentric to insist on a uniquely providential English translation being the exclusive basis for God's Word to reach the world. There was also a failure of historical understanding: it was belligerent to ignore the decidedly later and likely inferior character of the textual witnesses behind the King James, despite its legitimate importance. Insisting on the King James Version alone meant rejecting mainstream biblical scholarship while landing in fundamentalist legalism.

Late twentieth-century evangelicalism left behind that battle. Once most evangelicals opted for a composite text, with scholarly textual criticism reconstructing what was originally authored, then different translation philosophies came into play, especially "literal" or "formal equivalence" translations versus "functional" or "dynamic equivalence" translations. Such translations are distinct from "paraphrases" and other "free" renderings. None of these types is absolute; all of them represent points spread across a spectrum. No translation can be purely literal or functional. Absolute formal equivalence (matching word for word, syntactical structure for syntactical structure) is impossible. Dynamic equivalence (matching thought for thought) must reflect original structures to some degree. Nevertheless, versions like the King James, American Standard, Revised Standard, New American Standard, and English Standard (among others) aspire to formal equivalence, whereas versions like the New Revised Standard and New International espouse dynamic equivalence. The Living Bible is a paraphrase, and the New Living Translation is a rather free rendering; Eugene Peterson's *The Message* is a paraphrase, sometimes almost a commentary.

Contemporary Bible translation theory continues to evolve. Almost any communication may be translated, but not with exact thought structures intact. While translations have different aims, the "equivalence" spectrum may not capture all of their nuances. For theological purposes here, it is enough to celebrate textual reconstruction and translations that honor both divine and human authorship of the Scriptures. These are human texts, with traditions of transmission across time and place, as well as translation crossing linguistic and cultural barriers. Because these texts bear the divine Word, though, God has preserved reliable access to their saving message along with sufficient complexity to prevent false worship and false certainty.

The Attributes of Scripture as God's Word

For Christians, calling the Bible "Scripture" goes beyond the term's generic meaning in religious studies, where it designates a set of "sacred" texts for a particular community. The authority of Christian Scripture is rooted in dual authorship: God's "voice" is heard in and through human writers. The canonical status of Christian Scripture means that the texts' uniquely essential, faithful, and enduring witness to the gospel is recognized by the church as together presenting the Word of Jesus Christ, to hear and obey. Necessary processes of translation depend upon the Holy Spirit's guidance of human study and spiritual discernment as part of how God communicates personally. Building upon this Christian understanding of Scripture, the following five attributes further characterize God's written Word.

Inspiration

As already introduced from 2 Timothy 3:16–17, *inspiration indicates the divine authorship of the Scriptures: in them we hear God's Word. Although evangelical expositions vary, "inspiration" best refers to the books, not the writers—to the texts' God-spoken character (being identified as Scripture), not particular processes of composition (better treated under "inscripturation"). Inspiration means that every portion of Scripture bears the quality of having been breathed out by God, thereby having theological authority and spiritual profitability. Inspiration is *verbal*, involving the *words* as the texts' means of conveying their message. Inspiration is *plenary*, involving *all* the words. Verbal, plenary inspiration identifies the texts of Scripture as the written form of God's Word.[6] When Deuteronomy 4:2 and Revelation 22:18–19 forbid adding or subtracting from the Scriptures, and Jesus says that not one iota of God's Word will pass away (Matt. 5:18), they are not commending a magical approach to meanings hidden under particular words. Instead, they

---

6. In earlier days, "plenary" inspiration was sometimes pitted against "verbal" inspiration, to suggest that the text's message was inspired but not its words. Standard evangelical usage now widely affirms both: verbal, plenary inspiration. The primacy of divine speech as the biblical way of understanding Scripture may be helpful in overcoming the frequent dichotomy between "personal" and "propositional" aspects of divine revelation.

underscore that God communicates concretely through words; to hear what God has actually said—rather than abstracting a "message" that we might prefer—requires interpreting all the words of the texts that God has preserved.

One modern challenge to verbal, plenary inspiration concerns a "dictation" theory. Critics allege that verbal, plenary inspiration portrays God controlling the writers merely as impersonal instruments, negating genuinely human communication by directly dictating the exact words. Against this charge, the traditional doctrine of inspiration has a twofold defense. First, the human authorship of the biblical texts is acknowledged and even celebrated by responsible advocates of the doctrine. When others speak of divine dictation, they substitute claims about particular *processes* (as if all of Scripture came by prophetic oracle, for example) for the proper claim about the *product* of inspiration: God's Word in human words. Second, the doctrine of inspiration is an important test case for addressing divine providence generally. When mistaken advocates or critics speak of divine dictation, they fail to recognize the traditional emphasis upon God superintending creaturely processes. God can actively accomplish God's purposes without thwarting ours: while not just a function of generic providence, verbal, plenary inspiration involves "concursus" between divine and human action.

Another modern challenge to verbal, plenary inspiration concerns Scripture's diversity, not just its humanity. Critics allege that the Bible's content is theologically diverse to the point of contradiction. Often that allegation is linked with objections to biblical inerrancy, discussed below, and with competing authorities such as modern history or science. But advocates of verbal, plenary inspiration already acknowledge that Scripture's content is diverse, in at least two important ways. These forms of theological diversity are canonically complementary rather than contradictory, and therefore they nuance but do not preclude the traditional doctrine of inspiration.

First, Scripture's content is *historically* diverse: the biblical texts represent numerous authors, audiences, times, places, and, most importantly, acts within salvation history. To illustrate, different stances toward animal sacrifice, from the Pentateuch through the Prophets and the Gospels all the way to Hebrews, frequently reflect a combination of historical diversity and pastoral priorities. Yet Christian readers discern a developmental unity in this unfolding divine revelation: regarding sacrifices, they go from necessary shadows of a coming reality to fulfillment and therefore cessation; sometimes their necessity is already relativized in the Old Testament due to God's overarching priority upon justice and mercy.

Second, then, Scripture's content is *conceptually* diverse: the biblical texts reflect the varied wording and thought forms that historical development and pastoral contexts would suggest. To illustrate, the apparent differences between Paul in Romans 4 and James in James 2 reflect complementary priorities rather than contradictory claims: justification is by faith alone when Paul relates faith in a healthy, holistic sense to our standing before God; justification is not by faith alone when James critiques a dead, merely mental sense of "faith" and (possibly) focuses on the vindication of our works before other people. Scripture's historical and conceptual diversity enables the Word to journey with God's people across particular contexts: some people need the "faith alone" reassurance of God's favor in Christ from Paul; others need the confrontation of dead faith from James. The concepts of "justification" and "faith" in our systematic theologies will likely draw primarily on Paul's positive language use, but our pastoral theologies need to deal adequately with the dangers highlighted in James's critique. Verbal, plenary inspiration embraces legitimate diversity as part of how God speaks a perennially relevant Word.

Scripture even contains diverse models of authority.[7] Scripture conveys "revelation," as noted long ago regarding Psalm 19 and Romans 1:18–32. Yet Scripture also contains a "witnessing tradition," especially in narratives. Scripture constitutes an "authoritative canon," especially in legal codes and moral instruction. Scripture presents an "inspired word," especially in prophetic oracles. And Scripture offers "experienced revelation," especially in Psalms, apocalypses, Wisdom literature, and letters. Sometimes God addresses us in the first person (e.g., prophetic oracle); at other times God's "voice" is in the second person (e.g., a Psalm addressed to God); on still other occasions God appears in the third person (e.g., narratives). Noticing these diverse models of biblical authority respects the forms in which God has chosen to address us.

Nevertheless, in all of these models *God* addresses us. Sometimes Scripture itself appeals to nonprophetic texts as divine speech. Take Hebrews, for instance, which briefly acknowledges the human authorship of a narrative (4:4) and a psalm (4:7) but identifies these same portions as divine speech. Inspiration does not cancel out diverse literary models of authority. In the Psalms, for example, God may speak in first, second, or third person, and in any of these modes there may be fairly direct revelation of who God is. Simultaneously, the relative dominance of the second-person mode communicates indirectly that God presents the Psalms as models for our praying. Thus, God's people learn by listening to how God speaks, along with hearing what God says.

---

7. The models treated here come from Goldingay, *Models for Scripture*; Goldingay, *Models for Interpretation of Scripture*.

Infallibility

Verbal, plenary inspiration entails Scripture's infallibility: God does not fail. As God's Word, Scripture is *infallible because God does not fail to accomplish the sovereign purpose(s) for which God speaks (Isa. 55:11). Hebrews 4:12–13 conveys the inward reach of this "living and active" power, "sharper than any double-edged sword," relating this power to the all-knowing God, who speaks.

"Infallibility" was the historic Protestant term for the acknowledgment of Scripture's authoritative truth. Once the fundamentalist-modernist controversies emerged in the twentieth century, Protestant usage of "infallibility" began to shift. Some began to affirm Scripture's infallibility regarding only matters of faith and practice, not history and science. By contrast, traditionalists held to the Bible's comprehensive truthfulness, whatever it addresses. These traditionalists needed a new term, "inerrancy," to affirm Scripture's full truth once the reach of infallibility became restricted.

Despite these complexities, orthodox Christians across the various communions still agree: God's Word does not fail to achieve its end(s), bearing faithful witness to God's self-revelation and redemption in Jesus Christ. Indeed, as God's final Word, Christ in his prophetic office testifies of himself through the prophets and apostles. The Old Testament "prophets" anticipate, and the New Testament "apostles" proclaim, this divine Word that the Holy Spirit, in and through Scripture, powerfully ministers. For Scripture to be inspired means that the biblical texts are God's Word; for Scripture to be infallible means that, as God's Word, the biblical texts reflect the character of the Triune God.

Inerrancy

As an aspect of biblical infallibility, then, inerrancy has become the focus of modern Protestant controversy. One controversial factor is the term's relative newness. Though earlier theologians typically affirmed Scripture's trustworthy character and occasionally insisted that it did not contain error, they did not widely speak of inerrancy. As often happens, the term rose to prominence once the underlying concept was increasingly denied. A related factor concerning the term is its negative connotation, denying error rather than celebrating truth.

Another controversial factor involves a mixed hermeneutical legacy from inerrancy's adherents. For a classically problematic example, one proponent insisted that Peter must have denied knowing Jesus six times, not just three, in order to iron out a literalist chronological harmony between the Gospel accounts.[8] Fairly or not, biblical inerrantists have been charged with proof-texting out of context, trying to find Bible verses for everything, and producing absurd interpretations in order to harmonize details.[9]

Many global and some American evangelicals affirm Scripture's infallibility while denying its full inerrancy. Somewhat similarly, while the Catholic Church occasionally uses inerrancy-like language, the term has not been prominent enough to be controversial there, and its modern biblical scholars do not consistently operate on the basis of full inerrancy. Positions of *limited inerrancy affirm that Scripture is God's Word, but typically they limit the extent of its truthfulness to "matters of faith and practice" as the focus of God's speech. In particular, they exclude historical or scientific aspects from the comprehensive reach of verbal, plenary inspiration. An ensuing challenge, of course, is to delimit when a text's claim is merely historical or scientific, thus lacking import for faith or practice.

Limited inerrancy among evangelicals arose in the 1960s under the indirect influence of Karl Barth. Barth's approach to Scripture was often misunderstood, or at least presented in the worst possible terms, by conservative evangelical critics.[10] It is true that Barth rejected biblical inerrancy because he did not hold a traditional account of verbal, plenary inspiration. Instead he held that Scripture becomes God's Word in moments of personal divine self-revelation by the Spirit. This dynamic view of inspiration—though certainly not the verbal, plenary view—does not simply deny Scripture's authority in favor of religious subjectivity. Barth's "actualistic ontology" emphasized that Scripture "becomes" what God intends it to "be"—namely, a form of God's self-revelation. Barth emphasized Jesus Christ as God's "final Word," indicating that Scripture is a secondary form of the Word—indirectly identified with divine revelation. In contrast, some evangelical conceptions of Scripture

8. Lindsell, *Battle for the Bible*, 174–76.

9. The evangelical "biblicism" critiqued by C. Smith, *Bible Made Impossible*, is associated with inerrancy. For a response, see Treier, "Heaven on Earth?" The critique that inerrancy harms the faith of evangelical youth is pressed by Bovell, *Inerrancy*. For a spectrum of approaches, see Merrick and Garrett, *Five Views on Biblical Inerrancy*.

On "proof-texting," see briefly Treier, "Proof Text"; more extensively, Allen and Swain, "In Defense of Proof-Texting." More historical perspective is available in Treier, "Scripture and Hermeneutics" (2007); Vanhoozer and Treier, *Theology and the Mirror of Scripture*.

10. Both conservative evangelicals and many "liberal" theologians applied the label "neoorthodoxy" to a supposed family of thinkers including Emil Brunner, Rudolf Bultmann, Paul Tillich, and Dietrich Bonhoeffer. However, the label is problematic because this supposed family has substantial differences. Barth eschewed the label and emphasized fundamental differences from these other thinkers, with the possible exception of Bonhoeffer. For a sympathetic account of Barth's position vis-à-vis the traditional evangelical view, see McCormack, "Being of Holy Scripture."

overemphasized its cognitive content and neglected the biblical emphasis on Jesus Christ. In their view, however, Barth overemphasized one strand of the Bible's teaching and neglected its repeated, direct identification of Scripture with God's Word. Traditional evangelicals understandably worried that the dynamic Barthian view undermined the stability of Scripture's meaning and the fullness of its truth.

The fundamental argument for Scripture's full inerrancy, then, rests on verbal, plenary inspiration. God is, by definition, truthful. If Scripture is fully God's Word, then what Scripture says is trustworthy. Denials or limitations of biblical inerrancy limit inspiration's verbal character or else deny its plenary extent. Conversely, if Scripture is infallible, then telling the truth is one of its aims. On this basis, *inerrancy is "the view that when all the facts become known, they will demonstrate that the Bible in its original autographs and correctly interpreted is entirely true and never false in all it affirms, whether that relates to doctrine or ethics or to the social, physical, or life sciences."[11] The well-known Chicago Statement on Biblical Inerrancy sought to stabilize such a consensus, however much adherents quibble over details.

Biblical inerrancy heightens the necessity of interpretation, as reflected in the subsequent and less successful Chicago Statement on Biblical Hermeneutics. Scripture's inerrancy must be carefully indexed to the communicative focus of biblical texts and therefore the kind(s) of truth that they teach. Inerrancy does not require the Bible to speak with scientific precision and technical vocabulary; to have equal contemporary relevance in all portions; to contain verbatim quotation of the Old Testament in the New Testament or literalist agreement between parallel accounts; or to lack unclear passages, the recording of sinful acts or errant claims, quotations from noninspired sources, or historical investigation and perspective. The inerrancy of Scripture does not extend to its interpreters, who may not presently know all the answers to challenging questions. Accordingly, biblical inerrancy may not always require "traditional" views regarding the texts' dates or authors, depending on Scripture's own claims. But biblical inerrancy does entail that there can be no outright internal contradictions within Scripture's teaching, and no external contradictions between biblical teaching and genuine science or other forms of human knowledge.

God's *accommodation to human contexts and limits is traditionally part of Scripture's truthfulness, not an indication of error. Accommodation shows that apparent errors "properly understood . . . were not errors at all but were written in language adapted to the capacity of the common people." The

---

11. P. Feinberg, "Bible, Inerrancy and Infallibility of," 125.

incarnation, in which "God accommodated himself to human nature yet without in any way losing any of his divine nature," served as an analogy: "In the same way, Scripture is written by humans in human language accommodated to us and to our capacity and needs, as well as to the various time periods and cultures in which it was written, without in any way compromising its faithfulness to divine truth."[12] In other words, Scripture's truthfulness requires discerning its meaning carefully, respecting the texts' historical contexts—ancient and modern alike—their literary genres, and so forth, as aspects of *how* God has chosen to communicate the truth to us. In the eyes of traditional evangelicals, the complexity of biblical interpretation nuances but does not nullify the significance of Scripture's inerrancy.

Sufficiency

The sufficiency or "perfection" of Scripture again reflects God's communicative action. *Sufficiency insists that God communicates all the truth necessary for salvation and holy living. Second Timothy 3:14–17 speaks of Scripture making wise unto salvation, thoroughly equipping God's people for every good work. Second Peter 1:3–4 celebrates, "His divine power has given us everything we need for a godly life through our knowledge of him who called us by his own glory and goodness. Through these he has given us his very great and precious promises, so that through them you may participate in the divine nature." Of course, people need more than knowledge for godly living, and the "knowledge" of God addressed here is holistic and personal. Affirming Scripture's sufficiency does not mean that only the Bible—isolated from the Spirit's work in the church—meets our spiritual needs. Rather, Scripture's sufficiency means that apostolic teaching is one crucial part of God's spiritual provision, and Scripture is the church's sufficient source for that teaching.

Scripture is sufficient alongside genuine knowledge from other creaturely sources. Scripture's sufficiency does not entail the ludicrous claim that the Bible conveys all valuable knowledge. The crucial distinction concerns what is necessary for salvation and holy living. Much general knowledge, in psychology for instance, is worthwhile as part of God's creation, perhaps even contributing to Christian growth. Such contributions do not entail spiritual necessity, however. God's self-disclosure in Jesus Christ via Scripture is distinct from the wider knowledge that humans are free to pursue. Despite

---

12. Sunshine, "Accommodation Historically Considered," 264. Sunshine summarizes debate over Calvin's approach, showing how the doctrine of accommodation functioned until the rise of modern rationalism, when theologians began using the term differently, to suggest that the Scriptures contained error.

being valuable for exploring the beauty and addressing the brokenness of God's creation, extrabiblical knowledge is neither revelatory nor necessary in the same way as Scripture's spiritually sufficient testimony concerning Jesus Christ. What do we reveal about our expectations of God and aspirations for our lives if we treat Scripture as insufficient? In other words, *sola scriptura* focuses on the Bible's communication of the breadth and depth of God's love in the gospel.[13]

Clarity

Like sufficiency, Scripture's clarity or "perspicuity" is a Protestant doctrine that celebrates God's provision for salvation and holy living. Orthodoxy and Catholicism insist that Scripture must be interpreted through authoritative Tradition and/or the church's magisterial teaching office. Conversely, Protestant theologies acknowledge the clarity and sufficiency of Scripture's basic saving message.[14] Tradition plays an inevitable, often helpful, and "ministerial" role in Protestant interpretation, but is never a magisterial necessity for communicating the biblical gospel. The Spirit can use ordinary reading of the literal sense to help people hear this Word.

Scriptural support for this claim is indirect but real. The Bible opposes supplanting the divine Word with merely human and possibly mistaken tradition; for instance, consider how Jesus confronted such opponents in Mark 7:8–13. The Bible repeatedly makes direct claims to give light, to be pure, to provide guidance, and so on (see Ps. 119). More broadly, Scripture's clarity depends upon God's creation of language as a vehicle of communication with and among human beings. The gospel also supports Scripture's clarity with its verbal emphasis, declaring us forgiven in Christ and promising future resurrection. Hearing this Word in the Spirit, the church is called into existence and then into a mission of proclamation that shines the light with which the church has come to see.

Like sufficiency, Scripture's clarity requires a series of nuances. First, believers need the Holy Spirit to illuminate the text and its subject matter, as well as their own eyes (Eph. 1:17–18). Second, believers generally need teachers, along with the church's enduring history and catholic contexts. Teachers provide vernacular translations, read and proclaim the Word publicly, protect against error, and nurture life in the truth. Scripture's basic message is clear as people read with the Spirit's anointing (1 John 2:27), but the Spirit has given

13. Berkouwer, *Holy Scripture*, 299–326.
14. For a historical treatment, see Callahan, *Clarity of Scripture*; for a clearer theological treatment, see M. D. Thompson, *Clear and Present Word*.

teachers to the church (Eph. 4:7–16). Third, believing readers need to make "due use of ordinary means"; the biblical texts are human documents involving interpretation. While Scripture cannot be read like just any other book, it remains a collection of texts. Fourth, believers need the creedal, trinitarian "Rule of Faith" and the wider biblical "analogy of faith" to guide their reading of this collection as one Word. The Rule of Faith distills a coherent story of salvation from the Bible as a whole; the analogy of faith applies clearer teaching to understanding more difficult passages. Fifth, clarity focuses upon the gospel: Scripture shines its light to illuminate the path toward salvation. Thus, sixth, believers find difficulties in many biblical passages: Scripture is not clear concerning every question anyone might ask. Sometimes clarity requires acknowledging what Scripture does not clearly address!

Scripture's *clarity entails the basic claim that the Bible's central message—the Creator graciously redeeming a fallen world in Jesus Christ—can be understood personally and faithfully, through reading vernacular translations, with the Holy Spirit's help and without necessary interpretive reliance upon the institutional church. The preceding nuances oppose overextending this claim into individualism, naive literalism, and the like. The Rule of Faith, the Spirit's aid, the church's teachers, catechesis, prayerful reading, and clearer passages can guide interpretation and guard against heretical error. Scripture's clarity cautions us that difficulties in understanding arise from broken "subjectivity"—dullness of hearing, self-interest, intellectual selectivity—as much as ambiguities in the Bible itself. By the Holy Spirit, the Word is living and active, able to pierce through our defenses and point out the right path.

The Spirit's Accompaniment of the Word

Scripture's sufficiency and clarity establish the Word's primacy over the church, rooting the church's life in the saving history of Jesus Christ. The Spirit accompanies the Word from beginning to end: from election to prophetic inspiration to incarnation to apostolic mission, and then from inscripturation to preservation to illumination. The Spirit's illumination heals sinfully blind eyes, opens stubbornly closed hearts, and shines light upon shadowy nooks or neglected crannies of biblical texts. The Spirit leads hearers of the Word into the freedom of obedience. The Spirit's lordship over our hearing may involve supernatural intervention, but primarily enlivens our natural capacities for faithful and fruitful interpretation.

Evangelicals approach biblical hermeneutics with various accounts of the Spirit and the church. Some emphasize the Spirit's natural and institutional work, so they emphasize tradition and reason. Others emphasize the Spirit's supernatural and personal work, so they emphasize experience. The former groups emphasize the teaching authority of pastors and the value of academic training. The latter groups emphasize the practical piety of laypeople and the dangers of knowledge. Despite this variety, evangelicals together celebrate the "priesthood of all believers" and the freedom of the gospel when addressing how the Spirit accompanies the Word.

The Priesthood of All Believers

Protestants uphold Scripture's clarity and sufficiency by affirming the priesthood of all believers. This doctrine underscores that Jesus Christ is the sole Mediator between God and humanity; the Spirit's anointing gives every believer personal access to God in Christ. If Scripture were not clear, then Tradition and/or an infallible pope would be necessary to avoid interpretative chaos. Of course, Protestants have created plenty of chaos with the Bible, often failing to make the priesthood of all believers seem plausible. This doctrine never authorized individual Christians to function as their own popes, as if they could read the Bible alone on lots of spiritual islands. The *priesthood of all believers—not the "priesthood of the believer"—maintains that all who are baptized into Christ share immediate access to God. This priesthood involves personal participation in a collective identity. Therefore, all believers may call upon God in prayer, hear God in Scripture, and proclaim the divine Word to others, sharing in the ministry of Christ as our one true Mediator.

Along with Christ's mediation, believers' priestly ministry depends upon the empowering presence of the Holy Spirit, who teaches people to know Christ. Still, when 1 John 2:20–27 celebrates the Spirit's anointing of all believers as teachers, the text is *teaching* precisely about this reality! The Spirit's illumination does not contradict the inspired Scriptures or supplant the need for interpretation. Faithful reading is necessary because God has chosen to speak through written texts. Illumination does mean, though, that the scriptural texts are not timelessly self-interpreting. The reading of Scripture is a function of redemption, not just creation and providence. The priesthood of all believers presupposes *both* the clarity of Scripture's central message regarding Christ the Mediator *and* the Spirit's ministry of illumination.

From a Protestant perspective, Orthodoxy and Catholicism undermine the priesthood of all the baptized with their appeals to Tradition and the magisterium. Admittedly, Protestants often make the Spirit's illuminating work too individual, inward, and thus idiosyncratic. We need to learn from others' emphasis upon tradition as an enduring, institutional form of the Spirit's illuminating work. Yet the Protestant view recognizes Christ's unique mediation, the Word's objective priority, the Spirit's illuminating work among the whole people of God, and the church's ongoing sinfulness.[15] While tradition plays a ministerial role in biblical interpretation, nowhere does the biblical gospel suggest earthly perfection for any institutional aspect of the church. A remnant may always be protected against fundamentally abandoning the gospel (Matt. 16:17–20), but such indefectibility does not entail magisterial infallibility. Protestants affirm the priesthood of all believers in connection with the way *sola scriptura* follows from *sola gratia*: Scripture's final authority helps to minister the spiritually sufficient Word of Christ clearly to the church.

The Freedom of the Gospel

The Protestant Reformers championed *sola scriptura* in order to celebrate Christian freedom; their concerns about tradition focused on interpretations and practices that obscured the free grace of the biblical gospel.[16] In the Bible's own references to its writing, reading, and interpretation there is a dynamic relationship between the fixed nature of texts and appropriate freedom in understanding them. Interwoven with this dynamic relationship is oscillation between remembrance and renewal: the texts fix the memory and meaning of God's mighty acts, while interpretive freedom fosters the ongoing renewal of the covenant people. Accompanied by the Spirit, the Word incorporates hearers within salvation history—history that includes growth in understanding as both a gift and a necessity. Despite the fullness of revelation in Christ, the biblical witness does not instantly finalize the church's understanding: even in grasping the truth, the new humanity must grow in corresponding to Christ's fullness (Eph. 4:13–16).

God communicates for the sake of communion with the covenant people. This communion evokes genuine human freedom and corresponding growth in communal wisdom. Biblical wisdom makes space for human experience and reflection. Simultaneously, though, Christian virtue focuses on hearing God's voice, in a dynamic relationship between enduring tradition and ongoing inquiry. The Spirit helps believers in Christ to grow in spiritual wisdom through hearing the Word with gospel freedom—and vice versa. As God's self-communication establishes communion, the covenant people should neither

15. Neglected until recently, the priesthood of all believers has now received excellent dissertation-length treatments from Uche Anizor and Hank Voss, who have distilled their treatments in *Representing Christ*.

16. The following exposition draws upon Treier, "Freedom of God's Word," esp. 28–32, 38–39.

become autonomous nor remain infantile; as they dwell with God, they should grow into spiritual adulthood. On the one hand, freedom is not autonomy from God's Word; on the other hand, maturity rules out slavish literalism but instead reflects responsible interpretation of the texts as ultimately comprising one divine Word. Recognizing that true freedom lies in learning the mind of Christ by Word and Spirit, believers grow in understanding as part of their discipleship. Recognizing too that communion with God involves the body of Christ, believers seek to learn from others and to discern with others.

The Spirit grants freedom by making the Word of Christ present and powerful. In other words, the Spirit's illumination uses the process of interpretation as an ingredient in our sanctification. This gift of freedom in the gospel is integral to the Spirit's creation of one holy, catholic, and apostolic church—a new humanity that learns to hear and obey together. The authority of the Bible as Scripture, the attributes of Scripture as God's Word, and the Holy Spirit's accompaniment of the Word are thus integral to evangelical freedom.

— 14 —

Church

THESIS

The Bible identifies the church as God's people in Christ; the Spirit graciously uses various practices for shaping the church as a community of worship, nurture, and witness; along with Word and sacrament, institutional order marks the church, yet traditional models of polity require wise modern implementation and humble acknowledgment of communal brokenness.

LEARNING OBJECTIVES

After learning the material in this chapter, you should be able to:

1. *Define briefly* the key terms introduced here (marked with an asterisk and included in the glossary).
2. *List and recognize* the following: (a) the four marks of the church; (b) historic challenges that have shaped the doctrine of the church.
3. *Describe and compare* the following: (a) theological models for the church; (b) views of the rites of the church; (c) church polities.
4. *Identify and illustrate* the biblical images for the church and its missional identity.
5. *Explain* the modern complexities that the church faces in embodying its unity and possible approaches to addressing its brokenness.

Through the Word, the Holy Spirit is forming a new humanity in Jesus Christ. The *church is neither a building nor just an institution, but a regathered form of Israel incorporating people from every tribe, tongue, and nation. For the time being, the church grows in realizing its identity as God's people (the first subject of this chapter) through certain practices (second) and polity (third). The church is an embassy of God's kingdom: both an earthly sociocultural entity and a heavenly sign—anticipating a

319

community that will transcend human politics, enjoying the *shalom* of dwelling with God.[1]

Identity: God's People in Christ

The third article of the Nicene Creed confesses that the church is one, holy, catholic, and apostolic. *Oneness means that the church is fundamentally united in Jesus Christ, as his body; holiness, that the Holy Spirit has set apart this body for God's service; *catholicity, that this body has a universal embrace, with each member connected to the whole; *apostolicity, that this body has been sent into the world to extend faithfully the apostles' proclamation. Of course, these four *marks are true of the church only in a preliminary and partial, not a perfect, sense. Yet they identify core truths about the church that can be unpacked further in terms of key biblical teaching, historical challenges, and theological models.[2]

Biblical Teaching

The key New Testament term, *ekklēsia*, designates an assembly; from this term *ecclesiology names the doctrine of the church. Because of the root *kaleō*, "to call," Christians often speak of the church as a community "called out of" the world. Yet word meanings transcend their origins. True, Christ-followers are called out of the world; more centrally, though, we are called together, into communion with one another as we are united to God in Christ. In the Lord's Prayer, "hallowing"—honoring holiness—makes God's name central and not marginal, sacred and not just separate. In the church, likewise, Jesus followers are called to embody the healthy community for which God created all of humanity. The church ought to show the world what it means to be the world[3]—both what it should be and how far short of that ideal humanity currently is.

The church should be distinct from, albeit lovingly engaged with, the world. The church must not love "the world" in the sense of idolatrous cultural systems that war against God and God's people (1 John 2:15–17). Simultaneously, the church must love the world's people, whom God loves (John 3:16–17).

---

1. On the church as an embassy, see Leeman, *Political Church*; on the church as a postpolitical entity, see O'Donovan, *Ways of Judgment*, esp. part 3.

2. Portions of this chapter appear in Treier, "Who Is the Church?," used here with permission.

3. This aphorism reflects the thought of Stanley Hauerwas and William H. Willimon, as in *Resident Aliens*. In *Where Resident Aliens Live*, 58, for instance, they assert that "the church serves the world by helping the world know that it is the world."

The church must also love the world as the sum total of God's creatures, the theater of God's glory, in which God's preserving grace is present. The church is the primary sign, although not the exclusive site, of God's coming reign in Jesus. Think of the world as water and the church as a boat: the water always pushes on the boat, filling whatever space it finds. The church seems remarkably porous, with lots of holes that let the world in. Nevertheless, the world remains God's gift, essential to the creaturely life that the church seeks to rescue.[4] In the old covenant, Israel was both the people of God and a nation in the world. The nature of the unity and distinctions between "Israel" and "church" within the one people of God is disputed. This book's next chapter, on last things, details some aspects of that dispute, which affects what Pentecost means for the church's identity as well as how the community of the new covenant engages the present world in light of God's coming kingdom.

Those complications aside, the New Testament teaches about the church through a dazzling array of images.[5] The church is a temple (e.g., 1 Cor. 3:16–17), a household (1 Tim. 3:15), a bride (Eph. 5:22–33), a vineyard (John 15:1–8), and much more. Often these crucial images have Old Testament antecedents. Currently, then, the church is a regathered form of God's people— newly sharing in the life of Christ, as his body, by the Spirit. Hence the church has begun to enjoy what the Old Testament anticipates: "My dwelling place will be with them; I will be their God, and they will be my people" (e.g., Ezek. 37:27). Its members enjoy a human share in the fellowship that characterizes the Triune God as Father, Son, and Holy Spirit.

"Church" indicates not just what we do, but who we are. The church is a *missional community: as the Father sent the Son into the world, so now by the Spirit the Son gathers and sends us into the world. Christians are sent for relational purposes: to *worship* God, *nurture* one another, and bear *witness* to society in word and deed. Members of the church begin to fulfill these purposes simply by being God's people, celebrating the good news by being present in the world as forgiven and forgiving sinners. The mission is God's; the church is privileged to be a sign, pointing toward the coming of God's kingdom in fullness. Mission, then, involves not just one activity but rather the church's identity throughout its life: "being sent" as the people of the Triune God, whose self-giving in Christ they proclaim by the Spirit's powerful presence.

This identity entails holistic mission, which has been championed by the Lausanne Covenant, a globally evangelical and ecumenical movement

---

4. I heard this analogy in a sermon from my former pastor Jerry Andrews.
5. Notably, see Minear, *Images of the Church*.

galvanized by John R. W. Stott (1921–2011) in 1974. Lausanne was ahead of its time in highlighting Christianity's non-Western emergence, environmental stewardship, technological change, and other concerns of integral mission. Lausanne challenged evangelicals to continue verbal evangelism while organically connecting such proclamation with social action. Both are vital aspects of the church's mission; though they may be distinguished, they must not be separated. Their relationship is integral, not instrumental. The gospel goes beyond humanitarian deeds: contra the catchphrase "Proclaim the gospel, and use words if necessary," Romans 10:14 asks, "How, then, can they call on the one they have not believed in? And how can they believe in the one of whom they have not heard? And how can they hear without someone preaching to them?" The gospel proclaims Christ and urges people to call upon him for salvation. Yet good deeds do more than gain a hearing; they share the love of Jesus.

Beginning in the 1980s, Lesslie Newbigin (1909–98) further advanced missional thinking about the church. Newbigin was an Anglican missionary to India for several decades who, upon returning to England, was amazed at the cultural change during his absence. Christendom was ending, and acquaintance with the Christian faith rapidly declining. Returning home as if to a foreign country, Newbigin saw that churches must engage in cross-cultural interpretation of their local contexts in order to embody the gospel faithfully. The church is a "hermeneutic of the gospel"—a way for outsiders to understand the message of Jesus Christ by encountering church practices.[6]

An important caution regarding the church's missional character concerns the historic association of "mission" with crusading violence, religious coercion, and colonialism. For long periods the church failed to send people out proclaiming the good news, instead remaining comfortably at home in Europe. Christendom's preeminent "missions" were the Crusades, which left an ambiguous legacy at best. Then late medieval and early modern Catholic "missions" to the Americas and elsewhere used coercion to attain conversions. Protestants too have their share of colonialism—both literally and metaphorically—for which to repent. These associations of "mission" with cultural pride and colonial violence suggest humility and caution in using that word.

Nevertheless, mission is inescapable within the Bible—in its dramatic form as well as its content.[7] Despite its checkered history, "mission" names the

6. See especially Newbigin, *Gospel in a Pluralist Society*. For an overview of the "missional church" movement, see Guder, *Missional Church*.

7. C. Wright, "Mission as a Matrix," 103, tells of how teaching a course on mission in the Bible led him to recognize that the Bible itself is a missional phenomenon.

church as the people whom the Triune God has sent. Mission is not just one thing we do; it is not primarily something *we* do, even if it calls us to passionate activity. The church participates in the *missio Dei*, the mission of *God*. Biblical mission proclaims our Triune God's self-giving love while embodying the humility of Jesus Christ, in whose name we are sent.

Historical Challenges

The institutional possibilities of particular contexts have shaped the ecclesiological implications that Christians have drawn from Scripture. Four historical challenges have been especially important.[8]

First, early on: as the apostles began dying and the Lord's expected return was delayed, the church faced the challenge of *apostolic succession*. What principle(s) of authority would maintain Christian unity after the apostles passed from the scene? What practices would maintain the church's theological identity through the recognition and interpretation of canonical Scriptures? The Rule of Faith provided a vital answer. A formal concept of *apostolic succession offered a complementary answer. Yet strict claims about an unbroken line of bishops succeeding the apostles became difficult to maintain after various schisms.

Second, still within the patristic period: the church faced the challenge of *lapsed believers and priests*. Cyprian (200–258), bishop of Carthage, famously proclaimed that "outside the church there is no salvation" (*extra ecclesiam nulla salus*). He was dealing with those who denied Christ in the face of martyrdom. Could they be restored to the church, or did Hebrews 6:4–6 preclude their salvation? If restoration were impossible, would that stem from a divine mandate or human inability? What counted as such apostasy? Cyprian faced laxists (who favored full restoration without public penance) on one side and rigorists (who opposed any restoration) on the other; his own position (allowing for restoration while insisting on public penance) eventually gained mainstream support.

A subsequent iteration of this controversy involved the *Donatists. Their rigor involved church leaders: not simply whether lapsed priests could be restored but whether their sacramental actions could be effective. If North African priests were among the *traditores*, who escaped persecution or martyrdom by "handing over" sacred texts for public burning, could laypeople be confident of the sacrament's validity? The Donatists answered no, but Augustine answered yes, focusing upon God's grace rather than priests' spirituality.

---

8. This section reflects the helpful account in McKim, *Theological Turning Points*, chap. 3.

Augustine's response fostered the idea that the sacraments are effective *ex opere operato*, "in the very doing of the act." The goal was not to champion a magical view of ritual performance but rather to reassure troubled believers of available grace. Augustine also appealed to the parable of the wheat and the tares (Matt. 13:24–30) concerning the church's mixed character. On his view, if Jesus did not expect the church to be entirely pure until the eschatological future, then the Donatist desire to root out the tares should be resisted.

Third, over subsequent centuries: the church faced the challenge of *complex interactions with other monotheistic faiths*, Judaism and Islam. The New Testament already narrates a "parting of the ways," but unfortunately Christian apologists responded to Judaism with intensifying *supersessionism: "According to this teaching, God chose the Jewish people after the fall of Adam in order to prepare the world for the coming of Jesus Christ, the Savior. After Christ came, however, the special role of the Jewish people came to an end and its place was taken by the church, the new Israel."[9] With its negative connotations, "supersessionism" is a difficult label to apply precisely, since Christian faith makes claims about new covenant fulfillment based on Israel's Old Testament hopes. Christians do not encounter Judaism as another "religion" in the same way as other faiths;[10] in a sense, "Judaism" labels Hebrew faith after its separation from the Jesus movement and Rome's destruction of Jerusalem. Even so, the church has often been guilty of racially anti-Semitic or religiously anti-Judaic forms of supersessionism that simplistically displace Israel from God's favor, with tragic consequences.

"Christendom" persecuted Jews with embarrassing frequency. After the church's anti-Judaic tendencies exacerbated Western culture's anti-Semitism, the horror of the Holocaust forced Christians to grapple with this legacy. Gentile-dominant churches increasingly wrestle with their theological identity as a regathered form of Israel, rejecting simplistic accounts of the people of God in which a (gentile) "church" replaces Israel entirely or else remains completely separate (as if there were two ways of salvation). Meanwhile "messianic" communities are practicing Christian faith in distinctly Jewish ways. The mystery of Romans 9–11 remains, but in a post-Holocaust world the church has faced it anew.

Islam emerged from Christianity somewhat as Christian faith emerged from Judaism. This emergence is open to various interpretations. Speaking of a different "religion" invokes a modern category with debated features—sacred

9. Soulen, *The God of Israel*, 1–2.
10. On Judaism as the only non-non-Christian religion, see McDermott and Netland, *Trinitarian Theology of Religions*, 3n1.

texts, rituals, and so forth. Before Islam became a distinct religion, though, it could be seen as an ancient Christian "heresy"—an internal rejection of the trinitarian gospel. Islam worried about protecting the transcendence of the one God. The incarnation seemed scandalous—God having a Son! The Trinity seemed to violate monotheism—God as Father and Son and Holy Spirit. Islam can provoke the church to be vigilant about remaining monotheistic, but it rejects the Triune God and the biblical gospel. After Islamic persecution of Christians and medieval Crusades, tensions perennially arise. A contemporary ecclesiological question follows, concerning "Muslim background believers": Is it necessary for converts to separate fully from Muslim worship practices and to affiliate publicly with the Christian community? Or is it permissible, even contextually appropriate, for converts to remain within Muslim communities as Jesus followers? This issue remains debated in missiological circles.[11]

Fourth, notably in the Great Schism of 1054 and the Protestant Reformation: the church has faced the challenge of *formal schisms*. Each resulting "church" interprets the four marks in mutually exclusive ways. "Apostolic" designates, for Orthodoxy, communion with bishops tied to the great liturgical Tradition; for Catholicism, communion with bishops ordained in communion with the bishop of Rome; for Protestants, subjection to the apostles' teaching communicated in Scripture. Competing definitions of apostolicity put pressure on the other three marks: each church locates the others somehow outside the "one" true church or defers institutional unity to an eschatological hope. Now no church can be completely "catholic" or acknowledge the others as fully "holy." We all have failed to "keep the unity of the Spirit through the bond of peace" (Eph. 4:3); like holiness, unity and catholicity constitute a calling, a gift not yet fully enjoyed. Protestants naturally acknowledge this failure by defining apostolicity in biblical rather than institutional terms, a definition that can reduce the church's visibility. The church is the people of God in Christ, sent into the world to proclaim God's reign through word and deed, even our very presence—but we are present as a community of forgiven sinners.

Theological Models

Thus, different models have taken root in particular traditions.[12] In principle, the church could be virtually all that these models call for. But not all

11. For an introduction to six approaches, see Tennent, *Theology in the Context of World Christianity*, chap. 8. On Islam's emergence, see S. Griffiths, *Church in the Shadow of the Mosque*.

12. These six models stem from Dulles, *Models of the Church*. For evangelical overviews of the church, see B. Harper and Metzger, *Exploring Ecclesiology*; Husbands and Treier, *Community of the Word*.

of their respective truths can receive equal emphasis, especially given some mutually exclusive institutional claims.

Catholicism and Orthodoxy, along with some Protestants, treat the church as an *institution*. They highlight the apostolic succession of bishops, who connect congregations to the original community that Jesus founded and the apostles led. At the heart of this community is the Eucharist, but validity of the Eucharist depends upon celebrants who perpetuate the community's institutional essence.

These traditions also treat the church as a *mystical communion*. They highlight spiritual relationship in Christ—the *communion of saints—across time and place. This communion is with the Triune God and with others in Christ's body, even transcending death and enabling earthly believers to draw upon the intercession of already glorified saints.

Such traditions sometimes treat the church as a *sacrament* too. They highlight the ways in which the church mediates God's gracious presence to the world. This emphasis goes beyond celebrating sacraments to consider the church's existence itself as sacramental, perhaps continuing the incarnation—an emphatic appeal to the motif of the body of Christ.[13]

Many Protestants emphasize less vertical models. The Lutheran and Reformed traditions typically treat the church as a *herald*. They highlight proclamation of God's Word. Still fairly vertical, this model does not emphasize the church's institutional or mystical or sacramental being. Instead, crucial acts involve the Word being rightly preached and the sacraments, as visual words, being rightly administered. "Word and sacrament" become "marks" of the church as herald.

"Low-church" Protestants such as Anabaptists—along with some liberationist groups—treat the church as a *servant*. They highlight the work of local communities serving others, seeking justice, and promoting peace. Again, the focus rests upon acts that mark the church rather than something essential to its being.

Still other Protestants treat the church as a *community of disciples*. They highlight the pursuit of personal and/or social holiness. This model characterizes low-church Protestants, including Holiness groups and Baptists, as well as denominations like the Methodists.

If the first three models emphasize the institution that precedes new members and mediates divine grace to them, and the fourth emphasizes the proclamation of the Word that influences the next generation along with inviting

---

13. This model reflects Augustine's concept of the church as the *totus Christus*, the whole Christ. For an influential statement of this sacramental view, see Lubac, *Catholicism*, esp. 29.

new members, then the last two models emphasize the personal decision to join the community of Jesus followers. All of these models shape the ordinary lives of Christians and their congregations. Their concrete implications appear in shared practices that connect relationships and rituals.

Practices: The Spirit's Means of Grace

Christian *practices reflect and foster the church's conformity to Christ. These means of grace involve personal participation in communal activity.[14] Pneumatology introduced means of grace in the context of personal sanctification and thus spiritual disciplines. Even Scripture reading and prayer, though, are not ultimately practiced alone; such personal disciplines are extensions of communal practices, oriented by church teaching and public worship. God's grace works freely, not mechanically, within both personal disciplines and communal practices. Sometimes, of course, God works beyond or despite human activity, but church practices remain the ordinary means of sharing divine grace.

Worship, Nurture, and Witness

Church practices focus upon worshiping God, nurturing members' faith, and bearing witness to the world. Having addressed these relationships elsewhere, here we can focus briefly on how their purposes relate to the church's corporate worship.

Called by God, the covenant people gather. Praising God, we recognize our sinfulness. God receives our confession and restores fellowship, announcing again that we are forgiven. Then we greet one another, sharing God's peace. We continue our praise, we gratefully offer gifts to advance God's mission, and we intercede for one another and the world. We hear God's Word read and proclaimed. Often, we celebrate the Lord's Supper—remembering Christ's redemptive work, reaffirming our unity, and renewing our hope of a heavenly banquet. Finally, we receive God's blessing as we are sent out again to minister in the world.

14. On Christian practices generally, see Pohl, *Living into Community*; Volf and Bass, *Practicing Theology*; for a communal experiment in such practices, see Bonhoeffer, *Life Together*. For an illustrative treatment of a Christian practice, see Pohl, *Making Room*.

MacIntyre, *After Virtue*, 186–87, defines a practice in terms of social activity with internal goods rather than merely external products. For the church, then, a practice like prayer is more than a means to an external end; growing in the grace of prayer is an essential aspect of excellent Christian living.

Every church has a *liturgy: patterned movements of worship. Some liturgies are formal and planned; others are freer yet learned through repetition. Worship needs both form and freedom. Forms like written prayers, through the wisdom of past saints and present teachers, implant the gospel in hearts and minds. Freedom indicates the Holy Spirit in our midst, leading the church as a living tradition into the future. Formal elements of liturgy can actually free us to find God afresh with others. More than praise offered in song or feelings experienced in praise, worship involves a set of practices for offering ourselves to God while receiving grace anew—hearing, seeing, and tasting as well as speaking and singing. These practices express emotions while reshaping them through bodily rites.

In the gathered community and in daily life, worship bears witness to God's saving work via word and deed. In regathering us around the Word as well as sending us out in the Spirit, corporate worship regularly reorients the church toward living as God's covenant people.

Rites

Certain practices involve *rites, or ritual acts: "Rituals are regular, repetitive, rule-determined patterns of symbolic behaviour, performed by one or more people, that utilize any or all of the following components: language, action, visual imagery, personification and characterization, specific objects imbued with meaning, and music"—usually marking shared experiences.[15] Theological categories for certain rites are disputed. Speaking ecumenically of *sacraments celebrates the mysterious communication of God's grace through ritually embodied signs. Most Baptists and other low-church groups speak of ordinances instead, championing human obedience to God's command: the ritual remembrance does not offer unique divine presence.

In grouping such ritual practices together, Catholicism and Orthodoxy recognize seven sacraments: baptism, confirmation, Holy Eucharist, penance, anointing of the sick, holy orders, and matrimony. Aside from some Anglicans, Protestants generally recognize two sacraments or ordinances: baptism and the Lord's Supper. Before treating those two rites below, it is worth commenting briefly on the other five.

In Catholic and Orthodox contexts, confirmation completes the grace of baptism, anointing confirmands with the seal of the Holy Spirit so that they may begin receiving the Holy Eucharist.[16] When practiced in Protestant

---

15. Rambo, "Ritual," 509.
16. See *Catechism of the Catholic Church*, 325–32, §§1285–311, with differences between East and West usually treated in these sections.

contexts, confirmation has varied significance, initiating young people who were baptized as infants into full membership.

"Penance and reconciliation" is one of the Catholic sacraments of healing, distinct from the sacraments of initiation (baptism, confirmation, and Holy Eucharist). *Penance involves ongoing need for conversion, confession, and forgiveness, with means of satisfaction such as fasting, prayer, and almsgiving. Protestants object to the language of needing to "make satisfaction for" or "expiate" sins; even if recovering spiritual health after full absolution assumes the basis of Christ's work, practices like indulgences seem to hinder reliance upon the one Mediator.[17] Luther and other early Protestants allowed for private confession of sin, developing penitential manuals to guide confessors. These practices subsided among later Protestants, although the recent recovery of "spiritual direction" makes a gesture toward private confession (e.g., James 5:16). Many Protestant liturgies, of course, include communal confession.

Like confession, *anointing of the sick appeals to James 5:13–20. In Catholicism, despite popular perception, anointing is not solely for people at the threshold of death (as part of "viaticum" preparing them for heaven).[18] Protestant groups also anoint the sick, often after a personal appeal to church leaders.

In Catholicism, holy orders and matrimony are sacraments directed toward the salvation of others rather than oneself. These sacraments involve particular consecrations of "those already *consecrated* by Baptism and Confirmation for the common priesthood of all the faithful." *Holy orders, the sacrament of apostolic ministry, includes the three "degrees" of the episcopate, the presbyterate, and the diaconate (treated below under polity). This sacrament is limited to men, whom Catholicism calls to celibacy, whereas Orthodoxy opens the diaconate and the priesthood to married men (requiring celibacy of bishops and those who were celibate when ordained).[19] Protestants, aside from some Anglicans, do not treat ordination to ministry as sacramental; some do not practice ordination at all. Celibacy is not a Protestant requirement for ordained ministers, and Protestants differ about the propriety of women's ordination.

For Catholicism, matrimony confers grace, having a unitive aspect that establishes a covenant bond and a procreative aspect that enables the vocation of parenting. Unlike Catholicism, few Protestants (again aside from some Anglicans) treat marriage as a sacrament. A general challenge for sacramental theology concerns whether to start deductively (defining the category and then

---

17. See *Catechism of the Catholic Church*, 357–74, §§1420–98.
18. See *Catechism of the Catholic Church*, 375–82, §§1499–532.
19. See *Catechism of the Catholic Church*, 383–99, §§1533–600; on marriage, see 400–415, §§1601–66.

determining what rituals qualify) or inductively (examining biblical rites and then discerning commonalities).[20] Probably the former, deductive tendency favors the Catholic focus on mediating grace; the latter, inductive tendency favors the Protestant primacy of baptism and the Lord's Supper.

The use of "sacrament," conveying "mystery," emerged from Tertullian. Similarly, Augustine made the category "sign" prominent. Augustine addressed everything in terms of signs and things, with some things being signs. People ought to enjoy participating in God, the ultimate Good, using other things to enjoy God. Signs point to this Good. The sign's participation in the thing signified became an increasing medieval emphasis regarding Christ's body and blood in the Eucharist. Protestant Reformers rejected the eventual Catholic theology of the Mass, in which they perceived Jesus's sacrifice to be offered repeatedly. Still, many Protestants retained Christ's presence at the Lord's Supper; others focused instead on Christians' act of remembering Christ's work. The general approaches of most Western Christians, then, have fallen into five categories:

1. In the *Catholic* view, a sacrament is *both a sign and a sanctifier*. It confers grace *ex opere operato*: in the very doing of the act it is effective.

2. In the *Lutheran* view, a sacrament is an *efficacious sign*. It does not confer grace *ex opere operato* but it helps to incite faith through its relationship to the Word.

3. In the *Zwinglian* view, Luther's opposite among Protestants, a sacrament or ordinance is *only a sign*. It may help to confirm but not to give faith.

4. In the *Calvinist* view, a mediating position between Luther and Zwingli, a sacrament is *a sign and seal*. It helps to confirm and increase faith via the Word.

5. At a *popular evangelical* level, many do not hold even a Zwinglian view. For them, ordinances *do not distinctively* signal God's presence or confirm faith. That said, many people still treat these acts of remembrance as opportunities for obedience and spiritual meaning.

Baptism

*Baptism initiates believers into their priestly participation in Christ's body, identifying with his saving work and sharing in the Holy Spirit. Baptized believers may participate in the Lord's Supper, being subject to the church's

---

20. Catholicism, for instance, treats other rites, such as blessings, under the category of "sacramentals."

discipline. In Matthew 28:19–20 baptism identifies disciples with the name of the Triune God. In Romans 6:1–14 baptized believers participate in Christ's death and resurrection. In Romans 10:9–13 baptism identifies believers with others who publicly confess Jesus's lordship and personally celebrate his resurrection. In 1 Peter 3:18–22 baptism again unites the redeemed community with Christ's death and resurrection, especially with his victorious ascension and subjection of hostile powers. In short, baptism identifies people with the church's faith in Jesus so that they share in the Holy Spirit as members of Christ's body (1 Cor. 12:13).

This connection to faith generates debate over paedobaptism, the baptism of infants or others who are not able to exercise personal faith. Advocates of *credobaptism highlight the active confession of faith in New Testament baptism passages. Paedobaptists acknowledge this need for faith to be present, with the family and/or the Christian community confessing on the child's behalf. Credobaptists argue, though, that the basic meaning of *baptizō* involves dipping or immersing, not just sprinkling or other means commonly used to baptize infants.

Many paedobaptists connect baptism to Old Testament circumcision (citing Col. 2:11–15), applying the sign and seal of God's grace to children of covenant families before they personally confess faith. Paedobaptists further cite New Testament "household" texts (such as the Philippian jailer's conversion in Acts 16:16–40; also 1 Cor. 7:12–16) as evidence that baptism encompassed more than adult believers. Orthodox, Catholic, Lutheran, and some Anglican paedobaptists affirm baptismal regeneration, with baptism conferring new life in Christ and removing the guilt of original sin. Reformed and Methodist paedobaptists typically reject baptismal regeneration, with baptism confirming God's promises and anticipating the child's personal faith.

The beginnings of paedobaptism are disputed. If biblical household texts do not reflect paedobaptism, then the practice may have arisen after Christianity gained official status in the Roman Empire. Hence many who oppose "Constantinian" Christendom oppose paedobaptism, associating the practice with nominal faith. Yet credobaptists usually have their own ritual—the dedication of infants—that relies on indirect biblical support and presupposes the importance of Christian families. Meanwhile, nominalism and apostasy beleaguer every Christian community.

Baptism's basic purpose is clear: the public identification of people with Christ's body. This initiatory rite symbolizes the cleansing and the new life that are found in our crucified and risen Lord. Paedobaptists underscore the Triune God's gracious movement toward us; credobaptists underscore the human response of faith.

The Lord's Supper

Baptized believers celebrate the Lord's Supper (so named in 1 Cor. 11:20–34) as an ongoing rite of remembrance, unity, and anticipation. The Lord's Supper is also called the "Eucharist," to emphasize thanksgiving (Greek *eucharistia*) as the church *remembers* Jesus's saving work, and "Holy Communion," to emphasize present *unity* as the people enjoy Christ's presence together. The Lord's Supper further *anticipates* a future banquet (Rev. 19:9) celebrating the fullness of God's kingdom. The Catholic terminology of the "Mass" associates the Eucharist with sacrifice, although the primary liturgical association of *missa* involves sending the faithful into the world.[21] Protestants, except for some Anglicans, fear that the Catholic "re-presentation" of Jesus's sacrifice obscures its once-for-all character (Heb. 9:23–28).

The Lord's Supper originated in Jesus's final Passover meal with his disciples, at which he introduced a new-covenant meal, anticipating the eschatological banquet (e.g., Matt. 26:17–30).[22] John's Gospel associates the Last Supper with Jesus's washing of his disciples' feet. This foot washing had the double significance of celebrating their cleansing and calling them to servanthood (John 13:1–17). The description of early Christian practice in Acts 2:42–47 and Paul's instruction in 1 Corinthians 11 associate the Lord's Supper with a meal, which Jude 12 and early tradition label the *agapē*, the love feast. Both foot washing and the love feast underscore believers' present unity in Christ. In Corinth, by contrast, wealthier congregants apparently gorged themselves, getting drunk and leaving poorer congregants or slaves nothing to eat once they arrived. Taking bread and wine to remember Christ's sacrificial death was incompatible with such selfishness, and celebrating unity was inconsistent with the community's fundamental division.

As with baptism, so Christian traditions vary over the biblical emphasis concerning the Lord's Supper. Some emphasize an "ordinance" of human remembrance before God. Others emphasize a "sacrament" of divine grace. The element of obedience is biblically obvious from the commands of Jesus and Paul. The element of mystery is present in Scripture too, especially in 1 Corinthians 10–11 concerning participation. Of course, views of Christ's presence at the Lord's Supper have a complex history.

---

21. On the Catholic view, see below and *Catechism of the Catholic Church*, 334–56, §§1322–419.

22. A respected treatment of this transition (including historical complexities of Jesus's final week on earth) is I. Marshall, *Last Supper and Lord's Supper*; a recent treatment highlighting its importance in Jesus's ministry is Pitre, *Jesus and the Last Supper*. Some Anabaptist groups continue to practice foot washing and the love feast as ordinances, even as part of the "communion" service.

Augustine's vocabulary of signs elicited both realist and symbolic theories in the medieval church. Paschasius Radbertus (785–865) wrote the first substantial Western treatise on the Eucharist to champion a realist view: Jesus's historical body is present in the supper's elements. Christ spoke literally of the bread as his body and the wine as his blood, without which participants could not be certain of receiving grace. His flesh and blood save our bodies, which, though frail, are integral to the sanctification of our souls in God's image. Ratramnus (died c. 870), Radbertus's predecessor as abbot of Corbie (France), opposed the realist view. Ratramnus reworked Radbertus's distinction between "figure" and "truth," associating truth with sense perception and denying that Christ's body was present in that way; after all, the bread and wine undergo no perceptible change. Instead, on Ratramnus's symbolic view, Christ is spiritually present at the Lord's Supper but not physically present in the elements, which represent him figuratively.

Realism became the official *Catholic* view at the Fourth Lateran Council in 1215, with *transubstantiation* confirmed at Lyons in 1274. *Transubstantiation is the version of realism that Thomas Aquinas unfolded using newly recovered Aristotelian categories. Thomas distinguished between the *substance (the essential nature) and the *accidents (external properties that can change without altering the essential reality) of the bread and wine. So, for instance, my "substance" remains "human being" even as the "accidents" of my height and weight change. In the *epiclesis*, the eucharistic prayer that invokes the Spirit's blessed presence, the substance of the bread and wine is transformed into Christ's body and blood, while the accidental properties of physical bread and wine remain the same. This distinction enabled Thomas to maintain Radbertus's realism while addressing the lack of sensible change in the elements.

The *Lutheran* view, difficult to characterize, is frequently labeled *consubstantiation*, a label that many Lutherans reject because Luther gave no ontological explanation. He maintained Christ's real presence while attacking what he saw as speculation and superstition. The substance and not just the accidents remain bread and wine; although not localized, Christ is present "in, with, and under" the elements.

The *Zwinglian* view acknowledges *no distinctive presence* of Christ at the Lord's Supper. The elements symbolize Jesus's body and blood, enabling the congregation to remember his death and resurrection. But no special divine grace is present beyond the church's opportunity to respond in faith.

The *Calvinist* view again fits between the Lutheran and Zwinglian ends of the Protestant spectrum. Calvin acknowledged Christ's *real, spiritual presence*, mediated by the Spirit through faith. This "spiritual" presence nourishes union with Christ by confirming faith; physical presence would threaten the integrity of Jesus's bodily ascension and ongoing incarnation. Such presence would leave the Spirit's agency unclear, whereas for Calvin the Spirit gives the congregation an anticipatory encounter with the ascended Christ.

Popular evangelical views, again, may not match Zwingli's. As noted above, participants frequently treat this act of *obedience and remembrance* as an opportunity for spiritual experience. The emphasis upon remembrance is obviously biblical. However, unless we articulate how remembering Jesus's work consistently strengthens faith, God's "ordinance" can look arbitrary. The "thanksgiving" in the Lord's Supper should foster "communion" with God and with one another—or so biblical texts like 1 Corinthians 10–11 suggest.

CHRIST IN THE BODY

The passage in 1 Corinthians distinctively associates baptism (10:1–5) and the Lord's Supper (10:6–33; 11:17–34) as bodily rites related to Jesus's death. These rites are obligatory for all who can participate in the gathering of Christ's body. Most Protestants have resisted the Orthodox and Catholic idea that the church itself is sacramental or continues the incarnation: being called "the body of Christ" powerfully communicates the church's unity and members' equality, yet the body's head remains humanity's one Mediator before God.[23] Protestants can recognize baptism and the Lord's Supper as the two practices in which the church's identity is most fully realized: bearing witness to God's saving work.[24] These practices are the archetype of obedience in response to grace: remembering Christ's unique work, consecrating our bodies, making the church visible, and foreshadowing final redemption. Such holistic participation in Christ's reconciling work introduces the third major aspect of ecclesiology: the polity that orders life together.

Order: The Church's Institutional Structures

While polity divides churches, points of wide agreement exist, and without polity Christians cannot express unity in shared practice or ministry. Baptism calls the whole people of God into ministry.[25] Ordained ministry is a distinct,

---

23. Concerning the incarnation's uniqueness and well-meaning but misguided references to "incarnational ministry," see Billings, *Union with Christ*, 123–65.

24. Henri Blocher, a Reformed Baptist, made this suggestion in a seminar at Trinity Evangelical Divinity School (Deerfield, IL, Spring 1999). Baptist theologians have been retrieving sacramental strands in their tradition, as surveyed in Cortez, "Who Invited the Baptist?"

25. This summary reflects the *koinōnia* ecclesiology in the influential 1982 Lima document, "Baptism, Eucharist, and Ministry," from the Faith and Order Commission of the World Council of Churches.

but not more important, calling. The Lord's Supper remembers and/or communicates God's grace. At the church's heart is *koinōnia—fellowship with God and among believers. *Fellowship involves both a shared identity that stems from participation in Christ and relational interactions that stem from Christian affection in the Spirit. Such communion involves order: "God is not a God of disorder but of peace" (1 Cor. 14:33). *Polity—the structures by which the church orders its leadership to foster the *shalom* of its common life—is a divine gift by which Jesus Christ directs his body.

Polity

Along with "Word and sacrament," order marks the church, identifying its members and leaders. For the time being, in its geographical and theological variety "the church" exists in particular churches. At best, their polities reflect the church's creedal marks in the ministry of Word and sacrament. At worst, church order becomes idolatrous and divisive rather than ministering the good news of Christ's reconciling presence. The following are the chief ways in which churches order their leadership.

TRADITIONAL MODELS

Orthodox and *Catholic* polities emphasize *apostolic succession*. Each institution claims to be the truly one, holy, catholic, and apostolic church, because their bishops are the successors of the successors (etc.) of the apostles. Orthodox succession involves patriarchs handing down the apostolic Tradition expressed in the Sacred Liturgy. Catholic succession involves communion with the pope.

Some Protestant churches, *Lutheran* and *Anglican* in particular, have *episcopal* polity. As in Orthodoxy and Catholicism, Anglican bishops constitute a third order of ministry alongside pastors (called "priests" by some Anglicans) and deacons (who, for Anglicans, typically are training for priesthood, rather than focusing on service as they do in other polities). Lutherans and some other Protestants have bishops without a threefold order; in other words, their bishops are pastors and their deacons are not pastors in training. Episcopal structures foster ecumenical linkage, in principle being closer to reunion with Orthodoxy and Catholicism. Yet schism has broken any clear claim of apostolic succession.[26] "Established" episcopal churches have some official government affiliation, such as the Church of England, whereas others

26. Even Catholic claims must confront the medieval struggle between the Rome and Avignon popes. For a history, see Rollo-Koster, *Avignon and Its Papacy*.

do not. Still other groups, like the African Methodist Episcopal Church, blend elements from multiple polities, including bishops.

Presbyterian polity primarily characterizes *Reformed* churches. "Presbyters" or "elders" form a "session" that governs a local congregation. Elders from particular congregations gather to form "presbyteries" or "synods" that govern a denomination at various levels. Presbyterian polity distinguishes between deacons (focused on service, often appealing to Acts 6:1–7) and elders (focused on spiritual leadership), and further between teaching elders and ruling elders. In modern, Western contexts, teaching elders typically are ordained pastors with recognized professional roles, whereas ruling elders are laypersons. All elders must be able to teach the faith (1 Tim. 3:2), but teaching elders make teaching their focus whereas ruling elders focus upon other aspects (1 Tim. 5:17).

Free (nonstate) churches that are *Baptist or baptistic* usually have *congregational* polity. These groups may form *denominations, formal church associations based on historic (however brief) affinities of doctrine or ministry. Some denominations embrace that label, whereas other groups champion looser structures or titles to avoid jeopardizing local church autonomy. In congregational polity individual members together compose the final human authority through which Christ governs his church, while congregations have two "offices": deacons (focused on serving) and pastors (focused on teaching)—not bishops or elders, which are treated as synonymous with pastors in New Testament terminology.

The modern West has blurred these polities in practice. Many baptistic congregations have pastors as paid, professional leaders, and deacons as unpaid, lay leaders who nevertheless act as a spiritual governing body. Some baptistic congregations have begun to borrow from presbyterian polity, pursuing team leadership by having lay elders (distinct from deacons) who must be able to teach (yet are not called "ruling elders"). Still others have complicated these categories with sheer size, which makes frequent meetings for congregational decision-making practically impossible.

Ongoing Complexities

Some ongoing complexities of church polity reflect disputed biblical teaching, which can be summarized under four questions.

Does the allusion to Peter as the rock in Matthew 16:16–20 support Catholic claims for the papacy, or does the New Testament support another form of apostolic succession?

Does a threefold order of ministry rightly emerge from the diaconate (associated with Acts 6:1–7) and the early catholic rise of bishops as presbyters of presbyters (associated with leaders of leading cities)?

Does a plurality of elders appear at the congregational level or just at the city level, and does 1 Timothy 5:17 distinguish between teaching and ruling elders?

Do narratives of communal discernment support congregational government, and if so, how should individual congregations relate to one another (if the Jerusalem Council of Acts 15 is such a narrative)?

Other complexities of church polity reflect specifically modern contexts for implementing biblical teaching. The *nation-state* is a modern entity, arising in the wake of the Great Schism and the Protestant Reformation. Traditional polities have historic ties to Europe and the Americas, so emerging Christian movements in the Global South offer new contexts for discernment. Hermeneutically, many low-church and American Protestant groups have sought "maximal" conformity to New Testament structures (e.g., Anabaptists or nondenominational evangelicals), whereas European Protestants have sought more "minimal" conformity as long as polities fulfill biblical functions (e.g., Anglicans). Cultural complexity now favors minimalism; no modern polity can claim exact equivalence with early Christian practice or easy extraction from biblical texts.[27] But, for understandable reasons, many Christians around the world favor maximalism, and minimalism can easily become an excuse for cultural preferences.

The *family* likewise blends biblical commitments with cultural forms. In a sense, the household is the original "small group" of believers,[28] a primary New Testament analogy for the church. For much of history, the household included more than the nuclear family, containing other members of a clan and/or servants. Christianity has both adopted and adapted cultural institutions. The Lord's call for the church to be "first family" (e.g., Matt. 12:46–50) needs fresh attention, especially in the late modern West.[29] Aspirations of easily transposing family structures onto the church require caution due to cultural complexity and change.

The church also faces the challenge of relating *spiritual gifts* to special offices within diverse contexts. American evangelicals tend to treat spiritual

---

27. See, e.g., Fee, "Reflections on Church Order." The New Testament focuses on the loving humility of church leaders, while every modern version of the polities sketched here departs somewhat from the Bible's original contexts. Still, the debated polities may do better or worse at corresponding to biblical functions and fostering spiritual leadership.

28. A thought suggested by Icenogle, *Small Group Ministry*.

29. See Clapp, *Families at the Crossroads*, plus Hill, *Spiritual Friendship*.

gifts systematically and callings to church leadership individually. The resulting expectations for believers (finding God's unique will) and their gifts
(being uniquely effective) may unrealistically push beyond what the Bible
conveys, as noted above in chapter 12, on pneumatology. Scripture passages
concerning God's "will" did not assume the vocational autonomy that many
people have today, but rather the Holy Spirit's general direction for spiritual growth and faithful service. Ordinarily, then, spiritual gifts should be
recognized in practice and callings to church office should be recognized in
community.

Finally, *parachurch organizations* challenge contemporary ecclesiology regarding what counts as a church, since they often undertake the same practices. Catholicism has a similar concept, the "sodality"—an order that bands
together with episcopal permission for a particular ministry. The Domini-
cans, for instance, are an order of preachers. Protestant parachurch groups
likewise extend the reach of certain ministries beyond local congregations,
albeit usually without episcopal accountability. Banding together to do what
congregations cannot do alone, parachurch institutions embody an evangelical form of ecumenism.

Are extracongregational, extradenominational forms of Christian community—whether organizations like campus fellowships or home discipleship
groups—actually churches? Who decides what makes a community or an
organization a church, or what wider authority Christian leaders should have
beyond their congregations? Some groups (e.g., the Salvation Army) do not
practice the ordinances yet claim to be churches anyway. Other institutions
(e.g., Wheaton College) disavow being churches yet celebrate one or both
of the sacraments—typically the Lord's Supper—as an extracongregational
expression of evangelical ecumenism. The former groups risk ignoring the
New Testament's strong linkage of baptism and the Lord's Supper with the
church's very identity. The latter institutions risk ignoring the New Testament's strong linkage of baptism and Eucharist with ordered ministry, which
directs congregational discipline to honor the Lord's Table. As for leaders'
extracongregational influence, the diversity of spiritual gifts and implied flex-
ibility of biblical church structures make this frequent reality understandable.
Yet Jesus gave the "keys of the kingdom" to his apostles (Matt. 16:19) for
overseeing the church's ministry of reconciliation (Matt. 18:15–20). A Protestant "church" is distinct from "Christian community" due to the *ordered*
ministry of the Word and the sacraments or ordinances. In responding to
parachurch groups and leaders, evangelicals should recognize diverse gifts and
embrace genuine fruitfulness while respecting ordered ministry and celebrating ordinary congregations.

Brokenness and Wholeness

Ecclesiologies understandably highlight biblical concepts or creedal marks over the church's institutional and moral brokenness. The church is, however, a community of forgiven sinners.[30] Ironically, hungry for authenticity, late modern people become disillusioned with the very community that should be able to deal honesty with humans as we are. It is easy to be romantic in our hopes and individualistic in our evaluations—holding others to higher standards than ourselves. Profound experiences of Christian community happen outside local congregations, and painful experiences within them. Given church splits, clergy abuse scandals, declining denominations, segregated congregations, and "worship wars," it is tempting to retreat into a "personal relationship" with Jesus and perhaps "like-minded" community.

Warts and all, however, the church remains the preeminent sign of God's kingdom. Mutual love manifests our identity as Jesus's followers (John 13:34–35); "Lone Ranger Christians" cannot bear such witness. "Prayer closets" are vital, but they cannot fulfill the ultimate end of a community declaring God's glory among the nations (Ps. 96:3). Parachurch organizations extend ministries and enhance fellowship, but they cannot provide the long-term accountability that God locates in congregations. Christ promises in Matthew 18:20 to be distinctively present when two or three disciples gather in his name. The context involves discipline, when the church must prayerfully evaluate testimony from witnesses. Jesus promises to lead his gathered people even when facing their brokenness. Indeed, "temple" passages about the Holy Spirit's indwelling (e.g., 1 Cor. 3:16–17) may have congregations in view, not just individual persons. God is distinctively present when the Holy Spirit gathers the covenant people in Jesus's name.

Although God is distinctively present in the gathered community, concepts of the church must acknowledge sin and avoid triumphalism. Orthodoxy and Catholicism underscore the church's *indefectibility: the gates of hell shall not prevail; God has promised not to let the community of Christ-followers wither away to nothing (Matt. 16:18–19).[31] From a Protestant perspective, this promise does not guarantee the permanence or perfection of any particular institution. Christian communities, like their members, are simultaneously justified and sinful. If the church were not sinful, it would be empty.

---

30. G. Wainwright, "Ecclesial Scope of Justification," applies *simul iustus et peccator* to the church, not just individual Christians. Healy, *Church, World and the Christian Life*, exhorts ecclesiology to address actual churches, not just ideal characteristics.

31. As Gerrish, *Christian Faith*, 258, notes, it would be better to speak of indefectibility in relation to the Word rather than the church.

At our worst, evangelicals quickly flee broken institutions and start new ones. Hoping that they will be as pure as the primitive church, we are soon disappointed. At our best, however, we renew complacent forms of church life. Recent house church and new monastic movements champion small, dedicated groups that (they assume) characterized early Christianity. Any "charismatic" communities soon institutionalize, though, to endure across time and place—just as early Christianity moved toward "catholic" forms. Indeed, the New Testament portrays churches that were far from pure, full of moral chaos and leadership conflicts. No matter how charismatic or institutional, congregations point to Jesus's love through forgiveness, not perfection.

The New Testament not only is realistic about the church's brokenness but also distinguishes unity from uniformity. Galatians 3:28 and other texts suggest that true unity incorporates God-honoring diversity. We love one another—enemies and friends and neighbors—not because we are all the same but because we are bound together by the Spirit in Christ. Unity is no excuse for simply assimilating minority groups into majority-dominated cultures or accepting supposedly "separate but equal" tribalism. Given the legitimate diversity within biblical unity, however, not all institutional separation is tantamount to sinful brokenness. Nor does every formal affiliation manifest true oneness in Christ.

The New Testament portrays different kinds of divisions.[32] First, some concern *the gospel* itself. Separation may be necessary in resisting false teachers. Gospel-level divisions typically involve heretical Christology—denial of Jesus's divine lordship or full humanity. Second, other divisions concern *ministry*. Here separation may be necessary or at least inevitable due to differing approaches. Paul and Barnabas disagreed about whether to take Mark along on their missionary journey (Acts 15:36–41). Eventually, rather than remaining paralyzed in disagreement, they took different partners. Sometimes God multiplies ministry in this fallen world after charitable separation, a paradigm that addresses some denominational differences: Protestant churches often recognize others' baptisms, welcome one another to the Lord's Table, pray for other congregations, and cooperate in certain ministries. Third, still other potential divisions concern *adiaphora*, "disputable matters," with separation being unnecessary or inappropriate. According to passages like Romans 14:1–15:13, in many cases we should remain in community while, simultaneously, challenging one another and granting freedom to enact various understandings of God's Word. It can be challenging for local congregations to remain

---

32. For a fuller account of this biblical framework, see Vanhoozer and Treier, *Theology and the Mirror of Scripture*, chap. 5.

like-minded yet foster personal accountability before God, but that is the church's proper testimony concerning reconciliation in Christ.

Late modern Christianity is increasingly postdenominational, presenting new opportunities and challenges for church unity. Increasing individual autonomy accompanies decreasing denominational allegiance. Many groups face liberal-versus-conservative internal conflicts that run as deep as external divisions. Particular Christians may discern various callings when facing contemporary dilemmas of church affiliation. Western Christians will frequently be tempted to separate rather than stay, yet we must both resist unstable doctrine (Eph. 4:14) and "make every effort to keep the unity of the Spirit through the bond of peace" (4:3).

The church is both visible and invisible. The *visible church is an institution with sinful members, false confessors of faith, and disordered polity. The *invisible church is the company of those who are genuinely saved. As problematic as it can be, this distinction acknowledges, first, that not every member of every congregation is a true believer in Christ. Second, the invisible church includes the church "triumphant" (the dead who are with Christ awaiting their resurrection, having "fought the good fight") as well as the church "militant" (Christians still living on earth and facing spiritual struggle). Third, for whatever reason, some believers in Christ are not currently affiliated with a congregation.

These distinctions between visible and invisible notwithstanding, Christian unity remains important. Calvin was no friend to Catholic interpretations of Cyprian's dictum that "outside the church there is no salvation," yet he insisted that having God as our Father means having the church as our mother.[33] God can deal graciously with ignorance that complicates the church's visible identity, and its earthly unity remains imperfect. But salvation involves communion with the Triune God "in Christ," and the unity of his body is a crucial aspect of gospel witness. So "we believe in one holy, catholic, and apostolic church," acknowledging one baptism as we long for resurrection to make us whole.

---

33. Calvin, *Institutes* 4.1.1 (2:1012).

— 15 —

All Things New

THESIS

The vital Christian hope that God will make all things new has both cosmic and personal dimensions: cosmically, involving the return and reign of Christ as anticipated in biblical prophecy; personally, involving resurrection of the body and final judgment. This hope is already inaugurated but not yet completely fulfilled, thus serving as an impetus for mission and an incentive for martyrdom in whatever form becomes necessary.

LEARNING OBJECTIVES

After learning the material in this chapter, you should be able to:

1. *Define briefly* the key terms introduced here (marked with an asterisk and included in the glossary).
2. *List and recognize* the following: (a) approaches to the interpretation of biblical prophecy; (b) versions of dispensationalism; (c) views of other religions.
3. *Describe and compare* the following: (a) views of the return and reign of Christ; (b) covenant theology and dispensationalism; (c) views of final judgment.
4. *Identify and illustrate* the importance of maintaining a biblically nuanced account of Christian particularism.
5. *Explain* the following: (a) inaugurated eschatology; (b) the nature and importance of Christian hope for the resurrection of the body.

The *last things involve the historical end(s) of the present cosmos and its people before the eschaton, the new creation after the earthly last things. This area of doctrine, *eschatology, appears in the creedal article on the Holy Spirit: "We look for the resurrection of the dead and the life of the world to come." Of course, Christ's return is crucial: as the second article anticipates, "He will come again in glory to judge the living and the dead, and his kingdom will have no end." Yet the Spirit is already inaugurating aspects of the new creation, applying the power with which God raised Jesus from the dead. Eschatology belongs nearby but distinct from ecclesiology, since the Spirit uses Word and sacrament to prepare the church for the fullness of God's presence. The church is the primary sign and instrument of God's kingdom in the present age, but the Spirit bestows life when, where, and as God wills, bringing all things toward fullness in Christ.

Eschatology is a difficult, divisive, maybe even dangerous doctrine. The creedal affirmations are minimal; the biblical materials are complex. The theological history contains much speculation. However, we dare not become so embarrassed about the resulting aberrations that we say nothing. The Old Testament speaks volumes about the "day of the Lord," and the New Testament devotes entire epistles to the "last days": consider 1–2 Thessalonians, not just Revelation! Inaugurated by the incarnation, these last days stretch forward until Christ's kingdom comes in fullness. In order to number our days wisely (Ps. 90:12) and live in light of the new creation (2 Pet. 3:11–14), we must learn biblical hope.

That hope raises two sets of crucial issues. First, *cosmic* eschatology: the second coming of Christ and the end of the created world (at least of history as we know it). Second, *personal* eschatology: the resurrection of the dead and the final judgment. After surveying these issues, this chapter concludes by sketching key themes of Christian hope.

Cosmic Eschatology

Cosmic eschatology deals with the end of the *kosmos*, the world order that God created. This world has structural order: the matter and form of the solar system, the earth itself, and its "kinds" (Gen 1:21) of creatures. This world has historical order: a beginning and an end in time, with events and actions moving in between according to God's will. The human dimensions of this world have cultural order, so that sometimes in Scripture "the world" refers to a historical era or a social group. After the fall, earthly history has suffered from God's curse, reflecting human bondage to Satan and hostility toward God. Thus, the covenantal history of salvation begins with reconciling particular humans to God and one another. Ultimately, God will redeem the entire cosmos in Christ—"far as the curse is found." The following survey begins with views of Christ's return to establish his comprehensive reign; then we will examine underlying differences over biblical theology.

The Return and Reign of Christ

The basic views of cosmic eschatology focus on how Christ's return relates to God's present reign. Before delving into these views, it is worth noting the relational significance of Christ's return: "See what great love the Father has lavished on us, that we should be called children of God! . . . Dear friends, now we are children of God, and what we will be has not yet been made known. But we know that when Christ appears, we shall be like him, for we shall see him as he is" (1 John 3:1–2). We long to know our Savior face-to-face, to express our gratitude for God's great love, and to enjoy fully our inheritance as God's children.

The earliest Christian eschatologies have left few traces. There is some evidence of *chiliasm, the belief in a literal *millennium (the thousand-year earthly reign of Christ that is mentioned in Rev. 20). After Emperor Constantine's conversion and Christianity's Roman establishment in the fourth century AD, however, chiliasm was despised. Instead, optimism prevailed: Christ's rule would gradually increase via church and empire. Versions of amillennialism and periodic bursts of postmillennialism have characterized Orthodoxy and Catholicism ever since, as well as the Magisterial Reformation traditions. Free-church Protestants revived chiliasm in the 1800s. Its popularity increased steadily until it dominated major pockets of twentieth-century evangelicalism.

Rather than proceeding chronologically, the present survey is conceptual. Postmillennialism appears first, at the optimistic end of a cultural spectrum; premillennialism, its opposite, appears last because of its multiple varieties. The prefixes in the names of these millennial views (post-, a-, pre-) indicate when Christ's *parousia*, or second coming, will happen in relation to his earthly reign.

Postmillennialism. *Postmillennialism teaches that God's kingdom has been inaugurated by Jesus Christ at his first advent and grows progressively via the church. His second advent will happen *after* (hence "post-") his millennial reign extends over the entire earth. That reign may not constitute a literal one thousand years. Postmillennialism "looks for a fulfillment of the Old Testament prophecies of a glorious age of the church upon earth through the preaching of the gospel under the power of the Holy Spirit."[1] Postmillennialism has interpreted the church's progress in various ways, affected by cultural circumstances—from Christendom's official status to Jonathan Edwards's optimism about settling the Americas to the spread of a social gospel. Postmillennialism's most recent form, Christian reconstructionism,

---

1. Kik, *Eschatology of Victory*, 4.

or *dominion theology, encourages the church to extend God's kingdom via political influence, especially in America. Some versions of this view promote establishing biblical (especially Mosaic) law as society's civil code. Postmillennialism had a heyday in the optimistic late nineteenth and early twentieth centuries, followed by a sharp decline in the pessimistic wake of two world wars and other twentieth-century tragedies.

Amillennialism. *Amillennialism similarly teaches that God's kingdom has been inaugurated by Jesus Christ at his first advent. Satan is partially bound for the sake of God's work in the church. For amillennialism, Christ's reign through the church *is* what the millennial passages in Scripture are talking about. Hence the prefix "a-": Christians are not waiting for a distinct, future time period of the kingdom on this present earth before the eternal state. That aspect of the kingdom is already here; "the millennium of Revelation 20 is not exclusively future but is now in the process of realization."[2] Christ's second advent will fully extend the kingdom over the cosmos, ushering in the new heavens and earth. Amillennialism is the dominant view among Reformed and Wesleyan as well as Orthodox and Catholic Christians, not to mention contemporary biblical and theological scholars. Twentieth-century evangelicals sometimes confused amillennialism with the more "liberal" optimism of the social gospel, which actually reflected postmillennial tendencies. As conservative evangelicals championed "literal" interpretation of Scripture, they often understood that approach to require dispensational premillennialism—thus opposing the "figurative" or "spiritual" interpretation of certain passages that supported amillennialism.

Premillennialism. Premillennialists differ among themselves about whether Jesus Christ's first advent inaugurated God's kingdom. Many premillennialists, especially earlier dispensationalists, have emphasized that Israel rejected Jesus's offer of the kingdom. But others, more recently, have embraced inaugurated eschatology: Jesus already brought God's kingdom in his first advent, although the fullness of that reign is not yet realized; some promises to Israel are not yet fulfilled. Either way, Christ's second advent ends a distinctive time of tribulation for Israel and thereby the world. *Premillennialism holds that Christ's return *will initiate* (hence "pre-": happening before the millennium) an intermediate stage in which he reigns fully over the present, sin-cursed form of the cosmos. Typically, but not necessarily, this intermediate reign involves a literal one thousand years. This millennium fulfills Old Testament promises to Israel and corresponds to Revelation 20. As a transitional phase, the millennium leads into the eternal state. This phase will begin with Christ's second

2. Hoekema, "Amillennialism," 156.

coming to rule the nations. During the millennium all of Christ's enemies will be subjected to him; even the devil will be bound. God will demonstrate the extent of some creatures' hostility, though, by allowing a final rebellion to ensue briefly. After that rebellion God will abolish death and, with the final resurrection, introduce an eternally "new heaven and a new earth, where righteousness dwells" (2 Pet. 3:13).

Premillennialists agree that Christ's return will happen before he establishes his millennial reign on earth. But they vary over its timing: how the second coming relates to an earthly time of great *tribulation and whether there will be a distinct *rapture of the church—Christ snatching away living Christians from earth.[3]

The *posttribulational* view sees the rapture as part of Christ's return, when he comes to inaugurate the millennium. Hence, as the prefix "post-" suggests, the rapture happens *after* the "tribulation" mentioned in texts like Matthew 24:21. God preserves Christians through this distress, rather than removing them from the earth. A parallel was Israel's preservation in Goshen: plagues passed over them while causing Egypt to suffer. God's people may undergo earthly tribulation, but they will not directly experience God's wrath.

The *prewrath* view positions the rapture *right before* the portion of the tribulation in which God actively pours out wrath, at the unfolding of the very last days (beginning in Rev. 6:12 with the sixth seal). This relatively recent view agrees with the pretribulational and midtribulational views that God's people will not remain on earth during the direct outpouring of divine wrath. According to the prewrath view, only the last part of the tribulation contains this wrath; the rest of the period simply involves earthly suffering, during which believers remain present.

Like the preceding view, the older *midtribulational* view sees the rapture taking believers away before God's wrath comes: here, as the prefix "mid-" suggests, at the *middle* of the tribulation period. This view treats biblical passages with "time, times, and half a time" as dividing the tribulation into two three-and-a-half-year halves, with the latter (the "Great Tribulation") increasing in intensity. Believers endure some earthly suffering in the tribulation, but God removes them before the climactic events ensue.

Like the previous two views, the *pretribulational* view sees Christian believers being kept away from and out of God's wrath (appealing to Rev. 3:10 and other texts). Therefore, as the prefix "pre-" suggests, believers are

---

3. For longer, contemporary presentations of the views, see Hultberg, Blaising, and Moo, *Three Views on the Rapture.*

raptured *before* the tribulation begins, because the entire period contains God's wrath. The actions of the *antichrist, Satan's deceptive world ruler during the tribulation, are not directly divine. But they are an aspect of God's wrath, helping to unfold the extent of human and demonic wickedness.

Most premillennialists, but not all, treat the tribulation period as a literal seven years. Many who hold to the *imminence of Christ's return—in principle, it could happen at any time—argue for a pretribulational (or, recently, prewrath) rapture, to keep the timing unpredictable. If numbers in apocalyptic texts are nonliteral, then this argument weakens; it would not be possible to calculate Christ's return vis-à-vis exactly seven years of tribulation. Ironically, popular predictions of the Lord's return periodically surface anyway. In any case, such nuances among the views of Christ's return put a spotlight on hermeneutics.

The Interpretation of Biblical Prophecy

Prophetic material in Scripture is notoriously complex, generating significant distinctions—between types of literature, approaches to key texts, and larger-scale structures for biblical theology.

TYPES OF LITERATURE

First, modern scholarship frequently distinguishes between "apocalyptic" and "prophetic" literature (and underlying "schools"). *Apocalyptic literature arises from marginalized communities. This literature sharply divides between good and evil, urging the community to remain steadfast in adversity. Given this urgency, apocalyptic literature hopes for a dramatic unveiling of God's power, overturning present history. *Prophetic literature, by contrast, confronts God's people or their leaders about current patterns of unfaithfulness. Prophetic texts do not always make claims about the future; when they do, their promises may be conditional, indexed to whether or not the people repent. Anticipated deliverance has continuity with God's grace already working in history rather than simply overturning current structures.

Right or wrong, this contrast between apocalyptic and prophetic commonly appears in modern scholarship, along with the worry that older forms of premillennialism overinterpreted both types of literature. Apocalyptic literature was overinterpreted as providing largely literal rather than symbolic pictures of the future; prophetic literature was overinterpreted as providing largely future promises rather than contemporary confrontation. For simplicity's sake, though, the rest of this chapter refers more generically and popularly to the Bible's "prophetic" material regarding the future.

Approaches to Key Texts

Second, key eschatological texts have elicited several approaches. The *historicist interpretation of prophecy has periodically suggested that certain prophecies are fulfilled within the course of church history. As a popular example, each of the seven letters to the churches of Revelation 2–3 is connected to an epoch of the church's life. In modern times, historicism arose among some premillennialists. But such readings are increasingly rare among scholars. Historicism generates tension with both amillennial and some premillennial affirmations that Christ's return is imminent, in contrast with any prophetic necessity for certain events to happen first.

The *futurist interpretation of prophecy, in its most emphatic form, argues that "none of the prophecies of the 'last days' have been fulfilled in the history of the church"; all await the time of Christ's return.[4] More moderately, futurism applies only to certain prophetic texts or aspects. Futurism obviously appeals to premillennialism more than other views. Yet amillennialism can incorporate futurist elements, and many premillennial scholars today adopt moderate rather than exhaustive futurism.

The *preterist interpretation of prophecy maintains that prophetic literature addressed the original audiences entirely in terms of their immediate horizon. Hence the key eschatological texts addressed events that are now past, or initially fulfilled at any rate. Preterism characterizes postmillennialism and substantially shapes amillennialism. Many premillennialist scholars are now adopting eclectic approaches; in increasing convergence with moderate amillennialists, they incorporate preterist elements.

The *idealist interpretation of prophecy, which sometimes operates in tandem with preterism, focuses on the rhetoric of apocalyptic symbols rather than references to specific events.

Structures for Biblical Theology

Alongside prophetic interpretation, the structure of Scripture's story has eschatological impact. Evangelical debate has historically centered on "covenant" and "dispensational" theologies. Before expounding these two systems, we must heed two caveats. First, additional yet similar systems exist, such as the Lutheran contrast between law and gospel. Second, the modern discipline of biblical theology now includes evangelicals among its leaders, but it remains suspicious of both covenant and dispensational systems in their classic forms. Systematic proposals are controversial because they use an

---

4. Weber, *Shadow of the Second Coming*, 10.

anchoring concept to encompass the Bible's historical and literary diversity. Despite these caveats, though, covenant and dispensational systems remain influential forms of biblical theology; they offer melodic lines from which many evangelicals compose their harmonies.

COVENANT THEOLOGY

Covenant theology was a dominant Protestant position from the century after the Reformers until the rise of dispensationalism. Here the unity of the covenants is the organizing principle. Traditionally, Reformed covenant theology propounds two main covenants. First, God entered a *covenant of works with Adam on behalf of all humanity. This covenant required obedience in order to enjoy life, but Adam and Eve sinned and incurred a deadly curse. Second, God purposed to redeem the elect via the *covenant of grace in Jesus Christ. Behind this covenant stands the *pactum salutis, sometimes labeled the "covenant of peace"—an intratrinitarian agreement between Father, Son, and Holy Spirit regarding their externally undivided saving action. The logic of this eternal decree varies. According to *supralapsarianism, God decreed first to redeem the elect, then (logically, not temporally, speaking) to create and to allow the fall into sin. According to *infralapsarianism, God decreed first to create and to allow the fall, then to initiate the covenant of grace. Supralapsarianism focuses on the ultimate end of the history; infralapsarianism focuses on the natural order of the narrative.

In the twentieth century, Karl Barth promoted a one-covenant, supralapsarian model instead. Covenant and creation have been intertwined from the very beginning, according to Barth: creation is the external basis of the covenant, and the covenant is the internal basis of creation.[5] Another twentieth-century development came from George Ladd (1911–82), who proposed a form of *historic premillennialism that appealed to early, more generic chiliasm rather than adhering to later covenant theology or dispensationalism. Ladd's premillennialism championed inaugurated eschatology in a way that blurred lines between the reigning covenant and dispensational systems. Since then, other evangelicals have developed one-covenant forms of theology.[6] Accordingly,

---

5. See Barth, *CD* III/1, 94–228 and 228–329, respectively.

6. Ladd's view is sometimes called "covenant premillennialism"; to complicate the matter even more, other versions of historic premillennialism preceded his. For a one-covenant emphasis from within the Reformed tradition, see Holwerda, *Jesus and Israel*; from outside, see Hafemann, *The God of Promise*. Another one-covenant approach is the new "progressive covenantalism" of Gentry and Wellum, *Kingdom through Covenant*. Like progressive dispensationalism, they emphasize the progress of the covenant history toward the newness of the new covenant. Unlike progressive dispensationalism, they emphasize that biblical typology treats the land of Israel as

some versions of covenant theology now include ethnic Israel in the consummation of salvation history, rather than maintaining older views of the church simply being identified with or replacing Israel.

DISPENSATIONALISM

Dispensationalism is difficult to define, because it is not a confessional tradition but rather a cross-denominational form of futurist premillennialism. As the name implies, dispensations—eras in which God administers distinct forms of interaction with people—are the organizing principle. Dispensationalism maintains a distinct future for ethnic Israel as God's special people. The church era, inaugurated at Pentecost, does not end God's special commitment to the Jewish people, which returns to prominence in the tribulation and the millennium.

The Reformer John Calvin already spoke of "dispensations," which correspond to the "generations" within God's mysterious plan (Eph. 3:4–5). Covenant theology and other systems acknowledge historical unfolding within God's plan, but they focus more upon the unity than the distinctions between eras. Dispensationalism is typically traced to John Nelson Darby (1800–1882) in the nineteenth century, who claimed that Christ's second coming would occur in two phases—the first being the rapture. Bible conferences spread Darby's influence from Ireland to the United States. Dispensationalism then spread in the early twentieth century among fundamentalists, thanks to the *Scofield Reference Bible* and leaders of Dallas Theological Seminary such as Lewis Sperry Chafer (1871–1952).

Dispensationalists usually champion a pretribulational rapture. Historically, they have emphasized discontinuity between the Old and New Testaments, between ethnic Israel and the post-Pentecost church, and even between law and grace as organizing principles of the old and new covenants. Today their internal debate concerns how much discontinuity to maintain in these areas.

Classic dispensationalism was associated fundamentally with C. I. Scofield (1843–1921) and Chafer. Its most famous scheme contained seven dispensations: (1) innocence, involving Adam and Eve as created; (2) conscience, from the fall until the flood; (3) human government, from the flood until the tower of Babel; (4) promise, from Abraham until Moses; (5) law, from Moses until Jesus Christ; (6) grace, from the cross until the rapture of the church; and (7) the millennial kingdom. The classic version sharply distinguished between

---

a type of the new creation, so that those Old Testament promises do not await the same degree of Israel-specific fulfillment.

Israel (ethnic and political) and the church (spiritual), even separating them into two peoples of God. The church was an "intercalation," the present age a "parenthesis" within God's overall plan, which focused on Israel. Contrasting "law" and "grace" fed sharp contrasts between the two Testaments and two covenants. Occasionally Scofield seemed to suggest different ways of salvation: obedience for Israel in the Old Testament (but Israel failed), faith in Christ for the church in the New Testament. Hence "free grace" strands of dispensationalism and emphatic versions of a Lutheran contrast between law and gospel may sound similar. The Lutheran contrast does not run between the Old and New Testaments, though, but rather between aspects of any biblical passage's application.

Revised dispensationalism is associated preeminently with Charles Ryrie (1925–2016), who updated Scofield's and Chafer's positions. Like Scofield, Ryrie produced a study Bible; like Chafer, he wrote a systematic theology. In the mid-1960s he labored to identify dispensationalism's sine qua non, or nonnegotiable core.[7] Ryrie moderated the idea of two peoples of God and the distinctions between covenants, firmly rejecting two different ways of salvation. Indeed, revised dispensationalists tried to show that Scofield did not really hold such a sharp contrast between law and grace. Ryrie championed consistently "literal" interpretation as dispensationalism's distinctive essence. Prophecy—in fact, the Bible generally—should be read as literally as possible, except where "figurative" language must be acknowledged. By contrast, Ryrie alleged, covenant theology "spiritualizes" Old Testament promises, especially concerning the land of Israel, when it treats prophetic texts as already having fulfillment in the church.

Whereas revised dispensationalism initially moderated sharp distinctions, some traditionalists have recently reversed course by distinguishing two forms of the new covenant.[8] One new covenant, promised in the Old Testament, applies to Israel; its fulfillment awaits the future, tied to the earthly millennium. Another new covenant, an initial form or analogy of the one promised in the Old Testament, applies to the church. On this account, there has currently been no fulfillment of actual new-covenant promises. Although the distinction between law and grace concerns sanctification, not salvation, such traditionalists deny that the Torah exercises direct authority over Christians rather than, at most, broadly reflecting God's character.

Progressive dispensationalism emphasizes continuous development across salvation history, not these sharp distinctions between eras. Thus, not all

---

7. Ryrie, *Dispensationalism Today*.

8. E.g., Master, "New Covenant," claims that the new covenant has been formulated but not yet actualized. The church enjoys the same spiritual promises as Israel, but the prior covenants were for Israel alone while the new covenant is reserved for eschatological Israel.

Old Testament kingdom promises await strictly future fulfillment; some are initially fulfilled in the church. Having been inaugurated, God's kingdom progresses until all promises' complete fulfillment in either the millennium or the eternal state.[9] Fulfillment of the one new covenant has already begun, even if some aspects await the future. There is one way of salvation and of sanctification. Christ's coming and the Spirit's outpouring internalized the administration of God's grace, but grace remains the operative principle. So there is one people of God; the old and new eras are modestly distinguished by how they incorporate Israel's ethnic and political aspects.

Progressive dispensationalists depart from traditional dispensationalism in several ways. They deny watershed hermeneutical differences (over "consistently literal" interpretation) between dispensational and covenant theologies, despite disagreements over particular passages. They deny the impression that the church is a sidetrack in God's plan: God will never revoke the present union of Jews and gentiles in the church, which fulfilled a long-standing promise. They also moderate traditionalist expectations concerning Israel's future preeminence, such as the restoration of Old Testament sacrifices (which appeal to literal interpretation of Ezek. 40–48) as a way of remembering Christ. When "all Israel" is saved (whatever that exactly means in Rom. 11:25–26), redeemed Jews are incorporated into the church alongside gentiles. Yet unlike some forms of covenant theology, progressive dispensationalism still insists that not all Old Testament promises to ethnic Israel have spiritual fulfillment in Christ or the church.

It can be tricky to distinguish progressive dispensationalism from historic premillennialism. Progressive dispensationalism embraces inaugurated eschatology, reflecting Ladd's influence. Distinctions, however, typically remain: historic premillennialism tends toward a posttribulational rapture, phasing in Christ's *parousia* and the millennium; progressive dispensationalism tends toward a pretribulational rapture, retaining more emphasis on ethnic Israel's theological future.

Amid these complexities, it is worth celebrating the ecumenical contribution of evangelical scholarship. Disagreements between covenant and dispensational theologies have become milder. Common ground has appeared in versions of inaugurated eschatology, and new insights have emerged in biblical theology. Challenges remain, especially in the chaos of popular eschatology; overall, however, evangelical theology has begun to address the biblical "last days" more charitably and responsibly.

9. For progressive dispensationalism's reduced distinctions between the millennium and the eternal state in certain texts, see Turner, "New Jerusalem."

As discussed further below, Christian hope addresses both cosmic and personal eschatology. Cosmic eschatology's focus, the return and reign of Christ, involves a new heaven and a new earth, which biblical theology has freshly championed under the theme of new creation. Personal eschatology's focus, the resurrected and reconciled human being, involves union with God, which classic theology often championed in terms of beatific vision. Respective emphasis upon the cosmic (new creation) or the personal (beatific vision) is perhaps the most significant debate emerging in contemporary eschatology.

Personal Eschatology

Eschatology's personal significance focuses on resurrection of the body and final judgment—the end(s) of particular human beings. The Nicene Creed's second article affirms that Jesus Christ will come again in glory to judge the living and the dead, and his kingdom will have no end; the third article anticipates the resurrection of the dead and the life of the world to come.

Resurrection of the Body

Resurrection of the body, our ultimate participation in the Spirit's resurrection of Jesus, glorifies the new humanity for eternal life in God's kingdom. We initially participate when we are baptized into Christ's body (Rom. 6:1–14), so that his death, burial, and resurrection render us dead to sin and alive to God. The corpses in the valley of dry bones (Ezek. 37) have awakened to life, yet they await their glorified flesh.

Contra the frequent allegation that Christianity is body-denying, orthodox teachers actually resisted "gnostic" Greco-Roman tendencies. Christians championed the body by expecting its resurrection. Sometimes they failed to apply this hope consistently, not least in assumptions about gender and sexuality.[10] Nevertheless, by comparison, early Christian teaching valued the body remarkably. To be sure, understanding bodily resurrection was an immense challenge. In the key passage, 1 Corinthians 15, Paul makes Christ's bodily resurrection the first of many, using agricultural imagery: Jesus began God's harvest of the new humanity. In Paul's account of resurrection, continuity of identity persists between the seed, the original human body, and the fruit, the body raised to glory. Further explaining this continuity of

10. For constructively critical appropriation of traditional theology here, see B. Jones, *Marks of His Wounds*.

identity has vexed Christians for centuries—only underscoring the body's importance.[11]

The earlier chapter on theological anthropology introduced views of the intermediate state. That state between a person's earthly death and bodily resurrection is understandably mysterious. Even so, the Christian tradition has predominantly distinguished between the body and the soul in order to maintain the continuity of personal existence after bodily death. For those who are in Christ and thus have their names in the "book of life" (Rev. 20:12), being absent from the body will mean enjoying a new form of the Lord's presence (Phil. 1:21–23) while awaiting resurrection.

Final Judgment

Whatever the nature of the intermediate state, fallen humans face death and eventual judgment (Heb. 9:27). Judgment is not simply equal to punishment but involves laying bare truth.[12] Everyone, including believers in Christ, will somehow account for their earthly actions, good or bad (2 Cor. 5:10).[13] Yet Christians differ regarding the possible outcomes for those who die as unbelievers.[14]

The first possible outcome is *universal salvation*. Among early Christians, Origen championed *apokatastasis*—ultimate reconciliation of everyone to God. This universal reconciliation required that everyone pass through hell as purifying fire, with varying severity. Subsequently, most advocates of universal salvation have been modern. Karl Barth is often associated with this hope, yet he refused to affirm its certainty because of God's freedom. Universal salvation seems consistent with the extent of God's redeeming love revealed in Christ, and advocates highlight biblical passages that speak of cosmic reconciliation (e.g., Eph. 1:10; Col. 1:19–20). Pervasive and prominent judgment sayings, however—not least from Jesus himself (e.g., Luke 6:46–49; 13:1–9; 16:19–31)—have prevented most Christians, and nearly all evangelicals, from reading texts of cosmic reconciliation in terms of universal salvation.

A second possible outcome is *annihilation*—judgment being tempered with absolute destruction instead of eternal torment. In the early Christian material that is available, only Arnobius (died c. 330) is associated with this

---

11. To substantiate this point, see Bynum, *Resurrection of the Body*.

12. Rae, *Christian Theology*, 107.

13. Of course, Jesus's resurrection and ascension present an exceptional case. Those who affirm Mary's bodily assumption treat her as another exceptional case. Christian believers who are alive at the Lord's return present still another exception.

14. The following summary is indebted to Hunsinger, "Hellfire and Damnation," with some alterations.

view. Yet both Tertullian and Augustine refuted annihilation, which may indicate that the view was wider spread than current evidence shows. Some
evangelicals have recently embraced the position,[15] appealing to the biblical
language of destruction, which could imply extinction; biblical imagery, which
could imply nonliteral interpretation (since phenomena like fire and darkness apparently conflict); and claims about divine justice, which could imply
that the experience of punishment cannot be endless. Finally, annihilationism
claims to handle "universalism" texts better than other evangelical views, since
unredeemed humans cannot continue in rebellion, even passively. Biblical
objections to annihilationism are not as obvious as they are for universalism,
but most evangelicals do not believe that Scripture's judgment texts can all
be construed in terms of annihilation; at least some of them seem to depict
ongoing consciousness of punishment.

A third possible outcome is *postmortem repentance*—everyone receives
an opportunity clearly to accept or reject the gospel, including postmortem
encounters with God as needed. Such encounters would not guarantee universal salvation; people might persist in unbelief rather than responding to God's
love. At least some advocates of postmortem repentance conclude that any
remaining unbelievers face annihilation rather than eternal torment.[16] Clearly,
standing behind this position are particular interpretations of God's justice
and love along with human freedom. Appeals to biblical texts for support—
regarding, for instance, Christ descending into hell and preaching the gospel—
are relatively few and highly debated. Instead, most evangelicals believe that
Scripture's judgment texts leave no possibility of postmortem repentance;
"people are destined to die once and after that to face judgment" (Heb. 9:27).

A fourth possible outcome is *hell*, which evokes many images but is best
defined in terms of eternal and conscious punishment. The modern emphasis
upon hellfire has not always been dominant; within Christendom, most people
were baptized and expected the fire of purgatory to be spiritually refining, not

---

15. John Stott expressed openness to the view without definitively embracing it. For an
evangelical defense, see Wenham, "Case for Conditional Immortality." The terminology of
"conditional immortality" is potentially misleading. As Harmon, "Case against Conditionalism," shows in the same volume (a response to Edward William Fudge, perhaps its most detailed
proponent), the terms "annihilationism" and "conditionalism" have been preferred for different
reasons with different meanings in different contexts. Proponents also vary over timing: whether
annihilation is immediate or eventual.

Evangelical scholars increasingly hold that in Scripture immortality is not a native human
property but rather a conditional divine gift: granted provisionally prior to the fall, lost at the
fall, and granted again eschatologically. These scholars often deny annihilationism, though: eschatological immortality means "life" for the redeemed, the second "death" for the unredeemed.

16. See Pinnock, *Wideness in God's Mercy*, esp. 168–72; J. Sanders, *No Other Name*, esp.
chap. 6.

eternally punishing.[17] Images aside, *particularism believes that the Bible consistently depicts the fate of unbelievers in eternal and conscious terms: eternal, in a host of texts like Revelation 14:11; conscious, in texts like Luke 13:28 that refer to "weeping and gnashing of teeth." Particularists vary concerning how much God has revealed about the exact fate of everyone who does not name Jesus as Lord while on earth, but they agree that salvation is found in no other name (Acts 4:12) and that dying in unbelief brings punishment. The heart of this punishment is the pain of being separated from God's presence, excluded from the blessings of God's kingdom. Most evangelicals hold some version of particularism, which they find emerging from the plainest understanding of Scripture. Possible objections emerge from biblical texts involving universal reconciliation and from concerns over divine love and justice, as mentioned above; therefore, objectors believe that particularists overextend biblical judgment texts beyond what they firmly establish.

A fifth approach, though not a possible outcome, has been labeled *reverent agnosticism*—hopeful restraint about specifying the fate of apparent unbelievers. Among premodern precursors for this stance, Clement of Alexandria (150–215) expected remedial punishment, appealing for "holy silence" beyond that. Likewise, Gregory of Nazianzus and Maximus the Confessor probably did not affirm universal salvation, as sometimes thought. Instead, they restrained their hope from generating definitive claims; hence Barth probably fits here too.[18] Given the modest set of precursors, this approach characterizes few if any traditional evangelicals, although Barth's recent influence may increase its momentum. As with the first three possible outcomes above, this approach has some understandable arguments yet seems biblically vulnerable: hope for the salvation of all or nearly all seems to contradict the claim that only a few find the narrow road (Matt. 7:14) and the expectation that numerous judgment texts bear witness to a painful reality.

Other Religions

The possible outcomes of final judgment intersect somewhat with Christian approaches toward other religions. A threefold typology dominates the discussion, despite having widely recognized problems.

---

17. For example, Bynum, *Resurrection of the Body*, shows that medieval depictions of hell focused on bodily disintegration. For traditional evangelical discussions of the imagery's complexity, see Harmon, "Case against Conditionalism," 216–24; Blocher, "Everlasting Punishment," 304–7.

18. Hunsinger, "Hellfire and Damnation," 243; on 247 he notes that Barth also used language of annihilation.

The *pluralist approach to religions denies that the Christian faith presents distinctive truth about God and salvation in Christ. Pluralism treats all religions as providing partial perspectives for grasping whatever reality is sacred. A frequently used analogy speaks of parts of an elephant being grasped by blindfolded people: each person grasps only one part of the whole reality and would be wrong to assume that this one part represents the whole.

The *exclusivist approach to religions, by contrast, claims that only the God revealed in Jesus Christ is true, and only those who place explicit faith in Christ will be redeemed. Exclusivism and "particularism" are sometimes treated as identical, but their connotations vary.[19] Exclusivism connotes a focus on salvation's benefits, excluding those without personal faith in Jesus; particularism connotes a focus on salvation's accomplishment, tying it particularly to Christ's work, while acknowledging the alternative reality of punishment. Some conservative, nonuniversalist versions of inclusivism may count as particularist.

The *inclusivist approach to religions has become increasingly prominent in post–Vatican II Catholic, mainline Protestant, and progressive evangelical circles, despite lacking any direct premodern pedigree. Inclusivism claims that God is truly revealed in Jesus as the only way of salvation (John 14:6), but salvation's benefits may extend to those who lack explicit faith in Christ. If some or all of these "anonymous Christians" (as they are sometimes called) share in Christ's benefits, they are included by implicit faith—following "whatever light they have" in general revelation or the religion available to them.

These three categories can be misleading, given the variety of inclusivist and exclusivist positions. Several thinkers oppose any simple dilemma between inclusivism and exclusivism.[20] Another challenge involves the complexity of defining "religion," which affects criteria for wider inclusion in Christ's benefits. Addressing the destiny of the unevangelized should remain distinct from developing a theology of religion, since responses to general revelation may not correlate exactly with the practice of non-Christian religions. Biblical revelation involves particular times and places in salvation history; God's foundational covenant with Israel renders all other religion(s) idolatrous.

19. Another term is "restrictivism," which J. Sanders, *No Other Name*, treats as a synonym for "exclusivism" and "particularism" in contrast with "wider hope" views. But restrictivism is somewhat pejorative, and there are reasons for not entirely conflating exclusivism in the threefold typology of religions with particularism concerning the fate of the unevangelized.

20. See, e.g., works by Lesslie Newbigin. Okholm and Phillips, *Four Views on Salvation*, contains an essay by Alister E. McGrath that fits between clearly inclusivist and exclusivist accounts. Another complex evangelical discussion (Mangum, "Is There a Reformed Way to Get the Benefits?") suggests that biblical revelation may be underdetermined regarding the fate of the unevangelized. Indeed, Fackre, "Claiming Jesus as Savior," lists ten (!) different positions.

God's self-communication within Scripture's covenant history, though, may not address every question that Christians have about the reach of salvation, since religious pluralism operates differently in God's plan after Christ (Acts 17:30–31) and in contexts other than Christendom.

Full Reconciliation

When addressing final judgment and other religions, evangelical particularism bases its case on widespread biblical evidence that includes the Old Testament witness (plus its New Testament continuation in passages like Rom. 1:18–32), a host of Jesus's sayings from passages like Luke 13, and epistolary texts like 2 Thessalonians 1:6–10.[21] Yet questions remain for particularism to address.

First, particularism must address the promised fullness of cosmic reconciliation. Some accounts of final judgment seem to keep evil around—with sinners fighting against the comprehensive reign of God that the Lord's Prayer anticipates and 1 Corinthians 15:24–28 promises. Luke 16:19–31 and other passages portray *"both the extreme of vicious rebellion and the sinner's approval of his judgment as just"*: final judgment brings sinners to remorse-in-agreement-with-God. This ultimate remorse concerns only the past, not comprising repentance—a saving change toward sin that concerns a historical future.[22] Eternal life and death are asymmetrical; death means that sinners' rebellion is "history"—has ceased.

Second, particularism must address the scope of biblical texts regarding final judgment. While texts like John 14:6 and Acts 4:12 locate salvation only in Jesus Christ, other texts may suggest restraint about how comprehensively gentile pagans are addressed by judgment texts. For instance, Amos 9:7–8 indicates God's sovereign work in nations outside Israel,[23] while in Romans 1–3; 5:12–21, Paul argues from Israel's exclusive old-covenant relationship with God in a way that may simply leave pagans aside. To be sure, passages like Romans 3:25–26 and Acts 17:30–31 indicate that God's "overlooking" of prior ignorance has somehow changed with Christ's coming. Given such nuances, however, particularism must respect the contexts—and possibly limited scope—of biblical judgment sayings, rather than extracting universal principles too quickly.

Third, particularism must address the possibility of extraordinary divine revelation and saving faith beyond the church's apparent reach. For instance,

---

21. Such evidence is summarized in Demarest, *Cross and Salvation*, 28–31, for instance.

22. Blocher's point in "Everlasting Punishment," 302, 307 (emphasis original).

23. Lindbeck, *Nature of Doctrine*, 54.

anecdotal evidence suggests that Muslims and others have dreams of Jesus Christ.[24] At minimum, our accounts of election unto salvation, human depravity, and mission history must not portray God as ethnocentric: "God does not show favoritism" (Acts 10:34; Rom. 2:11). Thus, while divine election and foreknowledge are mysterious, it seems unbiblical to imagine salvation's reach staying altogether limited for long centuries by access to particular churches' gospel presentations. Perhaps bracingly, too, particularism can incorporate caution about the church's knowledge of others' saving faith—that is, how specifically to designate its required content or to discern its attachment to the true God.[25]

Fourth, particularism must address cultural pressure from two sides. Evangelical caution is appropriate about hastily departing from traditional views in pursuit of modern popularity. We must continue to proclaim the gospel in a way that understands eternal punishment as a possibility from which Christ's work saves people. We can trust God to be just and merciful: as Abraham rightly insisted, "Will not the Judge of all the earth do right?" (Gen. 18:25). Cultural pressure, however, can foster conservative, not just liberal, distortions.

One distortion portrays saving sinners from hell as the virtually exclusive motivation for evangelism. Reaching lost people is vital, yet God's glory among the nations should be preeminent.[26] Obeying the Great Commission (Matt. 28:18–20) expresses love for God in loving our neighbors. Having compassion upon "harassed and helpless" unbelievers (Matt. 9:36–38) concerns not just their final destinies but also their present bondage. Biblical missionary fervor does not emerge only from the most conservative exclusivism. Other forms of particularism foster active evangelism, whereas popular exclusivism can generate arrogant or overly aggressive evangelism if God's glory is not the overriding concern.

Another distortion portrays hell with excessive literalism. Biblical warnings of punishment are sobering indeed, yet the images are diverse. Wrongly pressed, they would conflict, as in darkness vis-à-vis fire. Some Scripture texts suggest degrees of punishment (notably, Matt. 11:20–24), which would be immaterial if hideous hellfire rhetoric were true. Indeed, God is a just judge, not a torturer. The focus of eternal conscious punishment is exclusion from God's gracious and glorious presence. The meanings of "conscious" and "punishment" remain somewhat unclear because the unredeemed will not enjoy resurrection "life" in Christ. Theirs is a second "death": their bodies

---

24. See, e.g., Trousdale, *Miraculous Movements*, esp. chap. 8. Qureshi, *Seeking Allah, Finding Jesus*, 65, notes the prominence of prophetic dreams within Muslim expectations.

25. See, e.g., the conservative discussion by Helm, "Are They Few That Be Saved?"

26. See Piper, *Let the Nations Be Glad!*

will not be "glorified"; while they will experience remorse, they will no longer add to a history of rebellion against God. Eternal punishment is, finally, the tragic consequence of rejecting communion with God and others.[27]

Still another distortion, though, portrays judgment in opposition to God's love. Martyrs cry out, "How long, Sovereign Lord?" (Rev. 6:9–11). Judgment comes to fulfill God's promise of a new creation—which infinite patience would jeopardize, since (as Revelation forcefully depicts) some earth-dwellers refuse to repent. Evangelical zeal flows from gratitude for the Triune God's loving mission—the Father having sent the Son, in the Spirit's power, to create "a people for his name" (e.g., Acts 15:14).[28] We prayerfully long for the covenant people to incorporate members from every nation. The gospel involves God's own loving satisfaction of God's justice, while judgment reflects the holiness of God's love: God has promised a new creation where only righteousness is at home (2 Pet. 3:13).

Christian Hope

Given all of our questions, it is important not to lose the unifying focus of biblical hope. Christian *hope* is not wishful thinking, but rather is the expectation of biblical *faith*—personal knowledge of God's *love* heralding good news about the future. As the future-oriented aspect of faith, Christian hope confidently anticipates fulfillment of God's promises. These promises anticipate the glorious wedding celebration of Christ and the church, orienting Christian hope toward love. Amid all their disagreements, evangelicals can celebrate together the inauguration of the new creation, with its promise of glory.

New Creation

Evangelical scholars widely agree that cosmic eschatology involves the Bible's two-age salvation history and the already inaugurated fulfillment of God's promised kingdom.[29] The Bible divides history into two eras: "this age" (in which evil has a partial reign on earth) and "the age to come" (when the Messiah comes to reign in righteousness and peace). Contrary to what God's people might have expected, these two periods are not neatly separated. Instead, they overlap because the "last days" have broken into the present,

27. See Volf, *Exclusion and Embrace*, esp. 299–301.
28. This theme is prompted by Beals, *A People for His Name*.
29. This paragraph is particularly indebted to Stephen R. Spencer.

beginning in Jesus the Messiah and continuing by his Spirit in the church. Since Christ's first coming, therefore, history is a mixture of the two ages, of evil and righteousness.[30]

God's redemptive reign was inaugurated in Jesus's ministry, particularly in his climactic victory over death, but is not yet consummated. We do not yet see all things subjected to the new humanity in Christ (Heb. 2:8). This already-and-not-yet tension may be illustrated with the Allies' successful landing at Normandy on June 6, 1944, which did not produce complete German surrender until April 1945.[31] The decisive battle was already won on D-Day, but resistance continued; victory was not immediately completed despite being secured. Likewise, Christ's first advent conquered sin, death, and the devil, yet we await the cessation of hostilities and enjoyment of divine rest.

World War II provided more than an illustration. Its horrors galvanized a scholarly recovery of biblical hope. Theologians of hope and liberation recognized that the Holocaust required fresh attention to God's covenant history with Israel. They also contemplated horrendous evil anew in light of the cross. At the same time, biblical scholars recognized that many Christians were losing the proper tension between already "realized" and still "futurist" elements of the last things; Jesus's presentation of God's kingdom in the Gospels incorporated both. Whereas optimistic postmillennial tendencies shaped the late nineteenth and early twentieth centuries, they gave way to two broad alternatives as the twentieth century unfolded. First, at elite levels, chastened amillennial tendencies still focused on already realized eschatology (whether or not Jesus's vision was seen as genuinely divine and successful). Second, at popular levels, pessimistic premillennial tendencies sometimes denied any realized eschatology at all. These polar opposites exert continuing influence, but they are increasingly overcome by inaugurated eschatology.

Theologians of hope and liberation complemented the emerging support for inaugurated eschatology from biblical scholarship. These theologians—notably Jürgen Moltmann—recovered the biblical emphasis upon eschatology, highlighting Jesus's resurrection: beyond indicating his divinity or vindicating his passion, the resurrection brought the climax of Christ's saving work, the dawn of the new creation.[32] This climax distinctively inaugurated the fulfillment of God's promise to make all things new. In some respects, this

30. For such a distinction, see, e.g., Matt. 12:32; Mark 10:30 // Luke 18:30; 20:34–35; Eph. 1:21; Heb. 6:5; for application of "last days" to the present, see Acts 2:17; 1 Cor. 10:11; Heb. 1:1–2; 9:26; 1 Pet. 1:20; 1 John 2:18.

31. See especially Cullmann, *Christ and Time*, 39, 72, 81–93.

32. Along with Moltmann, Wolfhart Pannenberg is credited with the postwar recovery of eschatology. Moltmann's *Theology of Hope* was influential among theologians of liberation as well.

inaugurated eschatology helped to recover an Augustinian definition of "the secular"—in terms of time rather than space. Contra modernity, the secular does not designate a realm that is neutral or nonreligious, the opposite of sacred; instead, the secular is a temporary era after Christ's decisive victory, in which God has reauthorized earthly powers to preserve social order for the sake of the church's mission.[33]

The new covenant celebrates "new" teaching, a "new" commandment, a "new" name, a "new" song—ultimately, a "new" heaven and earth for a "new" humanity.[34] Hosts do not put new wine into old wineskins, lest they burst; they put new wine into new wineskins, preserving both old and new properly (Matt. 9:14–17). Similarly, no one sews a patch of new, unshrunk cloth on an old garment, for that would simply make the tear worse. There is discontinuity: when the new reality arrives, the old forms cannot contain it. Yet there is also continuity: garments and wineskins are involved; the old is preserved. Christ's resurrection signaled that God would redeem rather than annihilate creation.

Hence, as mentioned above, contemporary biblical scholarship trumpets new creation.[35] Sometimes this theme is contrasted with beatific vision, which has been the traditional end of redeemed humanity, especially in Western Christianity. As a metaphor for *theosis*, beatific vision celebrates the personal, mystical union of the pure in heart seeing God (Matt. 5:8). Champions of new creation blame the "Platonic" tendencies of patristic and medieval Christianity for "gnostic" and "escapist" accounts of salvation. From the standpoint of new creation, the earthiness of Old Testament hope anticipates the New Testament witness regarding resurrection. Resurrection gives Christian hope an embodied, social dimension that the beatific vision minimizes. Popular distortions convey an association between beatific vision and the annihilation of the original cosmos rather than its purification.

New creation challenges such popular distortions. Biblical hope emphasizes Jesus's resurrection as the firstfruits: the bodies of those who are in Christ will likewise be raised and glorified for a new heaven and a new earth. Thus, individualistic or disembodied notions of the afterlife need correction. Yet defenders of the beatific vision highlight the biblical theme of rest, and the danger that advocates of new creation can ignore the end of history: "In their desire to preserve the worth and importance of the present life, they paint a picture of the next life nearly identical to this one, with the exception that

33. So O'Donovan, *Desire of the Nations*.
34. Emphasizing this theme is Hoch, *All Things New*.
35. See especially Middleton, *A New Heaven and a New Earth*, and numerous works by N. T. Wright, such as *Surprised by Hope*.

sin will have been eradicated."[36] New creation will not simply be more of the same; the rest that we enjoy will include the opportunity to reflect upon the completion of our historical action.[37]

Glorification

The beatific vision underscores that resurrected bodies—like Jesus's—are transformed, spiritual bodies, not exactly the same as we presently have. The ultimate focus of Christian love rests upon the One who gave himself for us. We long for more than the restoration of earthly life minus the evils of history after the fall; we await the immediate experience of God's loving presence in Christ.[38] The wholeness of human life involves embodiment and community—hence resurrection. Our primary sense of communion with one another, though, will involve the wonder of shared communion with the Triune God. Hence "glorification," a common Protestant word for "deification": the complete spiritual transformation of particular persons who gaze upon Jesus Christ.[39]

Speaking of "glory" ties together the content and the means of our true end: "to glorify God, and to enjoy him forever."[40] The content: the new heaven and new earth will be full of God's glory (Isa. 6:3; Hab. 2:14). The means: fully transformed "from glory to glory" (2 Cor. 3:18 KJV), humans will finally be ready to see God's glory as we were made to do—to know as we are fully known (1 Cor. 13:12–13). For the glory of the Triune God involves self-giving love, not unholy celebrity. New creation and beatific vision celebrate different but mutually essential aspects of this glorious consummation.

Mission and Martyrdom

In the meantime, Christian hope leads us into the loving obedience that springs from faith. The hope of new creation sends the church to embody integral mission—proclaiming the gospel, practicing the love of Christ, and

36. Morales, "'With My Body I Thee Worship,'" 355.
37. On this aspect of rest, see Heb. 4:9–10, and then O'Donovan, *Finding and Seeking*; O'Donovan, *Entering into Rest*.
38. For a speculative Catholic defense of the beatific vision, see P. Griffiths, *Decreation*; for a Protestant retrieval, see Allen, *Grounded in Heaven*.
39. See the historical corrections of common misconceptions in Mosser, "Deification." This notion appears early and widely throughout the Christian tradition, even among Protestants. Its eventual loss, especially among Protestants, partly stems from distortions that made its meaning more particular and controversial. Despite the ecumenical history, however, contemporary Protestants still might have biblical reasons for preferring to speak of glorification.
40. *The Shorter Catechism*, question 1, in *Book of Confessions*, 175.

pursuing the justice of God's kingdom. Integral mission reflects the gospel's holistic hope, rooted in the embodied and communal significance of the resurrection.

The hope of new creation is also personal, anticipating the beatific vision. This hope leads us to become martyrs—in the word's initial sense, "witnesses"—regarding the love of Jesus. Such hope enables us to endure suffering joyfully in a world that does not yet know the fullness of God's love. *Martyrdom means bearing witness with one's whole life concerning the costly price of redemption; awaiting in faith the ultimate vindication of love for God and neighbor, such witnesses are even willing to give up earthly life if necessary.[41] As Dietrich Bonhoeffer suggested, each follower of Christ receives "*their* own cross ready" to bear, "assigned by God and measured to fit."[42]

The souls of the martyrs, who are in God's presence at the heavenly altar, do not cry out asking whether God's promises will be fulfilled. They cry out, "How long, Sovereign Lord?" Our hope is secure in Christ, guaranteed by the Spirit's empowering presence among us. Evangelical faith obeys the missional imperative of Christian hope on account of the Triune God's love—truly good news.

---

41. See further Hovey, *To Share in the Body*; Vanhoozer, "Trials of Truth."
42. Bonhoeffer, *Discipleship*, 87 (emphasis original).

Glossary

accidents: external properties that can change without altering the substance, the essential reality.

accommodation: traditionally, God's use of human authors' language, cultural settings, and other limits to communicate understandably without compromising Scripture's truthfulness.

active obedience of Christ: Jesus's righteous fulfillment of God's law throughout his earthly life as our human representative.

ad extra: activity that is outside of the Triune God's immanent life, in engagement with creation.

adiaphora: from Romans 14, a matter that is biblically disputable within Christian faith and practice.

ad intra: the internal life of Father, Son, and Holy Spirit, without any necessary regard to the economy of God's relations with creation.

adoptionism: a cluster of heretical christological views holding that Jesus was only a human being who was given a unique role in God's plan (often with elevated status or power).

amillennialism: an eschatological view in which Christ's current reign through the church (instead of a distinct, future time period) is the subject of Scripture's millennial passages.

analogia entis / analogy of being: the view, most associated with Thomas Aquinas, that modest correspondence exists between creatures and the Creator (who also "exists," but necessarily so as the ground of creaturely being); thus, human language can communicate about God despite the distinction between Creator and creature.

analogia fidei / analogy of faith: the practice of relating difficult biblical texts to clearer ones and to the canonical message as a whole, trusting that God is the ultimate source of all Scripture.

analogical language: an approach to language in which concepts apply to God somewhat like they do to

---

Thanks to Jeremy Mann for laboring to compile an excellent first draft of this glossary.

creatures—neither equivocally nor univocally.

angels: spiritual beings created by God to serve as messengers.

anhypostatic Christology: the quality of Christ's incarnation whereby his human nature is without a personal *hypostasis* until being assumed by the divine Son.

animism: a worldview in which a multiplicity of spirits animates animals, plants, and inanimate objects.

annihilation: a position on the outcome of the final judgment involving absolute destruction instead of eternal torment.

anointing the sick: associated with James 5:13–20, an occasional Protestant practice and a Catholic sacrament to seek healing; despite popular perception, Catholic anointing is not solely for people at the threshold of death (as part of "viaticum" preparing them for heaven).

anthropology: the doctrine of human being.

anthropomorphism: the representation of God using human forms (e.g., body parts).

antichrist: in literal terms, Satan's deceptive world ruler during the tribulation.

apocalyptic literature: texts that typically present visions or other divine revelation, sharply dividing between good and evil, urging marginalized people to remain steadfast, and hoping for a dramatic unveiling of God's power to overturn present history.

Apocrypha: a collection of books focused on the interaction of intertestamental "Judaism" with its pagan environment; included in the canon of Scripture by Catholic and Orthodox Christians but not by Protestants.

apokatastasis: ultimate reconciliation of all things to God; universal salvation.

Apollinarianism: a christological heresy on the monophysite side that claimed Jesus could not have had a human mind, but only a human body and lower soul and a divine mind—thus denying his full humanity.

apologetics: defense of the Christian faith, often by disarming conceptual attacks or invalidating alternative viewpoints.

apophaticism: the view that humans cannot possess direct knowledge of the divine essence, since God is infinite and human concepts are limited.

apostolicity: one of the creedal marks of the church, involving its mission to extend faithfully the apostles' proclamation.

apostolic succession: an unbroken line of bishops succeeding the apostles as the earthly vehicle through which Christ administers his lordship over the church.

appropriation: association of properties and actions common to the Godhead with individual persons in the Trinity.

archetypal knowledge: God's self-knowledge as Creator of everything (the archetype for all true theology).

Arianism: an ancient christological heresy and recurring tendency on the adoptionist side; denial of the Son's self-existence and, accordingly, his eternity, holding instead that he was "begotten timelessly" as the first creature.

Arminianism: a soteriology that rejects elements of Calvinism associated with God's unconditional election of sinners to save; originally emerging within the Reformed tradition, this view emphasizes libertarian freedom instead.

articles, creedal: major sections of a creed.

arts: creative, skilled, human acts expressing both internal states and external realities.

ascension: the visible departure of Christ's body from the earth and exaltation to the right hand of the Father.

asceticism: a strain of Christian tradition that promotes self-denial, often through abstaining from physical comforts.

aseity: an element of classical theism, according to which God has no external cause and exists utterly independent of anything else.

assurance of salvation: confidence in being God's beloved child, awaiting a heavenly inheritance.

atonement: reconciliation, or restoring of peace, between offended parties.

authorship of Scripture: both divine and human; God's self-identification with the words of Scripture as the "voice" who is their ultimate source, speaking in and through them.

autographa: the initially authored manuscripts of the Scriptures.

baptism: using water, a rite that initiates Christian believers into their priestly participation in Christ's body, identifying with his saving work and joining the community indwelt by his Holy Spirit.

baptismal regeneration: God's creation, via baptism as the ordinary or required vehicle, of new life in a human being who was previously in bondage to sin and death.

baptism in the Holy Spirit: in classic Pentecostal and some Holiness theology, a postconversion second blessing of greater joy and power for ministry, initially manifested by speaking in tongues; otherwise, a metaphor for believers' indwelling by the Spirit from conversion onward.

beatific vision: the destiny of all the redeemed, a mystical union with God that transcends human cognition but still involves the mind's eye, as it were (Matt. 5:8).

Beatitudes: the blessings given by Jesus that begin the Sermon on the Mount.

biblical theology: a subdiscipline of theology that pursues historical and literary understanding of how Scripture's parts relate to its overall teaching.

blasphemy: scornful misuse of language about God, implying disgrace or unbelief.

calling: God's invitation in history for people to receive salvation.

Calvinism: a system of theology based on the work of John Calvin, often referring especially to soteriology that affirms unconditional election.

canon of Scripture: both a list and a rule, identifying which texts share divine authorship and what their authority involves.

cardinal virtues: prudence, justice, temperance, and fortitude—the four basic virtues that shape Catholic, along with some Orthodox and Protestant, accounts of the moral life.

catechesis: foundational instruction in essential Christian beliefs and practices.

catechism: an expression of a particular tradition's beliefs arranged in a question-and-answer format.

catholicity: one of the creedal marks of the church, involving its united fullness as Christ's body, bearing the Spirit's gifts, with each member connected to the whole.

celibacy: abstention from sexual activity out of submission and devotion to God.

cessationism: the view that treats certain sign gifts from the Holy Spirit, notably glossolalia, as special aspects of the old covenant and/or apostolic eras that have now ceased.

charismata: a Greek word meaning "spiritual gifts," involving God's blessing on certain talents or activities of particular persons through whom the Holy Spirit builds up the church's ministry.

chastity: the God-honoring state or practice of refraining from improper sexual activity.

chiliasm: belief in a literal millennium, the thousand-year reign of Christ on earth.

Christ: the Greek equivalent of Messiah ("anointed one") in Hebrew.

Christendom: the Christian synthesis of the church and the late Roman Empire that shaped the Catholic, Orthodox, and early Protestant traditions.

Christian perfection: according to Wesleyan teaching, "perfect love," in which the Spirit enables a person to live without committing voluntary sin.

Christian reconstructionism. *See* **dominion theology.**

Christology: the doctrine of Jesus Christ, focusing on the "person" who accomplished the "work" of salvation.

Christus Victor: a model of the atonement in which Christ defeated and rescued us from the hostile powers to which God subjected us after the fall.

church: neither a building nor just an institution, but a regathered form of Israel incorporating people from every tribe, tongue, and nation; its creedal "marks" are oneness, holiness, catholicity, and apostolicity.

clarity of Scripture: the Protestant view that the Bible's central message— the Creator graciously redeeming a fallen world in Jesus Christ—can be understood personally and faithfully, through reading vernacular translations, with the Holy Spirit's help and without necessary interpretive reliance upon the institutional church.

classic dispensationalism. *See* **dispensationalism, classic.**

common grace: God's kindness to everyone, both Christians and non-Christians, in providing for human life through nature and preserving human culture(s).

communicatio idiomatum / **communication of attributes:** the manner in which the attributes of Christ's two natures relate to each other.

communicative action: the conceptual integration of divine revelation with the rest of God's activity: God's speech actively establishes covenant relationship, while God's communion-establishing actions are communicative.

communicative praxis: the way in which Christian practices, directly and indirectly, enact a drama—learning and speaking of God in response to mighty acts of salvation.

communion of saints: the fellowship in Christ that all his followers share across time and place.

compatibilism: the view that divine sovereignty and human responsibility are both taught in Scripture and are somehow coherent.

complementarianism: the view that men and women are equal in human dignity but have different God-given roles in the human family and/or the church.

concept: a habitual, somewhat language-independent, means of relating words to objects or ideas.

concupiscence: corrupt human desire that, in Catholic and some other theologies, is not blameworthy until actualized, whereas in classic Protestant theologies it is already sinful.

concursus: God's providential cooperation with all that happens (as the primary cause undergirding secondary causes).

confession of sin: acknowledgment of wrongdoing, whether in thought, word, and/or deed, by things done and/or left undone—offending God and affecting neighbor(s).

confessions of faith: similar to but more comprehensive than ecumenical creeds, documents that express the foundational beliefs of particular Protestant churches.

confirmation: a process by which a baptized child personally affirms Christian faith and is acknowledged as a full member in a church.

congregational polity: church order in which members of local congregations together constitute the final human authority through which Christ governs.

consecration: the human response to God's sanctifying work; moment by moment setting apart of oneself to serve the living Christ in the power of the Holy Spirit.

consequentialist ethics: theories claiming that consequences are ethically fundamental; to act morally is to have one's act(s) produce maximal good and minimal or no harm.

conservatio: God's providential preservation of creation.

Constantinian paradigm: named after the emperor Constantine and also called "Christendom," a synthesis in which church and state rule society together.

constructive theology: an approach to theology that emphasizes creativity and cultural relevance.

Contemplative model of sanctification: the classic pursuit of mystical "union with Christ" in a transrational, not irrational, sense, often involving stages of self-denial and prayer.

continuationism: the opposite of cessationism; the view that all spiritual gifts in the New Testament, including special sign gifts, are operative after the apostolic era.

contraception: "birth control," typically referring to "artificial" or technical means of preventing pregnancy.

conversion: turning away from sin's mastery in repentance and turning to God in faith.

cosmos: a word, with Greek roots (kosmos), used for the orderly universe that God created.

counterfactuals of creaturely freedom: in God's middle knowledge, what could happen through human choices if particular circumstances occurred.

covenantal nomism: the idea that Second Temple Israelites saw themselves as already in covenant with God by grace, needing to respond with obedience to remain in covenant blessing.

covenant of grace: in Reformed theology, God's covenant to redeem the elect through Jesus Christ.

covenant of works: in Reformed theology, a covenant initiated by God with Adam, on behalf of all humanity, requiring obedience in order to enjoy life.

covenant theology: a dominant Protestant system of biblical theology from the century after the Reformers until the rise of dispensationalism, with the unity of the two major covenants as the organizing principle.

creatio ex nihilo: the doctrine that in creating, the Triune God did not use preexisting materials, face threatening chaos or opposing forces, or have the cosmos emanate from the divine being.

Creator Spiritus: the Spirit of creation, a title that emphasizes the Spirit's identity as the Giver of life.

credobaptism: the rejection of paedobaptism and insistence on believer's baptism.

creed: an ordered account of the fundamental beliefs of the Christian faith.

crisis experience: a decisive event in one's spiritual life, often a postconversion second blessing or particular filling with the Holy Spirit or moment of consecration.

cultural mandate: the human privilege and responsibility of filling the earth and representing God's rule (often grounded in Gen. 1:28–29).

culture: the expression(s) of meaning, both the seeds and the harvest of human freedom.

death: for humans, according to traditional Christianity, spiritual and/or physical; physically, not the cessation of all existence but only the temporary separation of body and soul.

deification: participation in the divine nature, emphasized in Orthodox accounts of salvation (in which humans participate in the divine energies but not the divine essence).

Deism: a type of theism that claims that God created the world and left it to run on its own.

demons: a minority of angels that joined the devil's rebellion.

denomination: a formal Protestant church association based on historic (however brief) affinities of doctrine and/or ministry.

deontological ethics: theories claiming that commands are ethically fundamental; to act morally is to have one's act(s) follow a rule.

descent into hell: an aspect of the Apostles' Creed referring to Christ's liberation of the realm of the dead; typically understood by classic Protestants in terms of Jesus's full identification with sinful humanity's plight—even, mysteriously, suffering our alienation from God.

devil: also called "Satan," a preeminent angel who pridefully rebelled and became God's chief adversary.

dichotomy: an approach to human constitution that distinguishes between body and soul, or humanity's material and immaterial aspects.

disenchantment of the universe: the deadening of a human sense of mystery and ultimate purpose in the natural world, introduced by modern science and skepticism about divine agency.

dispensationalism: a tradition that emphasizes the different ways in which God deals with human beings across the eras of salvation history.

dispensationalism, classic: associated with C. I. Scofield and Lewis Sperry Chafer, early forms of dispensationalism that sharply distinguished between Israel (ethnic and political) and the church (spiritual), "law" and "grace," and so forth.

dispensationalism, progressive: recent forms of dispensationalism that emphasize continuous development across salvation history, acknowledging that some Old Testament promises of God's kingdom are initially fulfilled in the church.

dispensationalism, revised: associated with Charles C. Ryrie, a modified but traditional form of dispensationalism that attempts to identify its core as consistently "literal" interpretation of Scripture (including prophecies), while diminishing some classical distinctions.

divine names: a cluster of proper names (e.g., "Yhwh"), metaphors (e.g., "rock"), and confessions (e.g., "compassionate and gracious, slow to anger, abounding in love") used to articulate God's perfection.

docetism: a family of early heresies that would not meaningfully acknowledge Christ's humanity.

dogma: authoritative church teaching.

dogmatic theology: an approach to theology that emphasizes the church's "Great Tradition" or a particular confessional tradition.

dominion theology: forms of theology, typically postmillennial, that encourage the church to extend God's kingdom via political influence, especially in America, perhaps by establishing biblical law as society's civil code.

Donatists: a sect in North Africa (opposed by Augustine) that opposed a mixed church (composed of unbelieving "tares" amid the "wheat" of genuine believers) and argued that lapsed priests invalidated the sacraments.

donum superadditum: a "superadded gift" above and beyond created nature yet independent of the fall, a point of Catholic theology disputed by most Protestants.

dualism: a hierarchical split between two fundamental aspects of reality, generally valuing spiritual or intellectual life over material things.

early high Christology: the demonstration that Christ's identity as the fully divine Son is present in the New Testament beyond John's Gospel, including early texts and the Synoptic Gospels.

Ebionism: an early christological heresy on the adoptionist side, likely shaped by Judaism, that claimed Jesus was a unique human but not fully divine.

ecclesiology: the doctrine of the church.

economy: God's well-planned administration of the world, like a beloved household, for the sake of divine self-revelation and creaturely reconciliation in Christ.

ectypal knowledge: creaturely correspondence, by revelation, to God's self-knowledge; true finite theology.

ecumenical (ecumenism): historically, referring to councils or statements representing broad, ideally universal, Christian consensus; also referring, today, to efforts at restoring the institutional unity of Christ's "one body," the church.

egalitarianism: the view that men and women are equal in both human dignity and God-given leadership roles.

election: God's eternal decision to redeem sinners.

enhypostatic Christology: the quality of Christ's incarnation whereby his human nature possesses a personal *hypostasis* (only) in the divine Son who assumed it.

envy: wanting others not to have what is theirs, or wanting to have it in their place.

episcopal polity: church order involving a threefold hierarchy of ministry, in which bishops oversee pastors and deacons.

epistemology: the study of knowledge.

equivocal language: an approach to language in which concepts apply to God in an entirely different way than creatures—neither analogically nor univocally, virtually nullifying divine revelation.

eschatology: the doctrine of last things.

eschaton: the final state to which redemption brings the cosmos and the new humanity in Christ.

eternal generation of the Son: the eternally "begotten," not "made," relation of the Son to the Father, with the begetting metaphorical rather than physical, introducing no subordination of the Son's being to the Father's being.

eternal security of the believer: a popular evangelical approach to assurance and perseverance that emphasizes "once saved, always saved," without an accompanying insistence on human discipleship and divine sovereignty.

eternity: the absence of limitation by time; for God, either "timeless eternity," in which God is outside of time, or "everlastingness," a modern view in which God exists at all times.

ethics: disciplined evaluation of the projects of human freedom— the rightness (or wrongness) of

particular decisions and the goodness (or evil) of ways of living.

ethnicity: an anthropological and theological category relating to ancestry, language, and culture.

eugenics: attempts to improve human traits such as intelligence by genetic means, including selective breeding and forms of population restriction.

Eutychianism: a christological heresy on the monophysite side that claimed that Jesus had one, mixed, "nature" as both divine and human.

evangelicalism: a historical movement and transdenominational subculture of Protestant Christianity that emphasizes the authority of Scripture, the need for personal conversion and renewal by the Holy Spirit, active participation in God's mission, and the atoning death of Christ.

evangelism: heralding in word and deed the good news that the Triune Creator has acted to redeem humanity and renew creation through Christ.

evil: the privation or pollution of that which God created good.

exaltation: in the traditional doctrine of the two states, the upward trajectory of Jesus's divinely vindicated mission, involving his resurrection and ascension to the right hand of God the Father.

exclusivist approach to religions: the view that only the God revealed in Jesus Christ is true, and only those who place explicit faith in Christ will be redeemed.

exegesis: the discipline of understanding "the way the words run," the meaning of the literal sense in Scripture texts.

ex opere operato: within Augustine's response to the Donatists, claiming effective validity for the sacraments "in the very doing of the act."

experience: the human encounter with raw sense perceptions, emotions, and thoughts, often deeply embedded with culture, language, and memory; the fourth theological "source" in the Wesleyan quadrilateral.

expiation: the bearing away of sin and its penalty.

extra Calvinisticum: the Calvinist view (as named by Lutheran opponents) that by virtue of his divine nature Jesus Christ shared in ruling the universe even while incarnate in Judea, and thus his divine lordship extended beyond his embodied human locale.

extra ecclesiam nulla salus: Latin for "outside the church there is no salvation," a famous proclamation of Cyprian (200–258).

extra nos: "outside us," a Latin phrase used by Protestants to note that Christ's righteousness remains ontologically outside of believers and becomes ours only in covenant union with Christ.

faith: personal knowledge of God's promised benevolence: personal, interacting with God as Creator and Redeemer; knowledge, revealing who God is and how humans should live.

fall, the: the willful rebellion of Adam and Eve against obedient fellowship with God, violating creation's original goodness, in response to which God placed the cosmos under a curse.

fallen human nature of Christ: the view that, while not actively sinful himself, God's Son embraced humanity's "fallen" condition in spiritual solidarity.

fellowship: both a shared identity that stems from participation in Christ and relational interactions that stem from Christian affection in the Spirit.

filioque: Latin for "and the Son," a clause inserted into the Nicene Creed by the Western church to indicate that the Holy Spirit proceeds not from the Father only but also from the Son—an insertion that contributed to formal division between the Eastern and Western churches.

finitude: the possession of inherent limits that render human beings incapable of knowing the Infinite God on their own, yet graciously free for interaction in various relational realms.

free-church polity: church order that involves no affiliation with an established state church; often associated with congregational polity.

freedom: opportunity for purposeful action in response to authoritative grounds that make our actions intelligible.

freedom, libertarian: a view that requires an agent to have the power of contrary choice, not simple volition.

freedom, volitional: a view that does not require the power of contrary choice but simply the will to choose according to the agent's nature (with such a will to choose, theologically, lying within God's overall determination).

freewill theism. *See* **open theism.**

futurist interpretation of prophecy: most emphatically, the view that all prophecies of the "last days" still await fulfillment upon Christ's return; more moderately, that certain prophetic texts or aspects await such future fulfillment.

gender: masculinity and femininity as distinct, lived, social constructs.

gender dysphoria: the condition of feeling dissonance between one's cultural gender expression and one's biological sex.

general revelation: God's self-disclosure in the gracious activity of creating and providentially sustaining the cosmos.

glorification: a term that many Protestants use to describe the removal of sin's presence, involving resurrected bodies, human hearts fully reconciled to God, and a redeemed cosmos.

glory: the dazzling revelation and reputation of God.

glossolalia: speaking in tongues.

gnosticism: ancient movement(s) influenced by Greek thought to denigrate materiality, often claiming special knowledge (*gnōsis*) about how spiritual people can escape the physical world's downward pull.

"God of the gaps": a term that describes the use of God to explain currently missing elements in a scientific account of causes.

gospel: good news—the joyful announcement that the Triune Creator has returned to redeem Israel in Christ, who bore human sin on the cross and was raised from the dead as the firstfruits of our new life; the Holy Spirit is regathering the covenant people around Jesus as Lord and is welcoming gentiles into this redeemed community; ultimately Christ will return to establish the *shalom* of God's comprehensive reign.

governmental model of atonement: a model, associated with Hugo Grotius, in which Jesus's death attains divine forgiveness while maintaining the world's moral order.

grounding objection: a challenge to Molinism that questions the basis on which God could have (middle) knowledge of counterfactuals of creaturely freedom if the humans and their circumstances are not actual.

***gubernatio*:** God's providential directing of all that happens.

hamartiology: the doctrine of sin (from the Greek *hamartia*, meaning "missing the mark").

healing: the restoration of wholeness (Ps. 41:3), making well—whether physically, mentally, or spiritually.

hell: eternal and conscious punishment from God.

Hellenization thesis: the theory that Greco-Roman philosophical ideals substantially (often, detrimentally) influenced early Christian theology.

heresy: the opposite of orthodoxy; the decisive rejection of basic, church-identifying dogma.

hermeneutics: the study of human understanding.

***hesed*:** the Hebrew word for "loyal covenant love."

historical theology: a subdiscipline of theology that studies the Christian tradition with interest in doctrinal formulation.

historic episcopate: the concept maintained by Catholicism and Orthodoxy (and a few Protestants) that the church is led by a chain of bishops who are the apostles' successors.

historicist interpretation of prophecy: the view that certain prophecies are fulfilled within the course of church history.

historic premillennialism: an eschatological view in which Christ's second coming occurs prior to a thousand-year reign of the saints but subsequent to the great apostasy (and any tribulation).

holiness: both a unique divine perfection and one of the creedal marks of the church, the latter involving the sacred identity of being God's people—set apart for service by the Holy Spirit.

holistic dualism: a version of dichotomy that defends the traditional distinction between body and soul while emphasizing the biblical unity of the human person during earthly and resurrected life.

holy orders: the Catholic or Orthodox sacrament that includes the threefold apostolic ministry of the episcopate, the presbyterate, and the diaconate.

homoousios: the Greek word specifying that the Son is of the *same*, not just a similar, being or essence as the Father.

hypocrisy: saying one thing but thinking and doing another.

hypostasis: a Greek word for the underlying substance or reality that grounds personal attributes.

hypostatic union: taken from *hypostasis*, the union of the divine and human natures in the one person of Jesus Christ.

icon: an object picturing Jesus Christ or Mary (or another saint) that is used as a vehicle for worship.

iconoclasts: those who claim that use of icons is idolatrous.

iconodules: those who defend "venerating" icons as a way of offering "worship" to God.

idealist interpretation of prophecy: sometimes operating in tandem with preterism, a view that focuses on the rhetoric of apocalyptic symbols rather than references to specific events.

idol: anything in life that draws allegiance away from the Creator.

imago Dei: the most fundamental concept of Christian theological anthropology for two millennia, despite mystery surrounding its precise meaning; the dominant views involve reason/righteousness, royalty, or relationship.

imitatio Christi: the imitation of Christ in all areas of life, while acknowledging his unique circumstances and redemptive work.

immanence, divine: God's nearness to creaturely life, radically expressed both by the incarnate Son's assumption of humanity in history and by the Spirit's empowerment of creaturely life and indwelling of God's people.

imminence of Christ's return: the possibility of Christ's return occurring, in principle, at any time.

immutability: the classical view that God does not change, at least remaining constant in personhood, perfections, and purposes.

impassibility: the classical view that God does not "suffer," not only undergoing no pain but not even being acted upon from outside.

impeccability: Christ's inability to sin.

inaugurated eschatology: the dialectical, "already and not yet," tension over God's kingdom *already* being present in the Creator's cosmic sovereignty, and anew with the first advent of Jesus Christ, but *not yet* in its ultimate fullness.

incarnation: to become embodied, referring theologically to the Son of

God becoming fully human in Jesus Christ.

inclusivist approach to religions: the view that God is truly revealed in Jesus as the only way of salvation (John 14:6), but salvation's benefits may extend to those who lack explicit faith in Christ.

indefectibility of the church: its certain endurance, at least in a faithful remnant, based on God's promise that the gates of hell will not prevail against it.

indulgences: in Catholicism, gifts through which purification is eased after death and penitential time is shortened on earth.

inerrancy of Scripture: the view that "when all the facts become known, they will demonstrate that the Bible in its original autographs and correctly interpreted is entirely true and never false in all it affirms, whether that relates to doctrine or ethics or to the social, physical, or life sciences" (P. Feinberg, "Bible, Inerrancy and Infallibility of," 125).

infallibility of Scripture: the view that as God's Word, Scripture does not fail to accomplish the sovereign purpose(s) for which God speaks (Isa. 55:11).

infinity: the perfection whereby God has no limitation (aside from God's own perfect being).

infralapsarianism: a Calvinist position (opposed to supralapsarianism) that God decreed first (logically speaking) to create and to allow the fall, then to initiate the covenant of grace.

initial evidence, tongues as: the Pentecostal doctrine that glossolalia is the normative manifestation of receiving the baptism with the Holy Spirit.

inspiration of Scripture: the divine authorship of the Scriptures; the process and/or status whereby in them we hear God speak (2 Tim. 3:16–17).

intelligent design: a theory that attempts to accept established evolutionary science while resisting philosophical materialism by highlighting gaps (as potentially normative) in current scientific explanations for creatures' complexity.

intermediate state: the period between a person's death and the general resurrection.

invisible church: Christ's body viewed in terms of those who are genuinely saved members.

irresistible grace: that which makes the general call(s) to salvation to be effectual for each particular member of the elect.

jealousy: wanting to have as much as possible, prompted by wanting things like others have.

Jehovah's Witnesses: a heretical sect that rejects the incarnation and trinitarian theology in favor of an Arianlike Christology.

Jesus: the given human name of the Incarnate Son, indicating his identity as Israel's Savior (Matt. 1:21).

judgment: a claim about reality; frequently, in the case of sin, a divine verdict of deserving punishment.

justice: rightly ordered relationships in which particular entities have their due.

justification by faith alone: the central position of Protestant soteriology, claiming that faith alone links those who are united with Christ to God's gracious verdict of forgiveness.

just war tradition: a set of criteria for determining a government's proper use of restraining or defensive force;

such criteria address *ius ad bellum*, the right to go to war, and *ius in bello*, right conduct in war.

kenotic Christology: models suggesting that in the incarnation Christ gave up or restricted the use of certain divine attributes, appealing to *kenōsis* ("emptied himself" or "made himself nothing") in Philippians 2:7.

Keswick model of sanctification: an approach that distinguishes between believers who are fully consecrated to God and those who are not—sometimes, between those who have made Jesus their Lord and those who have only received him as Savior—urging believers to pursue steps for letting go and being filled with the Holy Spirit.

kingdom of God: the cosmic blessedness—constant in principle, inaugurated in practice, to be fully consummated in the future—that involves God reigning over all things and people (ultimately, both willing and unwilling subjects) in heaven and earth.

koinōnia: a Greek word for "fellowship."

krypsis: a Greek word for "hidden," used in Christology to acknowledge some degree of hiddenness regarding the Son's divinity, without ontological or functional kenosis.

last things: the historical end(s) of the present cosmos and its people.

lex orandi lex credendi: Latin for "the law of prayer is the law of faith."

liberation: release from bondage, bringing restoration of justice and freedom.

liberation theology: a specific movement arising in Latin America, followed by subsequent movements among other marginalized groups, identifying Jesus with the broader biblical struggles of oppressed humanity, confronting structural evil along with personal sin.

limited atonement: the idea that Christ's atoning death is effective only for the elect.

limited inerrancy: the view that Scripture is God's Word, but its truthfulness extends only to "matters of faith and practice" as the focus of God's speech (not necessarily historical or scientific aspects).

literal sense: difficult to define, the church's traditional foundation for interpreting Scripture; "the way the words run."

liturgy: patterned movements of worship; some are formal and planned, others are freer yet learned through repetition.

Logos: in Greek thought, the rational structure that holds together the cosmos; in Christian theology, shaped especially by John's Gospel, this rational structure is the Second Person of the Trinity, the Son who is the Word the Father speaks in the Spirit.

Lord: in Greek, *kyrios*, typically a form of respectful address (something like "sir"); applied to the resurrected and ascended Jesus; however, its use as the Greek equivalent of the Old Testament's "YHWH" became significant.

love: the giving of oneself to enhance fellowship with, and the good of, another.

magisterium: the teaching office of the Roman Catholic Church, particularly the church's bishops and ultimately the pope.

marks of the church: characteristics of the true church in a preliminary and partial, not perfect, sense; according to the Nicene Creed, oneness, holiness, catholicity, and apostolicity.

marriage: the covenantal union of one male and one female to form a distinct household that may welcome new children.

martyrdom: bearing witness with one's whole life concerning the costly price of redemption, and awaiting the ultimate vindication of love for God and neighbor, even at the cost of earthly life.

means of grace: normative elements by which the Holy Spirit helps believers to grow in spiritual union with Christ, including the Word (hearing it preached, and reading it oneself), the sacraments, providence (God-given joys and trials), and prayer.

Messiah: the Hebrew name for one anointed by God (generally kings in the Old Testament, but also prophets and priests); ultimately, the promised royal deliverer awaited by Israel, who arrived as Jesus.

metaphor: thinking of what is difficult to name by bringing to mind features of more familiar terms.

middle knowledge: in contrast to God's "natural" knowledge, which involves self-knowledge and thus what is necessary and past, as well as God's "free" knowledge of the history God has chosen to actualize, this "middle" knowledge contains counterfactuals of creaturely freedom—states of affairs that would obtain in different circumstances.

midtribulational rapture: a premillennial view that sees the rapture taking believers away from earth at the middle of the tribulation; as the prefix "mid-" suggests, "time, times, and half a time" is taken as dividing that period into two three-and-a-half-year halves.

millennium: the thousand-year (if literal) earthly reign of Christ that is mentioned in Revelation 20.

missional community: the church being gathered by the Son and sent by the Spirit into the world, as the Father sent the Son.

modalism: a term for heretical views that deny trinitarian orthodoxy by treating the Father, Son, and Spirit not as distinct persons but only as forms of appearing in interaction with humans—thus treating only God's oneness as ontologically real.

model: a smaller-scale representation with which humans teach and learn aspects of revealed truth.

modernity: a time period characterized by a broad intellectual movement, emerging fully in the nineteenth century, that sought to overcome limitations of tradition and authority with appeal to reason—thus challenging Christianity with skepticism influenced by biblical criticism, evolutionary theory, and a scientific understanding of nature.

Molinism: a modern approach to divine providence based on the work of the Spanish Jesuit Luis de Molina, according to which God plans partly by using middle knowledge.

monarchianism: a view that elevates God the Father to such an extent that the Son and Spirit are not equally divine, or are considered mere derivations from the Father.

monism: the idea that there is only one ultimate kind of reality, whether material or spiritual (historically, more often spiritual).

monophysitism: a cluster of "one nature" Christologies that emphasize the divinity of Jesus and minimize his humanity.

monothelitism: referring to "one will" (*thelēma*), the view that Christ had only one will or principle of operation—condemned in 680 at the Third Council of Constantinople.

Mormonism: a heretical sect that historically teaches that God the Father has a body, the human fall into sin was necessary, and evolutionary eternal progression involves deified humanity.

mortification of sin: believers' active resistance to the devil by putting sin to death.

munus triplex: the threefold office of Christ, drawn from the anointing associated with prophets, priests, and kings in the Old Testament; also used to help those who are "in Christ" to understand their ministry.

naturalism: the view that the natural world and its laws are all that exist, with corresponding denial of the existence of God, the soul, and, in most cases, moral laws.

natural law: moral requirements that people of good conscience can or at least should discern from the nature of the world God created.

natural theology: conceptually developed knowledge of God that seeks to progress by means of general revelation; insufficient for salvation, but possibly preparing someone to seek salvation.

necessity, divine: an element of classical theism, maintaining that it is impossible for God not to exist.

neoorthodoxy: a label applied (often by conservatives) to a supposed family of thinkers, including Karl Barth, Dietrich Bonhoeffer, Emil Brunner, Rudolf Bultmann, Reinhold Niebuhr, and Paul Tillich; despite Barth's rejection of the label and their substantial differences, the label suggested that they sought to retain aspects of traditional orthodoxy in a new, modern way.

Nestorianism: a christological heresy on the adoptionist side that overemphasized Jesus's two natures, losing his ontological unity as one person; due to denying the title *Theotokos* to Mary, perceived as teaching that Jesus was born a man whose union with the divine was only relational.

new perspective on Paul: despite having its very definition contested, a set of hermeneutical approaches that understand Second Temple Judaism in terms of covenantal nomism, not justification by works, and therefore oppose classic Protestant analogies between Paul's opponents and medieval Catholicism.

Nicene Creed: the most ecumenical statement of orthodox faith from the early Christian church, first adopted at the Council of Nicaea (AD 325) in response to the "Arian" heresy, which denied the full deity of Jesus Christ, then expanded at the Council of Constantinople (AD 381) to acknowledge more fully the deity of the Holy Spirit.

nominalism: the view, presented with varying degrees of strength, that concepts lack real existence in the divine mind and are merely human names for things.

nonreductive physicalism: the view that human beings are essentially material, and personal qualities traditionally associated with the soul—language, feelings, and the like—emerge from a physical substrate, although without being explained solely in terms of sociobiological interactions.

nonresistance: an alternative to pacifism that allows for fulfilling military obligations and helping others without participating directly in killing.

nouvelle théologie: the new theology of Catholic figures like Henri de Lubac, who encouraged *ressourcement* and critiqued rigid neoscholasticism, especially its concept of "pure nature."

omnipotence: God's perfection of being all-powerful—having all the powers it is consistent with God's other perfections to exercise.

omnipresence: God's perfection of being present in all places; both ubiquity and immensity—granting various kinds of divine presence to creatures, not being localized but as Spirit being ontologically present with each point in space.

omniscience: God's knowledge of all things, past and present and future, divine and human and otherwise, as the perfectly wise Creator.

oneness: one of the creedal marks of the church, involving its fundamental unity in Jesus Christ despite its diversity of spiritual gifts, cultural contexts, human leaders, and so forth.

Oneness Pentecostalism: a contemporary, subtler, "Jesus-only" form of modalism that arose on the fringe of evangelicalism.

ontology: study of the being or natures or essences of things.

open theism: a view that denies that God has exhaustive foreknowledge, holding instead that God's foreknowledge is as comprehensive as possible given the world God chose to create (with libertarian human freedom).

ordinance: the baptistic name for baptism and the Lord's Supper as divinely commanded practices for symbolically remembering Christ, with no (sacramental) assumption of unique divine presence.

ordo salutis: Latin for "order of salvation," describing in sequence how the Spirit unites people to Christ and his saving benefits.

original sin: the doctrine concerning the historical fall of humanity from created goodness in the first sin of Adam and Eve—somehow, on an Augustinian account, involving all their descendants in original guilt and shared corruption.

orthodoxy: the basic, church-identifying dogma that the true God is Father, Son, and Holy Spirit, definitively revealed in the incarnation of Jesus Christ as the God-man.

ousia: a Greek word for "substance" or "essence."

pacifism: nonviolence, at least the avoidance of all participation in killing, including military combat.

pactum salutis: Latin for "covenant of peace"—an intratrinitarian agreement between Father, Son, and Holy Spirit regarding their externally undivided saving action.

paedobaptism: the baptism of infants.

panentheism: the view that the universe is in some sense ontologically "in" God, divine, yet there is more to God than just the universe (thus distinct from pantheism).

pantheism: the view that the entire world and the divine are simply the same thing.

papal infallibility: the Catholic dogma, officially adopted at Vatican I, that the pope cannot err when speaking *ex cathedra*, from his authoritative chair on behalf of the church, regarding matters of faith or practice.

parousia: the Greek word for "appearing"; theologically, the second coming of Christ.

particularism: often seen as Augustinian, the position that the Bible consistently depicts the fate of those who are not in Christ as eternal and conscious punishment.

passive obedience of Christ: Jesus's obedient act of suffering redemptive death ("passion") on a cross at human hands.

pastoral theology: a subdiscipline of theology that brings experience of Christian living and church ministry to bear on doctrinal concepts.

patriarchy: the headship of the male as father figure across all or significant parts of society.

patripassianism: the heresy that held the one God and Father suffered and died on the cross since the Son was not a distinct divine person.

Pelagianism: the view that by virtue of creation, apart from redeeming grace, humans can freely choose to obey God's commands rather than sinning.

penal substitution: a model of the atonement in which out of divine love Jesus underwent the penalty for sin (expiation), typically involving God's wrath (propitiation), on behalf of individual sinners.

penance: in Catholic teaching, a sacrament that addresses the ongoing need for conversion, confession, and forgiveness, with means of satisfaction such as fasting, prayer, and almsgiving.

perichōrēsis: a Greek word meaning "coinherence or mutual interweaving of being," used to express the three divine persons' communion.

perseverance of the saints: the Calvinist belief that the indwelling Holy Spirit preserves the elect so that they persevere in saving faith.

person: a "someone," not just a "something"—a someone who engages his or her shared nature and individual identity with understanding and freedom.

philosophical theology: a subdiscipline of theology that incorporates conceptual tools and engages questions from philosophy.

Platonism: a philosophical theory based on Plato's belief in the universal and unchanging ideas, or "forms," in which passing earthly objects participate.

pluralist approach to religions: the denial that the Christian faith presents distinctive truth about God and salvation in Christ, instead treating all religions as providing partial perspectives for grasping whatever reality is sacred.

pneumatology: the doctrine of the Holy Spirit.

polity: the structures by which the church orders its leadership to foster the *shalom* of its common life.

pope: the bishop of Rome, who, having gained prominence by association with Peter, is now the leader of the Catholic Church.

postmillennialism: an eschatological view in which God's kingdom has been inaugurated by Jesus Christ at his first advent and grows progressively via the church.

postmortem repentance: a possible outcome of the final judgment if everyone receives an opportunity clearly to accept or reject the gospel, including postmortem encounters with God as needed.

posttribulational rapture: a premillennial view that sees the rapture as part of Christ's return inaugurating the millennium; as the prefix "post-" suggests, the rapture happens after the "tribulation" mentioned in texts like Matthew 24:21.

power: the capacity to act and to realize successfully one's intentions in so acting.

practical theology: a subdiscipline of theology (roughly synonymous with pastoral theology) that brings experience of Christian living and church ministry to bear on doctrinal concepts.

practices: actions that reflect and foster the church's conformity to Christ; these means of grace involve personal participation in communally shared activities.

prayer: the heart's response to God, crying out for deeper communion in light of divine revelation.

preexistence (of the Son): a loose but standard term indicating that the Son of God lived—eternally, according to Christian orthodoxy—prior to becoming incarnate as Jesus Christ on earth.

premillennialism: an eschatological view in which Christ's return will initiate an intermediate stage (literally, one thousand years) of reigning fully over the present, sin-cursed form of the cosmos.

presbyterian polity: church order that characterizes Reformed churches, involving "presbyters" or "elders" who form a "session" that governs a local congregation, while "presbyteries" or "synods" govern a denomination at various levels.

preterist interpretation of prophecy: the view that prophetic literature addressed the original audiences entirely in terms of their immediate horizon; hence the key eschatological texts addressed events that are now past, or at least initially fulfilled.

pretribulational rapture: a premillennial view in which Christian believers are kept away from God's wrath by being raptured before the tribulation begins, since the entire period contains God's wrath.

prevenient grace: generally, grace that comes before and enables human response; specifically in Arminian and Wesleyan traditions, a universal work of the Holy Spirit that restores the possibility of freely willed faith.

prewrath rapture: a premillennial view that positions the rapture right before the portion of the tribulation (in the latter half) in which God actively pours out wrath.

priesthood of all believers: the view that all who are baptized into Christ share immediate access to God; through the one Mediator they may call upon God in prayer, hear God in Scripture, and proclaim the divine Word to others.

problem of evil: a perennial challenge about how there can be an all-good, all-powerful God yet considerable evil in the world.

process theology: a panentheist type of modern theology, sometimes portraying the world as God's body, in which God acts by subatomic and not necessarily personal persuasion.

progressive dispensationalism. *See* dispensationalism, progressive.

progressive sanctification: a Reformed emphasis, oriented around union with Christ, on the gradually forward movement of the true believer's spiritual maturity; no postconversion "crisis" experiences are necessary or normative.

prolegomena: literally, "the first words" on a subject, referring to how theology will proceed from faith toward understanding.

proof-texting: in its negative connotation, appealing to Scripture passages in support of a theological claim without adequately addressing their contexts.

prophetic literature: texts that confront God's people or their leaders about current patterns of unfaithfulness— sometimes, but not always, including an element of promise or prediction regarding the future.

propitiation: the appeasement of God's wrath.

proposition: a truth claim (which can be either true or false), often referring to cognitive content from divine revelation.

pseudepigrapha: writings with falsely presented authorship.

public: a community's context and goals that orient particular questions to which people of faith are responding.

pure act: the view that God is never inactive or vulnerable to unrealized potential.

purgatory: according to Catholicism (and Orthodoxy, though usually in other terms), an interim phase of purification between a person's death and glorified enjoyment of the beatific vision.

quests for the "historical Jesus": modern efforts to study Jesus historically, "from below," without necessarily affirming (and often opposing) the

"Christ of faith," conciliar Christology, "from above" as biblical dogma.

race: a modern social construct that separates ethnic groups along purportedly biological lines.

racialization: a term used by Michael Emerson and Christian Smith to describe differential effects of race in society even without overt racial prejudice.

racism: narrowly, overt hatred for all persons of a particular race; more broadly, covert prejudices about certain persons or tendencies representing a particular race; most broadly, power structures that contribute to disparate outcomes across racial lines.

radical orthodoxy: a recent, largely Anglican theological movement initiated by John Milbank that critiques secular social theory and champions the sacramental participation of all creation in God.

Rahner's Rule: "The economic Trinity is the immanent Trinity, and the immanent Trinity is the economic Trinity."

ransom: the liberation of humanity from captivity to sin, death, and the devil.

rapture of the church: an initial aspect of Christ's second advent in which he snatches away living Christians from earth.

realist view of original sin: an account that ties all humanity to Adam's sin through biological or otherwise direct presence and participation.

reason: a God-given cognitive and linguistic faculty by which we communicate and seek coherent understanding; the third theological "source" in the Wesleyan quadrilateral.

recapitulation: the view, associated with Irenaeus, that Jesus faithfully relived the fallen human story in his own redemptive life history.

reconciliation: all that God does in Christ to restore covenant fellowship with and among sinful humans, and eventually the entire cosmos.

redemption: a metaphor for the atonement, the "buying back" of humanity.

regeneration: the event or process of God making new those who belong to Christ, releasing them from sin's power.

regula fidei / Rule of Faith: an authoritative guide to Scripture's unified revelation, shaped by early church practice and precedent-setting until the development of dogma; a summary of the overall "scope" of the Bible's story, identifying the Creator God of Israel with the Redeemer God revealed in Jesus Christ.

religion: devotion to something sacred beyond oneself, typically involving shared rituals of some kind.

repentance: *metanoia* in Greek, the changing of mind and heart, especially turning away from sin's mastery.

representative view of original sin: an account that ties all humanity to Adam's sin through federal headship, analogous to God's imputation of Christ's righteousness to the redeemed.

ressourcement: creative retrieval of tradition through fresh historical study.

resurrection: not simply "life after death," but dead people returning to new bodily life.

revelation: God's self-disclosure, especially associated with speech and therefore having both personal and propositional dimensions.

reverent agnosticism: hopeful restraint about specifying the ultimate fate of apparent unbelievers.

revised dispensationalism. *See* dispensationalism, revised.

rite: a regular pattern of symbolic behavior that is performed by or on behalf of a community seeking shared religious experience.

Sabbath: the seventh day of the Jewish week; theologically, devoted to worship, rest, and mercy and justice.

Sabellianism: an early form of modalism that became associated with patripassianism.

sacrament: a ritually embodied sign that celebrates the mysterious communication of God's grace.

sacramental participation: the idea that created things are signs that mysteriously share in the life of the Creator.

sacrifice: the willing offering of oneself or one's possessions for a greater good.

saint: a believer recognized in Orthodox and Catholic traditions (plus by a few Protestants) as having attained a level of glorified sanctification through which others may be specially blessed.

salvation: deliverance from danger or bondage, healing from a deadly illness or wound; as an action of the Triune God, dependent upon the Father's loving initiative, the Son's ministry of reconciliation, and the Spirit's application of the Son's atoning work.

sanctification: the most common Protestant term for the process of becoming holy, conforming to the pattern of Jesus Christ.

Satan: also called "the devil," a preeminent angel who pridefully rebelled and became God's chief adversary.

satisfaction: the fulfillment of moral or legal demands on humanity due to sin.

Scripture: sacred writings; regarding the Christian Bible, the verbal witness of prophets and apostles concerning God's ultimate speech in Jesus Christ (Heb. 1:1–4; 4:12–13).

Scripture principle: a cornerstone of Protestantism, the belief that the Bible is the inspired, thereby canonically written and infallible record and channel of revelation so that it is the supreme authority for theology.

second blessing: according to Wesleyan teaching, a "second work of grace" that removes the inclination to sin and fills the heart with perfect love of God and neighbor.

self: a human person's individual and internal identity that distinguishes that person from others and grounds his or her engagement with the world.

sensus divinitatis: articulated by John Calvin, the idea of a seed of divinity—a religious sensibility—planted in the heart that should grow into faith yet is deadened by fallen human nature.

Septuagint (LXX): a Greek translation of the Old Testament that was prominent in early Christianity.

session: the heavenly ruling of the ascended Christ over his regathered form of Israel called "church," thereby advancing his earthly reign; in presbyterian polity, a group of elders.

seven deadly sins: chief or capital vices with which the devil tempts people to love the world rather than God.

sex: the biological reality of bodies, physically male or female.

shalom: a Hebrew word that signifies peaceful flourishing, the ultimate end of Christian worship, thought, and practice.

Shema: from the Hebrew word for "hear," an encapsulation of the divine uniqueness found in Deuteronomy 6:4: "Hear, O Israel: The LORD our God, the LORD is one."

simplicity: a specification of God's unity as the one, holy Creator that neither the three "persons" of the Trinity nor the divine "perfections" constitute "parts" of God, and there is no distinction between God's essence and God's existence.

simul iustus et peccator: a Latin phrase used by Luther to describe the Christian as simultaneously justified before God yet still sinful.

sin: any act—whether a thought, desire, emotion, word, or deed—or absence that displeases God and thus establishes guilt.

slavery: an attempt to own another human being, despite the fact that all belong to God as responsible agents.

social trinitarianism: an approach that emphasizes the mutuality of the three trinitarian persons as a model for human community, generally envisioned along democratic and egalitarian lines.

sola fide: one of five key slogans from developed Protestant theology, "faith alone," emphasizing that salvation is received through trust in Christ, not righteous works, or the sacramental system, and so forth.

sola gratia: one of five key slogans from developed Protestant theology, "grace alone," emphasizing that salvation depends entirely upon God's grace in a way that does not credit human cooperation but rather enables it.

sola scriptura: one of five key slogans from developed Protestant theology, "Scripture alone," emphasizing the Bible as the sole final arbiter of truth claims, the norming norm whose basic message—the gospel—is sufficiently clear that "Scripture interprets Scripture" and provides wisdom unto salvation with the "due use of ordinary means."

solo verbo: one of five key slogans from developed Protestant theology, "the Word alone," often paired with *sola scriptura*, emphasizing the proclamation of the Bible as the fundamental source for encountering the revelation of God's grace in Jesus Christ.

solus Christus: one of five key slogans from developed Protestant theology, "Christ alone," emphasizing that being united with Christ's righteousness alone, ultimately independent of other types of human mediation, gains sinners everlasting life.

Son of God: although not used to assert Christ's divinity in every case, this title gradually pointed in that direction, emphasizing, in the Gospels, Jesus's supernatural power over the spirit world; although not recorded as Jesus's own title, a favorite of the New Testament Epistles.

Son of Man: primarily designating humanity in the Old Testament, in the Gospels this title is associated with the entire Christ narrative, including Jesus's exaltation to eschatological glory.

soteriology: the doctrine of salvation.

special revelation: God's self-disclosure by means of the Spirit's ministry of the Word (through prophets and apostles, yet ultimately in Jesus Christ) to particular people at particular times, addressing our need to know God as Redeemer, not just Creator.

sphere sovereignty: a neo-Calvinist position that maintains that God's common grace authorizes the integrity of distinct areas of life within the created order.

Spirit: God's noncorporeal being, personal in an infinite sense, and not bound by a body in time and space.

Spirit Christologies: Christologies emphasizing that Jesus performed his earthly wonders as a faithful human being empowered by the Holy Spirit; some go further, rejecting Chalcedonian "Logos Christology" as incompatible with Jesus's full humanity.

spiritual gifts. *See charismata.*

status duplex: the twofold state of the incarnate Christ, involving humiliation and exaltation; these are both dialectically true at once and sequentially true in a narrative of descent and ascent (first suffering, then glory).

structural evil: the ways in which sin aggregates in social groups, and societal institutions oppress particular persons or foster communal evils (also called "systemic sin").

subsidiarity: a principle of Catholic social teaching in which higher-order (e.g., government) communities should support more local communities with coordination but as little interference as possible.

substance: the essential nature of something, as distinguished from its accidents.

substitution: the standing-in of Jesus for some aspect of humanity, the atoning nature of which is debated.

sufficiency of Scripture: also called perfection; the Protestant view that in the Word, God communicates all the truth necessary for salvation and holy living.

supersessionism: the view that God's special relationship with the Jewish people came to an end after the coming of Jesus Christ and the establishment of his church, which replaced Israel.

supralapsarianism: a Calvinist position that God decreed first (logically speaking) to redeem the elect, then to create and to permit the fall into sin.

system: in theology, a network of concepts and models that convey judgments about both particular truths and special emphases.

systematic theology: a culminating discipline (roughly equivalent to constructive or dogmatic theology) that emphasizes intellectual coherence in studying how the church may bear enduring, timely, and biblically truthful witness to the Triune God revealed in Jesus Christ.

systemic sin. *See* **structural evil.**

Tanakh: the Jewish Scriptures, in place by the early Christian era, containing the Torah, the Prophets, and the Writings.

Tetragrammaton: the four-consonantal name of God in Hebrew, YHWH, revealed as a personal proper name to the covenant people Israel.

textual criticism: the process of attempting to ascertain the original wording of an ancient manuscript.

Textus Receptus: the "Received Text" that stands behind the Authorized (King James) Version of 1611.

theodicy: a human attempt to vindicate divine goodness and providence in view of the existence of evil.

theological virtues: habitual dispositions toward human excellence; theologically, by divine grace, faith, hope, and charity (love).

theology: faith seeking understanding; in other words, the disciplined pursuit of Christian wisdom, the most germane biblical concept for knowledge of God.

theology of glory: a phrase employed by Martin Luther to critique speculatively projecting onto God a pagan notion of power, in contrast to a theology of the cross.

theology of the cross: a phrase employed by Martin Luther to champion focusing on the uniqueness of God's cruciform power, in contrast to a theology of glory.

theology proper: strictly speaking of God's character, distinct from the economy of divine activity that discloses God's character in the world.

theopneustos: a Greek term in 2 Timothy 3:16, referring to the "God-breathed" character of Scripture.

theosis: a view in which salvation involves "deification" or "divinization" through human participation in the divine nature, based on 2 Peter 1:4.

Theotokos: "God-bearer," used of Mary by the Alexandrian school and subsequent orthodoxy, but rejected by Nestorius.

Torah: the law, or divine instruction, revealed to Moses in the Pentateuch.

torture: inhumanely cruel treatment that uses physical pain and mental disorientation for breaking someone's will.

total depravity: the view that every aspect of human life after the fall is corrupted by sin (not that human life individually or overall is absolutely as evil as possible).

tradition: broadly, all Christian witness, verbal and nonverbal, faithful and false; somewhat more specifically, as the second theological "source" in the Wesleyan quadrilateral, the communal handing on of authentic Christian faith over time—and thus, for many Protestants, a "ministerial" guide or secondary norm (not a "magisterial" norm) for biblical interpretation.

transcendence, divine: God's utter blessedness and unique being, beyond finite knowing, so that divine action does not compete with ours but operates on a different plane, sustaining creaturely agency.

transcendentals: the ideals or orienting qualities of being (for classic Christian thought, divine perfections in which creatures participate): goodness, truth, and beauty.

transfiguration: a special occasion of the revelation of Christ's glory to and through his disciples.

translation of Scripture: both a literal, linguistic process and a metaphorical, mental aspect of hearing biblical texts with understanding.

transubstantiation: the Catholic position on the Lord's Supper, in which the substance of the bread and wine is transformed into Christ's body and blood, while the accidental properties of physical bread and wine remain the same.

tribulation: an eschatological period of suffering and judgment, mentioned in the Gospels and in Revelation and variously interpreted, that precedes the second coming of Christ.

trichotomy: an approach to human constitution that distinguishes between body, soul, and spirit.

trinitarian theology: the basic Christian orthodoxy that identifies the one true God as eternally existing in the three persons of the Father, the Son, and the Holy Spirit.

Trinity: from the Latin word *Trinitas*, designating the triunity of the Father, Son, and Holy Spirit in the one being of God.

tritheism: any heretical tendencies to posit three gods or even three separate "persons" (in the modern sense) that simply share a "divine" nature.

unconditional election: an element of Calvinistic soteriology according to which God has sovereignly chosen in eternity past particular persons for salvation, irrespective of any action or preexisting condition of their part.

union with Christ: the central, overarching category in Paul's theology, naming the covenant relationship in which we receive the benefits of salvation.

univocal language: an approach to language in which concepts apply to God and humans in the same way, neither analogically nor equivocally, jeopardizing the distinction between Creator and creature.

***via media*:** a middle way; associated especially with some Anglican claims, such as the claim to navigate between the Roman Catholic Church and Protestantism.

***via negativa*:** an approach to the divine attributes that proceeds by negating the application of creaturely limitations to God, who mysteriously transcends any human concepts.

virtue ethics: theories claiming that character is ethically fundamental; to act morally is to have one's act(s) produced by and producing virtues—enduring dispositions of the heart that provide the impetus for living well.

visible church: Christ's body viewed as a concrete, earthly institution, thus including sinful members, false confessors of faith, and disordered polity along with the marks of oneness, holiness, catholicity, and apostolicity.

visio Dei. See **beatific vision.**

voluntarism: an emphasis upon free will; in the case of God, emphasis upon divine freedom rather than any necessary or fitting relation between God's will and what is good.

Vulgate: an early composite translation of the Bible in Latin, dominant in Western Christianity for over one thousand years.

Wesleyan quadrilateral: the framework, attributed to John Wesley, that highlights Scripture, tradition, reason, and experience as key "sources" of Christian theology.

Western culture: a complex term frequently meaning "Northern" in contrast to the "Majority World" and the "Global South" Christianity rapidly growing today; often associated with Christian thought shaped by Greco-Roman categories, particularly the Latin tradition downstream from Augustine.

wisdom: the most germane biblical concept for the knowledge of God, and thus the goal of Christian theology—whole-personed, communally learned knowledge of God that is integrated with loving others and living well.

witness, Christian: communicative action—whatever believers in Christ say or do with reference to God, whether good or bad.

worship: proclamation of God's worth, via praise, thanksgiving, and service.

wrath, divine: God's just response to creatures' foolish, self-destructive refusal of love.

YHWH: Often translated as "the LORD" and pronounced as "Yahweh," the personal name with which the covenant people were invited to address God starting in Exodus 3.

Bibliography

Abasciano, Brian. "Clearing Up Misconceptions about Corporate Election." *Ashland Theological Journal* 41 (2009): 67–102.

Abraham, William J. "Church and Churches: Ecumenism." In *The Oxford Handbook to Evangelical Theology*, edited by Gerald R. McDermott, 296–309. Oxford: Oxford University Press, 2010.

Adam, Peter. "The Trinity and Human Community." In *Grace and Truth in the Secular Age*, edited by Timothy Bradshaw, 52–65. Grand Rapids: Eerdmans, 1998.

Alexander, Donald, ed. *Christian Spirituality: Five Views*. Downers Grove, IL: InterVarsity, 1989.

Allen, R. Michael. *Grounded in Heaven: Recentering Christian Hope and Life on God*. Grand Rapids: Eerdmans, 2018.

———. *Justification and the Gospel: Understanding the Contexts and Controversies*. Grand Rapids: Baker Academic, 2013.

Allen, R. Michael, and Scott R. Swain. "In Defense of Proof-Texting." *Journal of the Evangelical Theological Society* 54, no. 3 (September 2011): 589–606.

Allen, R. Michael, and Daniel J. Treier. "Dogmatic Theology and Biblical Perspectives on Justification: A Reply to Leithart." *Westminster Theological Journal* 70, no. 1 (2008): 105–10.

Anderson, Allan. *An Introduction to Pentecostalism: Global Charismatic Christianity*. 2nd ed. Cambridge: Cambridge University Press, 2014.

Anderson, Gary A., and Markus Bockmuehl, eds. *Creation ex nihilo: Origins, Development, Contemporary Challenges*. Notre Dame, IN: University of Notre Dame Press, 2017.

Anizor, Uche, and Hank Voss. *Representing Christ: A Vision for the Priesthood of All Believers*. Downers Grove, IL: IVP Academic, 2016.

Anselm of Canterbury. "Proslogion." In Anselm, *Basic Writings*, edited and translated by Thomas Williams, 75–99. Indianapolis: Hackett, 1997.

Athanasius. *On the Incarnation*. Translated by John Behr. Popular Patristics 44A. Yonkers, NY: St. Vladimir's Seminary Press, 2011.

Atkinson, D. J. "Divorce." In *Evangelical Dictionary of Theology*, edited by Daniel J. Treier and Walter A. Elwell, 249–51. 3rd ed. Grand Rapids: Baker Academic, 2017.

Augustine. *City of God*. Translated by Marcus Dods. In *The Nicene and Post-Nicene Fathers*, Series 1, edited by Philip Schaff, 2:1–512. 1886–89. Reprint, Peabody, MA: Hendrickson, 1994.

———. *Confessions*. Translated by Henry Chadwick. Oxford World Classics. Oxford: Oxford University Press, 1991.

———. "The Punishment and Forgiveness of Sins." In Augustine, *Answer to the Pelagians*, translated by Roland J. Teske, edited by John E. Rotelle, 18–139. Vol. 1/23 of *The Works of Saint Augustine: A Translation for the 21st Century*. Hyde Park, NY: New City Press, 1997.

———. "Tractate 29.6 [on John 7:14–18]." *Homilies on the Gospel of John*. Translated by John Gibb and James Innes. In *The Nicene and Post-Nicene Fathers*, Series 1, edited by Philip Schaff, 7:7–456. 1886–89. Reprint, Peabody, MA: Hendrickson, 1994.

———. *The Trinity*. Translated by Edmund Hill. Edited by John E. Rotelle. New York: New City Press, 1991.

Ayres, Lewis. *Nicaea and Its Legacy: An Approach to Fourth-Century Trinitarian Theology*. Oxford: Oxford University Press, 2004.

Badcock, Gary D. *Light of Truth and Fire of Love: A Theology of the Holy Spirit*. Grand Rapids: Eerdmans, 1997.

Baker, Mark D., and Joel B. Green. *Recovering the Scandal of the Cross: Atonement in New Testament and Contemporary Contexts*. 2nd ed. Downers Grove, IL: IVP Academic, 2011.

Barclay, John M. G. *Paul and the Gift*. Grand Rapids: Eerdmans, 2015.

Barnes, Michel René. "De Régnon Reconsidered." *Augustinian Studies* 26 (1995): 51–79.

———. "Rereading Augustine on the Trinity." In *The Trinity: An Interdisciplinary Symposium on the Trinity*, edited by Stephen T. Davis, Daniel Kendall SJ, and Gerald O'Collins SJ, 145–75. Oxford: Oxford University Press, 1999.

———. "The Use of Augustine in Contemporary Trinitarian Theology." *Theological Studies* 56 (1995): 237–51.

Barth, Karl. *Church Dogmatics*. Edited by G. W. Bromiley and T. F. Torrance. Translated by G. W. Bromiley, G. T.

Thomson, et al. Four volumes in 13 parts. Edinburgh: T&T Clark, 1936–77.

Basil the Great. *On the Holy Spirit*. Translated by Stephen Hildebrand. Popular Patristics 42. Yonkers, NY: St. Vladimir's Seminary Press, 2011.

Bass, Diana Butler. *Christianity after Religion: The End of Church and the Birth of a New Spiritual Awakening*. San Francisco: HarperOne, 2012.

Bauckham, Richard. *Jesus and the God of Israel: God Crucified and Other Studies on the New Testament's Christology of Divine Identity*. Grand Rapids: Eerdmans, 2008.

———. "Only the Suffering God Can Help?" *Themelios* 9, no. 3 (April 1984): 6–12.

Bavinck, Herman. *God and Creation*. Translated by John Vriend. Edited by John Bolt. Vol. 2 of *Reformed Dogmatics*. Grand Rapids: Baker Academic, 2003.

Beale, G. K. *The Temple and the Church's Mission: A Biblical Theology of the Dwelling Place of God*. New Studies in Biblical Theology. Downers Grove, IL: IVP Academic, 2004.

———. *We Become What We Worship: A Biblical Theology of Idolatry*. Downers Grove, IL: IVP Academic, 2008.

Beals, Paul A. *A People for His Name: A Church-Based Missions Strategy*. Rev. ed. Pasadena, CA: William Carey Library, 2013.

Bebbington, David W. "About the Definition of Evangelicalism . . ." Review of *Four Views on the Spectrum of Evangelicalism*, edited by Andrew David Naselli and Collin Hansen. *Evangelical Studies Bulletin* 83 (Fall 2012): 1–6.

———. *Evangelicalism in Modern Britain: A History from the 1730s to the 1980s*. London: Unwin Hyman, 1989.

Beckwith, Roger. *The Old Testament Canon of the New Testament Church*. Grand Rapids: Eerdmans, 1986.

Behe, Michael J. *Darwin's Black Box: The Biochemical Challenge to Evolution*.

10th anniversary ed. New York: Free Press, 2006.

Beilby, James K., and Paul R. Eddy, eds. *Divine Foreknowledge: Four Views.* Downers Grove, IL: InterVarsity, 2001.

Berkouwer, G. C. *Holy Scripture.* Edited and translated by Jack B. Rogers. Studies in Dogmatics. Grand Rapids: Eerdmans, 1975.

Bethge, Eberhard. *Dietrich Bonhoeffer: A Biography.* Rev. ed. Minneapolis: Fortress, 2000.

Betz, Hans Dieter. *The Sermon on the Mount: A Commentary on the Sermon on the Mount, Including the Sermon on the Plain (Matthew 5:3–7:27 and Luke 6:20–49).* Edited by Adela Yarbro Collins. Hermeneia. Minneapolis: Fortress, 1995.

Billings, J. Todd. *Union with Christ: Reframing Theology and Ministry for the Church.* Grand Rapids: Baker Academic, 2011.

Bird, Michael F. *Evangelical Theology: A Biblical and Systematic Introduction.* Grand Rapids: Zondervan, 2013.

Bishop, Robert. "God and Methodological Naturalism in the Scientific Revolution and Beyond." *Perspectives on Science and Christian Faith* 65, no. 1 (March 2013): 10–23.

Blocher, Henri. "Atonement." In *Dictionary for Theological Interpretation of the Bible*, edited by Kevin J. Vanhoozer, 72–76. Grand Rapids: Baker Academic, 2005.

———. "Everlasting Punishment and the Problem of Evil." In *Universalism and the Doctrine of Hell*, edited by Nigel M. de S. Cameron, 281–312. Grand Rapids: Baker, 1992.

———. *In the Beginning: The Opening Chapters of Genesis.* Translated by David G. Preston. Downers Grove, IL: InterVarsity, 1984.

———. *Original Sin: Illuminating the Riddle.* New Studies in Biblical Theology. Grand Rapids: Eerdmans, 1998.

Bloesch, Donald G. *God the Almighty: Power, Wisdom, Holiness, Love.* Christian Foundations 3. Downers Grove, IL: InterVarsity, 1995.

Bockmuehl, Markus. "*Creatio ex nihilo* in Palestinian Judaism and Early Christianity." *Scottish Journal of Theology* 65, no. 3 (2012): 253–70.

Boersma, Hans. *Heavenly Participation: The Weaving of a Sacramental Tapestry.* Grand Rapids: Eerdmans, 2011.

Boethius. "A Treatise against Eutyches and Nestorius." In Boethius, *The Theological Tractates* III.85, translated by H. F. Stewart, E. K. Rand, and S. J. Tester, 72–129. Loeb Classical Library 74. Cambridge, MA: Harvard University Press.

Bonhoeffer, Dietrich. *Discipleship.* Edited by Geffrey B. Kelly and John D. Godsey. Translated by Barbara Green and Reinhard Krauss. Dietrich Bonhoeffer Works in English 4. Minneapolis: Fortress, 2001.

———. *Letters and Papers from Prison.* Edited by John W. de Gruchy. Translated by Isabel Best et al. Dietrich Bonhoeffer Works in English 8. Minneapolis: Fortress, 2009.

———. *Life Together and Prayerbook of the Bible.* Edited by Geffrey B. Kelly. Translated by James H. Burtness. Dietrich Bonhoeffer Works in English 5. Minneapolis: Fortress, 1996.

———. "Natural Life." In Dietrich Bonhoeffer, *Ethics*, edited by Clifford J. Green, translated by Reinhard Krauss, Douglas W. Stott, and Charles C. West, 171–218. Dietrich Bonhoeffer Works in English 6. Minneapolis: Fortress, 2005.

The Book of Confessions. Louisville: Office of the General Assembly, Presbyterian Church (U.S.A.), 1999.

Bouteneff, Peter C. "Oriental Orthodox." In *Encyclopedia of Eastern Orthodox Christianity*, edited by John Anthony McGuckin, 2:427–28. 2 vols. Malden, MA: Wiley-Blackwell, 2011.

Bovell, Carlos R. *Inerrancy and the Spiritual Formation of Younger Evangelicals.* Eugene, OR: Wipf & Stock, 2007.

Boyd, Gregory A. *God at War: The Bible and Spiritual Conflict*. Downers Grove, IL: InterVarsity, 1997.

Brannan, Rick. "Writing a Systematic Theology? You Must Discuss These References." *theLAB* (blog). June 5, 2017. https://academic.logos.com/writing-a-systematic-theology-you-must-discuss-these-references/.

Brown, William P. *The Ethos of the Cosmos: The Genesis of Moral Imagination in the Bible*. Grand Rapids: Eerdmans, 1999.

Bruce, F. F. *The Canon of Scripture*. Downers Grove, IL: InterVarsity, 1988.

Buckley, Michael J. *At the Origins of Modern Atheism*. New Haven: Yale University Press, 1987.

Burgess, Stanley M., and Eduard M. van der Maas, eds. *The New International Dictionary of Pentecostal and Charismatic Movements*. Rev. ed. Grand Rapids: Zondervan, 2002.

Buschart, W. David. *Exploring Protestant Traditions: An Invitation to Theological Hospitality*. Downers Grove, IL: IVP Academic, 2006.

Bynum, Caroline Walker. *The Resurrection of the Body in Western Christianity, 200–1336*. New York: Columbia University Press, 1995.

Callahan, James. *The Clarity of Scripture: History, Theology and Contemporary Literary Studies*. Downers Grove, IL: InterVarsity, 2001.

Calvin, John. *Commentaries on the Epistle of James*. Calvin's Commentaries 22. Reprint, Grand Rapids: Baker, 1993.

———. *Institutes of Christian Religion*. Edited by John T. McNeill. Translated by Ford Lewis Battles. 2 vols. Library of Christian Classics. Philadelphia: Westminster, 1960.

Cameron, Nigel M. de S. "Revelation, Idea of." In *Evangelical Dictionary of Biblical Theology*, edited by Walter A. Elwell, 679–82. Grand Rapids: Baker, 1996.

Campbell, Douglas A. *The Deliverance of God: An Apocalyptic Rereading of Justification in Paul*. Grand Rapids: Eerdmans, 2009.

The Cape Town Commitment: A Confession of Faith and a Call to Action. Third Lausanne Congress. Didasko, 2011.

Carroll R., M. Daniel. *Christians at the Border: Immigration, the Church, and the Bible*. 2nd ed. Grand Rapids: Brazos, 2013.

Carson, D. A. *Christ and Culture Revisited*. Grand Rapids: Eerdmans, 2008.

———. "Domesticating the Gospel: A Review of Grenz's *Renewing the Center*." In *Reclaiming the Center: Confronting Evangelical Accommodation in Postmodern Times*, edited by Millard J. Erickson, Paul Kjoss Helseth, and Justin Taylor, 33–55. Wheaton: Crossway, 2004.

———, ed. *The Enduring Authority of the Christian Scriptures*. Grand Rapids: Eerdmans, 2016.

———. "God's Love and God's Sovereignty." *Bibliotheca Sacra* 156 (July/September 1999): 259–71.

———. "God's Love and God's Wrath." In *The Difficult Doctrine of the Love of God*, 65–84. Wheaton: Crossway, 2000.

———. "Reflections on Christian Assurance." *Westminster Theological Journal* 54 (1992): 1–29.

———. "Unity and Diversity in the New Testament: The Possibility of Systematic Theology." In *Scripture and Truth*, edited by D. A. Carson and John D. Woodbridge, 65–95. Grand Rapids: Baker, 1992.

———. "The Vindication of Imputation: On Fields of Discourse and Semantic Fields." In *Justification: What's at Stake in the Current Debates*, edited by Mark Husbands and Daniel J. Treier, 46–78. Downers Grove, IL: IVP Academic, 2004.

———. "The Wrath of God." In *Engaging the Doctrine of God: Contemporary Protestant Perspectives*, edited by Bruce L. McCormack, 37–63. Grand Rapids: Baker Academic, 2008.

Carter, Craig A. *Rethinking Christ and Culture: A Post-Christendom Perspective.* Grand Rapids: Brazos, 2006.

Carter, J. Kameron. *Race: A Theological Account.* New York: Oxford University Press, 2008.

Cary, Phillip. "Why Luther Is Not Quite Protestant: The Logic of Faith in a Sacramental Promise." *Pro Ecclesia* 14, no. 4 (Fall 2005): 447–86.

Catechism of the Catholic Church. 2nd ed. Washington, DC: United States Catholic Conference, 1997.

Chan, Simon. *Grassroots Asian Theology: Thinking the Faith from the Ground Up.* Downers Grove, IL: IVP Academic, 2014.

Chappell, P. G. "Heal, Healing." In *Evangelical Dictionary of Theology*, edited by Daniel J. Treier and Walter A. Elwell, 368–69. 3rd ed. Grand Rapids: Baker Academic, 2017.

Charry, Ellen T. *By the Renewing of Your Minds: The Pastoral Function of Christian Doctrine.* Oxford: Oxford University Press, 1997.

Clapp, Rodney R. *Families at the Crossroads: Beyond Traditional and Modern Options.* Downers Grove, IL: InterVarsity, 1993.

Clendenin, Daniel B. *Eastern Orthodox Christianity: A Western Perspective.* 2nd ed. Grand Rapids: Baker Academic, 2003.

Coakley, Sarah. *God, Sexuality, and the Self: An Essay "On the Trinity."* Cambridge: Cambridge University Press, 2013.

———. "*Kenōsis* and Subversion: On the Repression of 'Vulnerability' in Christian Feminist Writing." In *Powers and Submissions: Spirituality, Philosophy and Gender*, 3–39. Challenges in Contemporary Theology. Oxford: Blackwell, 2002.

———. "What Does Chalcedon Solve and What Does It Not? Some Reflections on the Status and Meaning of the Chalcedonian 'Definition.'" In *The Incarnation*, edited by Stephen T. Davis, Daniel Kendall, and Gerald O'Collins, 143–63. Oxford: Oxford University Press, 2004.

Cobb, John B., and Clark H. Pinnock, eds. *Searching for an Adequate God: A Dialogue between Process and Free Will Theists.* Grand Rapids: Eerdmans, 2000.

Collins, C. John. *The God of Miracles: An Exegetical Examination of God's Action in the World.* Wheaton: Crossway, 2000.

Cone, James H. *The Cross and the Lynching Tree.* Maryknoll, NY: Orbis, 2011.

Cooper, John W. *Body, Soul, and Life Everlasting: Biblical Anthropology and the Monism-Dualism Debate.* Rev. ed. Grand Rapids: Eerdmans, 2000.

Cortez, Marc. "Who Invited the Baptist? The 'Sacraments' and Free Church Theology." In *Come, Let Us Eat Together: Sacraments and Christian Unity*, edited by George Kalantzis and Marc Cortez, 200–218. Downers Grove, IL: IVP Academic, 2018.

Crisp, Oliver D. *Divinity and Humanity: The Incarnation Reconsidered.* Current Issues in Theology. Cambridge: Cambridge University Press, 2007.

———. "Original Sin and Atonement." In *The Oxford Handbook of Philosophical Theology*, edited by Thomas P. Flint and Michael C. Rea, 430–51. Oxford: Oxford University Press, 2009.

Crouse, Robert C. *Two Kingdoms and Two Cities: Mapping Theological Traditions of Church, Culture, and Civil Order.* Emerging Scholars. Minneapolis: Fortress, 2017.

Cullmann, Oscar. *Christ and Time: The Primitive Christian Conception of Time and History.* Translated by Floyd V. Filson. London: SCM, 1951.

Cunningham, David S. *These Three Are One: The Practice of Trinitarian Theology.* Challenges in Contemporary Theology. Oxford: Blackwell, 1998.

Cyprian. "Epistle LXXII: To Jubaianus, Concerning the Baptism of Heretics." *The Epistles of Cyprian.* Translated by Ernest Wallis. In *The Ante-Nicene Fathers*, edited by Alexander Roberts and James Donaldson, 5:379–86. 1885–87.

Reprint, Peabody, MA: Hendrickson, 1994.

Dalton, W. J. *Christ's Proclamation to the Spirits: A Study of 1 Peter 3:18–4:6*. 2nd rev. ed. Analecta Biblica 23. Rome: Editrice Pontifico Istituto Biblico, 1989.

Davies, Oliver. *A Theology of Compassion: Metaphysics of Difference and the Renewal of Tradition*. Grand Rapids: Eerdmans, 2003.

Dawn, Marva J. *Powers, Weakness, and the Tabernacling of God*. Grand Rapids: Eerdmans, 2001.

———. "Powers and Principalities." In *Dictionary for Theological Interpretation of the Bible*, edited by Kevin J. Vanhoozer, 609–12. Grand Rapids: Baker Academic, 2005.

"The Definition of Chalcedon (451)." In *Creeds of the Churches: A Reader in Christian Doctrine from the Bible to the Present*, edited by John H. Leith, 34–36. 3rd ed. Louisville: John Knox, 1982.

Demarest, Bruce A. *The Cross and Salvation*. Foundations of Evangelical Theology. Wheaton: Crossway, 1997.

Dembski, William A. *Intelligent Design: The Bridge between Science and Theology*. Downers Grove, IL: IVP Academic, 1999.

Dempster, Stephen G. "The Old Testament Canon, Josephus, and Cognitive Environment." In *The Enduring Authority of the Christian Scriptures*, edited by D. A. Carson, 321–61. Grand Rapids: Eerdmans, 2016.

DeYoung, Curtiss Paul, Michael O. Emerson, George Yancey, and Karen Chai Kim. *United by Faith: The Multiracial Congregation as an Answer to the Problem of Race*. New York: Oxford University Press, 2004.

DeYoung, Rebecca Konyndyk. *Glittering Vices: A New Look at the Seven Deadly Sins and Their Remedies*. Grand Rapids: Brazos, 2009.

Didache [*The Teaching of the Twelve Apostles*]. Translated by Isaac H. Hall and John T. Napier. In *The Ante-Nicene Fathers*, edited by Alexander Roberts and James Donaldson, 7:369–84. 1885–87. Reprint, Peabody, MA: Hendrickson, 1994.

Duby, Steven J. *Divine Simplicity: A Dogmatic Account*. Studies in Systematic Theology. New York: Bloomsbury T&T Clark, 2015.

Dulles, Avery. *Models of Revelation*. 2nd ed. Maryknoll, NY: Orbis, 1992.

———. *Models of the Church*. New York: Doubleday, 1983.

Dunbar, David G. "The Biblical Canon." In *Hermeneutics, Authority, and Canon*, edited by D. A. Carson and John D. Woodbridge, 295–360. Grand Rapids: Baker, 1995.

Dunn, James D. G. *Baptism in the Holy Spirit*. London: SCM, 1970.

Edwards, Jonathan. "A Treatise Concerning Religious Affections." In *A Jonathan Edwards Reader*, edited by John E. Smith, Harry S. Stout, and Kenneth P. Minkema, 137–71. New Haven: Yale University Press, 1995.

Emerson, Michael O., and Christian Smith. *Divided by Faith: Evangelical Religion and the Problem of Race in America*. New York: Oxford University Press, 2001.

Emery, Gilles. *The Trinity: An Introduction to Catholic Doctrine on the Triune God*. Translated by Matthew Levering. Washington, DC: Catholic University of America Press, 2011.

Endres, J. B. "Appropriation." In *New Catholic Encyclopedia*, 1:606. 2nd ed. 15 vols. Washington, DC: Catholic University of America; Detroit: Thomson/Gale, 2003.

Enns, Peter. *The Evolution of Adam: What the Bible Does and Doesn't Say about Human Origins*. Grand Rapids: Brazos, 2012.

Evagrius Ponticus. *Treatise on Prayer*. In *Evagrius of Pontus: The Greek Ascetic Corpus*. Translated by Robert E. Sinkewicz. Oxford Early Christian Studies. Oxford: Oxford University Press, 2003.

Evangelicals and Catholics Together. "The Gift of Salvation." *Christianity Today* 41, no. 14 (December 8, 1997): 35–38.

Evans, C. A. "Jesus' Self-Designation 'The Son of Man' and the Recognition of His Divinity." In *The Trinity: An Interdisciplinary Symposium on the Trinity*, edited by Stephen T. Davis, Daniel Kendall, and Gerald O'Collins, 29–47. Oxford: Oxford University Press, 1999.

Evans, C. A., and Emanuel Tov, eds. *Exploring the Origins of the Bible: Canon Formation in Historical, Literary, and Theological Perspective*. Acadia Studies in Bible and Theology. Grand Rapids: Baker Academic, 2008.

Evans, C. Stephen, ed. *Exploring Kenotic Christology: The Self-Emptying of God*. New York: Oxford University Press, 2006.

Fackre, Gabriel. "Claiming Jesus as Savior in a Religiously Plural World." *Journal for Christian Theological Research* 8 (2003): 1–17.

———. *The Doctrine of Revelation: A Narrative Interpretation*. Grand Rapids: Eerdmans, 1997.

Farley, Edward, and Peter C. Hodgson. "Scripture and Tradition." In *Christian Theology: An Introduction to Its Traditions and Tasks*, edited by Peter C. Hodgson and Robert H. King, 61–87. Rev. ed. Minneapolis: Fortress, 1994.

Faro, Ingrid. "The Question of Evil and Animal Death Before the Fall." *Trinity Journal* 36, no. 2 (September 2015): 193–213.

Farrow, Douglas. *Ascension and Ecclesia: On the Significance of the Doctrine of the Ascension for Ecclesiology and Christian Cosmology*. Grand Rapids: Eerdmans, 1999.

Fee, Gordon D. *God's Empowering Presence: The Holy Spirit in the Letters of Paul*. Peabody, MA: Hendrickson, 1994.

———. "Reflections on Church Order in the Pastoral Epistles, with Further Reflection on the Hermeneutics of *Ad Hoc* Documents." *Journal of the Evangelical Theological Society* 28, no. 2 (June 1985): 141–51.

Feenstra, Ronald J., and Cornelius Plantinga, Jr., eds. *Trinity, Incarnation, and Atonement: Philosophical and Theological Essays*. Notre Dame, IN: University of Notre Dame Press, 1990.

Feinberg, John S. "Evil, Problem of." In *Evangelical Dictionary of Theology*, edited by Daniel J. Treier and Walter A. Elwell, 294–95. 3rd ed. Grand Rapids: Baker Academic, 2017.

———. *No One Like Him: The Doctrine of God*. Foundations of Evangelical Theology. Wheaton: Crossway, 2001.

Feinberg, Paul D. "Bible, Inerrancy and Infallibility of." In *Evangelical Dictionary of Theology*, edited by Daniel J. Treier and Walter A. Elwell, 124–27. 3rd ed. Grand Rapids: Baker Academic, 2017.

Felder, Cain Hope, ed. *Stony the Road We Trod: African American Biblical Interpretation*. Minneapolis: Fortress, 1991.

Finney, Charles G. "Lectures on Revivals of Religion (1835)." In *The New England Theology: From Jonathan Edwards to Edwards Amasa Park*, edited by Douglas A. Sweeney and Allen C. Guelzo, 227–36. Grand Rapids: Baker Academic, 2006.

Ford, David F. *Self and Salvation: Being Transformed*. Cambridge Studies in Christian Doctrine. Cambridge: Cambridge University Press, 1999.

———. *The Shape of Living: Spiritual Directions for Everyday Life*. Grand Rapids: Baker, 1997.

Friesen, Garry, with J. Robin Maxson. *Decision Making and the Will of God: A Biblical Alternative to the Traditional View*. Critical Concern. Portland, OR: Multnomah, 1980.

Gagnon, Robert A. J. *The Bible and Homosexual Practice: Texts and Hermeneutics*. Nashville: Abingdon, 2002.

Galli, Mark. "The Great Divorce." *Christian History* 16, no. 2 (May 1997): 10–18.

Ganssle, Gregory, ed. *God and Time: Four Views*. Downers Grove, IL: IVP Academic, 2001.

Gathercole, Simon. *Defending Substitution: An Essay on Atonement in Paul*. Grand Rapids: Baker Academic, 2015.

Gentry, Peter J., and Stephen J. Wellum. *Kingdom through Covenant: A Biblical-Theological Understanding of the Covenants*. Wheaton: Crossway, 2012.

George, Timothy, ed. *God the Holy Trinity: Reflections on Christian Faith and Practice*. Grand Rapids: Baker Academic, 2006.

Gerrish, B. A. *Christian Faith: Dogmatics in Outline*. Louisville: Westminster John Knox, 2015.

Giberson, Karl W. *Saving the Original Sinner: How Christians Have Used the Bible's First Man to Oppress, Inspire, and Make Sense of the World*. New York: Beacon, 2015.

Girard, René. *I See Satan Fall Like Lightning*. Translated by James G. Williams. Maryknoll, NY: Orbis, 2001.

Goetz, Ronald. "The Suffering God: The Rise of a New Orthodoxy." *Christian Century* 103 (April 16, 1986): 385–89.

Goldingay, John. *Models for Interpretation of Scripture*. Grand Rapids: Eerdmans, 1995.

———. *Models for Scripture*. Grand Rapids: Eerdmans, 1994.

Goldstein, Valerie Saiving. "The Human Situation: A Feminine View." *Journal of Religion* 40, no. 2 (April 1960): 100–112.

González, Antonio. *The Gospel of Faith and Justice*. Translated by Joseph Owens. Maryknoll, NY: Orbis, 2005.

Green, Joel B. "Monism and the Nature of Humans in Scripture." *Christian Scholar's Review* 29, no. 4 (Summer 2000): 731–43.

Greenman, Jeffrey P., Timothy Larsen, and Stephen R. Spencer, eds. *The Sermon on the Mount through the Centuries: From the Early Church to John Paul II*. Grand Rapids: Brazos, 2007.

Gregory, Brad S. *The Unintended Reformation: How a Religious Revolution Secularized Society*. Cambridge, MA: Belknap, 2012.

Gregory of Nyssa. "On Not Three Gods." Translated by H. A. Wilson. In *The Nicene and Post-Nicene Fathers*, Series 2, edited by Philip Schaff and Henry Wace, 5:331–36. 1890–1900. Reprint, Peabody, MA: Hendrickson, 1994.

Grenz, Stanley J. "Evangelical Theological Method after the Demise of Foundationalism." In *Renewing the Center: Evangelical Theology in a Post-theological Era*, 192–225. 2nd ed. Grand Rapids: Baker Academic, 2006.

———. *Rediscovering the Triune God: The Trinity in Contemporary Theology*. Minneapolis: Augsburg Fortress, 2004.

———. *The Social God and the Relational Self: A Trinitarian Theology of the Imago Dei*. The Matrix of Christian Theology 1. Louisville: Westminster John Knox, 2001.

Griffiths, Paul J. *Decreation: The Last Things of All Creatures*. Waco: Baylor University Press, 2014.

———. *Lying: An Augustinian Theology of Duplicity*. Grand Rapids: Brazos, 2004.

Griffiths, Sidney H. *The Church in the Shadow of the Mosque: Christians and Muslims in the World of Islam*. Princeton: Princeton University Press, 2010.

Grillmeier, Aloys. *From the Apostolic Age to Chalcedon (451)*. Translated by John Bowden. Vol. 1 of *Christ in Christian Tradition*. Louisville: Westminster John Knox, 1975.

Grudem, Wayne A. *The Gift of Prophecy in the New Testament and Today*. Westchester, IL: Crossway, 1988.

Guder, Darrell L. *The Continuing Conversion of the Church*. Grand Rapids: Eerdmans, 2000.

———, ed. *Missional Church: A Vision for the Sending of the Church in North America*. Grand Rapids: Eerdmans, 1998.

Gundry, Robert H. "Grace, Works, and Staying Saved in Paul." *Biblica* 66, no. 1 (1985): 1–38.

———. "The Nonimputation of Christ's Righteousness." In *Justification: What's at Stake in the Current Debates*, edited by Mark Husbands and Daniel J. Treier, 17–45. Downers Grove, IL: IVP Academic, 2004.

Gundry, Stanley N., ed. *Five Views on Sanctification*. Counterpoints. Grand Rapids: Zondervan, 1996.

Gunton, Colin E. *Act and Being: Towards a Theology of the Divine Attributes*. Grand Rapids: Eerdmans, 2002.

———. "And in One Lord, Jesus Christ . . . Begotten, Not Made." In *Nicene Christianity: The Future for a New Ecumenism*, edited by Christopher R. Seitz, 35–48. Grand Rapids: Brazos, 2001.

———. *Christ and Creation: The Didsbury Lectures, 1990*. Reprint, Eugene, OR: Wipf & Stock, 2005.

———. "Indispensable Opponent: The Relations of Systematic Theology and Philosophy of Religion." *Neue Zeitschrift für Systematische Theologie und Religionsphilosophie* 38, no. 3 (1996): 298–306.

———. *The One, The Three, and the Many: God, Creation, and the Culture of Modernity*. Cambridge: Cambridge University Press, 1993.

———. "A Rose by Any Other Name? From 'Christian Doctrine' to 'Systematic Theology.'" *International Journal of Systematic Theology* 1, no. 1 (March 1999): 4–23.

———. *The Triune Creator: A Historical and Systematic Study*. Edinburgh Studies in Constructive Theology. Grand Rapids: Eerdmans, 1998.

Haarsma, Deborah B., and Loren D. Haarsma. *Origins: Christian Perspectives on Creation, Evolution, and Intelligent Design*. 2nd ed. Grand Rapids: Faith Alive, 2011.

Hafemann, Scott J. *The God of Promise and the Life of Faith: Understanding the Heart of the Bible*. Wheaton: Crossway, 2001.

Hall, Amy Laura. *Conceiving Parenthood: American Protestantism and the Spirit of Reproduction*. Grand Rapids: Eerdmans, 2007.

Hall, Christopher, and Roger Olson. *The Trinity*. Guides to Theology. Grand Rapids: Eerdmans, 2002.

Hamilton, Victor P. *The Book of Genesis Chapters 1–17*. New International Commentary on the Old Testament. Grand Rapids: Eerdmans, 1990.

Harmon, Kendall S. "The Case against Conditionalism: A Response to Edward William Fudge." In *Universalism and the Doctrine of Hell*, edited by Nigel M. de S. Cameron, 93–224. Grand Rapids: Baker, 1992.

Harper, Brad, and Paul Louis Metzger. *Exploring Ecclesiology: An Evangelical and Ecumenical Introduction*. Grand Rapids: Baker Academic, 2009.

Harper, Kyle. *From Shame to Sin: The Christian Transformation of Sexual Morality in Late Antiquity*. Cambridge, MA: Harvard University Press, 2013.

Harris, Paula, and Doug Schaupp. *Being White: Finding Our Place in a MultiEthnic World*. Downers Grove, IL: InterVarsity, 2004.

Hauerwas, Stanley, and William H. Willimon. *Resident Aliens: Life in the Christian Colony*. Nashville: Abingdon, 1989.

———. *Where Resident Aliens Live: Exercises for Christian Practice*. Nashville: Abingdon, 1996.

Healy, Nicholas M. *Church, World and the Christian Life*. Cambridge Studies in Christian Doctrine. Cambridge: Cambridge University Press, 2000.

Helm, Paul. "Are They Few That Be Saved?" In *Universalism and the Doctrine of Hell*, edited by Nigel M. de S. Cameron, 255–81. Grand Rapids: Baker, 1992.

Henry, Carl F. H. "The Evaporation of Fundamentalist Humanitarianism." In *The Uneasy Conscience of Modern*

Fundamentalism, 16–23. Grand Rapids: Eerdmans, 1947.

———. *God Who Speaks and Shows: Fifteen Theses, Part Two*. Vol. 3 of *God, Revelation, and Authority*. Waco: Word, 1979.

———. "The Method and Criteria of Theology (II): The Role of Reason, Scripture, Consistency and Coherence." In *God Who Speaks and Shows: Preliminary Considerations*, 225–44. Vol. 1 of *God, Revelation, and Authority*. Waco: Word, 1976.

Heschel, Abraham J. *The Prophets: An Introduction*. Vol. 1. New York: Harper, 1962.

Hexham, Irving. "Jehovah's Witnesses." In *Evangelical Dictionary of Theology*, edited by Daniel J. Treier and Walter A. Elwell, 438–39. 3rd ed. Grand Rapids: Baker Academic, 2017.

———. "Mormonism." In *Evangelical Dictionary of Theology*, edited by Daniel J. Treier and Walter A. Elwell, 563–64. 3rd ed. Grand Rapids: Baker Academic, 2017.

Hiebert, Paul G. "The Flaw of the Excluded Middle." *Missiology* 10, no. 1 (January 1982): 35–47.

Hill, Wesley. *Spiritual Friendship: Finding Love in the Church as a Celibate Gay Christian*. Grand Rapids: Brazos, 2015.

———. *Washed and Waiting: Reflections on Christian Faithfulness and Homosexuality*. 2nd ed. Grand Rapids: Zondervan, 2016.

Hoang, Bethany Hanke, and Kristen Deede Johnson. *The Justice Calling: Where Passion Meets Perseverance*. Grand Rapids: Brazos, 2016.

Hoch, Carl B., Jr. *All Things New: The Significance of Newness for Biblical Theology*. Grand Rapids: Baker, 1995.

Hoekema, Anthony A. "Amillennialism." In *The Meaning of the Millennium: Four Views*, edited by Robert G. Clouse, 155–87. Downers Grove, IL: InterVarsity, 1977.

Hoffmeier, James K. *The Immigration Crisis: Immigrants, Aliens, and the Bible*. Wheaton: Crossway, 2009.

Hoglund, Jonathan. *Called by Triune Grace: Divine Rhetoric and the Effectual Call*. Studies in Christian Doctrine and Scripture. Downers Grove, IL: IVP Academic, 2016.

Holmes, Christopher R. J. *The Holy Spirit*. New Studies in Dogmatics. Grand Rapids: Zondervan, 2015.

———. *The Lord Is Good: Seeking the God of the Psalter*. Studies in Christian Doctrine and Scripture. Downers Grove, IL: IVP Academic, 2018.

Holmes, Stephen R. "Of a Troublesome Comma in the Creed." *Shored Fragments* (blog). September 28, 2012. https://shoredfragments.wordpress.com/2012/09/28/of-a-troublesome-comma-in-the-creed/.

———. *The Quest for the Trinity: The Doctrine of God in Scripture, History and Modernity*. Downers Grove, IL: IVP Academic, 2012.

Holwerda, David E. *Jesus and Israel: One Covenant or Two?* Grand Rapids: Eerdmans, 1995.

Horan, Daniel P. *Postmodernity and Univocity: A Critical Account of Radical Orthodoxy and John Duns Scotus*. Minneapolis: Fortress, 2014.

Horton, Michael S. *Lord and Servant: A Covenant Christology*. Louisville: Westminster John Knox, 2005.

Hovey, Craig. *To Share in the Body: A Theology of Martyrdom for Today's Church*. Grand Rapids: Brazos, 2008.

Hughes, D. A. "Animism." In *New Dictionary of Theology: Historical and Systematic*, edited by Martin Davie, Tim Grass, Stephen R. Holmes, John McDowell, and T. A. Noble, 34. 2nd ed. London: InterVarsity, 2016.

Hultberg, Alan, Craig A. Blaising, and Douglas J. Moo. *Three Views on the Rapture: Pretribulation, Prewrath, or Posttribulation*. Counterpoints. Grand Rapids: Zondervan, 2010.

Humphrey, Edith M. "Called to Be One: Worshipping the Triune God Together." In *Grace and Truth in the Secular Age*, edited by Timothy Bradshaw, 219–34. Grand Rapids: Eerdmans, 1998.

———. "The Gift of the Father: Looking at Salvation History Upside Down." In *Trinitarian Theology for the Church: Scripture, Community, Worship*, edited by Daniel J. Treier and David Lauber, 79–102. Downers Grove, IL: IVP Academic, 2009.

Hunsinger, George. "Hellfire and Damnation: Four Ancient and Modern Views." In *Disruptive Grace: Studies in the Theology of Karl Barth*, 226–49. Grand Rapids: Eerdmans, 2000.

———. "Karl Barth's Christology: Its Basic Chalcedonian Character." In *Disruptive Grace: Studies in the Theology of Karl Barth*, 131–47. Grand Rapids: Eerdmans, 2000.

Hurtado, Larry W. *Lord Jesus Christ: Devotion to Jesus in Earliest Christianity*. Grand Rapids: Eerdmans, 2003.

Husbands, Mark, and Timothy Larsen, eds. *Women, Ministry and the Gospel: Exploring New Paradigms*. Downers Grove, IL: IVP Academic, 2007.

Husbands, Mark, and Daniel J. Treier, eds. *The Community of the Word: Toward an Evangelical Ecclesiology*. Downers Grove, IL: IVP Academic, 2005.

Icenogle, Gareth Weldon. *Biblical Foundations for Small Group Ministry: An Integrational Approach*. Downers Grove, IL: InterVarsity, 1994.

Irenaeus. *Against Heresies*. Translated by Alexander Roberts and W. H. Rambaut. In *The Ante-Nicene Fathers*, edited by Alexander Roberts and James Donaldson, 1:309–567. 1885–87. Reprint, Peabody, MA: Hendrickson, 1994.

Jacobs, Alan. *Original Sin: A Cultural History*. San Francisco: HarperOne, 2008.

Jaeger, Lydia. *What the Heavens Declare: Science in the Light of Creation*. Translated by Jonathan Vaughan. Eugene, OR: Cascade, 2012.

Jeffrey, David Lyle. "(Pre) Figuration: Masterplot and Meaning in Biblical History." In *"Behind" the Text: History and Biblical Interpretation*, edited by Craig Bartholomew, C. Stephen Evans, Mary Healy, and Murray Rae, 363–92. Scripture and Hermeneutics 4. Grand Rapids: Zondervan, 2003.

Jennings, Willie James. *The Christian Imagination: Theology and the Origins of Race*. New Haven: Yale University Press, 2011.

Jenson, Matt. *The Gravity of Sin: Augustine, Luther and Barth on "homo incurvatus in se."* New York: T&T Clark International, 2007.

Johnson, Alan F., and Dallas Willard, eds. *How I Changed My Mind about Women in Leadership: Compelling Stories from Prominent Evangelicals*. Grand Rapids: Zondervan, 2010.

Jones, Beth Felker. *Faithful: A Theology of Sex*. Ordinary Theology. Grand Rapids: Zondervan, 2015.

———. *Marks of His Wounds: Gender Politics and Bodily Resurrection*. New York: Oxford University Press, 2007.

———. *Practicing Christian Doctrine: An Introduction to Thinking and Living Theologically*. Grand Rapids: Baker Academic, 2014.

Jones, L. Gregory. *Embodying Forgiveness: A Theological Analysis*. Grand Rapids: Eerdmans, 1995.

Jüngel, Eberhard. "On the Doctrine of Justification." Translated by John Webster. *International Journal of Systematic Theology* 1, no. 1 (1999): 24–52.

Kalantzis, George. *Caesar and the Lamb: Early Christian Attitudes on War and Military Service*. Eugene, OR: Wipf & Stock, 2012.

Kapic, Kelly. "The Son's Assumption of a Human Nature: A Call for Clarity." *International Journal of Systematic Theology* 3 (2001): 154–66.

Kapuściński, Ryszard. *The Shadow of the Sun*. Translated by Klara Glowczewska. New York: Vintage International, 2001.

Kärkkäinen, Veli-Matti. *A Constructive Christian Theology for the Pluralistic World*. 5 vols. Grand Rapids: Eerdmans, 2013–17.

———. *The Doctrine of God: A Global Introduction*. Grand Rapids: Baker Academic, 2004.

———. *Pneumatology: The Holy Spirit in Ecumenical, International, and Contextual Perspective*. Grand Rapids: Baker Academic, 2002.

Kelsey, David H. *To Understand God Truly: What's Theological about a Theological School*. Louisville: Westminster John Knox, 1992.

Kevan, E. F. "Baptist Tradition, The." In *Evangelical Dictionary of Theology*, edited by Daniel J. Treier and Walter A. Elwell, 114–15. 3rd ed. Grand Rapids: Baker Academic, 2017.

Kik, J. Marcellus. *The Eschatology of Victory*. Nutley, NJ: Presbyterian & Reformed, 1971.

Kilby, Karen. "Perichoresis and Projection: Problems with Social Doctrines of the Trinity." *New Blackfriars* 81 (2000): 432–45.

Kimel, Alvin F., Jr., ed. *Speaking the Christian God: The Holy Trinity and the Challenge of Feminism*. Grand Rapids: Eerdmans, 1992.

Klein, William W. *The New Chosen People: A Corporate View of Election*. Grand Rapids: Zondervan, 1990.

Köstenberger, Andreas J., and Thomas R. Schreiner, eds. *Women in the Church: An Interpretation and Application of 1 Timothy 2:9–15*. 3rd ed. Wheaton: Crossway, 2016.

Kostlevy, William, ed. *Historical Dictionary of the Holiness Movement*. 2nd ed. Lanham, MD: Scarecrow, 2009.

Kreider, Alan. *The Change of Conversion and the Origin of Christendom*. Christian Mission and Modern Culture. Harrisburg, PA: Trinity Press International, 1999.

Laansma, J. C. "Lord's Day." In *Dictionary of the Later New Testament and Its*

Developments, edited by Ralph Martin and Peter H. Davids, 679–86. Downers Grove, IL: InterVarsity, 1997.

———. "Rest (Work)." In *New Dictionary of Biblical Theology*, edited by T. Desmond Alexander and Brian Rosner, 727–32. Downers Grove, IL: InterVarsity, 2000.

Laing, John D. "The Compatibility of Calvinism and Middle Knowledge." *Journal of the Evangelical Theological Society* 47, no. 3 (September 2004): 455–67.

Lane, Anthony N. S. "Scripture, Tradition and Church: An Historical Survey." *Vox Evangelica* 9 (1975): 37–55.

Langford, Thomas A. *Practical Divinity: Theology in the Wesleyan Tradition*. Rev. ed. Nashville: Abingdon, 1998.

Larsen, Timothy. "Defining and Locating Evangelicalism." In *The Cambridge Companion to Evangelical Theology*, edited by Timothy Larsen and Daniel J. Treier, 1–14. Cambridge: Cambridge University Press, 2007.

Leeman, Jonathan D. *Political Church: The Local Assembly as Embassy of Christ's Rule*. Studies in Christian Doctrine and Scripture. Downers Grove, IL: IVP Academic, 2016.

Leithart, Peter. *Delivered from the Elements of the World: Atonement, Justification, Mission*. Downers Grove, IL: IVP Academic, 2016.

Letham, Robert. *The Holy Trinity: In Scripture, History, Theology and Worship*. Phillipsburg, NJ: P&R, 2005.

Levering, Matthew. *Scripture and Metaphysics: Aquinas and the Renewal of Trinitarian Theology*. Challenges in Contemporary Theology. Oxford: Blackwell, 2004.

Lewis, C. S. *Mere Christianity*. Rev. ed. San Francisco: HarperOne, 2015.

———. *The Problem of Pain*. New York: Macmillan, 1962.

Lincoln, Andrew T. *Born of a Virgin? Reconceiving Jesus in the Bible, Tradition, and Theology*. Grand Rapids: Eerdmans, 2013.

Lindbeck, George A. *The Nature of Doctrine: Religion and Theology in a Postliberal Age.* Louisville: Westminster John Knox, 1984.

Lindsell, Harold. *The Battle for the Bible.* Grand Rapids: Zondervan, 1976.

Long, D. Stephen. *Theology and Culture: A Guide to the Discussion.* Cascade Companions. Eugene, OR: Cascade, 2008.

Long, Kathryn, and Mark Noll. "What Are the Varieties of Classical Protestantism and Why Are They Important for Christian Scholarship?" Unpublished paper.

Lubac, Henri de. *Catholicism: A Study of Dogma in Relation to the Corporate Destiny of Mankind.* Translated by Lancelot C. Sheppard. New York: Longmans, Green, 1950.

Luther, Martin. "The Disputation Concerning Justification." In *Career of the Reformer IV,* edited by Helmut T. Lehmann and Lewis W. Spitz, 176. Vol. 34 of *Luther's Works: American Edition.* Edited by J. Pelikan and H. Lehmann. Philadelphia: Fortress, 1960.

———. "Handbook: The Small Catechism [of Dr. Martin Luther] for Ordinary Pastors and Preachers." In *The Book of Concord: The Confessions of the Evangelical Lutheran Church,* edited by Robert Kolb and Timothy J. Wengert, 347–75. Minneapolis: Fortress, 2000.

———. "Judgment of Martin Luther on Monastic Vows." In *Christian in Society I,* edited by James Atkinson, 298. Vol. 44 of *Luther's Works: American Edition.* Edited by J. Pelikan and H. Lehmann. Philadelphia: Fortress, 1966.

———. "The Large Catechism." In *The Book of Concord: The Confessions of the Evangelical Lutheran Church,* edited by Robert Kolb and Timothy J. Wengert, 379–480. Minneapolis: Fortress, 2000.

———. "Preface to the Epistles of St. James and St. Jude." In *Word and Sacrament I,* edited by E. Theodore Bachmann, 395–98. Vol. 35 of *Luther's Works: American Edition.* Edited by J. Pelikan and H. Lehmann. Philadelphia: Fortress, 1960.

———. "Preface to the New Testament." In *Word and Sacrament I,* edited by E. Theodore Bachmann, 357–62. Vol. 35 of *Luther's Works: American Edition.* Edited by J. Pelikan and H. Lehmann. Philadelphia: Fortress, 1960.

———. "The Smalcald Articles." In *The Book of Concord: The Confessions of the Evangelical Lutheran Church,* edited by Robert Kolb and Timothy J. Wengert, 297–328. Minneapolis: Fortress, 2000.

———. "Theses Concerning Faith and Law." In *Career of the Reformer IV,* edited by Helmut T. Lehmann and Lewis W. Spitz, 124. Vol. 34 of *Luther's Works: American Edition.* Edited by J. Pelikan and H. Lehmann. Philadelphia: Fortress, 1960.

The Lutheran World Federation and the Roman Catholic Church. *Joint Declaration on the Doctrine of Justification.* Grand Rapids: Eerdmans, 2000.

MacDonald, Lee M., and James A. Sanders, eds. *The Canon Debate.* Peabody, MA: Hendrickson, 2001.

MacIntyre, Alasdair. *After Virtue: A Study in Moral Theory.* 2nd ed. Notre Dame, IN: Notre Dame University Press, 1984.

Macleod, Donald. *The Person of Christ.* Contours of Christian Theology. Downers Grove, IL: IVP Academic, 1998.

Madueme, Hans, and Michael Reeves, eds. *Adam, the Fall, and Original Sin: Theological, Biblical, and Scientific Perspectives.* Grand Rapids: Baker Academic, 2014.

Mangum, R. Todd. "Is There a Reformed Way to Get the Benefits of the Atonement to 'Those Who Have Never Heard'?" *Journal of the Evangelical Theological Society* 47, no. 1 (March 2004): 121–36.

Marpeck, Pilgram. "Exposé of the Babylonian Whore." In *The Exposé, A Dialogue, and Marpeck's Response to Caspar Schwenckfeld,* 21–48. Vol. 1 of *Later Writings by Pilgram Marpeck and His Circle.* Translated by Walter Klaassen, Werner Packull, and John Rempel.

Anabaptist Texts in Translation 1. Scottdale, PA: Herald, 1999.

Marshall, Bruce D. "Absorbing the World: Christianity and the Universe of Truths." In *Theology in Dialogue: Essays in Conversation with George Lindbeck*, edited by Bruce D. Marshall, 69–102. Notre Dame, IN: University of Notre Dame Press, 1990.

———. "Are There Angels?" In *Why Are We Here? Everyday Questions and the Christian Life*, edited by Ronald F. Thiemann and William C. Placher, 69–83. London: Bloomsbury T&T Clark, 1998.

———. "Trinity." In *The Blackwell Companion to Modern Theology*, edited by Gareth Jones, 183–203. Oxford: Blackwell, 2004.

———. *Trinity and Truth*. Cambridge Studies in Christian Doctrine. Cambridge: Cambridge University Press, 2000.

Marshall, I. Howard. *Last Supper and Lord's Supper*. Grand Rapids: Eerdmans, 1981.

Martin, Clarice J. "The *Haustafeln* (Household Codes) in African American Biblical Interpretation: 'Free Slaves' and 'Subordinate Women.'" In *Stony the Road We Trod: African American Biblical Interpretation*, edited by Cain Hope Felder, 206–31. Minneapolis: Fortress, 1991.

Master, John R. "The New Covenant." In *Issues in Dispensationalism*, edited by Wesley R. Willis and John R. Master, 93–110. Chicago: Moody, 1994.

McBrien, Richard P. *Catholicism*. 2 vols. Minneapolis: Winston, 1980.

McCabe, Herbert. *God, Christ and Us*. Edited by Brian Davies. London: Continuum, 2005.

McCormack, Bruce L. "The Actuality of God: Karl Barth in Conversation with Open Theism." In *Engaging the Doctrine of God: Contemporary Protestant Perspectives*, edited by Bruce L. McCormack, 185–242. Grand Rapids: Baker Academic, 2008.

———. "The Being of Holy Scripture Is in Becoming: Karl Barth in Conversation with American Evangelical Criticism."

In *Evangelicals and Scripture: Tradition, Authority and Hermeneutics*, edited by Vincent E. Bacote, Laura C. Miguélez, and Dennis L. Okholm, 55–75. Downers Grove, IL: InterVarsity, 2004.

———. "The Only Mediator: The Person and Work of Christ in Evangelical Perspective." In *Renewing the Evangelical Mission*, edited by Richard Lints, 250–69. Grand Rapids: Eerdmans, 2013.

McDermott, Gerald R. "The Emerging Divide in Evangelical Theology." *Journal of the Evangelical Theological Society* 56, no. 2 (2013): 355–77.

McDermott, Gerald R., and Harold A. Netland. *A Trinitarian Theology of Religions: An Evangelical Proposal*. Oxford: Oxford University Press, 2014.

McFadyen, Alastair. *Bound to Sin: Abuse, Holocaust, and the Christian Doctrine of Sin*. Cambridge Studies in Christian Doctrine. Cambridge: Cambridge University Press, 2000.

McFarland, Ian A. *In Adam's Fall: A Meditation on the Christian Doctrine of Original Sin*. Challenges in Contemporary Theology. Malden, MA: Blackwell, 2010.

McGuckin, John Anthony. *Saint Cyril of Alexandria and the Christological Controversy*. Reprint, Crestwood, NY: St. Vladimir's Seminary Press, 2010.

McIntyre, John. *The Shape of Pneumatology: Studies in the Doctrine of the Holy Spirit*. Edinburgh: T&T Clark 1997.

McKim, Donald K. *Theological Turning Points: Major Issues in Christian Thought*. Louisville: Westminster John Knox, 1989.

McMichael, Ralph, ed. *The Vocation of Anglican Theology*. London: SCM, 2014.

Meadors, Gary T. *Decision Making God's Way: A New Model for Knowing God's Will*. Grand Rapids: Baker Books, 2003.

Melanchthon, Philip. *The Loci Communes of Philip Melanchthon*. Translated by Charles Leander Hill. Boston: Meador, 1944.

Merrick, J., and Stephen M. Garrett, eds. *Five Views on Biblical Inerrancy*. Counterpoints. Grand Rapids: Zondervan, 2013.

Metzger, Paul Louis, ed. *Trinitarian Soundings in Systematic Theology*. London: T&T Clark, 2006.

Meyendorff, John. *Byzantine Theology: Historical Trends and Doctrinal Themes*. New York: Fordham University Press, 1974.

Middleton, J. Richard. *The Liberating Image: The* Imago Dei *in Genesis 1*. Grand Rapids: Brazos, 2005.

———. *A New Heaven and a New Earth: Reclaiming Biblical Eschatology*. Grand Rapids: Baker Academic, 2014.

Migliore, Daniel L. *Faith Seeking Understanding: An Introduction to Christian Theology*. Grand Rapids: Eerdmans, 1991.

Milbank, John. *Theology and Social Theory*. Oxford: Blackwell, 1990.

Miller, Paul E. *A Praying Life: Connecting with God in a Distracting World*. Colorado Springs: NavPress, 2009.

Minear, Paul. *Images of the Church in the New Testament*. Philadelphia: Westminster, 1960.

Moberly, R. W. L. *The Bible, Theology, and Faith: A Study of Abraham and Jesus*. Cambridge Studies in Christian Doctrine. Cambridge: Cambridge University Press, 2000.

Moltmann, Jürgen. *The Crucified God: The Cross as the Foundation and Criticism of Christian Theology*. Translated by R. A. Wilson and John Bowden. New York: Harper & Row, 1974.

———. *Theology of Hope: On the Ground and the Implications of a Christian Eschatology*. Translated by James W. Leitch. New York: Harper & Row, 1967.

Moltmann-Wendel, Elisabeth. *The Women around Jesus*. New York: Crossroad, 1993.

Morales, Isaac Augustine. "'With My Body I Thee Worship': New Creation, Beatific Vision, and the Liturgical Consummation of All Things." *Pro Ecclesia* 25, no. 3 (Summer 2016): 337–56.

Moreau, A. Scott. "Flaw of the Excluded Middle." In *Evangelical Dictionary of World Missions*, edited by A. Scott Moreau, 362. Grand Rapids: Baker, 2000.

Morrison, Larry. "The Religious Defense of American Slavery before 1830." *Journal of Religious Thought* 37 (1981): 16–29.

Mosser, Carl. "Deification: A Truly Ecumenical Concept." *Perspectives* (July/August 2015): 8–14.

Mouw, Richard J., and Douglas A. Sweeney. *The Suffering and Victorious Christ: Toward a More Compassionate Christology*. Grand Rapids: Baker Academic, 2013.

Muller, Richard A. *Divine Will and Human Choice: Freedom, Contingency, and Necessity in Early Reformed Thought*. Grand Rapids: Baker Academic, 2017.

Munday, John C., Jr. "Creature Mortality: From Creation or the Fall?" *Journal of the Evangelical Theological Society* 35, no. 1 (March 1992): 51–68.

Murphy, Nancey, Warren S. Brown, and H. Newton Malony, eds. *Whatever Happened to the Soul? Scientific and Theological Portraits of Human Nature*. Minneapolis: Fortress, 1998.

Nassif, Bradley. "Kissers and Smashers." *Christian History* 16, no. 2 (May 1997): 20–23.

Newbigin, Lesslie. *The Gospel in a Pluralist Society*. Grand Rapids: Eerdmans, 1989.

Nicole, Roger. "The Canon of the New Testament." *Journal of the Evangelical Theological Society* 40, no. 2 (June 1997): 199–206.

Niebuhr, H. Richard. *Christ and Culture*. London: Faber & Faber, 1952.

Nikodimos of the Holy Mountain and Makarios of Corinth, comps. *The Philokalia: The Complete Text*. 4 vols. in English. Edited and translated by G. E. H. Palmer, Philip Sherrard, and Kallistos Ware. Boston: Faber & Faber, 1979–95.

Noll, Mark A. *The Civil War as a Theological Crisis*. Chapel Hill: University of North Carolina Press, 2006.

———. "What Is 'Evangelical'?" In *The Oxford Handbook of Evangelical Theology*, edited by Gerald R. McDermott, 19–32. Oxford: Oxford University Press, 2010.

Noll, Mark A., and Bruce Hindmarsh. "Rewriting the History of Evangelicalism." *Books & Culture* 17, no. 2 (March/April 2011): 8.

Nussbaum, Martha. *Upheavals of Thought: The Intelligence of Emotions*. Cambridge: Cambridge University Press, 2003.

Oberman, Heiko A. "Quo Vadis? Tradition from Irenaeus to Humani Generis." *Scottish Journal of Theology* 16, no. 3 (September 1963): 225–55.

O'Donovan, Oliver. *The Desire of the Nations: Rediscovering the Roots of Political Theology*. Cambridge: Cambridge University Press, 1996.

———. *Entering into Rest*. Ethics as Theology 3. Grand Rapids: Eerdmans, 2017.

———. *Finding and Seeking*. Ethics as Theology 2. Grand Rapids: Eerdmans, 2014.

———. *On the Thirty-Nine Articles: Conversations with Tudor Christianity*. 2nd ed. London: SCM, 2011.

———. *Resurrection and Moral Order: An Outline for Evangelical Ethics*. 2nd ed. Grand Rapids: Eerdmans, 1994.

———. *Self, World, and Time*. Ethics as Theology 1. Grand Rapids: Eerdmans, 2013.

———. *The Ways of Judgment: The Bampton Lectures, 2003*. Grand Rapids: Eerdmans, 2005.

O'Donovan, Oliver, and Joan Lockwood O'Donovan, eds. *From Irenaeus to Grotius: A Sourcebook in Christian Political Thought*. Grand Rapids: Eerdmans, 1999.

Okholm, Dennis L., and Timothy R. Phillips, eds. *Four Views on Salvation in a Pluralistic World*. Rev. ed. Counterpoints. Grand Rapids: Zondervan, 2010.

Olson, Roger E. "(Fireworks Alert!) My Response to 'The Emerging Divide in Evangelical Theology' by Gerald McDermott (JETS 56:2 [June, 2013])." *Roger E. Olson* (blog). September 21, 2013. https://www.patheos.com/blogs/rogereolson/2013/09/fireworks-alert-my-response-to-the-emerging-divide-in-evangelical-theology-by-gerald-mcdermott-jets-562-june-2013/.

O'Neill, J. C. "How Early Is the Doctrine of *Creatio ex Nihilo*?" *Journal of Theological Studies* 53, no. 2 (October 2002): 449–65.

Otto, Randall E. "The Use and Abuse of Perichoresis in Recent Theology." *Scottish Journal of Theology* 54 (2001): 366–84.

Packer, J. I. "All Sins Are Not Equal." *Christianity Today* 49, no. 1 (January 2005): 65.

———. "Holiness Movement." In *New Dictionary of Theology*, edited by Sinclair B. Ferguson, David F. Wright, and J. I. Packer, 314–15. Downers Grove, IL: InterVarsity, 1988.

———. *Knowing God*. Downers Grove, IL: InterVarsity, 1973.

Palmer, Phoebe. "The Way of Holiness (1843)." In *Phoebe Palmer: Selected Writings*, edited by Thomas C. Oden, 165–84. Mahwah, NJ: Paulist, 1988.

Paris, Jenell Williams. *The End of Sexual Identity: Why Sex Is Too Important to Define Who We Are*. Downers Grove, IL: InterVarsity, 2011.

Peace, Richard V. *Conversion in the New Testament: Paul and the Twelve*. Grand Rapids: Eerdmans, 1999.

Pelikan, Jaroslav. *Acts*. Brazos Theological Commentary on the Bible. Grand Rapids: Brazos, 2005.

———. *The Emergence of the Catholic Tradition (100–600)*. Vol. 1 of *The Christian Tradition: A History of the Development of Doctrine*. Chicago: University of Chicago Press, 1971.

Perrin, Nicholas. "Gnosticism." In *Dictionary for Theological Interpretation of the Bible*, edited by Kevin J. Vanhoozer, 256–59. Grand Rapids: Baker Academic, 2005.

Peterson, David. *Possessed by God: A New Testament Theology of Sanctification and Holiness*. New Studies in Biblical Theology. Grand Rapids: Eerdmans, 1995.

Peterson, Eugene H. *Answering God: The Psalms as Tools for Prayer*. San Francisco: HarperOne, 1989.

Peterson, Ryan S. *The* Imago Dei *as Human Identity: A Theological Interpretation*. Journal of Theological Interpretation Supplements 14. Winona Lake, IN: Eisenbrauns, 2016.

Pierce, Ronald W., and Rebecca Merrill Groothuis, eds. *Discovering Biblical Equality: Complementarity without Hierarchy*. Downers Grove, IL: IVP Academic, 2005.

Pinnock, Clark H. *A Wideness in God's Mercy: The Finality of Jesus Christ in a World of Religions*. Grand Rapids: Zondervan, 1992.

Pinnock, Clark H., Richard Rice, John Sanders, William Hasker, and David Basinger. *The Openness of God: A Biblical Challenge to the Traditional Understanding of God*. Downers Grove, IL: InterVarsity, 1994.

Piper, John. *Let the Nations Be Glad! The Supremacy of God in Missions*. 3rd ed. Grand Rapids: Baker, 2010.

Piper, John, and Wayne Grudem, eds. *Recovering Biblical Manhood and Womanhood: A Response to Evangelical Feminism*. Wheaton: Crossway, 1991.

Pitre, Brant. *Jesus and the Last Supper*. Grand Rapids: Eerdmans, 2015.

Placher, William C. *The Domestication of Transcendence: How Modern Thinking about God Went Wrong*. Louisville: Westminster John Knox, 1999.

Plantinga, Alvin. *God, Freedom, and Evil*. Grand Rapids: Eerdmans, 1989.

Plantinga, Cornelius, Jr. *Not the Way It's Supposed to Be: A Breviary of Sin*. Grand Rapids: Eerdmans, 1996.

Pohl, Christine D. *Living into Community: Cultivating Practices That Sustain Us*. Grand Rapids: Eerdmans, 2011.

———. *Making Room: Recovering Hospitality as a Christian Tradition*. Grand Rapids: Eerdmans, 1999.

Power, Samantha. *"A Problem from Hell": America and the Age of Genocide*. New York: Basic Books, 2002.

Priest, Robert J., and Alvaro L. Nieves, eds. *This Side of Heaven: Race, Ethnicity, and Christian Faith*. New York: Oxford University Press, 2007.

Qureshi, Nabeel. *Seeking Allah, Finding Jesus: A Devout Muslim Encounters Christianity*. Grand Rapids: Zondervan, 2014.

Radner, Ephraim. *The End of the Church: A Pneumatology of Christian Division in the West*. Grand Rapids: Eerdmans, 1998.

———. *A Time to Keep: Theology, Mortality, and the Shape of a Human Life*. Waco: Baylor University Press, 2016.

Rae, Murray. *Christian Theology: The Basics*. New York: Routledge, 2015.

Rambo, Lewis R. "Ritual." In *Westminster Dictionary of Christian Theology*, edited by Alan Richardson and John Bowden, 509–10. Philadelphia: Westminster, 1983.

Ramm, Bernard. *The Christian View of Science and Scripture*. Grand Rapids: Eerdmans, 1954.

Richard of St. Victor. "Book Three of the Trinity." In *Richard of St. Victor*, translated by Grover A. Zinn, 371–97. Classics of Western Spirituality. Mahwah, NJ: Paulist, 1979.

Richter, Kent. *Religion: A Study in Beauty, Truth, and Goodness*. New York: Oxford University Press, 2017.

Ricoeur, Paul. *Oneself as Another*. Translated by Kathleen Blamey. Chicago: University of Chicago Press, 1992.

Rigby, Cynthia L., ed. *Power, Powerlessness, and the Divine: New Inquiries in Bible and Theology*. Scholars Press Studies in Theological Education. Atlanta: Scholars Press, 1997.

Rollo-Koster, Joëlle. *Avignon and Its Papacy, 1309–1417: Popes, Institutions, and Society*. Lanham, MD: Rowman & Littlefield, 2015.

Rosen, Christine. *Preaching Eugenics: Religious Leaders and the American Eugenics Movement*. New York: Oxford University Press, 2004.

Rowe, C. Kavin. "Biblical Pressure and Trinitarian Hermeneutics." *Pro Ecclesia* 11, no. 3 (Summer 2002): 295–312.

Ryrie, Charles C. *Dispensationalism Today*. Chicago: Moody, 1965.

Sanders, E. P. *Paul and Palestinian Judaism: A Comparison of Patterns of Religion*. Philadelphia: Fortress, 1977.

Sanders, Fred. *The Deep Things of God: How the Trinity Changes Everything*. Wheaton: Crossway, 2010.

———. "Oneness Pentecostalism: An Analysis." *The Scriptorium Daily*. May 3, 2014. http://scriptoriumdaily.com/oneness-pentecostalism-an-analysis/.

———. "The Trinity." In *The Oxford Handbook of Systematic Theology*, edited by John Webster, Kathryn Tanner, and Iain Torrance, 35–53. Oxford: Oxford University Press, 2007.

Sanders, John. *The God Who Risks: A Theology of Providence*. Downers Grove, IL: InterVarsity, 1998.

———. *No Other Name: An Investigation into the Destiny of the Unevangelized*. Grand Rapids: Eerdmans, 1992.

Sarisky, Darren. *Scriptural Interpretation*. Challenges in Contemporary Theology. Malden, MA: Wiley-Blackwell, 2013.

Schleiermacher, F. D. E. *The Christian Faith*. Edited by H. R. Mackintosh and J. S. Stewart. Edinburgh: T&T Clark, 1999. Originally published as *Der christliche Glaube nach den Grundsätzen der evangelischen Kirch im Zusammenhang dargestellt*. 2nd ed. Berlin, 1830.

Schreiner, Susan. *The Theater of His Glory: Nature and the Natural Order in the Thought of John Calvin*. Durham, NC: Labyrinth, 1991.

Sexton, Jason S., ed. *Two Views on the Doctrine of the Trinity*. Counterpoints. Grand Rapids: Zondervan, 2014.

Sharp, Douglas R. *No Partiality: The Idolatry of Race and the New Humanity*. Downers Grove, IL: InterVarsity, 2002.

Sider, Ronald J., ed. *The Early Church on Killing: A Comprehensive Sourcebook on War, Abortion, and Capital Punishment*. Grand Rapids: Baker Academic, 2012.

Smith, Christian. *The Bible Made Impossible: Why Biblicism Is Not a Truly Evangelical Reading of Scripture*. Grand Rapids: Brazos, 2012.

Smith, Christian, with Melinda Lundquist Denton. *Soul Searching: The Religious and Spiritual Lives of American Teenagers*. New York: Oxford University Press, 2005.

Smith, David L. *With Willful Intent: A Biblical Theology of Sin*. Wheaton: Victor, 1994.

Smith, James K. A. *Introducing Radical Orthodoxy: Mapping a Post-secular Theology*. Grand Rapids: Baker Academic, 2004.

Smith, Kay Higuera, Jayachitra Lalitha, and L. Daniel Hawk, eds., *Evangelical Postcolonial Conversations: Global Awakenings in Theology and Praxis*. Downers Grove, IL: IVP Academic, 2014.

Sokolowski, Robert. *The God of Faith and Reason: Foundations of Christian Theology*. Washington, DC: Catholic University of America Press, 1995.

Sonderegger, Katherine. *The Doctrine of God*. Vol. 1 of *Systematic Theology*. Minneapolis: Fortress, 2015.

Song, Robert. *Covenant and Calling: Towards a Theology of Same-Sex Relationships*. London: SCM, 2014.

Soskice, Janet Martin. "The Gift of the Name: Moses and the Burning Bush." In *Silence and the Word: Negative Theology and the Incarnation*, edited by Oliver Davies and Denys Turner, 61–75.

Cambridge: Cambridge University Press, 2002.

———. *Metaphor and Religious Language.* Oxford: Clarendon, 1985.

———. "Naming God: A Study in Faith and Reason." In *Reason and the Reasons of Faith,* edited by Paul J. Griffiths and Reinhard Hütter, 241–54. London: T&T Clark, 2005.

Soulen, R. Kendall. *Distinguishing the Voices.* Vol. 1 of *The Divine Name(s) and the Holy Trinity.* Louisville: Westminster John Knox, 2011.

———. *The God of Israel and Christian Theology.* Minneapolis: Fortress, 1996.

Spaemann, Robert. *Persons: The Difference between "Someone" and "Something."* Translated by Oliver O'Donovan. Oxford Studies in Theological Ethics. Oxford: Oxford University Press, 2007.

Springsted, Eric. *The Act of Faith: Christian Faith and the Moral Self.* Grand Rapids: Eerdmans, 2002.

Sprinkle, Preston, ed. *Homosexuality, the Bible, and the Church: Two Views.* Counterpoints. Grand Rapids: Zondervan, 2016.

Stackhouse, John G., Jr. "Generic Evangelicalism." In *Four Views on the Spectrum of Evangelicalism,* edited by Andrew David Naselli and Collin Hansen, 116–42. Counterpoints. Grand Rapids: Zondervan, 2011.

———. "The Hard Work of Holiness: Protestants and Purgatory." *Christian Century* 131, no. 12 (June 11, 2014): 26–29.

Stanton, G. N. "Sermon on the Mount/Plain." In *Dictionary of Jesus and the Gospels,* edited by Joel B. Green, Scot McKnight, and I. Howard Marshall, 735–44. Downers Grove, IL: InterVarsity, 1992.

Stassen, Glen H., and David P. Gushee. *Kingdom Ethics: Following Jesus in Contemporary Context.* Downers Grove, IL: IVP Academic, 2003.

Stendahl, Krister. "The Apostle Paul and the Introspective Conscience of the West."

Harvard Theological Review 56, no. 3 (1963): 199–215.

Stott, John R. W. *The Cross of Christ.* Downers Grove, IL: InterVarsity, 1986.

Sunshine, Glenn S. "Accommodation Historically Considered." In *The Enduring Authority of the Christian Scriptures,* edited by D. A. Carson, 238–65. Grand Rapids: Eerdmans, 2016.

Surin, Kenneth. *Theology and the Problem of Evil.* Oxford: Blackwell, 1986.

Swain, Scott R. "Divine Trinity." In *Christian Dogmatics: Reformed Theology for the Church Catholic,* edited by Michael Allen and Scott R. Swain, 78–106. Grand Rapids: Baker Academic, 2016.

Sweeney, Douglas A. *The American Evangelical Story.* Grand Rapids: Baker Academic, 2005.

Tanner, Kathryn. *Theories of Culture: A New Agenda for Theology.* Guides to Theological Inquiry. Minneapolis: Fortress, 1997.

———. "Trinity." In *The Blackwell Companion to Political Theology,* edited by William T. Cavanaugh and Peter Scott, 319–32. Oxford: Blackwell, 2003.

Taylor, Charles. *Sources of the Self: The Making of the Modern Identity.* Cambridge, MA: Harvard University Press, 1989.

Tennant, Agnieszka. "In Need of Deliverance." *Christianity Today* 45, no. 11 (September 3, 2001): 46–63.

Tennent, Timothy C. *Theology in the Context of World Christianity: How the Global Church Is Influencing the Way We Think about and Discuss Theology.* Grand Rapids: Zondervan, 2007.

Thiselton, Anthony C. *Interpreting God and the Postmodern Self: On Meaning, Manipulation, and Promise.* Grand Rapids: Eerdmans, 1995.

———. *Systematic Theology.* Grand Rapids: Eerdmans, 2015.

Thomas Aquinas. *Summa theologica.* 5 vols. Reprint, Allen, TX: Christian Classics, 1981.

Thompson, Marianne Meye. *The Promise of the Father: Jesus and God in the New Testament*. Louisville: Westminster John Knox, 2000.

Thompson, Mark D. *A Clear and Present Word: The Clarity of Scripture*. New Studies in Biblical Theology. Downers Grove, IL: IVP Academic, 2006.

Tiessen, Terrance. *Providence and Prayer: How Does God Work in the World?* Downers Grove, IL: InterVarsity, 2000.

Torrance, Alan. "Being of One Substance with the Father." In *Nicene Christianity: The Future for a New Ecumenism*, edited by Christopher Seitz, 49–61. Grand Rapids: Brazos, 2001.

Torrance, Thomas F. *Atonement: The Person and Work of Christ*. Edited by Robert T. Walker. Downers Grove, IL: IVP Academic, 2009.

———. *Incarnation: The Person and Life of Christ*. Edited by Robert T. Walker. Downers Grove, IL: IVP Academic, 2015.

Treier, Daniel J. "Concept." In *Dictionary for Theological Interpretation of the Bible*, edited by Kevin J. Vanhoozer, 129–30. Grand Rapids: Baker Academic, 2005.

———. "Creation and Evolution." In *Evangelical Dictionary of Theology*, edited by Daniel J. Treier and Walter A. Elwell, 218–21. 3rd ed. Grand Rapids: Baker Academic, 2017.

———. "Evangelical Theology." In *The Cambridge Dictionary of Christian Theology*, edited by Ian A. McFarland, David Fergusson, Karen Kilby, and Iain R. Torrance, 173–76. Cambridge: Cambridge University Press, 2011.

———. "Faith." In *Dictionary for Theological Interpretation of the Bible*, edited by Kevin J. Vanhoozer, 226–28. Grand Rapids: Baker Academic, 2005.

———. "The Freedom of God's Word: Toward an 'Evangelical' Dogmatics of Scripture." In *The Voice of God in the Text of Scripture*, edited by Oliver D. Crisp and Fred Sanders, 21–40. Grand Rapids: Zondervan, 2016.

———. "Heaven on Earth? Evangelicals and Biblical Interpretation." *Books & Culture Online*. January 2012. http://www.booksandculture.com/articles/webexclusives/2012/january/heavenonearth.html.

———. "I Feel Your Pain." *Books & Culture* 12, no. 2 (March/April 2006): 38–39.

———. "Incarnation." In *Christian Dogmatics: Reformed Theology for the Church Catholic*, edited by Michael Allen and Scott R. Swain, 216–42. Grand Rapids: Baker Academic, 2016.

———. "Jesus Christ, Doctrine of." In *Dictionary for Theological Interpretation of the Bible*, edited by Kevin J. Vanhoozer, 363–71. Grand Rapids: Baker Academic, 2005.

———. "The New Covenant and New Creation: Western Soteriologies and the Fullness of the Gospel." In *So Great a Salvation: Soteriology in the Majority World*, edited by Gene L. Green, Stephen T. Pardue, and K. K. Yeo, 14–37. Majority World Theology. Grand Rapids: Eerdmans, 2017.

———. "Person." In *Evangelical Dictionary of Theology*, edited by Daniel J. Treier and Walter A. Elwell, 656. 3rd ed. Grand Rapids: Baker Academic, 2017.

———. "Postcolonial Theory." In *Evangelical Dictionary of Theology*, edited by Daniel J. Treier and Walter A. Elwell, 681–82. 3rd ed. Grand Rapids: Baker Academic, 2017.

———. "Proof Text." In *Dictionary for Theological Interpretation of the Bible*, edited by Kevin J. Vanhoozer, 622–24. Grand Rapids: Baker Academic, 2005.

———. *Proverbs and Ecclesiastes*. Brazos Theological Commentary on the Bible. Grand Rapids: Brazos, 2011.

———. Review of *Original Sin: Illuminating the Riddle*, by Henri Blocher. *Trinity Journal* 21, n.s. (Fall 2000): 233–37.

———. "Scripture, Unity of." In *Dictionary for Theological Interpretation of the Bible*, edited by Kevin J. Vanhoozer, 731–34. Grand Rapids: Baker Academic, 2005.

———. "Scripture and Hermeneutics." In *The Cambridge Companion to Evangelical Theology*, edited by Timothy Larsen and Daniel J. Treier, 35–49. Cambridge: Cambridge University Press, 2007.

———. "Scripture and Hermeneutics." In *Mapping Modern Theology: A Thematic and Historical Introduction*, edited by Kelly M. Kapic and Bruce L. McCormack, 67–96. Grand Rapids: Baker Academic, 2012.

———. "Systematic Theology." In *Evangelical Dictionary of Theology*, edited by Daniel J. Treier and Walter A. Elwell, 853–55. 3rd ed. Grand Rapids: Baker Academic, 2017.

———. "Theological Hermeneutics, Contemporary." In *Dictionary for Theological Interpretation of the Bible*, edited by Kevin J. Vanhoozer, 787–93. Grand Rapids: Baker Academic, 2005.

———. "Theology on Fire." *Books & Culture* 22, no. 4 (July/August 2016): 27–28.

———. "Virgin Territory?" *Pro Ecclesia* 23, no. 4 (Fall 2014): 373–79.

———. *Virtue and the Voice of God: Toward Theology as Wisdom*. Grand Rapids: Eerdmans, 2006.

———. "Who Is the Church?" In *Theology Questions Everyone Asks: Christian Faith in Plain Language*, edited by Gary M. Burge and David Lauber, 156–67. Downers Grove, IL: IVP Academic, 2014.

———. "Wisdom." In *Dictionary for Theological Interpretation of the Bible*, edited by Kevin J. Vanhoozer, 844–47. Grand Rapids: Baker Academic, 2005.

Treier, Daniel J., and Walter A. Elwell, eds. *Evangelical Dictionary of Theology*. 3rd ed. Grand Rapids: Baker Academic, 2017.

Treier, Daniel J., with Daniel Hill. "Philosophy." In *Dictionary for Theological Interpretation of the Bible*, edited by Kevin J. Vanhoozer, 591–94. Grand Rapids: Baker Academic, 2005.

Treier, Daniel J., and David Lauber. Introduction to *Trinitarian Theology for the Church: Scripture, Community, Worship*,

edited by Daniel J. Treier and David Lauber, 7–21. Downers Grove, IL: IVP Academic, 2009.

Treier, Daniel J., with Darren Sarisky. "Model." In *Dictionary for Theological Interpretation of the Bible*, edited by Kevin J. Vanhoozer, 517–19. Grand Rapids: Baker Academic, 2005.

Trousdale, Jerry. *Miraculous Movements: How Hundreds of Thousands of Muslims Are Falling in Love with Jesus*. Nashville: Nelson, 2012.

Turner, David L. "The New Jerusalem in Revelation 21:1–22:5: Consummation of a Biblical Continuum." In *Dispensationalism, Israel, and the Church: The Search for Definition*, edited by Craig A. Blaising and Darrell L. Bock, 264–92. Grand Rapids: Zondervan, 1992.

Vanhoozer, Kevin J. "Ascending the Mountain, Singing the Rock: Biblical Interpretation Earthed, Typed, and Transfigured." *Modern Theology* 28, no. 4 (October 2012): 781–803.

———, ed. *Dictionary for Theological Interpretation of the Bible*. Grand Rapids: Baker Academic, 2005.

———. *The Drama of Doctrine: A Canonical-Linguistic Approach to Christian Theology*. Louisville: Westminster John Knox, 2005.

———. "Human Being, Individual and Social." In *The Cambridge Companion to Christian Doctrine*, edited by Colin E. Gunton, 158–88. Cambridge: Cambridge University Press, 1997.

———. *Remythologizing Theology: Divine Action, Passion, and Authorship*. Studies in Christian Doctrine. Cambridge: Cambridge University Press, 2010.

———. "Scripture and Hermeneutics." In *The Oxford Handbook of Evangelical Theology*, edited by Gerald R. McDermott, 35–52. Oxford: Oxford University Press, 2010.

———. "The Trials of Truth: Mission, Martyrdom, and the Epistemology of the Cross." In *To Stake a Claim: Mission and the Western Crisis of Knowledge*, edited by J. Andrew Kirk and Kevin J. Vanhoozer, 120–56. Maryknoll, NY: Orbis, 1999.

———. "Wrighting the Wrongs of the Reformation? The State of Union with Christ in St. Paul and Protestant Soteriology." In *Jesus, Paul and the People of God: A Theological Dialogue with N. T. Wright*, edited by Nicholas Perrin and Richard B. Hays, 235–59. Downers Grove, IL: IVP Academic, 2011.

Vanhoozer, Kevin J., and Daniel J. Treier. *Theology and the Mirror of Scripture: A Mere Evangelical Account*. Studies in Christian Doctrine and Scripture. Downers Grove, IL: IVP Academic, 2015.

Vatican Council II. "Decree on Ecumenism: *Unitatis Redintegratio*, 21 November 1964." In *Vatican Council II: The Basic Sixteen Documents; Constitutions, Decrees, Declarations*, edited by Austin Flannery, 499–523. Northport, NY: Costello, 1996.

Venema, Dennis R., and Scot McKnight. *Adam and the Genome: Reading Scripture after Genetic Science*. Grand Rapids: Brazos, 2017.

Visser 't Hooft, W. A. *The Kingship of Christ*. New York: Harper, 1948.

Volf, Miroslav. *After Our Likeness: The Church as the Image of the Trinity*. Sacra Doctrina. Grand Rapids: Eerdmans, 1997.

———. *The End of Memory: Remembering Rightly in a Violent World*. Grand Rapids: Eerdmans, 2006.

———. *Exclusion and Embrace: A Theological Exploration of Identity, Otherness, and Reconciliation*. Nashville: Abingdon, 1996.

Volf, Miroslav, and Dorothy C. Bass, eds. *Practicing Theology: Beliefs and Practices in Christian Life*. Grand Rapids: Eerdmans, 2001.

Wainwright, Geoffrey. "The Ecclesial Scope of Justification." In *Justification: What's at Stake in the Current Debates*, edited by Mark Husbands and Daniel J. Treier, 249–75. Downers Grove, IL: InterVarsity, 2004.

———. *For Our Salvation: Two Approaches to the Work of Christ*. Grand Rapids: Eerdmans, 1997.

Wainwright, William J., ed. *God, Philosophy, and Academic Culture: A Discussion between Scholars in the AAR and the APA*. Reflection and Theory in the Study of Religion 11. Atlanta: Scholars Press, 1996.

Walker, Williston, Richard A. Norris, David W. Lotz, and Robert T. Handy. *A History of the Christian Church*. 4th ed. New York: Scribner, 1985.

Walls, Andrew F. "Christianity in the Non-Western World: A Study in the Serial Nature of Christian Expansion." In *The Cross-Cultural Process in Christian History*, 27–48. Maryknoll, NY: Orbis, 2002.

Walls, Jerry L. *Purgatory: The Logic of Total Transformation*. New York: Oxford University Press, 2012.

Walton, John H. *Genesis*. NIV Application Commentary. Grand Rapids: Zondervan, 2001.

———. *The Lost World of Genesis One: Ancient Cosmology and the Origins Debate*. Downers Grove, IL: IVP Academic, 2009.

Ware, Kallistos. *The Orthodox Way*. Crestwood, NY: St. Vladimir's Seminary Press, 1993.

Warfield, B. B. *Evolution, Science, and Scripture: Selected Writings*. Edited by David N. Livingstone and Mark A. Noll. Grand Rapids: Baker Books, 2000.

———. "The Idea of Systematic Theology." In *The Princeton Theology, 1812–1921: Scripture, Science, Theological Method from Archibald Alexander to Benjamin Breckinridge Warfield*, edited by Mark A. Noll, 241–61. Grand Rapids: Baker, 1983.

———. *The Plan of Salvation*. Rev. ed. Grand Rapids: Eerdmans, 1935.

Webb, William J. *Slaves, Women and Homosexuals: Exploring the Hermeneutics of Cultural Analysis*. Downers Grove, IL: IVP Academic, 2001.

Weber, Timothy P. *Living in the Shadow of the Second Coming.* 2nd ed. Grand Rapids: Zondervan, 1983.

Webster, John. "Criticism: Revelation and Disturbance." *Stimulus* 7, no. 1 (February 1999): 1–6.

———. *Holiness.* Grand Rapids: Eerdmans, 2003.

———. "The Holiness and Love of God." In *Confessing God: Essays in Christian Dogmatics II,* 109–30. London: T&T Clark International, 2005.

———. "The Immensity and Ubiquity of God." In *Confessing God: Essays in Christian Dogmatics II,* 87–107. London: T&T Clark International, 2005.

———. "Jesus—God for Us." In *Anglican Essentials: Reclaiming Faith within the Anglican Church of Canada,* edited by George W. Egerton, 89–97. Toronto: Anglican Book Centre, 1995.

———. "Providence." In *Christian Dogmatics: Reformed Theology for the Church Catholic,* edited by Michael Allen and Scott R. Swain, 148–64. Grand Rapids: Baker Academic, 2016.

Welch, Claude. *In This Name: The Doctrine of the Trinity in Contemporary Theology.* Reprint, Eugene, OR: Wipf & Stock, 2005.

Welker, Michael. *God the Spirit.* Translated by John F. Hoffmeyer. Minneapolis: Fortress, 1994.

Wellum, Stephen J. *God the Son Incarnate: The Doctrine of Christ.* Foundations of Evangelical Theology. Wheaton: Crossway, 2016.

Wenham, John W. "The Case for Conditional Immortality." In *Universalism and the Doctrine of Hell,* edited by Nigel M. de S. Cameron, 161–91. Grand Rapids: Baker, 1992.

Wesley, John. "Christian Perfection." In *Sermons 34–70,* edited by Albert Outler, 97–121. Vol. 2 of *The Works of John Wesley.* Nashville: Abingdon, 1984.

———. *The Journal of John Wesley: A Selection.* Edited by Elisabeth Jay. New York: Oxford University Press, 1987.

West, Cornel. *Prophetic Fragments.* Grand Rapids: Eerdmans, 1988.

Westerholm, Stephen. *Perspectives Old and New on Paul: The "Lutheran" Paul and His Critics.* Grand Rapids: Eerdmans, 2004.

White, Lynn, Jr. "The Historical Roots of Our Ecological Crisis." *Science* 155 (1967): 1203–7.

White, Vernon. *Identity.* Society and Church. London: SCM, 2002.

Williams, A. N. *The Architecture of Theology: Structure, System, and Ratio.* Oxford: Oxford University Press, 2011.

Williams, Rowan. "Ecology and Economy." Dr Rowan Williams 104th Archbishop of Canterbury website. March 8, 2005. http://rowanwilliams.archbishopofcant erbury.org/articles.php/1550/ecology-and -economy-archbishop-calls-for-action-on -environment-to-head-off-social-crisis.

———. "A History of Faith in Jesus." In *The Cambridge Companion to Jesus,* edited by Markus Bockmuehl, 220–36. Cambridge: Cambridge University Press, 2001.

———. *On Christian Theology.* Challenges in Contemporary Theology. Oxford: Blackwell, 2000.

Wittmer, Michael. *Heaven Is a Place on Earth: Why Everything You Do Matters to God.* Grand Rapids: Zondervan, 2004.

Wolters, Albert M. *Creation Regained: Biblical Basics of a Reformational Worldview.* 2nd ed. Grand Rapids: Eerdmans, 2005.

———. "No Longer Queen: The Theological Disciplines and Their Sisters." In *The Bible and the University,* edited by David Lyle Jeffrey and C. Stephen Evans, 59–79. Scripture and Hermeneutics 7. Grand Rapids: Zondervan, 2007.

Woodhead, Linda. "Theology and the Fragmentation of the Self." *International Journal of Systematic Theology* 1, no. 1 (March 1999): 53–72.

Worthen, Molly. *Apostles of Reason: The Crisis of Authority in American*

Evangelicalism. New York: Oxford University Press, 2013.

Wright, Christopher J. H. "Mission as a Matrix for Hermeneutics and Biblical Theology." In *Out of Egypt: Biblical Theology and Biblical Interpretation*, edited by Craig Bartholomew, Mary Healy, Karl Möller, and Robin Parry, 102–43. Scripture and Hermeneutics 5. Grand Rapids: Zondervan, 2004.

Wright, N. T. *Justification: God's Plan and Paul's Vision*. Downers Grove, IL: IVP Academic, 2009.

———. *The Last Word: Beyond the Bible Wars to a New Understanding of the Authority of Scripture*. San Francisco: HarperSanFrancisco, 2005.

———. "Resurrection of the Dead." In *Dictionary for Theological Interpretation of the Bible*, edited by Kevin J. Vanhoozer, 676–78. Grand Rapids: Baker Academic, 2005.

———. *The Resurrection of the Son of God*. Christian Origins and the Question of God 3. Minneapolis: Fortress, 2003.

———. *Surprised by Hope: Rethinking Heaven, the Resurrection, and the Mission of the Church*. San Francisco: HarperOne, 2008.

———. *What Saint Paul Really Said: Was Paul of Tarsus the Real Founder of Christianity?* Grand Rapids: Eerdmans, 1997.

Yarhouse, Mark A. *Understanding Gender Dysphoria: Navigating Transgender Issues in a Changing Culture*. Downers Grove, IL: IVP Academic, 2015.

Yates, Jonathan. "Pelagius, Pelagianism." In *Evangelical Dictionary of Theology*, edited by Daniel J. Treier and Walter A. Elwell, 647–48. 3rd ed. Grand Rapids: Baker Academic, 2017.

Yeago, David S. "The New Testament and the Nicene Dogma: A Contribution to the Recovery of Theological Exegesis." *Pro Ecclesia* 3, no. 2 (Spring 1994): 152–64.

Yoder, John Howard. *The Politics of Jesus*. 2nd ed. Grand Rapids: Eerdmans, 1994.

Yong, Amos. *Beyond the Impasse: Toward a Pneumatological Theology of Religions*. Grand Rapids: Baker Academic, 2003.

———. *The Bible, Disability, and the Church: A New Vision of the People of God*. Grand Rapids: Eerdmans, 2011.

———. *The Future of Evangelical Theology: Soundings from the Asian American Diaspora*. Downers Grove, IL: IVP Academic, 2014.

———. *In the Days of Caesar: Pentecostalism and Political Theology*. Sacra Doctrina. Grand Rapids: Eerdmans, 2010.

Young, Frances. *God's Presence: A Contemporary Recapitulation of Early Christianity*. Current Issues in Theology. Cambridge: Cambridge University Press, 2013.

Zizioulas, John D. *Being as Communion: Studies in Personhood and the Church*. Crestwood, NY: St. Vladimir's Seminary Press, 1985.

Scripture Index

Name Index

Subject Index

ability, human, 157–58
abortion, 157–58
abuse, atonement and, 211–12
accidents, 333, 367
accommodation, 311–12, 367
accompaniment, scriptural, 314–17
active obedience of Christ, 208, 367
A-C-T-S acrostic, 67–68
actualism, 204n8
Adam and Eve, 142–43
addiction, sin and, 225
ad extra, 367
adiaphora, 367
ad intra, 367
adoptionism, 177, 182–83, 367
adoration, prayer and, 67–68
adultery, 45–46
agency, double, 122
agnosticism, reverent, 357, 386
Ahaz, 12–13
Alexandria, Christology and, 175–76
Amen, 76
amillennialism, 346, 367
Amish, 260
Anabaptists, 45, 259–62
analogia entis, 17, 367
analogia fidei, 25, 367
analogical language, 102–4, 367
analogy of being, 367
analogy of faith, 25, 367
ancient Near East (ANE), 141
angels, 135–36, 368
Anglicanism, 262–64, 335–36

anhypostatic Christology, 200n4, 368
animism, 129–30, 368
annihilation, 133–34, 144, 355–56, 368
anointing the sick, 329, 368
anthropology, 148–69, 186–90, 368
anthropomorphism, 368
antichrist, 348, 368
Antioch, Christology and, 175–76
apocalyptic, 53–54, 348, 368
Apocrypha, 301, 368
apokatastasis, 355, 368
Apollinarianism, 180–81, 368
apologetics, 19–20, 368
apophaticism, 103–4, 368
apostolicity, 302, 320, 323, 325, 368
appropriation, 86–87, 368
archetypal knowledge, 94–95, 368
Arianism, 179–80, 368
Arminianism
    providence and, 117–20
    salvation and, 234, 241, 258, 288
    sin and, 230, 368
articles, creedal, 369
arts, 131–32, 369
ascension, 217–18, 369
asceticism, 369
aseity, 112, 369
assurance of salvation, 287–91, 369
atheism, materialistic, 128–29
Athens, Christology and, 175
atonement
    the cross and, 209–14
    definition of, 369